Date Due

Best Short Plays

of the World Theatre

1958-1967

Also by STANLEY RICHARDS

BOOKS:

THE BEST SHORT PLAYS OF 1968
CANADA ON STAGE

PLAYS:

THROUGH A GLASS, DARKLY
AUGUST HEAT
TUNNEL OF LOVE
SUN DECK
O DISTANT LAND
JOURNEY TO BAHÍA
MOOD PIECE
MR. BELL'S CREATION
THE PROUD AGE
ONCE TO EVERY BOY
HALF-HOUR, PLEASE
KNOW YOUR NEIGHBOR
GIN AND BITTERNESS
THE HILLS OF BATAAN
DISTRICT OF COLUMBIA

Best Short Plays
of the World Theatre

1958-1967

EDITED WITH AN INTRODUCTION
AND PREFACES TO THE PLAYS BY

Stanley Richards

Crown Publishers, Inc., NEW YORK

For My Mother and Father
who originally set me
forth on a journey
that continues
to prove
wondrous
and
rewarding

EDITOR'S NOTE

THE PREPARATION of an anthology involves the cooperation, assistance, and generosity of spirit and deed of many hands. In particular, I should like to express my deepest gratitude to the authors and their representatives who have provided me with the substance and materials to assemble this collection. Their response to this project—as well as their contributions—was notable and inspiring. Firm achievement on stage, however, can be reached only by and with the assistance of many "backstage" hands; thus, I should also like to record my warmest appreciation to: Norman Holland, Margaret Sherman, Eileen O'Casey, M. Abbott Van Nostrand, Hamish Hamilton, Ninon Tallon-Karlweis, Carol Kaplan, Marilyn Phillips, Eric Bentley, Joan White, Otis Guernsey, Jr., Ernest Dobbs, Mona Coxwell, Sheila Rosenbaum, Naomi Gale, Bernard Silverman, F. Andrew Leslie, Bennett Cerf, Leah Daniels, Mary Ellen Wang, Maggie Abbott, Tom Grainger, Stephen Phillips, Edd Kaplan, Mae Nolan, Shirley Mitchell, Margery Vosper, Irving Levin, Joan Daves, Margaret Ramsay, Joe Toto, John Farrar, Robert Hogan, Tuni Berman, Herbert Michelman, Naomi Rosenbach, Leota Diesel, Warren Bayless, and Paul Slocumb-Rolley.

Gratefully,
STANLEY RICHARDS

CONTENTS

INTRODUCTION

THERE is one personal reflection that cannot be overlooked at this opening juncture. It concerns a remarkable coincidence that, you may be sure, was not engineered by my very pleased publishers. During the 1966–1967 New York theatre season, the identical period when this volume was being prepared, three of the reigning Broadway successes were productions of short plays: Robert Anderson's quartet, *You Know I Can't Hear You When the Water's Running;* Peter Shaffer's tandem, *Black Comedy* and *White Lies;* and the tripartite musical *The Apple Tree.* And to add fuel to the flame of this historic theatrical occasion, Off-Broadway's outstanding critical and box-office success was *America Hurrah,* Jean-Claude van Itallie's satiric triptych that witheringly reduced bits of contemporary Americana to pulp.

According to knowledgeable theatrical scorekeepers, this astonishing record—four enormously successful presentations of short plays running concurrently in New York—is unprecedented in the annals of the American professional theatre. True, in the past there have been other successful productions of short plays on the Broadway stage, but these stood isolated in the structure of their respective seasons. To mention just a few: Clifford Odets' *Waiting for Lefty* (combined with *Till the Day I Die*); William Saroyan's *My Heart's in the Highlands;* Irwin Shaw's *Bury the Dead;* Noël Coward's *Tonight at 8:30;* Peter Shaffer's *The Private Ear* and *The Public Eye;* Terence Rattigan's *The Browning Version* and *Harlequinade;* later, his *Separate Tables;* and Arthur Miller's *A View from the Bridge,* paired with *A Memory of Two Mondays.*

It is quite true that merit and quality do not always march hand in hand with commercial success. Yet, again, one cannot dispute the fact that commercial success is a barometrical measure of public acceptance and that the aforementioned quartet of thriving presentations do, to a discernible degree, manifest proof that audiences no longer are allergic to the short play.

To those of us who never wavered in our respect for, and dedication to, the short play, this recent "happening" was tantamount to a triumph; for, until this past season, the form had a singularly erratic career in the canon of American drama. To persons in and out of the realm of the professional theatre, it always seemed to be regarded as something of an enigma. With occasional prominent exceptions, it was a dramatic form that, by and large, begrudgingly was accepted and then, periodically, stored away until a new, unexpectedly explosive piece of work restored curiosity and generated renewed interest, if not always durable confidence, in the genre. On the other hand, the short play perpetually has enjoyed a respectable degree of popularity in other corners of the world: notably, in Great Britain and on the Continent where the dramatist is not subject to what Henry James once described as "the tyranny of the clock."

The history of the *one-act play*—and now that we're trudging back a bit into history, I suppose it may be appropriate and justifiable to refer temporarily to the form by its *classic* rather than *modern* designation—is as colorful and expressive as it is checkered.

Although the one-act play's origins may be traced back through the centuries, we shall commence our brief historical peregrinations in eighteenth-century England, where one-acters—invariably, short comedies or farces—were introduced to audiences as *afterpieces.* From the beginning of that century, and even earlier, playbills and notices contain references to supplementary "entertainments" for patrons relishing "some light diversion" after sitting glued through a five-act tragedy.

While these "diverting" afterpieces may well have had a therapeutically restorative effect upon the weary playgoer preparing to trail homeward after a long evening, there also happened to be a more practical issue involved in the development of the afterpiece. In order to keep their managerial heads above water—and from this we can gather that the basic economics and fiscal problems of the theatre haven't altered much through the centuries—managements threw in these end-of-the-evening dividends in an effort to lure audiences away from competitive playhouses. And further to swell their box-office coffers, they warmly welcomed latecomers who, at considerably reduced admission fees, came to catch the "afterpiece." Thus, and possibly sociologists will concur, the one-act play may safely be considered responsible for history's initial, direct cut-price bid to attract the middle class to the theatre—hitherto, primarily a diversion for the aristocracy—by providing them with a solid entertainment, however brief, and at the hour they could attend and afford. Apparently, the most eminent theatrical personages of the day offered their whole-hearted blessings and support to this revolutionary movement, for, among other period notables, David Garrick and Samuel Foote cheerfully wrote short plays *especially* for history's original late, late show.

Then, a funny thing happened to the afterpiece on its way into the nineteenth century: it was swung back from its customary perch as *show-closer* to *show-opener,* and in the process derived a new name: *curtain raiser.* The metamorphosis, however, chiefly was one of reversed placement, for, inherently, the malleable one-acter retained its farcical coat of arms. Its primary function still was to "divert and amuse": now, *before,* rather than *after,* the somber *pièce de résistance* took possession of the stage.

The curtain raiser continued as a theatrical staple into the early years of the twentieth century. Then, quite unexpectedly, it made the "big time" through vaudeville, the most popular entertainment of its day.

In order to draw "class" audiences into its variety houses, managements initially had to attract "class" performers to their boards. And they did. With guarantees of enormous salaries and accouterments fit for royalty, they succeeded in luring to their circuits such glittering legitimate stage luminaries as: Sarah Bernhardt, Lily Langtry, Mrs. Leslie Carter, Mrs. Patrick Campbell, James O'Neill, Arnold Daly, Otis Skinner, Alla Nazimova, and Ethel Barrymore. But even in the more informal ambiance of the variety house, it was a prerequisite that an established star come armed with a suitable vehicle, particularly one that could illuminate her magnificence within the time limitations imposed by the length of the bill. And this is how and where the one-acter finally came into its

own as an independent and dignified component of the drama.

The term *curtain raiser* no longer could be applied to the one-act play, for with such heady (and costly) glamour topping the casts, stars commanded stellar billing on the marquees of the nation's leading vaudeville emporiums. Some of the celebrated appeared in truncated versions of their old Broadway or international favorites. Others commissioned and starred in especially written playlets. This demand opened new avenues of profit and fame for both young and established dramatists who also welcomed a temporary freedom from the rigid conventions of the full-length play. Some of the future notables who created one-act plays specifically for vaudeville: George Kelly, Eugene Walter, Kenyon Nicholson, Edgar Allan Woolf, Edwin Milton Royle, Willard Mack, Arthur "Bugs" Baer, and the already prominent journalist-novelist Richard Harding Davis.

As the late chronicler Bernard Sobel pointed out: "With the appearance of legitimate stars in one-act plays, vaudeville took on its highest distinction. They gave dignity to the bills, Their artistry alerted audiences to the spell of drama. For example, Ethel Barrymore's performances in Sir James M. Barrie's *The Twelve Pound Look* were ceremonial occasions. Best of all, the legitimate stars inspired oncoming playwrights to turn out one-act plays or sketches . . . and inspired the national growth of Little and Community Theatres."

In 1915, the one-act play took an even more significant step forward when the Washington Square Players (later to become the nucleus of the Theatre Guild) inaugurated its career with a program of one-act plays at the Bandbox Theatre, New York. During the players' three-year tenure, they presented sixty-two one-act plays, many of them outstanding and now regarded as "modern classics." Authors who contributed to this prodigious repertoire included: Ben Hecht, Theodore Dreiser, Edward Goodman, Philip Moeller, George Cram Cook, Lawrence Langner (a founder and leading force in the subsequent Theatre Guild), Elmer Rice, Zoë Akins, Zona Gale, and Susan Glaspell. (The latter four later were awarded Pulitzer Prizes for full-length plays.)

Without a doubt, though, the major, most striking, influence on the American one-act play was Eugene O'Neill, whose initial work to be staged, *Bound East for Cardiff*, was presented by the Provincetown Players in 1916. Always an experimentalist and innovator, O'Neill brought the craft to a high point of development with his short plays of the sea, four of which eventually were collected under the title *S.S. Glencairn*. Not only did the future Noble Prize winner enjoy his first conspicuous success with the *Glencairn* plays—all drawn from firsthand knowledge from his days as a seaman—they also succeeded in attracting unprecedented critical attention to the form.

O'Neill, unquestionably, elevated the stature of the American one-act play to new artistic levels and serious consideration. This was fortunate, indeed, for until his emergence the field was overflowing with works of inconsequential nature and dubious craftsmanship. The majority dealt with a single, frequently contrived, incident rather than with themes of import and fully dimensioned characterizations. Most were constricted by the limitations of a single conventional setting. This rigid conformity largely was an obeisance to the mushrooming amateur market, sprung from the one-acter's popularity with vaudeville audiences. The Little Theatres sought uncomplicated, harmless offerings for the edification of its family patrons. Authors and publishers willingly—and profitably—bowed to their needs. But condescension in the arts, as with anything else, is not likely to impel much progress. And this is where a spirited woman, Margaret Mayorga, propelled herself into the center ring with all the fervor and dedication of an Evangelist.

As an early aficionado of the one-act form, she resented the contrivances that were passing as "drama" in the nation's Little Theatres. Now, cheered on by the widespread recognition of O'Neill, Miss Mayorga determined that here was the auspicious moment to introduce other outstanding short works of serious caliber and professional authority to the public. Thus, in 1919, she launched her initial collection, *Representative One-Act Plays by Amer-ican Authors*, the precursor of her influential series, *The Best One-Act Plays*.

In the four decades that followed, and until her retirement, Miss Mayorga—or, as she was designated by *The New York Times*: "the high priestess of the short play in America"—relentlessly pursued, and won, her campaign permanently to establish the one-act play as a consequential and honored branch of American drama.

In 1952, after having been represented with six of my own plays in Miss Mayorga's volumes, I felt secure enough to propose to this "high priestess" that—as time and tide indicated—she alter the title of her collections to *The Best Short Plays*.

To most persons lumbering through the second portion of the twentieth century, the appellative *one-act* evoked images of an earlier epoch. It also bore the curious stigma of amateurism: something hauled up from the lower reaches of a publisher's catalogue. Moreover, television put the finishing touches to the one-act play per se by conditioning millions of viewers to the more modern *short* play. And regardless of whether Madison Avenue cares to admit it, the bulk of the one-hour dramas seen on television are short works, divided into *three acts* to accommodate the purse-string advertisers.

Miss Mayorga adopted my suggestion and, in 1953, modernized the title of her annuals. By doing so, she gave renewed impetus and a wider latitude to the short dramatic form. Today it is linked in status with the short story or novella.

The contemporary dramatist, who now chooses to employ this form of expression, is free to portray consequential themes, on his own terms, untenanted by fusty restrictions. As the veteran New York drama critic Richard Watts, Jr., pointed out: "It is a form which tends to set free the imagination and the spirit of the playwright and to send it bounding through time and space, ignoring the customary fetters of convention and length. Almost any playwright can say what he wants to say in less time than the full-length play requires and the short work is joyously free of the usual padding. It is a sprightly form and a splendidly easygoing one."

No theme is too strong or too ample for

the short drama. If a theme is worthy of dramatic exploration, it is worth the telling in any form conceived by the writer. One cannot stretch a rubber band beyond its determined length. The same theory is applicable to drama: if an author has something important to say and it fits into the dimensions of the short play, then that is its rightful place. Padding often tends toward diffusion. To cite one major example: when Arthur Miller's *A View from the Bridge* was produced in expanded version in Chicago, a reviewer for a national trade paper noted: "The author has expanded what was originally a short play into two acts and lost considerable momentum in the process."

The short play is a form unto itself: it must be concise, stringent, and have instantaneous impact upon the viewer. After all, a short bell ring can be as effective as a protracted bell ring: its hearer is alerted in either case. The short play therefore can —and *must*—alert and stimulate audiences just as the long play purportedly does.

Edward Albee, whose short drama *The Zoo Story* initially elevated him to prominence, put it quite aptly when he declared: "They're *all* full-length plays. A play can be full-length be it three minutes or twelve hours long. It has its own duration and an audience should be able to receive gratification within any time limits."

The writer who embarks on the course of the short play must not compromise; his integrity is as valued and appreciated in this field as it is in any other field of writing. He must permit himself full freedom: in choice of theme, characterization, locale, and development. He must write with all the professionalism inherent in his makeup. Commercialism, at least during the creative period, must be ejected from his thoughts; indeed, often, it is the least suspected candidate for popularity that scoops up an author's most impressive profits. But that is because he firmly believes in what he is writing about.

In early life, one is advised not to discuss sex or religion, theoretically, man's two most contentious subjects. I should like to add a third: anthologies. For, invariably, two challenging questions are put before the house:

1. How did the editor ever fasten onto *that* selection?

2. How could he ever omit such an eminent, influential author as ———?

This questioning is anticipated, logical, and altogether human, for few of us ever are in *total* accord. Anyway, the omissions are a bit simpler to explain before controversy rages: insurmountable difficulties in obtaining clearances from the original publishers of several of the more "eminent" absentees. Regrettably, too, for, personally, they wished to be included in these pages, but contractual restrictions overruled them.

To remain in tune for another moment: any anthology bearing the somewhat embarrassingly lofty title of *Best Short Plays of the World Theatre* is bound to stir up some intriguing geographical questioning. Where, for instance, are the plays representative of Spain, Sweden, Russia, Poland, Mexico, Czechoslovakia? To assuage the interrogators: many of the foreign-language plays could not be suitably translated within the time limitations specified for the preparation of this volume. These and other vexatious omissions dutifully will be attended to in succeeding volumes, ultimately bringing a more copious international representation to the series.

Since, as some old sage once observed, "It takes all kinds to make up a world," similarly, it takes all types of plays to make up an anthology. First and foremost, however, I sought plays that spoke dramatically and effectively in an original and articulate voice to the world at large; not self-indulgent, obscure recitals performed by authors in front of distortive vanity mirrors.

The plays I have selected for inclusion in these pages either were written, performed, or published for the first time within the period covered in this anthology: 1958–1967. In addition to being eminently actable—and, after all, a play primarily is created for performance—they make some valid and pertinent statements about people and the world we live in, in a penetrative, stimulating way. Style without content is meaningless, just as polemics without pleasure or entertainment are soporiferous in the theatre.

Social frameworking is supposed to be a modern preoccupation, but this awareness of the everyday context is in reality a return to the theatre's ancient and continuing concern with portraying man in relation to his society. And while the plays that follow may be strikingly variegated in style—ranging from realism to surrealism—and perched on different social and psychological levels, all are deeply rooted in human truths. They restore a sense of *reality, immediacy,* and *personal involvement* to the theatre; and, unfashionable as it may sound to coterie audiences, the sheer storytelling aspect of each play comes through admirably, too.

While in some rarefied ateliers, these qualities may be looked upon with a sharply derisive eye, I am certain that most readers—perhaps like myself—warmly will welcome being reintroduced to plays that remain with you after the curtain has fallen.

STANLEY RICHARDS

New York, New York

Best Short Plays
of the World Theatre
1958-1967

THE ORCHESTRA

(L'Orchestre)

Jean Anouilh

Translated by MIRIAM JOHN

PATRICIA, *first violin*

PAMELA, *second violin*

MADAME HORTENSE, *double bass and leader of the orchestra*

SUZANNE DÉLICIAS, *cello*

EMMELINE, *viola*

LÉONA, *flute*

MONSIEUR LÉON, *piano*

MONSIEUR LEBONZE, *manager of the brasserie*

THE WAITER

THE DOCTOR

THE PLAYS of Jean Anouilh, France's most esteemed contemporary dramatist and one of the titans of the modern theatre, have been translated into many languages and have been produced in every conceivable theatrical corner of the world. Yet, in striking contrast to other notables of the international theatre, very little is known about the man personally. Adamantly reticent about private divulgences, M. Anouilh has immunized himself from all journalistic questionings and the granting of interviews: "I shall keep the details of my life to myself."

A few facts, however, have managed to seep through the scrim curtain that separates the man from the dramatist. Jean Anouilh was born at Bordeaux in 1910, and when still very young came to Paris. There he studied law for a short period, then washed his hands of briefs and legal documents, and joined forces with an advertising firm "where I learned to be ingenious and exact, lessons that took for me the place of literary studies." After two years of ministering to communications, his passionate interest in the theatre propelled him toward Louis Jouvet, the famous actor-manager, and in 1931 M. Anouilh became his secretary.

Whether by destiny or proximity to the great man of the theatre, one year later, Jean Anouilh himself was to become a public figure in France. The occasion: the presentation of his first play, *L'Hermine,* starring Pierre Fresnay. Though it disappeared from the boards after only thirty-seven performances, critics welcomed the young writer as "a promising avante-garde talent," and the play's *succès d'estime* launched him on his life's work.

The next five years were not exactly auspicious ones for M. Anouilh, but in 1937 the sun came blazingly through again with *Le Voyageur sans bagage.* Performed by the enormously influential theatre couple Georges and Ludmilla Pitoëff, the play transscended Jean Anouilh's erstwhile "avant-garde" status and became the inaugural link in a long chain of successes. To list some, in nonchronological order: *Becket; The Waltz of the Toreadors; The Lark; The Rehearsal; Legend of Lovers; Antigone; Traveller Without Luggage; Ring Round the Moon; Romeo and Jeannette; Médée; Mademoiselle Colombe; Ardèle; The Fighting Cock; Thieves' Carnival; Time Remembered;* and *The Cavern.*

The primary function of the theatre is, was, and forever will be entertainment. Even the most sublime poetry, the most noble thoughts, could not exist onstage without a concomitant quota of entertainment. If we strip bare the basic elements of drama, then we are left with nothing more provocative than disembodied speeches, routine propaganda, and platitudinous lectures. And Jean Anouilh fully realized this.

After serving two masters, Luigi Pirandello and Jean Giraudoux, Anouilh began to develop and perfect an individualistic style that even in its most bitter moments was eminently entertaining and irresistibly theatrical. The recurring theme of his many plays —the related axis upon which they dazzlingly revolve—is the quest for purity and happiness, deterred or frustrated by either a moral flaw in the central character's own nature or by the corruption of society. Anouilh has classified his plays in two groups: "Pièces roses," in which the theme is surveyed with illumining wit and comedy, and "Pièces noires," where it is interpreted through a bitter eye. Whichever mold he happens to select for his interpretation, invariably the dramatist's technical virtuosity and theatrical brilliance give stunning life to his premise, people, and plot.

The Orchestra accents Jean Anouilh's mastery of the stage. Almost a play within a play, or, to be more precise, a play within an orchestral recital, the author ingeniously juxtaposes fact and fancy in the lives of a group of mature, disillusioned—and, I suspect, not very gifted—musicians whose true souls and emotions must carefully be camouflaged from the public.

L'Orchestre was first presented at the Comédie des Champs-Elysées, on February 10, 1962. The production, with a musical score by Georges Van Parys, was directed by Jean Anouilh and Roland Piétri.

Jean Anouilh is represented again later in this anthology with *Madame de . . . ,* a dramatization of Louise de Vilmorin's novel. The translator: John Whiting.

Sparkling music from behind the lowered curtain, which then rises on an all-female orchestra on the platform of a spa town brasserie. The restaurant is not visible. The women are dressed in exactly similar bespangled black gowns with a single pink rose as ornament.

At the piano, with his back to the audience, is a rather wan, skinny little man, hardly noticeable at first. To one side is a stand with a card bearing the number 3. The lively piece comes to an end shortly after curtain rise. As soon as they finish playing, the musicians start talking.

———

PATRICIA. Then I add some shallots and leave it to marinate. Just two minutes—no longer. When I have my sauce ready, I cut the veal in small cubes. . . .

PAMELA. I put bacon with mine.

PATRICIA. For real *timbale Poitevine* you *never* use bacon, if you don't mind my saying so.

PAMELA. Well, I do, always.

PATRICIA (*thin-lipped*). Then it isn't *timbale Poitevine*, it's pig swill. I come from Loudun; I should know.

(*They hand their music sheets back to* MADAME HORTENSE, *who plays double bass and is leader of the orchestra.*)

PAMELA. Who's boasting? I come from Batignolles.

PATRICIA (*sourly*). Oh—Paris!

(MADAME HORTENSE, *still gathering up music, is speaking to* SUZANNE DÉLICIAS, *who is knitting away quietly between pieces behind her cello. They are continuing a conversation.*)

MADAME HORTENSE. Three plain, three purl, slip three, and the same again.

SUZANNE D. That's Japanese stitch.

MADAME HORTENSE. No. Japanese stitch has a wrong side, my dear; this has two right sides.

SUZANNE D. (*with a sour little laugh*). Excuse me, but if you loop it like that, your work has quite simply got two wrong sides! It must look horrible for a man's pull-over.

MADAME HORTENSE. Just as you like. Anyway, Japanese stitch looks vulgar.

EMMELINE (*finishing a conversation with* LÉONA, *who is slightly hunchbacked*). So I said to him, "Edmond," I said, "you can't make a woman suffer like this with impunity."

LÉONA. And what did he say to that?

EMMELINE. A foul word.

MADAME HORTENSE (*turns on the* PIANIST *as she continues her rounds*). Monsieur Léon in the clouds, as usual! Come along now, quickly. Ready with your "Gay Reverie," or we shall get all our parts mixed up again! What a dreamer you are! I think your dandruff's getting worse and worse.

PIANIST. All artists have it.

MADAME HORTENSE. Why don't you use that Pope's Lotion I advised you to try?

PIANIST. It smells oriental. I don't think it's very virile.

MADAME HORTENSE (*with a smile*). When I was with Monsieur Hortense, he used to use it. And I flatter myself that in all our twelve years of marriage I was the best-loved woman in the world. Monsieur Hortense performed three times a day—once in the afternoon. Ah! How he spoiled me!

PIANIST (*modestly*). He was a violinist, and violinists are . . .

MADAME HORTENSE (*significantly*). I've also known pianists with a fiery temperament.

PIANIST (*still modest*). It's rarer, though.

(MADAME HORTENSE *has gone to take her music back to the heap of sheet music on a table at the back of the stage.* SUZANNE D. *leaves her knitting and her cello and goes over to the piano.*)

SUZANNE D. She never stops, does she?

PIANIST. We were just chatting.

SUZANNE D. If you don't shut her up, I will.

PIANIST. It's difficult to stop her while the customers are here. After all, she's the leader, isn't she?

SUZANNE D. Coward! Coward! (*She sits down again.*)

PATRICIA (*continuing a conversation with* PAMELA *of which we have not heard the beginning*). Then I rub it with a bit of Kleenall and a really dry, soft rag.

PAMELA. I prefer a drop of ammonia.

PATRICIA (*acidly*). Ammonia removes the varnish, not the mark.

PAMELA (*also aggressive*). Each to her own method.

PATRICIA. Yes, but some methods are bad. Certain women have no pride in their homes.

PAMELA. My home looks just as good as yours. (*With a laugh.*) Maybe there aren't so many little mats and table runners and things.

PATRICIA. Well, not everyone has artistic taste, I mean, have they? I like my little soft, warm nest, with all my souvenirs around me. The mats and things make it cosy.

PAMELA. Dust traps. My little place is modern, I'm proud to say. Tubular furniture and formica surfaces. Everything neat and bright. No ornaments.

PATRICIA (*with a nervous little sneer*). Oh, I can just see it—a clinic! I'm not an invalid.

PAMELA. And I *am*, I suppose?

PATRICIA. Well, with those eyes . . .

PAMELA. My eyes may be a little haggard, my dear, but that's because I have a lover who adores me, and that's more than you can say. At least both *my* eyes look in the same direction.

PATRICIA (*squinting nervously*). Oh! What a thing to say about a physical handicap. Anyway, it's hardly noticeable. How low can you sink? And as for your lover, there's no need to boast about him. A bottle washer!

PAMELA (*laughing quite good-naturedly*). One does what one can. The great thing is to make a good job of it. I like a job well done. (*She is cooing insolently.*)

PATRICIA. You're unspeakable. I wonder women like you are tolerated in a respectable orchestra.

MADAME HORTENSE (*who has changed the number and is passing the music around*). Ladies! No arguments on the platform, please! Even when we stop playing, the customers don't stop looking. Smiles, please, charm . . . You can still say what you think with a smile. Your flower, Pamela.

PAMELA. What about my flower?

MADAME HORTENSE. It's drooping. I want all your roses looking fresh!

PATRICIA (*bitchily*). Like their wearers! (PAMELA *stamps angrily on her toe.*) Ouch!

MADAME HORTENSE. Ladies!

PATRICIA. Little bitch! She trod on my toe!

MADAME HORTENSE (*still smiling, but with a glint in her eye*). Manners now, whatever happens. You belong to your

public. That's the rule. The manager said to me at the audition, when we got the job in preference to Mag's Star and the Symphony Band—and you know they're both reputable orchestras—he said, "I'm taking you because I want women and charm! An orchestra that will catch my customers' imagination."

PATRICIA. Some hopes of catching imagination in a spa for the cure of constipation. Do you think they listen to us? They talk about it all the time. And tote up their bills. Some bills, too!

MADAME HORTENSE. It's not our concern what the customer is thinking, or whether or not he is constipated. Poise and elegance. That's what we were engaged for. And quantities of femininity. Now we're going to play "Impressions of Autumn" by Chandoisy, in the Goldstein arrangement. Lots of feeling and vibrato, if you please. (*She slides a finger in passing under* MONSIEUR LÉON'*s collar.*) Oh, Monsieur Léon, how warm you are! Your collar is quite damp.

PIANIST. I always bring two with me. I'll change during the intermission, after the March from *Tannhäuser*.

SUZANNE D. (*beside herself*). Stop it, stop it! Or I shall leave the platform.

PIANIST (*pitifully*). Please, don't let's have a scene. She said I was too warm. I can't very well tell her I'm not.

SUZANNE D. Monster! You're a monster of cruelty!

MADAME HORTENSE (*very much in command*). Careful of that sharp in the reprise during your solo, Mademoiselle Délicias, won't you, please?

EMMELINE (*finishing a conversation with* LÉONA). Everything! Everything! I told him everything! The rent not paid, my trouble with my poor mother, my period not coming . . .

LÉONA. So what did he say?

EMMELINE. Nothing. He was asleep.

LÉONA. Well! What an oaf! I'd never have stood that from André.

(MADAME HORTENSE *taps discreetly with her bow on her double bass. The music starts up. Very tender and tuneful. During the performance at chosen points in the music, the musicians talk as they play.*)

PATRICIA. I'm a woman. I'm probably more of a woman than you, even though

I don't throw myself on my back for anyone that happens along. I'm waiting for someone . . . someone I can . . . I want to be able to look deep down into his eyes.

PAMELA (*puffing out her cheeks as she plays*). You'll have difficulty doing that with both eyes at once.

PATRICIA (*stifling a sob at this second jab*). Oh!

PAMELA. He'll have to change sides from time to time.

PATRICIA (*another sob*). Oh! It's too much!

(MADAME HORTENSE *gives her a discreet tap on the head with her bow. She swallows her emotion and plays with a passionate abandon. Music.*)

EMMELINE (*continuing*). So then when we went into the restaurant, an extremely smart place where his friends had invited us, I said to him: "Where shall I sit, Edmond?"

LÉONA. And what did he say?

EMMELINE (*sniffing indignantly*). He said, sit where you f——

(*A tap on the head from* MADAME HORTENSE's *bow cuts the word off just as if by general consent the orchestra has drowned it. The piece comes to an end with much pathos and brilliance of technique. Once it is over,* MADAME HORTENSE *collects the music and changes the number.*)

PATRICIA. Why is the waiter hanging about with our refreshments? I'm dying of thirst. We have *some* rights!

PAMELA (*good-naturedly joining in*). He has customers to serve, so our glass of beer can wait, needless to say.

PATRICIA. Artists don't count, of course.

MADAME HORTENSE (*changing the number*). During the intermission, ladies. You know that's the usual thing. We have a right to refreshments during intermission.

PATRICIA. Yesterday they served us at midnight. Oh, he's quicker off the mark on Saturdays, he gets a tip. This week I shall give him ten centimes. What a life, among all these yokels. Some people find it quite natural, of course, to the point of taking them to bed. I was brought up differently. An officer's daughter in a clip joint!

MADAME HORTENSE (*vexed*). The Brasserie du Globe et du Portugal is a first-class establishment and you were very lucky to get in, my dear. Don't spit in your own soup.

PATRICIA. And with my gifts! Let me tell you, I've played at concerts and I've given recitals. Once, at a charity affair, Massenet, the great Massenet, was in the audience. At the end of the concert, he kissed my hand. I had been rendering an arrangement of something by Mignon. I'd really put the whole of myself into it. The Master had tears in his eyes. He was so moved, he could find nothing to say to me. Such an eloquent talker, too. . . . Obviously, you wouldn't understand.

MADAME HORTENSE. We all have our little successes. Monsieur Hortense was once first violin at the Brasserie Zurki in Saint Petersburg. I am speaking of the time before the revolution. He used to play to crowned heads. But there are always ups and downs. It didn't prevent him from doing his job conscientiously. He would say to me, "Zélie, music is like greens, it is always good for you."

PATRICIA. Giving all you have to the constipated!

MADAME HORTENSE. Constipation never prevented anyone from appreciating music. Just the contrary, I should say. We have some splendid music lovers here. Only yesterday a big Belgian industrialist came over to congratulate me. As a matter of fact, he mentioned you.

PATRICIA (*suddenly transformed*). Really? How amusing. What did he say?

MADAME HORTENSE. He asked me if you came from Ghent. It seems you remind him of someone from there. In charge of the cloakroom at the *Kursaal*.

EMMELINE (*continuing, to* LÉONA). So I said to him, "Edmond, maybe *you* don't like it, but don't put other people off!"

LÉONA. Just like that?

EMMELINE. Just like that. Short and to the point. And then I said, "I'm a woman, and you'll never stop a woman thinking and feeling like a woman." That, my dear, that little pay-off line went right home, I could see that.

LÉONA. What did he say?

EMMELINE. Nothing. He just went on brushing his teeth.

LÉONA. So what did you do?

EMMELINE. I put down my scissors—I

was cutting my toenails at the time—and went out of the bathroom.

LÉONA. Just like that?

EMMELINE. Just like that. You've got to admit he didn't get away with that! I put on my girdle and stockings. Still not a word, my dear. He was rinsing his teeth. So I put on my dress. I'd made up my mind. You know me. And I just went out and slammed the door. I was in such a rage! The first man, I assure you, the first man to be nice to me I was going to give myself to. Only there was nobody but the night watchman outside—an old Negro— and you know what Moulins is like in the morning! Not so much as a cat in sight. I walked as far as I could, just to frighten him. I went to have a look at the cathedral since everyone says it's so nice, but there was nothing to look at, and at a quarter past two I went back up. I'd had enough. I had those pink shoes on—the ones I gave you because they were too small and hurt my corns. And anyway, I'd shouted out when I left that we'd have to put an end to it once and for all, so I was afraid he might be frightened of the water and call the police.

LÉONA. Is he frightened of water, then?

EMMELINE. Don't be so stupid—there's a river running through Moulins. It's the first thing anybody thinks of in the state I was in—everyone knows that. I did go as far as the edge, too, but it was too dark, so I came back.

LÉONA. Oh, I see! He thought you were dead! So what did he say when he saw you?

EMMELINE. Nothing. He didn't see me. He'd gone out, too.

LÉONA. To fetch the police?

EMMELINE. No. To have a round with his pals at the all-night bar opposite the station.

SUZANNE D. (standing near the piano). I've put up with everything! Our secret rendezvous, our occasional meetings in that filthy little hotel where the manager talks to me as if I were a tart—me! who has always dreamed of the day when I could go around with my head high and be seen arm in arm with the man I love! But there is one thing I won't put up with, Léon—the advances of that horrible woman to the man I've chosen and given myself

to! Your poor, sick wife—that's another matter; I can understand pity even if I do find it cowardly and despise the degrading precautions you take. . . . But here, under my very nose, this exhibition of lust! Right here, in the orchestra!

PIANIST. Our relations are strictly limited to professional matters, my love.

SUZANNE D. Her finger around your collar just now—was that a professional matter? And what about when she ruffled your hair?

PIANIST. She was drawing my attention to the dandruff on the collar of my jacket. It was strictly her professional right as director of the orchestra.

SUZANNE D. (trembling). Your collar is mine, Léon, your hair is mine, even your dandruff is mine! I'm the only one who should be worrying about that little snowstorm! I'm the one who should be brushing your collar! I've given you everything —my saved-up virginity, my illusions, the good name of an irreproachable family— and then there's my religious sister, who'd die if she heard of this. Everything you are is mine now! I shall claw at her like a she-lion!

PIANIST (mildly). Lionesses bite. It's tigresses that claw—I've told you before, my love.

SUZANNE D. Right! Then I'll bite! (As MADAME HORTENSE passes near her, she suddenly shows her teeth with a lion-like roar as though she is about to take a bite at her.) Rrr-rr-rr!

MADAME HORTENSE (halting). Is something the matter?

(SUZANNE D. bursts into sobs.)

PIANIST (stammering). It's just nerves. Just nerves.

MADAME HORTENSE. Nerves or no nerves, my dear, not on the platform! We're the center of attention of the entire establishment. (To LÉON.) You! Give her a slap on the back; they'll think she was choking. We don't want a scandal in the orchestra!

PIANIST (doing so). My little lamb, my little bunny rabbit, my little stoat . . .

MADAME HORTENSE. Now, now. The Fables of La Fontaine can wait. During off hours, I don't care how you pass the time, the two of you!

SUZANNE D. (to LÉON, irritably). Stop slapping me like that. You're hurting. (To

MADAME HORTENSE, *pulling herself up*) I'm in love and I'm loved, if you want to know, madame!

MADAME HORTENSE. No, Mademoiselle Délicias. No. I do not want to know. We are in the temple of music here.

SUZANNE D. Oh no, that's too easy—trying to shut me up in the name of Art. Do you think I'm ashamed? I can hold my head up! Yes, I can hold my head up! (*She does so on the platform for a ridiculously long interval.*)

MADAME HORTENSE (*snatching the music* SUZANNE D. *is brandishing*). All I ask of you is that you don't ruin your music sheet. Don't you realize what it costs, this music? Just look at that. "Cockades and Cockcrows" all crumpled up. And it's an extremely rare piece!

SUZANNE D. (*with a contemptuous laugh*). Extremely rare—really, your taste for cheap music is deplorable, if I may say so, Madame Hortense. Extremely rare! Duverger!

MADAME HORTENSE. Arranged by Benoisseau, my dear! And he was a man who knew his job. I'm sorry I have to tell you that. I knew him at the Casino de Royan, in the good old days of the Symphony Orchestra. There was a musician for you!

SUZANNE D. I was brought up on the classics. Ah, Beethoven, Saint-Saëns . . . !

MADAME HORTENSE. In a place like this, the customer plays cards or dominoes to forget his health troubles. What he wants is a good background noise. This piece is gay, vibrant, lively. And it makes one think of France—that's always a good thing in a café.

SUZANNE D. Oh, I've sunk too low! All these humiliations will kill me! Such mediocrity—it's suffocating. I shan't sing the great aria from *La Vestale* this time. My voice is broken. I'm in no condition to sing.

MADAME HORTENSE (*severely*). The air from *La Vestale* is on the program. It's in print. A change of program always makes a bad impression. Monsieur Lebonze has absolutely forbidden it. It confuses his customers. You will sing it.

SUZANNE D. (*sits down suddenly, groaning*). No! No! This is too much. It's too much for my nerves. Help me, Léon! This woman is persecuting me!

MADAME HORTENSE. You are a small person. Monsieur Léon is a man and an artist. He will be obliged to agree with me. (*She continues on her Olympian way, distributing the music to the members of the orchestra.*)

EMMELINE. I'm saying nothing. It's not my lookout. But if anyone took it into their heads to take a tenth of the liberties with Edmond that she takes with that unfortunate boy, I should see red. Once, at the casino at Palavas, I go out for a moment during the interval. When I come back, he's not on the platform. You know where I find him?

LÉONA. No.

EMMELINE. With the lavatory attendant.

LÉONA. No!

EMMELINE. Oh, yes. A blonde creature with a horrible reputation. Can you imagine? A pee-pee girl!

LÉONA. What was he doing?

EMMELINE. He pretended afterward that he was asking her for some change, but he couldn't fool me. You know what I said to him?

LÉONA. No.

EMMELINE. Nothing. I just looked at them, like that, said, "Is there any paper?" and walked straight into the Ladies'.

LÉONA. Just like that. And what did he do?

EMMELINE. He went into the Gents', without a word. But let me tell you, he had turned quite pale. I could see he'd taken the snub.

LÉONA. You did quite right. Some people have to be put in their place.

MADAME HORTENSE (*suddenly, from the back*). Men! I've had dozens of them! Tall ones, handsome ones, well-set-up ones. Since Monsieur Hortense died, I've been taking a rest. But I just want you to know that if I needed one . . . !

SUZANNE D. May one know what would happen if you needed one, madame?

MADAME HORTENSE. I would choose a better-built one—there!

SUZANNE D. Léon is beautiful. He has a Grecian nose.

MADAME HORTENSE. Grecian nose or no Grecian nose, I couldn't care less. I believe in a chest measurement.

PIANIST. Ladies!

MADAME HORTENSE. Monsieur Hortense

was a wardrobe of a man. He crushed a woman in bed. That's love for you!

SUZANNE D. How crude you are, madame.

PIANIST. Ladies!

SUZANNE D. Keep your stevedores, your waiters, your brutes—I despise them. I vomit them! I'd die rather than let them come near me with their great fists. Léon has an Apollo's figure. Not a trace of a stomach. Show her, Léon! I will not have people say you aren't beautiful.

PIANIST (horrified). Suzanne! Not in the orchestra!

SUZANNE D. (atremble). Why not? I'm proud of our love! I want to brave everybody and their opinions—I want to brave the entire world!

MADAME HORTENSE (who has suddenly cast a terrified look at the end of the room). Suzanne Délicias, the manager is looking at us. You know he won't have gossiping in the orchestra. And our contract is renewable every two weeks. (She calls out obsequiously.) Right away, Monsieur Lebonze, right away! We're off! Are you ready, ladies? "Cockades and Cockcrows," smartly now. Very lively. Let's go, now, one, two, three, four. . . .

(The orchestra, everyone having scuttled back to position, attacks the glossy, heroic music. SUZANNE DÉLICIAS is muttering to herself meanwhile as she plays furiously on her cello.)

SUZANNE D. I shall kill myself.

PIANIST (groaning as he plays). Suzanne.

SUZANNE D. With laudanum.

PIANIST (as before, but with a different tone of voice each time). Suzanne.

(Music.)

SUZANNE D. I shall go and throw myself in the river.

PIANIST (distracted). Suzanne.

SUZANNE D. Or under a train.

PIANIST. Suzanne.

(With music still playing, SUZANNE suddenly bursts into derisive laughter.)

SUZANNE D. Not likely! That's just what she'd like. She'd have you at last! You know what I'm going to do tomorrow? I'm going to buy myself a new dress. The most expensive I can find at Petit Paris. I'll blow two weeks' pay on it and make her mad with my wasp waist—showing up her great, fat, undignified backside!

PIANIST. Suzanne!

SUZANNE D. (demands suddenly). Do you love me, Léon?

PIANIST. I adore you, my love. I shall never love anyone but you.

SUZANNE D. You're not afraid of death?

PIANIST. With you?

SUZANNE D. (beside herself). Yes!

PIANIST (with conviction). No!

SUZANNE D. So we shall die together if we are too unhappy. We'll have them all fooled.

PIANIST (lukewarm). Quite.

SUZANNE D. (gloomily, over her cello, while the music becomes more and more spirited). It's good to die!

PIANIST (halfhearted). Delicious!

(A flourish of chords as the music comes to an end. Applause here and there throughout the room. MADAME HORTENSE, delighted, acknowledges it discreetly and gestures toward the orchestra with her hand. MADAME HORTENSE goes around collecting the music.)

MADAME HORTENSE. You heard the way they applauded. So "Cockades and Cockcrows" arranged by Benoisseau is still cheap music, mm? What a reaction, my dears, what a reaction! Did you see that? That piece really penetrates the vitals! The Frenchman knows that it was written for him. (She throws this remark at SUZANNE.) You have to have turnip juice in your veins and no love for your country not to feel what that music has to give!

SUZANNE D. My answer to that is utter contempt!

MADAME HORTENSE. Now I have patriotism in my blood! During the war at the height of unemployment, I refused a season at Vichy. And I know some who wouldn't have had any scruples. Even played for the enemy!

SUZANNE D. Your insinuations leave me cold as marble. It is true that I played in a Paris brasserie in '40, but it was a resistance orchestra. Whenever there were German officers in the place, the word went around to play out of tune. That needed some courage! We could have been denounced—those people were all musicians!

MADAME HORTENSE (laughing unpleasantly). Knowing you, I should think playing out of tune came all too easily!

SUZANNE D. (*pulling herself up, pale*). Oh, this is too much! If you're going to insult my art, if nothing's to be sacred here, I'm leaving. . . .

(*She gets up and leaves the platform. The* PIANIST, *deathly pale, runs and catches her as she goes out.*)

PATRICIA (*to* PAMELA). There, you see! She's going too far, attacking her that way. Maybe she didn't play at Vichy, but she played over the radio.

PIANIST (*at floor level with* SUZANNE, *whom he is trying to deter*). This argument is ridiculous, like all arguments. Nobody's questioning your talent, Suzanne!

SUZANNE D. (*with a bitter laugh*). To hell with my talent! It's always possible I didn't even have that! And I thought I was making such a gift of myself! It's too funny. Don't you find it funny? So I've given nothing to Art, or to my country, or to you.

PIANIST (*wearily*). No, you haven't. . . . I mean, yes, you have! Now, please, Suzanne, don't let's have a scandal!

SUZANNE D. I'm beyond scandal now. I've been putting up with it for a long time, Léon. I've given myself to you in degrading conditions in furnished hotels! (*Shouting madly*) *Furnished* hotels!

PIANIST (*stammering pitifully*). Quiet, now, Suzanne, quiet. Hotels are always furnished . . . in Europe at least . . . and, anyway, when we were traveling . . .

SUZANNE D. (*with a prolonged nervous laugh*). Oh, yes, when we were traveling. Never got very far though, did we? The other side of the town—on foot! We were the sort of travelers who really didn't need luggage! I've suffered enough. Oh, the way the manager would look at me when we asked for our room, the look he gave me—sharing me with you in advance.

PIANIST. You exaggerate, Suzanne. He's a respectable married man. . . .

SUZANNE D. (*contemptuously*). That makes two of you—respectable married men—sharing me on my so very short travels. We made love with an eye on the time, Léon, so that your so dear and so pathetic invalid wife shouldn't go mad with your everlasting late home-comings. What about me—wasn't I as pathetic and ill as she was?

PIANIST. It wasn't the same thing, Suzanne!

SUZANNE D. (*with rising excitement*). Maybe we were traveling without baggage, but we did have watches. One each, on the bedside tables. Some lovers lie and play at listening to each other's hearts, to see if they beat in time. But we spent our time in bed checking whether we had the right time by our watches. Oh, that watch, that watch, I hate it. (*She throws it on the floor and stamps on it.*) I'm throwing it out; I'm stamping on it! Give me yours! (*She tries to snatch his watch.*)

PIANIST (*a pathetic figure, defending his own watch as he picks up the other*). My love, the whole place can see us! . . . The glass isn't broken, fortunately. . . . You're exaggerating, Suzanne. Everyone watches out for the time these days. Modern life is lived with an eye on the clock. . . .

SUZANNE D. Oh, yes, I've lived modern life all right. I've been a free woman, liberated from prejudice as they say. But they're in chains all the same, these free women. All tied up in watch chains! I've been a free woman weighed down with watch chains. Isn't that amusing?

PIANIST. I told you at the start that I couldn't risk killing my poor sick wife. And you told me our love would be so great!

SUZANNE D. (*still ridiculous, but with a sort of sincere misery*). Well, it wasn't—it wasn't big enough! It was murdered, murdered with the hands of a watch. It got drowned in the lavatory bowl along with the children I could have had. Ten times I suggested we should kill ourselves, Léon. Dying together would have been clean! To drown the lot, once and for all: father, mother, and children, instead of just the children. That would have been simple!

PIANIST (*stammering*). It only seemed simple, my love. . . . I had no right to leave her, either. . . .

SUZANNE D. (*shouting*). But me, you had the right to leave me at the end of my daily three quarters of an hour. I was a ridiculous old maid and I'd waited all that time just to be a woman three quarters of an hour a day! To the minute. Timed on two watches, if you please!

PIANIST (*correcting her idiotically*). An hour! An hour and a half! I'd told my wife I had to be on here a good hour later

—you know that!

SUZANNE D. (*also idiotic, but somehow touching as well*). Yes, but there was all that walking! And I only had the right to be your wife on the other side of the town. Someone might have seen us otherwise. We had to be good and just walk side by side—as though we didn't know each other!

PIANIST (*trying to be romantic*). What did it matter, so long as we loved each other! Does the time count?

SUZANNE D. (*serious*). Yes, I've finally decided that it counts terribly. And that that's just what life is made of. (*Stating*) I've wasted my time. Funny expression, isn't it? Wasted my time. No good praying to Saint Anthony to give it back to me. (*She suddenly bursts out.*) What time do you make it, Léon? Do we both make it the same? My watch says a quarter to eleven.

PIANIST (*mechanically consulting his*). Mine says quarter to twelve. We should be playing, Suzanne. Get up on the platform. We'll talk about it during the intermission —my love. We'll have a long quarter of an hour to ourselves.

SUZANNE D. (*haughtily*). Thanks. I've already finished here.

MADAME HORTENSE (*who has come down off the platform, in a low voice*). Now, have we finished with this scene? The manager's looking at us. Do you want to have us all thrown out? That's what you're trying to do, isn't it, you little sourpuss?

SUZANNE D. (*dignified*). No, madame. So far as I am concerned, I'm out already. I refuse once and for all to play out of tune. Good-by, madame. I leave him to you. But you were right—he's a runt. (*She turns haughtily.*) I hope you have a good watch at least? (*She bursts into a long, nervous laugh, and exits.*)

MADAME HORTENSE (*calls after her*). You'll get five hundred francs' fine, my girl. And I warn you, you'll be replaced on Saturday!

PIANIST (*who has gone back onto the platform, head lowered*). She's suffering, Madame Hortense. You are abusing your power. (*He groans as he sits down at his pathetic piano.*) You should be ashamed.

MADAME HORTENSE. It's you who should

be ashamed, Monsieur Léon, with your poor, sick wife. That hysterical creature will end up telling her everything to relieve her own feelings.

PIANIST (*desperate*). It's too much—too much!

MADAME HORTENSE. I know men, Monsieur Léon. I've managed other men besides you. A man has need of contentment, it's only human. No one will reproach you for that, in your situation. But entrust yourself to a proper woman, who knows what life is and who will have something to give. I was lying just now. I don't find you skinny at all. A little slender, perhaps, but for someone motherly, like me, that's just one of your charms. . . . (*She passes a finger around his collar again.*) Oh! How warm he is, how warm he is, the wicked man. And he doesn't like being petted. He does so need someone to look after him.

PIANIST (*weeping, his head in her arms*). These scenes destroy my nerves. I'm an artist. I'm not made for real life.

MADAME HORTENSE. We'll help you, we'll help you, my dear. I understand you so well. Why the need for scenes over every little thing? A little discreet pleasure— shouldn't that be enough to make for happiness? You're swimming. Change your collar, my poppet.

PIANIST (*broken but heroic*). After the March from *Tannhäuser*. No point in doing it before. (*Snivels*) You mustn't think I don't still love my wife. Twelve years— you can't forget that so easily. I could have put her in a home. She's incurable. Who would have blamed me? I've kept her at home, in spite of her insane jealousy. I've taken a housekeeper, a woman I can rely on. But all that costs money. Sometimes I feel so alone.

MADAME HORTENSE. You should have someone to help you instead of torturing you even more. That's all there is to it. Someone sensitive, like yourself.

PIANIST (*groaning*). I'm a harp. It takes nothing to break me.

MADAME HORTENSE. You are an artist. And artists don't need emotions outside their art. A little pleasure, yes. That's all. The rest goes into music. Haven't you noticed that that mad creature was the only one who caused us any trouble in the orchestra?

PIANIST. She's a harp too!

MADAME HORTENSE. Yes, but a broken-down harp. Leaving the orchestra like that, just for a whim! Just when we ought to be striking up "Cuban Delights." . . . Léona, be a good girl and go and see what she's doing, the little lunatic. She's probably sniveling away in the toilets! (LÉONA *gets up and goes.*) Sentiment is all very fine, but we have a job to do. We're in danger of losing our engagement as well. The manager's on the prowl. I don't know what's the matter with him this evening, he's so suspicious. (*She begins to busy herself with the parts.*)

PATRICIA (*pursuing a sudden friendly conversation with* PAMELA). All the same, she was absolutely horrible to her. First of all, people should stop talking about the war. I resisted, like anyone else. I listened to London radio every day. I did what I could. But I had my poor old mother. I had to see she had some comforts.

PAMELA. Does your old girl still live with you?

PATRICIA (*with a sour little laugh*). Sure. Poor Toots. That's what I call her. She's my baby now. I've decided to devote my life entirely to her. To her and my art. There's nothing else I can do with such a small place.

PAMELA. You know, I just couldn't do it. When I go to see mine at Batignolles—she's not badly off, she's a concierge—it's all right for a while: "Hullo, Maman . . . How are you, Maman? . . . I'm all right, Maman." Makes me feel I was a kid again. There'll be Irish stew waiting for me—it's her favorite vice, Irish stew. But by the third mouthful, without fail, we start bawling each other out. The plates start jumping around the table and off I go again home.

PATRICIA (*smiling slightly*). You mustn't think we don't have our little skirmishes, too, poor Toots and me. As she gets older, she gets more and more like a little girl. Whims and fancies at every turn. Oh, but I'm very severe with her! When she goes to steal a sweet, the rascal, smack! A good rap on the knuckles for her. "Ooh! Ooh!" she snivels, but after that, she's good. It's obviously boredom that accounts for all these little yearnings. And then again I've tried to train her to "ask," but it's no good; the wicked old thing always dirties herself.

PAMELA. It's just a bad phase. It'll probably adjust itself in time.

PATRICIA. She's getting on for eighty, so I don't hold out much hope any more. But there again I've decided to be absolutely inflexible. I change her three times a day, and if she forgets herself meanwhile, so much the worse for her. I often think she does it out of spite, you know. Sometimes, when I'm all rigged out ready to leave for work, she'll call out "caca" and start whimpering. My goodness—that's just too bad! I leave her until midnight to lie in her own mess. That teaches her.

PAMELA. You have to be firm with them. My girl, when I had her with me——

PATRICIA (*cutting in*). And you know what she's been trying ever since last winter? She's started sucking her thumb!

PAMELA. My mother used to smear mustard on mine, but I don't know what you'd do with old people.

PATRICIA. Mustard? She'd be only too happy! She adores mustard. She adores anything that's bad for her. Oh, if I were to let her eat what she wants! Any time I find her at it, she gets a jolly good rap. And no pudding. That's where it hurts most. Oh, the puddings and the sweets she'd have if I let her—all my pills would disappear, even! But I'm very firm about that. No sweets or sugary things in the house. If a visitor brings any, I hide them, and she can have one a week, on Sundays, if she's been good. You should hear her blubbering at the cupboard when I take them away from her. "Sweetie! Sweetie!" Just like a baby.

PAMELA. It's for their own good. They'd only get toothache.

PATRICIA (*with the same sour little smile*). Poor Toots! She hasn't got any teeth any more. But it's the principle of the thing, you see. Once you start giving way to them . . .

PAMELA. It can't be much fun having that sort of thing every day.

PATRICIA (*gravely*). There's a great satisfaction in knowing one is doing one's duty. *Maman* is everything to me, apart from my art. And I make the sacrifice cheerfully. Believe me, and I think I can say this without boasting, I am a model daughter. It's just that she must be straight with me.

PAMELA. I sent my daughter away to the country. What with my work and being separated from my husband, I just couldn't. And then, you know, I'm a real woman, I need men. And men can never get used to the child. And even if one did come along by chance who got used to her, you know how it is, sooner or later he'd change. Anyway, all I have goes for her clothes. I want her to be a real coquette, my Mouquette, a real little woman, I want her to be. On her fifth birthday I gave her a really sophisticated dress. Silk, you know, with the hooped petticoat and the ribbons . . . twelve thousand francs it cost me. You can see I'm not stingy over her. And I sent her some money for a perm and some nail varnish and lipstick. She looked so sweet! You should have seen her with her little nails all painted and her lips made up and everything. What a love! Me all over, she looked, my dear. That's what I adore about her. She's the absolute image of me. It was too bad I couldn't stay. I had a tiff with Fernand. He wouldn't get out of the car and kept sounding the horn continuously out in the street. And there she was calling out, *"Maman, Maman,* you haven't even given me a proper kiss." (*She sighs.*) It would be nice to see more of them! But what can you do? Life's like that. Anyway, she had her party frock. She'll remember that, later on.

PATRICIA. When you're an artist, you have heart. My friends keep telling me I should put her in a home, where she'd have all the attention she needs, poor Toots. True, she'd be better off than at home, where she's nearly always alone on account of my work. But I really couldn't. . . . I'd rather correct her firmly when she's naughty and know I've done my duty. She's my mother. My friends say, "You're a saint, Patricia," but I always say, "You never recover your losses!" The only thing I ask of her is that she's grateful. Otherwise, a good smack and no pudding.

PAMELA. But, you know, if you do recover them, you don't do so well! I could have stayed with her father and kept her. He found me with Georges, but he thought it was the first time. These things happen in any family and it gets forgotten, especially if there's a child. But Georges said he was leaving for Nice, and at the beginning I thought I couldn't do without the man. I was crazy about him. So I left the child. Mind you, two months later we parted, but how was I to know? That's life!

PATRICIA. Maybe your husband would have taken you back?

PAMELA. I thought about that, mostly because of the child. The divorce wasn't through and with that man I had only to appear and everything would have been settled in bed. So I packed my things and went back. But I met someone in the train —I was in funds at the time and had treated myself to first class—we were alone in the compartment. You know how it is! Ah! Night trains, my dear, they should be forbidden. (*She sighs.*) And to think I'd bought her the dearest little regional costume from Nice, with the matching hat and skirt—well, anyway, I had to send it to her. . . . She must have been thrilled with it, my little Mouquette. Apparently her friends at school were sick with envy. The kid told me in a letter that the other girls had said, "You're in luck, having a mother like that." Imagine—I'd brought her the prettiest model, with the apron in real silk. There's nothing I wouldn't do for my kid!

LÉONA (*returning*). I've looked everywhere; she's not in the toilets. There's one that's engaged, but I didn't dare bang on the door. I was afraid it might be a client.

MADAME HORTENSE. Bitch! Never mind! Let's tackle "Cuban Delights" just the same. Monsieur Lebonze has just looked at his watch. He must be thinking we're taking our time. Emmeline, be so kind as to leave your instrument and take the cello part. He may not notice the gap so much that way.

EMMELINE. What does he know about music?

MADAME HORTENSE. Nothing, but he can count. And there are only six of us now. We'll tell him she had food poisoning. It happened last week to a customer who ate the wrong sort of mushroom.

EMMELINE (*whom* LÉONA *is helping to the other seat while* MADAME HORTENSE *is distributing the parts*). She's suffering, that girl. I can understand it only too well —love's a killer. Once I told Edmond, right to his face, "Edmond," I said, "sentiment forgives nothing. If I find you with another woman, I shall shut my eyes and pull the trigger. A woman who has suffered what I've suffered—there are laws in this country—I'll get off."

PIANIST. So what did he say?

EMMELINE. Nothing. But he was yawning at the time. So he stopped and picked up the paper.

LÉONA. Just like that.

EMMELINE. Just like that. I could see it had gone home.

MADAME HORTENSE. Now, off we go. I want this very warm—very sensual.

(She has tapped discreetly on her music stand with her bow. She gives them one bar before starting and the orchestra then launches into "Cuban Delights," a syncopated piece heavy with sensuality. They have put on appropriate headgear and are throwing themselves heart and soul into their playing. LÉONA has left her flute for an exotic instrument. The piece has a refrain which everyone sings quietly as they play. It is a tradition. It suddenly makes itself heard during the muted passage at the second reprise.)

ORCHESTRA (singing). Delights, delights, Cuban delights! In Cuba, in Cuba! Delights, delights in Cuba!

(Music)

PAMELA (hollowly, to PATRICIA). This tune makes me feel quite peculiar. It's silly it should be so evocative!

PATRICIA (sourly, as she plays). Cheap music.

PAMELA. Yes, but it reminds you of love. You wouldn't understand, my dear. But when you have men in your blood, the way I have . . . Take Georges, for example. Oh! How I missed that man. He beat me and he was stupid, so stupid . . . a real moron. But in bed . . . After all, what is there to say to each other during the day, anyway? Have you really never made love, not even once?

PATRICIA. There are questions one woman should never even ask another. I told you I've given everything to my art, and to poor Toots!

(Music)

ORCHESTRA. Delights, delights . . . Cu-

ban delights! . . . (Et cetera)

MADAME HORTENSE (in a hollow whisper to the PIANIST). For one thing the girl is a skinny creature anyway. You need flesh for love-making. For small men like you, Monsieur Léon, the woman has to take care of you, wrap you around; men like you have to be kept warm, they must be able to bury themselves in the woman, hide themselves in her!

PIANIST (groaning suddenly). Oh, Mother, Mother! Maman was the only one who loved me!

MADAME HORTENSE. I'll be your maman, my chicken! You shall bury yourself in my bosom. Skinny women only think of themselves. They have nothing to give.

PIANIST. Oh, Maman!

ORCHESTRA. Delights, delights, Cuban delights! . . . (Et cetera)

PATRICIA (mournfully). Don't think I don't suffer! Sometimes when I'm undressing I look at myself in the glass. I'm beautiful! Really beautiful! My figure is nice and round and my legs are smooth, but I just can't!

PAMELA. It's not so difficult!

(Music)

ORCHESTRA. Delights, delights . . .

EMMELINE (to LÉONA). But, you know, Edmond's a real boor. I've never, but never, known such a pig. Never a kind word. Nothing. Dumb and clumsy as a carp!

LÉONA. A bull!

EMMELINE. But he's part of me. When that part's taken away, I'm not complete any more and there's nothing for it but to wait until he wants to come back—to finish me off, if you understand what I mean?

LÉONA. It's quite clear. It's no longer his; it's yours.

EMMELINE. That's why he'll get those six bullets in his head if he ever gets the idea of taking himself off with anyone! Bang, bang, bang, bang, bang, bang!

LÉONA. Just like that.

EMMELINE. That's love.

(Music)

ORCHESTRA. Delights, delights, Cuban delights! . . . (Et cetera)

(The piece comes to an end. Increasing applause. The PIANIST, still wearing his Mexican hat, suddenly turns on the piano *like a hunted animal and shouts:*)

PIANIST. I do not give a damn! My wife weeping away all the time in that armchair . . . and the other one as well with her tears and her emotions! Damn them both! (*He shouts wildly.*) Damn them! It's torture crying with both of them, suffering twice over! Once in the hotel room without any clothes and again at home fully dressed. I'm getting thin, losing weight, pining away; I've got acid stomach with it all, but deep down inside me I've got to admit that I don't give a damn! Sometimes I slip away all by myself and go down to the river where they've got that bathing place and I look at them, all those women in bikinis offering themselves to the sun. I look sort of preoccupied and you'd probably think I was just going for a walk, or looking for someone, but it's not true. I'm not looking for anyone. *I'm* the sun. I'm taking them —I'm taking the lot of them, one after the other! Slowly, thoroughly! And what's more, I ring the changes. Brunettes, blondes, redheads, coloreds, thin, fat, the lot! Just as the mood takes me! Young ones, that haven't got around to it yet, and matrons with rather riper pleasures to offer. And there they all are—spread out, bottoms up—you'd never think they were the same you can see so respectably sipping afternoon tea in the patisserie. There they are, offering everything to you with the best will in the world, their beauties and their secrets, offering you every inch of themselves, so as not to miss a single ray of sunshine. The magazines have told them it has to be nicely done all over! (*Shouting with unpleasant laughter:*) Done! Done! Done! On the spit! On the spit! With me as chef! I'm Nero! Tiberius! Farouk! All of them, all of them mine! One after the other—sometimes several at a time! Some of them I'm nice to, stroking them gently and putting some feeling into it. But there are others I take the whip to, and some I have killed off afterward! (*He is quite out of breath and exhausted, but he adds, lyrically:*) With tarts you knew you could have it, but you had to approach them and anyway it's expensive, and there was always the danger of disease, but these "nice" women's rumps, these really luscious ones—who'd

have thought we'd have the lot of them one day—all of them, for nothing! (*Yelling like a mad thing:*) Three cheers for the bathing stations! (*Adding sharply, cutting it short:*) An enormous Lido and everybody stark naked! Everybody! By law! On pain of death!

MADAME HORTENSE (*terrified*). Monsieur Léon, my poor lamb. You mustn't excite yourself so on duty. Come now, pull yourself together. There's the manager staring at us!

(*There is suddenly the noise of a pistol shot in the distance. The musicians look up uneasily. There is a flurry, which is quickly stifled.* MONSIEUR LEBONZE, *the manager, enters majestically, napkin in hand. A* WAITER *runs across the stage.*)

MONSIEUR LEBONZE. Who in God's name sent me such an orchestra! Is this what you think you're paid for, you litter of pigs? To go and commit suicide in the firm's toilets? And when we're busy, too. Just to put the customer off, I suppose! I'm sick of your scenes. I shall engage another orchestra tomorrow! Now, get going! Play! Play! Bunch of boneheads . . . Faster! Faster than that! And make it loud—and lively! We don't want the customers suspecting anything!

MADAME HORTENSE. Is she dead?

MONSIEUR LEBONZE. How do I know? They're just forcing the door. The doctor's coming. Let's have some music now! God in heaven! Music, immediately! We've told the customers at the other end that the percolator's exploded.

(*He goes off again in the direction of the toilets.* MADAME HORTENSE *rushes madly around changing the parts. The musicians get hopelessly involved, colliding with each other and knocking over music stands.*)

MADAME HORTENSE. Hurry, girls, hurry! We'll have to skip the aria from *La Vestale.* Number seven. We'll have to change the number. Let's take the "Little Marquis Gavotte." The fool! I said she'd bring us bad luck. What rhyme or reason does it make to kill yourself, except to annoy others? Hats on, everyone! Make it lively! (*The orchestra, distraught, hurl themselves to their seats. They have all put on ridiculous little Louis XV hats made of cardboard.*) Ready! One and two and three and . . . *Grazioso!*

(*They attack the genre piece, which is light and gay, playing it with spirit and making little simpering grimaces under the stern eye of the manager, who has by* this time returned. The WAITER comes running back, followed by the DOCTOR. The orchestra continues playing with many airs and graces.)

THE NEW HOUSE

A Play in Two Parts

Brendan Behan

JIM HANNIGAN
CHRIS, *his wife*
NOEL, *his son*
EILEEN, *his daughter*
SEAMUS, *his younger son, a schoolboy*
MRS. CARMODY, *an elderly neighbor*
MRS. HANRATTY
THE BARMAN
THE OLD MAN IN THE PUB

THE BUS CONDUCTOR
THE LADY IN THE SHOP
GABBLE GIBBON, *a neighbor*
A NEWSBOY
A POLICE GUARD
FINNEGAN, *a Civic Guard*
HEGARTY, *a Civic Guard*
CUSTOMERS IN THE PUB

SOME ARE BORN and die rebels, and so it was with Brendan Behan (1923–1964), the irrepressible native of Dublin whose brief candle burned at the middle as well as at both ends. Possessed and propelled by relentless vigor and rare ebullience, the Irish dramatist, author, poet, and raconteur charged through life and letters with equal passion and spirit. There was nothing moderate about Behan, and to quote a colleague: "His death in Dublin in 1964 has left an empty seat forever at the feast."

On the strength of his two full-length plays, *The Hostage* (1958) and *The Quare Fellow* (1956), it appeared for a time that Behan would fill the mantle left vacant by Sean O'Casey, but Fate decreed otherwise. Yet, his comparatively small legacy of dramatic and literary works offers permanent testimony that Brendan Behan was indeed a rare fellow of erratic but towering talent.

Behan's rebellious spirit was kindled early in life, and never wavered throughout his forty-one years, eight of which were spent in prison for "terrorist" activities on behalf of the Irish Republican Army. His early and often turbulent personal experiences are at the core of most of his writings, perceptibly in the autobiographical *Borstal Boy* and in his plays; though formless and undisciplined, they nonetheless ring strikingly with human truths.

The New House, published here as a unified play for the first time, is a rare "find" in the canon of modern dramatic literature, for it represents Behan's initial play to be produced professionally. There is added significance in its early autobiographical gleanings, for the play's factual roots are in the Behan family's move from a tenement in Dublin's Russell Street to a new housing development in Crumlin.

The play's journey from author's pen to these pages is as colorful and deviant, perhaps, as its creator's own passage through life. In the words of Radio Eireann's Micheál Ó hAodha, the man of whom it may be said ignited the fuse: "Knowing Brendan's gift for salty Dublin dialogue, I suggested to him that he should try his hand at a serial play for radio, based on the lives of the Dublin characters among whom he grew up in Russell Street. At this time, he had already written a few short stories, some poems, as well as some autobiographical excerpts, later incorporated in *Borstal Boy*. The result was two radio sketches, *Moving Out* and *The Garden Party,* both broadcast in 1952. Whatever their merit, this series of two must constitute the shortest radio serial on record. For even between scripts, Brendan was liable to disappear for weeks on end, for a sojourn in Paris, Connemara or Dunquin. . . ."

These two episodes later were staged by Alan Simpson at the Gate Theatre under the general title of *The New House*. In spite of their considerable success, they remained unknown outside Dublin until an enterprising scholar of Irish drama and literature, Robert Hogan, rediscovered them. In 1967, Mr. Hogan issued the two playlets in paperback edition under the imprint of his newly established Proscenium Press and, with an enthusiasm worthy of Behan himself, promptly brought them to the attention of this editor.

With the generous cooperation of the author's widow, Beatrice Behan, and, of course, Mr. Hogan, the erstwhile complemental radio sketches have been combined for this collection as "a short play in two parts."

Categorically, *The New House* represents the author at his earliest as a playwright, yet through it flow the same rich characterizations, colorfully demotic speech, and hearty exuberance that later was to be identified with Brendan Behan.

PART ONE

Moving Out

Scene One

*It is breakfast time in the Dublin tene-
ment flat of the Hannigan family. Chris,
the mother, is preparing the meal.*

CHRIS. Call that fellow, Jim, as you come
out.

JIM (*from another room*). Hey, Noel,
it's gone half-seven. Come on, get up, or
are you going to work at all today?

NOEL (*drowsily, offstage*). Right, Da, all
right.

JIM (*appearing at the kitchen door*). It's
not all right. You were lively enough last
night, going off to your hop.

CHRIS. Bedad, and it would be the bad
accident would keep you from a hop in
your day, Jim.

JIM. It didn't keep me out of my bed
till three in the morning.

CHRIS (*putting his breakfast on the
table*). Your breakfast is ready. Sit over.

JIM (*coming to the table*). Are you not
sitting down yourself?

CHRIS. In a minute. This fellow's fallen
off again. I'll go in and give him a shake.

JIM. Let him lie there if he wants to.

CHRIS. It's not you that would have to
be figuring out the loss of his day if I
did. (*She goes out.*) Noel, sit up, son.

NOEL (*drowsily, offstage*). All right, Ma,
all right.

JIM (*shouting in*). It's not all right!
You've the heart persecuted out of your
mother. Every morning it's the same.

CHRIS (*coming back to the doorway*).
Go on, you, Jim, with your breakfast.
Noel, let me see you sitting up. And don't
wake the other fellow. He can lie on another minute. It'll be hard enough to get
him out to school then. (*She comes into
the room.*)

SEAMUS (*appearing in the door and
moaning sleepily*). He did wake me, Ma.
There, he stuck his elbow in my ribs. (*He
goes off.*)

CHRIS (*sitting at the table*). Pour us out
a sup of tea, Jim. I declare to heaven,
you'd be worth nothing in this house after

getting you all out. Between cutting
lunches and everything. Sugar, Jim.

JIM. Amn't I fed up telling you to have
the lunches cut the night before.

CHRIS. Aye. Is it for them to go stale
and you to throw them away at one
o'clock? It's hard enough on men and
boys, out all day on building jobs with
the winter blowing through a half-built
house without giving them stale bread
with their sup of tea.

(NOEL *comes in.*)

NOEL. What class of a morning is it out?

JIM. You should know. You saw the
first of it.

NOEL. I was only asking to see if I'd use
the bike.

CHRIS. Sit over to your bit, Noel, and
don't mind him. He was the quare old
night-hawk himself in his day.

(NOEL *sits at the table.*)

JIM (*laughing*). Bedad and if them new
houses had have been the go when we
were courting, you could have walked
home to Ballyfermot on your own.

NOEL (*sullen*). Well, it wasn't Ballyfermot, if you want to know.

JIM. Well, Cabra West or wherever she
hangs out.

EILEEN (*entering and coming to the
table*). Better than these dirty holes anyway.

JIM. The dead arose and appeared to
many.

EILEEN. That egg is very hard-fried,
Mammy.

NOEL. Why didn't you get up when it
was first cooked?

EILEEN. You mind your own interfer-
ence, Mr. Bold-face. You're not so handy
at getting up yourself. (*To Chris*) But
they definitely are very bad for the diges-
tion, Mammy. Hard-fried.

CHRIS. And hard got. At seven-pence
each.

JIM. The cost of living. Are we to have
that old record again? Is there anything
any good on the other side of it? You
can't eat a bite these times but you nearly
hear it being counted as it goes into your
craw. "A penny, tuppence, another bit of
bread and sausage. That's a ha-penny."

NOEL. And go easy on the salt.

EILEEN. It doesn't seem to affect your
appetite anyway.

CHRIS. Don't mind them, Eileen. I'd like to give them the running of this place for awhile. They'd be above in Ridleys before the week was out.

NOEL. "And that, dearly beloved, finishes the sermon for this morning." Mother, hurry up with my lunch. I'm going out to that new job today on the boundary.

JIM. On the boundary? Sure, if you were any further out, you'd be in the Province of Connaught.

NOEL. It's all equal to me. I'm getting an hour's travelling time to it.

JIM. It's country money you should be getting to that place. It's all equal to you certainly. But what about the unfortunate people has to live in them? They'll be getting no travelling time when they have to come in and out.

NOEL. That's no skin off my nose. The city has to grow in some direction. It can't grow into the sea, can it? The Corporation has to put the people somewhere. We're not all going to spend our lives in slums the like of this.

EILEEN. For once in a way *you* said something sensible. Dirty filthy holes. Without proper light or anything. I wish *we* had a new house. I wouldn't care if it was on the top of Old Smoky.

NOEL. We'd get a bit of air, anyway, not like here. With a laundry throwing out smoke all day and the brewery taking over to gas us in our sleep. It's a wonder we're not all choked to death years ago.

JIM. It's a wonder, isn't it? Well, let me tell you, son, that better men nor you'll ever be came out of this ould street.

EILEEN. A pity *you* wouldn't turn the record, Da. You might get Elvis Presley on the other side.

JIM. You're all terrible smart. Yourself and your Mickey Dazzler of a brother here. I'm not in love with these houses, if you want to know, though there was good men reared in them, but I want to stay somewhere near to where I was born and reared and not shoved out to Siberia.

EILEEN. You'd have some way of keeping yourself decent with a bath and everything.

JIM. I don't care if they were giving television sets with them. I'm not going out to the Bog of Allen for a bath. Not if they filled it with asses' milk, like Pharaoh's daughter.

NOEL. Maybe if they filled it with porter it might tempt you.

JIM. You're terribly witty this morning. Are you taking anything for it?

(*A factory siren sounds.*)

CHRIS. There's the quarter to eight from the brewery.

JIM. Off in a minute, Chris. I was only telling this one—

EILEEN. Which one? There was three and sixpence paid for Miss Eileen Hannigan's name.

JIM. Well, there's always one way of getting out of here. Be changing it. If you can get anyone thicker than yourself to take you. And there was never such a shortage of thicks in this town. You and him can go and live on top of the Three Rock mountain for all I care. And the same goes for Head-the-Ball here. If he doesn't like this quarter, he can always go up to West Cabra with the mot.

NOEL. You're miles out. She doesn't live next or near it.

JIM. Well, wherever it is. You're out of your time now, or very near. And if you get spliced, maybe her ould wan would take you in. Give you the sumptuous front parlour. But as long as your mother and I are over the sod, we'd sooner be near what we're used to. Amn't I right, Chris?

CHRIS (*caustically*). Were you ever anything else but right, Jim?

JIM. You're quare and sharp this morning and all. Mind you don't cut yourself. I was right when I got you. But not in the head.

CHRIS. That old clock is right, and it says a minute to eight by it. It's all right for these, they have their bicycles.

(*From outside the hall door comes the old, quavering, and rather snuffy voice of* MRS. CARMODY.)

MRS. CARMODY. Mrs. Hannigan, ma'am, are you in or up, me jewel and darlin'?

JIM. Aw, good-night, Joe Doyle. I see that ould wan is on for an early start.

NOEL (*getting up*). Out of old Carmody's way.

MRS. CARMODY. Mrs. Hannigan, ma'am.

NOEL (*imitating* MRS. CARMODY's *voice*). Mrs. Hannigan, ma'am, would you ever have the lend of a loan of a small turn-over? The baker died on Tuesday.

EILEEN. Don't be jeering. We'll all live to be old if we can.

NOEL (*opening the hall door*). I'm off.

MRS. CARMODY (*appearing in the door*). Mrs. Hannigan, me jewel, is all your mankind gone out yet?

CHRIS. Come in, ma'am. They're just off.

EILEEN (*getting up hastily from the table and going for her coat*). Bye, Mammy. God bless.

JIM (*getting up also*). So long, Chris. I'll be in early.

CHRIS. God go with yous. I suppose you will, Jim, barring you meet an angel.

MRS. CARMODY. Good morning to you, Mr. Hannigan.

JIM (*brushing past her and going out*). Good morning, ma'am.

MRS. CARMODY. Good morning, Eileen.

EILEEN. Good morning, Mrs. Carmody. (*She goes out.*)

MRS. CARMODY. Morning, Noel.

NOEL. And good luck, Mrs. Carmody, ma'am, would you ever buy the ticket of an ass?

MRS. CARMODY. What's that, avic?

CHRIS. Go off to your work, you. Don't heed him, ma'am.

MRS. CARMODY. There's a letter for you, ma'am.

NOEL. Show us, maybe I'm after getting my double up. "Mr. J. Hannigan." It's for my da. I'll bring it to him at the bus stop. I'll catch him on the bike. It's from—

CHRIS (*opening the letter*). It's from the Corporation. I know what it is. You're not to go to work today.

NOEL. I have to. The job is only starting, and I've the key to the hut.

CHRIS. They'll have to break the lock then. I want you here. And I want Eileen. Go after her quick. She waits at the bottom of the street for some of the girls out of the buildings. Hurry down after her.

NOEL. But—but—what's up, Mother?

CHRIS. The sky is up. I'll tell you when you come back. Hurry up now, and get Eileen!

NOEL. All right, then, but I wish I knew what you're up to.

CHRIS. You'll know soon enough. And if you see your father tell him nothing. He'll know soon enough, too.

The lights come up on the same scene a few minutes later.

———

MRS. CARMODY. Says I, says I, it's a while now since we had a pig's cheek and himself was always partial to a bit, especially the ear, but there's pig's cheeks and pig's cheeks in it. The one old Daly handed me was the most ugly looking object you ever put an eye to. It was after being shoved up again the side of a barrel by all the other cheeks and was all twisted. A class of cock-eyed, ma'am, if you follow my meaning. "God bless us and save us," says I in my own mind, "if I put that up to him with the bit of cabbage, and that twisty look in his eye, when he goes to put a knife in it, he'll throw me out." So I says to old Daly, says I, "God bless us and save us, Mr. Daly," says I, "but that's a very peculiar looking pig's cheek." And says he, "What do you want for two shillings," says he, "Mee-hawl Mac Lillimore?" The impudent ould dog. Says he, "Hold on a minute, and I'll see if I can get you one that died with a smile."

CHRIS. Whist! Someone coming up. This'll be Noel and Eileen.

NOEL (*outside on the stairs*). The ould wan, still gabbling away.

EILEEN. Ah, God help her, she likes going in to Mammy for the bit of company. (NOEL *and* EILEEN *come in.*)

NOEL. Here we are, Mother.

EILEEN. What is it, Mammy? You're not sick or anything?

MRS. CARMODY. I'll be off, ma'am.

NOEL. Goodbye again, Mrs. Carmody. Don't take any bad money.

MRS. CARMODY. That's right, son. Good morning all.

NOEL. And good luck.

(MRS. CARMODY *goes out.*)

CHRIS. That letter this morning.

EILEEN. The arrears on my bike.

NOEL. Shaybo is being summonsed.

SEAMUS (*from the next room*). Oh, is he now? I won't get up at all, so I won't.

CHRIS. Get up this minute, Seamus.

NOEL. Get up at once when you're told.

EILEEN. You leave him alone. Get up, Shaybo, and be a good boy.

SEAMUS (*coming to the door*). I won't

be a good boy. I'll be a very bad one. What's the good of people being good boys and other people round saying they's summonsed.

CHRIS. You're not being summonsed.

SEAMUS. Well, anyway I've a desperate pain, and I'm too sick to get up.

CHRIS. Don't mind them, Seamus, and you can forget about your pain. You're not going to school today.

SEAMUS (*coming into the room*). No?

CHRIS. You can get your health back. And help me and Eileen and Noel shift the furniture. We're moving.

SEAMUS. Moving!!!

EILEEN. No, Mother!

NOEL. When, Mother?

SEAMUS. I'll be up in a minute! It was only a small pain anyway. (*He runs back into the bedroom.*)

CHRIS. We're moving this very day of Our Lord. I had a letter from the Corporation this morning. Here it is.

NOEL (*reading*). "Housing Department, Dublin Corporation. Mr. James Hannigan: You have been allocated the tenancy of 38, Ardee Road. Please call to Lord Edward Street, where the keys are. . . ."

CHRIS. Oh, we won't mind a little thing like that.

SEAMUS (*running back in with his clothes half-way on*). Here I am dressed and all.

EILEEN. My daddy will go mad.

CHRIS. Will he? Well, he can go sane again.

EILEEN. It'll be lovely. A new house and electric light and bath.

SEAMUS. And mountains and trees and sand-pits.

NOEL. What mountains? You little eedgit, you're as bad as my da. Anywhere an inch past the Circular Road and you think you're in Texas.

SEAMUS. It takes one eedgit to know another. And there will be mountains, won't there, Ma?

CHRIS. Well, there'll be plenty of good fresh air and fields for you to play in.

EILEEN. Of course, we don't have to mix with them, but I believe they're an awful clique up in that road. A girl in work moved up there, and she said they were desperate.

NOEL. I heard that myself all right. They play tag with hatchets.

CHRIS. That's the Dublin people all over. Never a good word for one another, from one street to the next. When I was going with your father, the people over our side of the city said to me, "Chris Coyle, don't say you're getting married to that clique over there. Sure, in that quarter they eat their dead." And your father told me years afterwards he was warned about our quarter in the same way, only they said that we eat our young.

NOEL. Convenient all the same. One side of the river you wanted no prams, and on the other there was no call for hearses.

CHRIS. The people in Ardee Road will be the same as ourselves. Pledging on Monday, releasing on Saturday, and trying to pull the divil by the tail the five days between.

MRS. CARMODY (*outside the hall door*). Mrs. Hannigan, me jewel and darling.

NOEL. I'm off. Where am I to go first?

CHRIS. Go down to Con Farrell and get the hiring of his yoke. Seamus can go with you if he's finished with his breakfast.

SEAMUS. I am, Ma. I am!

CHRIS. Eileen and I will go down town and see if we can get a few things.

MRS. CARMODY (*opening the door and peering in*). Mrs. Hannigan, me jewel.

CHRIS. Yes, Mrs. Carmody, come on in, ma'am, and Noel—

NOEL. Yes, Mother.

CHRIS. Be very careful with the wireless. And put straw, the Gem will give you some, round my little ornaments. Seamus can sit up on the lorry and hold the two dogs.

SEAMUS. I will, Ma, and I won't let them fall and break neither.

CHRIS. You better not. I had them before I had you. In Cole's Lane for one and six I got them.

NOEL (*sarcastically*). You got value for money in them times.

SEAMUS. Ma, I'm not going to go with bigmouth if he doesn't give over. First people is being summonsed, and then they're worth one and six.

MRS. CARMODY. Mrs. Hannigan, ma'am.

NOEL (*to Seamus*). Come on, Lightning. (*As they go out*) One thing about Ardee Road, we won't have to be listening to that old one.

EILEEN. But Mother, he'll rise murder. You heard him saying a hundred times that he'd never leave here, only for a flat in the city. And sure, where we're going now, he hardly knows what side of the town it's on.

CHRIS. Let him go and ask a Guard, then. He won't be long finding out. I've stood these dens long enough. His dinner will be cooking for him in 38, Ardee Road tonight. It better be coddle. He'd walk to Ardee—not to mind Ardee Road—for a good coddle. We'll leave a note for him. "Dear Jim, Just a line to let you know we moved today to number—"

EILEEN. Ah, no, Ma. Don't just write the number. Put first, "To new and commodious premises at number 38, Ardee Road—"

CHRIS. "Where a hot coddle has been cooked for you by—"

SCENE THREE

When the lights come up, Jim, finished work and home for his dinner, is standing outside the door of his former apartment, reading the note.

———

JIM. "—a hot coddle has been cooked for you, by your loving wife, Chris Hannigan." (*He rattles the door handle and the padlock on the door.*) Is she gone out of her mind or what? 38, Ardee Road— that's out in the new houses. Is that where I've to go for my bit of dinner? For a journey like that a man would want a sup of something to help him on his way. And when I see you again, Christina Hannigan, if it's above in Ardee Road itself, I'll give you a hot coddle. Hot coddle, indeed! (*He goes off.*)

SCENE FOUR

The lights come up on the pub. Several people are standing around the bar. There is a babble of talk and a rattle of glasses. Jim has just entered.

———

BARMAN. Me sound man, Jim. And how's the form?

JIM. Never was worse, Jerry. As sure as I'm standing here and you pulling that pint, evicted I am, deported and transported. Did you ever hear tell of Captain Boycott?

BARMAN. I did then. In old times. Putting the people out on the roads.

JIM. Well, you're looking at her husband.

BARMAN. I always thought it was a man.

JIM. Well, you needn't. It's a woman. And I'm married to her. At least I was. But seeing I was deserted, I'm not sure now, whether I am or not. (*Drinks.*) That was badly wanting. Give us a bottle of that, Jer.

BARMAN (*producing a bottle and drawing the cork*). Coming up, Jim. But where's she gone to?

JIM. Some place they call Ardee Road. It might as well be in Jiputty for all I know. The deceit of her. There I was this morning, going out to my hard day's work, little dreaming that before the day would be out, I'd be an—an—an orphan. And what nicer am I nor an orphan and exile with no place to lay my head?

BARMAN. It's no joke right enough.

JIM. I don't even know where Ardee Road is. Nor how to get to it.

BARMAN. Oh, I can tell you that.

JIM. I thought you were from Tipp. Is it that far out?

BARMAN. Ah, no, it's not that. We used to play hurling out there in the old days. And we used to go out there with long dogs, the greyhounds, for a bit of coursing. "The United Coursing and Sporting Grocers' Curates of Ireland."

JIM. I'm not a bit surprised to hear it. No, nor if you told me you shot wolves in it. But whatever about the coursing, be a sporting grocer's curate and tell me how I get to it.

BARMAN. When you get down as far as O'Connell Bridge, you get the Number Eighty-four bus. Go as far as you can on that and then ask the conductor to let you off at the Widow Clarkin's.

JIM. Is it bona-fide?

BARMAN. I don't know if it's there at all now. That was twenty-five years ago. (*Sentimental*) Myself, I was only a gossoon at the time. Just up. And poor Mick Ryan from Nenagh, and Sean Roche from the Galtees, and sure where would you leave poor Paddy Leahy? Hurled from Beherlahan and had more county medals then—

JIM. Jerry, keep that bit of Knockagow for the winter nights and concentrate your brains for the minute on my innocent children, kidnapped to the wilds of the bog by a faithless wife. Always the curse of Ireland, Jerry.

BARMAN. True for you.

JIM. Bad and all as she was, I didn't think she'd walk off with a man's house, home and habitation, without saying yes, aye or no.

BARMAN. And when you get to the Widow Clarkin's, it's out beyond where that new scheme is. Only a mile or two up the road.

JIM. Give us another there to help me along the road. And give Mrs. Hanratty a gin there as you're at it.

BARMAN. There you are, Jim, and it's on the house. You were always a good customer here, and a decent one.

CHORUS. Oh, bedad he was. No lie there. Good man, Jim.

MRS. HANRATTY. Good-b-b-b-bye, Mr. H-H-H-Hannigan. And you were always a good neighbor t-t-too. (*She sobs.*)

BARMAN. Arrah, cheer up, Mrs. Hanratty, ma'am, sure it's not to America he's going.

MRS. HANRATTY. Sure, if only it was, Jerry. Sure, there's parts of that's civilized. But amn't I after hearing you with your own lips saying that place is infested with wild greyhounds, that goes round eating people, even grocer's curates.

AN OLD MAN. Ah, she'll be all right, Jerry, it's only the few sups. It takes her that way, between. The day she stood in a tanner with me on the three cross double of the Aga Khan's across the board and anything to come on to Gordon in the last race, we had a few and all went well an' as merry as a wedding. But we went into Daughter's for a cup of tea and a bit of brawn, and she heard me grandchild reciting a poem he got for his exercise about the Battle of Clontarf. She broke down at the bit where the Danes cut the two legs off of Brian Boru and wanted to get the Guards for them.

JIM. Well, I better be making a start.

CHORUS. Good-bye, Mr. Hannigan. Good luck, Jim. A good road to you, Jim.

MRS. HANRATTY. Good-bye and God love you, Mr. Hannigan. Jim, I can tell you. I knew your poor mother, Mrs. Hannigan, in death. The Lord have mercy on her and on you and yours, going out to that mountain, with w-w-w-wild grocers—I mean—greyhound's curates—I mean—

JIM. There now, ma'am, I know what you mean, and it does you credit. Good luck, Jerry.

BARMAN. Goodbye, Jim, and don't forget to give us a call.

JIM. That I will, Jer, anytime I come to Dublin. (*He goes out.*)

BARMAN. And don't forget your road now. Eighty-four from O'Connell Bridge, all the way out, and then ask for the Widow Clarkin's.

CHORUS. Good luck, Jim. So long, old son. Mind yourself, Jim.

SCENE FIVE

Lights up. Jim has just alighted from the bus and is talking to the conductor.

CONDUCTOR. Right, the new houses. Anything to declare? Take it out and we'll eat it.

JIM. Is that the Widow Clarkin's there?

CONDUCTOR. I suppose it is, if her husband is dead.

JIM. I'm looking for the new houses.

CONDUCTOR. Well, this is as far as we go. You couldn't bring the buses up there yet. I only know that this is the terminus. Thus far shalt thou go and no further, as the man said. Try them in the shop there.

(*The light comes up on a door leading into a small shop.*)

JIM. I will. Good night. (*The light fades on the bus, and we hear the sound of it moving away.*) It's as black as my boot. I'll go over and see if this is it. (*As he goes into the shop, the bell on the door rings. A woman is standing behind the shop counter.*)

THE WOMAN. Good evening.

JIM. Good evening, ma'am. Any harm asking would you be the Widow Clarkin?

THE WOMAN. How dare you, sir! What do you mean?

JIM. Oh, it's all right. I was only asking. If you are, poor ould Clarkin is better off, whoever he was.

THE WOMAN (*outraged*). How dare you, sir. I'll have the Guards on you if you—

JIM. Bedad, and sorrow much loss if you did. I'd have a bed for the night, anyway. Instead of walking round this wilderness like poor dog Tray. (*He goes out and bangs the door behind him. The light fades on the shop.*) Where in the divil's name am I? If I could only see the stars through the fog. But I suppose the stars out here are not the same as the ones I was used to, back in the city. If I could only meet some other Christian itself. (*Steps are heard on the night air. A man appears.*) Maybe this fellow might have an idea where we are. Good night. Begging your pardon, could you ever tell me how to—

GIBBON (*disgusted*). You're asking the wrong man. I haven't a notion. No more than the newest child in the Rotunda. I was home from work today and I sees a notice on my own door, left there by my wife, saying she's after moving to—

JIM. I'm the very—

GIBBON. Just hold on a minute till I tell you this. You never heard the beatings of it since Chuckles Roshford fought the monkey in the dustbin and came out without a scratch. I was come home from work, and goes to my own back drawing-room—we had the pair for half nothing, pre-war, only she wasn't satisfied, neither was my eldest daughter. Wanted a nice house to bring her fellow, if you please. One of the reasons I didn't want to move. Same fellow would ate the side wall of Store Street Bus Station. Sit there all Sunday evening glutting himself, mangling mate the way you'd think he was in training to go back to Birmingham. Ate a child's leg through a chair. And the daughter one side of him, and her ma the other, like two seconds, wiping his forehead and egging him to savage a bit more. "Come on, Eamon, try another bit of the ham." "Eamon, just taste another pick of the corned beef." And me sitting there, like a half thick, watching me Monday's lunch going down his hungry-looking maw. Honest, I ask your pardon, do they ever get e'er a bit at home? And

now, today, I come home and there's a notice on the door, saying, "Gone to new house at—"

JIM. What nicer am I? Wasn't I just—

GIBBON. Just a minute, Mac, give me a chance, for only a second. Do you know where Ardee Road is? Or how I get to it?

JIM. Sure, isn't that where I'm going myself? I went home too, and they were moved out to Ardee Road.

GIBBON. What number are you?

JIM. Thirty-eight.

GIBBON. I'm right beside you. Thirty-seven. We'll be able to get together of an evening for a chat. Gabble Gibbon's the name. Course that doesn't mean I gabble all the time or anything like that. It's a name I got during the Trouble. All our squad had nicknames. To bluff the other crowd. I remember one night and I coming home. It'd be just after curfew—

JIM. You were never out here during the Trouble? I mean on reconnaissance, so as we could find our houses now?

GIBBON. Here's houses. Go up and ask. Maybe they'd know.

JIM. Chance it, anyway.

(*The light comes up on the house door. Jim walks up and knocks. He knocks again, and the door opens.*)

EILEEN. Come in, Da.

JIM. It's Eileen.

EILEEN. Come on in to our new house. Welcome to thirty-eight, Da.

NOEL. Welcome to thirty-eight, Da.

SEAMUS. Welcome to thirty-eight, Da.

EILEEN. Come on into the kitchen, Da.

(*Jim goes inside. The light comes up on the kitchen scene.*)

CHRIS. Jim! You must be lost.

JIM. Not your fault I'm not.

CHRIS. Now don't be giving out of you. I've the coddle hot for ye, and see what Seamus put up over the mantelpiece.

JIM (*reading*). "Cead Mile Failte" (*slowly, and "Failte" pronounced "Fawcha"*).

SEAMUS. It's supposed to be a Christmas decoration, Da, but sure this is a kind of Christmas.

CHRIS. And I kept a few ha'pence out of the linoleum money for a half dozen. You'd need it, God help you, after your wanderings. Sit over to the table now for a bit, and Noel, draw the cork of a bottle for your father, while I knock in to Mrs. Carmody.

JIM. M-M-M-*Mrs. who?*

CHRIS. *Mrs. Carmody,* she is moved out to the house this side of us.

JIM. And that Gabble merchant the other!

CHRIS (*knocking on the wall*). Who?

MRS. CARMODY (*from the next house*). I'll be in to you in one minute, Mrs. Hannigan, my jewel and darling.

JIM (*weakly*). Draw the cork of that bottle, Noel. It's badly wanting.

MRS. CARMODY. Out in a minute, Mrs. Hannigan, my jewel.

(*The lights fade as the cork is drawn and Part One is concluded.*)

PART TWO

A GARDEN PARTY

SCENE ONE

As the lights brighten again, it is tea time in the Hannigan house at 38, Ardee Road. The family is seated around the table.

———

CHRIS. Eileen, pass your father the pepper. Another bit of onion, Jim?

JIM. No thanks, Chris, I'm all right.

CHRIS. Are you ready for a cup of tea, Noel?

NOEL. Just about, Ma.

CHRIS. Pass Noel the milk and sugar, Seamus.

JIM. God between us and all harm, Chris, I had that Gabble fellow next door on the bus, beside me all the way home. I thought I'd go out of my mind.

NOEL. He'd put years on you, all right. He caught me one day on the bus and gave the father and mother of a lecture on the history of Ireland in one act. He told me about when he was in jail, and I said the best in the world could go wrong sometime and if he paid his debt to society no one should say anything to him. He near split me for insulting him, but sure I thought he was after doing a month over a bike or gas meters or something.

SEAMUS. Not at all. Old Gibbon was a Commander-in-Chief over all the rest of them. I gave Vincent Gibbon a dig today in the school yard over it. He said his fellow was Commander-in-Chief and my da wasn't. And you were one, weren't you, Da?

NOEL. He was a Colonel commanding a wheel barrow and a porter commando.

JIM. Never you mind what I was. And don't be so impudent or I'll give you commando.

CHRIS. You ought to tell Seamus not to be fighting, Jim. We don't want trouble and we only after arriving in the place.

JIM. If your Gibbon takes after his old fellow, the Gabble, it'd be an act of charity to the public to give him an odd stuff in the gob now and again, be way of no harm. It'd keep his trap shut for a bit.

CHRIS. Don't go putting that class of carrying on into his head. He'll be bad enough on his own forby your instigations.

NOEL. It does you no harm to be able to take your part. I hope you gave him a good one, Shaybo.

SEAMUS. I did, Noel. He says to me, "Your old fellow was a Commander-in-Chief, was he? Well, you're all wet, because there is only the one Commander-in-Chief in any army, and if my da was it how can your da be it too? And—" (*Pauses for breath.*)

NOEL. Go on, Shaybo, only another five furlongs.

SEAMUS (*indignant*). I got me mouth to talk, as well as what you did.

NOEL. You're getting the value of it anyway.

EILEEN. It's a shame for you and me da too, to be encouraging him at all to be going around fighting and making a little slag of himself. He'll get his name up at school and all, over the scheme.

CHRIS. Leave him be. Quarrelsome dogs get torn tails.

NOEL. It'd be no harm to shorten this tale a bit.

SEAMUS. You're that funny, it's a wonder you're not on the radio.

NOEL. Ah, go on, Shaybo, sure I'm only getting it up for you. I'm mad to get to the finish of this, as the navvy said to the bad pint.

EILEEN. Oh, we're on pints now, are we?

NOEL. It's only an expression. Either-ways, it'd be no skin off of your shiny nose.

EILEEN. Mother, did you hear what this eedgit is—

CHRIS. That's all right, Eileen, I've a little job for him and his father will take the energy out of them for the night. Just go out there a minute, Jim, and see if you have everything you want.

JIM. I want to finish my tea, if it's all the one to you. What are you talking about? Go out where?

CHRIS. Just open the back door.

JIM. Oh, it's out in the yard, is it?

EILEEN. The garden.

JIM (getting up and opening the door). Yard or garden is all— There's a shovel and some class of a pitchfork and— (Suddenly and vehemently) Sacred to the memory of Brian Boru, what's that smell? Oh!

SEAMUS. It's the manure, Da, the men left in today.

JIM. The sewers, I knew it. These new houses is all the same. Why did yous not get the sanitary man or the Civic Guards or someone? Oh, take me home and bury me decent.

SEAMUS. It's no sewers, it's the manure, Da.

JIM (shutting the door). Whatever it is, I'll take an hour off work tomorrow to go into the Housing about it. Dumping stuff like that in people's yards! Must be trying to give us all the fever. Oh, Mother call a cab. You'd no right to let him leave it out there.

SEAMUS. But we bought it, Da.

JIM. Yous what? Yous bought it! Are yous gone out of your mind or what? Yous bought it?

CHRIS. Thirty shillings, including carting to the door. And it's good manure.

JIM. Oh, I've no doubt. The real pre-war article. But would you mind telling me for the love and honour, before I go down as far as Butt Bridge and throw meself in the starboard side—

CHRIS. Listen here, Jim Hannigan, there's a spade and a fork and a good load of manure—

JIM. There's no getting away from that.

CHRIS. There's no getting away from that. And cabbage fourpence a head and sixpence a quarter for potatoes, it'd be a mortal sin to leave that big garden out there run to waste. You can dig, Noel can manure.

NOEL. Ah, Mother, have a heart. I'll be run off the job tomorrow. They'll say there's something the matter with me. How would you like to be working beside a fellow and the smell of that stuff coming off you?

CHRIS. Is Eileen and meself to go out there before the neighbours and disgrace yous? And two menkind in the house?

SEAMUS. Three, Ma, what about me?

NOEL. You'll be a man before your mother.

CHRIS. He's a sight more willing than you or your father, anyway. And he'd give me and Eileen a hand. That's if yous do want to be disgraced by us going and digging the garden. You could hardly sit looking at us through the window.

EILEEN. I wouldn't like to chance them, Ma. It wouldn't be their best.

JIM. All right, all right. Hold on a minute. Do yous know that that yard—

EILEEN. Garden.

JIM. All right, all right, garden! Anyone that would downface their own father will never have luck! That's well known.

CHRIS. And it's well known that the best time for planting a few vegetables for yourself and your family is in the long spring evenings.

JIM. All fine and large. But has it ever occurred to you that that ground out there is the property of the Dublin Corporation? And what call have we to go digging it up? If you went into Stephen's Green and started throwing muck, the like of what you paid—

CHRIS. Thirty shillings carted to the door.

JIM (heavily sarcastic). More nor reasonable. Cheap at half the price. There must be a sale on. Some knacker's yard selling out. But if you went to Fairview or Harold's Cross Park, all public parks, mind you, do you think you'd be entitled to dig them up and—

CHRIS. The garden goes with our house and we pay the rent of it.

JIM. That doesn't say. We pay for the house to live in. And the ground around it is to get in and out of it. But we can't go digging up the ground to feed ourselves anymore nor can we use the floorboards to warm ourselves or the bannisters for drumsticks.

NOEL. Number one for me da, sound man yourself.

EILEEN. Oh, yous are terrible well up and smart. But what about all the people round here that's growing all manner of vegetables and flowers?

JIM. That's a different thing. They must have got permission. But it's a very serious thing to interfere with municipal territory, so to speak, without permission. It's—it's a class of high treason. Come under the Abatement of Polygamy Act, I believe.

CHRIS (decisively). Right, your Worship can adjourn the proceedings to the back snug of the "Floating Ball Room." Go on quick, though! You'll have time for about forty fill-ups before ten o'clock. Eileen, go out and get the things. Seamus, get into them old trousers I couldn't get a patch on to.

JIM. Aw, Ma, listen. Chris, you know that it's not that I begrudge doing it. But we must go about it the right way. I'll get permission off the Corporation all right. I'll see about it tomorrow. A chap I knew in the old days will give me a letter, and I'll go down to the City Hall and—

CHRIS. Never you mind the City Hall. Didn't we hear on the wireless the Minister for Industry saying with his own lips that we had to grow more food?

JIM (fervently). God forgive him. It's the last vote of mine he'll ever get.

CHRIS. So you can start tonight before it gets too dark, and if the Corporation say anything to you, you can say I put you up to it.

JIM (a broken man). All right, as soon as I finish this cup of tea. Noel, get out them implements from behind the back door.

NOEL. Right, Da, in a minute, Eh— (Brightly as one inspired) But just let Shaybo finish his yarn first.

EILEEN. Don't take all night, Shaybo. Or it'll be too late to do anything in the garden.

NOEL. There's Miss Manners for you. Do you call that politeness? Must keep all your politeness for that crowd up in the tennis dance.

JIM (in a low voice). Oh, that's them

for you. House angels and street devils.

EILEEN. Listen here, Noel Hannigan—

NOEL. Just have a bit of manners and let Shaybo finish his yarn, can't you?

JIM (brightening up a bit). Eh, yes, Eileen, while I'm finishing the sup of tea.

CHRIS. It won't be light after eight o'clock.

JIM. That's all right, Chris, but we mustn't interrupt the boy when he's started to tell us something.

NOEL. Certainly not. By no manner of means.

JIM. You can't expect kids to have a bit of manners if you don't show them some. Go ahead, Shaybo, that's a most interesting yarn.

SEAMUS. Do you think so, Da?

JIM. Certainly and I do.

EILEEN. Seamus must be coming on. I never heard him get all this attention before.

JIM. Well, he's a big lad now.

NOEL. He's growing brains along with whiskers. Go ahead. Good little scrapper too. I heard the other kids say.

SEAMUS. Did you hear them say that, Noel?

NOEL. Certainly. Go ahead, Shay. Carry on with the coffin, the corpse can walk.

SEAMUS. Well, Vincent Gibbon comes over to me in the school yard.

NOEL. Now, let's get this straight, Shaybo. Which school yard?

SEAMUS. Behind the school.

NOEL. Well, of course it's behind the school. You don't expect to find it behind the chip shop, do you?

(The clock strikes.)

EILEEN. There's a quarter past six.

JIM. Yes, we better get a move on, eh, Seamus. You were in the school yard.

CHRIS. You're terrible interested in Seamus tonight, the pair of yous.

NOEL. And isn't he my brother, why wouldn't I be interested in him?

JIM. Do you take us for cannibals? Do you think I'm one of these fathers has no time for anything except swallowing down me tea and charging off to get me gut full of porter?

CHRIS. Go on, Seamus, with your story, and if you finish before half six, I'll give you a shilling for the pictures tomorrow.

JIM (piously). Isn't that a lovely way to

rear children? (*Eagerly*) Eh, remind me, Shay, Friday night, that I've a bit of overtime this week.

NOEL. I don't think I'll be using my bike all the weekend. One thing I hate is spoiling a yarn by rushing it.

EILEEN. I got two lovely ties in work, was only stamped backwards. Brand new, though. Anyway, Shay, me ma had you first.

SEAMUS. That's right, she had.

EILEEN. And first up is the best dressed with two massive Yankee ties—well, one at a time.

CHRIS. That's my good son.

SEAMUS. Right. (*At breakneck speed*) I was in the school yard today, and Vincent Gibbon said to me that his father was a Commander-in-Chief, and I said so was mine and had medals to prove it, and he said that his father was the Commander-in-Chief and there was only one of them in any army, and that if his da was it, how could my old fellow be, and I said my da was higher than that again and that eitherways he wasn't an old fellow not like his old Gabble of an old fellow anyway, and he says: "Will you stand out," and I showed him me spar and says I: "That's Glasnevin and that's Mount Jerome, and you needn't wait to stand out," and with that I drew out and gave him a belt that near put him in the middle of next week, he met himself coming back so he did, and he said he'd get his old fellow so he did, and I get me shilling, too, don't I, Ma?

(*The clock strikes half six.*)

CHRIS. That you do, my son.

EILEEN. And the ties too, if you'll just go out and get the gardening implements for—

NOEL (*mimicking*). "Gardening implements." Look now, what I brought you, and me only off the boat.

EILEEN. Look at here, you!

JIM (*wearily*). Get up, Noel, and out to the—the back of the house. I thought I'd have me tea digested before I started throwing that muck around. (*Shoving his chair back:*) Well, I suppose what it is to be will be.

(*A loud and fierce knocking is heard at the front door.*)

CHRIS. Save us and bless us.

JIM. Go and see who it is, Seamus.

SEAMUS. Right, Da. (*He goes out into the hall, and then calls back.*) It's Mr. Gibbon, Da.

GIBBON (*from the hall*). That's who it is all right, Stanislaus Aloysius Ignatius Gibbon, Commander. Only known to all and sundry as the gabbling gunman of the Dublin No. 1 Brigade. (*He comes into the kitchen.*)

NOEL (*murmurs*). Would it be the Fire Brigade by any chance?

GIBBON. And I'll give it to yous over my son being hit today in the school yard.

JIM (*jumping up from his chair*). You put a hand on my son, and you'll be only fit for the bone yard.

EILEEN. Oh, Daddy, Daddy, don't! (*Grabbing his arm.*)

CHRIS. For the love of heaven, Jim, have a bit of sense. (*Grabbing his other arm.*)

JIM. Noel, make them leave me go. Leave me go—Chris—and I'll show that—!

GIBBON. Be easy, madam. Gabble Gibbon makes no war on women and children. The Colonel of the Auxies says to me, "Gibbon, I can but admire your pluck, and I respect a brave enemy as well as the next. The exquisite tact which you told the lady to tell her husband to come down to the hall—there was a gentleman wished to shoot at him for a few minutes —can but command my respect. Efficiency can be had from an officer, but good breeding can only be had from one who is also a gentleman. If you didn't go to school, you met the scholars coming back." I cannot hit your son—

SEAMUS. You better not, or tomorrow morning I'll hit yours.

CHRIS. Seamus!

JIM. Let me go, will yous?

GIBBON. But I'll take the old fellow on.

JIM (*furiously*). Let me go. Let me at him.

CHRIS. For the love and honour, Jim, please!

MRS. CARMODY (*speaking through the wall from her own house next door*). Mrs. Hannigan, ma'am.

CHRIS. Eileen, there's Mrs. Carmody. She hears the row through the wall. Knock in there to her to come in. Surely they wouldn't fight in front of an old woman.

(EILEEN *knocks on the wall.*)

MRS. CARMODY. I'll be right in, ma'am.

GIBBON. I'm telling yous that—

JIM. And I'm telling you—

MRS. CARMODY (*entering from the back door*). Mrs. Hannigan, me jewel and darling, and Mr. Hannigan, me decent man, and the other gentleman that's lifting the chair, God between us and all harm, sir, I hope it's not to split someone with it.

GIBBON. Gibbon is the name, ma'am. Gabble to Ireland's friends in the old days, and to her enemies, "The horror of the North"—that's on account of me mother being from Amiens Street. You seem an honest old party. I advise you to withdraw unless this man whose offspring hit my offspring—

JIM. Come on out the road, it's wide enough for the two of us.

EILEEN. Daddy, Daddy, don't!

SEAMUS. Daddy, Daddy, do!

GIBBON. My son was hit by that—

JIM. He comes in here, and he starts—

GIBBON. Cease to come between us, I'm a man of few words. A couple of minutes out there is all I want, and I'll transmogrofy him.

JIM. Now let me—

MRS. CARMODY. Oh, Mrs. Hannigan, ma'am, I'm in a weakness! I'm—oh, oh— (*Moans.*)

CHRIS. It's the old heart. God forgive yous men.

MRS. CARMODY. A little sup of brandy—

GIBBON. At once, me good woman. Never let it be said. I'll belt down like a good one.

JIM. I'll be down with you!

GIBBON. I can carry the bottle myself!

JIM. Well, I'll carry the cork.

CHRIS. Hurry up, some of yous.

MRS. CARMODY. Ohhhhhhhhhhhhh.

CHRIS. The poor woman might die for the want of it.

MRS. CARMODY. Ohhhh. It was excitement. I'm gone for me chips. Ohhhhhh.

Scene Two

The light comes up on the pub scene. GIBBON *and* JIM *come in and hurry over to the bar.*

⸻

GIBBON. A glass of brandy, quick. It's for the old woman taken bad.

JIM. I'll pay for it.

GIBBON. You needn't bother. It'll never be said of Gabble Gibbon that he couldn't stand an old woman her last drink in this world. I suppose we might as well have one while we're waiting.

JIM. I'll get it then. What are you, having, Gibbon?

GIBBON. Gabble is the name. Sure, you couldn't keep up a fight, and we going back to the wake practically.

JIM. Hey, Mac, give us two—

Scene Three

Back in the Hannigan kitchen.

⸻

MRS. CARMODY (*whispering*). Mrs. Hannigan, are they back yet?

CHRIS. They won't be long now, ma'am. You'll be all right. It was them with their shouting and acting the tin jinnet.

MRS. CARMODY (*recovering her health*). Divil a thing was the matter with me, ma'am, only I heard the shouts and roars, and I says to myself, says I, "There's Mrs. Hannigan and himself hard at it and I never knew them to fight like that in the city, it must be the strong air up here is making them fight," and then I came in and thought it was the best of my play to throw a sevener and put the heart crossways in them, and anyway, the drop of brandy won't do me the least bit of harm —as my poor fellow used to say.

Scene Four

In the pub again.

⸻

JIM. . . . thirty shillings for manure, and I asks her—

GIBBON. Manure, manure, manure, don't give me manure, amn't I a martyr to manure? What am I getting for me breakfast, dinner and tea but manure?

JIM. The potatoes and cabbages, my one says, and the daughter backing her up—

GIBBON. Will you let someone else get a word in edgeways? Now and again. What am I nicer? You think you're bad with potatoes and cabbage, but look at me, I've had them to contend with and then there's the bulbs they want planted in the front. Says I, "Would yous want thirty-watt bulbs or hundred-watt bulbs?" They send off be post to some fellow down the country that sells rare and precious blooms. Bedad, I says to my one, "When I got you, I got a rare and precious bloom!" Do you know what I'm going to tell you? It'd be a charity of big dimensions if someone would get the Corporation to have the ground round the houses properly concreted in. It makes dirt and the little children picking up maggots and muck and—

JIM (*bitterly*). Manure.

GIBBON. Oh, the manure, where would you leave the manure?

(*Enter* MRS. HANRATTY.)

MRS. HANRATTY. Well, I ask your pardon, if it's not poor Jim Hannigan was moved up to the new houses, himself and his misfortunate wife and family. And how's all the care, Jim? Ah sure, I never thought I'd see you again in this world. But isn't me youngest daughter after getting married to a fellow that's on his mother's floor. They have the front parlour, and the poor old one is up for subletting, and we went down to the Corporation, and me daughter's fellow, he can't get anything to do this six year, but he's a lovely dancer and, sure, God help us all, it's nothing but a vale of tears when all is said and done.

GIBBON. True enough, ma'am. As I often said myself when I was in jail!

MRS. HANRATTY. Ah sure, God help you. We never done any harm, only what we lifted.

GIBBON. Look here, ma'am, I wasn't—

JIM. This is Gabble Gibbon. He was a patriot.

MRS. HANRATTY. Me poor fellow was in that too, but he was caught lifting, and he had to go back on the mail bags. It was the time he was in over a watch he got in the Shelbourne. He went to mend a burst pipe and only took it to keep it out of the wet. Did you know him at all, Mr. Gabble, sir? He was in the bag shop.

GIBBON. Madam, my name is Gibbon.

MRS. HANRATTY. Mr. Gibble, sir, it's a pleasure to meet you, sir.

GIBBON. We better be getting back with the brandy for the old one that's dying.

MRS. HANRATTY. Is there someone dying? Course they're doing that every minute of the day.

JIM. It's Mrs. Carmody that's taken bad. She's moved out beside us.

MRS. HANRATTY. Ah, don't say the like. Poor Anastasia Angelica Magdalen Carmody. "Duck the Bullet," we used to call her. Though I didn't talk to her this forty year over me beautiful glass ornament she pledged on me and sold the ticket of. Lovely flowers all colours, massive glass tulips and—

GIBBON (*with bitterness*). Rare and precious blooms?

MRS. HANRATTY. The very thing, sir. How did you know?

GIBBON. Me female family have a book about them. I've had it every night for that long that I have it be heart. I know every bloom and blossom from here to the top of India. There is, according to the book, "Johnstonii, Queen of Spain."

MRS. HANRATTY. Lovely, sir.

GIBBON (*quoting*). "I offer the true collected stock from Iberia, which must not be confused with—"

MRS. HANRATTY. Siberia.

GIBBON. "—with some of the spurious creatures I have seen masquerading in some gardens—"

MRS. HANRATTY. The cheek of them.

GIBBON. "—these last seasons. Ord. Iridaceae—"

MRS. HANRATTY. Oh, I love them!

GIBBON. "I offer you here a fine selection of the lovely species, Gladioli—"

MRS. HANRATTY (*with deep emotion*). The lovely species, Gladioli.

GIBBON. "In my opinion, far nicer in every way than the rather blowsy large flowered one that totters in our gardens in the July rains. The Tuber Gen'l Annum—"

MRS. HANRATTY. The Tuber Gen'l Annum—I love them!

GIBBON. "I must state quite frankly—"

MRS. HANRATTY. Oh, speak your mind, sir.

GIBBON. "That this is the finest of all the Muscari—"

MRS. HANRATTY. It's well known, sir, better than all the other Muscari put together.

GIBBON. "One of the finest spring flowers, true blue—"

MRS. HANRATTY. To the last, sir, no denying it.

GIBBON. "No trace of mauve or violet—"

MRS. HANRATTY. Oh, divil damn the trace! Deny it who may.

GIBBON. "—in existence. Herbertia Ord. Iridaceae. I could find no reference to this plant in any of the dozen contemporary hand books at my disposal and was almost giving up and describing it as unknown, when in the 1868 edition of *Paxton's Botanical Dictionary* I came across the following: Herbertia, in honour of the Honourable and Reverend William Herbert—"

MRS. HANRATTY. God bless him. Honourable and Reverend. A lovely man.

GIBBON. "—of Spofforth, and author of a monograph on Amaryllidaceae 1837."

MRS. HANRATTY. Poor old Amarayllidacea, a decent poor old sort when he had it, say what you like.

GIBBON. "Planted in loam, peat and sand—"

MRS. HANRATTY (*breaking down*). Is that where they planted her? Loam. Peat and sand. Ah, sure when you're dead they don't care where they put you.

GIBBON. "With a good bedding of manure—"

JIM. Manure!

MRS. HANRATTY. My lovely glass ornaments, but I forgive old Carmody. I'll go up along with you to pay my last respects to an old neighbour. They were always the best, even if there was nothing you could leave out of your hand with them. (*Weeps.*) And to think of her planted in loam, sand, peat—

JIM. And manure.

MRS. HANRATTY. We better have another one the time that's in it. Young fellow?

(*A newsboy comes in.*)

JIM. Here's the fellow with the late papers. Hey Mac, have you a full box?

NEWSBOY. Itbethehahado—eeeeeeeeeeeeeeee!

MRS. HANRATTY. God between us and all harm, what's the matter with him?

JIM. Here, give us a reader and go and roar at someone else.

NEWSBOY (*giving him a paper and some change*). Thanks.

JIM. Keep the ha'penny.

NEWSBOY. Thanks again. Itbethehahado—eeeeeeeeeeeeeeee!

GIBBON. Give us a paper, what's the idea of the roar?

NEWSBOY (*in a refined accent*). What? Itbethehahado—eeeeeeeeeeeeeeee! That merely tells the public the names of the journals I am selling. Itbethehahado—eeeeeeeeeeeeeeee. Final City Editions of the Evening Herald (Incorporating the Evening Telegraph). And the Evening Mail and Dublin Daily Express. Itbethehahado—eeeeeeeeeeeeeeee! (*He goes out.*) Itbethehahado—eeeeeeeeeeeeeeee!

GIBBON (*reading*). "Daring robbery in Dublin museum. National historical treasures stolen."

MRS. HANRATTY. Isn't that desperate? Go on, sir.

GIBBON. "Ten gold bracelets that belonged to Queen Maeve of Connacht—"

MRS. HANRATTY. Could you leave anything out of your hand! I could have warned her. After me lovely glass ornaments. Six and thruppence the pair in Cole's Lane. When six and thruppence was six and thruppence. Still maybe she had them insured.

GIBBON. "—were stolen today with valuable ornaments in Wicklow gold of the period three hundred B.C."

MRS. HANRATTY. None of your old B.P.N.S. there.

GIBBON. Wish I had the price of them. I'd be able to put something to it and pay what I owe.

MRS. HANRATTY. God help us all, what nicer am I? As me poor departed used to say, I owe that much, I have to go to Mass in a cab. But I suppose they'll get them robbers when they're taking all the gold things to the pawn.

JIM. They'll dump them more nor likely till all blows over.

MRS. HANRATTY. Behind the pictures maybe.

GIBBON. Under the floor boards.

JIM. Or buried in a garden.

GIBBON (*musing*). Or as you say yourself, buried in a garden. Buried in a garden. Oh, excuse me before it's too late. I must ring up about me aunt, she's bad in hospital.

MRS. HANRATTY. God send she gets over it. What's the matter with her? What hospital is she in?

GIBBON. She's above in Bricins, suffering

from digger's disease. Very common in gardeners.

JIM. Sure, that's the army hospital.

GIBBON. She was a cook with the Eighteenth and got her disability digging spuds for their dinner during the big manoeuvres.

MRS. HANRATTY. Poor creature. I hope she gets over it.

GIBBON. I'll go over and ring up and see how she is anyway. Here, Christy, give us threepence in coppers. (*He goes off.*)

MRS. HANRATTY. Digger's disease? I never heard of that before. Surprising what you can die of these times. They're always inventing new ones. The longer you live, the more you eat. I hope nothing happens to the poor creature anyway.

SCENE FIVE

The light comes up on GIBBON *at the telephone, and across the stage on a* POLICE GUARD *at the telephone.*

———

GIBBON (*with a heavy foreign accent*). . . . and at der moment der gold ornaments are lying in her garden, either front or back of either 37 or 38, Ardee Road.

GUARD. And what did you say the name was?

GIBBON. Ardee Road. In der new houses. Take der course by der Pole Star, Northeast by eastsouth a half west.

GUARD. No, there's a reward for this. Your own name.

GIBBON. Poppocoppolis. Ivan Giuseppe Mahomed Poppocoppolis. Mahomed is mine confirmation name.

GUARD. Poppocoppolis. Thank you, Mr. Poppocoppolis, there will be a squad car up there in five minutes.

GIBBON. Dat is gut. Tell them to bring their spades and pitchforks. Gut bye.

SCENE SIX

The lights come up on three guards in the police car. They are listening to a voice over the radio.

———

VOICE. Calling car twenty-five. Calling car twenty-five. Return at once to headquarters and pick up pitchforks and spades. And proceed to 37 and 38, Ardee Road. That is all.

GUARD. And about enough too. They must be going to put us on the turf. Let her in, Mike.

(*Sound of the car gathering speed and moving off as the lights fade out.*)

SCENE SEVEN

The lights come up on the pub scene.

———

MRS. HANRATTY. Here's Mr. Gibbons back from the phone. He looks as if he got good word about the aunt.

JIM. How is the aunt?

GIBBON. Oh, the aunt. Not too bad. They're going to amputate from above the neck. Nothing to worry about, though. The doctor says she'll be out in a day or two, if she lives. Give us a drink there, Christy.

SCENE EIGHT

The squad car pulls into Ardee Road.

———

GUARD. Pull in there, Mike. I think that's it. 38, Ardee Road. We'll do that one first. Jump out. (*They get out.*) Hey, Finnegan, I didn't ask you to cut the head off me with that spade. Come on, Hegarty, leap out there first.

FINNEGAN. I'll get out first, Sergeant. Hegarty wants the room of three men, he's that fat.

SERGEANT. This little job will do him all the good in the world, again we get the gold he'll be a bit slimmer. But when we get them, we'll get more promotion—

FINNEGAN. Pay—

HEGARTY. Pension.

SERGEANT. So, right lads, up to the front door! (*He goes up to the front door and knocks.*) Hey, there, open up, police on duty! (*He knocks.*) And let the people open the door, Hegarty. We're not here to spear the public with pitchforks. (*He knocks again.*) Come on, there. Open up!

Scene Nine

The lights come up on the pub again.

JIM. What are you having for the last?

GIBBON. I'll take a fifty.

MRS. HANRATTY. I'll have a half on account of the time that's in it, and poor old Carmody kicking out.

JIM. Christy, come down here a minute and pay more attention to the customers.

Scene Ten

The lights come up on the back garden of 38, Ardee Road.

FINNEGAN (*grunting as he shovels*). Oh, me guts is twisted in knots. I'll never do another day's good.

HEGARTY. Nor me, I'm swimming in sweat.

SERGEANT. Just swim on another bit, and you're made for life. (*Grunting as he shovels:*) Lads, we'll get the Scott medal for this.

HEGARTY. Oh. (*Groaning:*) They can pin it on me habit.

SERGEANT. Keep the old heart up, Hegarty. Remember you're digging for—

HEGARTY. Pay—

FINNEGAN. Promotion—

SERGEANT (*groaning wearily as he turns a stone*). And pension. Let's start on the garden next door. If it's not buried in one, it must be buried in the other.

HEGARTY (*wearily and despairingly*). Oh, then Sergeant a chroi, isn't it a pity to the heaven we didn't dig the other one first.

SERGEANT. It'll be soon over, boys. And think of the good you're doing your figure, Hegarty.

HEGARTY. I'd as soon be a fat guard as a dead mannequin. Never mind. Finnegan, lift me spade over that wall and into the next garden, will you? You're a younger man than me.

FINNEGAN. I'm not then. We were born the one year. Ninety-four.

HEGARTY. Yes, but I was born New Year's Day.

SERGEANT. Right, lads, into it. Your spade might hit the gold the first time you shove it into the ground.

FINNEGAN (*hitting something*). Mine didn't. That's a porter bottle.

Scene Eleven

The lights come up on the road in front of Number 38.

MRS. HANRATTY. Is your house far up this road, Jim? Me only hope is to hurry so that I can forgive poor old Carmody about me glass ornaments before she goes.

GIBBON. You're just here, ma'am. Go up and open the door, Jim. I'll carry the rest of the bottles.

JIM (*opening the front door*). Come on in, ma'am. Come on in, Gabble.

Scene Twelve

The lights come up on the Hannigan kitchen. JIM, MRS. HANRATTY, *and* GIBBON *come in.*

EILEEN (*excitedly*). Da, there's police and—

MRS. HANRATTY. How is she? I hope rigger mortar hasn't set in.

MRS. CARMODY. It that old one talking about me by any chance?

MRS. HANRATTY. Ah, there you are, ma'am. I came up to see the last of you.

CHRIS (*agitatedly*). Oh, Jim, I thought you'd never come. There were police—

SEAMUS (*excitedly*). They said we had the gold out in the garden. Or in Mister Gibbon's. They're still digging yours, Mr. Gibbon.

JIM. Gold—what gold?

GIBBON. Oh, you wouldn't be minding these fellows. They have to let on to be doing something.

MRS. HANRATTY. Never where they're wanted.

GIBBON. I wouldn't say that, ma'am.

SEAMUS. They nearly finished in your garden, Mr. Gibbon.

GIBBON. Just run out there, son, and tell them when they're finished to come in and have something. I dare say they need it. I wonder what put it into their heads we had gold up here?

SEAMUS. I'll run out now. Are we going to have a party, Da?

Scene Thirteen

The lights come up on the garden as SEAMUS *runs in.*

———

SEAMUS. Guards, me da wants to know will you come in before you go?

SERGEANT. Right, son. (*Wearily*) There's my last shovelful. If it was deep enough, I'd fall into it and stop there.

HEGARTY. If I make a—a crutch—out of me—spade—I might get as far—as the garden gate.

CURTAIN

THE WASTE DISPOSAL UNIT

Brigid Brophy

The Waste Disposal Unit was first presented by B.B.C. Radio, Great Britain, on April 9, 1964, with the following cast:

HOMER KNOCKERBICKER	Harry Towb	LIA-PIA	Nicolette Bernard
VIRGIL KNOCKERBICKER	Ronald Wilson	ANGELO LUMACA	John Baddeley
MERRY KNOCKERBICKER	Mavis Villiers	MRS. VAN DEN MOST	Mavis Villiers

(*Note:* The roles of MERRY and her mother, MRS. VAN DEN MOST, are performed by the same actress.)

SCENE: The *salone* of a *palazzo* in northern Italy. The time is the present.

WITHIN A COMPARATIVELY short period, the London-born (1929) Brigid Brophy has risen to major international status with her sharply honed essays, bristlingly perceptive reviews, and lauded novels. Her straightforward and entertaining criticisms of life and letters prompted *Time* magazine to enoble her as "The British Intelligentsia's Newest High Priestess." Close upon the heels of this accolade, another prominent journal characterized her as "A brilliant stylist with more brains than anyone deserves."

Miss Brophy began to gather laurels at the outset of her career when her first novel, *Hackenfeller's Ape*, received the top award at the 1954 Cheltenham (England) Festival. Ceremonies over, she buckled down and produced four subsequent novels: *The King of a Rainy Country; Flesh; The Finishing Touch;* and *The Snow Ball.* And to compound her diversity, there were the nonfiction works: *Black Ship to Hell; Mozart the Dramatist;* and *Fifty Works of English Literature We Can Do Without,* the latter in collaboration with Michael Levey and Charles Osborne.

An indefatigable contributor to leading international magazines and newspapers, Miss Brophy enjoyed "prime time" in the American press with the 1967 publication of *Don't Never Forget,* an assemblage of her more trenchant views and reviews.

The Waste Disposal Unit originally was performed on radio, then converted into stage form by Miss Brophy. Its publication in this anthology marks its debut in print, and to the editor, it reflects the authoress at her most amusingly irreverent as she aims her sardonic scalpel at "the American woman who would rather be a lovely person than be herself."

Her other works for the stage include *The Burglar,* produced in the West End, and the recently completed *Libretto.*

Brigid Brophy lives in London with her husband, Michael Levey, the art historian and Deputy Keeper of the National Gallery, and their young daughter.

The salone *of a* palazzo *in northern Italy.*

The room is marbled and splendid, but the splendour is of a cool and echoing kind because the place is simply not furnished at all, apart from a crate of Coca-Cola bottles—some full, some already used —that has been nakedly dumped in the middle of the intricately patterned floor.

Luckily there are two marble window-seats beneath the tall uncurtained windows.

On one of these VIRGIL KNOCKERBICKER *is lying reading a small black-bound notebook which is propped up on his humped knees. He is dressed in black himself— cashmere sweater, narrow trousers, black plimsolls; his soft dark hair is cropped to the point of seeming a mere continuance of the pile on his jumper. In his black costume and his complete absorption in his small volume, he resembles—no doubt on purpose—the young Lord Hamlet.*

HOMER KNOCKERBICKER, *a slightly older and considerably plumper American is walking echoingly up and down the room. He is as worried and hot as Virgil is cool and controlled—this despite the fact that his clothing, unlike Virgil's, is designed for coolness rather than picturesque effect. His light-coloured, loose cotton suit and his transparent nylon-seersucker shirt are already crumpled, though the day (some of whose brilliance spills in through the windows) is not yet far advanced. In patches, his shirt is already even more translucent than the manufacturer intended, where his sweat has affected it as grease affects paper. From time to time he takes a vast handkerchief from his breast pocket and uses it to wipe his spectacles.*

Doors to left and right of the salone *lead out to the rest of the* palazzo.

Through the window there are summer country Italian sounds: chickens, occasional cicadas, lambrettas.

———

HOMER. Virgil?

VIRGIL (*without looking up from his reading*). Homer?

HOMER. Virgil, you planning on lying around all day today, the way you did yesterday?

VIRGIL. Mm-hm. (VIRGIL *thinks he has now disposed of the subject.*)

HOMER. This heat's murder. Merry says it isn't any worse than Southern California, but I tell her it is, it carries a higher degree of humidity. Southern California, you get the ocean. (*After a pause*) Gee, it's hot. It's hot as hell.

VIRGIL. Maybe you should relax more.

HOMER. I guess one in the family is enough.

VIRGIL. One what?

HOMER. O, you know. You know what I mean, Virgil. It's hot enough so it even mists up my lenses. You're lucky you don't have to wear glasses. This heat, you wouldn't be able to see to write.

VIRGIL. I'm not writing. I'm reading back what I already did.

HOMER. That reminds me, sometime I got to talk with you—you want a drink, Virgil?

VIRGIL. Mm-hm. Whisky sour.

HOMER. I didn't mean hard liquor.

VIRGIL. O. No thanks.

HOMER. I wish we had a water cooler in this place. Guess I'll have myself a Coke. I wonder if Merry could use a Coke. You think Merry could use a Coke, Virgil?

(HOMER *alludes to the door at the left.*)

VIRGIL. How would I know? Go on in and ask her.

HOMER. O, I can't go in there right now. She isn't through fixing her face.

VIRGIL. O. Well yell.

HOMER (*as he helps himself to a bottle of Coca-Cola and removes the cap*). What?

VIRGIL. Yell. Ask her through the bedroom door.

HOMER. Yeh, I might *do* that. (*He drinks deep, directly from the bottle.*) I might *do* that. Sure.

VIRGIL. Well go ahead.

HOMER. Sure.

MERRY (*offstage, calling cooingly in a pretty, tinkling voice*). Ho-mer!

HOMER (*calling hastily back, towards the door at the left*). I'll be right in, honey. I just grabbed myself a Coke. I just gotta find some place to put it down. (*He crams it into the crate and runs over to the door at the left; but as his hand turns the knob:*)

MERRY. O, don't come *in*, Homer.

(HOMER *shuts the door hastily.*)

HOMER. I certainly am sorry, Merry.

MERRY. Why, that's perfectly all right, Homer, think no more of it. Homer?

HOMER. Yes, Merry?

MERRY. Would you take a look round the *palazzo* see if I left my Kleenex some place.

HOMER. Sure, Merry. (HOMER *returns to the middle of the room.*) I don't see too well, my lenses got misted up again. (*Calling:*) I don't see them any place, honey, but I'll keep right on searching. Virgil, you seen them?

VIRGIL. See what?

HOMER. Merry's Kleenex.

VIRGIL. Sure. (VIRGIL *pulls out a box from behind his back.*)

HOMER. Now why in the world would you want to do that?

VIRGIL. This window-seat isn't too soft, Homer.

HOMER. If you wouldn't lie around all day—

VIRGIL. Don't you want them?

HOMER. What?

VIRGIL. Merry's Kleenex.

HOMER. Wait a moment, can't you, I got to wipe off these lenses again.

VIRGIL. Don't *you* get steamed up, too.

HOMER. I'm not getting steamed up, but you don't seem to understand, I got to get those Kleenex to Merry. Give here. (*He takes the box from* VIRGIL.) Why, Virgil, you crushed in one whole side of the pack. I don't know how Merry's going to—

VIRGIL. Yeh, well, these sharp-angled packs aren't really any more comfortable than marble. I guess I really took Merry's Kleenex more as a kind of talisman. You know, like a chicken sits on a china egg. To inspire my work.

HOMER. Now that's something I have to talk with you about, Virgil. I'll just go give these to Merry. I'll be right back. (*Approaching the door at the left and calling:*) Merry! I found them, honey. But I'm afraid the pack didn't stand up too well—

MERRY. Now isn't that just too bad of me, Homer. I was just going to call out I didn't need them any more.

HOMER. O.

MERRY. Homer, don't be sore. I found another pack right in here.

HOMER. O, I'm not sore, Merry. I'm certainly glad you found another pack. That's

swell. You through yet, honey?

MERRY. Not yet, Homer.

HOMER. O. O.K.

VIRGIL (*as, without looking away from his book, he reaches a hand out towards the Kleenex*). Give here.

HOMER. What?

VIRGIL. If Merry doesn't want them, I may as well sit on them a while longer. You never know what might hatch. I'll take a look round later, see if I can find a pack that isn't crushed. You don't have any scatter cushions round the place, Homer, I guess you don't have the domesticated touch, but you have to hand it to Merry, she certainly does have scatter Kleenex.

HOMER. Now see here, Virgil—

MERRY (*offstage*). I don't hear you too well but you boys sound to be having a lot of fun out there. I'll be right along.

HOMER. That's swell, honey.

VIRGIL. I don't figure how it takes a woman that long to make up like she was twenty-five when she *is* twenty-five.

HOMER. Now wait a moment, Virgil—

VIRGIL. Mm-hm?

HOMER. Merry's a lovely person.

VIRGIL. Sure. Sure, Homer. Merry's just great. She's great material.

HOMER. What do you mean, "material"?

VIRGIL. You know how it is, Homer. I guess I have a professional attitude, that's all. I'm certainly glad you married Merry.

HOMER (*not sure whether to be angered*). I don't know just how you mean that, Virgil. Do you mean you're glad on account of your work?

VIRGIL. O, I don't separate my work from my life.

HOMER. Now that's something we have to talk about. I'll just have myself that Coke. . . .

VIRGIL. In fact, I don't separate my work from *your* life.

(HOMER *puts the bottle abruptly back into the crate, and prepares to be angry.*)

HOMER. I didn't hear you too well, Virgil, I was kind of swallowing, but did you say my life or my wife?

VIRGIL. O, I wouldn't dare—

HOMER. Let's leave Merry out of this, Virgil. I want to talk with you.

VIRGIL. Mm-hm?

HOMER. Don't you ever look up from

that book?

VIRGIL. I'm told I have very remarkable concentration.

HOMER. I guess you wouldn't break your concentration no matter what happened.

VIRGIL. Nothing does happen.

HOMER. Maybe not, but most of the time it sounds like it did. Know what I think, Virgil? I think Italy's the noisiest country I was ever in.

VIRGIL. It's no worse than Southern California.

HOMER. It is *so* worse than Southern California. Out here you got the cicadas. If it isn't the cicadas, it's the lambrettas. If it isn't the lambrettas, it's the doves. If it isn't the doves, it's those goddam chickens out there in the yard.

VIRGIL. I don't mind the chickens in the *yard* too much.

HOMER. Now see h—

VIRGIL. Cool off, Homer.

HOMER. How can I cool off, this heat? We ought to have drapes at those windows, cut out the sun, but I don't know the Italian for drapes, anyway Merry likes looking out the window. . . . I'm worried, Virgil. I don't know how Merry's going to take this kind of climatic conditions.

VIRGIL. Relax, Homer. Merry doesn't feel it at all.

HOMER. You don't know how Merry feels. Merry is a very delicate character. I don't see how I can ask Merry to live in a climate like this.

VIRGIL. You didn't ask her. It was Merry's idea.

HOMER. You know what I *mean,* Virgil. You know how it is. A guy has to look out for his wife, he has to make provision. If I'd have known there wouldn't even have been a shower in this *palazzo*—

VIRGIL. You had one fixed.

HOMER. Sure I had one fixed, and I'm going to have plenty else fixed, I'm going to make this old *palazzo* like so it won't know itself. . . . But Merry's a very sensitive person. She's delicate, Virgil, even though she doesn't make any song and dance—

MERRY (*calling musically from the next room*). Ho-mer!

HOMER. Yes, honey?

MERRY. Could you step in here for a moment, Homer?

HOMER. Sure, Merry. I'll be right in. You through now? (*A bell rings loudly.*)

HOMER. I'll get it. (*He stops making towards the door at the left, and sets out for the door at the right; checks himself; executes a step-dance of hesitation; and finally calls, in a despairing flurry, towards the door on the left:*) I'll be right back, Merry. I just got to go see to the front door bell.

VIRGIL. Let Lia-Pia get it.

HOMER. How can I let Lia-Pia get it? She doesn't speak English.

VIRGIL. So she doesn't speak English. Maybe it was an Italian dropped by.

HOMER. Are you crazy? How would an Italian drop by?

VIRGIL. Well, we're in Italy.

HOMER. Sure, I *know* we're in Italy, but—

MERRY. Ho-mer! Would you step along to the front door. The bell just rang.

HOMER. Sure, Merry, sure. I'll get it.

(*As* HOMER *leaves by the door at the right,* MERRY *trips in by the door at the left. She tiptoes on her sneakers across the room, comes up behind* VIRGIL *as he reads, and places her hands as a blindfold over his eyes.*)

MERRY. Morning, Virgil. Guess who?

VIRGIL (*sourly*). Merry.

MERRY (*releasing his eyes*). You're a good guesser, Virgil.

VIRGIL (*craning round and looking at her*). Mm-hm, Merry. Just like I thought. Morning, Merry. You look cute.

MERRY (*dropping him a mock curtsey*). Why, thank you, Virgil.

VIRGIL (*looking her up and down*). Sure, cute. Little pony tail, all done up in a tartan bow, and those long white knee-hose, and your Bermuda shorts, and that cute little—what you call it?

MERRY. Shirtwaister?

VIRGIL. Sure, shirtwaister. O, you look cute, Merry. You look like all the college girls in Southern California rolled into one.

MERRY. Why, Virgil, that's the darlingest thing you ever said to me, I guess you must be becoming a better integrated personality. I'm going to give you a little kiss on your brow, just for saying that. (*She bends over and neatly deposits the kiss.*)

VIRGIL. O, don't take any account of me, Merry, I'm just apple-polishing. There's something I want you to tell me.

MERRY. Well, I'll certainly tell you anything I can, Virgil, but Homer says you already know 'most everything. I'm going to just curl up alongside of you on this lovely *Renaissance* window-seat, and then you can ask me anything you want. (*Doing so.*) I guess wherever I am I find myself some corner I can curl up in. There now, Virgil. What's your problem? You know, Virgil, Homer has a very, very high regard for your intellectual integrity.

VIRGIL. Now how would he be able to judge, I wonder?

MERRY. Now, Virgil, Homer's—

VIRGIL. O sure, Homer's a lovely person.

MERRY (*subsiding*). I'm certainly glad you appreciate it. Now what is it I can tell you?

VIRGIL. Why don't you let your husband in your bedroom, Merry?

MERRY (*rising in fury*). Virgil Knockerbicker, how can you make such an absolutely awful insinuation? If you dare imply for one moment—

VIRGIL. Merry, I only asked—

MERRY. Virgil Knockerbicker, I'm going right back in the bou*doir* until Homer returns. (*She turns her back on Virgil.*)

VIRGIL. Merry, what did I do?

MERRY (*swinging on him*). What did you *do!* You were insinuating that my relationship with Homer is not perfectly adjusted on the physical side.

VIRGIL. Merry, I only—

MERRY. You as good as called me a frigid wife!

VIRGIL. Merry, I—

MERRY (*stamping*). I do so let him in my bedroom!

VIRGIL. He told me a while back he couldn't go in there.

MERRY (*losing all her anger, now the trouble is explained*). O sure, but that was in the morning.

VIRGIL. What's the difference?

MERRY. Virgil, you certainly seem a little naïve for your age. Homer comes in my room nights—*of* course—and then he always goes away while it's still dark. He promised me that's how it would always be, and I know Homer won't break his

promise. Then mornings he doesn't come in again before I got my face fixed.

VIRGIL. Is it that important he shouldn't see you without you got your face fixed?

MERRY. Well maybe it isn't that important right now, Virgil, but it will be. And the way Homer is, it could do a lot of damage to his feelings if I suddenly had to ask him to quit coming in when I got to be of age when it would matter. Right after Homer became my beau, I figured I ought to start right in planning for the future. It was our wedding night I asked him to give me this promise. That way I know he'll never break it.

VIRGIL (*laying his book down on his knees and surrendering himself to musing in wonder on Merry's revelation*). And you feel you couldn't possibly let him in till you're through fixing your face?

MERRY (*with quiet resolution*). No, I couldn't do that, Virgil. I just couldn't *do* that. (*Dreamily*) You see, Virgil, I have something I want to preserve.

VIRGIL. Your face?

MERRY (*gently*). No, Virgil, something intangible, something that's been kind of entrusted to me. I don't know that you can understand very well, Virgil. Although you and I are pretty much of an age, I guess a woman matures faster than a man. I doubt that you have achieved sufficient maturation yet to understand. But what I feel is—well, I guess I feel that romance is a very wonderful and a very fragile thing. (*She lets these words hang like a beautiful sunset in the air for a moment. Then she trips to the door at the right.*)

MERRY. I guess I'll just go along and see who it was dropped by. Maybe I can help Homer some. (*Opening the door and pausing.*) Well . . . I'm glad you talked with me about this, Virgil. I'm not going to tell Homer we talked about it, because I believe that even within the marital framework there ought to be areas of privacy. If you have some more problems, Virgil, I hope you will talk with me about them. I have a personal conviction that relationships can only achieve a completely adjusted orientation if problems are brought right out in the open. And I sincerely hope we can all three pass a wonderful vacation in this lovely old *palazzo.*

(MERRY *leaves by the door at the right.*
LIA-PIA *shuffles in by the door at the left.
She is a dear old thing in a black overall
and lopsided bedroom slippers. She is
ushering in a smartly dressed young
Italian.*)

LIA-PIA (*clucking comfortingly, like a
dove*). Si accomodi, signore, si accomodi,
si accomodi.

(LIA-PIA *shuffles out, leaving the visitor,
as he thinks, alone. He deposits his smart,
speckled-leather briefcase against his side
of the Coca-Cola crate, settles the sit of
his perfectly pressed suit, puts one foot
up on the side of the crate and bends to
pull up one of his quite unsagging thin-
nylon socks.*)

VIRGIL (*picking up his book to resume
reading and speaking without looking at
the stranger*). I don't know why the old
thing told you to accommodate yourself.
I don't see where you can.

THE VISITOR (*whirling round in surprise*). Ah, scusi, non avevo visto—

VIRGIL. O.K. maybe I *am* insignificant.
You could sit on the Coca-Cola crate but
I doubt that it's comfortable.

THE ITALIAN. Please, it is no matter. I am
come to work, not sit. You are Mr. Knockerbicker?

VIRGIL. Mm-hm.

ANGELO. I am the man who is come to
fix the—

VIRGIL. O, then I'm not the Mr. Knockerbicker you want. The Mr. Knockerbicker
you want, the Mr. Knockerbicker who
counts, will be along presently. Pardon me
if I catch up on some reading while you
wait. (*He begins to do so.*)

ANGELO. Please? The Mr. Knockerbicker who counts?

VIRGIL. Sure, who counts out the dough.
I'm just the kid brother. The Mr. Knockerbicker who counts went to meet you,
and the Mrs. Knockerbicker who counts
went right after him, but the way this
palace is constructed, if you miss somebody the first time round, you have to
go through the whole tour of the building
before you get back where you started. I
guess the *Renaissance* just wasn't *onto*
the principle of the corridor.

ANGELO (*with a self-introductory bow*).
Lumaca, Angelo.

VIRGIL (*with an inclination of his head,
sidelong, over his book*). Knockerbicker,
Virgil.

ANGELO. You are reading?

VIRGIL (*continuing to do so*). Mm-hm.

ANGELO. I, too, read very often. It is
being very hot. I take off my coat. This is
not a nuisance?

VIRGIL (*without attending*). Go right
ahead.

(ANGELO *takes off coat, folds it inside
out, removes his wallet, hangs his coat on
a knob of the shutters at the window not
occupied by* VIRGIL *and returns to talk to*
VIRGIL.)

ANGELO. Ah, that is better. You are not
being too hot, dressed all in black?

VIRGIL. Black is the coolest colour there
is. And I am one of the coolest characters
there is.

ANGELO. I am sorry. I have been bad to
ask that question.

VIRGIL. How so?

ANGELO. Probably you are wearing the
black because you are being bereaved.

VIRGIL. No, I wasn't bereaved recently,
but now you come to mention it I'm prepared.

ANGELO. You are reading a book which
is interesting?

VIRGIL (*still reading*). Enthralling.

ANGELO. Love story, police story, es-
pionage, *Reader's Digest,* Science Fiction?

VIRGIL. Poetry.

ANGELO. Ah, I, too, am loving poetry.
Even though I am being an engineer, I
am loving poetry. You know what I am
thinking, Mr. Knockerbicker junior? I am
thinking in life today there is not being
enough poetry. I am loving beauty in all
its forms. I love poetry, music, paintings—
I am loving all the arts. And you know
why, Mr. Knockerbicker junior? Because
they are so beautiful. To me, they are so
beautiful. I am loving all the beautiful
things—including the women, yes?

VIRGIL (*without interest*). That so?

ANGELO. I think you are feeling the
same, eh, Mr. Knockerbicker junior?

VIRGIL. Mm-hm. (*As an afterthought.*)
All except the women.

ANGELO (*astounded*). How is this? You
are not loving the women?

VIRGIL (*without emphasis*). I'm homo-
sexual.

ANGELO (*completely taken aback*). O. (*After a pause of swallowing the information.*) I am begging your pardon.

VIRGIL (*without looking up*). Don't mention it. (*Musing.*) What a *peculiar* conversation.

ANGELO. Mr. Knockerbicker junior, this poem you read, who is the author?

(VIRGIL *reads to the end of the page before replying.*)

VIRGIL. I am.

(ANGELO *laughs politely.* VIRGIL *continues to read.*)

ANGELO. You are meaning this is true? Really you have written a poem?

VIRGIL. Am writing. I didn't finish it yet.

ANGELO. And you are beginning it when?

VIRGIL. When I was ten.

ANGELO. You are writing since you have been ten one poem? So many years, one poem?

VIRGIL. I'm not that old.

ANGELO. No, but—

VIRGIL. I guess it was the romantic movement spread the idea a poem has to be a lyric.

ANGELO. Without the lyric feeling, where is the poetry?

VIRGIL. Before romanticism was invented, there were plenty of long poems. My namesake Virgil, who was born not too far from here, wrote an extremely long poem. My brother's namesake wrote two of them. Dante and Milton also wrote long poems, but as my parents didn't have any more sons they are not commemorated in our family.

ANGELO. Dante, Milton, that was long ago. Modern life moves with more pace, Mr. Knockerbicker junior. How did you find rhymes for a long poem? It is difficult, yes?

VIRGIL. I don't use rhyme.

ANGELO. Without the rhyme, how is it poetry? You are writing the blank verses?

VIRGIL. I don't use meter.

ANGELO. What can it be like, your poem?

VIRGIL. My poem is kind of an American Song of Songs.

ANGELO. But without the rhyme, without the meter, where is the poetry?

VIRGIL. The poetry is in the subject.

ANGELO. Mr. Knockerbicker junior, what *is* the subject of your poem?

VIRGIL. The subject of my poem is the American Woman.

ANGELO. Ah, now I am understanding. The American Woman, she is poetry herself.

VIRGIL (*prosaically agreeing*). Yes, I include her among the ideas which have a sufficient poetic content in themselves, along with the collision of planets and the copulation of dinosaurs.

ANGELO (*overwhelmed*). You must be a very poetical person, Mr. Knockerbicker junior.

VIRGIL. Fortunately I don't have to reply to that compliment because I hear the other Mr. Knockerbicker on his way back. He has a very weighty tread. Come to think of it, Homer must weigh all of a hundred and sixty.

(HOMER *comes worriedly through the door at the left.*)

VIRGIL. Meet Mr. Homer Knockerbicker. Homer, meet Mr. Angelo Lumaca.

HOMER (*politely, but too distractedly worried to pay attention*). Mr. Lumaca.

ANGELO. Call me Angelo.

HOMER. Sure. (*Worry bursting out of him.*) Virgil, did you see Merry any place? Lia-Pia was saying something about the *signora*, but I didn't follow her too well—

VIRGIL. Merry went right after you. She'll be back. (*Virgil resumes his reading.*)

HOMER. I certainly hope she will. This *palazzo*. . . . (*Sighs, and wipes his spectacles.*) A person as delicate as Merry could easily get lost in a *palazzo* like this. Pardon me, Angelo, I'm sorry I had to keep you waiting, I got snarled up with the hired help, she only speaks Italian, I didn't get what she was trying to tell me. . . .

(MERRY *comes through the door at the left.*)

MERRY. O, Homer, there you are. I was— (*Stopping and dimpling prettily*) Why, I didn't know we had company.

HOMER. Honey, I'd like to have you meet Mr. Angelo Lumaca.

ANGELO. Call me please Angelo.

MERRY. Angelo? Why, that must mean angel. That's a perfectly darling name. I'd certainly feel very privileged to call you by a name like that. Welcome to our *palazzo*, Angelo. I certainly never thought

I'd be welcoming a real Italian to a real Italian *palazzo*.

ANGELO. Welcome to Italy, Mrs. Knockerbicker. (*He kisses her hand.*)

MERRY (*delighted*). You certainly have *palazzo* manners.

VIRGIL. Now she'll want us all to kiss her hand every morning. It'll become a ritual, like the breakfast food.

HOMER. Now see here, Virgil—

MERRY. Now, Homer, quit picking on Virgil. You know he can't help himself.

ANGELO (*conversationally, trying to help them steer past a family row*). You hired this *palazzo*, Mr. Knockerbicker?

HOMER (*distractedly*). What? O yeh, sure. For our vacation.

ANGELO. You have a very old *palazzo* here, Mr. Knockerbicker. *Cinquecento.*

VIRGIL. And boy is it hideous.

MERRY (*deeply reproachful*). Why, Virgil, how can you *say* such a thing?

ANGELO. O, no, Mr. Knockerbicker junior, you must be mistaken. This *palazzo* is very old, it is of the *rinascimento,* you understand? of the sixteenth century. So it *cannot* be hideous.

MERRY. O, don't take any account of Virgil. Have you looked out the window, Angelo? We have a real Italian yard out there, a *giardino*.

ANGELO. La signora parla italiano!

MERRY (*almost ecstatic with pleasure*). O, no, not really, just a word or two I picked up from the hired help, but I certainly hope to learn a lot more. Yes, we have a real Italian *giardino*, and real Italian doves and real Italian chickens. I didn't learn the Italian for doves and chickens yet. But I get a big thrill just from watching those chickens and knowing every one of them is a real Italian chicken.

ANGELO (*with a glance through the window*). You have twenty, thirty hens out there and only two cocks. Nice life for the cocks, eh?

VIRGIL. If you like responsibility.

HOMER (*belatedly understanding some at least of Angelo's remark*). O, you mean roosters.

ANGELO. Please?

VIRGIL. Somebody sold you English English instead of American English, Angelo. In the United States we have to call them roosters, because American women have such effortlessly sexual trains of thought.

MERRY (*very rappingly*). Virgil, will you please be quiet?

HOMER. What'd he say, Merry? I didn't get it.

MERRY. Don't let's any of us pay any attention to Virgil. He certainly has some anti-social compulsions this morning. But I'm not going to let anything spoil this wonderful place. D'you know, Angelo, living here, I can just imagine I'm back in those old days, with knights and cardinals and poison and frescoes and illuminated manuscripts. . . . O, I was just wild to get here. Last fall, I said to Mr. Knockerbicker "Homer, if it's the last thing you ever do for me, take me to Italy."

HOMER (*worrying*). Yeh, I know, honey, but in those days they didn't have too good a concept of hygiene, and an old place like this . . .

MERRY. Homer, quit worrying. We're making out fine.

HOMER. So far honey. Knock on wood. (*Casting about anxiously.*) Where *is* some wood? Hell, this *palazzo's* all marble.

VIRGIL. There's the Coca-Cola crate.

HOMER. O, sure. (*He knocks on it.*) Thanks, Virgil.

MERRY. Now, Homer, quit fussing. What *could* happen?

HOMER (*putting an arm round her, drawing her convulsively to him and drooling a little over her hair*). You're a brave little person, Merry. D'you know, Angelo, when we came here, they didn't even have a *shower* in this *palazzo,* only a tub.

MERRY. Relax, Homer, will you. You'll get yourself a duodenal. Just relax, and let the lovely Italian culture just seep into you.

HOMER. Maybe I'll get around to that, baby, when I got this place fixed so it's good enough for you.

MERRY. O, you take marvellous care of me, Homer. D'you know, Angelo, Homer had a shower fitted.

HOMER. Yeh, I had this shower fitted, and I installed another icebox—

MERRY. Why, yes, Angelo, Homer had a complete kitchen installed right here (*She points to the door at the right.*)—

it's right through there just next door to the living room, so we don't have to have our food cooked by the hired help any more—

HOMER. When we first came, the hired help wanted to cook everything, but she was operating under pretty primitive conditions—

MERRY. O, it wasn't just the conditions, Homer dear, it was the calories. I don't know, Angelo, if you ever saw a breakdown of the calorific content of olive oil, but believe you me it would horrify you. Well, the first thing Homer did, he imported a stock of low-calory cooking medium from the States, and then he fixed up this little kitchen right out there—

HOMER. Yeh, well, we have this kitchen, but there are some gadgets I wasn't yet able to find in Italy, and some we have that I imported but they're not yet operational—

ANGELO (*excitedly trying to get a word in*). But, Mr. Knockerbicker, listen, *please*. This is why I am here.

HOMER. Why you are—I don't get it. Pardon me a moment, Angelo, I have to wipe off my lenses again. (*He does so.*)

ANGELO (*pleadingly*). *Please*, Mr. Knockerbicker. I am the man who has come to fix the waste disposal unit!

HOMER (*amazed*). No-o-o? (*Putting on his now wiped spectacles and stepping forward.*) Well, how do you like that? Hullo there again.

ANGELO. Hullo.

HOMER. Hi.

ANGELO. Ciao.

HOMER (*laughing*). We-ell. I guess that just about takes care of it. You know, I guess I thought that as you aren't an American you wouldn't know how to fix a waste disposal unit.

ANGELO. I am the accredited Italian agent. I have here my card. (*He proffers it, then reads it aloud.*) You see. I am the accredited agent of the Atlantic Seaboard Waste Disposal Unit Corporation of New York, NY, USA.

HOMER. Well, what do you know? Isn't that swell, Merry? Now we can have that waste disposal unit operational.

ANGELO (*with self-assurance*). You certainly can, Mr. Knockerbicker.

MERRY (*graciously social*). Homer, would you take Angelo through there and show him where it has to be connected?

HOMER (*happily*). I sure will. (*He ushers* ANGELO *across the room and opens the door at the right for him.*) Right through here, Angelo.

ANGELO (*pausing at the door to make a declaration*). You are going to enjoy this waste disposal unit, Mrs. Knockerbicker. (*Reciting.*) This is the finest waste disposal unit on the market, a triumph of American technical know-how. This unit will dispose of *anything*. Say goodbye forever to malodorous, unhygienic, germbreeding, squelchy bundles. The Atlantic Seaboard waste disposal unit takes over. Soggy, crunchy, pulpy, bony, mushy, spiny—it's all one to the Atlantic Seaboard waste disposal unit.

VIRGIL. The guy certainly is accredited.

MERRY (*on a sudden thought*). Say, Homer, ask him if he ever fixed one before.

HOMER. You got something there, Merry. They told me this was the first they imported into Italy. Say, Angelo, did you ever fix one before?

ANGELO (*pained, and holding up his hand like a traffic policeman*). Mr. Knockerbicker. Mrs. Knockerbicker. Please. I am the accredited agent. I fix it.

(HOMER *and* ANGELO *go through the door at the right.* MERRY, *swinging her pony tail, trips her way to the unoccupied window-seat, perches one urchin knee on it and looks out of the window.* VIRGIL *reads for a moment, then without looking up:*)

VIRGIL. You mad at me, Merry?

MERRY. Why, no, Virgil. I guess I maybe would be, if I didn't know you had problems.

VIRGIL. I got problems O.K. How'm I going to end this poem?

MERRY. Maybe it'd help you feel less mixed-up, Virgil, if you kind of explained your problem to me.

VIRGIL. I guess it's easier for composers. They just come back to the key note, and it sounds swell.

MERRY. And you want kind of a key note for your poem?

VIRGIL. It's not that simple. I need a climax—something terrible and tragic:

and then a resolution: and then some kind of final chorus, to round the thing off.

MERRY. I'll keep it in mind, Virgil. Maybe I'll come up with something we can kick around together.

(HOMER *returns, much less worried than usual.*)

HOMER. He's making out fine in there. We'll soon have that unit operational. (*Going up to her and giving her a squeeze.*) And how're *you* making out, Merry? (*He places an infatuated kiss on top of her head.*) Still looking out that window?

MERRY. O, I'm as happy as I can be just so I can watch those romantic old doves and those quaint little old chickens.

HOMER (*sifting her pony tail through his fingers*). You're just a lovely little person, Merry. You're just so satisfied with the simple things in life.

MERRY (*suddenly freezing with horror as she gazes through the window*). Homer!

HOMER. Why, Merry! Hey, Merry! Merry, what's your problem? Merry, look at me! Virgil! She's gone quite rigid, like she was in shock. I guess I ought to pat her cheeks. Hey, Merry, Merry! (HOMER *nervously pats her cheeks.*)

MERRY. Homer, I been watching those roosters—

HOMER. Sure, Merry, I know it—

MERRY. Homer, *one of those roosters is a degenerate.*

HOMER (*agonisedly, very gently*). My poor little Merry, my poor little Merry, why did you have to be born so sensitive? Now, listen, Merry, you quit thinking of it right now. You start right in thinking about something beautiful. You start thinking about music or lovely old paintings or beautiful literature. . . .

VIRGIL. Why don't you tell her go take a look at the waste disposal unit?

HOMER. Why, Merry, you hear what Virgil said? I think that's a swell idea. Come along now. (*He leads her across the room to the door at the right.*) If there's one thing that ought to take your mind off all the ugly, unclean things that happen in this world, it's that waste disposal unit. (*Opening the door for her.*) You go right on in there, Merry, and see how the project's making out. (HOMER *tenderly closes the door after Merry and then marches back across the room.*)

HOMER. Now what're we going to do?

VIRGIL. I don't know why, but that question always panics me. Do about what, anyway?

HOMER. That rooster, of course. I can't ask Merry to share the premises with a rooster that's a degenerate.

VIRGIL. I don't see why it's any worse than asking her to share them with a brother-in-law that's a degenerate.

HOMER (*angrily*). Will you quit talking that way? You'd be a perfectly healthful American boy, if you'd only try.

VIRGIL. I guess that's what's unhealthful about me. I can't even try to try.

HOMER. Why not, for pity's sakes? Don't I have enough on my mind as it is?

VIRGIL. Maybe I'm afraid it would spoil my work.

HOMER. Now that's another thing. I keep trying to get round to talking with you about that. How much longer is your work going to take?

VIRGIL. I can't say. I'm kind of held up for a climax.

(HOMER *deliberates, then:*)

HOMER. You know, Virgil, I sometimes get to wondering if you wrote anything at all.

VIRGIL (*deliberates, then deciding to take up the challenge*). O.K. I'll read it to you.

HOMER. Right now?

VIRGIL. Mm-hm.

HOMER. But you didn't finish it yet.

VIRGIL. I'll read it as far as I went. Maybe you'll come up with something for the ending.

HOMER. I don't think I have any talent.

VIRGIL. Then sit down, brother, and listen to mine.

HOMER. How can I sit, there's no place to—I guess I can stand. It won't take that long, will it?

VIRGIL. Why didn't you hire some furnishings for this *palazzo*?

HOMER. That's a very selfish request, Virgil. You're the one that sits around all day. Maybe I'll hire some furnishings when I get round to it, but the first problem is to make the basic living conditions fit for Merry.

VIRGIL. O.K. brother, you stand. But

don't move around any, you could distract me.

HOMER. O.K. O.K. Quit stalling, Virgil. Shoot.

VIRGIL (*turns back to the beginning of his book, clears his throat, then breaks off for a preliminary*). Say, Homer. I hope you know this isn't going to be poetry like you mean poetry. It's more like—did you ever read any Chinese poetry?

HOMER. Sure, I guess I read some Chinese poetry some place, some magazine or something. In English.

VIRGIL. O, my poetry's in English, too. I just wanted you to know the opening sequences are modelled on Chinese poetry.

HOMER. Virgil, do you figure you can sell this? Is there a market for it? I don't know that the Chinese market's too easy to break into. I don't know, but it could even be that poetry is scheduled.

VIRGIL. Scheduled?

HOMER. Schedule of prohibited exports. I mean, if you're thinking of *Red* China.

VIRGIL. Brother!

HOMER. O.K. O.K., I didn't say a thing, go right ahead.

VIRGIL (*announcing*). Section One. (*Reading:*)

The American Woman
Is strange, terrible and beautiful,
Like fruits from the sea.
There is nothing she would not ask her
    husband to do for her.
For this reason
She appears to be the most independent
    woman in the world,
Just as aristocrats are said to be "of
    independent means"
When in fact they are supported by
    slave labour.

(*There is a pause.*)

HOMER. Is that all?

VIRGIL. That's all of Section One.

HOMER. Maybe I'll get to see more in it when I become better accustomed to it.

VIRGIL (*reading*).
Section Two.
The American Woman has grown
Like a cactus
In a place where there is no water.
The American Woman would rather be
    a lovely person
Than be herself.
The American Woman would rather be

a lovely, warm, genuine, sincere
    person
Than simply be.

(VIRGIL *leaves a brief pause.*)

HOMER. Say, Virgil, do you think Merry's making out O.K. in there? Suppose this guy Angelo makes a pass at her?

VIRGIL. Homer, quit worrying and concentrate. Merry can handle it.

HOMER. I doubt that she can. That guy's a Latin, he's hot-blooded—

VIRGIL. You don't seem too well acquainted with Latin mores. If he does make a pass, he'll just pinch her fanny. That's the climactic act for Latins. Merry'll just think a mosquito got her.

HOMER. I don't know that she—

VIRGIL. Of *course* she can handle it, Homer, she'll handle it with a flit gun. Now can I read the third *canto*?

HOMER. Third what? Sounds like you were going horseback riding.

VIRGIL. Homer, you're not *that* illiterate. Or maybe you meant it as a gag. The third *canto* is freer and more rhapsodic in style.

HOMER. O.K. O.K. I guess we'll get to hear of it if Merry has problems.

VIRGIL. (*reading*). There is only one American Woman but she has two faces: one young, one old.

When she is young, she is younger than you would have thought possible. When she is old, she is older than the rocks she has persuaded her husband to buy for her.

The young American Woman is like an ad in a magazine of a glass of milk fresh from the icebox. She looks thirst quenching. But when you taste her, she tastes of wood-pulp.

The young American Woman is a wax apple. She is flawless. But she has no sap. Except her husband.

When you have talked with her a little while, you realise she was not begotten by sexual intercourse. Therefore:

When she grows old, she becomes a goddess. I love her best when she is old. For then she commands me more.

(*Aside*) You know, I really mean that, Homer. I'm determined to live to be a very old man, because I want to see Merry grow old. (*Resuming:*)

I followed the American goddess

Through the beautiful shrines of Europe.
I shadowed her through the Louvre,
I nearly caught up with her in the Rue de la Paix;
I watched her buying leather goods from a tiny but very expensive basement shop in Florence;
I dodged between her and the sunlight in Roman colonnades;
I glimpsed her in Castile;
When I stood in the Parthenon she was there.
She loves all that is old and said to be beautiful.
She has no taste.
But she has attended many seminars on good taste.

The old American Woman
Is all locust and no wild honey.
She is dry and mottled, like peanut brittle.
If you held her and bent her, she would snap.
But you do not lay hands on a cult object.
The strands of her hair are one with the spun gold she wears at her wrists and neck;
Her eyes are one with the topazes she wears on her knucklebones;
The skin of her forearms is one with the alligator hide that makes her purse.
I followed the tinkle of her charms on her charm bracelet
And the tinkle of her beaten metal hair.
I followed the clacking of her heels
And the clacking of her voice,
Which is an almost perfect imitation of the human voice.
I followed. I am unnatural; I am perverse.

The American Woman is more strange and more bizarre
Than the art of the mummy-maker.
And she is more old.
Organic in form, she is not created by life,
But is slowly deposited, like a tree of crystals
Imitating a baroque pearl.
The American Woman is a wax avocado pear
From a desert under the sea

(ANGELO *bursts in from the door at the right and flings himself, across the doorway, into the posture of the blinded Oedipus.*)

ANGELO (*sobbing and groaning*). O no no no no no no no no no. Orrore! (*He falls silent; his groans are quietly reiterated by a soft mechanical chug-chug from the next room. For a second everyone is too shocked to show reaction. Then* HOMER *dashes across the room towards* ANGELO, *who compassionately bars the way.*)

HOMER (*trying desperately to get past*). What happened? What happened to Merry? Let me in there, Angelo, I got to get in there and see what happened to Merry.

ANGELO. Non c'è niente da vedere.

HOMER (*distractedly over his shoulder*). What'd he say, Virgil?

VIRGIL (*threnodically*). He says there is nothing to see.

HOMER (*in a groan of horror*). What?

ANGELO (*pleading distressfully*). Mr. Knockerbicker, I *tell* her not to lean over it and peer down it, but she wants to check I fixed it right—

HOMER (*beside himself*). Can't you reverse the machinery or something? (*Bursting past* ANGELO.) Let me *in* there—

ANGELO (*appealing to Virgil*). Mr. Knockerbicker junior, *you* are understanding, are you not? I *did* fix it right. If only she had believed me. Of *course* I reverse the machinery, but this is a very efficient unit. In thirty seconds, everything is—you understand, Mr. Knockerbicker junior?— *everything* . . .

(*The noise of the machinery is switched off.* HOMER *plods brokenly back into the* salone.)

HOMER. My little Merry! My little Merry! She was such a dainty little person, the last thing she would have wanted was to get mixed up with the garbage.

(*There is a moment's respectful silence.*) Virgil, I know you will never forget that just before—why, it could even have been at the very moment—(HOMER *nearly breaks down.*) Well, anyhow, that you were just saying you wanted to live to see what a lovely lovely old lady Merry was going to grow into.

(LIA-PIA *shuffles unperturbedly into the room by the door at the left. She is followed by* MRS. VAN DEN MOST—*an older Merry and taken, of course, by the same actress.*)

LIA-PIA. Signori, ho incontrato queste signore davanti alla casa, non so cosa vuole. . . .

(LIA-PIA *shuffles out by the route she came, closing the door behind her.*)

HOMER (*horrified to reeling point*). Mrs. van den *Most!*

MRS. VAN DEN MOST (*waggishly reproachful*). Now, Homer. You know I asked you to call me something more intimate, such as Mom, because I think it will be so lovely for Merry to feel her family has been really integrated into her marriage.

HOMER. I didn't know—

MRS. VAN DEN MOST (*wagging a waggish finger at him*). I know it, Homer, you didn't even know I was in Europe. Well, I figured I'd just hop over and see how you were taking care of my little girl. (HOMER *hides his face, and groans.*) I was counting on giving you a real surprise, and I must say you certainly seem to have gotten one. I wasn't even going to ring the doorbell, I was just snooping around outside, when your lovely old Italian hired help came out to feed your chickens. Those certainly are lovely chickens, Homer, I can just guess how Merry loves those chickens. And your lovely old Italian hired help brought me right along in. (*Noticing, with displeasure.*) O. Virgil's here. Hi, Virgil. I certainly hope you're beginning to get a hold on those problems of yours. (*Noticing, with pleasure.*) Why, we have company, I didn't notice.

VIRGIL. This is Signor Angelo Lumaca.

MRS. VAN DEN MOST. Why, you must be an Italian! I just love Italians, I love your *Ren*aissance, I feel sure you must be a very good friend of my little girl, because she just loves your *Ren*aissance too. Now where *is* my little girl? No, don't tell me. I can guess. Merry always takes such good care of her husband, Signor Lumaca, she's a real homebody, I don't have to ask where she is. I feel positive she's right along in the kitchen. Homer just loves her homebody ways, don't you, Homer?

Right from the start, that girl loved to be in the kitchen. She has such a happy temperament, she makes everyone happy. Well, I should know. Right from the start she made *me* happy. Why, d'you know, Signor Lumaca, that little girl was toilet-trained before she was one year old. It was on account of she had such a happy temperament I persuaded Mr. van den Most to let me call her Merry. Lots of folks, when they first meet her, they think she's called Mary—Maria, as you would say it, Signor Lumaca—but no, her name is really Merry, M-E-double-R-Y, because, I always tell them, she *is*. Now where *is* the kitchen? No, naughty me, I don't need to ask. I didn't pass it on my way along, so I guess it must be right through here. (*She opens the door at the right.*) I'll just go give Merry a little surprise. (*Calling:*) Merry! Merry dear! (*Popping her head back into the* salone) I didn't find Merry yet, Homer, but I saw you had a waste disposal unit installed. Now that's very thoughtful of you, Homer, I'm sure Merry appreciates that. I wouldn't have thought you could obtain one over here. Well, I guess you imported it, but I reckon it was quite a problem for you getting it operational. I wonder if you got it fixed right. I'll just go take a quick look.

(MRS. VAN DEN MOST *hurries out. At once, the machinery noise begins again.*)

ANGELO (*lunging after her*). No! Mrs. van den Most, no! Come back! No!

HOMER (*dashing across the room*). Stop her, Angelo! I'm coming! Stop her!

(ANGELO *and* HOMER *sprint through the door at the right. Even* VIRGIL *is sufficiently anxious to discard his book, rises from the window-seat, and stands tense while he awaits the outcome.*)

(*The noise of the W.D.U. rises to a climax, and stops.* HOMER *and* ANGELO *return to the* salone.)

ANGELO (*with an explanatory, proving-his-point gesture*). You see, Mr. Knockerbicker—

HOMER. Virgil—

VIRGIL (*incredulously*). No?

HOMER. } Yes.
ANGELO. }

HOMER (*with deep, plodding philosophy*). The way I look at it, God proposes—

VIRGIL. And the Atlantic Seaboard waste disposal unit disposes.

HOMER (*with not altogether reluctant resignation*). Well, everything has come to an end—

VIRGIL (*rising to exultation*). And the Atlantic Seaboard waste disposal unit is the American male's best friend.

HOMER ⎱(*beginning a stomping dance
VIRGIL ⎰with one another*).

Soggy crunchy
Pulpy bony
Mushy spiny

VIRGIL. Mottled shiny

HOMER.⎱ Pulpy bony
VIRGIL. ⎰

ANGELO (*trying a last plea*). Signori Knockerbicker, *please*—

VIRGIL (*stomping gaily*). How're you feeling now, brother?

HOMER (*likewise*). How'm I feeling now? (*As in a college cry*) M-E-double-R-Y.

HOMER ⎱ (*in a shout in unison*).
VIRGIL ⎰ Merry!

VIRGIL. Say goodbye forever to squelchy bundles!

ANGELO (*giving up restraint and joining the dance with a wild, free-lance fling, as he sings in a bold tenor*). La donna è mobile! La donna è mobile!

HOMER ⎫
VIRGIL ⎬ (*stomping and chanting*).
ANGELO ⎭

Soggy crunchy
Honeybunchy
Sodden dry
Sweetiepie
Say goodbye
Mushy spiny
Dainty tiny
Lovely happy
Minced-up pappy
Very merry

ANGELO (*floating his tenor above the stomp*). La donna è mobile.

VIRGIL (*basso profondo*). E disponibile!

(*There is a general, happy, panting collapse onto the floor.*)

VIRGIL (*happily*). Angelo, did it take but *everything*?

ANGELO (*with happy assurance*). Every single thing, Mr. Knockerbicker junior.

HOMER. Even the second time round?

ANGELO. Second time round was even more efficient, Mr. Knockerbicker. That machine likes something tough to bite on.

VIRGIL (*solemnly*). Angelo, Homer, I guess we have witnessed the ultimate triumph of American technology.

CURTAIN

COME INTO THE GARDEN MAUD

A Light Comedy in One Act and Two Scenes

Noël Coward

Come into the Garden Maud was first presented by H. M. Tennent, Ltd., at the Queen's Theatre, Ltd., on April 14, 1966, with the following cast:

ANNA-MARY CONKLIN   Irene Worth   VERNER CONKLIN   Noël Coward
FELIX, *a waiter* Sean Barrett   MAUD CARAGNANI   Lilli Palmer

Directed by Vivian Matalon
Setting by Brian Currah
Costumes by Molyneux-Paris
Lighting by Joe Davis

The time is the present. The action of the play passes in the course of one evening. The scene is the sitting room of a private suite at the Hotel Beau Rivage, Lausanne-Ouchy, Switzerland.

SINCE 1924, when he sprang to international prominence with *The Vortex,* Noël Coward has symbolized glistening sophistication, trenchant wit, and impeccable style in the theatre. Few can match his prolificacy as dramatist, composer, lyricist, director, and performer.

Born near London in 1899, Mr. Coward made his stage debut at the age of ten. At twenty-one, his first produced play, *I'll Leave It to You,* opened in the West End. As he personally has described the event: "The first night was a roaring success, and I made a boyish speech. The critics were mostly very enthusiastic, and said a lot about it having been a great night, and that a new playwright had been discovered, etc., but unfortunately their praise was not potent enough to lure audiences to the New Theatre for more than five weeks; so the run ended rather miserably. . . ."

In the four decades that followed, however, the unique theatrical wizardry of Noël Coward *did* lure hundreds of thousands into theatres in many parts of the world. Among his forty plays, musicals, and revues are such landmarks of their respective eras as: *This Year of Grace; Hay Fever; Fallen Angels; Private Lives; Design for Living; Cavalcade; Bitter Sweet; Conversation Piece; Set to Music; Quadrille; Present Laughter; Blithe Spirit;* and the memorable series of nine short plays, *Tonight at 8:30,* which brightened a depression-shaded world in the mid-1930's with the author and radiant Gertrude Lawrence as co-stars.

A Renaissance man of the theatre, Mr. Coward also has made some notable contributions to films (*In Which We Serve; Brief Encounter; This Happy Breed*) and has added substantially to international library shelves with four volumes of memoirs, several collections of short stories, a popular novel, *Pomp and Circumstance,* and, of course, his forty or so published plays.

In spite of the fact that he occasionally has come under critical fire from some disciples of the "new wave" for persistently clinging to traditional, and eschewing exploratory, forms in the theatre, Mr. Coward still maintains his undeniable status as one of the giants of the twentieth-century theatre. This was affirmed unequivocally in 1964, when Britain's celebrated National Theatre Company, under the leadership of Sir Laurence Olivier, triumphantly revived Mr. Coward's indestructible comedy, *Hay Fever,* with Dame Edith Evans as star. Its success with press and public sparked an extraordinary resurgence of interest in the author and his plays, with additional West End revivals coming close upon the heels of the precursive *Hay Fever.*

In 1966, London again welcomed him as author and co-star of *Suite in Three Keys.* Lauded by the London *Daily Express* as "Coward at his zenith," *Suite in Three Keys* represents the omnibus title for three individual plays designed to be performed by the same players in two evenings. The program consists of the full-length *A Song at Twilight,* and the brace of short plays, *Shadows of the Evening* and *Come into the Garden Maud,* and while they are entitative, they are linked together by a mutual frame of action: the sitting room of a private suite in a luxury hotel in Switzerland.

The inclusion of *Come into the Garden Maud* in this anthology marks the first time the play has been published separately.

Noël Coward frequently has been likened to the nineteenth-century master of "artificial comedy," Oscar Wilde; for he, too, is a supreme precisionist at entertainingly tearing away at social pretensions. Yet, beneath the surface of his characteristically witty, cutting, and pointed dialogue, invariably there is a flow of pertinent commentary on contemporary society and its values.

SCENE ONE

The action of the play passes in the sitting room of a private suite of a luxurious hotel in Switzerland.

On stage Left there is a door leading into the bedroom. There are double doors at the back which open into a small lobby, from which open other rooms and the corridor.

The time is about seven o'clock on an evening in Spring. The windows opening onto a balcony on stage Right are open, disclosing a view of the lake of Geneva with the mountains of France on the opposite shore.

When the curtain rises, ANNA-MARY CONKLIN *is seated at the writing desk. Standing near her is* FELIX, *a handsome floor-waiter.* ANNA-MARY CONKLIN *is an exceedingly wealthy American matron in her late forties or early fifties. At the moment she is wearing an elaborate blue peignoir, blue ostrich-feather "mules" and a hairnet through which can be discerned blue hair tortured in the grip of a number of metal curlers. Her expression is disagreeable because she happens to be talking to a member of the lower classes.*

———

ANNA-MARY. And another thing, young man. When I ask for a bottle of Evian water bien glacée to be put by my bed every night, I *mean* a bottle of Evian water bien glacée, and not a bottle of Perrier water which is not glacée at all, and gazoz into the bargain.

FELIX. I am most sorry, madame. It shall not occur again.

ANNA-MARY. And you might also explain to that chambermaid, Caterina or whatever her damn' name is, that for my breakfast I take prune juice, not orange juice, toast Melba, and not rolls, and good American coffee with cream, not that thick black French stuff served with lukewarm milk.

FELIX. Very well, madame.

ANNA-MARY. And you can tell her as well that I don't like being nattered at the first thing in the morning in a language that I can't understand. Neither Mr. Conklin nor I speak Italian and the sooner the staff of this hotel realises it, the better it will be for everybody concerned.

FELIX (*blandly*). Va bene, signora.

ANNA-MARY. Are you being impertinent?

FELIX. Oh, no, madame. I most humbly beg your pardon. It's just a question of habitude.

ANNA-MARY. It may interest you to know that Mr. Conklin and I have stayed in most of the finest hotels in Europe and when we pay the amount we do pay for the best service, we expect to get it.

FELIX. Very good, madame.

ANNA-MARY. That will be all for the moment. You'd better bring some ice later. Mr. Conklin takes his Scotch with lots of ice and plain water.

FELIX. Madame.

ANNA-MARY. Is the water here all right?

FELIX (*puzzled*). I fear I do not quite understand, madame.

ANNA-MARY. The drinking water? I mean it isn't just pumped up out of that lake without being properly filtered?

FELIX. There have been no complaints as far as I know, madame.

ANNA-MARY. All right. You can go now.

FELIX (*bowing*). A votre service, madame. (*He goes.*)

ANNA-MARY (*raising the telephone*). Hallo . . . Operator . . . Ici, Mrs. Conklin . . . Oui, Mrs. Verner Conklin, suite 354. Voulez vous me donner le numero de André's, le coiffeur? No. I don't know the number, that's why I'm asking you for it . . . the place is way up in the town somewhere not far from that big bridge, I was there this afternoon. All right I'll hold on. (*There is a pause during which she scrutinizes her fingernails with an expression of distaste. She continues in her execrable French accent.*) 'Allo . . . Je voudrai parler avec Monsieur André lui meme . . . oui, de la part de Mrs. Conklin . . . pardon . . . il est parti? Vous parlez anglais? Oh, bon . . . Well I'd like you to tell Monsieur André from me that the girl he gave me this afternoon has absolutely ruined my nails. I asked for Carmine foncee and what I got is tangerine foncee and they look terrible. I never noticed until I got out into the daylight. I had to take the stuff all off, and what is more she cut my cuticles, and if there's one thing I can't stand it is to have my cuticles cut, I like them pushed back gently with an orange stick and you can also explain to him that when I say I want a blue rinse I *mean* a blue rinse and not a purple dye. I've been under the shower for forty minutes trying to tone it down and—what? Well, I can't help who you are, you just give him those messages from Mrs. Conklin . . . Yes, Conklin . . . CONKLIN. Thank you. (*She slams down the receiver, rises irritably, takes a cigarette out of a box on the table and lights it. She paces up and down the room for a moment or two and then returns to the telephone, lifts the receiver and jiggles the machine impatiently.*) 'Allo, 'allo . . . Operator . . . *Donnez moi* . . . hold on a minute . . . (*She consults a pad on the desk.*) *Donnez moi vingt-trois-trente-six—vingt-deux—merci.* (*A moment's pause*) 'Allo, 'allo. *Ici,* Mrs. Conklin . . . *Je veux parler avec la comtesse s'il vous plait* . . . *Oui* . . . *Conklin* . . . (*Another pause*) 'Allo, Mariette? Yes it's me, Anna-Mary! Why, it's just wonderful to hear your voice—I can't believe we're actually here at last, I just keep pinching myself. I tried to call you this morning but your number was busy. First of all I want to thank you for those gorgeous flowers; it was just darling of you to send us such a lovely welcome—my dear, they light up the whole room, they literally do—I'm looking at them at this very minute. Oh, Verner? He's all right, he's out playing golf somewhere as usual. Now listen, honey, about tonight—you know about the etiquette of these sort of things much better than I do—ought I to go outside and *wait* for the Prince or will it be all right to have him sent to the bar where we're having cocktails? Oh, he likes things to be informal! Well, all I can say is thank God for that because I simply wouldn't know how to be anything else—I don't have to curtsey to her too do I—I do? Whatever for? I mean she was only a commoner after all before he married her . . . Oh, I see . . . Very well, I'll do what you say, but for heaven's sakes get here early to give me moral support . . . You're an angel! How's dear Henri? Out playing golf too! Well I suppose it gives them something to do. *Au revoir* darling, *à ce soir.* (*She hangs up the telephone and heaves a sigh.*)

(*At this moment* VERNER CONKLIN *comes into the room. He is a tall, pleasant-looking man in his late fifties. There is little remarkable about him beyond the fact that he has spent the major portion of his life making a great deal of money. He is carrying a bag of golf clubs which he flings onto the sofa.*)

ANNA-MARY (*ominously*). So you're back, are you?

VERNER. Yeah, sweetheart.

ANNA-MARY. You know, Verner, try as I may I just *do not* understand you.

VERNER. What's wrong?

ANNA-MARY. Well, to start with it's past six o'clock and we've got to be down in the bar and dressed by eight.

VERNER. What for? You said nobody was coming before eight-thirty.

ANNA-MARY. Did you remember about the cigars?

VERNER. Yes, I remembered about them.

ANNA-MARY. Well, thank heaven for small mercies.

VERNER. But the store was shut.

ANNA-MARY (*exasperated*). Verner!

VERNER. Sorry, sweetheart.

ANNA-MARY. Why didn't you call in on the way *out* to the golf course?

VERNER. I did. That was when the store was shut.

ANNA-MARY. I only have to ask you to do the smallest thing . . .

VERNER. All the stores shut in this lousy town from twelve until three.

ANNA-MARY. Clare Pethrington told me that the Prince likes a special sort of cigar which can only be got at one particular place here, and I, thinking it would be a nice gesture to have them served to him after dinner, am fool enough to ask you to take care of it for me—and what happens . . . ?

VERNER. Nothing happens. He does without 'em.

ANNA-MARY. Now, look here, Verner . . .

VERNER. There's no sense in working yourself up into a state. I guess the cigars you get in this hotel are liable to be good enough for anybody, and if His Royal Highness doesn't fancy 'em he can smoke his own, can't he?

ANNA-MARY (*bitterly*). You wouldn't care if the first dinner party we give in this "lousy town," as you call it, were a dead failure, would you?

VERNER. Calm down, sweetheart—it won't be. Our parties ain't ever failures; they cost too damn much.

ANNA-MARY. You know, Verner, that's one of the *silliest* things I've ever heard you say. The sort of people we're entertaining tonight are interested in other things besides money.

VERNER. Like hell they are!

ANNA-MARY. I can't think what you came on this trip at all for. You can play golf in Minneapolis.

VERNER. And on a damn' sight better course, too.

ANNA-MARY. You just about sicken me, Verner, you really do. Don't you get any kick at all out of travelling to new places and meeting distinguished people?

VERNER. What's so distinguished about 'em?

ANNA-MARY. Wouldn't you consider a Royal Prince distinguished?

VERNER. How do I know? I haven't met him yet.

ANNA-MARY. He just happens to be one of the most fascinating men in Europe, and one of the most sought after.

VERNER. Except in his own country, which he got thrown out of.

ANNA-MARY. You make me ashamed saying things like that.

VERNER. Listen, sweetheart. How's about you just stopping bawling me out and ringing for some ice. I want a drink.

ANNA-MARY. Ring for it yourself.

VERNER (*equably*). Okay . . . Okay . . . (*He rings the bell.*)

(*At this moment the telephone rings.*)

ANNA-MARY (*answering it*). Hallo . . . what . . . Who? . . . She's on her way up? Thank you. (*She hangs up.*) Oh, my God!

VERNER. What's wrong?

ANNA-MARY. It's Maud—Maud Caragnani—I invited her to come and have a drink, and it went completely out of my head.

VERNER. Well—we'll give her a drink. We can afford it.

ANNA-MARY. Here am I with so much on my mind that I'm going crazy and all you can do is try to be funny.

VERNER. Sorry, sweetheart.

ANNA-MARY. And take those dirty old golf clubs off the couch. This is a private sitting room, not the hotel lobby.

VERNER. I'll take 'em away when I've had my drink. She's the one we had dinner with that night in Rome, isn't she?

ANNA-MARY. She certainly is, in that stuffy little apartment that smelled of fish. I thought I'd die. No air-conditioning and all those ghastly stairs.

VERNER. I thought it was quite a cute little place, kinda picturesque. I liked her too; as a matter of fact she was the only one we met in Rome that I did like.

ANNA-MARY (*with an unpleasant little laugh*). Only because she made a play for you. Why, she practically threw herself at your head; it would have been embarrassing if it hadn't been so funny. I remember catching Lulu Canfield's eye across the table and it was as much as we could do not to burst out laughing.

VERNER. Well, it made a change anyway. Most of the characters we seem to pick up along the line don't even trouble to speak to me.

ANNA-MARY. You've only got yourself to blame for that, Verner. It's just that you happen to be a "taker" and not a "giver." You won't make an *effort* with people. You just sit there looking grouchy and don't say a word.

VERNER. Maybe. But I do say the five most important words of the evening. "*Garçon*, bring me the cheque!"

ANNA-MARY. You know something, Verner? It's just that very attitude of mind that makes Europeans despise us Americans. Can't you think of anything but dollars and cents?

VERNER (*mildly*). They're my dollars and cents, sweetheart, and I've spent the best part of my life pilin' 'em up, and if there didn't happen to be a hell of a lot of 'em you can bet your sweet ass we shouldn't be sitting here worrying about special cigars for Royal Princes and giving dinner parties to people who despise us.

ANNA-MARY. I wish you wouldn't use vulgar expressions like that.

VERNER. And I'll tell you something else. This dame who's on her way up, the one that handed you and Lulu Canfield such a good laugh by "throwing herself at my head." She at least took the trouble to give *us* dinner.

ANNA-MARY. Of course she did. It was a sprat to catch a whale. Even I could see that. She hasn't got a cent to her name. She's one of those social parasites who go about living off rich people.

VERNER. Well, at least she can't be lonely; the woods are full of 'em. Anyway, if you think so badly of her why the Hell did you ask her round for a drink?

ANNA-MARY. After all, she knows everybody, and she goes everywhere. She phoned me this morning and I had to think of something.

VERNER. She happens to be a Princess too, doesn't she? That's always a help.

ANNA-MARY (loftily). Only a Sicilian one. Princes in Sicily are a dime a dozen. (She glances at herself in the mirror.) My God, I can't receive her looking like this! I must put something in my hair.

VERNER. Try a crash-helmet, sweetheart. You're sure in a fighting mood.

(ANNA-MARY shoots him a withering look and goes hurriedly into the bedroom.

(There is a knock at the door. VERNER goes to open it. MAUD CARAGNANI comes into the room. She is an attractive-looking woman of about forty-seven or eight. Her appearance is a trifle "baroque." She has style, but it is a style that is entirely her own. She wears no hat and a number of heavy gold bracelets. She is English born and bred and has acquired much of the jargon of what is known as "The International Set." Beneath this, however, she is a woman of considerable intelligence. She greets VERNER by taking both his hands in hers.)

MAUD. It's lovely to see you again, Verner. I hoped you'd be here but I wasn't sure. Anna-Mary sounded a bit affolée on the telephone this morning. I gather she's giving a dinner party this evening for our portly Prince.

VERNER. Do you know the guy?

MAUD. Oh, yes, he's a horror. A great one for lavatory jokes and a bit of bottom-pinching on the side. The new wife's quite sweet and lovely to look at; she used to be a model I believe. He insists on everyone bobbing to her, and when they do she's liable to giggle. You'll like her.

VERNER. Did Anna-Mary ask you tonight?

MAUD. Yes, a little half-heartedly I thought. (She laughs.) Not that I blame her; she's probably got all the "placements" set. In any case I couldn't possibly have come even if I had wanted to. I'm driving back to Rome.

VERNER. It's the hell of a long trip. Are you driving yourself?

MAUD. Oh, yes. I love driving alone, particularly at night. I shall see the dawn come up over the Simplon Pass and probably get as far as Como for breakfast.

VERNER. What kind of a car?

MAUD. Rather a common little Volkswagen; you know, the type that looks as if it were sticking its tongue out, but it goes like a bird.

VERNER (admiringly). You certainly are quite a gal!

(At this moment FELIX comes in with a bucket of ice. He sees MAUD, and bows.)

FELIX. Buona sera, Principessa.

MAUD. Buona sera, Felix. Come sta?

FELIX. Molto bene grazie, e lie?

MAUD. Bene come sempre. Partiro stanotte a Roma.

FELIX. Che belleza! Come la invidio.

MAUD. Evero.

FELIX. Buon viaggo Principessa e arrividerci. (He bows and goes out.)

VERNER. What was all that about?

MAUD. Nothing much. I just told him I was going back to Rome and he said how he envied me and wished me well. He's a nice boy. We're quite old friends. I knew him first when he was at the Excelsior.

VERNER (at drink table). What shall it be? Scotch, gin, vodka? Or would you like some champagne?

MAUD. No, thanks. Vodka would be lovely, with a little tonic and lots of ice.

(While he is mixing the drinks, ANNA-MARY comes out of the bedroom. She is still in her "peignoir" but she has wound a blue scarf round her head. She kisses MAUD effusively on both cheeks.)

ANNA-MARY. Why, Maud, isn't this just wonderful? I'd no idea you were here. When you phoned this morning I couldn't believe it. I had to pinch myself. My! But you look cute as a June bug with all those gorgeous bangles. Come and sit down right here and tell me all the gossip. How's dear Lulu?

MAUD (sitting). I don't know. I haven't seen her for ages. I've been here for the last two weeks staying with my son and his wife.

ANNA-MARY. Why, Maud! You take the breath right out of my body! Nobody ever told me you had a son!

MAUD. It isn't exactly a topic of universal interest.

ANNA-MARY. But how old is he? What does he *do*? Is he handsome? Do you adore him? I've just got to meet him.

MAUD. I don't think he's really your cup of tea. He paints abstract pictures and he's a Communist.

ANNA-MARY (*shocked to the marrow*). A Communist!

MAUD. I don't mean that he's actually a member of the "party" but he's terribly Red-minded. He's also going through a grubby phase at the moment. They have a ghastly little flat in Pully and a lot of Beatnik cronies. It's all quite fun, really.

VERNER (*handing her a vodka and tonic*). Here's your booze, Princess.

MAUD (*taking it*). Thanks, pal.

ANNA-MARY. And you say he's got a wife?

MAUD. Yes, she's small and sharp, like a little needle. She used to be a dancer in the Festival ballet and she's just had a baby. That's why I've been here for so long; it sort of hung back. All those *Giselles* and *Swan Lakes* make childbearing a little complicated.

ANNA-MARY. And she had the baby? (*Offering a cigarette*)

MAUD. Yes. No, thank you. (*Refuses it.*) Late last night, in the hospital. It's a boy and it weighed exactly what it ought to weigh and was bright red, possibly out of deference to its father's political views. Anyhow, I am now a grandmother, which is a sobering thought.

ANNA-MARY. No one would believe it. You look sensational!

MAUD (*sipping her drink*). So do you, Anna-Mary; so do you. That particular colour is very becoming.

ANNA-MARY. Yes, nice, isn't it?

MAUD. Now I come to think of it, you wore blue that night in Rome when you came to dine.

ANNA-MARY. And how is that *divine* little apartment? I was saying to Clare Pethrington at lunch today that it was just *the* most picturesque place I ever saw,

wasn't I, Verner?

VERNER (*laconically*). Yes, sweetheart.

MAUD. Clare hates it. She says there are too many stairs and that it smells of fish. Which is only to be expected, really, because there happens to be a fishmonger on the ground floor. I keep on burning incense and dabbing the light bulbs with "Miss Dior," but it doesn't do any good.

ANNA-MARY. You know I'm just heartbroken that you can't come to dinner tonight. It's going to be loads of fun. I've got Mariette and Henri; the Pethringtons, of course; Sir Gerard and Lady Nutfield—he was the Governor of somewhere or other and he looks so British you just want to stand up and sing "God Save the Queen" the moment he comes into the room! Then there are the Carpinchos; they're Brazilian and as cute as they can be, and Bobo Larkin who's promised to play the piano in the bar afterwards providing we keep everybody out, and darling old Irma Bidmeyer who lives in this very hotel and plays bridge with the Queen of Spain, and, last but not least, Their Royal Highnesses!

MAUD. Not Royal, dear, just Serene.

ANNA-MARY (*visibly shaken*). Maud! Is that really true? Are you positive?

MAUD. Quite. But you needn't worry about it; it doesn't make any difference. So long as everybody calls him "Sir" and bobs up and down like a cork, he's as happy as a clam.

ANNA-MARY. But I could have *sworn* that Mariette said . . .

MAUD (*laughing*). Mariette's terribly vague about that sort of thing. She once lost her head at an official reception in Geneva and addressed poor old Prince Paniowtovski as "Ma'am!" She wasn't far out at that.

VERNER (*with a guffaw*). You know that's funny! That's very funny!

ANNA-MARY (*ignoring this*). Do you mean I have to *introduce* him as His Serene Highness?

MAUD. You don't have to introduce him at all. You just take people up to him and say: "Sir—may I present so-and-so." He may buck a bit at Irma Bidmeyer; he's notoriously anti-Semitic, but you can always mumble.

VERNER. Well—what do you know?

ANNA-MARY (crossly). Do be quiet, Verner, and stop interrupting.

VERNER. Okay, sweetheart.

ANNA-MARY. Why don't you make yourself useful for once and go down to the bar and ask if they've got any of those cigars? I want to have a little private visit with Maud.

VERNER. Okay, sweetheart.

ANNA-MARY. And for heaven's sakes take those golf clubs with you.

MAUD. Oh, don't send him away. I've hardly talked to him at all.

VERNER. Don't worry, Princess. I'll just set the table, fix the flowers, give a hundred dollars to each of the waiters, and be right back. (He winks at her, picks up his golf bag, and goes out.)

(ANNA-MARY sighs heavily.)

ANNA-MARY. Verner really gets on my nerves sometimes.

MAUD (quizzically). Yes. I see he does.

ANNA-MARY. He's just plain stubborn. He refuses to be interested in any of the things I'm interested in; he doesn't like any of the people I like.

MAUD. He doesn't seem to mind me.

ANNA-MARY. Only because you lay yourself out to be nice to him.

MAUD. Perhaps that's what he needs.

ANNA-MARY. You were just darling to him that night we dined with you. I remember saying to Lulu afterwards, "Maud's just wonderful, she's warm; she's human; and what's more, she's a giver and not a taker."

MAUD. You mustn't overrate me, Anna-Mary. I'm a taker all right when I get the chance.

ANNA-MARY. Why, Maud Caragnani, that's just plain nonsense, and you know it! You can't fool me. The one thing I flatter myself I'm never wrong about is people. Why do you suppose it is that you're so popular? That everybody's running after you and asking you everywhere?

MAUD. It's very sweet of you to say so, but I'm afraid you exaggerate my social graces.

ANNA-MARY. I'm not talking about social graces, honey. I'm talking about "character" and "heart"! You're just basically sympathique, and there's no getting away from it! And above all you go through life

making an effort! Now, Verner just will not make an effort. He just stands around waiting for people to come to him, instead of him going to them. Do you see what I mean?

MAUD. Perfectly. But I find it difficult to believe that he could have made the enormous fortune he has, if he were all that lackadaisical.

ANNA-MARY. Oh, he's sharp enough in business, I'll grant you that, but he just won't open his arms out to experience. I mean he deliberately shuts his eyes to the beauty of things. You'd never credit it, but in the whole five months we've been in Europe this trip, he's only been inside three churches!

MAUD (laughing). Perhaps he doesn't like churches.

ANNA-MARY. I managed to drag him into Saint Peter's in Rome, and all he did was stomp around humming "I Like New York in June" under his breath. I was mortified.

MAUD. Oh, poor Buffalo Bill!

ANNA-MARY. What on earth do you mean by that?

MAUD. It's how I see Verner in my mind's eye. A sort of frustrated Buffalo Bill who's had his horse taken away from him.

ANNA-MARY (snappily). Verner can't ride horseback.

MAUD. There's still time for him to learn.

ANNA-MARY. He's turned fifty-five. His arteries wouldn't stand it.

MAUD. There are different sorts of horses. Pegasus, for instance. He had wings.

ANNA-MARY. You know something, Maud? I just haven't the faintest idea what you're talking about.

MAUD. Verner. We're both talking about Verner. But from different points of view.

(The telephone rings. ANNA-MARY, with an exclamation of irritation, gets up and goes over to it.)

ANNA-MARY (lifting the receiver). Hallo . . . Yes, speaking . . . Bobo! My dear . . . I never recognized your voice. What! You can't mean it . . . you can't be serious! But when did it happen . . . I mean you sounded perfectly all right on the phone this morning . . . Oh, my God! (There is an anguished pause while she *listens.*) But Bobo you can't do this to me, at the very last minute. I just can't stand it . . . But if you don't come we shall be thirteen at table . . . But Bobo, honey, I was *counting* on you! I've made all the arrangements about the piano in the bar after dinner and everything . . . Well, all I can say is that it's just disaster that's all, absolute disaster . . . Couldn't you just manage to come for dinner? That would be better than nothing . . . A hundred and two! Are you *sure* it's a hundred and two? When did you take it? What—the doctor says you're not to talk any more on the phone—but Bobo—Bobo—(*She closes her eyes in despair and hangs up the receiver.*) He hung up on me. He just hung up on me! After dealing me the worst blow in my life, he has the nerve to hang up on me. I'll never speak to that God-damned little pansy again as long as there's breath left in my body.

MAUD. Be reasonable, Anna-Mary. You can't expect the poor beast to come to dinner if he's got a temperature of a hundred and two.

ANNA-MARY. Reasonable! Seven o'clock, thirteen at table, and you ask me to be reasonable!

MAUD. Can you think of anyone else?

ANNA-MARY. Of course I can't. We only got here last night. You'll have to come, Maud, you'll just *have* to. It'll make one woman too many, but that can't be helped.

MAUD. I really can't possibly. I haven't even got an evening dress with me, and I have to drive to Rome.

ANNA-MARY. Oh, Maud, go to Rome later; go to Rome any time but just help me out tonight. You don't have to worry about an evening dress. I can lend you a divine Balenciaga model I've only worn twice. Oh, Maud, for heaven's sakes I don't know where I'm at. This is a ghastly situation. I think I'm going crazy.

MAUD. Why don't you call up Mariette? She might have somebody on tap for just this sort of crisis.

ANNA-MARY. You really won't come? I'd bless you until my dying day if only you would.

MAUD (*shaking her head*). It's quite out of the question.

ANNA-MARY. You mean you don't *want* to come.

MAUD. To be perfectly frank, I don't. In the first place I haven't spoken to either of the Pethringtons for three years, I can't stand the sight of dear old Irma Bidmeyer and I think the Prince is the most lascivious, vulgar old bore it has ever been my misfortune to meet.

ANNA-MARY (*outraged at such* lèse-majesté). Maud!

MAUD. But leaving all that aside, I've promised to pick up my son at the hospital and take him to dine at the Grappe d'Or. They probably won't let him in if he looks anything like he looked earlier in the day, but it's the last chance I shall have of seeing him for a long time. Why don't you call up Mariette as I suggested?

ANNA-MARY (*going to the telephone*). This is ghastly—just ghastly!

MAUD. Don't take it so hard, Anna-Mary. I'm quite sure the Prince would waive the most atavistic superstition for the sake of a free meal.

ANNA-MARY. I just don't know how you can sit there, Maud, and say such terrible things.

MAUD. We just happen to be talking about the same person from different points of view again, don't we? Only in this case I happen to know him and you don't.

ANNA-MARY (*at the telephone*). Operator . . . Operator . . . *Donnez moi* . . . (*She glances at the pad again.*) *Donnez moi vingt-trois-trente-six-vingt-deux s'il vous plait et aussi vite que possible* on account of *je suis pressé.* (*Balefully to* MAUD:) The next time I see that Bobo Larkin, I'll just make him wish he'd never been born.

MAUD. He's probably wishing that at this very moment if he's got a temperature of a hundred and two.

ANNA-MARY (*at the telephone again*). 'Allo . . . 'Allo . . . *Ici, Mrs. Conklin, je veux parler avec la comtesse s'il vous plait* . . . what? I mean *comment?* (*She listens for a moment or two.*) *Je ne comprends pas—parlez vous Anglais?* (to MAUD) It's a different man from the one I talked to before. I can't understand a word he's saying . . .

MAUD (*rising*). Give it to me. (*She takes the telephone.*) 'Allo . . . *C'est de la part de Madame Conklin; est ce que Madame la comtesse est là? Oui . . . Elle est sortie? Depuis quand? Vous savez ou? . . . Oui j'écoute, un cocktail chez Madame de Vosanges . . . Oui . . . Vous ne savez pas le numero par hazard . . . Ah, bon, je vais le chercher . . . Merci beaucoup. (She hangs up.)* She left ten minutes ago to go to a cocktail party and she's not coming back before dinner.

ANNA-MARY. I think I'm going out of my mind!

MAUD. Somebody called Vosanges. I don't know them, but they're sure to be in the book. (*She starts to look in the telephone book when* VERNER *comes into the room.*)

VERNER. What's cooking?

ANNA-MARY. The most terrible thing's happened.

MAUD (*looking up from the telephone book*). Bobo Larkin's got a temperature of a hundred and two.

VERNER. Well—what do you know? Who the hell's Bobo Larkin?

ANNA-MARY (*with dreadful patience*). It doesn't matter *who* he is, Verner. But what does matter is *where* he is. And *where* he is is in bed with a fever which means that he can't come to dinner, nor can he play the piano in the bar *after* dinner.

VERNER. Poor guy. Probably a virus of some sort.

ANNA-MARY. It can be a virus or bubonic plague for all I care, but what it means is that we shall be thirteen at table.

VERNER. Well—well—well! Boy, are we in trouble? (*He laughs.*)

ANNA-MARY (*icily*). There's nothing to laugh about, Verner. It'll *ruin* the whole evening.

VERNER. Sorry, sweetheart. It's just nerves. (*To* MAUD) What about you, Princess? How about you pinch-hitting for this Bozo what's his name?

MAUD. Not even for you, Verner. Also, I can't play the piano, in the bar or anywhere else. I've found the number, Anna-Mary. Do you want me to ring it and see if I can get hold of Mariette?

ANNA-MARY. No, it's too late. And anyway I couldn't have her just dragging *anyone* along to meet Royalty. There's only one thing to be done. Verner, you must have your dinner up here.

VERNER. Huh?

MAUD. Won't that seem a little odd?

ANNA-MARY. It can't be helped. We'll pretend you're sick or something.

VERNER. You can say I've got a temperature of a hundred and three!

ANNA-MARY. You *could* be waiting for an important business call from New York.

MAUD. No, Anna-Mary. I don't think that would do. A high fever would be more convincing. You can't fob off a Serene Highness with a mere business call. It would be *lèse-majesté*.

VERNER. You could always say I've got a galloping hernia.

ANNA-MARY (*losing her temper*). You think this is very funny, don't you? Both you and Maud? Well, all I can say is I'm very, very sorry I can't share the joke. Mariette's been just wonderful making arrangements for this dinner for me tonight. We've been phoning each other back and forth for weeks. She's the only one who has taken the trouble to plan it all for *my* sake, and if only for *her* sake I'm going to see that it's a success if it's the last thing I do. And I'd like to say one thing more because I just can't keep it in any longer. I'm bitterly disappointed in you, Maud, and it's no use pretending I'm not. I think it's real mean of you not to stand by me tonight and help me out of this jam. You could perfectly easily come to dinner if you wanted to.

MAUD (*calmly*). Certainly I could, but, as I have already explained to you, I don't want to, and, as you may remember, I also explained why.

ANNA-MARY. I can remember that you were insulting about my guests and said the Prince was vulgar, and I just don't happen to think that's a nice way to talk.

VERNER. Listen, sweetheart, let's not have a brawl, shall we?

ANNA-MARY (*ignoring him, to* MAUD). You've hurt me, Maud, more than I can say. You've let me down. And I thought you were a friend.

MAUD (*coldly*). Why?

VERNER. Holy mackerel!

MAUD (*inexorably to* ANNA-MARY). We have met casually three or four times and you have dined with me once. Is that, according to your curious code of behaviour, sufficient basis for a life-long affection?

ANNA-MARY (*with grandeur*). I do not give my friendship as easily as you seem to think, Maud, and when I do it is only to those who are truly sincere and willing to stand by me in time of trouble. After all, that is what friendship is for, isn't it? It's a question of give-and-take. However, I do not wish to discuss the matter any further. I am sorry that there should have been this little misunderstanding between us, and I can only hope that the next time our paths cross, the clouds will have rolled away and everything will be forgiven and forgotten. If you will excuse me now, I must go and dress and do my hair. Verner, you will have your dinner up here, and can ring for the waiter and order it whenever you feel like it. And I'd be very glad if you would ring down to the Maître d' and tell him I'll be in the dining room at eight o'clock to rearrange the place cards. (*She bows coldly to* MAUD *and goes into the bedroom.*)

MAUD (*after a pause*). Well, that's that, isn't it?

VERNER. She sure is good and mad.

MAUD. Oh, I'm sorry. I'm afraid it's partly my fault. I was rather beastly to her.

VERNER. Forget it. Anna-Mary's tough; she can take it.

MAUD. Yes, I'm sure she can. But I hate being beastly to people. It's only that she made me suddenly angry. I wish I hadn't been.

VERNER. Have another drink.

MAUD. No, thank you. I really must go now.

VERNER. Come on, just a small one.

MAUD (*glancing at her watch*). Very well, but make it a really small one. I must leave at a quarter past.

VERNER (*going to the drink table*). Atta girl!

MAUD (*sitting down*). What an idiotic little drama. (*She sighs.*) Oh, dear!

VERNER. Snap out of it, Princess. It ain't worth worrying about. Anna-Mary always raises hell when things don't happen to go just the way she wants.

MAUD. Yes. I expect she does.

VERNER. I don't pay no mind to it any more.

MAUD. Are you disappointed? About being forbidden to go to your own dinner party, I mean?

VERNER. It's just about breaking my heart.

MAUD (*with a smile*). Yes. I suspect it is. (*She raises her glass to him.*) Well, here's to the next time we meet. When all those clouds have rolled away and everything is forgiven and forgotten.

VERNER (*raising his glass*). Here's to the next time we meet anyway, whether everything's been forgiven and forgotten or not.

MAUD. Thank you, Verner. I'll remember that.

VERNER. Do you want to know something?

MAUD. Shoot, pal.

VERNER. That evening we had with you in Rome was the high spot of our whole trip—for me.

MAUD. Only because I "laid myself out to be nice to you." That's what Anna-Mary told me earlier on this evening.

VERNER. Well, Momma was dead on the nose for once. You sure did.

MAUD. And it worked, apparently.

VERNER. Princess, it worked like a charm.

MAUD. Would you mind if I asked you a very personal question, almost an impertinent one, as a matter of fact?

VERNER. Go right ahead.

MAUD. You really are a very, very rich man, aren't you?

VERNER. If that's the question, I guess the answer's yes.

MAUD. It isn't. The question is more complicated than that, and I wouldn't even ask it if I didn't like you enough to be genuinely interested. (*She pauses.*)

VERNER (*sipping his drink and looking at her*). Well?

MAUD. Why, when you can easily afford to do whatever you like, do you allow yourself to be continually bullied into doing what you don't like?

VERNER. That sure is a sixty-four-thousand-dollar question all right.

MAUD. You must have asked it to yourself occasionally. You're nobody's fool.

VERNER (*looking down*). Maybe I have, Princess. Maybe I have.

MAUD. And did you give yourself the sixty-four-thousand-dollar answer?

VERNER (*looking down*). No, Princess,

I guess I goofed it.

MAUD. Yes, dear Buffalo Bill. I'm sadly afraid you did.

VERNER. Hey! What's this Buffalo Bill bit?

MAUD. Just one of my little personal fantasies. I puzzled Anna-Mary with it a short while ago. I said you needed a horse.

VERNER. A horse! Are you out of your mind? What the hell should I do with a horse?

MAUD (laughing). Jump on its back and gallop away on it. Failing a horse, a dolphin would be better than nothing. There was a little boy in Greek mythology I believe who had an excellent seat on a dolphin. It took him skimming along over the blue waves of the Aegean, and he never had to go to any dinner parties or meet any important people, and whenever they came to rest on a rock or a little white beach, the dolphin would dive deep deep down and bring him up a golden fish. It's high time somebody gave you a golden fish, Verner. It would mean nothing on the Stock Exchange but it might light up your whole sad world.

VERNER (astonished). Well, I'll be God damned!

MAUD (rising purposefully). I must go now. I promised my son I'd be at the hospital at seven-thirty.

VERNER (with feeling). Don't go yet, Princess. Please don't go yet.

MAUD. I can't. I really can't. But we'll meet again. (She unexpectedly kisses him on the cheek.) Good-bye for the moment, dear Buffalo Bill. Don't forget me too soon.

(She goes swiftly out of the room as the lights fade.)

SCENE TWO

Several hours have passed and it is now about eleven o'clock in the evening.

When the lights fade in on the scene, VERNER is stretched out on the sofa reading an Ian Fleming novel. He has taken off his tie and his shirt is open at the neck. On stage Right there is a table with the remains of his dinner on it.

There is a discreet knock on the door.

——

VERNER. Come in. Entrez.

(FELIX comes in bearing a bottle of Evian water in a large bucket of ice.)

FELIX. I hope I do not intrude, monsieur, but Madame requested a bottle of Evian bien glacée to be put by her bed.

VERNER. Okay. Go right ahead.

(FELIX takes the Evian into the bedroom. After a moment he reappears.)

FELIX. I regret not having taken away the table before, monsieur, but I am singlehanded on this floor tonight and there has been much to do.

VERNER. Don't worry, that's all right with me.

FELIX. Monsieur has need of anything?

VERNER (thoughtfully). Yeah, it seems that I have. I have need of a golden fish.

FELIX. Pardon, monsieur?

VERNER. Never mind. Skip it. Give me a bourbon on the rocks.

FELIX. Bien, monsieur. (He goes to the drink table.)

VERNER. Princess Caragnani said she knew you before. In Rome, wasn't it?

FELIX. Yes, sir. I served in the bar at the Excelsior for several months. Only as third barman, though. The Princess often was there with friends.

VERNER. She has a lot of friends in Rome, hasn't she?

FELIX (with enthusiasm). Ah, si signore, e una donna molto incantevole, tutto il mondo . . .

VERNER. Hey, none of that; stick to English.

FELIX. I was saying that she is a lady much enchanted and that all the world are most fond of her.

VERNER (a little wistfully). Yeah, I'll bet they are.

FELIX (handing him his drink). Your drink, monsieur.

VERNER. Thanks. (He takes it.) Molto gratzie!

FELIX (delighted). Ah, bravo! Il signore comincia imparare l'Italiano! Monsieur is beginning to learn my language.

VERNER. I guess it's never too late to try—to try to learn someone else's language.

FELIX. It is difficult at first, but here in La Suisse there is much opportunity because there are so many languages spoken.

VERNER (with a little laugh). You're telling me! Have you got a girl?

FELIX. Oh, yes, monsieur.

VERNER. Is she here in Lausanne?

FELIX. No, signore. She is in Italy.

VERNER. What's her name?

FELIX. Renata.

VERNER. Are you crazy about her?

FELIX. No, signore. But we are most fond. I have taught her to water-ski.

VERNER. Are you going to marry her?

FELIX (*with a slight shrug*). *Che sa?* One day, perhaps, but first I must make the money to afford it.

VERNER. Can you ride horseback?

FELIX (*puzzled*). No, signore. But in the village where I was born my uncle had a mule which I used to ride in the mountains. *Era un animale molto cattivo.* It was a most angry animal.

VERNER. And a dolphin, did you ever try a dolphin, when you were a kid?

FELIX. I fear I do not understand.

VERNER. You know, a porpoise—a kinda fish—(*He makes a gesture illustrating a porpoise jumping.*)

(FELIX *looks at him in some dismay.*)

FELIX. *Ah, si—un porco marino—un delfino!* Monsieur makes the little joke?

VERNER. Yeah. I guess you're right. It was only a little joke.

FELIX. Is there anything more that Monsieur requires?

VERNER. Yeah, Felix. I'm beginning to think there is. You can take away the table now.

FELIX. *Bien, monsieur.*

(VERNER *takes a roll of bills from his pocket and gives one to* FELIX.)

VERNER. Here. Buy a present for Renata.

FELIX (*looking at it*). Monsieur has made a mistake. This is fifty dollars.

VERNER. No, Felix. It ain't no mistake. I guess the only thing that Monsieur never makes a mistake about is money. Have yourself a ball. Good night, Felix.

FELIX (*overwhelmed*). *Mille mille grazie, signore* . . . Monsieur is most generous. *A domani, signore, a domani.*

(FELIX *bows, and wheels the dinner table from the room.* VERNER, *left alone, returns to his book, tries to read it for a moment or two, and then flings it down. He is about to light a cigarette when the telephone rings. He goes to it.*)

VERNER (*at the telephone*). Hallo . . .

Yes, speaking. (*His voice lightens.*) Oh, it's you! Where are you? Here in the lobby? Yeah . . . come on up . . . come right on up.

(VERNER *replaces the receiver and sits staring at the telephone for a second with a beaming smile. He then jumps to his feet, runs to the mirror, smooths his hair and straightens his tie. Then he hurriedly puts on his shoes and his coat, goes back again to the mirror to reassure himself, gulps down the remainder of his bourbon and lights, with a slightly trembling hand, the cigarette he was going to light when the telephone rang. After a few moments there is a knock at the door. He goes swiftly to open it, and* MAUD *comes into the room. She stands looking at him for a moment with a slight smile.*)

MAUD. Hallo, Buffalo Bill. How was your lonely bivouac?

VERNER (*grinning with pleasure*). Hi!

MAUD. I'm sure you say that to every taxi you see.

VERNER. Come right in, Princess. Come right on in and put your feet up.

MAUD (*sitting on the sofa*). I think it would be more discreet to leave them down.

VERNER. This is great! Just great! I nearly flipped when I heard your voice on the phone just now. I didn't think I was going to see you again for quite a while.

MAUD. No. Neither did I. It seemed a pity.

VERNER. I'd just been talking about you, only a few minutes ago . . .

MAUD. Talking about me? Who to?

VERNER. Felix, the waiter. He's just crazy about you.

MAUD. Is he indeed?

VERNER. He said that you were a lady much enchanted.

MAUD. Italians have a flair for romantic exaggeration. Aren't you going to offer me a drink?

VERNER. You bet. What'll it be?

MAUD. Brandy, I think, only very little. I have a long drive ahead of me.

VERNER (*going to the drink table*). You really are going to drive all through the night?

MAUD. Yes. I'm looking forward to it. There's a moon and there's not much snow left on the pass; the road will be fairly clear.

VERNER. Do you want anything with the brandy? Soda or water or ice?

MAUD. No, nothing, thanks, just neat. (*A slight pause*) Why were you talking about me to Felix?

VERNER. I don't know. You said you'd known him in Rome.

MAUD (*taking the glass he hands her*). I see.

VERNER. And I guess you were on my mind.

MAUD. You were on my mind too. I talked about you to my son at dinner.

VERNER. What did you say?

MAUD. I can't remember. Nothing very much. Just that I liked you.

VERNER. And what did *he* say?

MAUD. He asked me how long it was before babies started to talk. I replied that in some cases it took a lifetime. (*She laughs.*)

VERNER. Why are you laughing?

MAUD. It's been quite a funny evening one way and another. He's in a state of blissful euphoria. The fact of becoming a father has completely transformed him. He had his beard shaved off this afternoon and his hair cut. He even put on a coat and tie for dinner. He had a bottle of champagne, and he babbled away like a brook.

VERNER. Are you very close, you and your son?

MAUD. Not really. But we seemed to be tonight. I don't much care for his wife, and I think he knows it. She's actually not a bad little thing *au fond* but she's a bit neurotic. I expect having the baby will steady her.

VERNER. What's his name? Your son, I mean?

MAUD. Faber. His father's name was Fabrizio, and Faber was the nearest I could get to it in English.

VERNER. This Fabrizio—what was he like?

MAUD. Handsome, vain, charming, and badly mother-ridden. She was an old devil and hated me like the plague. I rather see her point now. Being a mother-in-law isn't all jam.

VERNER. Were you in love with him?

MAUD. Oh, yes. But it didn't last long. We'd only been married for a year when he was killed in a car crash. That was in 1940. I managed to get myself onto a ship going to Lisbon, and from there back to England. Faber was born in Cornwall.

VERNER. Did you ever see any of them again?

MAUD. Oh, yes. After the war was over I came back to Italy to live. I made the old girl fork out enough money to pay for Faber's education. In the last years of her life we almost became friends.

VERNER (*after a pause*). Why did you come back to see me tonight?

MAUD. A sudden impulse. I was on my way to Pully to pick up my suitcase from Faber's flat and I was driving along, just out there by the lake, and I thought of you sitting up here all by yourself, so I turned the car round and came back. I thought you might be lonely.

VERNER. That was mighty kind of you, Princess. (*He looks at her intently.*) I was.

MAUD. Aren't you going to have a drink? To keep me company?

VERNER. Yes, in a minute, after I've asked *you* the sixty-four-thousand-dollar question.

MAUD. Shoot, pal.

VERNER. Why did you kiss me like you did when you went away before dinner?

MAUD. Another sudden impulse. I'm a very impulsive character. It's often got me into trouble.

VERNER. And you came back because you thought I might be lonesome?

MAUD. Yes. That was one of the reasons.

VERNER. There were others?

MAUD. Yes.

VERNER. What were they?

MAUD. They're difficult to put into words. You have to be a master psychologist to dissect an emotional impulse successfully. Just as you have to be an expert watchmaker to be able to take a watch to pieces and put it together again. I'm not an expert in either of those fields. I'm afraid of being clumsy and making a botch of it.

VERNER. I don't reckon you could ever be clumsy.

MAUD (*with a slight smile*). Thank you, Verner. Let's hope your reckoning is accurate.

VERNER. You said "emotional impulse."

Was that right?

MAUD. Yes. Up to a point.

VERNER. Do you class "pity" as an emotion?

MAUD. Yes. But it was more than pity that made me turn the car round.

VERNER. That's what I was aiming to find out.

MAUD. Well, now that you've found out, you can get yourself a drink and let me out of the witness box.

VERNER (*going to the drink table*). Okay, lady. You're the boss.

(VERNER *pours some bourbon into a glass, adds ice to it and comes back to her.*)

MAUD. That remark is sadly significant.

VERNER. How come?

MAUD. I've never been to America.

VERNER. It's a great country.

MAUD (*thoughtfully*). I suppose American men must like being bossed by their women; otherwise they wouldn't put up with it.

VERNER (*a little defensive*). You can't judge Americans by the ones you meet in Europe.

MAUD. I've heard that said before. I'm not quite sure that I believe it. After all, the English and French and Italians seem to retain their basic characteristics wherever they are. I can't see why it should be only the Americans who are geographically unstable.

VERNER. You know, Princess, you sure do say the damnedest things.

MAUD (*repentant*). I know I do. That's what I meant just now by being clumsy. Please forgive me.

VERNER. There ain't nothing to forgive.

MAUD. I really came back to be a comfort, not an irritant.

VERNER (*looking at her intently*). The fact that you came back at all is good enough for me.

MAUD (*meeting his eye*). Is it, Verner? Is it really?

VERNER. You know damn well it is.

(*He puts down his drink, takes her drink carefully out of her hand and places it on a table; then he lifts her gently to her feet, puts his arms round her and presses his mouth onto hers. They stand quite still for a few moments, locked in their embrace; then she draws away.*)

MAUD. I knew perfectly well that that was going to happen, and yet somehow it was a surprise.

VERNER (*a little huskily*). I guess I knew too. But I wasn't quite sure, and I reckon I was a bit scared.

MAUD. Scared?

VERNER. Scared that you'd give me the brush-off, or laugh at me.

MAUD. Why should I laugh at you?

VERNER. I don't mean that I really thought you would. You're too kind to do that, but—well—I'm not the sort of guy who likes to kid himself.

MAUD (*gently*). No. I don't think you are.

VERNER. I mean I've seen too many fellars of my age suddenly go berserk and get themselves into trouble, bad trouble.

MAUD. Would you describe that kiss you gave me just now, as going berserk?

VERNER (*ruefully*). Now you *are* laughing at me.

MAUD. These fellows of your own age you talk about. How old are they?

VERNER (*grinning*). Old enough to know better.

MAUD. And this trouble their sudden madness gets them into, this bad trouble —what does it consist of?

VERNER. Oh, all kinds of things, making fools of themselves, getting in wrong with everyone, waking up one fine morning and realising that they've been played for a sucker.

MAUD. Do you consider, off hand, that I'm playing you for a sucker?

VERNER (*hurriedly*). No, Princess, you know damn well I don't—I didn't mean that at all.

MAUD. How old are you anyhow?

VERNER. Fifty-five, pushing fifty-six.

MAUD. Well, I'm forty-four and a grandmother. I'm ashamed of you, Buffalo Bill, running around making passes at grandmothers.

VERNER (*worried*). What are we going to do?

MAUD. What are we going to do about what?

VERNER. About this! About us?

MAUD (*putting her arms round his neck*). We could always go berserk again.

VERNER (*after another long embrace*). You're sensational. D'you know that?

You're just sensational.

MAUD. I believe you really mean it.

VERNER. Mean it! I'm crazy about you!
(*He moves towards her.*)

MAUD (*backing away*). No, really,
Verner, dear Verner, this has gone far
enough. We're both behaving very fool-
ishly. . . .

VERNER. What's so foolish about it?

MAUD. It's my own fault, I know. I
should never have let it get to this point.

VERNER. Why?

MAUD. Because nothing can come of it,
there's no sense in us allowing ourselves
to get emotionally involved with each
other. There's too much in the way. You
know that as well as I do.

VERNER. I don't know any such thing.
All I know is I've fallen in love with
you, and all I *want* to know is whether
you've fallen in love with me. It's as simple as that. Once that's clear, all the other
complications can be taken care of. Have
you?—or rather could you—do you think
—be in love with me?

MAUD (*looking at him*). Yes, Verner. I
think I could, and I think I am. Falling
in love sounds so comprehensive and all-
embracing and violent. It's the stuff of
youth, really, not of middle-age, and yet
—and yet . . .

VERNER (*urgently*). And yet—what?

MAUD (*genuinely moved*). I don't know.
I'm feeling suddenly conscience-stricken.

VERNER. About Anna-Mary?

MAUD. No, not about Anna-Mary. You
said yourself earlier this evening that she
was tough and could take it. You're dead
right, she's tough as old boots. If any
woman in the whole world asked for this
situation to happen to her, she did. I have
no conscience whatever about Anna-Mary,
but you . . . It's you I'm worrying about.

VERNER. Why?

MAUD. I wouldn't like you to get hurt.
As a matter of fact, I'm not any too anxious to get hurt myself.

VERNER. There's no fun in gambling on
certainties.

MAUD. What exactly do you want of me?
Have you thought?

VERNER. No. I haven't had time to think.
I only know I want you.

MAUD. You don't know me really at all.
You don't know anything about me.

VERNER. So what? Come to that, you
don't know so much about me.

MAUD. I think I know enough.

VERNER. That goes for me too.

MAUD. It's not quite so simple as that.
We've lived in completely separate worlds,
you and I. The standards and codes of behaviour and moral values on this side of
the Atlantic aren't the same as those you've
been brought up to believe in. I'm not
saying that they're either better or worse,
but they are profoundly different.

VERNER. It semes to me that people are
much the same all the world over, once
you get below the surface.

MAUD. That, darling Buffalo Bill, is a
platitude and an inaccurate one at that.
People are *not* the same all the world over.
When you get below the surface of an
American you can still find a quality of
innocence. There is no innocence left in
Europe.

VERNER. What are you trying to say?

MAUD. I'm trying to warn you, really. I
could never have lived the sort of life I've
lived in your country. It wouldn't have
been possible.

VERNER. How do you mean "the sort
of life" you've lived? You're scaring the
hell out of me.

MAUD (*with a slight laugh*). Oh, it
hasn't been as bad as all that, but I am,
I suppose, what the old-fashioned novelists
would describe as "A Woman with a
Past."

VERNER (*drily*). I hate to have to admit
it, Princess, but we have had just one or
two of those in the United States.

MAUD. Oh, I know—I know. But it still
isn't quite the same thing. (*She pauses.*)

VERNER. Okay—Okay—let's let it go at
that.

MAUD. Nor do I wish to give you the
impression that my life has been one long,
promiscuous orgy.

VERNER. Bully for you, Princess.

MAUD (*determined to be honest*). But I
have had lovers—here and there along the
line.

VERNER. If you'd been in America they'd
have been husbands and you could have
soaked them for alimony and been a damn'
sight better off.

MAUD. Oh, Verner! You really are very
sweet. (*She kisses him.*)

VERNER. C'mon. (*Holding her*) What's all this about?

MAUD. I just don't want you to be disillusioned.

VERNER. That'll be the day.

MAUD. I don't want you to wake up one morning like those other fellows, those other romantic innocents, and find that you've been played for a sucker.

VERNER (*shaking her gently*). Once and for all will you lay off that kind of talk!

MAUD. Okay, pal. I was only trying to be honest.

VERNER (*letting her go*). And get it into your head that it ain't your past I'm interested in, but your future. And that includes me. Do I make myself clear?

MAUD (*looking down*). Yes, Verner. Quite clear.

VERNER. Well, that being settled, where do we go from here?

MAUD (*suddenly laughing*). What about Rome? It's as good a jumping-off place as anywhere!

VERNER. Whatever you say, Princess.

MAUD. When will you come? This week? Next month? When?

VERNER. This week, next month my foot! I'm coming with you tonight.

MAUD. Verner!

VERNER. In that God-damned Volkswagen.

MAUD. It's very small, and your legs are so long. I'm afraid you'll be miserably uncomfortable.

VERNER. The seats slide back, don't they?

MAUD. Yes. I'm sure they do. . . . (*She breaks off and looks at him.*) Oh, Verner, do you really mean this?

VERNER. You bet I mean it. What time do we start?

MAUD (*suddenly turning away*). I can't let you do this, Verner; I really can't. It's —it's too sudden. You must give yourself more time to think. . . .

VERNER. Are you chickening out on the deal?

MAUD. No. It isn't that; really it isn't. I'm thinking of you, not of myself. I meant what I said just now. You haven't any idea what I'm really like. All you know for certain is that I married a Sicilian, had a son in Cornwall, and a grandson in Lausanne.

VERNER. I know what Felix said.

MAUD (*almost crossly*). Did you consult the nearest floor-waiter before you took on Anna-Mary?

VERNER (*dryly*). Maybe it would have been better if I had.

MAUD (*bursting out laughing*). Oh, darling Buffalo Bill, this is ridiculous; it really is. Everything's got out of hand.

VERNER. Now, see here, Princess. It was you who went on about the horse and the dolphin and the golden fish. How can I get the golden fish if I'm scared of taking the ride?

MAUD. But you must have loved Anna-Mary once, in the very beginning, I mean?

VERNER. I guess I kidded myself that I did, but not for long. She got me on the rebound anyway.

MAUD. The rebound?

VERNER. I was married before, to a girl I was crazy about. (*He pauses.*) Then, just after Pearl Harbor, when I'd been drafted into the Navy, she got stuck on another guy and went off with him to Mexico. The divorce was fixed up while I was in the Pacific. When I got home to Minneapolis in 1946, my old man died and I took over the business. Anna-Mary was there, waiting to greet the conquering hero; I'd known her since she was a kid.

MAUD. Was she pretty?

VERNER. Yeah. That's just about what she was, pretty. Her mother and my mother had been in school together. Everybody put their shoulders to the wheel; it was a natural. We got married and lived happily ever after for all of seven months. There was a good deal of dough around even in those days. Then she got pregnant and had herself an abortion without telling me. I'd wanted a kid more than anything, so it was a kind of disappointment. She pretended at the time that it was a miscarriage, but I found out the truth later.

MAUD. What did she do that for?

VERNER. I don't know. She was scared I guess. Also, she didn't want to spoil her figure. She was always mighty concerned about her figure. I reckon Anna-Mary's eaten enough lettuce in her life to keep a million rabbits happy for a hundred years.

MAUD. Oh, Verner! What a dismal waste

of time.

VERNER. You can say that again.

MAUD. And it never occurred to you to break away?

VERNER. Oh, yes. It occurred to me once or twice, but it never seemed worth the trouble. We've led our own lives—Anna-Mary and me. She's had her social junketings and I've had my work, and a couple of little flutters on the side every now and again.

MAUD. Well, I'm glad to hear that, anyhow.

VERNER. We might have jogged along all right indefinitely if we hadn't started taking these trips to Europe. Europe plays all hell with women like Anna-Mary; it gives 'em the wrong kind of ambitions.

MAUD. I belong to Europe, Verner. I'm a European from the top of my head to the soles of my feet. That's why I said just now that you ought to give yourself time to think—before you burn your boats.

VERNER. My boats wouldn't burn, honey; they're right down on the waterline anyways. What time do we leave?

MAUD (glancing at her watch). It's now twenty to twelve. I've got to pick up my suitcase at Faber's flat.

VERNER. I'll pack a few things and meet you in the lobby downstairs at twelve-thirty. The rest of my stuff can be sent on.

MAUD. You're sure? You're absolutely dead sure?

VERNER. Just as sure as I've ever been of anything in my whole life.

MAUD (going to him). Oh, Verner!

(He takes her in his arms again.)

VERNER. As soon as I can get a divorce fixed up, we'll be married and . . .

MAUD (breaking away). O, no—don't say that!

VERNER. How come?

MAUD. I don't want there to be any set plans or arrangements or contracts. . . . This isn't a business deal. Come and live with me and be my love for just so long as it works, for just so long as it makes us both happy.

VERNER. But honey . . .

MAUD. Please, darling Buffalo Bill. We don't want to shackle ourselves with promises before we start. Don't let any sense of moral responsibility rub the gilt off our gingerbread. You do realise, don't you,

what a shindy there's going to be? Anna-Mary will scream blue murder. It will be all over Europe and America that Verner Conklin, the millionaire, has left his wife and run off with a dubious Italian Princess who runs a shop in Rome and hasn't a penny to her name.

VERNER. I didn't know you ran a shop.

MAUD. Didn't you? It's quite a success, really. We sell curious, rather out-of-the-way things, furniture and what-nots and peculiar jewellery. It's called La Boutique Fantasque. That's one of the reasons I have to be back tomorrow. (She looks at her watch again.) I must go, darling—I must fly like the wind, if I'm to be back by twelve-thirty. Don't forget your passport. Oh! (She looks suddenly stricken.) What about Anna-Mary? What are you going to say to her?

VERNER. Nothing much. Just "good night, sweetheart." It's what I've been saying to her for nineteen years.

MAUD. You're not going to explain? You're not going to tell her anything?

VERNER. What would be the sense of explaining? She'll find out in good time.

MAUD (conscience-stricken again). Will she mind? Really mind, I mean?

VERNER. You bet your sweet ass she'll mind. She'll be so hopping mad she'll eat up the furniture.

MAUD. Oh, Verner!

VERNER. Don't you worry about Anna-Mary. It's about time she had a real problem to yak about. Get going, baby, and be back in that little old Volkswagen at twelve-thirty sharp.

MAUD. Okay, pal! Oh, a thousand times okay! (She kisses him and goes swiftly out of the room.)

(VERNER, left alone, walks up and down the room for a moment or two with a springy step. Then he goes to the mirror and examines his face critically. He slaps his hand sharply under his chin in reproval of extra fleshiness. Then, with a sigh, he goes to the desk and sits down by the telephone.)

VERNER (lifting the receiver). Hallo . . . Operator . . . Give me the bar, please. (He waits for a moment or two, biting his lip thoughtfully.) Hallo, is that the bar? This is Mr. Conklin in 354 . . . Yeah, I know she's there but I don't want you to disturb her . . . No, there's no need to say I phoned . . . Is the party still going on? . . . Uh-uh . . . The Prince left over an hour ago? . . . I see . . . It's breaking up right now? . . . Thanks . . . thanks a lot.

(VERNER *hangs up the receiver and sits thinking for a minute. Then he quickly takes off his coat and tie, kicks off his shoes, rumples his hair, takes his book from the table where he left it, and stretches out on the sofa. He cocks his ear and listens for a moment; then, apparently hearing footsteps in the corridor, he puts his head back, lets the book fall from his hand, and starts snoring gently.*)

ANNA-MARY *comes in. She is resplendent in a gown of sapphire-blue satin. She is also wearing a sapphire necklace, earrings and a thick bracelet to match. She is carrying a handbag and a pair of long white gloves. Her expression is grim. She stops short on seeing* VERNER *asleep, and it becomes grimmer.*)

ANNA-MARY (*sharply, stamping her foot*). Verner!

VERNER (*waking elaborately*). Why, sweetheart—are you back already?

ANNA-MARY (*disagreeably*). What do you mean, "already"? It's five to twelve.

VERNER (*sitting up*). Well, who'd have thought it? I guess I must have dropped off.

ANNA-MARY. Dropped off! You were snoring like a bull moose.

VERNER. I must have been on my back, then. I always snore when I sleep on my back.

ANNA-MARY (*with sarcasm*). That's very interesting, Verner, very interesting indeed. But you'd better go and snore in your own room now; I'm tired.

VERNER. Can I fix you a drink?

ANNA-MARY (*sinking down into a chair*). Yes. A bourbon on the rocks. (*She kicks off her shoes and wriggles her toes.*) These shoes have been murder all the evening. They get me right across the instep.

VERNER (*at drink table*). How was the party?

ANNA-MARY. I just wouldn't know, Verner. I'm so darned mad I can't see straight.

VERNER. What's wrong?

ANNA-MARY. Mariette! That's what's wrong. I'll never speak to her again as long as I live. She's nothing more nor less than a snake-in-the-grass.

VERNER (*handing her her drink*). What did she do?

ANNA-MARY (*taking it*). Do? She just monopolized the Prince all evening long. I put him on my right, naturally, and her on the other side of him, and she never gave me the chance to say two words to him.

VERNER. Who did you have on your other side?

ANNA-MARY. That stuffed shirt Sir Gerard Nutfield. He's got one of those British accents that I just can't stand. He kept asking me where I *came* from. (*She gives him her glass.*) Put some more water in that; it's too strong.

VERNER (*taking it to the drink table*). Okay, sweetheart.

ANNA-MARY. My, you look terrible! With no tie on and your hair all mussed up.

VERNER. I'll have it set and waved first thing in the morning.

ANNA-MARY. I suppose that was meant to be funny.

VERNER (*chuckling*). Yes, Anna-Mary, that was supposed to be funny. But, oh, boy! There's better to come!

ANNA-MARY. Have you been drinking?

VERNER. Yeah. Like a fish. A golden fish.

ANNA-MARY (*coldly*). And what, may I ask, does that mean?

VERNER. It means a hell of a lot of things. A kid riding on a dolphin, for instance.

ANNA-MARY. *What?*

VERNER (*pursuing his dream*). And a flat rock and a little white beach and no tie and my hair mussed up.

ANNA-MARY. You've just gone clean out of your mind.

VERNER (*cheerfully*). Way, way out. (*He brings her her glass.*) Drink up your booze, ma'am, and enjoy yourself.

ANNA-MARY (*taking it*). How often have I got to tell you that I just can't stand the word "booze," Verner? It's vulgar and it grates on my nerves. You said it to Maud this evening, and I was mortified.

VERNER. *She* didn't seem to mind. Maybe her nerves ain't as sensitive as yours.

ANNA-MARY. I should think not, considering the sort of life she leads. You should have heard what Clare Pethrington was telling me about her tonight. I just couldn't believe my ears.

VERNER. That's the one with buck teeth that we had lunch with today, isn't it?

ANNA-MARY. Verner!

VERNER. She looked as if she could eat an apple through a tennis racquet.

ANNA-MARY. I'll have you know that Clare Pethrington is a highly cultured woman. She comes from one of the finest families in England. Her grandfather was the Earl of Babbercombe, and her great-grandfather was a close friend of Queen Victoria's. He used to stay at Balmoral every year, regular as clockwork.

VERNER. Bully for him.

ANNA-MARY. Just because she didn't throw herself at your head and butter you up and make you think how wonderful you were like Maud did, you think it's funny to make snide remarks about her.

VERNER (*with deceptive gentleness*). I wouldn't like to make any snide remarks about any of your friends, Anna-Mary, but I would like to say, kind of off the record, that in my opinion this dame we happen to be talking about, is a snooty, loud-mouthed, bad-mannered bitch.

ANNA-MARY. Verner Conklin. I just *don't want* to talk to you any more. And that's

the truth. I just don't want to talk to you *any more!* I come back worn out after an exhausting evening and find you lying here drunk. Then you start making silly jokes and saying mean things about people I respect and admire. I'll tell you here and now I've had just about enough of it. You've changed lately, Verner, and it's no use pretending you haven't; you've changed beyond all recognition.

VERNER. You hit it right on the nose, baby. I sure have.

ANNA-MARY. You'd better go to your room, order some black coffee, and take an Alka-Seltzer.

VERNER (*gaily*). Did His Serene Highness enjoy his God-damned cigars?

ANNA-MARY (*furiously*). Go away, Verner. Go away and leave me alone.

VERNER. Okay . . . Okay . . . That's just exactly what I'm going to do. Good night, sweetheart.

VERNER *picks up his tie and shoes, flings his coat over his arm, looks at her quizzically for a split second, and goes swiftly out of the room.* ANNA-MARY *sits glaring after him balefully as*

THE CURTAIN FALLS

CRAWLING ARNOLD

Jules Feiffer

Crawling Arnold was first presented at Gian Carlo Menotti's "Festival of Two Worlds," Spoleto, Italy, on June 27, 1961.

Subsequently, *Crawling Arnold* was presented by the London Playgoers Club and Theatre Perimeter at the New Arts Theatre, London, on February 17, 1965, with the following cast:

BARRY ENTERPRISE   Bill Maynard
GRACE ENTERPRISE   Doreen Mantle
MISS SYMPATHY   Avril Elgar

MILLIE   Helen Dowling
ARNOLD ENTERPRISE   David Healy

Directed by Charles Marowitz
Designed by Tony Leah

Jules Feiffer appositely has been captioned by the British critic and essayist Kenneth Tynan: "One of the best cartoonists now writing, and certainly the best writer now cartooning." This encomium is neatly substantiated in Mr. Feiffer's comedy *Crawling Arnold,* wherein he unleashes a stage full of his favorite social targets, all of them ripe for his inimitable satiric pulverizations.

The man who later was to be hailed as "the most talented social commentator in cartooning in our generation" stepped into the world he so deftly satirizes in an eventful year, 1929, preceding the historic Wall Street debacle by a mere matter of months.

A dedicated native of New York, Mr. Feiffer attended schools in three different boroughs (including the Art Students League of New York and Pratt Institute, Brooklyn). Then, acceding to the wishes of his local draft board, he joined forces with the United States Army's Signal Corps, and it was during this period—while working with a cartoon-animation unit—that he conceived the character of *Munro,* the four-year-old who inadvertently is drafted into the service.

Restored to civilian life after two years, Mr. Feiffer was determined to see his drawings in print, but apparently the publishers he had managed to track down did not share this determination. Consequently, he turned his sights toward Greenwich Village, and offered his drawings without reimbursement to *The Village Voice.* That was in 1956. Today, his work still appears regularly in the weekly *Village Voice* as well as in eighty other newspapers and magazines in the United States and abroad.

Although primarily celebrated for his cartoons and popular books—from *Sick, Sick, Sick* to the recent *Feiffer's Marriage Manual*—the author is not exactly a stranger to the theatre. In addition to *Crawling Arnold,* he has contributed a revue, *The Explainers,* staged at Chicago's Second City; and a full-length comedy, *Little Murders,* briefly seen on Broadway in 1967, but later a success in London as the first American play to be produced by the Royal Shakespeare Company. As an appendage: Mr. Feiffer's comic fable, *Passionella,* provided the source material for the final segment of Sheldon Harnick and Jerry Bock's tripartite Broadway musical *The Apple Tree.*

The author-cartoonist has been the recipient of many awards, notably the George Polk Memorial Award in journalism and Hollywood's Academy Award (1961) for his animated cartoon *Munro.*

The curtain rises on a projection: an enormous color slide of a smiling baby. The stage is dark, and voices come out of the darkness. Everybody "oohs" and "ahhhs" at the projection.

———

BARRY. That's little Will at six months.

GRACE. Eight months, dear. Even little Will wasn't that big at six months.

BARRY. Seven months, then. What a big bad bandit of a boy, eh, Miss Sympathy?

MISS SYMPATHY. An alert child.

BARRY (*clicks slide changer*). Next slide please. (*The projection changes.*) There he is at only one year! Did you ever see such a rough and tough customer, Miss Sympathy?

GRACE. Fourteen months, dear.

BARRY. Thirteen months.

MISS SYMPATHY. He does seem like an alert child.

BARRY. Alert? You should see him crawl around down in the shelter. Arnold just goes down when the siren sounds and sits there. But little Will! He has to touch everything. Won't keep out of anything—the oxygen tank, the gas masks, the plastic bombs—

MISS SYMPATHY. The shelter? (*The lights come up slowly to reveal the expensively bedecked patio of the* ENTERPRISE *home.* BARRY *and* GRACE ENTERPRISE, *a vigorous, athletic couple in their seventies are sitting with* MISS SYMPATHY, *a young and pretty social worker, in deck chairs facing the slide screen. The projector is behind them, being operated by* MILLIE, *the Negro maid. She, expressionlessly, begins to wheel it off.*)

BARRY. Our *fallout* shelter! Wait till you see it! (*To* MILLIE) You can serve our helmets now, Millie.

(MILLIE *coolly exits.* BARRY *and* GRACE *look hostilely after her.*)

GRACE. It's the only shelter in the country that has a television set and a whatayoucall them, dear?

BARRY. Stereo rig.

GRACE. Stereo rig. (*She begins to fuss with the baby, making small gurgling noises at it.*)

MISS SYMPATHY. A television set? But what good would a—

BARRY. It's not a real television set. It's the frame of one, and then I have a

sixteen-millimeter movie projector and a library of films—*Tim McCoy, Our Gang* —a variety of fare. The idea, you understand, is that under enemy attack the family can survive down there for *weeks,* while being able to simulate normal conditions of living. For example, I've had cards made up with the names of our favorite shows, and at the time they would ordinarily go on, we run a picture—a slide picture on the screen showing the title of the show—

GRACE. *Lassie—Ben Casey*—

BARRY. And during the half-hours those shows normally run, we sit and reminisce about our favorite episodes.

MISS SYMPATHY. You've *done* this?

BARRY. Several times. Before Little Will was born, Mrs. Enterprise and I—*and Arnold*—used to spend many happy weeks —many happy weeks in our shelter.

GRACE. One gets to *know* Ben Casey so much more deeply after one has talked about him in a fallout shelter for two weeks.

(MILLIE *enters with four air-raid helmets on a serving tray. There is evident tension between herself and the* ENTERPRISES. BARRY *and* GRACE *each sullenly take a helmet.*)

You may serve cocktails now, Millie. (GRACE *places a helmet in baby carriage.* MISS SYMPATHY *quietly demurs.*)

BARRY. You're making a mistake, Miss Sympathy. Today's drill begins pretty soon.

(MILLIE *exits, with* MISS SYMPATHY *looking after her, curiously.*)

You should see our library down there! Four years' worth of back copies of the *Reader's Digest.* I didn't know how long we'd be down there, so I wanted to get articles of *lasting* interest. (*He takes the baby carriage from* GRACE *and begins to fuss with the baby, making small gurgling noises.*)

GRACE (*proudly*). It's the only shelter in the country to be written up in *Good Housekeeping.*

MISS SYMPATHY. Little Will is how old?

GRACE (*proudly*). He'll be—

BARRY (*jealously*). He'll be two in September. (*He buries his face in the blankets of the carriage, muffling the sound of his voice.*) Isn't this the biggest, baddest, toughest little fellow who ever lived? I'll tell the world this is the biggest, baddest, toughest little fellow who ever lived!

MISS SYMPATHY (*peering into the carriage*). My, he's a *large* baby.

BARRY. Arnold was half his size at that age. Arnold couldn't crawl until he was almost *two*. Little Will's been crawling for four months now. *Four* months.

MISS SYMPATHY. And Arnold?

BARRY (*nervously*). Wasn't Millie supposed to bring us some drinks?

GRACE. Well, that's why we asked you to come, Miss Sympathy.

BARRY (*embarrassed*). Yes. Arnold is crawling again too. For four months.

GRACE (*sadly*). Regressed.

MISS SYMPATHY (*taking out a pad and making notes*). That sometimes happens when the first child feels overcompetitive with the second child. *Sibling rivalry.*

GRACE. Crawl. As soon as he enters the house he falls on all fours and crawls, crawls, crawls. I say to him, "Arnold, you *know* you can walk beautifully. At business you walk beautifully—"

MISS SYMPATHY. At business?

BARRY (*embarrassed*). Arnold is thirty-five. (*He fusses with the carriage.*)

MISS SYMPATHY (*making a long note*). *Advanced* sibling rivalry.

GRACE (*distressed*). That's what we wanted to talk to you about. I know there's nothing seriously wrong with Arnold. He's always been a good boy. Done everything we told him. Never talked back. Always well-mannered. Never been a show-off.

MISS SYMPATHY (*taking notes*). He's never had any previously crawling history?

GRACE. I'm afraid he took the news of Little Will's birth rather hard. I imagine when one has been raised as an only child and has lived happily all one's years in one's parents' home, it's hard to welcome a little stranger.

BARRY (*buries his head in the blankets, muffling his voice*). Who's Daddy's brave big bandit of a man! Little Will's Daddy's brave big bandit of a man.

GRACE. Please, dear. Don't talk with your mouth full.

(MILLIE *enters with three drinks on a*

platter. A coolness immediately settles on the patio. BARRY *and* GRACE *lapse into a sullen silence.* GRACE *coldly receives her drink.*)

Thank you, Millie.

(BARRY *grumbles something under his breath as he receives his.* MISS SYMPATHY *is obviously perturbed.*)

MISS SYMPATHY (*whispers to* MILLIE *as she is served her drink*). I strongly sympathize with the aspirations of your people.

(MILLIE *exits.*)

BARRY (*rocking the carriage*). A nationwide alert! All the American people mobilized as one, sitting it out in shelters all over the country. That's what I'd like Little Will to grow up to see. I guess it's just an old man's dream.

GRACE. Here's Arnold! Please, Miss Sympathy, don't tell him you're here because we asked—

ARNOLD (*enters crawling. He is an attractive young man in his thirties. He wears a hat and a business suit and carries an attaché case*). Father—Mother— (*He notices* MISS SYMPATHY, *sizes her up for a long moment, then coolly turns to his mother.*) Company?

GRACE. Arnold, dear, this is Miss Sympathy, this is our son, Arnold Enterprise.

MISS SYMPATHY. I'm pleased to meet you.

ARNOLD (*turning away*). That's O.K. (*To his mother*) Dinner ready?

BARRY. You're being damned rude, Arnold!

ARNOLD. I apologize. I have things on my mind. Are you having drinks?

GRACE. Oh, I'm sorry, dear. With you on the floor that way I forgot that you drink.

ARNOLD. Occasionally to excess. (*Crawls around.*) Did anyone see my coloring book?

GRACE. Millie!

(ARNOLD *crawls around. There is an awkward pause.* MILLIE, *finally, enters with a drink.* MISS SYMPATHY *leans forward, examining everyone's reaction.*)

ARNOLD (*accepting the drink*). It's got an olive in it!

GRACE. Please, dear.

ARNOLD (*to* MILLIE). You know I drink martinis with a lemon peel!

GRACE (*placating*). Millie—would you

mind—

(MILLIE *coolly takes back the glass and starts off.*)

MISS SYMPATHY (*whispers to* MILLIE *as she exits*). I have great regard for the aspirations of your people!

GRACE (*to* ARNOLD). Did you have to—

ARNOLD (*to himself*). When I began drinking martinis ten years ago I ordered them with an olive. I didn't know any better, I guess. They always came back with a lemon peel. (*To* MISS SYMPATHY) There was something so garbagey about a lemon peel lying at the bottom of my martini.

BARRY (*angry*). Arnold! I'm sorry, Miss Sympathy.

MISS SYMPATHY (*waving* BARRY *off*). No. No. I understand. (*To* ARNOLD) Please go on.

ARNOLD (*shrugs*). There's nothing to go on. I got used to it. I got to like it. I got to *want* lemon peels in my martinis. It still looked garbagey, but I found that *exciting!* I've always been surrounded by lots of money, cut off from life. That lemon peel floating there in its oil slick that way was to me my only contact with The People. It reminded me of East *River* movies—the Dead End Kids. Remember the Dead End Kids?

MISS SYMPATHY. No, I'm afraid not—

ARNOLD (*suspiciously*). What do you *do*?

(BARRY *and* GRACE *look distressed.* MISS SYMPATHY *warns them off with her eyes.*)

MISS SYMPATHY. I'm a social worker.

ARNOLD (*astonished*). And you don't remember the Dead End Kids?

MISS SYMPATHY. A *psychiatric* social worker.

ARNOLD. Oh, *you'd* remember Ingrid Bergman movies. Where's my coloring book, Mother?

GRACE. Where did you leave it yesterday, dear?

ARNOLD (*restlessly*). I've got to find my coloring book. I feel in the mood for coloring.

GRACE. I'll help you look, Arnold, if you'll just tell me where you think you left it.

(ARNOLD, *perturbed, crawls around the patio looking for his coloring book.* GRACE *follows him anxiously.* BARRY, *flushed with*

embarrassment, rocks the baby carriage al-most violently.*)

BARRY. That's a good boy, Little Will; that's a nice, big good boy, Little Will.

ARNOLD. I found it! (*He crawls off in a corner with the coloring book.* GRACE *follows him. As he begins coloring, she looks over his shoulder.*)

BARRY (*miserably, to* MISS SYMPATHY). I've tried to know that boy.

MISS SYMPATHY. Communications between the generations is never easy, Mr. Enterprise.

BARRY. We wrote away to Dear Abby about him. She was snotty.

MISS SYMPATHY. I'm not sure you acted wisely. She's not licensed, you know.

BARRY. I tried in every way to get close to him, like a father should.

MISS SYMPATHY. Perhaps if you had been a bit more patient—

BARRY. I've tried, believe me, I've tried. I introduced him into my way of life—my friends—I even got him accepted into my athletic club, and they don't usually take Jews.

MISS SYMPATHY. Arnold's Jewish?

BARRY. *That* week. It's not worth discussing. The next week he converted to Buddhism. They don't take Buddhists at my club either. But I got him in. It didn't do any good. All he ever did was go down to the gym and ride one of those vibrating horses for hours. He'd just sit there and ride till closing time. And he'd have a far-away look in his eyes. It became the scandal of the club.

GRACE (*to* ARNOLD). The sky is blue, dear. Not red; *blue.*

ARNOLD. Picasso colors it red.

GRACE. Picasso is an artist, dear. Artists can color the sky red because they *know* it's blue. Those of us who aren't artists must color things the way they really are or people might think we're stupid.

BARRY (*flushed, strides over to* ARNOLD). For Christ's sake, stop embarrassing us in front of the woman! Color the goddamn sky blue! (*He glares over* ARNOLD'S *shoulder.* GRACE *flutters nervously over to* MISS SYMPATHY.*)

GRACE. Another drink perhaps, Miss Sympathy?

MISS SYMPATHY. I'm fine, thank you. You mustn't allow yourself to get too depressed, Mrs. Enterprise.

GRACE (*hopefully*). I manage to keep myself busy. Organizational work. I'm the block captain of the "Let's Be a Friend of Our Children Society." It's made up of mothers who've had somber histories with their children and are trying to profit others with their experience.

MISS SYMPATHY. That sounds very ambitious.

GRACE. And I'm chairman of the Gratification Committee of the Husband's Fulfillment League. We prepare and distribute many useful pamphlets based on lessons learned from many somber experiences with fufillment. And, of course, there's still tennis.

MISS SYMPATHY. It all sounds very ambitious.

GRACE. But primarily my life has been my husband's. When he's happy, I try to be happy. When he's unhappy, I try to be unhappy. When he wants me, I try to want him. The key to a successful marriage is giving. *I've* given. Everything.

(MILLIE *enters and serves* ARNOLD *his drink.*)

ARNOLD. That's it. A lemon peel! (*He drops coloring book and examines the martini.*) I can't tolerate a martini without a lemon peel. (*To* MILLIE) Have you been back to the UN, Millie?

MILLIE (*coolly*). Not since last time.

ARNOLD (*to* MISS SYMPATHY). Millie was on television at the UN. We all watched her.

MISS SYMPATHY (*interested*). Oh, what were you doing there?

(GRACE *and* BARRY *writhe uncomfortably.*)

MILLIE. Rioting. (*She exits.*)

BARRY (*furious*). I swear we've got to replace that girl.

GRACE. It doesn't do any good. Any of the girls you get these days, they're all the same. One time or another they've *all* rioted at the UN.

MISS SYMPATHY. I, naturally, don't agree with her means, but if we examine her motivation we should be able to understand why she may have felt that such a form of protest was in order. A misguided protest, I admit, but—

BARRY. She wants her own shelter!

MISS SYMPATHY. What?

BARRY. When I started work on the shelter, I was going to build two of them. One for us and one for Millie and any friends she'd want to invite. Same dimensions, same material, exactly like ours in every way.

GRACE. Millie resented the idea.

BARRY. That girl has been with us ten years, hardly a peep out of her in all that time. Before her, the girl we used to take in was Millie's mother. When Millie's mother was ill, her *grandmother* would come in to clean.

GRACE. Millie's grandmother was a *good* girl.

BARRY. We never had any trouble before. But when I tell Millie I'm building her a shelter—same dimensions, same material, exactly like ours in every way—she nearly quits!

MISS SYMPATHY. I sympathize with her aspirations. She wanted to share *your* shelter of course.

BARRY (*outraged*). *Yes!*

MISS SYMPATHY. You see, while on the surface it would seem that the two shelters are alike in every way, the simple fact that Millie is excluded from one of them can have a devastating psychological effect on her. I have always been opposed to separate but equal fallout shelters.

BARRY. But now she *wants* one!

MISS SYMPATHY. Oh?

BARRY. She comes back from the UN and we're having a practice air-raid drill— and you understand we're all Americans here, *we* accept the law of the land—so we invite Millie into our shelter. And she refuses! Suddenly she wants her *own* shelter!

MISS SYMPATHY. But why? For what reason?

GRACE (*distraught*). She says she's a neutralist!

ARNOLD. She's a hypocrite. A real neutralist wouldn't take shelter at all.

BARRY. Do you hear that kid? He's worse than she is!

MISS SYMPATHY. Are you a neutralist, Arnold?

ARNOLD. No, the neutralists are too extreme. I'm neutral.

GRACE (*maneuvering to leave* MISS SYMPATHY *alone with* ARNOLD). Barry, dear, don't you think we should make a final check of the shelter? The drill should start any time now.

BARRY. Good thinking. I wonder what the delay is. The block captain mentioned last week that they were having a little trouble with the siren.

(*They exit wheeling the baby carriage.*)

MISS SYMPATHY (*There is an awkward silence. She decides to get right to it*). Don't you know how to walk?

ARNOLD. That's a funny question. Why do you ask?

MISS SYMPATHY. Well, you're not walking.

ARNOLD. I'm not smoking, either. Why don't you ask me if I know how to smoke?

MISS SYMPATHY (*containing herself*). That's very good. (ARNOLD *shrugs.*) Do you mind if I crawl with you?

ARNOLD (*hotly*). Yes, I do!

MISS SYMPATHY. But *you* do it!

ARNOLD. I do it because I believe in it. You do it because you think you're being therapeutic. You're not. You're only being patronizing. I realize that in your field it's sometimes difficult to tell the difference.

MISS SYMPATHY (*with difficulty*). That's very good.

ARNOLD. If you really feel the urge to crawl with me—*really* feel it, I mean—then you'll be most welcome. Not any more welcome or unwelcome than you are now by the way. I am by no means a missionary. Did you see my coloring book?

MISS SYMPATHY. When anyone says anything you don't like, you retreat into that coloring book.

ARNOLD. I admit it's rude. I shouldn't do it unless I have a coloring book for you too. (*He studies her.*) Do you wear glasses?

MISS SYMPATHY. Contact lenses.

ARNOLD (*suddenly shy*). You'd be prettier with glasses. Or rather *I* think you'd be prettier with glasses. I like the way a girl looks with glasses. It makes her face look—less undressed.

MISS SYMPATHY. You think contact lenses make me look naked?

ARNOLD. I think the more people have on, the better they get along with each other. If everybody in the world wore big hats, thick glasses, and dark overcoats they'd all pass each other by thinking, "What an interesting person must be inside all that." And they'd be curious, but

they wouldn't ask questions. Who'd dare ask questions like "What are you really like?" to a person in a big hat, thick glasses, and a dark overcoat? The desire to invade privacy rises in direct proportion to the amount of clothing a person takes off. It's what we call "communication." Take off the big hat, and they say, "Good morning, sir!" Take off the thick glasses, and they say, "My, don't you have *haunted* eyes!" Take off the overcoat, and they say, "Tell me *everything!*" So there you have intimacy, followed by understanding, followed by disillusion, followed by— (*shrugs*). If only everybody wore more clothing, we wouldn't have wars.

MISS SYMPATHY. You're saying you'd like to wear an overcoat with me. Is that it?

ARNOLD. I'd feel better if one of us at least wore a big hat. Do you ever have fantasies?

MISS SYMPATHY. Aren't you getting intimate?

ARNOLD. *You* decided to wear the contact lenses.

MISS SYMPATHY. Everybody has fantasies.

ARNOLD. What are yours about?

MISS SYMPATHY. Being a better social worker.

ARNOLD. Dear God.

MISS SYMPATHY (*sadly*). I used to have fantasies about Adlai Stevenson. But that's all over now.

ARNOLD. I have fantasies all the time. When I'm awake, when I'm asleep, I *live* with them. I embellish them. Polish them day after day. You cultivate a good fantasy long enough, and soon it can seep out into the real world. Do you know how old my parents are?

MISS SYMPATHY. I hadn't thought of it. Middle fifties?

ARNOLD. They're both over seventy.

MISS SYMPATHY. And they had a *baby?*

ARNOLD (*shrugs, reaches for the coloring book, changes his mind*). My father doesn't look very much older than me, does he?

MISS SYMPATHY (*evasive*). I don't know if I noticed.

ARNOLD. You're kind. But that's how it's been always. They're both alert, involved, aggressive people. So while I'm out trying, unsuccessfully, to make it with a girl and I come home, mixed up and angry and feeling like not much of anything, what are they waiting up proudly to tell me? *They're* having a baby. I'll try to say this in as uninvolved and unneurotic a way as I know how—it's hard to face a daily series of piddling, eroding defeats and, in addition, have the fact thrown in your face that your *father* at *age seventy* can still do better than you can.

(*There is a long pause.* ARNOLD *fishes a ball out from under a chair and tosses it to* MISS SYMPATHY. *She one-hands it.*)

You catch pretty good.

(*She cocks her arm back.* ARNOLD *throws out one hand defensively.*)

No, don't throw it. I'm not ready to compete yet.

MISS SYMPATHY. These fantasies—were any of them about crawling?

ARNOLD. In my fantasies, it was everyone else who crawled. For instance, in one of them I had this uncle. Uncle Walter—

(*A weak siren begins to wail erratically.*)

BARRY (*enters, running with the baby carriage*). That's it! The alert! Down to the shelter, everyone!

GRACE (*enters with a fire extinguisher and shopping bag*). Oh, it's so exciting! It's so exciting!

(BARRY *switches on a transistor radio.*)

RADIO VOICE. Stay tuned to this frequency. All other frequencies have left the air. This is Conelrad!

BARRY (*listening intently*). I met that fellow down at civil-defense headquarters once. You'd be surprised. He's just like you and me.

(GRACE *is in a sudden, heated conversation with* ARNOLD.)

GRACE. But you *have* to go down! You went down with us last year!

RADIO VOICE. It is the law that everyone on the street take shelter—

ARNOLD. We're *not* on the street. We're on the patio.

BARRY (*exasperated*). You think the Russians give a damn we're not on the street?

GRACE. It's the spirit of the law one should follow, dear.

BARRY. Arnold, I've had enough of this nonsense! Downstairs! That's a parental order!

ARNOLD (*hotly*). I colored the sky blue, didn't I? Why don't *you* ever meet *me* halfway?

BARRY (*exits wheeling the baby carriage*). I can't do anything with him.

GRACE. We can't leave our oldest out on the patio!

BARRY (*reenters with the baby carriage*). He's the one who's breaking the law. Let's go! (*He exits with the carriage.*)

GRACE. You'd better follow me, Miss Sympathy. It's dark in the basement.

MISS SYMPATHY (*weakly, to* ARNOLD). It *is* the law.

ARNOLD. I told you I'm not asking for converts.

GRACE. For the last time, won't you come, Arnold? It's not going to be any fun without you.

ARNOLD. I'm doing something *else,* Mother.

BARRY (*reenters with the baby carriage*). The hell with him. The law doesn't mean a thing to *our* son. Come on!

(*He exits with the baby carriage.* GRACE *exits.*)

MISS SYMPATHY (*to* ARNOLD). I, as do you, question the sense of such a drill, but objecting to this law by defying it robs *all* laws of their meaning. Now, I can see working for its reform while continuing to *obey* it, but to be both against it and defy it at the same time seems to me to weaken your position.

ARNOLD. They're all downstairs. You'd better go.

MISS SYMPATHY (*starting away*). You do understand?

ARNOLD (*dryly*). I think I hear planes.

(*She exits running. Sound of offstage pounding*)

BARRY (*offstage*). Goddamit, Millie! What are you doing in there? Unlock the door!

GRACE (*offstage*). That's not nice, Millie! Let us into our fallout shelter!

(*Sound of pounding*)

BARRY (*offstage*). Millie! There is such a thing as the laws of trespass! You're in *my* shelter!

(*Sound of pounding.* MISS SYMPATHY *enters.*)

ARNOLD (*grinning*). Millie locked herself in the shelter?

MISS SYMPATHY. She says, "Let the white imperialists wipe each other out."

ARNOLD (*laughs*). I can appreciate her sensitivity and support her aspirations, but

I reject the extremes to which she's gone. (*Brightly*) But I do understand her motivations.

(*Sound of pounding*)

BARRY (*offstage*). Millie, you're not playing fair!

ARNOLD. You really shouldn't be up here, you know.

MISS SYMPATHY. I thought we were having an all clear by default.

ARNOLD. I doubt it.

BARRY (*offstage*). All right, Millie. We'll stay down here anyway! We'll use the basement as our shelter! Down on your stomach, Grace. Where's Miss Sympathy? Miss Sympathy!

MISS SYMPATHY (*yelling*). Upstairs! I thought it was over!

BARRY (*offstage*). The law's the law, Miss Sympathy. We can't come up till we hear the all clear. Otherwise we'd be making Khrushchev happy!

ARNOLD. It *is* the law.

MISS SYMPATHY. What if I lay on my stomach up here? It's so dusty down there.

ARNOLD. I guess that would be *semi*-compliance.

MISS SYMPATHY. Does it seem within the spirit of the law to you?

ARNOLD. Well, I know lying on your stomach *is* the accepted crisis position. I don't imagine you'd be penalized because of location.

(*She lies on her stomach.* ARNOLD *views her with wry amusement.*)

Don't you know how to stand?

MISS SYMPATHY (*dryly*). That's quite witty. You were telling me about your fantasy.

ARNOLD. Which one?

MISS SYMPATHY. Your uncle. (*Checks notes.*) Walter.

ARNOLD. Well, in a fantasy it's you who are in control, isn't it? So you can make things any way you want them. So I wanted an uncle. I guess I was eight or nine at the time. So I made him up. Uncle Walter. Uncle Walter was a mess. His eyes were very bad, and he wore big, thick bifocals—about this size—half the size of his face, and he had a beard. Hair all over. I mean it started with his nose hairs and blended with his ear hairs and went all the way down to his chest hairs. Except I never saw his chest. He was frail and he always wore a scarf. And a big heavy black overcoat. Even inside the house. It used to shed. *He* used to shed. My mother and father were always embarrassed when he came to visit. And I was too—but for *them*, not for him. I kept hoping Uncle Walter would understand that I was as normal as he was and that it wasn't my fault my parents were a little strange. He would never let me near him. He *hated* children. So *I* hated children. Anything Uncle Walter did I wanted to do. I tried to get bad eyes. I'd let them blur out of focus until they'd tear. I began seeing my parents as Uncle Walter saw them. I don't mean I began to understand them the way Uncle Walter did. I mean I *became* Uncle Walter looking at my parents. I became Uncle Walter looking at *me!* Then—I don't know how it happened—my father talked Uncle Walter into joining his athletic club. I thought it was a big joke—that in a week Uncle Walter would have them all wearing overcoats, bifocals, and beards—(*Mimes sign.*) "The Unhealthy Athletic Club." But all that happened was that Uncle Walter got healthy. He got rid of his overcoat. He shaved his beard. He took pills for his vitamin deficiency, and his eyes became twenty-twenty. He began to smile at me and say, "Howsa boy!" He talked business with the family. It was *my* fantasy, and he had sold me out! He died a month later. Never trust a grown-up.

MISS SYMPATHY. Will you tell me why you're crawling?

(ARNOLD *crawls over to* MISS SYMPATHY.)

ARNOLD. I find that in crawling like a child I begin to act like a child again.

MISS SYMPATHY. Is that why you started?

ARNOLD. Possibly. I did a very childlike thing on the way home. I never would have thought of doing such a thing before I crawled. As an adult my values encompassed a rigid good, a rigid evil, and a mushy everything-in-between. As a child I've rediscovered one value I had completely forgotten existed.

MISS SYMPATHY. What's that?

ARNOLD. Being naughty.

MISS SYMPATHY. You did something naughty on the way home. Is that what you're telling me?

ARNOLD. I don't think I want to talk

about it right now. I want to enjoy it by myself for a little while longer.

MISS SYMPATHY (*exasperated*). God, you're as hard to reach as a child! (*Quickly*) I understand why, of course.

ARNOLD. Why?

MISS SYMPATHY. First you tell me what you did today that was naughty.

ARNOLD. First you tell me why I'm as hard to reach as a child.

MISS SYMPATHY (*as if to a child*). First you tell me what you did that was naughty.

ARNOLD (*kidding*). You first.

MISS SYMPATHY (*as if to a child*). Oh, no, you!

ARNOLD (*kidding*). I asked you first.

MISS SYMPATHY (*as if to a child*). Then will you tell me?

ARNOLD (*trying to withdraw*). Yes.

MISS SYMPATHY (*very arch*). Promise?

ARNOLD (*serious*). Yes.

MISS SYMPATHY (*very arch*). Cross your heart and hope to die?

ARNOLD (*stares at her, unbelieving*). I can understand why you have trouble reaching children.

BARRY (*offstage*). Hey, up there. Have you heard the all-clear sound yet?

MISS SYMPATHY (*yelling angrily*). No, it hasn't, Mr. Enterprise!

BARRY (*offstage*). Funny. It should have sounded by now.

GRACE (*offstage*). I'm getting a chill lying on my stomach this way.

BARRY (*offstage*). It's the proper position, Grace.

GRACE (*offstage*). Can't we go up soon, Barry?

BARRY (*offstage*). When the all clear sounds we'll go up. That's the law. Is that Millie yelling something?

GRACE (*offstage*). Yell louder, Millie. We can't hear you—(*Pause*) She wants to know if the all clear sounded yet.

BARRY (*offstage*). Tell her to go to hell.

ARNOLD (*after a long study of* MISS SYMPATHY). Do you really want me to get up?

MISS SYMPATHY (*petulantly*). It's not what *I* want. It's what's best for yourself.

ARNOLD. You mean if I got up I'd be doing it for myself.

MISS SYMPATHY (*petulantly*). Not for me. Not for your mother. Not for your father. Strictly for yourself.

ARNOLD. That's too bad. I don't care

much about getting up for myself. I would have liked to have done it for you, though.

MISS SYMPATHY (*with sudden warmth*). I *would* be very pleased.

ARNOLD. If I got up right now?

MISS SYMPATHY (*warmly*). Yes.

ARNOLD (*begins to rise*). Okay.

MISS SYMPATHY (*tackles him*). No.

ARNOLD. But you said—

MISS SYMPATHY. Not *now*. *Later!* (*Whispers*.) It's against the law!

ARNOLD (*shrugs. Returns to his crawling position*). Did you see my coloring book?

MISS SYMPATHY (*furious*). You're not being *honest!* You blame me for accepting the rules of society. Well, without those rules we'd have anarchy. Every mature person has to operate within the warp and woof of society. You want to operate outside that warp and woof, to return to a *child's* world—to start all over again!

ARNOLD (*appreciatively*). Yeah! (*From his pocket he plucks a lollipop.*)

MISS SYMPATHY (*impatiently*). Well, you *can't* start all over again. It will all come out the *same way!*

ARNOLD (*sucking the lollipop*). Then I'll start all over again, again.

MISS SYMPATHY. But it will all come out the same way *again!*

ARNOLD. Then I'll start all over again, again, again. It's *my* game. (*He takes a long, loud suck on the lollipop.*)

BARRY (*offstage*). Wasn't that the all clear?

MISS SYMPATHY. I'm afraid not, Mr. Enterprise.

GRACE (*offstage*). I'm catching cold.

BARRY (*offstage*). Let me put my jacket under you.

GRACE (*offstage*). I'm *tired* of this.

BARRY (*offstage*). But it's only a few minutes. We've spent over two weeks in our shelter.

GRACE (*offstage*). But we had television.

BARRY (*offstage*). The law is there for the citizens to obey. If *we* are irresponsible, how can we attack *others* for being irresponsible?

MISS SYMPATHY (*coldly, to* ARNOLD). You have a very irresponsible attitude.

ARNOLD. "Naughty" is the word I prefer.

MISS SYMPATHY. You were going to tell me something.

ARNOLD. I forgot.

MISS SYMPATHY. What you did on the way home from work—(*with sarcasm*) Something *naughty*.

ARNOLD. Do you find me attractive, Miss Sympathy?

MISS SYMPATHY (*a long pause. She begins to sniffle*). Yes, I do.

ARNOLD (*surprised*). You can say it just like that?

MISS SYMPATHY (*barely restraining tears*). Because I do. I know I do. You're the kind of person I find attractive *always*. From previous examples I know you fall into my spectrum of attractiveness. Actually, it's because I find you so attractive that I'm having trouble with you. If I didn't find you attractive I could explain your problem without the slightest difficulty.

ARNOLD. Everything's so complicated.

MISS SYMPATHY. We live in a complex world.

ARNOLD. *Children* are complex. Adults are just complicated.

MISS SYMPATHY. Why did you ask if I found you attractive?

ARNOLD. Because we've been alone for a while and we'll be alone for a while longer. I thought it was the right thing to say.

MISS SYMPATHY. We have a time limit. The all clear will probably sound any minute.

ARNOLD. Four months ago you wouldn't have found me attractive.

MISS SYMPATHY. Why do you say that?

ARNOLD. Because four months ago I didn't crawl. Crawling has made me a more attractive person.

MISS SYMPATHY. It has? How?

ARNOLD. Well, for one thing I'm conspicuous now. I never used to be. There's a certain magnetism conspicuous men have for women. (*More cautiously*) I *think* conspicuous men have for women.

MISS SYMPATHY. No, don't stop. In some ways you're right.

ARNOLD. I'm more assertive now. Everybody used to have *their* road. My mother, my father, my friends, Millie—with me the question was Whose road would I take? Whose side was I on? Now I have *my* road, *my* side.

MISS SYMPATHY. You're terribly sweet. Do you mind if I crawl over to you?

ARNOLD. I'd like it.

(*She does. For a while they stare wistfully at each other. Then* ARNOLD *drops to his stomach and kisses her.*) I'm on my stomach now.

MISS SYMPATHY. Yes.

ARNOLD. I'm not even crawling any more. That's *real* regression.

MISS SYMPATHY. Yes. (*He kisses her.*) Before we do anything I want to tell you—

ARNOLD. What?

MISS SYMPATHY. Before—when I was feeling sorry for you—I felt you'd rejoin society if you were only made to feel like a man.

ARNOLD. An expert analysis.

MISS SYMPATHY. I was going to offer to go to bed with you to make you feel like a man. I couldn't offer myself in that spirit now.

ARNOLD. I'm glad you told me. The social worker my folks had in last month went to bed with me because she wanted to make me feel like a man. I think she got more out of it than I did.

MISS SYMPATHY. How many have there been?

ARNOLD. One a month for four months. My parents keep bringing them around. They're very nervous about me.

MISS SYMPATHY (*doubtfully*). You're not just using me, Arnold—

ARNOLD. We're using each other, Miss Sympathy. That's what using's for. (*He begins to unbutton the back of her blouse.*)

MISS SYMPATHY. The all clear—What if the all clear should sound?

ARNOLD. It won't. It's broken. That's what I did that was naughty today. (*They embrace as lights dim.*)

BARRY (*offstage*). Was that the all clear?

CURTAIN

THE ACADEMY

Mario Fratti

Translated by RAYMOND ROSENTHAL

THE PROFESSOR	*CORSO
THE SIGNORA	*DONATO
*AFRO	*ELIO
*BENITO	FORTUNATO

TIME: The present.
PLACE: Venice.

---

    * During Benito Mussolini's Fascist regime (1922–1945) it was common practice to give children born in that period names that glorified Mussolini's dreams of conquest: Afro (Africa); Benito; Corso (Corsica); Donato (gift of Providence); Elio (place in the sun).

MARIO FRATTI was born in L'Aquila, Italy, in 1927. He studied in Venice, where he received his doctorate in languages and literature, and though he presently lives in New York (his American base as correspondent and feature writer for several Italian newspapers), his plays continue to shed light upon some shadowy corners of life in postwar Italy.

As a dramatist, Mr. Fratti eschews the obscure and the enigmatic. A principled advocate of directness and immediate communication in the theatre even when exploring a somewhat bizarre premise as he does in *The Academy,* the author's tenets are admirably stated in a personal note: "The playwright must be clear to himself, clear to the actor, clear to the audience. A human being should never try to resist the temptation of communicating as clearly as possible. After all, there is a reason why playwrights choose dialogue as their working tool. Dialogue means an attempt to reach another human being. That's my purpose in the theatre. At the risk of being considered conservative and traditional, my only purpose is to 'communicate' my thoughts and emotions. I write about man, to be *understood* by men."

Fratti's plays are governed by a fine and firm creative hand that precludes ambiguity as it sets an instantaneous and coadjutant wave surging between stage and spectator.

Considered one of Italy's foremost contemporary dramatists, Mr. Fratti's plays have been produced on stage and television in many corners of the world and have garnered twenty-six awards for their prolific creator. His most recent full-length play, *Eleanora Duse,* dealing with the legendary Italian tragedienne who died in Pittsburgh in 1924, was commissioned and produced by the Asolo Theatre Festival, Sarasota, Florida, in July, 1967.

SCENE. *A large, striking poster with the words THE ACADEMY.*

A dusty classroom; stage left, a dais with two chairs, a blackboard, a map of the United States, the Italian and the American flags; stage right, some school benches.

AFRO *and* FORTUNATO *enter from left; they are two modestly dressed, virile young men; short hair, sweaters, the relaxed, easygoing attitudes of the American one sees in the movies.*

———

AFRO (*with a gesture, pointing to the room*). This is the classroom. You'll be glad you came. I've already begun to work. I average three hundred dollars a month. Because I'm just a beginner, not too experienced. You know English better than I do, so he'll let you take care of more important clients (*Pointing to the two chairs on the dais:*) "She" sits here. Still young, an attractive woman. Everything's up to the wife, remember. So give it your best, a little finesse, you understand. If she flunks you, you're finished here. You can't try again.

(BENITO *enters. A young man very much like the other two.*)

AFRO. Ask him. He brought his brother. He flunked.

BENITO (*languidly*). Ciao. A new one? (*Shakes* FORTUNATO's *hand.*)

FORTUNATO. Yes, new.

AFRO (*to* BENITO, *insistently*). Tell him about your brother.

BENITO (*reluctantly*). Who knows what was going on in her head? My brother's just like me. Better, perhaps. Sometimes— who knows?—it's a question of incompatibility.

(CORSO *and* DONATO *enter; two more students.* CORSO *is very tall and robust.*)

CORSO. Hi.

DONATO. Hi.

(CORSO *and* DONATO *sit down on the benches and begin talking in the background.*)

AFRO. Give her a big smile as soon as she comes in. Everything hinges on the first impression. He doesn't count at all. An ex-Fascist, they say. A sucker for American culture, now.—"If you can't beat them, join them."—Americans are the greatest, the best, tops in everything. They'll save

us from the Reds, etcetera. A regular ass-licker, a beaten dog who likes to butter up his master. Unemployed, just like us. He's satisfied with his ten percent. He did a good job of organizing here, and that's good for us. I'll loan you the ten thousand lire for the registration fee.

(AFRO *hands him the money; the* SIGNORA *enters; she has a sad air.*)

CORSO *and* DONATO (*who, being the first to notice her enter, get to their feet respectfully*). Buon giorno, signora.

SIGNORA. *Buon giorno.*

AFRO (*apologizing for not having noticed her immediately*). I didn't see you come in, signora. *Buon giorno.* May I introduce a new applicant, Fortunato.

FORTUNATO (*trying to hide the money he's holding and stretching out his hand embarrassedly*). Enchanted.

SIGNORA (*with detachment*). Pleased to meet you. (*As* FORTUNATO *is staring at her admiringly:*) Where is Elio? There's mail for him. (*Holds up a letter.*)

CORSO. He hasn't come yet. I'll give it to him. (*He takes the letter from her.*)

SIGNORA (*to* FORTUNATO, *making a gesture for him to follow her*). Come.

(*They go out together, to stage right.*)

CORSO (*looking at the envelope against the light*). There's fifty dollars in this. A fortune! Not a week goes by . . .

AFRO (*looking enviously at the door through which his friend and the* SIGNORA *have gone*). There's the fortunate one. He was christened Fortunato, and right now he's proving it. This audition is his most beautiful moment, here. . . .

(ELIO *enters, the same age as the others, but more elegant.*)

ELIO (*catching the last sentence on the fly and motioning with his head toward the door at stage right*). A new one?

AFRO. A new one.

ELIO (*ironically*). Still in love with our signora?

AFRO. Frustrated, perhaps. Only once, it whets the appetite. A woman sticks right here . . . (*pointing to his throat:*) if you don't have her completely.

CORSO. Mail.

ELIO (*takes letter*). Oh, my granny!

DONATO. The usual fifty bucks.

ELIO (*kissing letter*). *Mia divina!* If her venerable age allowed her to come back to

Italy, I would treat her better. (*Ironically*) Tell me, Afro, how would you treat our signora if she gave you another session?

AFRO. With kid gloves. So would you if given the chance. None of us have really had her.

ELIO. Could be . . . (*Reads letter that came with the fifty dollars.*) She's dreaming about me, desires me . . . hopes to come back. . . . Let's hope to God she won't be able to move. . . . Her pains are soothed. . . . She's hungry for tenderness . . . "Hunger," they say. It's really incredible, the stamina of these American grandmas. . . .

(*The* PROFESSOR *enters from stage left; he is about forty-five, lean, severe. They all rise to their feet.* ELIO *hides the letter with the money.*)

ALL. *Buon giorno,* Professor.

PROFESSOR (*formally*). Be seated. (*A moment of silence. To* ELIO, *taking him by surprise with his unexpected question:*) How much did she send you?

ELIO (*surprised*). Fifty . . . fifty dollars.

PROFESSOR. Turn over the percentage.

(ELIO *reluctantly goes to the dais and hands over the money.*)

ELIO (*as he goes back to the seat, nastily; getting revenge for having to pay*). There's a new applicant in the next room, with your wife.

PROFESSOR (*unconcerned, not giving it any importance*). Let's review a few things from the preceding lesson. Donato, you. What is the capital of Maryland? (*He points with pointer to the state on the map, which does not have the names of the cities.*)

DONATO. Annapolis.

PROFESSOR. Of Alabama?

DONATO. Montgomery.

PROFESSOR. Of Kentucky?

DONATO. Frankfort.

PROFESSOR. You, Benito. Which are the thirteen states that first joined the republic?

BENITO (*slowly, counting on his fingers*). Connecticut, Delaware, Georgia, Maryland, Massachusetts, New Hampshire, New Jersey, New York . . . Pennsylvania . . . South Carolina, North Carolina . . . Virginia . . . (*He can't think of the last one.*)

PROFESSOR. You're one short.

ELIO. Rhode Island.

PROFESSOR. Right. (*To* ELIO) When was Washington born?

ELIO. February 22, 1732.

PROFESSOR. Lincoln?

ELIO. February 12, 1809.

PROFESSOR (*to* CORSO). How many calories does a glass of carrot juice contain?

CORSO. Fifty.

PROFESSOR. A hamburger?

CORSO. Two hundred.

PROFESSOR. A yogurt?

CORSO. One hundred and sixty-five.

PROFESSOR (*to* AFRO). An example of high-calorie food?

AFRO. Caviar, anchovies, spaghetti . . .

PROFESSOR. Low calorie?

AFRO. Celery, jello . . .

PROFESSOR (*to* ELIO). How many calories should a tall, rawboned American woman ingest per day?

ELIO. Minimum, 1845. Maximum, 2580.

PROFESSOR. Good. (*Turns to* CORSO) Vitamin A is good for . . .

CORSO. Eyesight and glandular functions.

PROFESSOR (*to* DONATO). Vitamin C?

DONATO. Bones, teeth, gums, skin.

PROFESSOR. Good, You've not wasted your time or your money. Thanks to our Academy you are always ready to perform with éclat for our guests from across the sea. For the glory of our nation. Now . . .

(*The* SIGNORA *enters, followed by* FORTUNATO; *all eyes are on the woman, who hands a test paper to the* PROFESSOR. FORTUNATO *sits down next to* AFRO, *who questions him in a whisper.* FORTUNATO *continues to look at the* SIGNORA, *who sits down on the dais; and he answers* AFRO's *questions by nodding his head in a distracted manner.*)

PROFESSOR (*after a short consultation with the* SIGNORA). My wife's report: favorable. You've passed. (*To* FORTUNATO) Can you speak English?

FORTUNATO. Yes.

PROFESSOR. This is a bad start. When I say "can you" you must answer "I can." If I say "do you" you must answer "I do."

FORTUNATO. I'm sorry. You are right.

PROFESSOR. Now translate: *"Le piace l' Italia?"*

FORTUNATO. Do you like Italy?

PROFESSOR. *Passeggiare.*

FORTUNATO. To walk.

PROFESSOR. *Amare.*

FORTUNATO. To love.

PROFESSOR. *Dormire.*

FORTUNATO. To sleep.

PROFESSOR. *Labbra.*

FORTUNATO. Lips.

PROFESSOR. *Carezza.*

FORTUNATO. Caress.

PROFESSOR. *Capezzolo.*

FORTUNATO. Nipple.

PROFESSOR. *Pelle liscia.*

FORTUNATO. Baby skin.

PROFESSOR. *Sangue ardente.*

FORTUNATO. Hot blood.

PROFESSOR. *Luna di miele.*

FORTUNATO. Honeymoon.

PROFESSOR. *Tenerezza.*

FORTUNATO. Tenderness.

PROFESSOR. *Desiderio.*

FORTUNATO. Desire.

PROFESSOR. *Sogno.*

FORTUNATO. Dream.

(*A pause. The* PROFESSOR *looks for other questions, reads the name on the test paper.*)

PROFESSOR. Translate: *"Mi chiamo Fortunato. Lo sono veramente, oggi. Ho incontrato lei."*

FORTUNATO (*very sure of himself, with a good accent*). My name is Fortunato. I am really fortunate today. I met you.

PROFESSOR (*pleased*). Good. Did you free-lance?

FORTUNATO. Yes, whenever I hit on one of them.

PROFESSOR. Do you receive money?

FORTUNATO. No.

PROFESSOR. You see. What you lacked is organization. The seed was there, your good will; it did not, however, bear fruit. (*He points to* ELIO.) Today he received fifty dollars. All of them receive dollars, every now and then. One of them . . . (*making a vague gesture:*) one whom none of you remembers . . . once received a pair of ruby cuff links, as a present. He resold them for two thousand five hundred dollars. A fortune.

AFRO (*whispering to* FORTUNATO). It's not true. He read it in a novel by Tennessee Williams.

PROFESSOR (*taking note of the whispering*). What's that he's telling you? Don't listen to him. He reads too much. And his imagination runs away with him. All right, Fortunato. (*He looks at the* SIGNORA, *who nods in agreement.*) You're accepted. Let's have the registration fee: ten thousand lire. (*To the* SIGNORA) Collect the homework.

(*As* FORTUNATO *takes the ten thousand lire to the dais and signs a paper, the* SIGNORA, *with the students staring at her morbidly, collects the homework. After signing,* FORTUNATO *receives a list which he takes back to the bench and reads.*)

PROFESSOR (*after having waited for silence, in a professorial tone, savoring his words*). You see, my dear Fortunato— you are indeed fortunate to be with us —I used the word *"Organization"* not by chance. (*Scanning his words:*) This is in fact a first-class organization, just ask. (*A vague gesture to the other students*) Our Academy was conceived with love, vision, imagination. To attain—even though we suffered and lost the war—a lofty aim. We will fortify—thanks to our pure Latin blood—the other races. (*He takes a deep breath.*) Which is today the race to whom the destiny of the world is entrusted? The American race. They are the receptacle of all culture, the refined masters of every art, the original worshipers of *real* democracy. No civilization can be compared to *their* civilization. No society has ever reached such a standard of affluence. They're the most perfect embodiment of real accomplishment, the quintessence of progress, the synthesis of the best achievements. Their culture is on the highest level in every field. *They'll* save Europe from the Reds. We must therefore strengthen their race, improve it; we must contribute somehow to the noble task of defending civilization. (*Speaking in a less rhetorical tone:*) Therefore I am here in a school founded with inspired insight to give you an American culture, to put you in the position to exploit to the full your—our— best qualities. In fact the Academy develops the intensive and rational application of our masculine, virile patrimony. The Germans possess a splendid steel industry; the Americans have a first-class missile industry; we . . . we have created a new industry: the American woman, the American tourist. . . . (*Going into details, in a less heroic tone:*) On the sheet I have just handed to you are listed our branches in other cities, the stores that give us discounts: florists, photographers, bookstores, etc. Memorize it. Now let's get to the essentials. Where do you live?

FORTUNATO. Via Garibaldi.

PROFESSOR. A working-class neighborhood, not suitable. You must move around here, to this section. (*To* ELIO) Is the room near the square available?

ELIO. Yes.

PROFESSOR. You'll introduce him to Madame Lucia later. (*To* FORTUNATO) A pleasant, well-equipped room. A double bed, liquor, music, telephone, a good and convenient address in this section. She won't take you to her hotel. She'd be ashamed. She won't go to a place far away. Distrust. The premises have to be very nearby. And already *paid for.* In fact during the first few hours the whole subject of money must be handled with kid gloves, with tact. (*Pointing at him, imperiously:*) You must pay. At the restaurant, at the café, everywhere. We have the reputation of being after money. This way, you'll show that you're above all that, completely disinterested. (*Lingering over the words, understandingly:*) Certainly you're asking yourself, so where's the profit? Don't jump to conclusions. We get a daily report from the hotels. They only give us the names of the ladies who stay at least *four days* (*stressing*). Four, at least. (*To* DONATO) Why, Donato? Explain it to him.

DONATO (*standing up, repeating lesson by heart*). The first day we pay for everything. The second day we permit a very small expenditure. The third day we tell our little story.

PROFESSOR. What little story? Explain it to him.

DONATO (*to* FORTUNATO). The third day we will appear putting on the gloomy face, very, very sad. . . . "What's the matter, darling?"—the old girl, by now head over heels in love, will ask us. "My father has gone bankrupt." A disastrous crash. We've lost everything. Money, home, and honor. She will pay for lunch, then for dinner; she will reimburse us for everything we paid out before this. One ten-thousand-lire note leads to another.

PROFESSOR. Be seated. (*To* FORTUNATO)

It always works. The first day you must make sure to take her address in the States and give her yours. Desperate letters after she has left . . . I'll write or correct them for you; your English is not perfect. . . . Ingenious, isn't it? If it seems advisable, you will also follow them to the nearby cities. After the announcement of bankruptcy, they will foot all bills. For you it is an agreeable vacation. (*To* CORSO) Telephone number in Milan?

CORSO. 482559.

PROFESSOR. In Florence?

CORSO. 53771.

PROFESSOR. In Rome?

CORSO. 815683.

PROFESSOR (*to* FORTUNATO). Memorize these. The address of headquarters will, however, always be the most important. They will all write to you here.

AFRO. Not all of them, unfortunately.

PROFESSOR. It's your fault. (*To* FORTUNATO) He's referring to the fact that some don't answer. That will be entirely your fault. It will mean that you haven't done your work with enough tact, sensitivity, intelligence. To conquer a human being is not easy. (*Continuing with lesson, which he knows by heart:*) Our raw material, the American Woman, can be of two types: the woman who *knows* and pays, and the woman who does *not* know and pays anyway. The first is the astute type, usually the wife of some big industrialist accustomed to buying everything. She buys the merchandise on the spot, pays, does *not* want to pay at a distance for something she no longer has in hand. Contrary to what one might think, she is actually the most difficult client. It's a matter of convincing her that she can get more and better of the same merchandise. On the last day, the demanding fiancée whom you were forced to see at brief moments, which were denied to her, will be introduced. You'll bring up the subject with regret, irritation. At that moment she will understand that you're capable of more and better services. You will also stress your revulsion at having to live here, your yearning to go to America, to accept from her *any sort* of position. Even the position of personal attendant. Only if you have been endearing, persuasive, will you get mail. An invisible thread will bind her to you, compel her to pay. (*Pointing to* BENITO:) Benito, who is so quiet, so apparently reserved, inspires a feeling of confidence and security. He is very successful with this type. We have then the type that doesn't know, the romantic type. These are the ones who produce the best results, even if, quite obviously, the initial overtures are more delicate and difficult. Donato, will you describe these initial overtures?

DONATO (*standing up*). We get the report from the hotel, the snapshot from the photographer. Depending on how tall she is, either Corso or I go. Waiting around the hotel, shadowing, choice of the most propitious moment for the first act of politeness. Rescue from a wolf—whom we, of course, pay; intervention as an interpreter when she cannot understand why she must pay that particular amount of money in a store, and so on. In desperate cases, when, for instance, we have seen one or two free-lancers firmly repulsed, we make friends with an American male, get him to approach her in some way, and to introduce us. . . . We pay for a drink, then for another, and then for the dinner. Detachment, elegance, display of at least a bit of American culture, interest in and admiration for their world. Finally we ask her to come for a ride in a gondola—I'll point out to you the gondoliers who work with us—the real siege begins—"The gondolier is blind and deaf."—This must be said jokingly, to reassure her. An arm around her shoulders, a caress. After so many courtesies and such behavior, she won't dare to object.

PROFESSOR. "A patronizing attitude."

DONATO. A protective, tender, still discreet attitude. Then, slowly . . .

PROFESSOR (*breaking in*). We must trust our personal instincts, our physical appeal, the aggressiveness which is peculiar to us, us Latins. If you succeeded in the gondola, all the better. Everything will become much, much easier. She will never again recover from the shock—the swift transition from thinly veiled detachment to feverish assault—she'll accept everything, your room, the night, your problems, and then your desperation when your father goes bankrupt. . . . Ask my wife. (*Turning to* SIGNORA) Isn't it true that "afterward" it is too late? That no woman has the courage to turn back, to refuse?

SIGNORA. It's true.

AFRO (*jumping at the chance*). You, signora, are the living example of just the contrary. You never gave us a second chance. Why do you refuse?

PROFESSOR (*firmly*). We are talking about American women, another race, another mentality. (*Changing the subject*) Donato has mentioned culture, before. This is why besides English and sex psychology (*pointing to the* SIGNORA, *as the teacher of this subject*) we teach history, geography, religion, hygiene, diet, politics, sociology, *et similia*. To make sure that you're up to your job, well prepared and more interesting. Benito, tell our new student the names of the two Presidents whom it is not advisable to praise.

BENITO (*standing up*). Lincoln, because from the Southerner's point of view, he wronged the South, and Roosevelt, because he inflicted heavy taxes.

PROFESSOR. Elio, what question must never be put to a client from Washington, D.C.?

ELIO (*without standing up*). Whether it is true that in Washington they don't vote because the majority of the population is Negro.

PROFESSOR. Who are the most famous Italians every client will know?

AFRO. The Fontana sisters, Sophia Loren . . . Renata Tebaldi.

PROFESSOR. And who are the men?

AFRO. Pucci, Marcello Mastroianni, Volare—I mean Modugno—Moravia.

PROFESSOR. And Tomasi di Lampedusa: author of *The Leopard*. It was a best seller. (*To* CORSO) People best to ignore?

CORSO. Charlie Chaplin and Howard Fast.

AFRO (*correcting him*). Howard Fast is now in the clear. He denounced the Reds —years ago.

PROFESSOR. It would still be best to ignore him. He does have a past. (*To* DONATO) What poet should never be quoted to Jewish clients because of his collaboration with the German Reich?

DONATO (*diligently*). Ezra Pound. Born in 1885. Still alive. A good friend of Italy.

PROFESSOR (*to* FORTUNATO). To appear

informed on the subject of poetry *The Pocket Book of Modern Verse* will do. It contains all the poetry of the last hundred years. The least boring. If you go to our bookstore (*points to list*) they'll charge you only four hundred lire. Learn by heart a poem by Frost and one by Sandburg. You'll astound them. Among the authors to be read and quoted:

Thomas Wolfe	1900	1938
William Faulkner	1897	1962
Ernest Hemingway	1898	1961
Truman Capote	1924	alive

Then there are the touchy subjects. Afro, you list them.

AFRO. Segregation, Missiles, Politics, Religion.

PROFESSOR. Ignore segregation and the South. Missiles are not so touchy now. It is again possible to speak about them. They've regained some ground. Two years ago it would have been an unforgivable *faux pas.*

AFRO. Politics and religion.

PROFESSOR. What's your line in politics?

AFRO. If I absolutely must talk about it —when all other subjects have been exhausted—to fill up the gaps between one session and the next—(*all laugh*) I tell her that I had a slight interest in Socialism, which I am now losing.

PROFESSOR (*to* FORTUNATO). Understand? You never miss. They have some vague notion what it is. If they respect it they'll try to bring you back to the "democratic variety." Otherwise, they'll be happy to help you get away from the devil. (*To* AFRO) Be seated. Religion is another big headache. What with Baptists,* Jews, Protestants, Disciples of Christ, Catholics, Presbyterians, Episcopalians, Methodists, and Mormons, it's impossible to make head or tail of the whole thing. What is the wisest behavior, Benito?

BENITO (*standing up, recites*). "I am a Catholic; I'm somewhat discouraged by certain political interferences on the part of the Vatican; nevertheless I still go to church. . . ."

PROFESSOR (*to* FORTUNATO). Do you understand? If the client isn't a Catholic, she will like your veiled reproach; if she

---
* Substitute religions: Unitarians, Adventists, Christian Scientists, Zen-Buddhists, Evangelists, Spiritualists, Lutherans, etc.

is Catholic she will not feel too insulted, because she knows that in Italy the relationship between Church and State is completely different from theirs. (*Telephone on the dais rings. The* PROFESSOR *answers, takes notes.*)

Yes . . .

Yes . . .

Good . . .

Age? (*He writes.*) Height? (*He writes.*) Yes . . . A widow . . . (*He writes.*)

Good . . . Did you develop it? . . .

I'll send the man to get them . . .

Yes . . .

Thank you . . . (*Puts down receiver. Turning again to students*) Bleached blonde, medium height, widowed eight months ago. Has inherited a number of meat-processing plants. Has taken a luxurious suite. Age fifty-seven. Who wants to go?

DONATO. I'll go.

PROFESSOR. Do you need some money in advance?

DONATO. Fifty thousand lire.

PROFESSOR (*to* SIGNORA). Thirty thousand lire. Get them from my wife. (*As the* SIGNORA *hands over money and makes* DONATO *sign receipt:*) Now, don't forget. First you get the photograph—which you will carefully conceal in your wallet— then you order the flowers. Don't let her spend a single lira. In the gondola—detachment, melancholy, flashes of culture. And during the last half hour, helped by the moon, the lagoon, the night . . .

DONATO. Certainly. (*He has collected the money, goes stage left; turning to fellow students:*) Ciao. So long.

FELLOW STUDENTS *and* PROFESSOR. Good luck.

(DONATO *exits.*)

PROFESSOR (*moved, looking after him affectionately*). One of my creations goes forth. A part of myself. As are all of you. And each of your conquests is mine. I love through you, with you. Any questions, Fortunato?

FORTUNATO (*slowly*). If we succeed the first evening, in the gondola, why should we continue to pay the second day, too?

PROFESSOR. We know from experience that they are more generous if they are absolutely untouched by doubt. Paying for a few drinks even after having possessed and conquered is proof of impeccable morality. Anything else?

FORTUNATO. The flowers, who pays for the flowers?

PROFESSOR. I have arranged for a discount. It's up to you to pay. Don't forget that I receive only ten percent on all earnings.

(FORTUNATO *sits down again, whispers to* AFRO.)

PROFESSOR: Any more questions? (*No answer*) Now I must make the rounds of the hotels. To get a list of arrivals. I'll leave you with my wife. For the psychosexual questions. (*To* BENITO) You have learned enough. Come with me. We'll be back soon.

BENITO (*to fellow students*). Bye bye.

(PROFESSOR *and* BENITO *exit stage left. The four remaining students stare at the* SIGNORA. *A silence.*)

AFRO (*aggressively, ruthless*). You said before that after a session with each one of us, you can't forget. This is difficult for a woman. Is it true, even now that your husband isn't here to prompt you?

SIGNORA. It is true.

AFRO. That a man *can never be forgotten*?

SIGNORA. It is true.

AFRO. That no woman has the courage to say no?

SIGNORA (*a bit unsure*). It is true.

AFRO. So where do you get the courage to reject us and to prefer that old man?

CORSO. Does our profession disgust you?

AFRO. What about the first time? You realized even then that we did it just professionally, didn't you? If we come here it's because we've accepted "the organization" and its rules.

CORSO. Are we any worse than your husband? After all, he is the organizer! If we were able to get jobs . . .

FORTUNATO. And if one could survive on what they pay . . .

SIGNORA. He has taught you everything. You owe him everything.

AFRO. And what about you? What do you owe him?

(*A pause; the* SIGNORA *looks at him sternly, trying to understand the real meaning of his questions.*)

SIGNORA (*coldly*). I owe him what every wife owes her husband. Any other ques-

tions?

ELIO (*after a short pause*). I'm sick and tired of old women. I want something young. Do I have any hope, ever, with you? Or must I look for a sweet little fiancée?

(*The* SIGNORA *throws him a very stern look*.)

ELIO (*intimidated*). Forget I said it.

(*Another embarrassing pause*)

FORTUNATO (*gathering courage*). What's your personal opinion of guys like us? That we're whores?

SIGNORA. I don't have opinions. It is a profession like any other. If each of you were given the chance to do something more respectable, you would behave better. These are the consequences of our defeat.

ELIO. That's what your husband says. (*To the others*) She's just repeating him, like a parrot. She's in love with him.

CORSO. Incredible.

FORTUNATO. What does a woman expect from a man?

SIGNORA (*changing the subject, which is too personal*). What does an American woman expect? Perhaps a Latin Adventure. Perhaps escape. Perhaps a little companionship.

FORTUNATO. And what if the one I hit on does not belong to these categories? What if she's a good girl, like you?

SIGNORA. Don't talk so recklessly. You don't know anything about me. And you won't know anything about that client.

FORTUNATO. How can one get to know a woman well?

SIGNORA. One lets her talk, and waits.

FORTUNATO. If she is the serious, clean sort—there are some—she won't feel like talking. She'll wait in silence, studying me. How should I behave?

SIGNORA. It will be up to you then to talk about yourself. At length. So she'll get to know you. And you must be patient if she is silent or sarcastic.

FORTUNATO. What do I talk about?

SIGNORA. He'll teach you. (*Points to the door through which the* PROFESSOR *left.*) Hundreds of topics, as the time goes by. For the present, with your first clients rely on inspiration. Various subjects, your life . . .

FORTUNATO (*interrupting*). My troubles . . .

SIGNORA. You have no troubles. Don't forget you're a rich boy, with a father who can afford to go bankrupt.

(*Brief pause*)

FORTUNATO. Is it advisable to make advances . . . the first evening?

SIGNORA. Why not? Delicately, tenderly. Women like men who are proper, tender and at the same time skillful. The man who is sure of himself, who seems detached, unconcerned about the conquest for its own sake, the sexual act in itself. You can. With discretion. Pretending to be uninterested, at the beginning. As a result, taking her by surprise.

FORTUNATO. But at a certain point she can't help but realize that that's our aim . . . that all the talk merely hides that goal.

SIGNORA. Don't give her time to think, to react. She'll immediately adapt herself, adjust to the new situation.

FORTUNATO (*after a short pause*). Is a woman able to sense hate, irritation, revulsion? One can't like all of them. And these feelings come to the surface.

SIGNORA. Disguise them with a scene of jealousy, a fit of rage, even a promise of marriage. A lonely, tired woman responds very easily to this sort of thing. She will never forget a spontaneous proposal, a burst of tears, an avowal of love in the Latin manner. . . . Even later, months later, when she'll be about to mail you the money, she'll remember that spontaneity, that violence, the flowers with which you filled her room, "afterward." She will go back to the hotel, dazed, surprised; the flowers will move her more than anything else. He knows it. (*She alludes to the* PROFESSOR.) And phone her often, with desire in your voice. And remember, you must give her your address, your telephone number, at the beginning, when you're still a "rich" man. It will burn a hole in her bag. She will *have* to call you sooner or later. Or write to you. She's lonely, don't forget. (*Caught up in what she's saying:*) To be a lonely woman is a devastating thing. You will never understand this, you men.

(*A short pause*)

FORTUNATO. You're talking with great feeling. You're taking their side.

SIGNORA (*smiling sadly*). Female solidarity.

AFRO. It's your fault if I have failed in some of my jobs. I was so haunted by memory of you that I let someone else steal a client right from under my nose. What's your advice on how to win back a woman?

SIGNORA. You must be a good sport, a good loser. (*Staring at him:*) No woman forgets the man who can love, wait, accept her life, her *choice*. To know how to lose enhances us in everyone's eyes. Even in the eyes of your clients: of those women.

(PROFESSOR *enters.* BENITO *isn't with him. He shows some slips of paper.*)

PROFESSOR. Benito has found his ideal. They're already at the apéritif. (*Pointing to slips:*) It isn't too bad, today. (*He hands* CORSO *descriptive note and photograph.*) Well suited for you. Look at her front window. Some knockers! And just read what her bank account is. (*Handing slip to* AFRO:) This one is slim, hieratic. Just right for you. You have an Oedipus complex; white hair doesn't upset you. (*Handing slip to* ELIO:) Take this . . . the most difficult one. We know how good you are. She is distrustful, prejudiced. She drove one of our men in Rome crazy. If you can't do it . . . Gentlemen, good luck. (*He dismisses them.*)

STUDENTS (*ad lib*). Thank you, Professor.

So long, Professor.

Goodbye, Signora.

Until tomorrow.

(*The three "students" exit stage left.*)

PROFESSOR (*paternally to* FORTUNATO, *the last to leave*). You take this, Fortunato. The best one . . . a thirty-year-old Calvinist from Illinois . . . This is your "first." You don't yet have the stomach for the wrecks. (*Shows him photograph.*) Still young. Look what sad, beautiful eyes . . . intelligent, sensitive, majored in Fine Arts. . . . You will combine business with pleasure. . . . She is divorced. (*He pats him on the shoulder.*) Ciao. (*Looks after him with fondness as he starts to leave.*)

(FORTUNATO *goes out slowly, looking at the* SIGNORA *without daring to say goodbye to her.*) Say goodbye to my wife, come on. (*Points to her.*)

FORTUNATO (*timidly*). Goodbye, signora.

SIGNORA. Goodbye.

(FORTUNATO *exits stage left.*)

PROFESSOR. You can see, they are all happy! Give an Italian a taste of erotic adventure and you make him feel triumphant. Italians are children. They like forbidden fruit. It's a religious complex they can never free themselves of. They are intrigued by frustrated wives, rejected wives, divorcées. As long as she belongs to someone else. To an Italian a divorcée is still somehow considered married. An ex-wife. He feels like a hero if he can invade someone else's territory. (*A pause.* PROFESSOR *goes to window, lifts curtain, turning his back to the* SIGNORA *who gazes at him intensely. Without turning*) How do you like the new one, little wife? (*A silence*) Why don't you answer, little wife?

SIGNORA. After so many . . . They are all alike.

PROFESSOR. I have the feeling that *this* one will do brilliantly and he'll bring in a good percentage. (*A pause; he studies her reaction.*) He makes a good impression. (*A slight pause*) Even on you, little wife. I noticed it.

SIGNORA (*always sad, impenetrable*). You're losing your intuition.

(*Another brief pause; he studies her.*)

PROFESSOR (*from his window, he can still see* FORTUNATO *walking away*). He's built like an athlete. Strong, broadshouldered . . . (*Brief pause*) Do you like athletes, little wife?

SIGNORA (*after a pause; in a burst of desperation*). "Wife, wife" . . . why do you insist on claiming for yourself a woman like me . . . a . . . a whore? I'm *not* your wife. (*Sorrowfully*) Why do you continue to humiliate yourself? . . . You've already done too much for me by taking me off the streets. . . .

PROFESSOR (*without turning around*). It's I who's indebted to you. (*Turning around slowly to her as she stares at him with curiosity:*) The whole world is one big screwing. (*He stares at her, explains.*) They wouldn't part with the ten thousand lire for the registration if I didn't give them something in return, something which is mine by law . . . "my wife!" (*Pointing to where* FORTUNATO *is headed.*) His gait is confident, you see. He's happy. He's had his boss's "wife." Now with some luck he'll get another. He has found a pleasant, steady profession. He goes to meet the great adventure. . . . (*Ironic, loftily*) Will he fill the great void in the life of a desperate woman? Will he change someone's fate? (*Shrugging:*) For us, what's important is the ten thousand lire of today and the percentage of tomorrow. For him, the new industry: the AMERICAN WOMAN . . .

THE CURTAIN FALLS

THE FIREBUGS

(*Herr Biedermann und die Brandstifter*)

A Learning-Play Without a Lesson

Max Frisch

Translated by MORDECAI GORELIK

GOTTLIEB BIEDERMANN
BABETTE, his wife
ANNA, a maidservant
SEPP SCHMITZ, a wrestler
WILLI EISENRING, a waiter

A POLICEMAN
A PH.D.
MRS. KNECHTLING
THE CHORUS OF FIREMEN

SCENE. A simultaneous setting, showing the living room and the attic of BIEDERMANN's house.
TIME. Now.

Born in Zurich in 1911, Max Frisch is one of Europe's outstanding literary figures of the post–World War II generation. As a dramatist, he is linked with Peter Weiss and Friedrich Dürrenmatt as one of the three "giants" of today's German-speaking world. Paradoxically, Mr. Frisch remains little known outside the more advanced theatre circles in the United States. Partially, this may be due to the writer's own admitted lack of interest in pursuing a worldwide reputation. More significantly, perhaps, his persistent experimentalism and indifference to commercial considerations have constrained the less than intrepid managements from staging his works in this country.

An architect by profession, Mr. Frisch considers writing an avocation. After abandoning his formal studies for a while, he became a free-lance journalist, then, after a period of travel in Eastern Europe, returned to Switzerland to resume at the University of Zurich. Though the academic path led to architecture, he continued writing, and in 1943 he published a novel that attracted the attention of the director of the Zurich *Schauspielhaus*, who suggested that he try his hand at playwriting. That same year, he won an architectural prize for the design of a municipal swimming bath in Zurich; flushed with this success, he was able to launch out on his own as an architect, and devote more time to his "avocation."

Although Frisch had written several plays, novels, and stories before he created *The Chinese Wall*, it was this allegorical "dramatic farce" dealing with power and guilt that brought him his initial fame outside Switzerland.

One of the most consistently moralistic of modern European playwrights, Mr. Frisch's experimentalism and varying patterns of dramatic expression have likened him to the late Bertolt Brecht, whose influence he duly and publicly has acknowledged.

The Firebugs is considered by many to be Max Frisch's masterpiece. An entry in his diary reveals that the idea for what later was to develop into *Herr Biedermann und die Brandstifter* germinated in 1948, although it was not produced onstage until ten years later. Originally conceived as a radio play, it was revised and adapted for the stage in 1958. As *The Fire Raisers*, it had a successful run at the Royal Court Theatre, London, in 1961.

Alternately described by its author as "a morality without a moral" or "a didactic play without a lesson," *The Firebugs*, with ironic wit and superb theatrical technique, hypogenuously propounds the dangers of man's indifference to the world crisis. (According to the British essayist Frederick Lumley: "Frisch noted the idea for the play immediately after the Communist *coup d'état* in Czechoslovakia when the Fire Raisers were the Communist infiltrators whose aim was to overthrow the West. Through credulity and appeasement we were all victims in spite of the dire warnings of the chorus of firemen.")

Max Frisch's other stage works include: *Graf Oederland; Don Juan, oder die Liebe zur Geometrie;* and *Andorra*. The latter was a sensational success throughout Europe in 1961–1962, but inexplicably, a 1963 failure on the New York stage, where it expired after nine performances.

In addition to his plays, Mr. Frisch has published several novels, two of which, *Stiller* and *Homo Faber,* have been translated into English. A recipient of many international literary awards, the author is presently living near Zurich.

Mordecai Gorelik, translator of *The Firebugs,* is a prominent American scenic designer, educator, and author. Presently in residence at Southern Illinois University, Mr. Gorelik has designed many memorable Broadway productions, including the Group Theatre's *Men in White, Golden Boy, Rocket to the Moon,* and *Thunder Rock*. He is the author of *New Theatres for Old,* originally published in 1940, now a classic in its field. In 1935 and again in 1937 Mr. Gorelik was awarded a Guggenheim Fellowship, and since then his work and dedication to the theatre have been honored internationally.

Scene One

The stage is dark; then a match flares, illuminating the face of GOTTLIEB BIEDER-MANN. *He is lighting a cigar, and as the stage grows more visible he looks about him. He is surrounded by firemen wearing their helmets.*

————

BIEDERMANN. You can't even light a cigar any more without thinking of houses on fire. . . . It's disgusting! (*He throws away the burning cigar and exits.*)

(*The* FIREMEN *come forward in the manner of an antique* CHORUS. *The town clock booms the quarter hour.*)

CHORUS. Fellow citizens, we,
    Guardians of the city.
    Watchers, listeners,
    Friends of the friendly town.
LEADER. Which pays our salaries.
CHORUS. Uniformed, equipped,
    We guard your homes,
    Patrol your streets,
    Vigilant, tranquil.
LEADER. Resting from time to time,
    But alert, unsleeping.
CHORUS. Watching, listening,
    Lest hidden danger
    Come to light
    Too late.

The clock strikes half hour.

LEADER. Much goes up in flames,
    But not always
    Because of Fate.
CHORUS. Call it Fate, they tell you,
    And ask no questions.
    But mischief alone
    Can destroy whole cities.
LEADER. Stupidity alone—
CHORUS. Stupidity, all too human—
LEADER. Can undo our citizens,
    Our all-too-mortal citizens.

The clock strikes three quarters.

CHORUS. Use your head;
    A stitch in time saves nine.
LEADER. Exactly.
CHORUS. Just because it happened,
    Don't put the blame on God,
    Nor on our human nature,
    Nor on our fruitful earth,
    Nor on our radiant sun . . .
    Just because it happened,
    Must you call the damned thing Fate?

The clock strikes four quarters.

LEADER. Our watch begins.

The CHORUS *sits. The clock strikes nine o'clock.*

Scene Two

The Living Room. BIEDERMANN *is reading the paper and smoking a cigar.* ANNA, *the maidservant, in a white apron, brings him a bottle of wine.*

————

ANNA. Mr. Biedermann? (*No answer*) Mr. Biedermann—
(BIEDERMANN *puts down his paper.*)
BIEDERMANN. They ought to hang them! I've said so all along! Another fire! And always the same story: another peddler shoehorning his way into somebody's attic —another "harmless" peddler— (*He picks up the bottle.*) They ought to hang every one of them. (*He picks up the corkscrew.*)
ANNA. He's still here, Mr. Biedermann. The peddler. He wants to talk to you.
BIEDERMANN. I'm not in!
ANNA. Yes, sir, I told him—an hour ago. He says he knows you. I can't throw him out, Mr. Biedermann.
BIEDERMANN. Why not?
ANNA. He's too strong.
BIEDERMANN. Let him come to the office tomorrow.
ANNA. Yes, sir. I told him three times. He says he's not interested. He doesn't want any hair tonic.
BIEDERMANN. What *does* he want?
ANNA. Kindness, he says. Humanity.
BIEDERMANN (*sniffs at the cork*). Tell him I'll throw him out myself if he doesn't get going at once. (*He fills his glass carefully.*) Humanity! (*He tastes the wine.*) Let him wait in the hall for me. If he's selling suspenders or razor blades . . . I'm not inhuman, you know, Anna. But

they mustn't come into the house—I've told you that a hundred times! Even if we have three vacant beds, it's out of the question! Anybody knows what this sort of thing can lead to, these days—

(ANNA *is about to go, when* SCHMITZ *enters. He is athletic, in a costume reminiscent partly of the prison, partly of the circus; his arms are tattooed and there are leather straps on his wrists.* ANNA *edges out.* BIEDERMANN *sips his wine, unaware of* SCHMITZ, *who waits until he turns around.*)

SCHMITZ. Good evening. (BIEDERMANN *drops his cigar in surprise.*) Your cigar, Mr. Biedermann. (*He picks up the cigar and hands it to* BIEDERMANN.)

BIEDERMANN. Look here—

SCHMITZ. Good evening.

BIEDERMANN. What is this? I told the girl distinctly to have you wait in the hall.

SCHMITZ. My name is Schmitz.

BIEDERMANN. Without even knocking!

SCHMITZ. Sepp Schmitz. (*Silence*) Good evening.

BIEDERMANN. What do you want?

SCHMITZ. You needn't worry, Mr. Biedermann. I'm not a peddler.

BIEDERMANN. No?

SCHMITZ. I'm a wrestler. I mean I *used* to be.

BIEDERMANN. And now?

SCHMITZ. Unemployed. (*Pause*) Don't worry, sir. I'm not looking for a job—I'm fed up with wrestling. I came in here because it's raining hard outside. (*Pause*) It's warm in here. (*Pause*) I hope I'm not intruding. . . . (*Pause*)

BIEDERMANN. Cigar? (*He offers one.*)

SCHMITZ. You know, it's awful, Mr. Biedermann—with a build like mine, everybody gets scared. . . . Thank you. (BIEDERMANN *gives him a light.*) Thank you. (*They stand there, smoking.*)

BIEDERMANN. Get to the point.

SCHMITZ. My name is Schmitz.

BIEDERMANN. You've said that. . . . Delighted.

SCHMITZ. I have no place to sleep. (*He holds the cigar to his nose, enjoying the aroma.*) No place to sleep.

BIEDERMANN. Would you like—some bread?

SCHMITZ. If that's all there is.

BIEDERMANN. A glass of wine?

SCHMITZ. Bread and wine . . . If it's no trouble, sir; if it's no trouble. (BIEDERMANN *goes to the door.*)

BIEDERMANN. Anna! (*He comes back.*)

SCHMITZ. The girl said you were going to throw me out personally, Mr. Biedermann, but I knew you didn't mean it. (ANNA *has entered.*)

BIEDERMANN. Anna, bring another glass.

ANNA. Yes, sir.

BIEDERMANN. And some bread.

SCHMITZ. And if you don't mind, miss, a little butter. Some cheese or cold cuts. Only, don't go to any trouble. Some pickles, a tomato or something, some mustard —whatever you have, miss.

ANNA. Yes, sir.

SCHMITZ. If it's no trouble.

(ANNA *exits.*)

BIEDERMANN. You told the girl you know me.

SCHMITZ. That's right, sir.

BIEDERMANN. How do you know me?

SCHMITZ. I know you at your best, sir. Last night at the pub—you didn't see me; I was sitting in the corner. The whole place liked the way you kept banging the table.

BIEDERMANN. What did I say?

SCHMITZ. Exactly the right thing, Mr. Biedermann! (*He takes a puff at his cigar.*) "They ought to hang them all! The sooner the better—the whole bunch! All those firebugs!"

BIEDERMANN (*offers him a chair*). Sit down.

SCHMITZ (*sits*). This country needs men like you, sir.

BIEDERMANN. I know, but—

SCHMITZ. No "buts," Mr. Biedermann, no "buts." You're the old-time type of solid citizen. That's why your slant on things—

BIEDERMANN. Certainly, but—

SCHMITZ. That's why.

BIEDERMANN. Why what?

SCHMITZ. You have a conscience. Everybody in the pub could see that. A solid conscience.

BIEDERMANN. Naturally, but—

SCHMITZ. Mr. Biedermann, it's not natural at all. Not these days. In the circus, where I did my wrestling, for instance— before it burned down, the whole damned circus—our manager, for instance; you know what he told me? "Sepp," he says, "you know me. They can shove it. What do I need a conscience for?" Just like that! "What my animals need is a whip," he says. That's the sort of guy he is! "A conscience! If anybody has a conscience, you can bet it's a bad one." (*Enjoying his cigar:*) God rest him!

BIEDERMANN. Is he dead?

SCHMITZ. Burned to a cinder, with everything he owned.

(*A pendulum clock strikes nine.*)

BIEDERMANN. I don't know what's keeping that girl so long.

SCHMITZ. I've got time (*Their eyes meet.*) You haven't an empty bed in the house, Mr. Biedermann. The girl told me.

BIEDERMANN. Why do you laugh?

SCHMITZ. "Sorry, no empty bed." That's what they all say. . . . What's the result? Somebody like me, with no place to sleep —Anyway I don't want a bed.

BIEDERMANN. No?

SCHMITZ. Oh, I'm used to sleeping on the floor. My father was a miner. I'm used to it. (*He puffs at his cigar.*) No apologies necessary, sir. You're not one of those birds who sounds off in public—when *you* say something I believe it. What are things coming to if people can't believe each other anymore? Nothing but suspicion all over! Am I right? But *you* still believe in yourself and others. Right? You're about the only man left in this town who doesn't say right off that people like us are firebugs.

BIEDERMANN. Here's an ashtray.

SCHMITZ. Or am I wrong? (*He taps the ash off his cigar carefully.*) People don't believe in God anymore—they believe in the Fire Department.

BIEDERMANN. What do you mean by that?

SCHMITZ. Nothing but the truth.

ANNA (*comes in with a tray*). We have no cold cuts.

SCHMITZ. This will do, miss; this will do fine. Only, you forgot the mustard.

ANNA. Excuse me. (*Exits.*)

BIEDERMANN. Eat. (*He fills the glasses.*)

SCHMITZ. You don't get a reception like this every place you go, Mr. Biedermann, let me tell you! I've had some experiences! Somebody like me comes to the door—no necktie, no place to stay, hungry; "Sit down," they say, "have a seat"—and mean-

while they call the police. How do you like that? All I ask for is a place to sleep, that's all. A good wrestler who's wrestled all his life—and some bird who never wrestled at all grabs me by the collar! "What's this?" I ask myself. I turn around just to look, and first thing you know he's broken my shoulder! (*Picks up his glass.*) Prosit! (*They drink, and* SCHMITZ *starts eating.*)

BIEDERMANN. That's how it goes, these days. You can't open a newspaper without reading about another arson case. The same old story: another peddler asking for a place to sleep, and next morning the house is in flames. I mean to say . . . well, frankly, I can understand a certain amount of distrust. . . . (*Reaches for his newspaper.*) Look at this! (*He lays the paper next to* SCHMITZ's *plate.*)

SCHMITZ. I saw it.

BIEDERMANN. A whole district in flames. (*He gets up to show it to* SCHMITZ.) Just read that! (SCHMITZ *eats, reads, and drinks.*)

SCHMITZ. Is this wine Beaujolais?

BIEDERMANN. Yes.

SCHMITZ. Could be a little warmer. (*He reads, over his plate.*) "Apparently the fire was planned and executed in the same way as the previous one." (*They exchange a glance.*)

BIEDERMANN. Isn't that the limit?

SCHMITZ. That's why I don't care to read newspapers. Always the same thing.

BIEDERMANN. Yes, yes, naturally . . . but that's no answer to the problem, to stop reading the papers. After all, you have to know what you're up against.

SCHMITZ. What for?

BIEDERMANN. Why, because.

SCHMITZ. It'll happen anyway, Mr. Biedermann: it'll happen anyway. (*He sniffs the sausage.*) God's will. (*He slices the sausage.*)

BIEDERMANN. You think so?

(ANNA *brings the mustard.*)

SCHMITZ. Thank you, miss, thank you.

ANNA. Anything else you'd like?

SCHMITZ. Not today. (ANNA *stops at the door.*) Mustard is my favorite dish. (*He squeezes mustard out of the tube.*)

BIEDERMANN. How do you mean, God's will?

SCHMITZ. God knows. . . . (*He contin-*

ues to eat with his eye on the paper.) "Expert opinion is that apparently the fire was planned and executed in the same way as the previous one." (*He laughs shortly, and fills his glass.*)

ANNA. Mr. Biedermann?

BIEDERMANN. What is it now?

ANNA. Mr. Knechtling would like to speak to you.

BIEDERMANN. Knechtling? Now? Knechtling?

ANNA. He says—

BIEDERMANN. Out of the question.

ANNA. He says he simply can't understand you.

BIEDERMANN. Why must he understand me?

ANNA. He has a sick wife and three children, he says—

BIEDERMANN. Out of the question! (*He gets up impatiently.*) Mr. Knechtling! Mr. Knechtling! Let Mr. Knechtling leave me alone, dammit! Or let him get a lawyer! Please—let him! I'm through for the day. . . . Mr. Knechtling! All this to-do because I gave him his notice! Let him get a lawyer, by all means! I'll get one, too. . . . Royalties on his invention! Let him stick his head in the gas stove or get a lawyer! If Mr. Knechtling can afford indulging in lawyers! Please—let him! (*Controlling himself, with a glance at* SCHMITZ:) Tell Mr. Knechtling I have a visitor. (ANNA *exits*). Excuse me.

SCHMITZ. This is your house, Mr. Biedermann.

BIEDERMANN. How is the food? (*He sits, observing* SCHMITZ, *who attacks his food with enthusiasm.*)

SCHMITZ. Who'd have thought you could still find it, these days?

BIEDERMANN. Mustard?

SCHMITZ. Humanity! (*He screws the top of the mustard tube back on.*) Here's what I mean: you don't grab me by the collar and throw me out in the rain, Mr. Biedermann. *That's* what we need, Mr. Biedermann! Humanity! (*He pours himself a drink.*) God will reward you! (*He drinks with gusto.*)

BIEDERMANN. You mustn't think I'm inhuman, Mr. Schmitz.

SCHMITZ. Mr. Biedermann!

BIEDERMANN. That's what Mrs. Knechtling thinks.

SCHMITZ. Would you be giving me a place to sleep tonight if you were inhuman? Ridiculous!

BIEDERMANN. Of course!

SCHMITZ. Even if it's a bed in the attic. (*He puts down his glass.*) Now our wine's the right temperature. (*The doorbell rings.*) Police?

BIEDERMANN. My wife. (*The doorbell rings again.*) Come along, Mr. Schmitz. . . . But mind you, no noise! My wife has a heart condition.—

(*Women's voices are heard offstage.* BIEDERMANN *motions to* SCHMITZ *to hurry. They pick up the tray, bottles, and glasses and tiptoe toward stage right, where the* CHORUS *is sitting.*)

BIEDERMANN. Excuse me! (*He steps over the bench.*)

SCHMITZ. Excuse me! (*He steps over the bench. He and* BIEDERMANN *disappear.*)

(BABETTE BIEDERMANN *enters, left, accompanied by* ANNA, *who takes her packages.*)

BABETTE. Where's my husband?—You know, Anna, we're not narrow-minded, and I don't mind your having a boyfriend. But if you're going to park him in the house—

ANNA. But I don't have a boyfriend, Mrs. Biedermann.

BABETTE. Then whose rusty bicycle is that, outside the front door? It scared me to death!

The Attic. BIEDERMANN *switches on the light, and gestures for* SCHMITZ *to come in. They speak in whispers.*

BIEDERMANN. Here's the light switch. If you get cold, there's an old sheepskin around here somewhere. Only, for heaven's sake be quiet! Take off your shoes! (SCHMITZ *puts down the tray, takes off one shoe.*) Mr. Schmitz?

SCHMITZ. Mr. Biedermann?

BIEDERMANN. You promise me, though, you're not a firebug? (SCHMITZ *starts to laugh.*) Sh!! (*He nods good night, and exits, closing the door.* SCHMITZ *takes off his other shoe.*)

The Living Room. BABETTE *has heard something; she listens, frightened. Then, relieved, she turns to the audience.*

BABETTE. Gottlieb, my husband, promised to go up to the attic every evening, personally, to see if there is any firebug up there. I'm so thankful! Otherwise I'd lie awake half the night. (*Exits.*)

The Attic. SCHMITZ, *now in his socks, goes to the light switch and snaps out the light.*

Below.

CHORUS. Fellow citizens, we,
　Shield of the innocent,
　Guardians ever tranquil,
　Shield of the sleeping city.
　Standing or
　Sitting,
　Ever on guard.
LEADER. Taking a quiet smoke, now and again, to pass the time.
CHORUS. Watching,
　Listening,
　Lest malignant fire leap out
　Above these cozy rooftops
　To undo our city.

The town clock strikes three.

LEADER. Everyone knows we're here,
　Ready on call. (*He fills his pipe.*)
CHORUS. Who turns the light on at this wee, small hour?
　Woe!
　Nerve-shattered,
　Uncomforted by sleep,
　The wife appears.

(BABETTE *enters in a bathrobe.*)
BABETTE. Somebody coughed! (*A snore*) Gottlieb, did you hear that? (*A cough*) Somebody's there! (*A snore*) That's men for you! A sleeping pill is all they need!

The town clock strikes four.

LEADER. Four o'clock. (BABETTE *turns off the light again.*)
　We were not called. (*He puts away his pipe. The stage lightens.*)
CHORUS. O radiant sun!
　O godlike eye!
　Light up the day above our cozy

roofs!
　Thanks be!
　No harm has come to our sleeping town.
　Not yet.
　Thanks be! (*The* CHORUS *sits.*)

SCENE THREE

The Living Room. BIEDERMANN, *his hat and coat on, his briefcase under his arm, is drinking a cup of coffee standing up, and is speaking to* BABETTE, *who is off-stage.*

———

BIEDERMANN. For the last time—he's not a firebug!
BABETTE's VOICE. How do you know?
BIEDERMANN. I asked him myself, point-blank— Can't you think of anything else in this world, Babette? You and your fire-bugs—you're enough to drive a man in-sane!
BABETTE (*enters with the cream pitcher*). Don't yell at me.
BIEDERMANN. I'm not yelling at you, Ba-bette, I'm merely yelling. (*She pours cream into his cup.*) I have to go. (*He drinks his coffee. It's too hot.*) If every-body goes around thinking everybody else is an arsonist— You're got to have a little trust in people, Babette, just a little! (*He looks at his watch.*)
BABETTE. I don't agree. You're too good-hearted, Gottlieb. You listen to the prompt-ings of your heart, but I'm the one who can't sleep all night. . . . I'll give him some breakfast and then I'll send him on his way, Gottlieb.
BIEDERMANN. Do that.
BABETTE. In a nice way, of course, with-out offending him.
BIEDERMANN. Do that. (*He puts his cup down.*) I have to see my lawyer. (*He gives* BABETTE *a perfunctory kiss. They do not notice* SCHMITZ, *who enters, the sheepskin around his shoulders.*)
BABETTE. Why did you give Knechtling his notice?
BIEDERMANN. I don't need him anymore.
BABETTE. But you were always so pleased

with him!

BIEDERMANN. That's just what he's presuming on, now! Royalties on his invention—that's what he wants! Invention! Our Hormotone hair tonic is merchandise, that's all—it's no invention! All those good folk who pour our tonic on their domes could use their own piss for all the good it does them!

BABETTE. Gottlieb!

BIEDERMANN. It's true, though. (*He checks to see if he has everything in his briefcase.*) I'm too good-hearted—you're right. But I'll take care of this Knechtling! (*He is about to go when he sees* SCHMITZ.)

SCHMITZ. Good morning, everybody.

BIEDERMANN. Mr. Schmitz—(SCHMITZ *offers his hand.*)

SCHMITZ. Call me Sepp.

BIEDERMANN (*ignores his hand*). My wife will speak with you, Mr. Schmitz. I have to go, I'm sorry. Good luck . . . (*Changes his mind and shakes hands.*) Good luck, Sepp. (BIEDERMANN *exits.*)

SCHMITZ. Good luck, Gottlieb. (BABETTE *looks at him.*) That's your husband's name, isn't it—Gottlieb?

BABETTE. How did you sleep?

SCHMITZ. Thank you, madam—kind of freezing. But I made use of this sheepskin. Reminded me of old days in the mines. I'm used to the cold.

BABETTE. Your breakfast is ready.

SCHMITZ. Really, madam! (*She motions for him to sit.*) No, really, I—(*She fills his cup.*)

BABETTE. You must pitch in, Sepp. You have a long way to go, I'm sure.

SEPP. How do you mean? (*She points to the chair again.*)

BABETTE. Would you care for a soft-boiled egg?

SCHMITZ. Two.

BABETTE. Anna!

SCHMITZ. I feel right at home, madam. (*He sits.*)

(ANNA *enters.*)

BABETTE. Two soft-boiled eggs.

ANNA. Yes, ma'am.

SCHMITZ. Three and a half minutes.

(ANNA *starts to leave.*)

SCHMITZ. Miss—(ANNA *stops at the door.*) Good morning.

ANNA. Morning. (*She exits.*)

SCHMITZ. The look she gave me! If it was up to her I'd still be out there in the pouring rain.

BABETTE (*fills his cup*). Mr. Schmitz—

SCHMITZ. Yeah?

BABETTE. If I may speak frankly—

SCHMITZ. Your hands are shaking, madam.

BABETTE. Mr. Schmitz—

SCHMITZ. What's troubling you?

BABETTE. Here's some cheese.

SCHMITZ. Thank you.

BABETTE. Marmalade.

SCHMITZ. Thank you.

BABETTE. Honey.

SCHMITZ. One at a time, madam, one at a time. (*He leans back, eating his bread and butter; attentively.*) Well?

BABETTE. Frankly, Mr. Schmitz—

SCHMITZ. Just call me Sepp.

BABETTE. Frankly—

SCHMITZ. You'd like to get rid of me.

BABETTE. No, Mr. Schmitz, no! I wouldn't put it that way—

SCHMITZ. How would you put it? (*He takes some cheese.*) Tilsit cheese is my dish. (*He leans back, eating; attentively.*) Madam thinks I'm a firebug.

BABETTE. Please don't misunderstand me. What did I say? The last thing I want to do is hurt your feelings, Mr. Schmitz. . . . You've got me all confused now. Who ever mentioned firebugs? Even your manners, Mr. Schmitz; I'm not complaining.

SCHMITZ. I know. I have no manners.

BABETTE. That's not it, Mr. Schmitz—

SCHMITZ. I smack my lips when I eat.

BABETTE. Nonsense.

SCHMITZ. That's what they used to tell me at the orphanage: "Schmitz, don't smack your lips when you eat!" (BABETTE *is about to pour more coffee.*)

BABETTE. You don't understand me. Really, you don't in the least!

SCHMITZ (*places his hand over his cup*). I'm going.

BABETTE. Mr. Schmitz.

SCHMITZ. I'm going.

BABETTE. Another cup of coffee? (*He shakes his head.*) Half a cup? (*He shakes his head.*) You mustn't take it like that, Mr. Schmitz. I didn't mean to hurt your feelings. I didn't say a single word about you making noises while you eat. (*He gets up.*) Have I hurt your feelings? (*He folds his napkin.*)

SCHMITZ. It's not your lookout, madam, if I have no manners. My father was a coal miner. Where would people like us get any manners? Starving and freezing, madam—that's something I don't mind; but no education, madam, no manners, madam, no refinement—

BABETTE. I understand.

SCHMITZ. I'm going.

BABETTE. Where?

SCHMITZ. Out in the rain.

BABETTE. Oh, no!

SCHMITZ. I'm used to it.

BABETTE. Mr. Schmitz . . . don't look at me like that. Your father was a coal miner—I can understand it. You had an unfortunate childhood—

SCHMITZ. No childhood at all, madam. (*He looks down at his fingers.*) None at all. My mother died when I was seven. . . . (*He turns away to wipe his eyes.*)

BABETTE. Sepp!— But Sepp—

ANNA (*brings the soft-boiled eggs*). Anything else you'd like? (*She gets no answer; exits.*)

BABETTE. I haven't ordered you to leave, Mr. Schmitz. I never said that. After all, what did I say? You misunderstand me, Mr. Schmitz. Really, I mean it—won't you believe me? (*She takes his sleeve—with some hesitation.*) Come, Sepp—finish eating! (SCHMITZ *sits down again.*) What do you take us for? I haven't even noticed that you smack your lips. Honestly! Even if I did—we don't care a bit about external things. We're not like that at all, Mr. Schmitz. . . . (*He cracks his egg.*)

SCHMITZ. God will reward you!

BABETTE. Here's the salt. (*He eats the egg with a spoon.*)

SCHMITZ. It's true, madam, you didn't order me away. You didn't say a word about it. That's true. Pardon me, madam, for not understanding.

BABETTE. Is the egg all right?

SCHMITZ. A little soft . . . Do pardon me, won't you? (*He has finished the egg.*) What were you going to say, madam, when you started to say, very frankly—

BABETTE. Well, I was going to say . . . (*He cracks the second egg.*)

SCHMITZ. God will reward you. (*He starts on the second egg.*) My friend Willi says you can't find it anymore, he says.

Private charity. No fine people left; everything State-controlled. No real people left, these days . . . he says. The world is going to the dogs—that's why! (*He salts his egg.*) Wouldn't he be surprised to get a breakfast like this! Wouldn't he open his eyes, my friend, Willi! (*The doorbell rings.*) That could be him. (*It rings again.*)

BABETTE. Who is Willi?

SCHMITZ. You'll see, madam. Willi's refined. Used to be a waiter at the Metropol. Before it burned down . . .

BABETTE. Burned down?

SCHMITZ. Headwaiter.

(ANNA *enters.*)

BABETTE. Who is it?

ANNA. A gentleman.

BABETTE. What does he want?

ANNA. From the fire insurance, he says. To look over the house. (BABETTE *gets up.*) He's wearing a frock coat—

SCHMITZ. My friend Willi!

CHORUS. Now two of them dismay us—
  Two bicycles, both rusty.
  To whom do they belong?

LEADER. One yesterday's arrival.
  One today's.

CHORUS. Woe!

LEADER. Night once again, and our watch.

The town clock strikes.

CHORUS. How much the coward fears
    where nothing threatens!
  Dreading his own shadow,
  Whirling at each sound,
  Until his fears overtake him
  At his own bedside!

The town clock strikes.

LEADER. They never leave their room, these two.
  What is the reason?

The town clock strikes.

CHORUS. Blind, ah, blind is the weakling!
  Trembling, expectant of evil,
  Yet hoping somehow to avoid it!
  Defenseless!

Ah, weary of menacing evil,
With open arms he receives it!

The town clock strikes.

Woe! (*The* CHORUS *sits.*)

SCENE FOUR

The Attic. SCHMITZ *is dressed as before.*
EISENRING *has removed the jacket of his
frock coat and is in a white vest and shirt
sleeves. He and* SCHMITZ *are rolling tin
barrels into a corner of the attic. The barrels are the type used for storing gasoline.
Both vagabonds are in their socks and are
working as quietly as they can.*

———

EISENRING. Quiet! Quiet!
SCHMITZ. Suppose he calls the police?
EISENRING. Keep going.
SCHMITZ. What then?
EISENRING. Easy! Easy!
(*They roll the barrels up to those already
stacked in the shadows.* EISENRING *wipes
his fingers with some cotton waste.*)
EISENRING. Why would he call the po-
lice?
SCHMITZ. Why not?
EISENRING. Because he's guilty himself—
that's why. (*He throws away the rag.*)
Above a certain income every citizen is
guilty one way or another. Have no fear.
(*Doves are heard cooing.*) It's morning.
Bedtime! (*There is a sudden knocking on
the locked door.*)
BIEDERMANN'S VOICE. Open up! Open up,
there! (*He pounds on the door and shakes
it.*)
EISENRING. That's no call for breakfast.
BIEDERMANN'S VOICE. Open, I say! Imme-
diately!
SCHMITZ. He was never like that before.
(*The banging on the door gets louder.
Without haste, but briskly,* EISENRING *puts
on his jacket, straightens his tie and flicks
the dust from his trousers. Then he opens
the door.* BIEDERMANN *enters. He is in his
bathrobe. He does not see* EISENRING, *who
is now behind the open door.*)
BIEDERMANN. Mr. Schmitz!
SCHMITZ. Good morning, sir. I hope this

noise didn't wake you.
BIEDERMANN. Mr. Schmitz—
SCHMITZ. It won't happen again, I assure
you.
BIEDERMANN. Leave this house! (*Pause*)
I say leave this house!
SCHMITZ. When?
BIEDERMANN. At once!
SCHMITZ. But—
BIEDERMANN. Or my wife will call the
police. And I can't and won't stop her.
SCHMITZ. Hm . . .
BIEDERMANN. I said right away, and I
mean it. What are you waiting for?
(SCHMITZ *picks up his shoes.*) I'll have
no discussion about it!
SCHMITZ. Did I say anything?
BIEDERMANN. If you think you can do as
you like here because you're a wrestler—
A racket like that, all night— (*Points to
the door.*) Out, I say! Get out!
SCHMITZ (*turns to* EISENRING). He was
never like that before. . . . (BIEDERMANN
sees EISENRING *and is speechless.*)
EISENRING. My name is Eisenring.
BIEDERMANN. What's the meaning of
this?
EISENRING. Willi Maria Eisenring.
BIEDERMANN. Why are there two of you
suddenly? (SCHMITZ *and* EISENRING *look
at each other.*) Without even asking!
EISENRING. There, you see!
BIEDERMANN. What's going on here?
EISENRING (*to* SCHMITZ). Didn't I tell
you? Didn't I say it's no way to act, Sepp?
Where are your manners? Without even
asking! Suddenly two of us!
BIEDERMANN. I'm beside myself!
EISENRING. There, you see! (*He turns to*
BIEDERMANN.) That's what I told him!
(*Back to* SCHMITZ) Didn't I?
(SCHMITZ *hangs his head.*)
BIEDERMANN. Where do you think you
are? Let's get one thing clear, gentlemen
—I'm the owner of this house! I ask you—
where do you think you are? (*Pause*)
EISENRING. Answer when the gentleman
asks you something! (*Pause*)
SCHMITZ. Willi is a friend of mine. . . .
BIEDERMANN. And so?
SCHMIDT. We were schoolmates together.
BIEDERMANN. And so?
SCHMITZ. And so I thought . . .
BIEDERMANN. What?
SCHMITZ. I thought . . . (*Pause*)

EISENRING. You didn't think! (*He turns to* BIEDERMANN.) I understand fully, Mr. Biedermann. All you want to do is what's right—let's get that clear! (*He shouts at* SCHMITZ.) You think the owner of this house is going to be pushed around? (*He turns to* BIEDERMANN *again.*) Sepp didn't consult you at all?

BIEDERMANN. Not a word!

EISENRING. Sepp—

BIEDERMANN. Not one word!

EISENRING (*to* SCHMITZ). And then you're surprised when people throw you out in the street! (*He laughs contemptuously.*)

BIEDERMANN. There's nothing to laugh at, gentlemen! I'm serious! My wife has a heart condition—

EISENRING. There, you see!

BIEDERMANN. She didn't sleep half the night because of your noise. And anyway, what are you doing here? (*He looks around.*) What the devil are these barrels doing here? (SCHMITZ *and* EISENRING *look hard where there are no barrels.*) If you don't mind—what are these? (*He raps on a barrel.*)

SCHMITZ. Barrels . . .

BIEDERMANN. Where did *they* come from?

SCHMITZ. Do you know, Willi? Where they came from?

EISENRING. It says "Imported" on the label.

BIEDERMANN. Gentlemen—

EISENRING. It says so on them somewhere! (EISENRING *and* SCHMITZ *look for a label.*)

BIEDERMANN. I'm speechless! What do you think you're doing? My whole attic is full of barrels—floor to ceiling! All the way from floor to ceiling!

EISENRING. I knew it! (EISENRING *swings around.*) Sepp had it figured out all wrong. (*To* SCHMITZ) Twelve by twenty feet, you said. There's not two hundred square feet in this attic!—I couldn't leave my barrels in the street, Mr. Biedermann; you can understand that—

BIEDERMANN. I don't understand a thing! (SCHMITZ *shows him a label.*)

SCHMITZ. Here, Mr. Biedermann—here's the label.

BIEDERMANN. I'm speechless.

SCHMITZ. Here it says where they come from. Here.

BIEDERMANN. Simply speechless. (*He inspects the label.*)

The Living Room. ANNA *leads a* POLICEMAN *in.*

ANNA. I'll call him. What's it about, Officer?

POLICEMAN. Official business. (ANNA *exits. The* POLICEMAN *waits.*)

The Attic.

BIEDERMANN. Is it true? Is it true?

EISENRING. Is what true?

BIEDERMANN. What's printed on this label? (*He shows them the label.*) What do you take me for? I've never in my life seen anything like this! Do you think I can't read? (*They look at the label.*) Just look! (*He laughs sarcastically.*) Gasoline! (*In the voice of a district attorney*) What is in those barrels?

EISENRING. Gasoline!

BIEDERMANN. Never mind your jokes! I'm asking you for the last time—what's in those barrels? You know as well as I do—attics are no place for gasoline! (*He runs his finger over one of the barrels.*) If you don't mind—just smell that for yourselves! (*He waves his finger under their noses.*) Is that gasoline or isn't it? (*They sniff, and exchange glances.*)

EISENRING. It is.

SCHMITZ. It is.

BOTH. No doubt whatever.

BIEDERMANN. Are you insane? My whole attic full of gasoline—

SCHMITZ. That's just why we don't smoke up here, Mr. Biedermann.

BIEDERMANN. What do you think you're doing? A thing like that—when every single newspaper is warning people to watch out for fires! My wife will have a heart attack!

EISENRING. There, you see!

BIEDERMANN. Don't keep saying, "There, you see!"

EISENRING. You can't do that to a lady, Sepp. Not to a housewife. I know housewives.

ANNA (*calls up the stairs*). Mr. Biedermann! Mr. Biedermann! (BIEDERMANN *shuts the door.*)

BIEDERMANN. Mr. Schmitz! Mr.—

EISENRING. Eisenring.

BIEDERMANN. If you don't get these barrels out of the house this instant—and I mean this instant—

EISENRING. You'll call the police.

BIEDERMANN. Yes!

SCHMITZ. There, you see!

ANNA (*calls up the stairs*). Mr. Biedermann!

BIEDERMANN (*lowers his voice*). That's my last word.

EISENRING. Which word?

BIEDERMANN. I won't stand for it! I won't stand for gasoline in my attic! Once and for all! (*There is a knock at the door.*) I'm coming! (*He opens the door.*) (*The* POLICEMAN *enters.*)

POLICEMAN. Ah, there you are, Mr. Biedermann! You don't have to come down; I won't take much of your time.

BIEDERMANN. Good morning!

POLICEMAN. Good morning!

EISENRING. Morning!

SCHMITZ. Morning!

(SCHMITZ *and* EISENRING *nod courteously.*)

POLICEMAN. There's been an accident.

BIEDERMANN. Good heavens!

POLICEMAN. An elderly man. His wife says he used to work for you. . . . An inventor. Put his head inside his kitchen stove last night. (*He consults his notebook.*) Knechtling, Johann. Number 11 Ross Street. (*He puts his notebook away.*) Did you know anybody by that name?

BIEDERMANN. I—

POLICEMAN. Maybe you'd rather we talked about this privately, Mr. Biedermann?

BIEDERMANN. Yes.

POLICEMAN. It doesn't concern these employees of yours.

BIEDERMANN. No . . . (*He stops at the door.*) If anyone wants me, gentlemen, I'll be at the police station. I'll be right back.

(SCHMITZ *and* EISENRING *nod.*)

POLICEMAN. Mr. Biedermann—

BIEDERMANN. Let's go.

POLICEMAN. What have you got in those barrels?

BIEDERMANN. These?

POLICEMAN. If I may ask?

BIEDERMANN. . . . Hair tonic . . . (*He looks at* SCHMITZ *and* EISENRING.)

EISENRING. Hormotone. Science's gift to the well groomed.

SCHMITZ. Try a bottle today.

EISENRING. You won't regret it.

BOTH. Hormotone. Hormotone. Hormotone. (*The* POLICEMAN *laughs.*)

BIEDERMANN. Is he dead? (*He and the* POLICEMAN *exit.*)

EISENRING. A real sweetheart!

SCHMITZ. Didn't I tell you?

EISENRING. But he didn't mention breakfast.

SCHMITZ. He was never like that before. . . .

EISENRING (*reaching in his pocket*). Have you got the detonator?

SCHMITZ (*feeling in his pocket*). He was never like that before.

Below.

CHORUS. O radiant sun!
    O godlike eye!
    Light up the day again above our cozy roofs!

LEADER. Today same as yesterday.

CHORUS. Hail!

LEADER. No harm has come to our sleeping city.

CHORUS. Hail!

LEADER. Not yet . . .

CHORUS. Hail!

Traffic noises offstage; honking, streetcars.

LEADER. Wise is man,
    And able to ward off most perils,
    If, sharp of mind and alert,
    He heeds signs of coming disaster
    In time.

CHORUS. And if he does not?

LEADER. He, who
    Attentive to possible dangers,
    Studies his newspaper daily—
    Is daily, at breakfast, dismayed
    By distant tidings, whose meaning
    Is daily digested to spare him
    Fatigue of his own muddled brainwork—
    Learning daily what's happened, afar—
    Can he so quickly discern
    What is happening under his roof?
    Things that are—

CHORUS. Unpublished!

LEADER. Disgraceful!

CHORUS. Inglorious!
LEADER. Real!
CHORUS. Things not easy to face!
For, if he—

The LEADER *interrupts with a gesture.*

LEADER. He's coming.

The CHORUS *breaks formation.*

CHORUS. No harm has come to the sleeping city.
No harm yesterday or today.
Ignoring all omens,
The freshly shaven citizen
Speeds to his office. . . .

(*Enter* BIEDERMANN *in hat and coat, his briefcase under his arm.*)
BIEDERMANN. Taxi! . . . Taxi! . . . Taxi!
(*The* CHORUS *is in his way.*) What's the trouble?
CHORUS. Woe!
BIEDERMANN. What's up?
CHORUS. Woe!
BIEDERMANN. You've said that already!
CHORUS. Three times woe!
BIEDERMANN. But why?
LEADER. All too strangely a fiery prospect
Unfolds to our eyes.
And to yours.
Shall I be plainer?
Gasoline in your attic—
BIEDERMANN (*shouts*). Is that *your* business? (*Silence*) Let me through—I have to see my lawyer— What do you want of me? I'm not guilty. . . . (*Unnerved*) What's this—an inquisition? (*Masterfully*) Let me through, please!

The CHORUS *remains motionless.*

CHORUS. Far be it from us, the Chorus,
To judge a hero of drama—
LEADER. But we *do* see the oncoming peril,
See clearly the menacing danger!
CHORUS. Making a simple inquiry
About an impending disaster—
Uttering, merely, a warning—
Civic-minded, the Chorus comes forward,

Bathed, alas, in cold sweat,
In half-fainting fear of that moment
That calls for the hoses of firemen!
(BIEDERMANN *looks at his wristwatch.*)
BIEDERMANN. I'm in a hurry.
CHORUS. Woe!
LEADER. All that gasoline, Gottlieb Biedermann!
How could you take it?
BIEDERMANN. Take it!
LEADER. You know very well,
The world is a brand for the burning!
Yet, knowing it, what did you think?
BIEDERMANN. Think? (*He appraises the* CHORUS.) My dear sirs, I am a free and independent citizen. I can think anything I like. What are all those questions? I have the right, my dear sirs, not to think at all if I feel like it! Aside from the fact that whatever goes on under my own roof— Let's get one thing clear, gentlemen: I am the owner of the house!
CHORUS. Sacred, sacred to us
Is property,
Whatever befall!
Though we be scorched,
Though we be cindered—
Sacred, sacred to us!
BIEDERMANN. Well, then— (*Silence*) Why can't I go through? (*Silence*) Why must you always imagine the worst? Where will that get you? All I want is some peace and quiet, not a thing more. . . . As for those two gentlemen—aside from the fact that I have other troubles right now . . . (BABETTE *enters in street clothes.*) What do *you* want here?
BABETTE. Am I interrupting?
BIEDERMANN. Can't you see I'm in conference? (BABETTE *nods to the* CHORUS, *then whispers in* BIEDERMANN's *ear.*) With ribbons, of course. Never mind the cost. As long as it's a wreath. (BABETTE *nods to the* CHORUS.)
BABETTE. Excuse me, sirs. (*She exits.*)
BIEDERMANN. To cut it short, gentlemen, I'm fed up! You and your firebugs! I don't even go to the pub any more—that's how fed up I am! Is there nothing else to talk about these days? Let's get one thing straight—if you go around thinking everybody except yourself is an arsonist, how are things ever going to improve? A little trust in people, for heaven's sake! A little good will! Why keep looking at the bad

side? Why go on the assumption that everybody else is a firebug? A little confidence, a little— (*Pause*) You can't go on living in fear! (*Pause*) You think I closed my eyes last night for one instant? I'm not an imbecile, you know! Gasoline is gasoline! I had the worst kind of thoughts running through my head last night. . . . I climbed 'up on the table to listen—even got up on the bureau and put my ear to the ceiling! They were snoring, mind you—snoring! At least four times I climbed up on that bureau. Peacefully snoring! Just the same I got as far as the stairs, once—believe it or not—in my pajamas— and frantic, I tell you—frantic! I was all ready to wake up those two scoundrels and throw them out in the street, along with their barrels. Single-handedly, without compunction, in the middle of the night!

CHORUS. Single-handedly?

BIEDERMANN. Yes.

CHORUS. Without compunction?

BIEDERMANN. Yes.

CHORUS. In the middle of the night?

BIEDERMANN. Just about to! If my wife hadn't come after me, afraid I'd catch cold— (*Embarrassed, he reaches for a cigar.*)

LEADER. How shall I put it?
    Sleepless he passed the night.
    That they'd take advantage of a
        man's good nature—
    Was that conceivable?
    Suspicion came over him. Why?

(BIEDERMANN *lights his cigar.*)

CHORUS. No, it's not easy for the citizen,
    Tough in business
    But really soft of heart,
    Always ready,
    Ready always to do good.

LEADER. If that's how he happens to feel.

CHORUS. Hoping that goodness
    Will come of goodness.
    How mistaken can you be?

BIEDERMANN. What are you getting at?

CHORUS. It seems to us there's a stink of gasoline.

(BIEDERMANN *sniffs.*)

BIEDERMANN. I don't smell anything.

CHORUS. Woe to us!

BIEDERMANN. Not a thing.

CHORUS. Woe to us!

LEADER. How soon he's got accustomed to bad smells!

CHORUS. Woe to us!

BIEDERMANN. And don't keep giving us that defeatism, gentlemen. Don't keep saying, "Woe to us!" (*A car honks offstage.*) Taxi!—Taxi! (*A car stops offstage.*) If you'll excuse me— (*He hurries off.*)

CHORUS. Citizen—where to?

(*The car drives off.*)

LEADER. What is his recourse, poor
        wretch?
    Forceful, yet fearful,
    Milk-white of face,
    Fearful yet firm—
    Against what?

(*The car is heard honking.*)

CHORUS. So soon accustomed to bad
        smells!

(*The car is heard distantly honking.*)
    Woe to us!

LEADER. Woe to you!

(*The* CHORUS *retires. All but the* LEADER, *who takes out his pipe.*)
    He who dreads action
    More than disaster,
    How can he fight
    When disaster impends? (*He follows
        the* CHORUS *out.*)

SCENE FIVE

The Attic. EISENRING *is alone, unwinding cord from a reel and singing "Lili Marlene" while he works. He stops, wets his forefinger, and holds it up to the dormer window to test the wind.*

The Living Room. BIEDERMANN *enters, cigar in mouth, followed by* BABETTE. *He takes off his coat and throws down his briefcase.*

———

BIEDERMANN. Do as I say.

BABETTE. A goose?

BIEDERMANN. A goose! (*He takes off his tie without removing his cigar.*)

BABETTE. Why are you taking off your necktie, Gottlieb?

BIEDERMANN. If I report those two . . . to the police, I'll make them my enemies. What good will that do me? Just one match and the whole house is up in flames! What good will that do us? On the other hand, if I go up there and invite them to dinner, why—

BABETTE. Why, what?

BIEDERMANN. Why, then we'll be friends. (*He takes off his jacket, hands it to* BABETTE, *and exits.*)

BABETTE (*speaking to* ANNA, *offstage*). Just so you'll know, Anna: you can't get off this evening—we're having company. Set places for four.

The Attic. EISENRING *is singing "Lili Marlene." There is a knock at the door.*

EISENRING. Come in! (*He goes on singing. No one enters.*) Come in! (BIEDERMANN *enters in shirt sleeves, holding his cigar.*) Good day, Mr. Biedermann!

BIEDERMANN (*tactfully*). May I come in?

EISENRING. I hope you slept well last night?

BIEDERMANN. Thank you—miserably.

EISENRING. So did I. It's this wind. (*He goes on working with the reel.*)

BIEDERMANN. If I'm not disturbing you—

EISENRING. This is your house, Mr. Biedermann.

BIEDERMANN. If I'm not in the way— (*The cooing of doves is heard.*) Where is our friend?

EISENRING. Sepp? He went to work this morning. The lazy dog—he didn't want to go without breakfast! I sent him out for some sawdust.

BIEDERMANN. Sawdust?

EISENRING. It helps spread the fire. (BIEDERMANN *laughs politely at what sounds like a poor joke.*)

BIEDERMANN. I came up to say, Mr. Eisenring—

EISENRING. That you still want to kick us out?

BIEDERMANN. In the middle of the night —I'm out of sleeping pills—it suddenly struck me: you folks have no toilet facilities up here.

EISENRING. We have the roof gutter.

BIEDERMANN. Well, just as you like, of course. It merely struck me you might like to wash or take a shower—I kept thinking of that all night. . . . You're very welcome to use my bathroom. I told Anna to hang up some towels for you there. (EISENRING *shakes his head.*) Why do you shake your head?

EISENRING. Where on earth did he put it?

BIEDERMANN. What?

EISENRING. You haven't seen a detonator cap? (*He searches around.*) Don't trouble yourself, Mr. Biedermann. In jail, you know, we had no bathrooms either.

BIEDERMANN. In jail?

EISENRING. Didn't Sepp tell you I just came out of prison?

BIEDERMANN. No.

EISENRING. Not a word about it?

BIEDERMANN. No.

EISENRING. All he likes to talk about is himself. There *are* such people!— Is it our fault, after all, if his youth was tragic? Did *you* have a tragic youth, Mr. Biedermann? *I* didn't. I could have gone to college; my father wanted me to be a lawyer. . . . (*He stands at the attic window murmuring at the doves.*) Grrr! Grrr! Grrr!

BIEDERMANN (*relights his cigar*). Frankly, Mr. Eisenring, I couldn't sleep all night. Is there really gasoline in those barrels?

EISENRING. You don't trust us.

BIEDERMANN. I'm merely asking.

EISENRING. Mr. Biedermann, what do you take us for? Frankly, what sort of people—

BIEDERMANN. Mr. Eisenring, you mustn't think I have no sense of humor. Only your idea of a joke—well—

EISENRING. That's something we've learned.

BIEDERMANN. What is?

EISENRING. A joke is good camouflage. Next best comes sentiment: like when Sepp talks about childhood in the coal mines, orphanages, circuses, and so forth. But the best camouflage of all—in my opinion—is the plain and simple truth. Because nobody ever believes it.

The Living Room. ANNA *shows in the* WIDOW KNECHTLING, *dressed in black.*

ANNA. Take a seat, please. (*The* WIDOW *sits.*) But if you are Mrs. Knechtling, it's no use. Mr. Biedermann wants nothing to do with you, he said. (*The* WIDOW *gets up.*) Do sit down, please! (*The* WIDOW *sits down again.*) But don't get up any hopes. (ANNA *exits.*)

The Attic. EISENRING *busies himself stringing out the fuse.* BIEDERMANN *is smoking.*

EISENRING. I wonder what's keeping Sepp. Sawdust can't be so hard to find. I hope they haven't nabbed him.

BIEDERMANN. Nabbed?

EISENRING. Why do you smile?

BIEDERMANN. When you use words like that, Mr. Eisenring, it's as though you came from another world. Nab him! Like another world! *Our* kind of people seldom get nabbed! ——

EISENRING. Because your kind of people seldom steal sawdust. That's obvious, Mr. Biedermann. That's the class difference.

BIEDERMANN. Nonsense!

EISENRING. You don't mean to say, Mr. Biedermann—

BIEDERMANN. I don't hold with class differences—you must have realized that by now, Mr. Eisenring. I'm not old-fashioned —just the opposite, in fact. And I regret that the lower classes still talk about class differences. Aren't we all of us—rich or poor—the creation of one Creator? The middle class, too. Are we not—you and I —human beings, made of flesh and blood? . . . I don't know, sir, whether you smoke cigars— (*He offers one, but* EISENRING *shakes his head.*) I don't mean reducing people to a common level, understand me. There will always be rich and poor, of course—but why can't we just shake hands? A little good will, for heaven's sake, a little idealism, a little—and we'd all have peace and quiet, both the poor and the rich. Don't you agree?

EISENRING. If I may speak frankly, Mr. Biedermann—

BIEDERMANN. Please do.

EISENRING. You won't take it amiss?

BIEDERMANN. The more frankly, the better.

EISENRING. Frankly speaking, you oughtn't to smoke here. (BIEDERMANN, *startled, puts out his cigar.*) I can't make rules for you here, Mr. Biedermann. After all, it's your house. Still and all—

BIEDERMANN. Of course.

EISENRING (*looking down*). There it is! (*He takes something off the floor and blows it clean before attaching it to the fuse. He starts whistling "Lili Marlene."*)

BIEDERMANN. Tell me, Mr. Eisenring, what is that you're doing? If I may ask? What is that thing?

EISENRING. A detonator.

BIEDERMANN. A —?

EISENRING. And this is a fuse.

BIEDERMANN. A —?

EISENRING. Sepp says they've developed better ones lately. But they're not for sale to the public. Anyway, buying them's out of the question for us. Anything that has to do with war is frightfully expensive. Always the best quality . . .

BIEDERMANN. A fuse, you say?

EISENRING. A time fuse. (*He hands* BIE-DERMANN *one end of the cord.*) If you'd be kind enough, Mr. Biedermann, to hold this end— (BIEDERMANN *holds it for him.*)

BIEDERMANN. All joking aside, my friend—

EISENRING. One second— (*He whistles "Lily Marlene," measuring the fuse.*) Thank you, Mr. Biedermann. (BIEDERMANN *suddenly laughs.*)

BIEDERMANN. Ha, ha! You can't put a scare into me, Willi! Though I must say, you do count on people's sense of humor. The way you talk, I can understand your getting arrested now and then. You know, not everybody has my sense of humor!

EISENRING. You have to find the right man.

BIEDERMANN. At the pub, for instance— just say you believe in the natural goodness of man, and they have you marked down.

EISENRING. Ha! (*He puts down the fuse.*) Those who have no sense of humor get what's coming to them just the same when the time comes—so don't let *that* worry you. (BIEDERMANN *sits down on a barrel. He has broken into a sweat.*) What's the trouble, Mr. Biedermann? You've gone quite pale. (*He claps him on the shoulder.*) It's the smell. I know, if you're not used to it . . . I'll open the window for you, too. (*He opens the door.*)

BIEDERMANN. Thanks . . .

(ANNA *calls up the stairs.*)

ANNA'S VOICE. Mr. Biedermann! Mr. Biedermann!

EISENRING. The police again? It's a police state!

ANNA'S VOICE. Mr. Biedermann—

BIEDERMANN. I'm coming! (*They both whisper from here on.*) Mr. Eisenring, do you like goose?

EISENRING. Goose?

BIEDERMANN. Roast goose.

EISENRING. Why?

BIEDERMANN. Stuffed with chestnuts?

EISENRING. And red cabbage?

BIEDERMANN. Yes . . . I was going to say: my wife and I—I, especially—if we may have the pleasure . . . I don't mean to intrude, Mr. Eisenring, but if you'd care to join us at a little supper, you and Sepp—

EISENRING. Today?

BIEDERMANN. Or tomorrow, if you prefer—

EISENRING. We probably won't stay until tomorrow. But today—of course, Mr. Biedermann, with pleasure.

BIEDERMANN. Shall we say seven o'clock? (*They shake hands.* BIEDERMANN *at the door:*) Is it a date? (*He nods genially, then stares once more at the barrels and the fuse.*)

EISENRING. It's a date.

(BIEDERMANN *exits.* EISENRING *goes to work again, whistling. The* CHORUS *enters below as if for the end of the scene. They are interrupted by the sound of a crash, of something falling in the attic.*)

EISENRING. You can come out, Professor. (*A* PH.D., *wearing horn-rimmed glasses, crawls out from behind the barrels.*) You heard: we're invited to dinner, Sepp and me. You'll keep an eye on things. Nobody's to come in here and smoke, understand? Not before we're ready. (*The* PH.D. *polishes his glasses.*) I often ask myself, Professor, why in hell you hang around with us. You don't enjoy a good crackling fire or flames or sparks. Or sirens that go off too late or dogs barking—or people shrieking—or smoke. Or ashes . . . (*The* PH.D. *solemnly adjusts his glasses.* EISENRING *laughs.*) Do-gooder! (*He whistles gently to himself, surveying the professor.*) I don't like you eggheads—I've told you that before, Professor. You get no real fun out of anything. You're all so idealistic, so solemn. . . . Until you're ready to sell out. That's no fun either, Professor. (*He goes back to his work, whistling.*)

Below.

CHORUS. Ready for action,
　　Axes and fire hose;
　　Polished and oiled.

Every brass fitting.
　　Every man of us tested and ready.

LEADER. We'll be facing a high wind.

CHORUS. Every man of us tested and ready.
　　Our brass fire pump
　　Polished and oiled,
　　Tested for pressure.

LEADER. And the fire hydrants?

CHORUS. Everything ready.

LEADER. Tested and ready for action.

(*Enter* BABETTE *with a goose, and the* Ph.D.)

BABETTE. Yes, Professor, I know, but my husband . . . Yes, I understand it's urgent, Professor. I'll tell him— (*She leaves the professor and comes to the footlights.*) My husband ordered a goose. See, this is it. And I have to roast it, so we can be friends with those people upstairs. (*Churchbells ring.*) It's Saturday night—you can hear the bells ringing. I have an odd feeling, somehow, that it may be the last time we'll hear them. (BIEDERMANN *calls* "BABETTE!") I don't know, ladies, if Gottlieb is always right. . . . You know what he says? "Certainly they're scoundrels, Babette, but if I make enemies of them, it's good-bye to our hair tonic!" (BIEDERMANN *calls,* "BABETTE!") Gottlieb's like that. Good-hearted. Always too good-hearted! (*She exits with the goose.*)

CHORUS. This son of good family,
　　A wearer of glasses,
　　Pale, studious, trusting,
　　But trusting no longer
　　In power of goodness,
　　Will do anything now, for
　　Ends justify means.
　　(So he hopes.)
　　Ah, honest-dishonest!
　　Now wiping his glasses
　　To see things more clearly,
　　He sees no barrels—
　　No gasoline barrels!
　　It's an idea he sees—
　　An abstract conception—
　　Until it explodes!

PH.D. Good evening . . .

LEADER. To the pumps!
　　The ladders!
　　The engines!

(*The* FIREMEN *rush to their posts.*)

LEADER. Good evening. (*To the audience, as shouts of* "Ready!" *echo through the theatre.*) We're ready.

SCENE SIX

The Living Room. The WIDOW KNECHTLING *is still there waiting. Outside, the bells are ringing loudly.* ANNA *is setting the table.* BIEDERMANN *brings in two chairs.*

———

BIEDERMANN. You can see, can't you, Mrs. Knechtling? I haven't time now— no time to think about the dead. . . . I told you, go see my lawyer. (*The* WIDOW KNECHTLING *leaves.*) You can't hear yourself think, with that noise. Close the window. (ANNA *shuts the window. The sound of the bells is fainter.*) I said a simple, informal dinner. What are those idiotic candelabra for?

ANNA. But, Mr. Biedermann, we always have those!

BIEDERMANN. I said, simple, informal— no ostentation. Fingerbowls! Knife-rests! Nothing but crystal and silver! What are you trying to do? (*He picks up the knife-rests and shoves them into his pants pocket.*) Can't you see I'm wearing my oldest jacket? And you . . . leave the carving knife, Anna—we'll need it; but away with the rest of this silver! Those two gentlemen must feel at home!— Where's the corkscrew?

ANNA. Here.

BIEDERMANN. Don't we have anything simpler?

ANNA. In the kitchen. But that one is rusty.

BIEDERMANN. Bring it here. (*He takes a silver ice bucket off the table.*) What's this for?

ANNA. For the wine.

BIEDERMANN. Silver! (*He glares at the bucket, then at* ANNA.) Do we always use that, too?

ANNA. We're going to need it, Mr. Biedermann.

BIEDERMANN. Humanity, brotherhood— that's what we need here! Away with that thing! And what are those, will you tell me?

ANNA. Napkins.

BIEDERMANN. Damask napkins!

ANNA. We don't have any others. (BIEDERMANN *shoves the napkins into the silver bucket.*)

BIEDERMANN. There are whole nations, Anna, that live without napkins! (BABETTE *enters with a large wreath.* BIEDERMANN, *standing in front of the table, does not see her come in.*) And why a cloth on the table?

BABETTE. Gottlieb?

BIEDERMANN. Let's have no class distinctions! (*He sees* BABETTE.) What is that wreath?

BABETTE. It's what we ordered— Gottlieb, what do you think? They sent the wreath here by mistake! And I gave them the address myself—Knechtling's address —I wrote it down, even! And the ribbon and everything—they've got it all backward!

BIEDERMANN. What's wrong with the ribbon?

BABETTE. And the clerk says they sent the bill to Mrs. Knechtling! (*She shows him the ribbon.*) "To Our Dear, Departed Gottlieb Biedermann." (*He considers the ribbon.*)

BIEDERMANN. We won't accept it, that's all! I should say not! They've got to exchange it! (*He goes back to the table.*) Don't upset me, will you, Babette? I can't think of everything—

(BABETTE *exits.*)

BIEDERMANN. Take that tablecloth away. Help me, Anna. And remember—no serving! You come in and put the pan on the table.

ANNA. The roasting pan? (*He takes off the tablecloth.*)

BIEDERMANN. That's better! Just a bare table, for a plain and simple supper. (*He hands* ANNA *the tablecloth.*)

ANNA. You mean that, Mr. Biedermann —just bring in the goose in the pan? (*She folds up the tablecloth.*) What wine shall I bring?

BIEDERMANN. I'll get it myself.

ANNA. Mr. Biedermann!

BIEDERMANN. What now?

ANNA. I don't have any sweater, sir— any old sweater, as if I belonged to the family.

BIEDERMANN. Borrow one of my wife's.

ANNA. The yellow or the red one?

BIEDERMANN. Don't make a fuss! No apron or cap, understand? And get rid of these candelabra. And make sure especially, Anna, that everything's not so neat! —I'll be in the cellar. (BIEDERMANN *exits*.)

ANNA. "Make sure especially, Anna, that everything's not so neat!" (*She throws the tablecloth down on the floor and stomps on it with both feet*.) How's that?

(SCHMITZ *and* EISENRING *enter, each holding a rose*.)

BOTH. Good evening, miss.

(ANNA *exits without looking at them*.)

EISENRING. Why no sawdust?

SCHMITZ. Confiscated. Police measure. Precaution. They're picking up anybody who sells or owns sawdust without written permission. Precautions all over the place. (*He combs his hair*.)

EISENRING. Have you got matches?

SCHMITZ. No.

EISENRING. Neither have I. (SCHMITZ *blows his comb clean*.)

SCHMITZ. We'll have to ask him for them.

EISENRING. Biedermann?

SCHMITZ. Don't forget. (*He puts away his comb, and sniffs*.) Mmm! That smells good!

SCENE SEVEN

BIEDERMANN *comes to the footlights with a bottle*.

———

BIEDERMANN. You can think what you like about me, gentlemen. But just answer one question— (*Laughter and loud voices offstage*) I say to myself: as long as they're laughing and drinking, we're safe. The best bottles out of my cellar! I tell you, if anybody had told me a week ago . . . When did *you* guess they were arsonists, gentlemen? This sort of thing doesn't happen the way you think. It comes on you slowly—slowly, at first—then sudden suspicion! Though I was suspicious at once— one's always suspicious! But tell me the truth, sirs—what would *you* have done? If you were in my place, for God's sake? And when? *When* would you have done it? At what point? (*He waits for an answer. Silence*) I must go back up. (*He leaves the stage quickly*.)

SCENE EIGHT

The Living Room. The dinner is in full swing. Laughter. BIEDERMANN, *especially, cannot contain himself at the joke he's just heard. Only* BABETTE *is not laughing.*

———

BIEDERMANN. Oil waste! Did you hear that, Babette? Oil waste, he says! Oil waste burns better!

BABETTE. I don't see what's funny.

BIEDERMANN. Oil waste! You know what that is?

BABETTE. Yes.

BIEDERMANN. You have no sense of humor, Babette. (*He puts the bottle on the table*.)

BABETTE. All right, then, explain it.

BIEDERMANN. Okay!— This morning Willi told Sepp to go out and steal some sawdust. Sawdust—get it? And just now, when I asked Sepp if he got any, he said he couldn't find any sawdust—he found some oil waste instead. Get it? And Willi says, "Oil waste burns better!"

BABETTE. I understood all that.

BIEDERMANN. You did?

BABETTE. What's funny about it? (BIEDERMANN *gives up*.)

BIEDERMANN. Let's drink, men! (BIEDERMANN *removes the cork from the bottle*.)

BABETTE. Is that the truth, Mr. Schmitz? Did you bring oil waste up to our attic?

BIEDERMANN. This will kill you, Babette! This morning we even measured the fuse together, Willi and I!

BABETTE. The fuse?

BIEDERMANN. The time fuse. (*He fills the glasses*.)

BABETTE. Seriously—what does that mean? (BIEDERMANN *laughs*.)

BIEDERMANN. Seriously! You hear that? Seriously! . . . Don't let them kid you, Babette. I told you—our friends have their own way of kidding! Different company, different jokes—that's what I always say. . . . All we need now is to have them ask me for matches! (SCHMITZ *and* EISENRING *exchange glances*.) These gentlemen took me for some Milquetoast, for some dope without humor— (*He lifts his glass*.) Prosit!

EISENRING. Prosit!

SCHMITZ. Prosit!

BIEDERMANN. To our friendship! (*They drink the toast standing up, then sit down again.*) We're not doing any serving. Just help yourselves, gentlemen.

SCHMITZ. I can't eat any more.

EISENRING. Don't restrain yourself, Sepp; you're not at the orphanage. (*He helps himself to more goose.*) Your goose is wonderful, madam.

BABETTE. I'm glad to hear it.

EISENRING. Roast goose and stuffing! Now all we need is a tablecloth.

BABETTE. You hear that, Gottlieb?

EISENRING. We don't have to have one. But one of those tablescloths, white damask, with silverware on it—

BIEDERMANN (*loudly*). Anna!

EISENRING. Damask, with flowers all over it—a white flower pattern—we don't have to have one. We didn't have any in prison.

BABETTE. In prison?

BIEDERMANN. Where is that girl?

BABETTE. Have you been in prison?

(ANNA *enters. She is wearing a bright red sweater.*)

BIEDERMANN. A tablecloth here—immediately!

ANNA. Yes, sir.

BIEDERMANN. And if you have some fingerbowls or something—

ANNA. Yes, sir.

EISENRING. Madam, you may think it's childish, but that's how the little man is. Take Sepp, for instance—he grew up in the coal mines, but it's the dream of his miserable life, a table like this, with crystal and silver! Would you believe it? He never heard of a knife-rest!

BABETTE. But, Gottlieb, we have all those things!

EISENRING. Of course we don't *have* to have them here—

ANNA. Very well.

EISENRING. If you have any napkins, miss, out with them!

ANNA. But Mr. Biedermann said—

BIEDERMANN. Out with them!

ANNA. Yes, sir. (*She starts to bring back the table service.*)

EISENRING. I hope you won't take it amiss, madam, but when you're just out of prison—months at a time with no refinement whatever— (*He shows the tablecloth to* SCHMITZ.) You know what this is? (*To* BABETTE) He never saw one before!

(*He turns back to* SCHMITZ.) This is damask!

SCHMITZ. What do you want me to do with it? (EISENRING *ties the tablecloth around* SCHMITZ's *neck.*)

EISENRING. There— (BIEDERMANN *tries to find this amusing. He laughs.*)

BABETTE. Where are the knife-rests, Anna?

ANNA. Mr. Biedermann—

BIEDERMANN. Out with them!

ANNA. But you said "Take them away!" before!

BIEDERMANN. Bring them here, I tell you! Where are they, goddammit?

ANNA. In your pants pockets. (BIEDERMANN *reaches in his pants pocket and finds them.*)

EISENRING. Don't get excited.

ANNA. I can't help it!

EISENRING. No excitement, now miss— (ANNA *bursts into sobs and runs out.*)

EISENRING. It's this wind. (*Pause*)

BIEDERMANN. Drink up, friends! (*They drink. A silence*)

EISENRING. I ate roast goose every day when I was a waiter. I used to flit down those corridors holding a platter like this. . . . How do you suppose, madam, waiters clean off their hands? In their hair, that's how—while there's others who use crystal fingerbowls. That's something I'll never forget. (*He dips his fingers in the finger-bowl.*) Have you ever heard of a trauma?

BIEDERMANN. No.

EISENRING. I learned all about it in jail. (*He wipes his fingers dry.*)

BABETTE. And how did you happen to be there, Mr. Eisenring?

BIEDERMANN. Babette!

EISENRING. How did I get into jail?

BIEDERMANN. One doesn't ask questions like that!

EISENRING. I wonder at that myself. . . . I was a waiter—a little headwaiter. Suddenly they made me out a great arsonist.

BIEDERMANN. Hm.

EISENRING. They called for me at my own home.

BIEDERMANN. Hm.

EISENRING. I was so amazed, I played along.

BIEDERMANN. Hm.

EISENRING. I had luck, madam—seven really charming policemen. I said, "I have no time—I have to go to work." They answered, "Your restaurant's burned to the ground."

BIEDERMANN. Burned to the ground?

EISENRING. Overnight, apparently.

BABETTE. Burned to the ground?

EISENRING. "Fine," I said. "Then I *have* time. . . ." Just a black, smoking hulk— that's all that was left of that place. I saw it as we drove by. Through those windows, you know, the little barred windows they have in those prison vans— (*He sips his wine delicately.*)

BIEDERMANN. And then? (EISENRING *studies the wine label.*)

EISENRING. We used to keep this, too: '49, Cave de l'Echannon . . . And then? Let Sepp tell you the rest— As I was sitting in that police station, playing with my handcuffs, who do you think they brought in?— That one, there! (SCHMITZ *beams.*) *Prosit,* Sepp!

SCHMITZ. *Prosit,* Willi! (*They drink.*)

BIEDERMANN. And then?

SCHMITZ. "Are you a firebug?" they asked him, and offered him cigarettes. He said, "Excuse me, I have no matches, Mr. Commissioner, although you think I'm a firebug—" (*They laugh uproariously and slap each other's thighs.*)

BIEDERMANN. Hm.

(ANNA *enters, in cap and apron again. She hands* BIEDERMANN *a visiting card.*)

ANNA. It's urgent, he says.

BIEDERMANN. When I have visitors— (SCHMITZ *and* EISENRING *clink glasses again.*)

SCHMITZ. *Prosit,* Willi!

EISENRING. *Prosit,* Sepp! (*They drink.* BIEDERMANN *studies the visiting card.*)

BABETTE. Who is it, Gottlieb?

BIEDERMANN. It's some PH.D. . . . (ANNA *is busy at the sideboard.*)

EISENRING. And what are those other things, miss—those silver things?

ANNA. The candlesticks?

EISENRING. Why do you hide them?

BIEDERMANN. Bring them here!

ANNA. But you said, yourself, Mr. Biedermann—

BIEDERMANN. I say bring them here! (ANNA *places the candelabra on the table.*)

EISENRING. What do you say to that, Sepp? They have candlesticks and they hide them! Real silver candlesticks—what more do you want?— Have you a match? (*He reaches into his pants pocket.*)

SCHMITZ. Me? No. (*He reaches into his pants pocket.*)

EISENRING. Sorry, no matches, Mr. Biedermann.

BIEDERMANN. I have some.

EISENRING. Let's have them.

BIEDERMANN. I'll light the candles. Let me—I'll do it. (*He begins lighting the candles.*)

BABETTE (*to* ANNA). What does the visitor want?

ANNA. I don't know, ma'am. He says he can no longer be silent. And he's waiting on the stoop.

BABETTE. It's private, he says?

ANNA. Yes ma'am. He says he wants to expose something.

BABETTE. Expose something?!

ANNA. That's what he keeps saying. I don't understand him. He wants to disassociate himself, he says. . . . (BIEDERMANN *is still lighting the candles.*)

EISENRING. It creates an atmosphere, doesn't it, madam? Candlelight, I mean,

BABETTE. Yes, it does.

EISENRING. I'm all for atmosphere. Refined, candlelight atmosphere—

BIEDERMANN. I'm happy to know that. (*All the candles are lit.*)

EISENRING. Schmitz, don't smack your lips when you eat! (BABETTE *takes* EISENRING *aside.*)

BABETTE. Let him alone!

EISENRING. He has no manners, madam. Excuse me—it's awful. But where could he have picked up any manners? From the coal mines to the orphanage—

BABETTE. I know.

EISENRING. From the orphanage to the circus.

BABETTE. I know.

EISENRING. From the circus to the theatre—

BABETTE. I didn't know.

EISENRING. A football of fate, madam. (BABETTE *turns to* SCHMITZ.)

BABETTE. In the theatre! Were you, really? (SCHMITZ *gnaws on a drumstick, and nods.*) Where?

SCHMITZ. Upstage.

EISENRING. Really talented, too! Sepp as a ghost! Can you imagine it?

SCHMITZ. Not anymore, though.

BABETTE. Why not?

SCHMITZ. I was in the theatre only a week, madam, before it burned to the ground.

BABETTE. Burned to the ground?

EISENRING (*to* SCHMITZ). Don't be diffident!

BIEDERMANN. Burned to the ground?

EISENRING. Don't be so diffident! (*He unties the tablecloth* SCHMITZ *has been wearing and throws it over* SCHMITZ's *head.*)Come on! (SCHMITZ *gets up with the tablecloth over him.*) Doesn't he look like a ghost?

ANNA. I'm frightened!

EISENRING. Come here, little girl! (*He pulls* ANNA *onto his lap. She hides her face in her hands.*)

SCHMITZ. Who calleth?

EISENRING. That's theatre language, madam. They call that a cue. He learned it in less than a week, before the theatre burned down.

BABETTE. Please don't keep talking of fires!

SCHMITZ. Who calleth?

EISENRING. Ready— (*Everybody waits expectantly.* EISENRING *has a tight grip on* ANNA.)

SCHMITZ. EVERYMAN! EVERYMAN!

BABETTE. Gottlieb?

BIEDERMANN. Quiet!

BABETTE. We saw that in Salzburg!

SCHMITZ. BIEDERMANN! BIEDERMANN!

EISENRING. He's terrific!

SCHMITZ. BIEDERMANN! BIEDERMANN!

EISENRING. You must say, "Who are you?"

BIEDERMANN. Me?

EISENRING. Or he can't say his lines.

SCHMITZ. EVERYMAN! BIEDERMANN!

BIEDERMANN. All right, then—who am I?

BABETTE. No! You must ask him who *he* is.

BIEDERMANN. I see.

SCHMITZ. DOST THOU HEAR ME?

EISENRING. No, no, Sepp—start it again. (*They change their positions.*)

SCHMITZ. EVERYMAN! BIEDERMANN!

BABETTE. Are you the Angel of Death, maybe?

BIEDERMANN. Nonsense!

BABETTE. What else *could* he be?

BIEDERMANN. Ask him. He might be the ghost in *Hamlet.* Or that other one—what's-his-name—in *Macbeth.*

SCHMITZ. WHO CALLS ME?

EISENRING. Go on.

SCHMITZ. GOTTLIEB BIEDERMANN!

BABETTE. Go ahead, ask him. He's talking to you.

SCHMITZ. DOST THOU HEAR ME?

BIEDERMANN. Who are you?

SCHMITZ. I AM THE GHOST OF—KNECHTLING. (*He throws the tablecloth over* BIEDERMANN. BABETTE *jumps up with a scream.*)

EISENRING. Stop! (*He pulls the tablecloth off* BIEDERMANN.) Idiot! How could you do such a thing? Knechtling was buried today!

SCHMITZ. That's why I thought of him. (BABETTE *hides her face in her hands.*)

EISENRING. He's not Knechtling, madam. (*He shakes his head over* SCHMITZ.) What crudeness!

SCHMITZ. He was on my mind.

EISENRING. Of all things—Knechtling! Mr. Biedermann's best old employee! Imagine it: buried today—cold and stiff —not yet moldy—pale as this tablecloth—white and shiny as damask— To go and act Knechtling— (*He takes* BABETTE *by the shoulder.*) Honest to God, madam, it's Sepp— it's not Knechtling at all. (SCHMITZ *wipes off his sweat.*)

SCHMITZ. I'm sorry. . . .

BIEDERMANN. Let's sit down again.

ANNA. Is it over?

BIEDERMANN. Would you care for cigars, sirs? (*He offers a box of cigars.*)

EISENRING (*to* SCHMITZ). Idiot! You see how Mr. Biedermann is shaking! . . . Thank you, Mr. Biedermann!—You think that's funny, Sepp? When you know very well that Knechtling put his head inside the gas stove? After everything Gottlieb did for him? He gave this Knechtling a job for fourteen years—and this is his thanks!

BIEDERMANN. Let's not talk about it.

EISENRING (*to* SCHMITZ). And that's your thanks for the goose! (*They attend to their cigars.*)

SCHMITZ. Would you like me to sing

something?

EISENRING. What?

SCHMITZ. "Fox, you stole that lovely goosie . . . (*He sings loudly.*)
Fox, you stole that lovely goosie,
Give it back again!"

EISENRING. That's enough.

SCHMITZ. "Give it back again!

EISENRING. That's enough.

SCHMITZ. "Give it back again!
Or they'll get you in the shnoosie—"

EISENRING. He's drunk.

SCHMITZ. "With their shooting gun!"

EISENRING. Pay no attention to him.

SCHMITZ. "Give it back again!
Or they'll get you in the shnoosie
With their shooting gun!"

BIEDERMAN. "Shooting gun!" That's good!

(*The Men all join in the song.*)

THE MEN. "Fox, you stole that lovely goosie . . ."

(*They harmonize, now loudly, now softly. Laughter and loud cheer. There is a pause, and* BIEDERMANN *picks up again, leading the hilarity until they've all had it.*)

BIEDERMANN. So— *Prosit!* (*They raise their glasses. Fire sirens are heard nearby.*) What was that?

EISENRING. Sirens.

BIEDERMANN. Joking aside—

BABETTE. Firebugs! Firebugs!

BIEDERMANN. Don't yell like that!

(BABETTE *runs to the window and throws it open. The sound of the sirens comes nearer, with a howl that goes to the marrow. The fire engines roar past.*)

BIEDERMANN. At least it's not here.

BABETTE. I wonder where?

EISENRING. From where the wind is blowing.

BIEDERMANN. Not here, anyway.

EISENRING. That's how we generally work it. Lure the Fire Department out to some cheap suburb or other, and then, when things really let loose, they can't get back in time.

BIEDERMANN. No, gentlemen—all joking aside—

SCHMITZ. That's how we do it—joking aside—

BIEDERMANN. Please—enough of this nonsense! Don't overdo it! Look at my wife—white as chalk.

BABETTE. And you too!

BIEDERMANN. Besides, a fire alarm is nothing to laugh at, gentlemen. Somewhere some place is burning, or the Fire Department wouldn't be rushing there. (EISENRING *looks at his watch.*)

EISENRING. We've got to go now.

BIEDERMANN. Now?

EISENRING. Sorry.

SCHMITZ. "Or they'll get you in the shnoosie . . ." (*The sirens are heard again.*)

BIEDERMANN. Bring us some coffee, Babette! (BABETTE *goes out.*)And you, Anna —do you have to stand there and gape? (ANNA *goes out.*) Just between us, gentlemen: enough is enough. My wife has a heart condition. Let's have no more joking about fires.

SCHMITZ. We're not joking, Mr. Biedermann.

EISENRING. We're firebugs.

BIEDERMANN. No, gentlemen, quite seriously—

EISENRING. Quite seriously.

SCHMITZ. Yeah, quite seriously. Why don't you believe us?

EISENRING. Your house is very favorably situated, Mr. Biedermann; you must admit that. Five villas like yours around the gasworks. . . . It's true they keep a close watch on the gasworks. Still, there's a good stiff wind blowing—

BIEDERMANN. It can't be—

SCHMITZ. Let's have plain talk! You think we're firebugs—

BIEDERMANN (*like a whipped dog*). No, no, I don't think you are! You do me an injustice, gentlemen—I don't think you're firebugs. . . .

EISENRING. You swear you don't?

BIEDERMANN. No! No! No! I don't believe it!

SCHMITZ. What *do* you think we are?

BIEDERMANN. You're my friends. . . . (*They clap him on the shoulder and start to leave.*)

EISENRING. It's time to leave.

BIEDERMANN. Gentlemen, I swear to you by all that's holy—

EISENRING. By all that's holy?

BIEDERMANN. Yes. (*He raises his hand as though to take an oath.*)

SCHMITZ. Willi doesn't believe in anything holy, Mr. Biedermann. Any more than you do. You'll waste your time swearing. (*They go to the door.*)

BIEDERMANN. What can I do to make you believe me? (*He blocks the doorway.*)

EISENRING. Give us some matches.

BIEDERMANN. Some—

EISENRING. We have no more matches.

BIEDERMANN. You want me to—

EISENRING. If you don't think we're firebugs.

BIEDERMANN. Matches—

SCHMITZ. To show your belief in us, he means. (BIEDERMANN *reaches in his pocket.*)

EISENRING. See how he hesitates?

BIEDERMANN. Sh! Not in front of my wife . . . (BABETTE *returns.*)

BABETTE. Your coffee will be ready in a minute. (*Pause*) Must you go?

BIEDERMANN (*formally*). At least you've felt, while here, my friends . . . I don't want to make a speech on this occasion, but may we not drink, before you go, to our eternal friendship? (*He picks up a bottle and the corkscrew.*)

EISENRING. Tell your very charming husband, madam, that he needn't open any more bottles on our account. It isn't worth the trouble anymore.

BIEDERMANN. It's no trouble, my friends, no trouble at all. If there's anything else you'd like—anything at all— (*He fills the glasses once more and hands them out.*) My friends! (*They clink glasses.*) Sepp— Willi— (*He kisses them each on the cheek. All drink.*)

EISENRING. Just the same, we must go now.

SCHMITZ. Unfortunately.

EISENRING. Madam— (*Sirens*)

BABETTE. It's been such a nice evening. (*Alarm bells*)

EISENRING. Just one thing now, Gottlieb—

BIEDERMANN. What is it?

EISENRING. I've mentioned it to you before.

BIEDERMANN. Anything you like. Just name it.

EISENRING. The matches.

(ANNA *has entered with coffee.*)

BABETTE. Why, what is it, Anna?

ANNA. The coffee.

BABETTE. You're all upset, Anna!

ANNA. Back there—Mrs. Biedermann—

the sky! You can see it from the kitchen —the whole sky is burning, Mrs. Biedermann!

(*The scene is turning red as* SCHMITZ *and* EISENRING *make their bows and exit.* BIEDERMANN *is left pale and shaken.*)

BIEDERMANN. Not our house, fortunately . . . Not our house . . . Not our . . . (*The* PH.D. *enters.*) Who are you, and what do you want?

PH.D. I can no longer be silent. (*He takes out a paper and reads.*) "Cognizant of the events now transpiring, whose iniquitous nature must be readily apparent, the undersigned submits to the authorities the subsequent statement . . ." (*Amid the shrieking of sirens he reads an involved statement, of which no one understands a word. Dogs howl, bells ring, there is the scream of departing sirens and the crackling of flames. The* PH.D. *hands* BIEDERMANN *the paper.*) I disassociate myself.

BIEDERMANN. But—

PH.D. I have said my say. (*He takes off and folds up his glasses.*) Mr. Biedermann, I knew everything they were doing in your attic. What I didn't know was— they were doing it just for kicks.

BIEDERMANN. Professor— (*The* PH.D. *removes himself.*) What will I do with this, Professor?

(*The* PH.D. *climbs over the footlights and takes a seat in the audience.*)

BABETTE. Gottlieb—

BIEDERMANN. He's gone.

BABETTE. What did you give them? Matches? Not matches?

BIEDERMANN. Why not?

BABETTE. Not matches?

BIEDERMANN. If they really were firebugs, do you think they wouldn't have matches? Don't be foolish, Babette!

(*The clock strikes. Silence. The red light onstage begins deepening into blackness. Sirens. Bells ring. Dogs howl. Cars honk. . . . . A crash of collapsing buildings. A crackling of flames. Screams and outcries . . . fading. The* CHORUS *comes on again.*)

CHORUS. Useless, quite useless.
　　And nothing more useless
　　Than this useless story.
　　For arson, once kindled,

Kills many,
Leaves few,
And accomplishes nothing.
                First detonation.
LEADER. That was the gasworks.
                Second detonation.
CHORUS. Long foreseen, disaster
    Has reached us at last.
    Horrendous arson!
    Unquenchable fire.

Fate—so they call it!
                Third detonation.
LEADER. More gas tanks.
There is a series of frightful explosions.
CHORUS. Woe to us! Woe to us! Woe!
                The house lights go up.

                        CURTAIN.

THE DISPOSAL

William Inge

THE CHAPLAIN
JESS, *a young prisoner*
ARCHIE, *a young prisoner*
LUKE, *a middle-aged prisoner*
A GUARD

MONA, *Luke's wife*
JESS'S FATHER
JOE RUSELLI, *a young prisoner*
ANOTHER GUARD

For NEARLY A decade, William Inge personified that elusive ideal of the theatre: a playwright with an unblemished record of success. Esteemed by most professional drama arbiters, widely applauded by audiences and envied by his contemporaries, it struck one for a while that Mr. Inge's true ancestry lay not back in Kansas (where he was born in 1913), but in Phrygia, the legendary habitat of another celebrant of the golden touch, King Midas.

The gilt-edged chain began to assemble for the erstwhile St. Louis *Star-Times* stage-and-screen reviewer in 1950, when the Theatre Guild introduced to Broadway his deeply affecting domestic drama *Come Back, Little Sheba.* A second and more conspicuous link was added in 1953 with Joshua Logan's mounting of *Picnic.* Although the author personally was discontent with the comprissary "romantic" ending, the play won him both the New York Drama Critics Circle Award and the Pulitzer Prize.

In 1955, Mr. Inge again defied Shubert Alley's traditional sybilic prognostications and came blazingly through with his third successive hit: *Bus Stop.* Two years later, the prestigious chain was lengthened by *The Dark at the Top of the Stairs,* a variation of a play he had written some years earlier.

Legend insinuates that whatever goes up eventually must come down: in the theatre perhaps more precipitously than elsewhere. And it happened to William Inge with the dampening dismissals of his subsequent plays: *A Loss of Roses; Natural Affection; Where's Daddy?;* and *Hot September,* an abortive musical variation of his prize-winning *Picnic.* This temporary setback, however, could not alter his established rating as one of the mid-century's foremost and appreciably perceptive American dramatists.

The Disposal—here published for the first time—reveals William Inge under a bulb of different voltage as he potently and unequivocally strips bare the emotions and attitudes of three condemned men.

A collection of Mr. Inge's earlier short plays was published in 1962, and in the same year the author, who now makes his home in California, won an Academy Award for his screenplay *Splendor in the Grass.*

PROLOGUE

A PRIEST, *a man in his thirties, kneels in prayer. The light is dim.*

CHAPLAIN. Dear God, one of the men on Death Row goes to the chair tonight. To die. I don't know how I can face him today. I don't know how I can face *any* of them. I go to them and feel my own guilt in watching them suffer. Their vile language would shock me if I didn't know what they know they are facing. Their personal morals in the prison, their crude disrespect of one another, the graffiti scrawled on their walls . . . Still, I feel they are men more sacred than I, for they have felt the wrath of man, and the abuse of man as I have not, in ways in which I have been spared. So who am I, I must always ask myself, to try to bring faith into the hearts of men who have been used by life so badly? *You,* Holy Father, are but a joke to them, and *faith* a foolish myth.

This particular young man has been on Death Row for two years, confined inside of a narrow cell . . . dear God, even a lion in a zoo has more freedom . . . that even cheats him of seeing the day. And hope! What a curse hope can be! I've had to watch him live through three promises of freedom when his lawyer sought to get his sentence changed . . . and watch his hopes rise, only to fall again when the governor refused to recognize his appeal. We are not to torture them, the law states. But who would not rather take lashes or be maimed than to have to sit for two years and wait for death? The very waiting is the most cunning torture even a devil could devise.

Help me, Holy Father. I need courage to face this day before me.

(*He gets to his feet and exits. Blackout.*)

SCENE ONE

Death Row in a State Penitentiary in the Midwest. Three cells are shown on stage. In the center cell is a young man of about thirty who, despite his mature years, still acts like a boy, seems to us like a boy. His name is JESS. *On his right is a fat, screechingly effeminate young man in his early twenties named* ARCHIE. *On his left, a middle-aged man named* LUKE.

It is very early morning. The sun is just beginning to rise, but we can see only a glimpse of it through the tiny, rectangular window in JESS's *cell, too high for him to look through unless he stands on his cot.* ARCHIE *and* LUKE *sleep soundly, snoringly.* JESS *sits on his cot, his head in his hands. He sits thus in total silence, in deep, troubled thought for several long moments. Then he stands on his cot and looks out of his window.*

———

JESS (*to himself, softly*). Day.

(*He stands thus several moments, looking out on the new day, trying to fill his lungs with the fresh air. Then he jumps down off his cot and rushes to the bars of his cell, calling loudly.*)

JESS. Guard! Bring me m'breakfast. It's day! I want a cuppa coffee fer Christ's sake! Bring me m'coffee. I need m'coffee like a man needs his blood. It's day.

ARCHIE (*without rousing from his cot*). Shut up.

LUKE (*same*). Let a man get his sleep.

(*Both* ARCHIE *and* LUKE *return to sleep,* LUKE *snoring heavily.*)

JESS (*to* LUKE, *who sleeps on*). I don't make as much noise talkin' as you do snoring. You snore like a goddamn buzz saw! There's nights when you kep' me awake all night with your goddamn snorin'. You got no right t'object if I holler for my breakfast.

ARCHIE. Shut up, you bitch!

LUKE. Go back to sleep.

JESS (*to* ARCHIE). Don't call me a bitch, you faggot. A bitch is what you call a woman. You talk like everyone in the whole goddamn world was a woman. But *I'm* no woman, see?

ARCHIE (*still without rousing*). Fuck you!

JESS. Fuck you, too. I may be a lotta things in this life, but I'm no goddamn faggot.

ARCHIE. Fuck you!

LUKE (*finally sitting up, speaking loud*). Will you two kids stop hollerin' and let a man get his rest?

ARCHIE. See there? She wants her beauty

sleep. You are interfering with Princess Lukemia's beauty sleep.

LUKE (*with disgust*). Oh shit! (*He lies back down and tries to return to sleep*).

JESS (*to* ARCHIE). Can't you ever call a man by his name, without calling him Princess this or Madame that? Do you have to make the whole world sound like faggots?

ARCHIE. Fuck you! (*He tries to return to sleep, huddling the covers around his shoulders.*)

JESS (*to himself, dreamily*). I always did like the early morning. When I was a kid back on the farm, Pa used to get me outa bed every morning at five o'clock. Yes sir. Five o'clock. Goddamn, some a those black winter mornings were cold as a bear's ass, and Pa 'n I'd make our way out to the barn to begin the chores, with Ma behind in the warm kitchen, and it'd be so cold and black, sometimes with the stars still in the sky, sometimes a little sliver of moon'd still be there, and we couldn't see anything in front of us except our breath. Our breath looked like fog steamin' up off the ground, or smoke out of a chimney. And it'd be so fuckin' cold, our noses'd be numb by the time we got to the barn to do the milkin'.

ARCHIE (*half-asleep*). Shut up.

JESS. But I remember spring mornings, too. Goddamn, they was pretty. After that long, freeze-ass winter, it was like Mama had taken you in her arms again, and smiled at you, and hugged you, when spring came again. And the sun came out early, and there'd just be a little chill in the air, enough to make you feel peppy 'n glad to be alive. And then we'd see the trees begin to sprout green buds, and a few weeks later they'd be full of leaves. And the fields would look like a green ocean, and around the house, the flowers Ma had planted would bring little spots of pretty colors to the front yard. Jesus! The world looked pretty then.

ARCHIE. Shut up, girl.

(*Now* JESS *goes suddenly wild with fear and panic and dread. He runs around his cell, shaking the bars, pounding them, as if he might contain the physical energy to break his way into freedom.*)

JESS. I don't wanna die. I don't wanna die. God, please! I don't wanna die. Do

something, God. Don't let 'em send me to the chair. Gimme a miracle or somethin', God! Make the governor decide to save me. Let him think of some of the good things I done in this life. I saved a little calf once. No shit. I saved its life when it was gonna die of pneumonia. I nursed that li'l calf every morning and kept her warm under her blankets, and made sure the vet gave me the right kinda medicines for her, and I *saved* her. She got well. In another six months, she was sassy and fat and Pa got a good price off her, when he sold her to . . . (*He thinks.*) . . . to be slaughtered. Jesus! After all that work I done savin' her life, Pa sold her to be slaughtered. (*He laughs cynically.*) Yah. That poor li'l calf grew up nice and fat finally and then they slaughtered her for veal chops. Jesus! What'd I go t'all that trouble for? Why'd I feel so proud at the time, proud of savin' her? When all they did was slaughter her? (*Screams*) Christ! I wanna live! I wanna see more summer mornings. I wanna see the leaves come in leaf again. I wanna see the calves and lambs born and grow. And I want corn-on-the-cob again, and strawberries, and the smell of honeysuckle. I wanna feel a girl's soft boobs again 'n get laid. I wanna see movies again, and eat ice cream. Christ! Let me into the world again. Please!

(ARCHIE *sits up in his cot, bristling with indignation.*)

ARCHIE. Look, *Mary!* Just because you're making your grand exit tonight is no sign the rest of us have to suffer the tortures of the damned.

JESS. Shut your dirty-sewer mouth, *Mary!*

(*The* GUARD *appears with trays. He wears a black shirt, and black trousers that are tucked inside his shiny black half-boots.*)

GUARD (*full voice*). Breakfast!

JESS. It's about time.

(*The* GUARD *sets a tray inside* LUKE's *cell but* LUKE *continues to sleep and snore Then he gets to* JESS's *cell.*)

GUARD. How'd ya sleep?

JESS. How ya think? (*He grabs for his coffee.*) Coffee and a butt. Thass all I been cravin' for the past two hours. (*He starts gulping his coffee as the* GUARD *leaves a tray in* ARCHIE's *cell.*)

ARCHIE. Bless you, Grosvenor, my good man. The Duchess is ready for her *petit déjeuner.*

(ARCHIE *takes the coffee and rolls and sips and nibbles with some elegance.*)

GUARD. Pretty fancy talk for a guy that killed his mama and his grandma.

ARCHIE. Judge not lest ye be judged, Grosvenor, dear. After all, "there are crimes and crimes."

GUARD. Well, you committed your share.

ARCHIE. And I shall receive due punishment, too, just like *Miss Jess* is going to get tonight, at the stroke of ten.

GUARD. You sure will.

ARCHIE. Meanwhile, I intend to enjoy life to the utmost, within the confines allowed me in this morbid environment.

GUARD. You're still gettin' your kicks, huh?

ARCHIE. Fortunately, man has not yet discovered any means of imprisoning the imagination. I read, I have my fantasies, occasionally I hear some lovely music on my hi-fi, and I always have *you,* dear, to come stalking down the corridors to greet me every morning in those crazy boots.

GUARD. You *like* the boots, huh?

ARCHIE. Mad for them.

GUARD. If you're a good boy, I'll come around some time and let ya lick 'em.

ARCHIE. Promise?

(*The* GUARD *laughs.*)

JESS. Hey, Guard! Any mail?

ARCHIE. Oh God! We're going to go through that routine again.

GUARD. You know it's not in yet, Jess.

JESS. No telegrams come during the night?

GUARD. Nope.

ARCHIE. Any *billet-doux* by carrier pigeon?

JESS. Don't pay no 'tention to him. You'll keep special watch for me, won't ya?

GUARD. I bring ya every bit of mail that comes with *your* name on it, Jess.

JESS. Goddamn it, there's gotta be a letter down there someplace.

GUARD. There's nothin' down there now.

JESS (*pulling a wrinkled post card from his pocket*). But the Ole Man wrote me this, see? He wrote me this card from Spokane and said he'd get here to see

me before it happened. Now, you may not know something about my old man, but *I* happen to know he's a man of his goddamned word, and if he says he's gonna get here, that means he's gonna get here.

GUARD. Sorry.

JESS. Okay, then. Are ya sure there's been no telephone calls?

GUARD. No telephone calls.

JESS. Look, maybe the telephone rang sometime when you guys in the office or wherever you hang out were too busy to notice.

GUARD. There's a woman on the switchboard, Jess. She gets every call that comes in.

JESS. And there's been no call from my old man?

GUARD. Nope. No call from your old man.

JESS. Okay.

GUARD. Wanna gimme your menu now, Jess?

JESS. Menu?

GUARD. Yah. The chef fixes ya anything ya want tonight. Remember?

JESS. Oh yeah.

GUARD (*pencil in hand*). What'll it be?

JESS. I dunno. I don't feel hungry now. It's hard to think of what you're gonna wanna eat at night when ya don't feel hungry in the morning.

ARCHIE. Order the grandest spread you can imagine, *honey.* Make that lousy chef get off his ass and work a little.

GUARD. Whatta ya like best to eat? It's as simple as that. Whatever it is, the chef'll fix it.

JESS. Lemme think. I allus liked fried chicken. I can't think of anything I ever liked better 'n fried chicken.

ARCHIE. What a dreary lack of imagination!

JESS (*to* ARCHIE). Okay. *You* tell me, *Duchess.* What's better 'n fried chicken?

ARCHIE. Fried chicken, although I admit it can be succulent, is a peasant dish. Make the chef come through with a little *haut cuisine.*

JESS. I never had any *o kwizeen.* What's it taste like?

ARCHIE. *Haut cuisine* is not a dish. It is the highest form of culinary accomplishment. *Haut cuisine* raises cooking to an art.

JESS. Yah? Where'd you ever have any?

ARCHIE. I admit I have not traveled enough to enjoy the world's great restaurants, but I have read about them.

JESS. What are they like?

ARCHIE. Well . . . if it were *I* ordering my last meal, I think I might ask for *filet mignon* with *Béarnaise* sauce.

JESS. I know what *filet mignon* is.

ARCHIE. The Duke de Guermantes in Proust discusses the *Béarnaise* sauce that was served him once on a trip from London. It had not been prepared to his liking. He complained, "Devil of a *Béarnaise* sauce," and it ruined his entire day.

JESS. Fuck that shit. What is it?

ARCHIE. Order it and find out.

JESS. Maybe I wouldn't like it.

ARCHIE. Somehow, I'm certain I would.

JESS. Suggest something else.

ARCHIE. Well . . . there's always *Lobster Thermidor*. It's a tasty concoction.

JESS. I've had lobster tails down in Florida.

ARCHIE. *My dear girl,* lobster tails are not to be compared with cold water lobster.

JESS. Yah?

ARCHIE. Of course not. Order *Lobster Thermidor* made with *Maine lobster*.

GUARD. Look. You gotta be reasonable. We don't have time to fly in any Maine lobster.

ARCHIE. Well, there's *Chicken Tarragon, Salmon Mousse, Pompano en Papillote, Sole Marguery, Beef à la Stroganov, Duck à l'Orange, Turkey stuffed with Paté de Foie Gras* . . .

JESS. I never heard of any of that shit.

ARCHIE. It's your last chance for a new "taste thrill."

JESS. Okay, *Mary.* You order my dinner for me, you know so much.

ARCHIE. Are you serious?

JESS. Sure. Go ahead and order.

ARCHIE. Very well. Guard, are you ready?

GUARD. Shoot.

ARCHIE. I think he should have a fragrant cold soup for an appetizer. *Vichyssoise?* Or perhaps a cold curry soup. Yes. Tell the chef he will begin with a cold *Sénégalese* soup.

GUARD. Jesus!

ARCHIE. S-É-N-É-G-A-L-E-S-E soup. Cold.

GUARD (*writing it down*). Okay.

ARCHIE. And I think perhaps a light *Mimosa Salad,* of limestone lettuce, chopped egg and artichoke hearts. (*He discerns the* GUARD's *confusion.*) Mimosa. M-I-M-O-S-A. The recipe should be in any reputable cook book.

GUARD. I'll write it down, but I'm not makin' any promises.

ARCHIE. And *Chicken Paprikash* on homemade noodles, remember. Homemade noodles make all the difference in the world.

GUARD. The chef knows how to make noodles.

ARCHIE. Chicken P-A-P-R-I-K-A-S-H. Got it?

GUARD. Got it. What's it mean?

ARCHIE. Paprika.

GUARD. Then why the fuck din ya say *paprika?*

ARCHIE. On proper menus, it's always listed *paprikash.*

GUARD. What else?

ARCHIE. Well . . . I think some asparagus might be tasty.

GUARD. Okay. Asparagus.

JESS. I don't like asparagus. I hate asparagus. It's the only vegetable I hate.

ARCHIE. Very well. Inasmuch as I was going to suggest a *Hollandaise* sauce with it, which really wouldn't go well with the rich paprika sauce, maybe we can dispense with the asparagus. (*To* JESS) Would you like to express a preference of any kind?

JESS. I like hash-browns.

ARCHIE. When you're already having rich noodles?

JESS. Yah. I want some hash-browns.

ARCHIE. That's a lot of starch in one meal.

JESS. I don't have to watch my diet now.

ARCHIE. Very well, give *her* some hash-browns, since she insists. And maybe some *Brussel sprouts,* in a light butter sauce.

GUARD. Brussel sprouts.

ARCHIE. That should make up the main course. Now for dessert. Let me think.

JESS (*with a sudden idea*). I know what I want for dessert. I want Cherries Jubilee.

ARCHIE. Where, pray tell, did *you* ever

hear of *Cherries Jubilee?*

JESS. I had 'em once, when I was in the Navy. A restaurant in San Francisco.

ARCHIE. I was going to suggest a lemon soufflé with brandy sauce.

JESS. *I want Cherries Jubilee!*

ARCHIE. It's a very *bourgeois* dessert.

JESS. I don't care if it's *bourgeois!* I want it.

ARCHIE (*to the* GUARD). Very well. Give her *Cherries Jubilee.*

GUARD. I got it.

JESS. And bring it to me flaming, so I can blow out the flame before I eat it.

GUARD. Okay. Cherries Jubilee. Coffee?

JESS. Yah. Lotsa coffee.

ARCHIE. And I do hope you'll be able to spare him a bottle of champagne. *Dom Pérignon '57.*

GUARD. Sorry. No booze.

ARCHIE. But no meal is complete without a proper wine.

GUARD. You know the rules. No *booze.*

ARCHIE. Wine is not booze.

GUARD. It is in this hotel. That all, Jess?

JESS. I guess so.

GUARD. Cake? Macaroons?

JESS. Yah. Maybe some macaroons.

ARCHIE. Tell the chef to put a little almond flavoring in them. Otherwise, they're like wet straw.

GUARD. I'll take the menu to him. He'll do the best he can.

JESS. And watch for the mail, Guard. Or a telegram. The Ole Man said he'd be here. I know I'll hear from him today.

GUARD. The mail don't come for another half hour. If there's any messages, you'll get 'em. That's for sure. (*The* GUARD *starts off.*) Luke. Wake up. Your breakfast's gettin' cold.

(*The* GUARD *goes off.* LUKE *slowly comes to. Rises to a sitting position, and finally gets out of bed to pick up his tray as* ARCHIE *and* JESS *talk.*)

ARCHIE. You're too much. Honestly, you're a hoot. What makes you think your old man is gonna come to see you fry?

JESS. Because I got a card from him, see? (*He holds the card outside his bars.*) And he says on this card, he's gonna be here to see me before I . . . (*He can't bring himself to say it.*)

ARCHIE (*sadistically*). What's the matter? The cat got your tongue?

JESS. Shut up.

ARCHIE (*laughing maniacally*). Before you *fry.* Why don't you say it?

(JESS *is silent. He can't say it.*)

ARCHIE. Come on and say it. I dare you. "Before I fry."

JESS. Why should I?

ARCHIE. Because that's what you're gonna do, isn't it? (JESS *is silent.*) Isn't it?

JESS. . . . I guess so. . . .

ARCHIE. *Guess* so! That's a hoot. You *know* so. (JESS *is silent.*) At least, you *should* know so. You don't honestly believe the governor is going to come through with a pardon, do you?

JESS. It's happened before.

ARCHIE. Oh shit, *Mary!* Sometimes you're too much. Sometimes I think you're a schizo. You believe things you see in movies. Quit trying to kid yourself, girl. You're gonna fry. And you're gonna crap your pants when they drag you off, just like the others.

JESS. Wanna bet?

ARCHIE. What?

JESS. That I don't crap my pants like the others.

ARCHIE. What's the use of betting? You won't be around to pay off.

JESS. Oh! I hadn't thought a . . .

ARCHIE. You'll be *gone,* Mary.

JESS. Look, goddamn it! I'm not a girl. I'm a man, you fuckin, lousy faggot. And if you call me *Mary* once more, I swear to Christ, I'm gonna get a crack at you before they send me up and choke that sewer throat of yours. . . .

ARCHIE. My sewer throat! That's a vivid metaphor.

JESS. You're a disgrace to human nature, even if you do have brains.

ARCHIE. Brains alone are, if not a disgrace, certainly an embarrassment to human nature. . . .

JESS. I admit you're smart. But you're still a faggot.

ARCHIE. Yes. And I am also a realist.

JESS. Whatta ya mean?

ARCHIE. I can face what's ahead of me.

JESS. I can, too.

ARCHIE. I heard you ranting a while ago, praying for God or the governor to intervene and save you from frying tonight.

JESS. I suppose you're looking forward

to when it happens to you?

ARCHIE. I'm really not very concerned.

JESS. That's because you're a goddamn psycho, on top of being a faggot, and you've got no human feelings about *any-thing.*

ARCHIE. What you call "human feelings" are only the product of centuries of conventional thinking that society has in-stilled in us in order to divert us from discovering the real crimes that they per-form in the name of *law.*

JESS. I don't know what you're talking about.

ARCHIE. The world itself is the great criminal.

JESS. Bullshit!

ARCHIE. And we are like insects that got caught in the world's web, and had to commit some violent act to get out. I feel no guilt whatever for my supposed *crimes.* And I regard my rapidly approaching death philosophically.

JESS. You're a freak.

ARCHIE. Perhaps it takes a freak to face reality. For instance, just look at the freak-ish irony of our situation. If we had the forethought to *plan* our murders across the border in one of our neighboring states, we would not now be on Death Row, but serving life sentences, working content-edly at some usual craft or employment to keep our evil minds occupied.

JESS. A lotta good it does to think about that now.

ARCHIE. True. It's merely an idle thought that sheds some light upon the incongrui-ties of human justice.

JESS. I wanna see my old man!

ARCHIE. Why can you not admit to your-self by this time that your old man is not going to show up, anymore than Christ is going to appear out of the clouds with a band of angels and carry us all up to heaven?

JESS. I hate talk like that.

ARCHIE. You hate it because it's true.

JESS. *You* say it's true. But you don't know *everything.*

ARCHIE. Oh, I humbly admit that.

JESS. Then admit that you don't know whether my old man is coming or not.

ARCHIE. If he comes, I'll say a thousand *Hail, Mary's!* (*Pause*) *Princess Lukemia!* Do *you* want to place a bet with me?

LUKE. What on?

ARCHIE. That *Miss Jessica* doesn't crap her pants tonight when they take her off to fry!

(LUKE *is silent for several long mo-ments.*)

JESS. Take the sonuvabitch up on it, Luke, I'm not gonna. You can count on *that!*

LUKE. Sure. I'll take your bet . . . *Dragon Lady.* (ARCHIE *laughs.*) How much do ya wanna bet?

ARCHIE. Anything you say, *Dearest.*

LUKE. I've got five bucks.

ARCHIE. It's a deal. I'll bet five bucks *she* does.

LUKE. Okay.

JESS (*under his breath*). Dirty . . . !

ARCHIE. What's that, *Sweetie?*

JESS. *You* heard me.

ARCHIE. Mad?

JESS. I hate guys like you, think they know everything.

LUKE (*sitting on his cot, eating his breakfast with the calm of one who has accepted his fate*). Pay no 'tention to him, Jess.

JESS. He riles me.

LUKE. That's all he wants to do. Don't give him the satisfaction of payin' any 'tention to him.

JESS. You're right, Luke.

ARCHIE. Holy Mother! All I'm trying to do is to drill an ounce or two of realism into your immature brain. It'll be so much easier tonight, when the guards come and lead you away. . . .

JESS. Shut up, Goddamn you!

ARCHIE. It'll be so much easier if you just admit that that's what's gonna hap-pen, and neither the governor, nor God, nor Jesus, nor the Holy Virgin is going to come down and stop it.

JESS. Shut up, Just shut up, will ya? That's all I ask, is just shut up!

ARCHIE. Very well.

JESS. I'll face . . . whatever I've got to face . . . my own way.

ARCHIE. I never tried to kid myself. After I shot my old lady and Gran', I just sat down and said, "Well, I've done it. I had to do it some time. There's no point in running away because *Miss Lily Law* would catch up with me in time. So I'll call them and tell them." That's what I did. I picked up the telephone and called the sheriff's office and said: "Mary, I've done it. Come on out and get me. And bring a couple of stretchers to carry them away in." And then I sat down and waited. They could hardly believe I'd really done it, I'd always been known around home as such a goody-good. But I *had* done it. Finally, they came to their senses and realized I wasn't kidding. Jesus! When they got a look at those bloody corpses in the kitchen, there was no denying anything. (*He laughs.*) One of the cops was a young fellow, new on the force. He vomited when he saw them. Oh dear! I've never had much patience with squeamish people.

JESS. You wanna know something. *I* wanna vomit, just listening to you talk.

LUKE. Me, too.

ARCHIE. Well! Forgive me for being here, please! I would gladly remove myself from your sensitive presence, but I'm afraid it's impossible under the circumstances.

LUKE. Pay no 'tention to him, Jess.

JESS. I won't.

LUKE. He's plain abnormal.

ARCHIE. *I'm* abnormal. *I* am. That's a hoot. (*He laughs uproariously.*) I suppose you two are *4-H Club winners!*

JESS. I *was.*

ARCHIE. It *can't* be.

JESS. I was a 4-H Club winner when I was seventeen.

ARCHIE. Well, congratulations, *Duckie!* It is very heartening to realize that a 4-H Club winner had the guts to kill his young wife just before she had a baby. That is the most delicious irony I've digested since reading Kafka. If I were in your cell, I would kiss both your cheeks for congratulations.

JESS. Which cheeks?

ARCHIE (*laughing even harder*). Oh, that's marvelous! You're honestly showing a little wit before they take you off to fry. Thank God. I hate to see a man lose all sense of humor, regardless how sordid the situation.

JESS (*looking at his watch*). The mail oughta be here.

LUKE. Relax, Jess.

JESS. There's *gotta* be a letter there. The Old Man *knows* this is the day.

LUKE. Look at it this way, Jess. His car may have stalled on the road. It's a long way 'tween here and Spokane. Yah. And he's gotta travel through the desert. He may be stalled some place where he can't even get in touch with you.

JESS. I hadn't thought of that.

ARCHIE. He's stalled some place in a bar, so drunk he can't get a dime into a phone booth. That's where he's stalled.

LUKE (*softly*). Pay no 'tention.

JESS. I won't.

LUKE. Ya got a mother, Jess?

JESS. No. She died.

LUKE. Any other kin?

JESS. A sister somewhere.

LUKE. She know?

JESS. I dunno. I ain't seen her since I was a kid.

LUKE. Oh.

JESS. I don't see no reason to beat around the bush about it. She was a whore.

LUKE. Shit, when I was a kid, I used to watch my old lady screw every man that came to the house. The plumber, the ice man, the electrician . . . Any man knocked on the door, she'd have him in bed in less time than it took her to put on her lipstick.

JESS. My old lady was very religious. I dunno which is worse. To have a mother that's a whore or one that's crazy religious. I think prob'ly one's as bad as the other.

LUKE. My wife's real religious. I din wanna marry anyone like my old lady.

JESS. No, I didn't, either. Wanda's no whore but we both had played around some before we got married.

LUKE. All kids do, these days.

JESS. Yah.

LUKE. When I was a kid, I din lose my cherry 'till I was eighteen.

JESS. No shit?

LUKE. Yah. I was shy.

JESS. Jesus, I lost mine when I was twelve.

ARCHIE. I was *eight.* That was undoubtedly the happiest day of my life. You'd both be appalled to hear the details.

LUKE. Save them.

ARCHIE. On technical grounds, however, some would consider me still a virgin. (*Begins to quote.*) "What lips my lips have kissed, and where, and why I have forgotten, and what arms have lain under my head till morning; but the rain is full of ghosts tonight that tap and sigh upon my glass and listen for reply. And in my heart there stirs a quiet pain . . ."

JESS. Turn off, fer Christ sakes!

ARCHIE. I think it's a lovely poem.

JESS. From you, it *stinks*.

LUKE. From you, *any*thing stinks.

ARCHIE. I can only admit that I am not admired in this company.

LUKE (*in a serious voice*). How ya feel, Jess?

JESS. You mean . . . about tonight?

LUKE. Yah.

JESS. I . . . I'm beginnin' to get scared, Luke.

LUKE. Ya.

JESS. Yah. I never really believed it 'till this morning. I went to sleep last night the same as any other night. But I woke up in an hour or two, and then I began to realize, this is *it*. This is really *it*. I couldn't kid myself any longer.

LUKE. I been wonderin' about that day. Wonderin' how I'll face it, myself.

JESS. My heart's been pounding ever since I woke up. I'm sweatin' like a stuck pig. My stomach's in knots. My throat's dry as sand. I wish it could happen now and I could get it over with.

LUKE. The way I look at it, Jess, death is just as . . . (*He searches for the right word.*) as *ordinary* as anything else. I mean . . . well, shit . . . if you was free now, you could get killed tonight out on the freeways just as easy as in the chair, and . . .

JESS. I know.

ARCHIE. Kierkegaard says that life itself is a prison and we all want to get out.

LUKE. What's *she* talkin' about?

JESS. I dunno.

ARCHIE. "Therefore, since the world has still much good, but much less good than ill, I'd face it as a wise man would and train for ill and not for good."

LUKE. That one's got a quotation for *every*thing.

ARCHIE. Never expect anything good to happen. That's my motto. Then you're never disappointed.

JESS. I hate t'admit it, but maybe the son of a bitch is right.

LUKE. I hate faggots.

JESS. I knew one in reform school was a nice guy. Smart, too. Used to help me with my lessons.

LUKE. They're all smart.

JESS. I guess so.

LUKE. I allus beat the shit out of 'em when they came hangin' round me.

JESS (*reading his post card*). "Dear Son Jess. I'll be leaving Spokane tomorrow morning. It may take me five or six days to make the trip as my old car is pretty run down. But I'll get there or bust."

ARCHIE. He's busted. Send someone out to pick up the pieces.

LUKE. When did you get that, Jess?

JESS. Three weeks ago.

LUKE. And no word of any kind since?

JESS. No.

LUKE. Ya ask the warden to try to get in touch with him?

JESS. They looked all over Spokane. No one could find him.

LUKE. Too bad, kid, I know how ya feel. It'd be kinda nice to have your kin come see ya before it happens. On the other hand, sometimes they only make ya feel worse. Like my wife. Every time she comes to visit, I feel lower'n whale shit the rest a the day.

JESS. If I could just talk to *some*one that . . . maybe cared something about me . . . I'd feel better.

LUKE. Ya like your old man?

JESS. Yah. He was a great guy . . . mosta the time.

LUKE. That's good.

JESS. He used to beat hell outa me once in a while, but I got so, I could give it back to him, good as I got.

LUKE. When's the last ya seen him?

JESS. 'Bout five years ago, when I left home.

LUKE. A man can change a lot in five years.

JESS. Wanda and I got married two years ago. We had a real nice letter from him when we wrote him we were gonna have a baby. He sent us ten bucks to put aside for the kid. Pretty nice of him, wasn't it?

LUKE. Yah. Does he drink?

JESS. Some times.

LUKE. Every one drinks some times.

JESS. After he lost his farm, he started

drinkin' pretty heavy. But he was depressed. He din know what he was gonna do. He still has a hard time makin' a living for hisself.

LUKE. I see.

JESS. But he's no alcoholic or anything. He's got too much strength a character fer that.

LUKE. Maybe he just don't have the guts to come see ya . . . here on Death Row. Maybe he just couldn't bring hisself to face it.

JESS. Shit! My old man's not afraid a *anything*. Still it must be pretty hard to go talk with someone that's gonna fry. What could a person say? (*Eyes off left*) Jesus! Here's the mail! (*Hollering:*) Bring me that letter, Guard! Let's have it now!

(*The* GUARD *appears stage left, carrying a few pieces of mail.*)

GUARD. Here y'are, Luke.

LUKE (*taking the letter*). Thanks.

JESS (*anxiously*). Give it to me, Guard. I know ya got *some*thing there for me. Let's have it!

GUARD. Yah, here's *some*thing, but I don't know *what*. (*Passes a letter to* JESS.)

JESS. Le's see! Le's see . . .

(JESS *tears open the letter anxiously*.)

GUARD (*to* ARCHIE). Nothing for you, *Gloria*.

ARCHIE. What? I didn't get a letter from Alain Delon? *Quel dommage!*

LUKE. What is it, Jess?

JESS (*ripping it up*). An advertisement for a gas furnace.

ARCHIE (*after a wild fit of laughter*). A lot of need you'll have for a furnace where you're going!

LUKE. Sorry.

JESS. They forwarded it from the address Wanda and I lived at, two years ago. It got sent to two other addresses before it got here.

LUKE. One thing you can allus depend on in this life. The crap allus comes through.

JESS. Yah. The crap allus comes through.

(*The* CHAPLAIN *appears stage right, dressed in a long black skirt.*)

CHAPLAIN. Good morning, Luke.

LUKE. Morning, Father.

CHAPLAIN. Good morning, Jess.

JESS. Hi!

CHAPLAIN. I'm sorry you didn't hear from your father.

JESS. It don't matter.

CHAPLAIN. I wish you felt like talking to *me*, Son.

JESS. Don't call me son. You're not my father.

CHAPLAIN. Maybe I could be if you'd let me.

JESS. I don't understand that shit.

CHAPLAIN. You could look upon me as a father. You could talk to me as one.

JESS. But you *ain't* my father. What's the good of pretending?

CHAPLAIN. We all of us share the same Father, Jess. In heaven.

JESS. I want my father here on *earth*.

CHAPLAIN. I wish you'd reconsider me.

JESS. What for?

CHAPLAIN. Maybe I could give you confidence in what you have to face. Maybe I could make it easier. Maybe I could give you faith.

JESS. What in?

CHAPLAIN. The life everlasting.

JESS. I don't want the life everlasting. I want life *now*.

CHAPLAIN. I could help you accept death.

JESS. I don't *wanna* accept it. Death is an enemy. I hate it!

CHAPLAIN. I wish I could bring you solace.

JESS. Bring me what?

CHAPLAIN. Solace, peace.

JESS. Peace! When I know that in a few more hours I'll be in the chair? Do you expect me to feel peace when I know that?

CHAPLAIN. I could help you face death.

JESS. How?

CHAPLAIN. The true Father can forgive us any of our sins, and help us face death peacefully.

(JESS *thinks it over*.)

JESS. I want my ole man to forgive me. I want to tell him just how it was. Why I done what I done. I want to make him under*stand*.

CHAPLAIN. Our heavenly Father can understand *all* our sins.

JESS. Well . . . I want my earthly father to talk to. He's the only father I ever knowed.

CHAPLAIN. Sometimes those we love disappoint us, Jess.

JESS. What do you mean?

CHAPLAIN. Few humans can help us face eternity.

JESS. I still wanna talk to him!

CHAPLAIN. He has failed you. Our holy Father never fails us.

JESS. Then why am I here?

CHAPLAIN. You transgressed.

JESS. So they're gonna kill *me* to make things right.

CHAPLAIN. That's *man's* law.

JESS. But it ain't right I should die.

CHAPLAIN. I cannot dispute that.

JESS. They could keep me here, couldn't they? And give me some kinda work to do. I wouldn't be no threat to anyone. Why do they have to treat me like a . . . like a calf . . . in a slaughter-house?

CHAPLAIN. God can even help us to accept injustice, and still love those who would destroy us.

JESS. I can't see it that way. I just know it's not right I should have to die.

CHAPLAIN. We must abide by man's law, too, while we're on earth.

JESS. But man's law and God's aren't the same. How can we abide by both when they're not the same?

CHAPLAIN (*gently*). You committed a grievous sin.

JESS. I had reasons for doin' what I done. I ain't saying I was right to do it. I *wasn't* right. But it's not right to kill *me*, either. It's not gonna bring my wife and kid back to life for them to kill *me*, is it?

CHAPLAIN. I'm not here to argue the laws of man. We have to accept them as they are for the time being. I can only help you to face the fate that man has decreed for you, with courage and faith, and peace in your heart when that last moment comes.

JESS. What difference does it make? It don't take long, anyway. You walk into the room and sit down and in a few seconds, it's all over. So what difference does it make how I face it?

CHAPLAIN. The noblest thing man can do is to face his own death with faith and love in his heart.

JESS. I'm no hypocrite! I'm not gonna get down on my knees *now*, and say "I'm sorry, God," when all my life I never done any praying, never paid any 'tention to God, din even know whether I believed in Him or not, and what's more, din even care. No. I'm not gonna be a goddamn hypocrite and start praying now!

CHAPLAIN. It wouldn't be hypocrisy if you could really find Him now, in your heart, and pray to Him. (*Pause;* JESS *listens.*) Some of us never find Him until we face death, or some other crisis. But He always welcomes us, no matter when we find Him, or how.

JESS. You're wasting your time, mister.

CHAPLAIN. Very well, Jess. I'll be back again this evening. Maybe you'll feel differently then. Would you like to talk to me, Luke?

LUKE. Not now, Father.

CHAPLAIN. Archibald?

ARCHIE. I'm getting along just beautifully, thank you, *Dear*.

CHAPLAIN. Very well. Good day, men.

ALL. { So long.
{ Good day, Father.

(*The* CHAPLAIN *goes off left.*)

ARCHIE. It's basic black for that *girl* every season. Why doesn't *she* liven up that *drag* with a few emeralds?

LUKE. You oughta call him *Father*, Jess.

JESS. Why?

LUKE. A body just does. Whether he's a Catholic or not.

JESS. But he *ain't* my father.

LUKE. It's just a sign of respect.

JESS. I'll call him *mister*. That's enough respect. He's just another man to me.

ARCHIE. You said Death is an enemy. I'd say Life was *my* enemy. I gave up my belief in God and all that hogwash the same time I gave up playing with dolls.

JESS. You don't b'lieve in nothin'.

ARCHIE. I suppose that's true.

JESS. You believe in God, Luke?

LUKE. Oh sure, Jess. I b'lieve in God.

JESS. I dunno if I do or not.

LUKE. I heard ya prayin' this morning.

JESS. Yah?

LUKE. Din you hear yourself?

JESS. I guess it's just habit, left over from childhood.

LUKE. I never think to pray like my wife's allus tellin' me to, but I *b'lieve.* Yes sir!

JESS. I guess I pray lots of times without knowing it. I allus prayed when I was a kid. Th'old lady brought me up that way. I find myself . . . sometimes . . . just outa habit . . . praying. Like, I'll say: "Dear God, please do this for me, or that." But I'm not too sure there's anyone up there listening.

LUKE. Oh, there's a God, all right, Jess. Course there is. I dunno if he's gonna do *me* any good, but he's *there.*

ARCHIE (*singing gaily*). "Somebody up there *hates* me! Somebody up there *hates* me!"

JESS. A memory came to me this morning, Luke.

LUKE. Yah?

JESS. The time I nursed a sick calf back to health. The vet had told my old man there was no use tryin' to save her. But I din want her to die. I nursed her all night and all day and I saved her, Luke. No shit. I saved her life.

LUKE (*touched*). Yah?

JESS. But they . . . (*He begins to choke up.*) Jesus, what's the matter with me?

LUKE. You cryin'?

JESS. Yah. For *some* reason. I dunno why.

LUKE. Your feelings are on edge.

JESS. No. I know why I'm cryin'. They sent her to the slaughter-house that next spring.

LUKE. Oh!

JESS. I never realized how bad that made me feel, Luke. Jesus! I hated my old man then. I begged him to let me keep the calf after I'd nursed her the way I done. We got to be real friends, that calf 'n me. She'd kiss me. No shit. I'd go out to the barn every morning bright 'n early, 'n feed her, and she'd kiss me, like she knew I'd helped save her life.

ARCHIE. Was that your *first* girl friend?

JESS (*infuriated*). You really *are* a pervert! You got no human feelings. You can't let a decent thing exist in the whole damn world, can you? No! You gotta make everything dirty. *Dirty!* Jesus, you disgust me!

ARCHIE. My! *She's* in a rage.

LUKE. Pay no 'tention, Jess.

JESS (*Pause: to* LUKE). I remember now . . . I brooded a long time after the old man sent her away. He tried to reason with me. "That's the way of life, my boy. Man kills to live." But I couldn't see it that way.

ARCHIE. Get you! *You* killed, didn't you?

JESS (*slowly*). . . . . I admit it.

ARCHIE. You killed your wife when she was pregnant, for Christ sake, and now you're carrying on like *Hecuba* because of a calf! The calf was killed for a reason. You killed your wife and unborn child for *no* reason.

JESS. How do *you* know?

ARCHIE. Oh, I heard about the testimony at the trial. You killed them with no reason at all. Then you tried to kill yourself and chickened out.

JESS. Shut up!

ARCHIE. You even said you loved your wife.

JESS. I did.

ARCHIE (*in a sing-song, mocking voice*). "Yet each man kills the things he loves. By all let this be heard. Some do it with a . . ."

JESS. Maybe I had reasons I din wanna talk about.

ARCHIE. You call *me* a pervert, and say I've got no human feelings, while you're crying about a calf that gets slaughtered after you yourself slaughtered your wife and child. And the calf was slaughtered for a perfectly good reason. I happen to like veal, as do many other people. But you killed your wife and kid for no god-damn reason, at all!

JESS. I had my reasons.

ARCHIE. All right, what were they?

JESS. You wouldn't understand.

ARCHIE. Dear boy! I happen to have an I.Q. of one hundred and forty-five. If *I* cannot understand, whom, pray tell, can you expect to?

JESS. Maybe no one. Whatta I care?

ARCHIE. If you could have come up with a reason for killing them, you might not be here today, at the *Death Row Hilton.*

JESS. It's too late to worry 'bout that now.

(*There is a silence.*)

LUKE. Why *did* you kill her, Jess? Do you know?

JESS. Maybe.

LUKE. Did you talk it over with the headshrinker here?

JESS. Yah.

LUKE. Ya figure it out?

JESS. Oh . . . it's all kinda complicated. I . . . I just don't wanna talk about it,

Luke.

LUKE. To tell the truth, it allus puzzled *me* . . . why you done it. I mean, I killed a man in an armed robbery. I had to kill him, or he'd kill me. There was never any two ways about it. I was scared, shitless. That's th' oney reason I killed. But . . . why would *you* come home one night and kill your wife just a few weeks before she was to have her kid? It beats me.

JESS. It beats me, too. I'm not sure I really know.

LUKE. You seem like a *nice* kid to *me*, in most ways. But I got a long record. I got a wife 'n' two kids. We din' always get along too great, but I never wanted to kill 'em.

JESS. I dunno, Luke. I guess I just went off my nut when I done it. Ya wanna *know* something? I'd never planned to kill *them*, or anyone else. It'd never even occurred to me. And then one night, I found myself doin' it. And I couldn't believe it when I found myself doin' it. I couldn't believe it.

ARCHIE. You were probably subconsciously afraid the kid would look like somebody's else's kid. That's my guess.

JESS. Turn off, creep!

ARCHIE. You had to have *some* reason. No one kills without *some* reason. Even the *joy* of killing is a reason. Jesus! I enjoyed killing Granny and the Old Lady. I loved it! God, how I loved it. (*He gives an imitation of his mother and grandmother getting stabbed by him.*) "My God, Bess! Archie-boy is stabbing me. Oh! My God! Archie-boy! I'm your mother. Archie-boy! I'm your darling grandmother. I love you, Archie-boy. I love you!" (*He laughs like a fiend.*) *Love.* The more they used that horseshit word, the deeper I struck. Love. Those old crows, talking about *love*. Love is *shit*. Love is *shit*.

JESS (*quietly*). I din enjoy killing.

LUKE. How'd ya do it, Jess?

JESS. I woke up one night. Wanda was sleeping beside me. Very sound. And I leaned over her and looked her full in the face, and I kissed her on the lips, and then . . .

LUKE. Yah?

JESS. I put my hands around her throat, and pressed the breath out of her. That's all.

LUKE. Simple as that, huh?

JESS. Simple as that. And then I kissed her again, and told her I was sorry. But she didn't hear.

LUKE. Hmmmmmmmm.

JESS. And then, like *Mary* says, I tried to kill myself and couldn't do it.

LUKE. Why?

JESS. I just couldn't do it. That's all.

LUKE. I mean, why did you intend to in the first place?

JESS. I was tired, trying to live.

LUKE. Yah.

JESS. It was hard.

LUKE. *I* know.

JESS. Ya know something? I was never pre*pared* to live. I was green. No one ever told me what it was like when you were out on your own, with no way of making a living except . . . with your hands. Labor. Common labor. That's all I was good for.

LUKE. I was trained as a mechanic, and I made a living that way.

JESS. I shoulda trained to be a mechanic or something like that while I was in high school, but I spent all my time in sports, to make m' old man proud of me.

LUKE. I made a *purty* good living, but a man allus wants to do *better*. People look down on him if he's just a mechanic.

JESS. Yah. I felt like I had to make it *big*, for some goddamn reason. I felt I had to drive a Caddy, 'n' wear neat clothes, make people notice me.

LUKE. That's a bait we all swallow.

JESS. Jesus, I got to the place where I'd do *anything* fer money! Do things I din like doin', just to make out.

LUKE. Yah.

JESS. I used to hate m'self fer some a the things I done.

LUKE. Tell the truth, I never *had* to rob to make a living. But it seemed so easy, to get that extra bread and buy yourself some a the trimmings of life. Just to make yourself feel you're doin' as well as the next fella.

JESS. Yah. I guess we're all that way.

ARCHIE. I never fell for that crap of making it *big*, and driving a Caddy. I killed because I hated. Pure and simple. I hated those hypocritical old biddies, and couldn't stand to be around them anymore. I wouldn't mind staying in prison forever, because it's a *man's* world, and you don't have to try and get along with women. I suppose what I should have done is go to Denmark and have one of those operations and become a woman, myself. I had a friend in Chicago who did that. *She* came back from Denmark looking like *Brigitte Bardot*. Tits and everything! She had one man who wanted to marry her. Honestly!

LUKE. Yah, but could she have kids?

ARCHIE. Who cares? The world's most serious problem now is overpopulation.

JESS. There's gonna be one less by to-morrow.

LUKE. But you said you *wanted* to die.

JESS. It's one thing for a man to kill his-self because he don't *wanna* live, and an-other thing entirely to have others kill you because they don't think you got a right to live. That's what hurts most! Other men are making me die. And I don't feel that's their right.

LUKE. I still can't unnerstand a young fella like *you* wantin' t' die.

JESS. To tell the truth, life didn't seem *worth* living to me at the time, Luke. The whole world looked so ugly to me then, I thought life wasn't worth the effort.

LUKE. Yah!

JESS. And after killing *them,* my wife and kid, I found out *I* didn't have the guts to kill myself. I turned out to be a real chicken-shit, after all. I was gonna do away with *all* of us, but didn't have the guts to kill myself. What a chicken-shit I turned out to be. What an A Number One Chicken-shit I was!

ARCHIE. I have no regrets at all. But I had no intention of killing myself. I'd do the same thing over again. I only wish I had the *chance* to do it over again. Too bad. You can have the pleasure of killing someone only once. I'd like nothing better than to kill those old bitches every day, and watch them moan, and cry, and holler about *love.* Love, love, love, love, love! *Shit!*

(*The* GUARD *comes on from Left, shout-ing.*)

GUARD. Shut up, *Duchess.* There's a real lady outside.

ARCHIE. Oh, of course! Let's not offend the *fair* sex.

GUARD. Your wife, Luke.

LUKE. Mona? Today?

(*The* GUARD *returns off Left.*)

ARCHIE. Oh Christ, it's *pious Penelope,* come to bring us her blessings.

LUKE. You shut up, Faggot! I happen to love and respect my wife.

ARCHIE. I was sure you *would.*

(*The* GUARD *returns with* MONA, *a drab woman in her forties.*)

LUKE. Oh . . . hi, Mona. Golly, this is a surprise.

(*The* GUARD *unlocks the cell door and* MONA *enters. Throughout this scene,* ARCHIE *listens and reacts with occasional grimaces.*)

GUARD. Twenty minutes, Ma'm.

(*The* GUARD *exits.* MONA *stands looking upon* LUKE *with pious sweetness.*)

LUKE. I . . . I wasn't expecting you to-day, Mona.

MONA (*somewhat too compassionate*). Did you think I would let a week go by without coming to see my husband?

LUKE. No, but you usually come on Thursday afternoons, so I . . .

MONA. This Thursday, I'm meeting Mama at the airport. She's coming to visit. So I decided to come see you today.

LUKE. Oh, well that's *great.* Yah! It sure is good to see you, Mona.

MONA. You know you can always count on *me,* Luke. I'm not the kind of wife who deserts her husband in a time of need.

LUKE. Yah. Well . . . thanks, Mona. Uh . . . you're very thoughtful.

MONA. And I still pray for you every night, Luke.

LUKE (*more and more uncomfortable*). Thanks.

MONA. We may have had our disagree-ments at times, Luke, and there may have been many times when I disapproved of your life, but I'm not one to hold grudges now.

LUKE (*offering a chair*). Here, Mona. If you're gonna stay a while, ya might as well sit down and be comfortable.

MONA (*sitting*). Thank you, Luke.

LUKE. How are the kids?

MONA. Oh, they're fine. They send you their love, of course.

LUKE. That's nice. Tell 'em I think of 'em.

MONA. Of course.

LUKE. Uh . . . Mona, I . . . I never ast ya, but I've been wondering all this time . . . Do the kids look down on me? You know how I mean.

MONA (*stoically*). I have told them they must *still* honor their father, like the Bible says.

LUKE. Oh . . . thanks.

MONA. Of course, it's not easy. Some of the other school children look down on them.

LUKE. Yah . . . I suppose. (*He appears mournful.*) I'm sorry.

MONA. It's hard for them.

LUKE. Yah.

MONA. I wish I could bring them with me some time, but somehow I don't feel it's right for them to see you here.

LUKE. No. I don't want them to see me.

MONA. Now let's talk about something more cheerful, shall we?

LUKE (*delayed reaction*). Oh sure . . . anything you say.

MONA. I saw the sweetest movie last night. A Walt Disney, about three pet animals, the cutest little dog, and a Siamese cat, and a tame raccoon, and they made their way all through miles of forest to find their master. It was *so* dear. I went with Jeanette and we both sat there and cried and cried.

LUKE. I saw a good show on TV the other night. An old Cagney film. One I'd missed before. It was great.

MONA. I always liked Spencer Tracy.

LUKE. Yah! He was great, too.

(*There is a long, uncomfortable silence between them now; both of them search their minds desperately for conversation material.*)

MONA. Lorna had her first date the other night.

LUKE. Oh, that right?

ARCHIE (*under his breath*). How *sweet!*

MONA. Yes. I hesitated to let her. Only *fourteen.* But other girls her age are dating now. And I don't want to be too strict with her.

LUKE. No. Course not.

ARCHIE (*very sotto voce*). Of course not! Let her get laid like all the other little darlings.

MONA (*after another uncomfortable pause*). Children are growing up awfully fast today.

LUKE. Yah. Sure are.

ARCHIE. Yes, they sure are! They're growing up fast enough, to know what a bitch *you* are.

MONA. Junior is smoking.

ARCHIE. Pot or hashish?

MONA. He denies it, but I always smell it on him.

LUKE. Sorry to hear that.

MONA. I just pray to God that they stay away from that marijuana and L.S.D. They're having lots of trouble with some of the children in school with things like that.

LUKE. Yah. You tell 'em to keep away from things like that.

MONA. I do my best with them, Luke. You can depend on that.

LUKE. Sure. Of course ya do, Mona. I'm not worried 'bout that.

MONA. But it's not easy.

LUKE. I s'pose not.

MONA. They feel they have something to live *down* now.

LUKE. Yah. I s'pose I've been a bad influence.

MONA. Oh, I don't look at it that way, I tell myself we all have our crosses to bear.

LUKE. Yah. I guess we do.

MONA (*suddenly*). Oh! (*Begins looking through her handbag.*) I brought you a little booklet. Here it is. Jeanette gave me a copy and I just live by it. *"A Prayer to Greet the Day With."* I can't tell you what a blessing this little book has been to me. So I got one for you, too, Luke. A different prayer for every day of the year. Now if you'll read one of these each morning just as soon as you awaken, it's going to help you get through the day. I just know it will. Here, dear.

LUKE (*accepting the little booklet*). Thank you.

MONA. Well, I . . . suppose I may as well be going now.

LUKE. Well . . . no need to rush off.

ARCHIE. No. Just get on that broom and start flying pronto!

MONA. My twenty minutes is about up, anyway.

LUKE. Okay.

MONA. I just wanted you to know that I still care.

LUKE. Yeah . . . thanks, Mona.

MONA. And you can bet, I'm still holding my head high whenever I go out anywhere, Luke. I'm not going to let anyone think I'm *ashamed.*

LUKE. Yeah . . . that's fine.

MONA. There are some people in town who won't speak to me anymore, but I know that their lives are not without fault, either.

LUKE. You bet.

MONA. There are lots of people in that town who . . . who've done things just as bad as . . . as bad as anyone else . . . who are in no position to criticize *any*one.

LUKE. Yeah. Sure.

MONA. "Let him who is without sin cast the first stone." That's the attitude *I* take.

LUKE. Yeah.

MONA. So I still hold my head high when I walk down the aisle at church, and keep a smile on my face just to show people that I still have my pride.

LUKE. Yeah. Good for you, Mona.

MONA. Well . . . goodby, dear.

(*She stands.* LUKE *kisses her on the cheek.*)

LUKE. 'Bye, Mona.

MONA. And I'll be back again next week. You can depend on that. I'm not going to let my husband down.

ARCHIE. Bring him some dirty pictures, Honey, and we'll *all* have fun.

LUKE. Yeah. Fine, Mona. See ya next week. Fine. (*Calling:*) Guard!

(*The* GUARD *hurries on, unlocking the door.*)

MONA. Next week, I'll bring you some Brownies. I didn't have time to make any for today.

LUKE. Yah. They allus taste good.

(MONA *walks out of the cell.*)

MONA. Goodby!

LUKE. 'Bye, Mona!

(*She is off.* LUKE *remains motionless.*)

ARCHIE. My god, what a *ghoul!*

LUKE (*suddenly fierce*). You shut up, you dirty faggot! My wife's a fine woman!

ARCHIE. Sorry.

(LUKE *sits now with his hands over his face. We hear him begin to sob softly.*)

JESS. Whatsa matter, Luke?

LUKE. She talks to me . . . like I was already dead.

THE LIGHTS FADE

SCENE TWO

Night. JESS *sits on his bunk, his head in his hands.* ARCHIE *is finishing up the splendid repast that he ordered for* JESS. LUKE *sits idly, an expression on his face of one who has given up all hope.*

———

ARCHIE. A splendid repast. I shall recommend the chef to St. Peter, after I have my turn in the chair. I am most grateful to you, Jess.

JESS. You're welcome.

ARCHIE. There are few things in life more gratifying than a good meal.

JESS. I couldn't touch it.

ARCHIE. If only you hadn't insisted on those *hash-browns!* I feel bloated.

LUKE. Very hospitable of them, ain't it? The day you're gonna die, they fix you a grand meal and who can enjoy it, knowing it's his last? Why don't they give us better grub when we can enjoy it?

ARCHIE. One man's loss is another's gain. "Devil of a *Béarnaise* sauce!" I relished every morsel. The Mimosa salad was from heaven!

LUKE. Why did you give it to *him?* The pig.

JESS. *You* din want it.

LUKE. No. That rich food never agreed with me.

JESS. I din want it to go to waste. I hate to see things go to waste.

LUKE. I wouldn't feed horse-turds to that freak.

JESS. *She* enjoyed it.

ARCHIE. Indeed I did. It was a *Lucullan* feast. Now I should like to spend the evening out. Maybe the theatre. Yes. It would be pleasant now to see a lovely performance of *Swan Lake,* or attend an elegant masquerade ball at the *Plaza,* dancing with all the *haut monde* of society.

LUKE (*to* JESS). That one can sure dream up big ideas.

ARCHIE. But, under the circumstances, I suppose I shall remain *in* tonight. Besides, the weather is a little inclement. I'll read a little Nietzsche, perhaps, until *Miss Jessica* takes her leave of us, and then curl up in bed with some delicious dirty fantasies, and fall into a deep slumber. (*To* JESS) I'll miss you in the morning, *Jessica dear.*

JESS. I won't miss you.

ARCHIE. Sorry!

LUKE. That's one thing you got to be thankful for, Jess. You won't be waking up anymore with that morphidite beside you.

ARCHIE. *Princess Lukemia,* I hate to trouble the shallow waters of your ignorance, but I am *not* a morphidite.

LUKE. Whatever the hell you call yourself, you're not made like other men.

ARCHIE. You are inferring then that all men are made *alike?*

LUKE. Yes.

ARCHIE. That's medieval.

LUKE. It's *what?*

ARCHIE. Medieval. It's the kind of thinking that belongs in the Dark Ages.

LUKE. Thanks for telling me.

ARCHIE. There are no two men on the face of the earth who are made *exactly* alike. Think of it! It's almost incredible, isn't it? You'd think that, out of accident if nothing else, it would happen sometimes that two people were identical.

LUKE. I just hope there's no more like you, *dearie.*

ARCHIE. I'm sure there isn't.

LUKE. It's men like you that cause all the trouble in the world. You with all your smart-ass thinking. You make all kinds of trouble. You're a morphidite and a Red.

ARCHIE. *What?*

LUKE. You heard me!

ARCHIE. Why do you assume that because I'm a faggot I'm a Communist?

LUKE. The two go together.

ARCHIE *(to himself).* To think that I have to endure the society of such *primitive* mentalities.

LUKE. Well, maybe you're not a Red, but I know damn well you're a *morphidite.*

ARCHIE. I assure you, I am made just as other men, even though, as I said before, no two of us are identical.

LUKE. I don't believe you've got a cock and balls like other men. You couldn't, and talk and act the way you do.

ARCHIE. But I do. More's the pity. For the little good they do me here.

LUKE. Well, I know this much. There's something wrong with you *somewhere.* I may not know where. But *some*where, there's something very wrong about the way you're made.

ARCHIE. My physical examination showed me to be normally made and in excellent health.

LUKE. Maybe on the outside, but I bet that *inside* your organs are all mixed up somehow, and you've got a vagina stuck away somewhere up in your esophagus.

ARCHIE. Oh dear, I should give anything to find it.

JESS. Cut out this kinda talk a while, will ya, fellas? *(Silence)* It's makin' me kinda sick. . . .

ARCHIE. Pity!

JESS. I'd like to be kinda silent for a while, if ya don't mind.

LUKE. Sure, Jess.

JESS. I'm just tryin' to get used to the fact that . . . in another hour or so . . . I'll be gone.

LUKE. Yah. I think about it, too.

JESS. I never thought I'd be so scared . . . until this morning, when I woke up and knew the day was here.

LUKE. I guess no one knows exactly how he's gonna feel about death, until he faces it.

JESS. Jesus, I'm scared, Luke!

LUKE. I don't blame ya, kid.

JESS. Are ya sure it don't hurt much, Luke?

LUKE. It ain't happened to me yet, Jess, but they say it just lasts a few minutes, and then you're gone.

JESS. Gone. *(He thinks a moment.)* Gone where?

LUKE. That's something I never figured out, Jess.

JESS. Ya s'pose people like us, really go down to hell and burn . . . for*ever?*

LUKE. I dunno, Jess.

ARCHIE. Hell! That's a hoot. Why don't you boys bring your minds up to date? There's no more *hell* than there is a *heaven.*

JESS. My old lady was allus filling me and my sis with stories about *hell-fire-and-damnation.* She went nuts on that religious shit, though! They finally had to take her away to the asylum.

ARCHIE. She'd have to be nuts to believe it in the first place.

JESS. I just wonder . . . if I *have* got a soul . . . where's it goin'?

ARCHIE. No place, *honey.* This is the end of the line.

JESS. I can't help wondering.

LUKE. Why don't you talk to the priest, Jess?

JESS. What for?

LUKE. He might help you to feel better about it.

JESS. He can't stop it from happening.

LUKE. No. But he can give ya a li'l courage, maybe.

JESS. How?

LUKE. I dunno, but . . .

JESS. The oney thing that'd help would be to talk to m' old man a little while.

LUKE. It don't look like he's gonna make it now, Jess. Ya may as well try the priest.

JESS. I don't see the point.

LUKE. You can't lose anything by tryin'.

ARCHIE. Any kind of talk about God absolutely gives me the creeps.

LUKE. Try it, Jess.

JESS. Well . . . shit! I don't mind talkin' to him. But if he expects me to get down and pray, and make-believe like I was holy or somethin', it's no good.

LUKE. He don't expect ya to say anything you don't believe.

JESS. I don't have anything against the guy, but I wanna talk to my *own* father. That's who I really wanna talk to!

LUKE. He's not gonna make it, Jess.

ARCHIE (*singing*). Fare thee well,
Daddy's gone goodbye.
No need to sigh.
No need to cry . . .

LUKE. Shut up, faggot!

ARCHIE. Jesus, the last person in the world I'd ever wanna talk to would be *my* old man!

JESS. You'n I are two *different* people!

ARCHIE. He was a total stranger around the house. I never could believe he was really my father. We never had two words to say to each other. Whenever he did come home, he'd look at me like I was something that had been dropped down the chimney by a *flamingo*.

JESS. My ole man and me used to fight sometimes, but he liked me. I know he did.

ARCHIE. When I was twelve years old, my old man took one look at me, with red nail polish on and mascara, and said, "Jesus Christ! Is that what I brought into the world?" And then he took out and never came back. (*Laughs*.) What a hoot!

LUKE. I don't blame him!

JESS. I made my ole man proud of me . . . two or three times. I was a good basketball player . . . and once I won the broad jump in the all-state track meet.

ARCHIE. How many *broads* did you jump, *honey*?

LUKE. A guy can't even make an ordinary kind of remark without him twistin' it into somethin' dirty!

ARCHIE. *So* sorry, *Princess Lukemia*, if I have offended your sensibilities again.

JESS. My ole man was awful proud of me then. He went all over town braggin' about "my son's a champ." On th' other hand, though, he sure could gimme hell when I done something bad. Jesus, he beat the shit outa me when I stole a motorcycle once! Damn near killed me! He knocked three teeth out. And one eye was swollen shut for about a month afterwards. He sure had a temper, my ole man.

LUKE. Look at it this way, Jess. What good would it do if he did come see you now?

JESS. I'd like to talk to him.

LUKE. What'd ya talk about?

JESS. I'd like to tell him . . . how it happened.

LUKE. Yah?

JESS. I'd like to tell him . . . I'm sorry.

LUKE. Then what?

JESS. I just think I'd feel better. That's all.

LUKE. You could tell that to the priest.

JESS. But he ain't my *father*!

LUKE. You could pretend he was.

JESS. No, I couldn't. That priest is nothin' like my ole man. Nothin' at all.

ARCHIE (*looking off left*). Well, here she comes now in *full drag*, so be prepared to tell her something, or she's gonna be awful disappointed.

LUKE. Try to talk to him, Jess. *Try*.

(*The* CHAPLAIN *comes on hurriedly, accompanied by a* GUARD. *They stop before* JESS's *cell*.)

CHAPLAIN (*enthused*). I've wonderful news for you, Jess.

JESS. Yah?

CHAPLAIN. Your father has arrived.

JESS (*almost dumb*). Huh?

CHAPLAIN. Your father finally came. He's just outside now. I wanted to come and prepare you first.

(JESS *becomes very excited, jumping up and down, shouting*.)

JESS. Then show him in, fer Chris' sakes! Show him in!

CHAPLAIN. Just a minute, Jess. Let me say a few words first.

JESS. What for? My old man is *here*. I wanna see him!

CHAPLAIN. Quiet for a minute, Jess. Please.

JESS (*puzzled*). What's the matter?

CHAPLAIN. Remember my warning.

JESS. What about?

CHAPLAIN. Humans sometimes don't live up to all we expect of them.

JESS (*very excited*). To hell with all that! My old man is *here*. I wanna see him!!

CHAPLAIN. Very well, Jess. (*He signals Left.*)

JESS. Jesus, I can't believe it!

CHAPLAIN. You'll have ten minutes with him, Jess.

ARCHIE. Hail, Mary! Hail, Mary! Hail, Mary! Hail, Mary! . . . etc.

ARCHIE'S *voice slowly fades as the* GUARD *leads on a tired, bedraggled-looking middle-aged man. The man appears intimidated by the environment, and frightened, too. Obviously he has fortified himself with liquor in order to face this situation, and now his steps are uncertain. The* GUARD *brings him before* JESS'S *cell, and father and son stare at each other silently while the* GUARD *unlocks* JESS'S *cell.*)

FATHER (*finally, in a very meek voice*). Hi, Jess!

JESS. Pa!

GUARD (*admitting the man into the cell*). You have ten minutes, Mister.

FATHER. Thanks.

(CHAPLAIN *and* GUARD *exit Left.* JESS *grabs his father in an embrace.*)

JESS. Pa! You made it!

(*The* FATHER *is too awed and frightened to be able to respond to* JESS'S *great emotional need of him. He feels awkward in* JESS'S *embrace.*)

FATHER (*trying to affect a little laugh to show good nature*). Yah . . . I made it.

JESS (*eagerly*). Sit down, Pa. (*The* FATHER *sits.*) Jesus, I'm glad you came, Pa!

FATHER. Yah, well I . . . I wasn't gonna let ya down, Jess. No sir. I wasn't gonna let ya down.

(*But he looks about him fearfully, uncomfortably.*)

JESS. Jesus, Pa . . . there was so much

I wanted to say to ya and . . . now you're here, I . . . I can't think of what it was.

FATHER. Yah . . . Well, I feel the same, Jess. All the way here, I kept thinkin' of all the things I'd say to ya, and now . . . Well, I guess they're all gone.

JESS. Yah.

FATHER. Just lemme say this, though, Jess. I'da got here sooner but the old car, she kep' breakin' down.

JESS. Yah.

FATHER. I'll get me a good job soon and get me a new car.

JESS. Pa?

FATHER. . . . yah, Jess?

JESS. Pa, are ya . . . very mad at me?

FATHER. No. I'm not mad at ya, Jess. I'm not mad. *I* know ya never done what they accused ya of. Course ya never. Don't worry, Jess. (*He pats* JESS'S *knee feebly.*) *I* know you're innocent.

(*There is a long silence.* JESS *does not know how to respond to his father's inability to face the truth.*)

JESS. Pa!

FATHER (*after a few moments*). Yah, Jess?

JESS. Pa . . . I ain't innocent.

FATHER (*trying to laugh it off*). Aw now, come on, Jess-boy, I'm your old man. You can't expect me to believe you're guilty. No sir-ee. I tol' all my friends how it was. That gal you married was a chippie, Jess. I knowed that the first time I laid eyes on her. She had some other fella with her when it happened and you jest wanta protect her 'cause you . . .

JESS (*This is his most hopeless moment*). Pa! (*A long silence*) Wanda wasn't no chippie. Wanda was Okay. I *done* it, Pa. I *done* it!

(*There is another long silence. The* FATHER *squirms and clears his throat.*)

FATHER (*finally*). Now Jess, you know what *I* think? I think they've had ya in here so long you're wrought up. Sure. Thass all's the matter with you now. They just got you thinkin' you done . . . you done what they say you done 'cause . . .

JESS (*crying out in despair*). Pa! *I'm guilty!* Can't ya unnerstand? I did do it! *I'm guilty!*

(*Another long silence*)

FATHER. Well now, Jess, I'm your pa. And I'm not gonna believe you done what they say you done. I'm not gonna believe it. No use in tryin' to make me, cause I jest won't believe it.

JESS. Pa, you've *got* to b'lieve it! You've got to! You've got to try to unnerstand.

FATHER. Like I said, Jess, you're jest overwrought.

JESS (*crying out*). I'm *guilty!*

FATHER. You're jest overwrought.

JESS (*subsiding now*). No . . . I'm guilty.

FATHER. No you ain't, Jess. No you ain't.

JESS (*a soft, unconscious prayer of helplessness*). Oh God!

FATHER. You're my son and I'll never believe you're guilty. No sir-ee. And I'll stand up for ya to my friends as long as I live. You can bet your boots on that.

JESS (*giving up*). Holy Christ!

FATHER (*looks at his watch*). I think I better be goin' now, Jess.

JESS (*humbly*). Pa . . . I'm guilty.

FATHER (*ignoring* JESS). I . . . I guess I better not try to stay for . . . any longer cause I gotta go t' another town to find myself a place to stay. These motels around here cost too much. I . . . I better be goin' now, Jess.

JESS (*a cry for help*). Pa!

FATHER. And jest remember, I'll never believe anything else 'cept my boy was innocent.

JESS (*crying out*). Pa! Help me face my guilt! Help me, Pa! Help me!

FATHER. I gotta go, Jess.

JESS. Help me! Help me!

FATHER. Uh . . . Jess, do ya think I could pick up your belongings now? (JESS *looks at his father dumbly.*) Whatever you got you're having to leave behind. Personal things, and . . .

JESS. Everything's down there in your name.

FATHER. Is there any . . . *money* there, Jess?

JESS. Some.

FATHER. I can use it, Jess. Uh . . . 'bout how much money d'ya think is there, Jess?

JESS. 'Bout sixty bucks.

FATHER. That'll sure come in handy.

JESS. It's all yours.

FATHER. It may seem mean of me to ask ya, Jess . . . but . . . *I* still gotta live and as long as a person lives, a person's gotta think about money.

JESS. I understand, Pa.

FATHER. Thank you, Jess.

JESS. No need to thank me. I got no one else to leave it to.

FATHER. Uh . . . how do I get outa here now? (*Calling:*) Guard!

(*The* GUARD *appears immediately and unlocks the cell door.*)

FATHER. Well . . . g'by, son.

JESS. G'by!

(*The* GUARD *escorts* JESS's *father out, the* FATHER *walking faster and faster to get away from the atmosphere of death.* JESS *sits for several moments, looking totally desolate. Then he cries out in need:*)

JESS. Guard! (*Pause*) Guard! Tell the Chaplain to come here. *Please!*

(*The* CHAPLAIN *comes on briskly, followed by a* GUARD.)

CHAPLAIN. I'm here, Jess.

JESS. Talk to me! Will ya talk to me?

CHAPLAIN. That's what I'm here for.

(*The* GUARD *unlocks the cell door and admits the* CHAPLAIN.)

CHAPLAIN. What is it, Jess?

JESS. Talk to me like a man! Talk to me like another human being! Tell me you understand why I done it . . .

CHAPLAIN. I'm only a priest, Jess. I can only *help* you to face your sins. I can't face them *for* you.

JESS (*thinking*). Yeah. That's right. What you said this morning was right.

CHAPLAIN. How do you mean?

JESS. Sometimes . . . people . . . disappoint us.

CHAPLAIN. Yes.

JESS. My ole man drove all that distance . . . and it was no use.

CHAPLAIN. I'm sorry. Still . . . it was good of him to make the effort.

JESS. Yah. Maybe I was expectin' *too much.* After all, I guess there's some things we have to face *alone.*

CHAPLAIN. There are some things we can face only with *God.*

JESS. Don't talk to me about God now! I'm so scared, I feel like I'm gonna puke . . . my knees are bucklin' so bad, I don't see how I can even walk.

CHAPLAIN. I implore you, let me help you find peace before they take you away.

JESS. I never felt any peace while I was living. Why should I feel any now?

CHAPLAIN. Because you need it now to

face what's ahead of you.

LUKE. Just tell him you're sorry, Jess. That's *all* he's askin'.

JESS (*in a full voice*). Of course I'm sorry. Who wouldn't be sorry? I din wanna kill my wife 'n kid. I don't even know what made me do it. I just went wild for a minute, because I was so scared. I din wanna *see* my kid. Can't anyone understand that? I was scared to look at him after he was born. I didn't have the guts to look at any life that came from *me*. Because you wanna know something? (*He becomes louder and more violent.*) *I'm a no-good son of a bitch and I know it!* Is that what God wants to hear me say? Okay! I've said it! It's true. So how could I look at a kid I brought into the world? How could I believe that anything good could ever come outa *me*?

CHAPLAIN. What makes you think so poorly of yourself? And call yourself such a vile name?

JESS. I've robbed. I've lied. I've stolen. I've pushed dope. I've murdered. I've committed *every* sin in the book!

CHAPLAIN. God can *still* forgive you.

JESS. I've already said I'm sorry . . .

CHAPLAIN. Say it to *Him*.

JESS. I don't even know who He is.

CHAPLAIN. He is your true Father. It is only He who can understand all that is in your heart.

JESS. How can I believe in a heavenly Father when I never knowed one on earth?

CHAPLAIN. If man has destroyed God's name for you, can you bring yourself to believe in some positive force out there in the void? Some universal spirit so much greater than ourselves that all our transgressions are absolved, and blended into the elements, which may be neither good nor bad, but only vital to existence.

JESS. That talk's too deep for *me*.

CHAPLAIN. If you cut your finger, the wound heals, doesn't it?

JESS. . . . sometimes.

CHAPLAIN. Our wounded souls heal, too, Jess. If you can believe in that great healing power, you needn't be afraid.

JESS. I don't have the faith that anything's *ever* gonna heal.

CHAPLAIN. I'm sorry. (*He looks at the clock.*) The time has come now, Jess.

(JESS *is silent. The* CHAPLAIN *steps out and signals to the two* GUARDS *who appear immediately, unlocking the cell.* JESS *steps out first.*)

JESS. So long, Luke. (*He tosses* LUKE *a pack of cigarettes.*) I guess I've had my last butt. I guess you're not afraid of a little thing like cancer.

(LUKE *can not face* JESS. *He waves goodby to him and turns away.*)

JESS. So long, Archie.

ARCHIE. Save a nice warm seat for *me*, Girl.

(*The two* GUARDS *flank* JESS.)

CHAPLAIN. Have you anything final to say?

JESS. Yah. I got all kinds of feelings inside me I'd like the world to know about.

CHAPLAIN (*after a pause*). I'm ready to hear them.

JESS (*after a hopeless struggle*). . . . I guess I just can't find the words to explain them.

CHAPLAIN. Very well. God have mercy on you, Jess!

ARCHIE (*to himself*). Mercy! That's a hoot.

CHAPLAIN. We must go now, Jess.

JESS (*suddenly violent*). No! I don't wanna die! I wanna find some piece a heaven here on earth before I die! I wanna find some little piece of happiness in *this* life before I look for it in another!

(*The two* GUARDS *have seized* JESS *by the arms now, beginning to carry off his kicking, protesting body as the* CHAPLAIN *offers a prayer.* JESS *loses control of his bowels.* ARCHIE *holds his nose and moves to the back of his cell, away from the bad odor.*)

ARCHIE. Pee-u! He did the same as all the others.

JESS (*violently*). Git away from me you sons a bitches! Get away! Ya got no right to make me die! *You* ain't no rightful judge a anything I done. Take your hands off me, ya dirty mother-fuckers! I hate your goddamn guts! I hate all of you! I got enough hate inside me now to rile up heaven forever! I got hate enough now to turn heaven into hell!

CHAPLAIN (*as* JESS *is speaking*). Deliver me, O Lord,
From eternal death
In that awful day
When Heaven and earth

shall be moved,
When Thou shall come to judge
The world by fire.
Full of terror am I
And I fear the trial
and wrath to come.
That day shall be a day
of wrath,
Of calamity and misery;
That day shall be a
mighty one,
And exceedingly bitter.
Grant them eternal rest,
O Lord,
And let perpetual light
shine on them.
Deliver me, O Lord,
deliver me.
Amen.

(*We can still hear* JESS's *wildly protesting voice after the procession has disappeared. There is a long silence on the stage. Finally,* ARCHIE *speaks.*)

ARCHIE. When the Chaplain comes around to me, I'm just gonna say, "Look, *Girl,* save your wind to fart with. I'm gonna die. Let's get it over with."

LUKE. You fuckin' fairy, you don't know what you'll say. You'll probably shit your pants like everyone else!

ARCHIE. . . . maybe you're right. Who knows? Maybe I'll bawl. You wanna know something? I've never cried in my *entire life.* Never! Not even one tiny, salty little teardrop. I just never learned *how,* I guess. (*He laughs.*)

LUKE. You're a fucking psychopath! I don't care if ya got an I.Q. of fifty thousand.

ARCHIE. Why should *you* want to live?

LUKE. I don't know whether I do or not. All this time, I've been feelin' resigned to what's gonna happen. But who knows *how* I'll feel when they come and get me?

ARCHIE. Anyway, I won my bet. You pay me tomorrow at recreation.

LUKE. Okay. You know where you can stuff it . . .

(ARCHIE *laughs. Another* GUARD *brings in a new prisoner,* JOE, *a young man about* JESS's *age, and puts him in* JESS's *cell.*)

ARCHIE. Oh, you're cute. Wanna share my cell, *honey?*

JOE (*takes one look at* ARCHIE). Not with *you* in it.

ARCHIE. You'd come to like me . . . in time.

(*The* GUARD *locks* JOE *in* JESS's *cell and departs, taking* JESS's *few remaining personal belongings with him.*)

LUKE. My name's Luke.

ARCHIE. I'm Archie.

JOE. I'm Joe.

ARCHIE. Oh, are you Joe Ruselli?

JOE. Right.

ARCHIE. Oh, this is a big moment! Do you remember, *Princess Lukemia?* He's the one who entered a sorority house and raped three girls and killed almost a dozen. Oh, I think you're *divine!*

JOE. Save the compliments!

(*Suddenly the lights go dim. The three prisoners hold an awed silence until the lights come on again in full force.*)

ARCHIE. I guess that means the end for *Miss Jessica.*

LUKE. . . . Hard to believe, isn't it? That just a few minutes ago, he was here, alive and screaming his lungs out.

ARCHIE. *She's* quiet now.

(*The two* GUARDS *who took* JESS *to the chair return now, passing before the cells, going off Left.*)

ARCHIE. They've done their duty now. Bless their black hearts.

JOE. Was this Jess's cell?

LUKE. Yah.

ARCHIE. Did you know Jess?

JOE. Yah. We worked together in the machine shop before they brought him up here.

ARCHIE. She was a nice *girl,* but I guess we won't be seeing *her* anymore.

LUKE. How long ya got here, Joe?

JOE. Maybe a year. How 'bout you?

LUKE. Six months.

ARCHIE. I'm next. I go a week from tomorrow. You know something? I never think about it. I'm like *Scarlett O'Hara.* I never worry about tomorrow. I just let tomorrow take care of itself. . . .

(*He laughs. Now the* CHAPLAIN *appears, coming from the scene of* JESS's *death. His head hangs down. He looks grieved. His pace is slow and ponderous. The men in their cells watch him silently. When he gets as far as* LUKE's *cell,* LUKE *speaks.*)

LUKE. How'd he finally take it, Father?

CHAPLAIN. Like a man.

LUKE. That's good.

CHAPLAIN. Maybe I don't mean what you think I mean, Luke.

LUKE. Huh?

CHAPLAIN. I said, he took it like a man. He shook, and screamed, and defecated. He was unconscious with terror when they finally had to strap him into the death chair.

ARCHIE (*satanically*). O God that madest this hideous earth, when will it be ready to receive Thy demons? (*He laughs.*)

CHAPLAIN. What do we expect of man? To accept our reckless judgment of him willingly and glad? No. It is *man's* judgment that makes us cower. Not God's. I am proud of the boy that he behaved as he did. We have waited too long for heroes. Let us love man as he is, with his weaknesses and fears. I am sick of the world's cynics and detractors. I am proud that men are as good as they *are,* and have come as far as they have from their humble origin. No. Jess took his destruction as any man might. . . . (*As he turns to go:*) Good night, men. God bless us all!

(*The* CHAPLAIN *exits quickly.*)

CURTAIN

GREAT GOODNESS OF LIFE

(A "coon" show)

LeRoi Jones

VOICE OF THE JUDGE
COURT ROYAL, *middle-aged Negro man, gray hair, slight*
ATTORNEY BRECK, *middle-aged Negro man*
YOUNG MAN'S VOICE

HOODS 1 and 2, *K.K.K.-like figures*
YOUNG WOMAN, *25-year-old colored woman*
HOODS 3 and 4, *more refined than first two; wear business suits*
YOUNG MAN, *black boy of 20 or so*

SCENE: A log cabin. The outside front.

WHEN LEROI JONES's short play *Dutchman* opened at the Cherry Lane Theatre, New York, on March 24, 1964, it was glaringly evident that a new and impassioned playwright had vaulted into theatrical view. Alternately hailed by the press as "a fierce and blazing talent" and "an original and dangerous young playwright," with *Dutchman* and his subsequent works Mr. Jones substantiated that he is indeed "a man of shattering fury." He also happens to be a man of exceptional creative power whose plays are illuminated by flashes of lightning accompanied by the thunder of his anger. Undeniably a controversial figure and writer, his uncompromising works may shock and infuriate, but rarely will they induce apathy.

Born in Newark, New Jersey, in 1934, Mr. Jones was educated at Rutgers and Howard University and completed his graduate studies at Columbia. His interest in poetry took hold during his college days, and by the time he entered the United States Air Force in 1954, he already considered himself "a kind of poet."

Palpably, this view was generously shared, for, later, his poetry was to appear with remarkable frequency in many "reviews" and "little magazines." To name just a few: *Partisan Review; The Nation; Evergreen Review; Provincetown Review;* and *Kulchur.*

A provocative stylist and a facile adapter to the form that best suits his immediate needs, Mr. Jones has left no literary stone unturned. His published works include: two volumes of poetry, *Preface to a 20-Volume Suicide Note* and *The Dead Lecturer; Blues People* and *Black Music,* nonfiction works; and *Tales,* a recent compilation of short fiction concerned with the racial ferment in contemporary society.

In *Great Goodness of Life,* which marks its first publication anywhere in this collection, Mr. Jones again reflects his prevailing and total repudiation of "Uncle Tom." Subtitled, "A 'coon' show," outwardly it has the dimensions and sheen of a fable. Inwardly, it is something else again, with its dramatic exploration of an acquiescent stereotype who combustibly ignites the soul and fury of the author.

To this editor, *Great Goodness of Life* is less vehement, more dramatically controlled, than Mr. Jones's previous theatre pieces, and, consequently, more compelling and affecting, with its permeant subtleties and ineluctable symbolism. Here, harsh truths glimmer and impress through dramatic objectivity rather than overwhelm by reinless subjectivity.

LeRoi Jones's earlier plays—including *Dutchman; The Slave; The Toilet; The Eighth Ditch;* and *The Baptism*—have been presented Off-Broadway and in many national and international theatre centers. The film version of *Dutchman* was released in 1967.

In 1961–1962, Mr. Jones was awarded a John Hay Whitney Fellowship for poetry and fiction. In 1964, *Dutchman* brought him an "Obie Award" as the best American play presented Off-Broadway that year.

Married and the father of two girls, the prolific author is working concurrently on a new play, a novel, and a social critique.

THE SCENE. *An old house, with morning frost letting up a little.*

————

A VOICE. "Court."

(*A Negro man comes out, gray but still young looking. He is around fifty. He walks straight, though he is nervous. He comes uncertainly. Pauses.*)

"Come on."

(*He walks right up to the center of the lights.*)

"Come on."

COURT. I don't quite understand.

"Shutup, nigger."

COURT. What? (*Meekly, then trying to get some force up:*) Now what's going on? I don't see why I should . . .

"I told you to shutup, nigger."

COURT. I don't understand. What's going on?

"Black lunatic. I said shutup. I'm not going to tell you again!"

COURT. But . . . Yes.

"You are Court Royal, are you not?"

COURT. Yes. I am. But I don't understand.

"You are charged with shielding a wanted criminal. A murderer."

COURT. What? Now I know you have the wrong man. I've done no such thing. I work in the Post Office. I'm Court Royal. I've done nothing wrong. I work in the Post Office and have done nothing wrong.

"Shutup."

COURT. But I'm Court Royal. Everybody knows me. I've always done everything . . .

"Court Royal, you are charged with harboring a murderer. How do you plead?"

COURT. Plead? There's a mistake being made. I've never done anything.

"How do you plead?"

COURT. I'm not a criminal. I've done nothing . . .

"Then you plead, not guilty?"

COURT. Of course I'm not guilty. I work in the Post Office. (*Tries to work up a little humor.*) You know me, probably. Didn't you ever see me in the Post Office? I'm a supervisor; you know me. I work at the Post Office. I'm no criminal. I've worked at the Post Office for thirty-five years. I'm a supervisor. There must be some mistake. I've worked at the Post

Office for thirty-five years.

"Do you have an attorney?"

COURT. Attorney? Look, you'd better check you got the right man. You're making a mistake. I'll sue. That's what I'll do.

(*The* VOICE *laughs long and cruelly.*)

COURT. I'll call my attorney right now. We'll find out just what's going on here.

"If you don't have an attorney, the court will assign you one."

COURT. Don't bother. I have an attorney. John Breck's my attorney. He'll be down here in a few minutes—the minute I call.

"The court will assign you an attorney."

COURT. But I have an attorney. John Breck. See, it's on this card.

"Will the legal aid man please step forward?"

COURT. No. I have an attorney. If you'll just call, or adjourn the case until my attorney gets here.

"We have an attorney for you. Where is the legal aid man?"

COURT. But I have an attorney. I want my attorney. I don't need any legal aid man. I have money, I have an attorney. I work in the Post Office. I'm a supervisor; here, look at my badge.

(*A baldheaded smiling house slave in a wrinkled dirty tuxedo crawls across the stage; he has a wire attached to his back leading offstage. A huge key in the side of his head. We hear the motors "animating" his body groaning like tremendous weights. He grins and slobbers, turning his head slowly from side to side. He grins. He makes little quivering sounds.*)

"Your attorney."

COURT. What kind of foolishness is this? (*He looks at the man.*) What's going on? What's your name?

ATTORNEY. (*His "voice" begins sometime after the question; the wheels churn out his answer, and the deliberating motors sound throughout the scene.*) Pul . . . lead . . . errrr . . . (*As if the motors are having trouble starting:*) Pul-Pul- . . . lead . . . er . . . err Guilty!! (*Motors get it together and move in proper synchronization.*) Pul-Plead Guilty; it's your only chance. Just Plead Guilty, brother. Just Plead Guilty. It's your only chance. Your only chance.

COURT. Guilty? Of what? What are you talking about? What kind of defense attorney are you? I don't even know what I'm being charged with, and you say Plead Guilty. What's happening here? (*At* voice) Can't I even know the charge?

"We told you the charge. Harboring a murderer."

COURT. But that's an obvious mistake.

ATTORNEY. There's no mistake. Plead Guilty. Get off easy. Otherwise *thrrrrit* (*Makes throat-cutting gesture, then chuckles.*) Plead Guilty, brother, it's your only chance. (*Laughs.*)

"Plea changed to Guilty?"

COURT. What? No. I'm not pleading guilty. And I want my lawyer.

"You have your lawyer."

COURT. No. My lawyer is John Breck.

ATTORNEY. Mr. Royal, look at me. (*Grabs him by the shoulders.*) I am John Breck. (*Laughs.*) Your attorney, and friend. And I say, Plead Guilty.

COURT. John Bre . . . what? (*He looks at* ATTORNEY *closely.*) Breck. Great God, what's happened to you? Why do you look like this?

ATTORNEY. Why? Haha, I've always looked like this, Mr. Royal. Always.

(*Now another voice, strong, young, begins to shout in the darkness at* COURT ROYAL.)

YOUNG MAN'S VOICE. Now will you believe me, stupid fool? Will you believe what I tell you, or your eyes? Even your eyes. You're here with me, with us, all of us, and you can't understand. Plead Guilty; you are guilty, stupid nigger. You'll die; they'll kill you, and you don't know why. Now will you believe me? Believe me, half-white coward. Will you believe reality?

"Get that criminal out of here. Beat him. Shut him up. Get him."

(*Now sounds of scuffling come out of darkness. Screams. Of a group of men subduing another man.*)

YOUNG MAN'S VOICE. You bastard. And you, Court Royal, you let them take me. You liar. You weakling. You woman in the face of degenerates. You let me be taken. How can you walk the earttttt . . . (*He is apparently taken away.*)

COURT. Who's that? (*Peers into darkness.*) Who's that talking to me?

"Shut up, Royal. Fix your plea. Let's get on with it."

COURT. That voice sounded very familiar. (*Caught in thought momentarily.*) I almost thought it was . . .

"Since you keep your plea of Not Guilty, you won't need a lawyer. We can proceed without your services, Counselor."

ATTORNEY. As you wish, Your Honor. Goodbye, Mr. Royal. (*He begins to crawl off.*) Goodbye, dead sucker! Hahahaha (*Waving hands as he crawls off, laughing*) Hahahaha, ain't I a bitch? . . . I mean, ain't I? (*Exits.*)

COURT. John, John. You're my attorney, you can't leave me here like this. (*Starts after him . . . shouts:*) JOHN!!

(*A siren begins to scream, like in jailbreak pictures . . . "Arrrrrrrrerrrrr." The lights beat off, on, in time with the metallic siren shriek.* COURT ROYAL *is stopped in his tracks, bent in anticipation; the siren continues. Machine guns begin to bang, bang, as if very close to him; cell doors slamming, whistles, yells, "Break . . . Break," the machine guns chatter.* COURT ROYAL *stands frozen, half-bent arms held away from his body, balancing him in his terror. As the noise, din, continues, his eyes grow until he is almost going to faint.*)

COURT. Ahhhhhhgggg. Please . . . please don't kill me. Don't shoot me; I didn't do anything. I'm not trying to escape. Please . . . please . . . PLEEEEEAS . . .

(*The* VOICE *begins to shriek almost as loud with laughter as all the other sounds, and jumping lights stop as* VOICE *starts to laugh. The* VOICE *just laughs and laughs, laughs until you think it will explode or spit up blood. It laughs long and eerily out of the darkness.*)

COURT. (*Still dazed and staggered. He looks around quickly, trying to get himself together. He speaks now very quietly, and shaken*). Please. Please.

(*The* VOICE *begins to subside, the laughs coming in sharp cutoff bursts of hysteria.*)

"You donkey. (*Laughs*) You piece of wood. You shiny shuffling piece of black vomit."

(*The laughter quits like the tide rolling softly back, to silence. Now there is no sound, except for* COURT ROYAL's *breathing, and shivering clothes. He whispers.*)

COURT. Please? (*He is completely shaken*

and defeated, frightened like a small animal, eyes barely rolling.) Please. I won't escape. (*His words sound corny, tinny, stupid dropped in such silence.*) Please, I won't try again. Just tell me where I am?

(*The silence again. For a while no movement.* COURT *is frozen, stiff, with only eyes sneaking; now they stop, he's frozen, cannot move staring off into the cold darkness.*)

(*A chain, slightly, more, now heavier, dragged bent, wiggled slowly, light now heavily in the darkness, from another direction. Chains. They're dragged, like things are pulling them across the earth. The chains. And now low chanting voices, moaning, with incredible pain and despair; the voices press just softly behind the chains, for a few seconds, so very very briefly, then gone. And silence.*)

(COURT *does not move. His eyes roll a little back and around. He bends his knees, dipping, his head bending. He moans.*)

COURT. Just tell me where I am?

(*The* VOICE *is cool and businesslike.*) "HEAVEN."

(COURT's *eyes, head, raise an imperceptible trifle. He begins to pull his arms slowly to his sides, and claps them together. The lights dim, and only* COURT *is seen in dimmer illumination. The* VOICE *again.*)

"HEAVEN. (*Pause*) WELCOME."

COURT. (*mumbling*). I never understood . . . these things are so confusing. (*His head jerks like he's suddenly heard Albert Ayler. It raises; his whole body jerks around like a suddenly animate ragdoll. He does a weird dance like a marionette jiggling and waggling.*) You'll wonder what the devil meant. A jiggedly bobbidy fool. You'll wonder what the devil sent. Diggedy dobbidy cool. Ah man. (*Singing.*) Ah man, you'll wonder who the devil sent. And what was heaven heaven heaven. (*This is like a funny joke-dance, with sudden funniness from* COURT, *then suddenly as before he stops frozen again, eyes rolling, no other sound heard.*)

(*Now a scream, and two white hooded men,* HOODS 1 AND 2, *push a greasy head colored* YOUNG WOMAN *across in front of* COURT. *They are pulling her hair and feeling her ass. One whispers from time to time in her ear. She screams and bites occa-*sionally, occasionally kicking.*)

HOOD 1 (*To the* VOICE). She's drunk. (*Now to* COURT) You want to smell her breath?

COURT (*frightened, also sickened, at the sight, embarrassed*). N-No. I don't want to. I smell it from here. She drinks and stinks and brings our whole race down.

HOOD 2. Ain't it the truth!

"Grind her into poison jelly. Smear it on her daughter's head."

HOOD 1. Right, Yr Honor. You got a break, sister. (*They go off.*) Hey, Uncle, you sure you don't want to smell her breath?

(COURT *shivers "No."*)

"Royal, you have concealed a murderer, and we have your punishment ready for you. Are you ready?"

COURT. What? No. I want a trial. Please, a trial. I deserve that. I'm a good man.

"Royal, you're not a man!"

COURT. Please . . . (*Voice breaking*), Your Honor, a trial. A simple one, very quick, nothing fancy . . . I'm very conservative . . . no frills or loud colors, a simple concrete black-toilet-paper trial.

"And funeral."

(*Now two other men in hoods, white work gloves, and suits, very sporty,* HOODS 3 AND 4, *come in with a stretcher. A black man is dead on it. There is long very piped* applause. "Yea. Yea.")

HOOD 3. It's the Prince, Yr Honor. We banged him down.

"He's dead?"

HOOD 4. Yes. A nigger did it for us.

"Conceal the body in a stone. And sink the stone deep under the ocean. Call the newspapers and give the official history. Make sure his voice is in that stone too, or (*heavy nervous pause*) . . . just go ahead."

HOOD 3. Of course, Your Honor. (*Looks to* COURT, *almost as an afterthought.*) You want to smell his breath? (*They go out.*)

COURT (*mumbling, still very frightened*). No . . . no . . . I have nothing to do with any of this. I'm a good man. I have a car. A home. (*Running down:*) A club. (*Looks up, pleading.*) Please, there's some mistake. Isn't there? I've done nothing wrong. I have a family. I work in the Post Office. I'm a supervisor. I've worked for thirty-five years. I've done nothing wrong.

"Shutup, whimpering pig. Shutup and get ready for sentencing. It'll be hard on you, you can bet that."

COURT (*A little life, he sees he's faced with danger*). But tell me what I've done. I can remember no criminal, no murderer I've housed. I work eight hours, then home, and television, dinner, then bowling. I've harbored no murderers. I don't know any. I'm a good man.

"Shutup liar. Do you know this man?"

(*An image is flashed on the screen behind him. It is a rapidly shifting series of faces. Malcolm. Patrice. Robert Williams. Garvey. Dead nigger kids killed by the police. Medgar Evers.*)

COURT. What?

"I asked you, Do you know this man? I'm asking again, for the last time. There's no need to lie."

COURT. But this is many men, many faces. They shift so fast I cannot tell who they are . . . or what is meant. It's so confusing.

"Don't lie, Royal. We know all about you. You are guilty. Look at that face. You know this man."

COURT. I do? (*In rising terror*) No. No. I don't. I never saw that man; it's so many faces; I've never seen those faces . . . never. . . ."

"Look closer, Royal. You cannot get away with what you've done. Look more closely. You recognize that face . . . don't you? The face of the murderer you've sheltered all these years. Look, you liar, look at that face."

COURT. No, no, no . . . I don't know them. I can't be forced into admitting something I never did. Uhhh . . . I have worked. My God, I've worked. I've meant to do the right thing. I've tried to be a . . .

(*The faces shift; a long slow wail, like a moan, like secret screaming, has underscored the flashing faces. . . . Now it rises sharply to screaming point thrusts.* COURT *wheels around to face the image on the screen, directly. He begins shouting as loud as the voices.*)

COURT. No, I've tried . . . please, I never wanted anything but peace . . . please. I tried to be a man. I did. I lost my . . . heart . . . please, it was so deep.

I wanted to do the right thing, just to do the right thing. I wanted . . . everything to be . . . all right. Oh, please . . . please.

"Now tell me whether you know that murderer's face or not. Tell me before you die!"

COURT. No, no. I don't know him. I don't. I want to do the right thing. I don't know them. (*Raises his hands in his agony.*) Oh, son . . . son . . . dear God, my flesh, forgive me. . . . (*Begins to weep and shake.*) My sons. (*He clutches his body shaken throughout by his ugly sobs.*) Dear God . . .

"Just as we thought. You are the one. And you must be sentenced."

COURT. I must be sentenced. I am the one. (*Almost trancelike*) I must be sentenced. With the murderer. I am the one.

"The murderer is dead. You must be sentenced alone."

COURT (*as first realization*). The murderer . . . is . . . dead?

"And you must be sentenced. Now. Alone."

COURT (*voice rising, in panic, but catching it up short*). The murderer . . . is dead.

"Yes. And your sentence is—"

COURT. I must be sentenced . . . alone. Where is the murderer? Where is his corpse?

"You will see it presently."

COURT (*head bowed*). God. And I am now to die like the murderer died?

"No. (*Long pause.*) We have decided to spare you. We admire your spirit. It is a compliment to know you can see the clearness of your fate, and the rightness of it. That you love the beauty of the way of life you've chosen here in the anonymous world. No one beautiful is guilty. So how can you be? All the guilty have been punished. Or are being punished. You are absolved of your crime, at this moment, because of your infinite understanding of the compassionate God of the Cross. Whose head was cut off for you, to absolve you of your weakness. The murderer is dead. The murderer is dead."

(*Applause from the darkness*)

COURT. And I am not guilty now?

"No, you are free. Forever. It is asked only that you give the final instruction."

COURT. Final instruction . . . I don't understand.

"Heroes! bring the last issue in."

(HOODS 3 AND 4 *return with a* YOUNG MAN, *a black boy of about twenty. The boy does not look up. He walks stiff-legged to the center in front of* COURT ROYAL. *He wears a large "ankh" around his neck. His head comes up slowly. He looks into* COURT's *face.*)

YOUNG MAN. Peace.

(COURT *looks at his face; he begins to draw back.* HOOD 3 *comes and places his arms around* COURT's *shoulders.*)

"Give him the instruction instrument."

(HOOD 3 *takes a pistol out of his pocket and gives it with great show to* COURT.)

HOOD 3. The silver bullet is in the chamber. The gun is made of diamonds and gold.

HOOD 4. You get to keep it after the ceremony.

"And now, with the rite of instruction, the last bit of guilt falls from you as if it was never there, Court Royal. Now, at last, you can go free. Perform the rite, Court Royal, the final instruction."

COURT. What? No. I don't understand.

"The final instruction is the death of the murderer. The murderer is dead and must die, with each gift of our God. This gift is the cleansing of guilt, and the bestowal of freedom."

COURT. But you told me the murderer was dead, already.

"It *is* already. The murderer has been sentenced. You have only to carry out the rite."

COURT. But you told me the murderer was dead. (*Starts to back away.*) You told me . . . you said I would be sentenced alone.

"The murderer *is* dead. This is his shadow. This one is not real. This is the myth of the murderer. His last fleeting astral projection. It is the murderer's myth that we ask you to instruct. To bind it forever . . . with death."

COURT. I don't . . . Why do . . . You said I was not guilty. That my guilt had fallen away.

"The rite must be finished. This ghost must be lost in cold space. Court Royal, this is your destiny. This act was done by you a million years ago. This is only the memory of it. This is only a rite. You cannot kill a shadow, a fleeting bit of light and memory. This is only a rite, to show that you would be guilty but for the cleansing rite. The shadow is killed in place of the killer. The shadow for reality. So reality can exist beautiful like it is. This is your destiny, and your already lived-out life. Instruct, Court Royal, as the centuries pass, and bring you back to your natural reality. Without guilt. Without shame. Pure and blameless, your soul washed (*Pause*) white as snow.

COURT (*falling to his knees, arms extended as in loving prayer to a bright light falling on him, racing around the space*). Oh, yes . . . I hear you. And have waited for this promise to be fulfilled.

"This is the fulfillment. You must, at this moment, enter into the covenant of guiltless silence. Perform the rite, Court Royal."

COURT. Oh, yes, yes . . . I want so much to be happy . . . and relaxed.

"Then carry out your destiny."

COURT. Yes, yes . . . I will . . . I will be happy. (*He rises, pointing the gun straight at the* YOUNG MAN's *face.*) I must be . . . fulfilled . . . I will. (*He fires the weapon into the boy's face. One short sound comes from the boy's mouth.*)

YOUNG MAN. Papa! (*He falls.*)

(COURT *stands looking at the dead boy, with the gun still up. He is motionless.*)

"Case dismissed, Court Royal . . . you are free."

COURT (*now suddenly to life, the lights go up full; he has the gun in his hand. He drops it, flings it away from him*). My soul is as white as snow. (*He wanders up to the body.*) My soul is as white as snow. (*He starts to wander off the stage.*) White as snow. I'm free. I'm free. My life is a beautiful thing.

(*He mopes slowly toward the edge of the stage; then suddenly a brighter mood strikes him.*)

COURT (*raising his hand as if calling someone*). Hey, Louise, have you seen my bowling bag? I'm going down to the alley for a minute. (*He is frozen; the lights dim to . . .*

BLACK

BENITO CERENO

Robert Lowell

Benito Cereno was first presented at the American Place Theatre, New York, on November 1, 1964, with the following cast:

CAPTAIN AMASA DELANO Lester Rawlins
JOHN PERKINS Jack Ryland
DON BENITO CERENO Frank Langella
BABU Roscoe Lee Browne
ATUFAL Clayton Corbin
FRANCESCO Michael Schultz
AMERICAN SAILORS Conway W. Young, Robert Tinsley, Richard Kjelland, E. Emmet Walsch, Howard Martin

SPANISH SAILORS Luke Andreas, William Jacobson, James Zaferes
NEGRO SLAVES Woodie King, Lonnie Stevens, George A. Sharpe, Hurman Fitzgerald, Ernest Baxter, Aston Young, June Brown, Mary Foreman, Gene Foreman, Judith Byrd, M. S. Mitchell, Lane Floyd, Paul Plummer, Walter Jones, Ethan Courtney

Directed by Jonathan Miller

ROBERT LOWELL came to the theatre bearing exceptional credentials. By rare critical consensus, he is rated as the finest American poet of his generation. Of the scores of contemporary poets who now stir the nation's campuses and enliven bookshop sales, he surpasses all others as the most read, sought, and admired.

Though his verse translation of Racine's classic tragedy *Phèdre* was published in 1961, Mr. Lowell's true emergence as a practicing and professionally produced dramatist occurred in 1964, with the American Place Theatre's presentation of two parts of his dramatic trilogy, *The Old Glory*. A chronicle of the American character, the three individual plays are held together by the unifying symbol of the flag. *Endecott and the Red Cross* and *My Kinsman, Major Molineux* owe their source to Nathaniel Hawthorne and Thomas Morton, while the third and finest play of the trilogy, *Benito Cereno,* was inspired by Herman Melville's novella.

Benito Cereno excels with its inherent theatrical power, strong, suspenseful narrative, and the author's richly evocative dialogue. On the occasion of the play's New York premiere, the poet Randall Jarrell wrote: "I have never seen a better American play than *Benito Cereno.* The play is a masterpiece of imaginative knowledge."

In his short drama, Mr. Lowell carries us back to the early nineteenth century and allegorically proceeds to dig up the roots of our present-day clashes and tensions as he dramatically probes the ambiguous American attitude toward slavery and servitude.

The American Place Theatre's presentation of *The Old Glory*, as staged by Jonathan Miller, captured five Off-Broadway "Obie Awards" for the 1964–1965 season, including Best Play honors. It also won the Vernon Rice Award, presented by the Drama Desk (New York critics and editors), for distinguished achievement in playwriting for the 1964–1965 season.

In 1967, Mr. Lowell's new play, *Prometheus Bound,* was produced at the Yale School of Drama.

Robert Lowell was born in Boston in 1917. After two years at Harvard, he transferred to Kenyon College, where he studied poetry under John Crowe Ransom. During World War II, Lowell served a prison sentence as a conscientious objector, and many of his antiwar poems explaining his revulsion against war and the inhuman bombing of cities were written soon after he was released from jail. Collected and published under the title of *Lord Weary's Castle,* they won him the 1946 Pulitzer Prize for poetry. (*Land of Unlikeness,* his first volume of poems, was privately printed, though some of its contents were incorporated in the subsequent prize collection.) In 1951, Mr. Lowell published *The Mills of the Kavanaughs,* and eight years later his *Life Studies* won the National Book Award.

A consistent accumulator of honors and awards, his 1962 book, *Imitations,* shared the Bollingen Prize for the best translation of poetry into English. This was followed by *For the Union Dead,* in 1964.

In 1954, Robert Lowell was elected by the American Academy of Arts and Letters to the chair vacated by Robert Frost. He has also served as a Consultant in Poetry at the Library of Congress, and was the recipient of both a Guggenheim Fellowship and an Institute of Arts and Letters grant.

A great-grandnephew of poet James Russell Lowell, the contemporary poet also happens to be related to the colorfully eccentric poetess Amy Lowell (1874–1925), whose penchant for cigar smoking and assorted didoes brought her as much—if not more, attention than her "imagist" verse.

Mr. Lowell lives with his wife, authoress Elizabeth Hardwick, and their ten-year-old daughter, in New York City. Weekly, though, the celebrated New Englander (whose latest collection of poems, *Near the Ocean,* was published in 1967) makes a pilgrimage to home soil; specifically, Harvard, where he teaches poetry to eager and hopeful aspirants of the younger generation.

SCENE. *About the year 1800, an American sealing vessel, the* President Adams, *at anchor in an island harbor off the coast of Trinidad. The stage is part of the ship's deck. Everything is unnaturally clean, bare and ship-shape. To one side, a polished, coal-black cannon. The American captain,* AMASA DELANO, *from Duxbury, Massachusetts, sits in a cane chair. He is a strong, comfortable-looking man in his early thirties who wears a spotless blue coat and white trousers. Incongruously, he has on a straw hat and smokes a corncob pipe. Beside him stands* JOHN PERKINS, *his bosun, a very stiff, green young man, a relative of* DELANO's. *Three sailors, one carrying an American flag, enter.* EVERYONE *stands at attention and salutes with machinelike exactitude. Then the* THREE SAILORS *march offstage.* DELANO *and* PERKINS *are alone.*

———

DELANO

There goes the most beautiful woman in
  South America.

PERKINS

We never see any women, Sir;
just this smothering, overcast Equator,
a seal or two,
the flat dull sea,
and a sky like a gray wasp's nest.

DELANO

I wasn't talking about women,
I was calling your attention to the American flag.

PERKINS

Yes, Sir! I wish we were home in Duxbury.

DELANO

We are home. America is wherever her
  flag flies.
My own deck is the only place in the
  world
where I feel at home.

PERKINS

That's too much for me, Captain Delano.
I mean I wish I were at home with my
  wife;
these world cruises are only for bachelors.

DELANO

Your wife will keep. You should smoke,
  Perkins.
Smoking turns men into philosophers
and swabs away their worries.
I can see my wife and children or not see
  them
in each puff of blue smoke.

PERKINS

You are always tempting me, Sir!
I try to keep fit,
I want to return to my wife as fit as I left
  her.

DELANO

You're much too nervous, Perkins.
Travel will shake you up. You should let
a little foreign dirt rub off on you.
I've taught myself to speak Spanish like
  a Spaniard.
At each South American port, they mis-
  take me for a
Castilian Don.

PERKINS

Aren't you lowering yourself a little, Captain?
Excuse me, Sir, I have been wanting to
  ask you a question.
Don't you think our President, Mr. Jefferson, is lowering himself
by being so close to the French?
I'd feel a lot safer in this unprotected place
if we'd elected Mr. Adams instead of Mr.
  Jefferson.

DELANO

The better man ran second!
Come to think of it, he rather let us down
by losing the election just after we had
  named this ship,
the *President Adams*. Adams is a nervous
  dry fellow.
When you've travelled as much as I have,
you'll learn that that sort doesn't export,
  Perkins.
Adams didn't get a vote outside New England!

PERKINS

He carried every New England state;
that was better than winning the election.
I'm afraid I'm a dry fellow, too, Sir.

DELANO

Not when I've educated you!
When I am through with you, Perkins,
you'll be as worldly as the Prince Regent
   of England,
only you'll be a first-class American officer.
I'm all for Jefferson, he has the popular
   touch.
Of course he's read too many books,
but I've always said an idea or two won't
   sink our Republic.
I'll tell you this, Perkins,
Mr. Jefferson is a gentleman and an American.

PERKINS

They say he has two illegitimate Negro
   children.

DELANO

The more, the better! That's the quickest
   way
to raise the blacks to our level.
I'm surprised you swallow such Federalist
   bilge, Perkins!
I told you Mr. Jefferson is a gentleman and
   an American;
when a man's in office, Sir, we all pull behind him!

PERKINS

Thank God our Revolution ended where
   the French one began.

DELANO

Oh, the French! They're like the rest of
   the Latins,
they're hardly white people,
they start with a paper republic
and end with a toy soldier, like Bonaparte.

PERKINS

Yes, Sir. I see a strange sail making for the
   harbor.
They don't know how to sail her.

DELANO

Hand me my telescope.

PERKINS

Aye, aye, Sir!

DELANO

(With telescope)

I see an ocean undulating in long scoops
   of swells;
it's set like the beheaded French Queen's
   high wig;
the sleek surface is like waved lead,
cooled and pressed in the smelter's mould.
I see flights of hurried gray fowl,
patches of fluffy fog.
They skim low and fitfully above the
   decks,
like swallows sabering flies before a storm.
This gray boat foreshadows something
   wrong.

PERKINS

It does, Sir!
They don't know how to sail her!

DELANO

I see a sulphurous haze above her cabin,
the new sun hangs like a silver dollar to
   her stern;
low creeping clouds blow on from them to
   us.

PERKINS

What else, Sir?

DELANO

The yards are woolly
the ship is furred with fog.
On the cracked and rotten head-boards,
the tarnished, gilded letters say, the San
   Domingo.
A rat's-nest messing up the deck,
black faces in white sheets are fussing with
   the ropes.
I think it's a cargo of Dominican monks.

PERKINS

Dominican monks, Sir! God help us,
I thought they were outlawed in the new
   world.

DELANO

No, it's nothing. I see they're only slaves.
The boat's transporting slaves.

PERKINS

Do you believe in slavery, Captain Delano?

DELANO

In a civilized country, Perkins,
everyone disbelieves in slavery,

everyone disbelieves in slavery and wants
 slaves.
We have the perfect uneasy answer;
in the North, we don't have them and
 want them;
Mr. Jefferson has them and fears them.

PERKINS
Is that how you answer, Sir,
when a little foreign dirt has rubbed off on
 you?

DELANO
Don't ask me such intense questions.
You should take up smoking, Perkins.
There was a beautiful, dumb English ac-
 tress—
I saw her myself once in London.
They wanted her to look profound,
so she read Plato and the Bible and Ben-
 jamin Franklin,
and thought about them every minute.
She still looked like a moron.
Then they told her to think about nothing.
She thought about nothing, and looked
 like Socrates.
That's smoking, Perkins, you think about
 nothing and look deep.

PERKINS
I don't believe in slavery, Sir.

DELANO
You don't believe in slavery or Spaniards
or smoking or long cruises or monks or
 Mr. Jefferson!
You are a Puritan, all faith and fire.

PERKINS
Yes, Sir.

DELANO
God save America from Americans!

(*Takes up the telescope*)

I see octagonal network bagging out
from her heavy top like decayed beehives.
The battered forecastle looks like a raped
 Versailles.
On the stern-piece, I see the fading arms
 of Spain.
There's a masked satyr, or something
with its foot on a big white goddess.
She has quite a figure.

PERKINS
They oughtn't to be allowed on the ocean!

DELANO
Who oughtn't? Goddesses?

PERKINS
I mean Spaniards, who cannot handle a
 ship,
and mess up its hull with immoral statues.

DELANO
You're out of step. You're much too dry.
Bring me my three-cornered hat.
Order some men to clear a whaleboat.
I am going to bring water and fresh fish
 to the *San Domingo*.
These people have had some misfortune,
 Perkins!

PERKINS
Aye, aye, Sir.

DELANO
Spaniards? The name gets you down,
you think their sultry faces and language
make them Zulus.
You take the name *Delano*—
I've always thought it had some saving
Italian or Spanish virtue in it.

PERKINS
Yes, Sir.

DELANO
A Spaniard isn't a Negro under the skin,
particularly a Spaniard from Spain—
these South American ones mix too much
 with the Indians.
Once you get inside a Spaniard,
he talks about as well as your wife in Duxbury.

PERKINS

(*Shouting*)

A boat for the captain! A whaleboat for
Captain Delano!

(*A bosun's whistle is heard, the lights
dim. When they come up, we are on
the deck of the* San Domingo, *the
same set, identical except for litter
and disorder.* THREE AMERICAN SAILORS

climb on board. They are followed by
PERKINS *and* DELANO, *now wearing a
three-cornered hat. Once on board, the*
AMERICAN SAILORS *salute* DELANO *and
stand stiffly at attention like toys.* NE-
GROES *from the* San Domingo *drift
silently and furtively forward.*)

DELANO
I see a wen of barnacles hanging to the
waterline of this ship.
It sticks out like the belly of a pregnant
woman.
Have a look at our dory Bosun.

PERKINS
Aye, aye, Sir!

(*By now, about twenty blacks and
two Spanish sailors have drifted in.
They look like some gaudy, shabby,
unnautical charade, and pay no attention to the Americans, until an unseen
figure in the rigging calls out a single
sharp warning in an unknown tongue.
Then they all rush forward, shouting,
waving their arms and making inar-
ticulate cries like birds. Three shrill
warnings come from the rigging.
Dead silence. The men from the* San
Domingo *press back in a dense semi-
circle. One by one, individuals come
forward, make showy bows to* DE-
LANO, *and speak.*)

FIRST NEGRO
Scurvy, Master Yankee!

SECOND NEGRO
Yellow fever, Master Yankee!

THIRD NEGRO
Two men knocked overboard rounding
Cape Horn,
Master Yankee!

FOURTH NEGRO
Nothing to eat, Master Yankee!

NEGRO WOMAN
Nothing to drink, Master Yankee!

SECOND NEGRO WOMAN
Our mouths are dead wood, Master Yankee!

DELANO
You see, Perkins,
these people have had some misfortune.

(*General hubbub, muttering, shouts,
gestures, ritual and dumbshow of distress. The rigging, hitherto dark,
lightens, as the sun comes out of a
cloud, and shows* THREE OLD NEGROES,
*identical down to their shabby patches.
They perch on cat's-heads; their heads
are grizzled like dying willow tops;
each is picking bits of unstranded rope
for oakum. It is they who have been
giving the warnings that control the
people below. Everyone,* DELANO *along
with the rest, looks up.* DELANO *turns
aside and speaks to* PERKINS.)

It is like a Turkish bazaar.

PERKINS
They are like gypsies showing themselves
for money
at a county fair, Sir.

DELANO
This is enchanting after the blank gray roll
of the ocean!
Go tell the Spanish captain I am waiting
for him.

(PERKINS *goes off. Sharp warnings
from the* OAKUM-PICKERS. *A big black
spread of canvas is pulled creakingly
and ceremoniously aside.* SIX FIGURES
*stand huddled on a platform about
four feet from the deck. They look
like weak old invalids in bathrobes
and nightcaps until they strip to the
waist and turn out to be huge, shining
young Negroes. Saying nothing, they
set to work cleaning piles of rusted
hatchets. From time to time, they turn
and clash their hatchets together with
a rhythmic shout.* PERKINS *returns.*)

PERKINS
Their captain's name is Don Benito Cereno,
he sends you his compliments, Sir.
He looks more like a Mexican planter than
a seaman.
He's put his fortune on his back:

he doesn't look as if he had washed since
they left port.

DELANO
Did you tell him I was waiting for him?
A captain should be welcomed by his fel-
low-captain.
I can't understand this discourtesy.

PERKINS
He's coming, but there's something wrong
with him.

> (BENITO CERENO, *led by his Negro
> servant,* BABU, *enters.* BENITO, *looking
> sick and dazed, is wearing a sombrero
> and is dressed with a singular but
> shabby richness. Head bent to one
> side, he leans in a stately coma against
> the rail, and stares unseeingly at* DE-
> LANO. BABU, *all in scarlet, and small
> and quick, keeps whispering, pointing
> and pulling at* BENITO's *sleeve.* DELANO
> *walks over to them.*)

DELANO
Your hand, Sir. I am Amasa Delano,
captain of the *President Adams,*
a sealing ship from the United States.
This is your lucky day,
the sun is out of hiding for the first time
in two weeks,
and here I am aboard your ship
like the Good Samaritan with fresh food
and water.

BENITO
The Good Samaritan? Yes, yes,
we mustn't use the Scriptures lightly.
Welcome, Captain. It is the end of the day.

DELANO
The end? It's only morning.
I loaded and lowered a whaleboat
as soon as I saw how awkwardly your ship
was making for the harbor.

BENITO
Your whaleboat's welcome, Captain.
I am afraid I am still stunned by the storm.

DELANO
Buck up. Each day is a new beginning.
Assign some sailors to help me dole out my
provisions.

BENITO
I have no sailors.

BABU

> (*In a quick singsong*)

Scurvy, yellow fever,
ten men knocked off on the Horn,
doldrums, nothing to eat, nothing to drink!
By feeding us, you are feeding the King
of Spain.

DELANO
Sir, your slave has a pretty way of talking.
What do you need?

> (DELANO *waits for* BENITO *to speak.
> When nothing more is said, he shifts
> awkwardly from foot to foot, then
> turns to his* SAILORS.)

Stand to, men!

> (*The* AMERICAN SAILORS, *who have
> been lounging and gaping, stand in a
> row, as if a button had been pressed.*)

Lay our fish and water by the cabin!

> (*The* SAILORS *arrange the watercans
> and baskets of fish by the cabin. A
> sharp whistle comes from the* OAKUM-
> PICKERS. *Almost instantly, the provi-
> sions disappear.*)

Captain Cereno, you are surely going to
taste my water!

BENITO
A captain is a servant, almost a slave, Sir.

DELANO
No, a captain's a captain.
I am sending for more provisions.
Stand to!

> (*The* AMERICAN SAILORS *stand to.*)

Row back to the ship. When you get there,
take on five hogsheads of fresh water,
and fifty pounds of soft bread.

> (FIRST SAILOR *salutes and goes down
> the ladder.*)

Bring all our remaining pumpkins!

    (SECOND *and* THIRD *salute and go
    down the ladder.*)

My bosun and I will stay on board,
until our boat returns.
I imagine you can use us.

BENITO
Are you going to stay here alone?
Won't your ship be lost without you?
Won't you be lost without your ship?

BABU
Listen to Master!
He is the incarnation of courtesy, Yankee
    Captain.
Your ship doesn't need you as much as we
    do.

DELANO
Oh, I've trained my crew.
I can sail my ship in my sleep.

    (*Leaning over the railing and call-
    ing:*)

Men, bring me a box of lump sugar,
and six bottles of my best cider.

    (*Turning to* BENITO:)

Cider isn't my favorite drink, Don Benito,
but it's a New England specialty;
I'm ordering six bottles for your table.

    (BABU *whispers and gestures to* DON
    BENITO, *who is exhausted and silent.*)

BABU
Une bouteille du vin.

    (*To* NEGROES)

My master wishes to give you a bottle
of the oldest wine in Seville.

    (*He whistles. A Negro woman rushes
    into the cabin and returns with a dusty
    beribboned bottle, which she holds
    like a baby.* BABU *ties a rope around
    the bottle.*)

BABU
I am sending this bottle of wine to your
    cabin.
When you drink it, you will remember us.
Do you see these ribbons? The crown of
    Spain is tied to one.
Forgive me for tying a rope around the
    King of Spain's neck.

    (*Lowers the wine on the rope to the
    whaleboat.*)

DELANO

    (*Shouting to his* SAILORS:)

Pick up your oars!

SAILORS
Aye, aye, Sir!

DELANO
We're New England Federalists;
we can drink the King of Spain's health.

    (BENITO *stumbles offstage on* BABU's
    arm.*)

PERKINS
Captain Cereno hasn't travelled as much
    as you have;
I don't think he knew what you meant by
    the New England
Federalists.

DELANO

    (*Leaning comfortably on the rail; half
    to himself and half to* PERKINS:)

The wind is dead. We drift away.
We will be left alone all day,
here in this absentee empire.
Thank God, I know my Spanish!

PERKINS
You'll have to watch them, Sir.
Brown men in charge of black men—
it doesn't add up to much!
This Babu, I don't trust him!
Why doesn't he talk with a Southern ac-
    cent,
Like Mr. Jefferson? They're out of hand,
    Sir!

DELANO

Nothing relaxes order more than misery.
They need severe superior officers.
They haven't one.
Now, if this Benito were a man of en-
ergy . . .
a Yankee . . .

PERKINS

How can a Spaniard sail?

DELANO

Some can. There was Vasco da Gama and
Columbus . . .
No, I guess they were Italians. Some can,
but this captain is tubercular.

PERKINS

Spaniards and Negroes have no business
on a ship.

DELANO

Why is this captain so indifferent to me?
If only I could stomach his foreign reserve!
This absolute dictator of his ship
only gives orders through his slaves!
He is like some Jesuit-haunted Hapsburg
king
about to leave the world and hope the
world will end.

PERKINS

He said he was lost in the storm.

DELANO

Perhaps it's only policy,
a captain's icy dignity
obliterating all democracy—

PERKINS

He's like someone walking in his sleep.

DELANO

Ah, slumbering dominion!
He is so self-conscious in his imbecil-
ity . . .
No, he's sick. He sees his men no more
than me.
This ship is like a crowded immigration
boat;
it needs severe superior officers,
the friendly arm of a strong mate.
Perhaps, I ought to take it over by force.

No, they're sick, they've been through the
plague.

(BENITO *and* BABU *return.*)

I'll go and speak and comfort my fellow
captain.
I think you can help me, Captain. I'm feel-
ing useless.
My own thoughts oppress me, there's so
much to do.
I wonder if you would tell me the whole
sad story of your voyage.
Talk to me as captain to captain.
We have sailed the same waters.
Please tell me your story.

BENITO

A story? A story! That's out of place.
When I was a child, I used to beg for
stories in Lima.
Now my tongue's tied and my heart is
bleeding.

(*Stops talking, as if his breath were
gone. He stares for a few moments,
then looks up at the rigging, as if he
were counting the ropes one by one.*
DELANO *turns abruptly to* PERKINS.)

DELANO

Go through the ship, Perkins,
and see if you can find me a Spaniard who
can talk.

BENITO

You must be patient, Captain Delano;
if we only see with our eyes,
sometimes we cannot see at all.

DELANO

I stand corrected, Captain;
tell me about your voyage.

BENITO

It's now a hundred and ninety days. . . .
This ship, well manned, well officered,
with several cabin passengers,
carrying a cargo of Paraguay tea and Spanish cutlery.
That parcel of Negro slaves, less than four
score now,
was once three hundred souls.
Ten sailors and three officers fell from the
mainyard off the Horn;

part of our rigging fell overboard with
   them,
as they were beating down the icy sail.
We threw away all our cargo,
Broke our waterpipes,
Lashed them on deck
this was the chief cause of our suffering.

DELANO

I must interrupt you, Captain.
How did you happen to have three officers
   on the mainyard?
I never heard of such a disposal,
it goes against all seamanship.

BABU

Our officers never spared themselves;
if there was any danger, they rushed in
to save us without thinking.

DELANO

I can't understand such an oversight.

BABU

There was no oversight. My master had
   a hundred eyes.
He had an eye for everything.
Sometimes the world falls on a man.
The sea wouldn't let Master act like a
   master,
yet he saved himself and many lives.
He is still a rich man, and he saved the
   ship.

BENITO

Oh, my God, I wish the world had fallen
   on me,
and the terrible cold sea had drowned me;
that would have been better than living
   through what I've
lived through!

BABU

He is a good man, but his mind is off;
he's thinking about the fever when the
   wind stopped—
poor, poor Master!
Be patient, Yankee Captain, these fits are
   short,
Master will be the master once again.

BENITO

The scurvy was raging through us.
We were on the Pacific. We were invalids
and couldn't man our mangled spars.

A hurricane blew us northeast through the
   fog.
Then the wind died.
We lay in irons fourteen days in unknown
   waters,
our black tongues stuck through our
   mouths,
but we couldn't mend our broken waterpipes.

BABU

Always those waterpipes,
he dreams about them like a pile of
   snakes!

BENITO

Yellow fever followed the scurvy,
the long heat thickened in the calm,
my Spaniards turned black and died like
   slaves,
The blacks died too. I am my only officer
left.

BABU

Poor, poor Master! He had a hundred
   eyes,
he lived our lives for us.
He is still a rich man.

BENITO

In the smart winds beating us northward,
our torn sails dropped like sinkers in the
   sea;
each day we dropped more bodies.
Almost without a crew, canvas, water, or
a wind,
we were bounced about by the opposing
   waves
through cross-currents and the weedy
   calms,
and dropped our dead.
Often we doubled and redoubled on our
   track
like children lost in jungle. The thick fog
hid the Continent and our only port from
   us.

BABU

We were poor kidnapped jungle creatures.
We only lived on what he could give us.
He had a hundred eyes, he was the master.

BENITO

These Negroes saved me, Captain.
Through the long calamity,

they were as gentle as their owner, Don
Aranda, promised.
Don Aranda took away their chains be-
fore he died.

BABU

Don Aranda saved our lives, but we
couldn't save his.
Even in Africa I was a slave.
He took away my chains.

BENITO

I gave them the freedom of my ship.
I did not think they were crates or cargo
or cannibals.
But it was Babu—under God, I swear I
owe my life to Babu!
He calmed his ignorant, wild brothers,
never left me, saved the *San Domingo*.

BABU

Poor, poor Master. He is still a rich man.
Don't speak of Babu. Babu is the dirt
under your feet.
He did his best.

DELANO

You are a good fellow, Babu.
You are the salt of the earth. I envy you,
Don Benito;
he is no slave, Sir, but your friend.

BENITO

Yes, he is salt in my wounds.
I can never repay him, I mean.
Excuse me, Captain, my strength is gone.
I have done too much talking. I want to
rest.

(BABU *leads* BENITO *to a shabby straw
chair at the side.* BENITO *sits.* BABU
fans him with his sombrero.)

PERKINS

He's a fine gentleman, but no seaman.
A cabin boy would have known better
than to send his three officers on the mainyard.

DELANO

(*Paying no attention:*)

A terrible story. I would have been un-
hinged myself.

(*Looking over toward* BABU *and*
BENITO)

There's a true servant. They do things
better
in the South and in South America—
trust in return for trust!
The beauty of that relationship is unknown
in New England. We're too much alone
in Massachusetts, Perkins.
How do our captains and our merchants
live,
each a republic to himself?
Even Sam Adams had no friends and only
loved the mob.

PERKINS

Sir, you are forgetting that
New England seamanship brought them
their slaves.

DELANO

Oh, just our Southern slaves;
we had nothing to do with these fellows.

PERKINS

The ocean would be a different place
if every Spaniard served an apprenticeship
on an American ship
before he got his captain's papers.

DELANO

This captain's a gentleman, not a sailor.
His little yellow hands
got their command before they held a
rope—
in by the cabin-window, not the hawse-
hole!
Do you want to know why
they drifted hog-tied in those easy calms—
inexperience, sickness, impotence and aristocracy!

PERKINS

Here comes Robinson Crusoe and his good
man Friday.

DELANO

We don't beat a man when he's down.

(BENITO *advances uncertainly on*
BABU'S *arm.*)

I am glad to see you on your feet again,
That's the only place for a Captain, sir!
I have the cure for you, I have decided
to bring you medicine and a sufficient supply of water.
A first-class deck officer, a man from Salem,
shall be stationed on your quarter deck,
a temporary present from my owners.
We shall refit your ship and clear this mess.

BENITO
You will have to clear away the dead.

BABU
This excitement is bad for him, Yankee
Master.
He's lived with death. He lives on death
still;
this sudden joy will kill him. You've heard
how thirsty men die from overdrinking!
His heart is with his friend, our owner,
Don Aranda.

BENITO
I am the only owner.

(*He looks confused and shaken.* BABU
*scurries off and brings up the straw
chair.* BENITO *sits.*)

DELANO
Your friend is dead? He died of fever?

BENITO
He died very slowly and in torture.
He was the finest man in Lima.
We were brought up together,
I am lost here.

DELANO
Pardon me, Sir. You are young at sea.
My experience tells me what your trouble
is:
this is the first body you have buried in the
ocean.
I had a friend like yours, a warm honest
fellow,
who would look you in the eye—
we had to throw him to the sharks.
Since then I've brought embalming gear
on board.
Each man of mine shall have a Christian
grave on land.
You wouldn't shake so, if Don Aranda
were on board,

I mean, if you'd preserved the body.

BENITO
If he were on board this ship?
If I had preserved his body?

BABU
Be patient, Master!
We still have the figurehead.

DELANO
You have the figurehead?

BABU
You see that thing wrapped up in black
cloth?
It's a figurehead Don Aranda bought us
in Spain.
It was hurt in the storm. It's very precious.
Master takes comfort in it,
he is going to give it to Don Aranda's
widow.
It's time for the pardon ceremony, Master.

(*Sound of clashing hatchets*)

DELANO
I am all for these hatchet-cleaners.
They are saving cargo. They make
an awful lot of pomp and racket though
about a few old, rusty knives.

BENITO
They think steel is worth its weight in
gold.

(*A slow solemn march is sounded on
the gongs and other instruments. A
gigantic coal-black* NEGRO *comes up
the steps. He wears a spiked iron
collar to which a chain is attached
that goes twice around his arms and
ends padlocked to a broad band of
iron. The* NEGRO *comes clanking forward and stands dumbly and like a
dignitary in front of* BENITO. *Two
small black boys bring* BENITO *a frail
rattan cane and a silver ball, which
they support on a velvet cushion.*
BENITO *springs up, holds the ball, and
raises the cane rigidly above the head
of the Negro in chains. For a moment,
he shows no trace of sickness. The
assembled blacks sing, "Evviva, Benito!" three times.*)

BABU

(*At one side with the Americans, but keeping an eye on* BENITO:)

You are watching the humiliation of King Atufal,
once a ruler in Africa. He ruled as much land there as your President.
Poor Babu was a slave even in Africa,
a black man's slave, and now a white man's.

BENITO

(*In a loud, firm voice.*)

Former King Atufal, I call on you to kneel!
Say, "My sins are black as night,
I ask the King of Spain's pardon
through his servant, Don Benito."

(*Pause.* ATUFAL *doesn't move.*)

NEGROES

Your sins are black as night, King Atufal!
Your sins are black as night, King Atufal!

BENITO

What has King Atufal done?

BABU

I will tell you later, Yankee Captain.

BENITO

Ask pardon, former King Atufal.
If you will kneel,
I will strike away your chains.

(ATUFAL *slowly raises his chained arms and lets them drop.*)

Ask pardon!

WOMAN SLAVE

Ask pardon, King Atufal.

BENITO

Go!

(*Sound of instruments. The* BLACK BOYS *take* BENITO's *ball and cane. The straw chair is brought up.* BENITO *sits.* FRANCESCO *then leads him offstage.*)

BABU

Francesco!
I will be with you in a moment, Master.
You mustn't be afraid,
Francesco will serve you like a second Babu.

BENITO

Everyone serves me alike here,
but no one can serve me as you have.

BABU

I will be with you in a moment.
The Yankee master is at sea on our ship.
He wants me to explain our customs.

(BENITO *is carried offstage.*)

You would think Master's afraid of dying,
if Babu leaves him!

DELANO

I can imagine your tenderness during his sickness.
You were part of him,
you were almost a wife.

BABU

You say such beautiful things,
the United States must be a paradise for people like Babu.

DELANO

I don't know.
We have our faults. We have many states,
some of them could stand improvement.

BABU

The United States must be heaven.

DELANO

I suppose we have fewer faults than other countries.
What did King Atufal do?

BABU

He used the Spanish flag for toilet paper.

DELANO

That's treason.
Did Atufal know what he was doing?
Perhaps the flag was left somewhere it shouldn't have been.
Things aren't very strict here.

BABU
I never thought of that.
I will go and tell Master.

DELANO
Oh, no, you mustn't do that!
I never interfere with another man's ship.
Don Benito is your lord and dictator.
How long has this business with King
    Atufal been going on?

BABU
Ever since the yellow fever,
and twice a day.

DELANO
He did a terrible thing, but he looks like
    a royal fellow.
You shouldn't call him a king, though,
it puts ideas into his head.

BABU
Atufal had gold wedges in his ears in
    Africa;
now he wears a padlock and Master bears
    the key.

DELANO
I see you have a feeling for symbols of
    power.
You had better be going now,
Don Benito will be nervous about you.

(BABU goes off.)

That was a terrible thing to do with a
    flag;
everything is untidy and unravelled here—
this sort of thing would never happen on
    the President Adams.

PERKINS
Your ship is as shipshape as our country,
    Sir.

DELANO
I wish people wouldn't take me as repre-
    sentative of our country:
America's one thing, I am another;
we shouldn't have to bear one another's
    burdens.

PERKINS
You are a true American for all your talk,
    Sir;

I can't believe you were mistaken for a
Castilian Don.

DELANO
No one would take me for Don Benito.

PERKINS
I wonder if he isn't an impostor, some
traveling actor from a circus?

DELANO
No, Cereno is a great name in Peru, like
    Winthrop or Adams with us.
I recognize the family features in our
    captain.

(An OLD SPANISH SAILOR, grizzled and
dirty, is seen crawling on all fours
with an armful of knots toward the
Americans. He points to where BENITO
and BABU have disappeared, and whistles. He holds up the knots as though
he were in chains, then throws them
out loosely on the deck in front of
him. A GROUP OF NEGROES forms a
circle around him, holding hands and
singing childishly. Then, laughing,
they carry the SPANIARD offstage on
their shoulders.)

These blacks are too familiar!
We are never alone!

(Sound of gongs. Full minute's pause,
as if time were passing. DELANO leans
on the railing. The sun grows
brighter.)

This ship is strange.
These people are too spontaneous—all
    noise and show,
no character!
Real life is a simple monotonous thing.
I wonder about that story about the calms;
it doesn't stick.
Don Benito hesitated himself in telling it.
No one could run a ship so stupidly,
and place three officers on one yard.

(BENITO and BABU return.)

A captain has unpleasant duties;
I am sorry for you, Don Benito.

BENITO
You find my ship unenviable, Sir?

DELANO
I was talking about punishing Atufal;
he acted like an animal!

BENITO
Oh, yes, I was forgetting. . . .
He was a King,
How long have you lain in at this island,
Sir?

DELANO
Oh, a week today.

BENITO
What was your last port, Sir?

DELANO
Canton.

BENITO
You traded seal-skins and American muskets
for Chinese tea and silks, perhaps?

DELANO
We took in some silks.

BENITO
A little gold and silver too?

DELANO
Just a little silver. We are only merchants.
We take in a dollar here and there. We
have no Peru,
or a Pizarro who can sweat gold out of
the natives.

BENITO
You'll find things have changed
a little in Peru since Pizarro, Captain.

(*Starts to move away.* BABU *whispers
to him, and he comes back abruptly,
as if he had forgotten something important.*)

How many men have you on board, Sir?

DELANO
Some twenty-five, Sir. Each man is at his
post.

BENITO
They're all on board, Sir, now?

DELANO
They're all on board. Each man is working.

BENITO
They'll be on board tonight, Sir?

DELANO
Tonight? Why do you ask, Don Benito?

BENITO
Will they all be on board tonight, Captain?

DELANO
They'll be on board for all I know.

(PERKINS *makes a sign to* DELANO.)

Well, no, to tell the truth, today's our
Independence Day.
A gang is going ashore to see the village.
A little diversion improves their efficiency,
a little regulated corruption.

BENITO
You North Americans take no chances.
Generally, I suppose,
even your merchant ships go more or less
armed?

DELANO
A rack of muskets, sealing spears and cutlasses.
Oh, and a six-pounder or two; we are a
sealing ship,
but with us each merchant is a privateer—
only in case of oppression, of course.
You've heard about how we shoot pirates.

BABU
Boom, boom, come Master.

(BENITO *walks away on* BABU's *arm
and sits down, almost offstage in his
straw chair. They whisper. Meanwhile, a* SPANISH SAILOR *climbs the
rigging furtively, spread-eagles his
arms and shows a lace shirt under
his shabby jacket. He points to* BENITO
and BABU, *and winks. At a cry from*
ONE OF THE OAKUM-PICKERS, THREE

NEGROES *help the* SPANIARD *down with servile, ceremonious attentions.*)

PERKINS
Did you see that sailor's lace shirt, Sir?
He must have robbed one of the cabin
  passengers.
I hear that people strip the dead
in these religious countries.

DELANO
No, you don't understand the Spaniards.
In these old Latin countries,
each man's a beggar or a noble, often both;
they have no middle class. With them it's
  customary
to sew a mess of gold and pearls on rags—
that's how an aristocracy that's going to
  the dogs
keeps up its nerve.

DELANO
It's odd, though,
that Spanish sailor seemed to want to tell
  me something.
He ought to dress himself properly and
  speak his mind.
That's what we do. That's why we're
  strong:
everybody trusts us. Nothing gets done
when every man's a noble. I wonder why
the captain asked me all those questions?

PERKINS
He was passing the time of day, Sir;
It's a Latin idleness.

DELANO
It's strange. Did you notice how Benito
  stopped rambling?
He was conventional . . . consecutive for
  the first time since we met him.
Something's wrong. Perhaps, they've men
  below the decks,
a sleeping volcano of Spanish infantry.
  The Malays do it,
play sick and cut your throat.
A drifting boat, a dozen doped beggars on
  deck,
two hundred sweating murderers packed
  below like sardines—
that's rot! Anyone can see these people are
  really sick,
sicker than usual. Our countries are at
  peace.

I wonder why he asked me all those questions?

PERKINS
Just idle curiosity. I hear
the gentlemen of Lima sit at coffee-tables
  from sun to sun,
and gossip. They don't even have women
  to look at;
they're all locked up with their aunts.

DELANO
Their sun is going down. These old em-
  pires go.
They are much too familiar with their
  blacks.
I envy them though, they have no character,
they feel no need to stand alone.
We stand alone too much,
that's why no one can touch us for sailing
  a ship;
When a country loses heart, it's easier to
  live.
Ah, Babu! I suppose Don Benito's indis-
  posed again!
Tell him I want to talk to his people;
there's nothing like a well man to help the
  sick.

BABU
Master is taking his siesta, Yankee Master.
His siesta is sacred, I am afraid to dis-
  turb it.
Instead, let me show you our little enter-
  tainment.

DELANO
Let's have your entertainment;
if you know a man's pleasure
you know his measure.

BABU
We are a childish people. Our pleasures
  are childish.
No one helped us, we know nothing
about your important amusements,
such as killing seals and pirates.

DELANO
I'm game. Let's have your entertainment.

(BABU *signals. The gong sounds ten
times and the canvas is pulled from
the circular structure. Enclosed in a*

triangular compartment, an OLD SPAN-
ISH SAILOR *is dipping naked white
dolls in a tarpot.*)

BABU
This little amusement keeps him alive,
Yankee Master.
He is especially fond of cleaning the dolls
after he has dirtied them.

> (*The* OLD SPANISH SAILOR *laughs hys-
> terically, and then smears his whole
> face with tar.*)

OLD SPANISH SAILOR
My soul is white!

BABU
The yellow fever destroyed his mind.

DELANO
Let's move on. This man's brain,
as well as his face, is defiled with pitch!

BABU
He says his soul is white.

> (*The structure is pushed around and
> another triangular compartment ap-
> pears. A* NEGRO BOY *is playing chess
> against a splendid Spanish doll with
> a crown on its head. He stops and
> holds two empty wine bottles to his
> ears*).

This boy is deaf.
The yellow fever destroyed his mind.

DELANO
Why is he holding those bottles to his
ears?

BABU
He is trying to be a rabbit,
or listening to the ocean, his mother—
who knows?

DELANO
If he's deaf, how can he hear the ocean?
Anyway, he can't hear me.
I pass, let's move on.

> (*The structure is pushed around to
> a third compartment. A* SPANISH

SAILOR *is holding a big armful of
rope.*)

What are you knotting there, my man?

SPANISH SAILOR
The knot.

PERKINS
So I see, but what's it for?

SPANISH SAILOR
For someone to untie. Catch!

> (*Throws the knot to* DELANO.)

BABU

> (*Snatching the knot from* DELANO:)

It's dirty, it will dirty your uniform.

PERKINS
Let's move on. Your entertainment
is rather lacking in invention, Babu.

BABU
We have to do what we can
We are just beginners at acting.
This next one will be better.

> (*The structure is pushed around and
> shows a beautiful* NEGRO WOMAN. *She
> is dressed and posed as the Virgin
> Mary. A Christmas crèche is arranged
> around her. A* VERY WHITE SPANIARD
> *dressed as Saint Joseph stands behind
> her. She holds a Christ-child, the same
> crowned doll, only black, the* NEGRO
> BOY *was playing chess against.*)

She is the Virgin Mary. That man is not
the father.

PERKINS
I see. I suppose her son is the King of
Spain.

BABU
The Spaniards taught us everything,
there's nothing we can learn from you,
Yankee Master.
When they took away our country, they
gave us a better world.

Things do not happen in that world as
  they do here.

PERKINS
That's a very beautiful,
though unusual Virgin Mary.

BABU
Yes, the Bible says, "I am black not white."
When Don Aranda was dying,
we wanted to give him the Queen of
  Heaven
because he took away our chains.

PERKINS
The Spaniards must have taught them
  everything;
they're all mixed up, they don't even
  know their religion.

DELANO
No, no! The Catholic Church doesn't just
  teach,
it knows how to take from its converts.

BABU
Do you want to shake hands with the
  Queen of Heaven, Yankee Master?

DELANO
No, I'm not used to royalty.
Tell her I believe in freedom of religion,
if people don't take liberties.
Let's move on.

BABU

  (*Kneeling to the Virgin Mary:*)

I present something Your Majesty has
  never seen,
a white man who doesn't believe in taking
  liberties,
Your Majesty.

  (*The structure is pushed around and
  shows* ATUFAL *in chains but with a
  crown on his head.*)

BABU
This is the life we believe in.
Ask pardon, King Atufal!
Kiss the Spanish flag!

DELANO
Please don't ask me to shake hands with
  King Atufal!

  (*The canvas is put back on the structure.*)

BABU
You look tired and serious, Yankee Master.
We have to have what fun we can.
We never would have lived through the
  deadly calms
without a little amusement.

  (*Bows and goes off. The* NEGROES
  gradually drift away. DELANO *sighs
  with relief.*)

DELANO
Well, that wasn't much!
I suppose Shakespeare started that way.

PERKINS
Who cares?
I see a speck on the blue sea, Sir,
our whaleboat is coming.

DELANO
A speck? My eyes are speckled.
I seem to have been dreaming. What's
  solid?

  (*Touches the ornate railing; a piece
  falls onto the deck.*)

This ship is nothing, Perkins!
I dreamed someone was trying to kill me!
How could he? Jack-of-the-beach,
they used to call me on the Duxbury
  shore.
Carrying a duck-satchel in my hand, I
  used to paddle
along the waterfront from a hulk to school.
I didn't learn much there. I was always
  shooting duck
or gathering huckleberries along the marsh
  with Cousin Nat!
I like nothing better than breaking myself
  on the surf.
I used to track the seagulls down the five-
  mile stretch of beach for eggs.
How can I be killed now at the ends of
  the earth
by this insane Spaniard?

Who could want to murder Amasa Delano?
My conscience is clean. God is good.
What am I doing on board this nigger-
pirate ship?

PERKINS
You're not talking like a skipper, Sir.
Our boat's a larger spot now.

DELANO
I am childish.
I am doddering and drooling into my sec-
ond childhood.
God help me, nothing's solid!

PERKINS
Don Benito, Sir. Touch him,
he's as solid as his ship.

DELANO
Don Benito? He's a walking ghost!

(BENITO *comes up to* DELANO. BABU *is
a few steps behind him.*)

BENITO
I am the ghost of myself, Captain.
Excuse me, I heard you talking about
dreams and childhood.
I was a child, too, once, I have dreams
about it.

DELANO

(*Starting:*)

I'm sorry.
This jumping's just a nervous habit.
I thought you were part of my dreams.

BENITO
I was taking my siesta,
I dreamed I was a boy back in Lima.
I was with my brothers and sisters,
and we were dressed for the festival of
Corpus Christi
like people at our Bourbon court.
We were simple children, but something
went wrong;
little black men came on us with beetle
backs.
They had caterpillar heads and munched
away on our fine clothes.
They made us lick their horned and var-

nished insect legs.
Our faces turned brown from their spit,
we looked like bugs, but nothing could
save our lives!

DELANO
Ha, ha, Captain. We are like two dreams
meeting head-on.
My whaleboat's coming,
we'll both feel better over a bottle of cider.

(BABU *blows a bosun's whistle. The
gongs are sounded with descending
notes. The* NEGROES *assemble in
ranks.*)

BABU
It's twelve noon, Master Yankee.
Master wants his midday shave.

ALL THE NEGROES
Master wants his shave! Master wants his
shave!

BENITO
Ah, yes, the razor! I have been talking too
much.
You can see how badly I need a razor.
I must leave you, Captain.

BABU
No, Don Amasa wants to talk.
Come to the cabin, Don Amasa.
Don Amasa will talk, Master will listen.
Babu will lather and strop.

DELANO
I want to talk to you about navigation.
I am new to these waters.

BENITO
Doubtless, doubtless, Captain Delano.

PERKINS
I think I'll take my siesta, Sir.

(*He walks off.* BENITO, BABU, *and*
DELANO *walk toward the back of the
stage. A scrim curtain lifts, showing
a light deck cabin that forms a sort
of attic. The floor is matted, parti-
tions that still leave splintered traces
have been knocked out. To one side,
a small table screwed to the floor; on
it, a dirty missal; above it, a small*

*crucifix, rusty crossed muskets on one
side, rusty crossed cutlasses on the
other.* BENITO *sits down in a broken
throne-like and gilded chair.* BABU
*begins to lather. A magnificent array
of razors, bottles and other shaving
equipment lies on a table beside him.
Behind him, a hammock with a pole
in it and a dirty pillow.*)

DELANO

So this is where you took your siesta.

BENITO

Yes, Captain, I rest here when my fate
will let me.

DELANO

This seems like a sort of dormitory, sitting-
room,
sail-loft, chapel, armory, and private bedroom all together.

BENITO

Yes, Captain: events have not been favorable
to much order in my personal arrangements.

(BABU *moves back and opens a locker.
A lot of flags, torn shirts and socks
tumble out. He takes one of the flags,
shakes it with a flourish, and ties it
around* BENITO's *neck.*)

BABU

Master needs more protection.
I do everything I can to save his clothes.

DELANO

The Castle and the Lion of Spain.
Why, Don Benito, this is the flag of Spain
you're using!
It's well it's only I and not the King of
Spain who sees this!
All's one, though, I guess, in this carnival
world.
I see you like gay colors as much as Babu.

BABU

(*Giggling:*)

The bright colors draw the yellow fever
from Master's mind.

(*Raises the razor.* BENITO *begins to
shake.*)

Now, Master, now, Master!

BENITO

You are talking while you hold the razor.

BABU

You mustn't shake so, Master.
Look, Don Amasa, Master always shakes
when I shave him,
though he is braver than a lion and
stronger than a castle.
Master knows Babu has never yet drawn
blood.
I may, though, sometime, if he shakes so
much.
Now, Master!
Come, Don Amasa, talk to Master about
the gales and calms,
he'll answer and forget to shake.

DELANO

Those calms, the more I think of them
the more I wonder.
You say you were two months sailing
here;
I made that stretch in less than a week.
We never met with any calms.
If I'd not heard your story from your lips,
and seen your ruined ship,
I would have said something was missing,
I would have said this was a mystery ship.

BENITO

For some men the whole world is a mystery;
they cannot believe their senses.

(BENITO *shakes, the razor gets out of
hand and cuts his cheek.*)

Santa María!

BABU

Poor, poor Master, see, you shook so;
this is Babu's first blood.
Please answer Don Amasa, while I wipe
this ugly blood from the razor and strop
it again.

BENITO

The sea was like the final calm of the
world

On, on it went. It sat on us and drank
  our strength,
crosscurrents eased us out to sea,
the yellow fever changed our blood to
  poison.

BABU
You stood by us. Some of us stood by you!

BENITO
Yes, my Spanish crew was weak and
  surly, but the blacks,
the blacks were angels. Babu has kept
  me in this world.
I wonder what he is keeping me for?
You belong to me. I belong to you forever.

BABU
Ah, Master, spare yourself.
Forever is a very long time;
nothing's forever.

  (*With great expertness, delicacy and
  gentleness,* BABU *massages* BENITO's
  *cheeks, shakes out the flag, pours
  lotion from five bottles on* BENITO's
  *hair, cleans the shaving materials, and
  stands off, admiring his work.*)

Master looks just like a statue.
He's like a figurehead, Don Amasa!

  (DELANO *looks, then starts to walk out,
  leaving* BENITO *and* BABU. *The curtain drops upon them.* DELANO *rejoins*
  PERKINS, *lounging at the rail.*)

PERKINS
Our boat is coming.

DELANO

  (*Gaily*)

I know!
I don't know how I'll explain this pomp
and squalor to my own comfortable family of a crew.
Even shaving here is like a High Mass.
There's something in a Negro, something
that makes him fit to have around your
  person.
His comb and brush are castanets.

What tact Babu had!
What noiseless, gliding briskness!

PERKINS
Our boat's about alongside, Sir.

DELANO
What's more, the Negro has a sense of
  humor.
I don't mean their boorish giggling and
  teeth-showing,
I mean his easy cheerfulness in every
  glance and gesture.
You should have seen Babu toss that Spanish flag like a juggler.
and change it to a shaving napkin!

PERKINS
The boat's here, Sir.

DELANO
We need inferiors, Perkins,
more manners, more docility, no one has
  an inferior mind in America.

PERKINS
Here is your crew, Sir.

  (BABU *runs out from the cabin. His
  cheek is bleeding.*)

DELANO
Why, Babu, what has happened?

BABU
Master will never get better from his sick-
  ness.
His bad nerves and evil fever made him
  use me so.
I gave him one small scratch by accident,
the only time I've nicked him, Don Amasa.
He cut me with his razor. Do you think
  I will die?
I'd rather die than bleed to death!

DELANO
It's just a pinprick, Babu. You'll live.

BABU
I must attend my master.

  (*Runs back into cabin*)

DELANO
Just a pinprick, but I wouldn't have

thought

Don Benito had the stuff to swing a razor.

Up north we use our fists instead of knives.

I hope Benito's not dodging around some old grindstone

in the hold, and sharpening a knife for me.

Here, Perkins, help our men up the ladder.

(*Two immaculate* AMERICAN SAILORS *appear carrying great casks of water. Two more follow carrying net baskets of wilted pumpkins. The* NEGROES *begin to crowd forward, shouting, "We want Yankee food, we want Yankee drink!"* DELANO *grandiosely holds up a pumpkin; an* OLD NEGRO *rushes forward, snatches at the pumpkin, and knocks* DELANO *off-balance into* PERKINS' *arms.* DELANO *gets up and knocks the* NEGRO *down with his fist. All is tense and quiet. The* SIX HATCHET-CLEANERS *lift their hatchets above their heads.*)

DELANO

(*Furious*)

Americans, stand by me! Stand by your captain!

(*Like lightning, the* AMERICANS *unsling their muskets, fix bayonets, and kneel with their guns pointing at the* NEGROES. BENITO *and* BABU *appear.*)

Don Benito, Sir, call your men to order!

BABU

We're starving, Yankee Master. We mean no harm;

we've never been so scared.

DELANO

You try my patience, Babu.

I am talking to Captain Cereno;

call your men to order, Sir.

BENITO

Make them laugh, Babu. The Americans aren't going to shoot.

(BABU *airily waves a hand. The* NE-GROES *smile.* DELANO *turns to* BENITO.)

You mustn't blame them too much; they're sick and hungry.

We have kept them cooped up for ages.

DELANO

(*As the* NEGROES *relax*)

Form them in lines, Perkins!

Each man shall have his share.

That's how we run things in the States

to each man equally, no matter what his claims.

NEGROES

(*Standing back, bleating like sheep:*)

Feed me, Master Yankee! Feed me, Master Yankee!

DELANO

You are much too close.

Here, Perkins, take the provisions aft.

You'll save lives by giving each as little as you can,

Be sure to keep a tally.

(FRANCESCO, *a majestic, yellow-colored mulatto, comes up to* DELANO.)

FRANCESCO

My master requests your presence at dinner, Don Amasa.

DELANO

Tell him I have indigestion.

Tell him to keep better order on his ship.

It's always the man of good will that gets hurt;

my fist still aches from hitting that old darky.

FRANCESCO

My master has his own methods of discipline

that are suitable for our unfortunate circumstances.

Will you come to dinner, Don Amasa?

DELANO

I'll come. When in Rome, do as the Ro-

mans.
Excuse my quick temper, Sir.
It's better to blow up than to smoulder.

(The scrim curtain is raised. In the cabin, a long table loaded with silver has been laid out. The locker has been closed and the Spanish flag hangs on the wall. DON BENITO *is seated,* BABU *stands behind him. As soon as* DELANO *sits down,* FRANCESCO *begins serving with great dignity and agility.)*

FRANCESCO
A fingerbowl, Don Amasa.

(After each statement, he moves about the table.)

A napkin, Don Amasa.
A glass of American water, Don Amasa.
A slice of American pumpkin, Don Amasa.
A goblet of American cider, Don Amasa.
*(*DELANO *drinks a great deal of cider,* BENITO *hardly touches his.)*

DELANO
This is very courtly for a sick ship, Don Benito.
The Spanish Empire will never go down, if she keeps her chin up.

BENITO
I'm afraid I shan't live long enough to enjoy your prophecy.

DELANO
I propose a toast to the Spanish Empire on which the sun never sets;
may you find her still standing, when you land, Sir!

BENITO
Our Empire has lasted three hundred years,
I suppose she will last another month.
I wish I could say the same for myself.
My sun is setting,
I hear the voices of the dead in this calm.

DELANO
You hear the wind lifting;
it's bringing our two vessels together.

We are going to take you into port, Don Benito.

BENITO
You are either too late or too early with your good works.
Our yellow fever may break out again.
You aren't going to put your men in danger, Don Amasa?

DELANO
My boys are all healthy, Sir.

BENITO
Health isn't God, I wouldn't trust it.

FRANCESCO
May I fill your glass, Don Amasa?

BABU
New wine in new bottles,
that's the American spirit, Yankee Master.
They say all men are created equal in North America.

DELANO
We prefer merit to birth, boy.

*(*BABU *motions imperiously for* FRANCESCO *to leave. As he goes, bowing to the* CAPTAINS, FOUR NEGROES *play the "Marseillaise.")*

Why are they playing the "Marseillaise"?

BABU
His uncle is supposed to have been in the French Convention,
and voted for the death of the French King.

DELANO
This polite and royal fellow is no anarchist!

BABU
Francesco is very *ancien regime,*
he is even frightened of the Americans.
He doesn't like the way you treated King George.
Babu is more liberal.

DELANO
A royal fellow,
this usher of yours, Don Benito!

He is as yellow as a goldenrod.
He is a king, a king of kind hearts.
What a pleasant voice he has!

BENITO

(*Glumly*)

Francesco is a good man.

DELANO

As long as you've known him,
he's been a worthy fellow, hasn't he?
Tell me, I am particularly curious to
know.

BENITO

Francesco is a good man.

DELANO

I'm glad to hear it, I am glad to hear it!
You refute the saying of a planter friend
of mine.
He said, "When a mulatto has a regular
European face,
look out for him, he is a devil."

BENITO

I've heard your planter's remark applied
to intermixtures of Spaniards and Indians;
I know nothing about mulattoes.

DELANO

No, no, my friend's refuted;
if we're so proud of our white blood,
surely a little added to the blacks improves
their breed.
I congratulate you on your servants, Sir.

BABU

We've heard that Jefferson, the King of
your Republic,
would like to free his slaves.

DELANO

Jefferson has read too many books, boy,
but you can trust him. He's a gentleman
and an American!
He's not lifting a finger to free his slaves.

BABU

We hear you have a new capital modelled
on Paris,
and that your President is going to set up
a guillotine on the Capitol steps.

DELANO

Oh, Paris! I told you you could trust Mr.
Jefferson, boy,
he stands for law and order like your mulatto.
Have you been to Paris, Don Benito?

BENITO

I'm afraid I'm just a provincial Spaniard,
Captain.

DELANO

Let me tell you about Paris.
You know what French women are like—
nine parts sex and one part logic.
Well, one of them in Paris heard
that my ship was the *President Adams*.
She said,
"You are descended from Adam, Captain,
you must know everything,
tell me how Adam and Eve learned to
sleep together."
Do you know what I said?

BENITO

No, Captain.

DELANO

I said, "I guess Eve was a Frenchwoman,
the first Frenchwoman."
Do you know what she answered?

BENITO

No, Captain Delano.

DELANO

She said, "I was trying to provoke a philosophical discussion, Sir."
A philosophical discussion, ha, ha!
You look serious, Sir. You know, something troubles me.

BENITO

Something troubles you, Captain Delano?

DELANO

I still can't understand those calms,
but let that go. The scurvy,
why did it kill off three Spaniards in
every four,
and only half the blacks?
Negroes are human, but surely you
couldn't have favored them
before your own flesh and blood!

BENITO

This is like the Inquisition, Captain Delano.
I have done the best I could.

> (BABU *dabs* BENITO's *forehead with
> cider.*)

BABU

Poor, poor Master; since Don Aranda died,
he trusts no one except Babu.

DELANO

Your Babu is an uncommonly intelligent
fellow;
you are right to trust him, Sir.
Sometimes I think we overdo our talk of
freedom.
If you looked into our hearts, we all want
slaves.

BENITO

Disease is a mysterious thing;
it takes one man, and leaves his friend.
Only the unfortunate can understand misfortune.

DELANO

I must return to my bosun;
he's pretty green to be left alone here.
Before I go I want to propose a last toast
to you!
A good master deserves good servants!

> (*He gets up. As he walks back to*
> PERKINS, *the scrim curtain falls, con-
> cealing* BENITO *and* BABU.)

That captain must have jaundice,
I wish he kept better order.
I don't like hitting menials.

PERKINS

I've done some looking around, Sir. I've
used my eyes.

DELANO

That's what they're for, I guess. You have
to watch your step,
this hulk, this rotten piece of finery,
will fall apart. This old world needs new
blood
and Yankee gunnery to hold it up.
You shouldn't mess around, though, it's
their ship;

you're breaking all the laws of the sea.

PERKINS

Do you see that man-shaped thing in canvas?

DELANO

I see it.

PERKINS

Behind the cloth, there's a real skeleton,
a man dressed up like Don Benito.

DELANO

They're Catholics, and worship bones.

PERKINS

There's writing on its coat. It says,
"I am Don Aranda," and, "Follow your
leader."

DELANO

Follow your leader?

PERKINS

I saw two blacks unfurling a flag,
a black skull and crossbones on white silk.

DELANO

That's piracy. We've been ordered
to sink any ship that flies that flag.
Perhaps they were playing.

PERKINS

I saw King Atufal throw away his chains,
He called for food, the Spaniards served
him two pieces of pumpkin,
and a whole bottle of your cider.

DELANO

Don Benito has the only key to Atufal's
padlock.
My cider was for the captain's table.

PERKINS

Atufal pointed to the cabin where you
were dining,
and drew a finger across his throat.

DELANO

Who could want to kill Amasa Delano?

PERKINS

I warned our men to be ready for an emergency.

DELANO
You're a mindreader,
I couldn't have said better myself;
but we're at peace with Spain.

PERKINS
I told them to return with loaded muskets
and fixed bayonets.

DELANO
Here comes Benito. Watch how I'll humor
him
and sound him out.

(BABU *brings out* BENITO's *chair.*
BENITO *sits in it.*)

It's good to have you back on deck, Cap-
tain.
Feel the breeze! It holds and will increase.
My ship is moving nearer. Soon we will
be together.
We have seen you through your troubles.

BENITO
Remember, I warned you about the yellow
fever.
I am surprised you haven't felt afraid.

DELANO
Oh, that will blow away.
Everything is going to go better and
better;
the wind's increasing, soon you'll have no
cares.
After the long voyage, the anchor drops
into the harbor.
It's a great weight lifted from the cap-
tain's heart.
We are getting to be friends, Don Benito.
My ship's in sight, the *President Adams!*
How the wind braces a man up!
I have a small invitation to issue to you.

BENITO
An invitation?

DELANO
I want you to take a cup of coffee
with me on my quarterdeck tonight.
The Sultan of Turkey never tasted such
coffee
as my old steward makes. What do you
say, Don Benito?

BENITO
I cannot leave my ship.

DELANO
Come, come, you need a change of climate.
The sky is suddenly blue, Sir,
my coffee will make a man of you.

BENITO
I cannot leave my ship.
Even now, I don't think you understand
my position here.

DELANO
I want to speak to you alone.

BENITO
I am alone, as much as I ever am.

DELANO
In America, we don't talk about money
in front of servants and children.

BENITO
Babu is not my servant.
You spoke of money—since the yellow
fever,
he has had a better head for figures than
I have.

DELANO
You embarrass me, Captain,
but since circumstances are rather special
here,
I will proceed.

BENITO
Babu takes an interest in all our expenses.

DELANO
Yes, I am going to talk to you about your
expenses.
I am responsible to my owners for all
the sails, ropes, food and carpentry I give
you.
You will need a complete rerigging, almost
a new ship, in fact,
You shall have our services at cost.

BENITO
I know, you are a merchant.
I suppose I ought to pay you for our lives.

DELANO

I envy you, Captain. You are the only owner
of the *San Domingo,* since Don Aranda died.
I am just an employee. Our owners would sack me,
if I followed my better instincts.

BENITO

You can give your figures to Babu, Captain.

DELANO

You are very offhand about money, Sir;
I don't think you realize the damage that has been done to your ship.
Ah, you smile. I'm glad you're loosening up.
Look, the water gurgles merrily, the wind is high,
a mild light is shining. I sometimes think such a tropical light as this must have shone
on the tents of Abraham and Isaac.
It seems as if Providence were watching over us.

PERKINS

There are things that need explaining here, Sir.

DELANO

Yes, Captain, Perkins saw some of your men
unfurling an unlawful flag,
a black skull and crossbones.

BENITO

You know my only flag is the Lion and Castle of Spain.

DELANO

No, Perkins says he saw a skull and crossbones.
That's piracy. I trust Perkins.
You've heard about how my government blew
the bowels out of the pirates at Tripoli?

BENITO

Perhaps my Negroes . . .

DELANO

My government doesn't intend

to let you play at piracy!

BENITO

Perhaps my Negroes were playing.
When you take away their chains . . .

DELANO

I'll see that you are all put back in chains,
if you start playing pirates!

PERKINS

There's something else he can explain, Sir.

DELANO

Yes, Perkins saw Atufal throw off his chains
and order dinner.

BABU

Master has the key, Yankee Master.

BENITO

I have the key.
You can't imagine how my position exhausts me, Captain.

DELANO

I can imagine. Atufal's chains are fakes.
You and he are in cahoots, Sir!

PERKINS

They don't intend to pay for our sails and service.
They think America is Santa Claus.

DELANO

The United States are death on pirates and debtors.

PERKINS

There's one more thing for him to explain, Sir.

DELANO

Do you see that man-shaped thing covered with black cloth, Don Benito?

BENITO

I always see it.

DELANO

Take away the cloth. I order you to take away the cloth!

BENITO

I cannot. Oh, Santa María, have mercy!

DELANO

Of course, you can't. It's no Virgin Mary.
You have done something terrible to your
    friend, Don Aranda.
Take away the cloth, Perkins!

> (*As* PERKINS *moves forward,* ATUFAL
> *suddenly stands chainless and with
> folded arms, blocking his way.*)

BABU

> (*Dancing up and down and beside
> himself*)

Let them see it! Let them see it!
I can't stand any more of their insolence;
the Americans treat us like their slaves!

> (BABU *and* PERKINS *meet at the man-
> shaped object and start pulling away
> the cloth.* BENITO *rushes between them,
> and throws them back and sprawling
> on the deck.* BABU *and* PERKINS *rise,
> and stand hunched like wrestlers,
> about to close in on* BENITO, *who draws
> his sword with a great gesture. It is
> only a hilt. He runs at* BABU *and
> knocks him down.* ATUFAL *throws
> aside his chains and signals to the
> HATCHET-CLEANERS. They stand behind
> BENITO with raised hatchets. The
> NEGROES shout ironically, "Evviva
> Benito!"*)

You too, Yankee Captain!
If you shoot, we'll kill you.

DELANO

If a single American life is lost,
I will send this ship to the bottom,
and all Peru after it.
Do you hear me, Don Benito?

BENITO

Don't you understand? I am as powerless
as you are!

BABU

He is as powerless as you are.

BENITO

Don't you understand? He has been hold-
    ing a knife at my back.
I have been talking all day to save your
    life.

BABU

> (*Holding a whip:*)

Do you see this whip? When Don Aranda
    was out of temper,
he used to snap pieces of flesh off us with
    it.
Now I hold the whip.
When I snap it, Don Benito jumps!

> (*Snaps the whip.* DON BENITO *flinches.*)

DELANO

> (*Beginning to understand*)

It's easy to terrorize the defenseless.

BABU

That's what we thought when Don
Aranda held the whip.

DELANO

You'll find I am made of tougher stuff
than your Spaniards.

ATUFAL

We want to kill you.

NEGROES

We want to kill you, Yankee Captain.

DELANO

Who could want to kill Amasa Delano?

BABU

Of course. We want to keep you alive.
We want you to sail us back to Africa.
Has anyone told you how much you are
    worth, Captain?

DELANO

I have another course in mind.

BENITO

Yes, there's another course if you don't
like Africa, there's another course.
King Atufal, show the Yankee captain

the crew that took the other course!

(*Three dead* SPANISH SAILORS *are brought onstage.*)

ATUFAL
Look at Don Aranda?

BABU
Yes, you are hot-tempered and discourteous, Captain.
I am going to introduce you to Don Aranda.
You have a new command, Captain. You must meet your new owner.

(*The black cloth is taken from the man-shaped object and shows a chalk-white skeleton dressed like* DON BENITO.)

Don Amasa, Don Aranda!
You can see that Don Aranda was a white man like you,
because his bones are white.

NEGROES
He is a white because his bones are white!
He is a white because his bones are white!

ATUFAL

(*Pointing to the ribbon on the skeleton's chest:*)

Do you see that ribbon?
It says, "Follow the leader."
We wrote it in his blood.

BABU
He was a white man
even though his blood was red as ours.

NEGROES
He is white because his bones are white!

BABU
Don Aranda is our figurehead,
we are going to chain him to the bow of our ship
to scare off devils.

ATUFAL
This is the day of Jubilee,
I am raising the flag of freedom!

NEGROES
Freedom! Freedom! Freedom!

(*The black skull and crossbones is raised on two poles. The* NEGROES *form two lines, leading up to the flag, and leave an aisle. Each man is armed with some sort of weapon.*)

BABU
Spread out the Spanish flag!

(*The Lion and Castle of Spain is spread out on the deck in front of the skull and crossbones.*)

The Spanish flag is the road to freedom.
Don Benito mustn't hurt his white feet on the splinters.

(*Kneeling in front of* BENITO:)

Your foot, Master!

(BENITO *holds out his foot.* BABU *takes off* BENITO's *shoes.*)

Give Don Benito back his sword!

(*The sword-hilt is fastened back in* BENITO's *scabbard.*)

Load him with chains!

(*Two heavy chains are draped on* BENITO's *neck. The cane and ball are handed to him.*)

Former Captain Benito Cereno, kneel!
Ask pardon of man!

BENITO

(*Kneeling*)

I ask pardon for having been born a Spaniard.
I ask pardon for having enslaved my fellow man.

BABU
Strike off the oppressor's chain!

(*One of* BENITO's *chains is knocked off, then handed to* ATUFAL, *who dashes it to the deck.*)

Former Captain Benito Cereno,
you must kiss the flag of freedom.

(*Points to* DON ARANDA:)

Kiss the mouth of the skull!

(BENITO *walks barefoot over the Spanish flag and kisses the mouth of* DON
ARANDA.)

NEGROES
Evviva Benito! *Evviva* Benito!

(*Sounds are heard from* PERKINS,
*whose head has been covered with
the sack.*)

ATUFAL
The bosun wants to kiss the mouth of
freedom.

BABU
March over the Spanish flag, Bosun.

(PERKINS *starts forward.*)

DELANO
You are dishonoring your nation, Perkins!
Don't you stand for anything?

PERKINS
I only have one life, Sir.

(*Walks over the Spanish flag and
kisses the mouth of the skull.*)

NEGROES
Evviva Bosun! *Evviva* Bosun!

DELANO
You are no longer an American, Perkins!

BABU
He was free to choose freedom, Captain.

ATUFAL
Captain Delano wants to kiss the mouth
of freedom.

BABU
He is jealous of the bosun.

ATUFAL
In the United States, all men are created
equal.

BABU
Don't you want to kiss the mouth of freedom, Captain?

DELANO

(*Lifting his pocket and pointing the
pistol:*)

Do you see what I have in my hand?

BABU
A pistol.

DELANO
I am unable to miss at this distance.

BABU
You must take your time, Yankee Master.
You must take your time.

DELANO
I am unable to miss.

BABU
You can stand there like a block of wood
as long as you want to, Yankee Master.
You will drop asleep, then we will tie you
up,
and make you sail us back to Africa.

(*General laughter. Suddenly, there's
a roar of gunfire. Several* NEGROES,
mostly women, fall. AMERICAN SEA-
MEN *in spotless blue and white throw
themselves in a lying position on deck.*
MORE *kneel above them, then* MORE
*stand above these. All have muskets
and fixed bayonets. The First Row
fires. More* NEGROES *fall. They start to
retreat. The Second Row fires. More*
NEGROES *fall. They retreat further.
The Third Row fires. The Three*
AMERICAN LINES *march forward, but
all the* NEGROES *are either dead or in
retreat.* DON BENITO *has been wounded.
He staggers over to* DELANO *and shakes
his hand.*)

BENITO
You have saved my life.

I thank you for my life.

DELANO
A man can only do what he can,
We have saved American lives.

PERKINS

(*Pointing to* ATUFAL's *body:*)

We have killed King Atufal,
we have killed their ringleader.

(BABU *jumps up. He is unwounded.*)

BABU
I was the King. Babu, not Atufal,
was the king, who planned, dared and carried out
the seizure of this ship, the *San Domingo*.
Untouched by blood myself, I had all
the most dangerous and useless Spaniards
killed.
I freed my people from their Egyptian
bondage.
The heartless Spaniards slaved for me like
slaves.

(BABU *steps back, and quickly picks
up a crown from the litter.*)

This is my crown.

(*Puts crown on his head. He snatches*
BENITO's *rattan cane.*)

This is my rod.

(*Picks up silver ball.*)

This is the earth.

(*Holds the ball out with one hand
and raises the cane.*)

This is the arm of the angry God.

(*Smashes the ball.*)

PERKINS
Let him surrender. Let him surrender.
We want to save someone.

BENITO
My God how little these people understand!

BABU

(*Holding a white handkerchief and
raising both his hands:*)

Yankee Master understand me. The future
is with us.

DELANO

(*Raising his pistol:*)

This is your future.

(BABU *falls and lies still.* DELANO
*pauses, then slowly empties the five
remaining barrels of his pistol into
the body. Lights dim.*)

CURTAIN

MONICA

Pauline Macaulay

The first performance of *Monica* was given on B.B.C. Television, Great Britain, in November, 1965. The play was directed by Naomi Capon and the cast was as follows:

SIMON ELLIOTT Gary Bond
LEONARD Peter Cushing

PORTER Anthony Sagar

The stage premiere of *Monica* took place on October 17, 1966, at the New Arts Theatre, London. The production was directed by David Calderisi, with David Baxter as SIMON ELLIOTT and Christopher Tranchell as LEONARD.

Pauline Macaulay was born in Derbyshire, England, and after leaving school at fifteen, served for a while as a children's nurse in Nottingham. The theatre beckoned, however, and brought her to Brighton, where she joined a repertory company. As she recalls, there was more promise than fulfillment in the experience: "I worked around-the-clock as a general 'dogsbody,' but never was given the opportunity to act." Pride in hand, she departed from the company and for the next two years was employed as a model at the Brighton Art School.

Because the drama continued to beckon, she proceeded to London, where, between poses as a Chelsea model, she managed to write a radio play that was accepted with unusual alacrity by the British Broadcasting Corporation. Several subsequent radio scripts were commissioned and written before her first melodrama, *The Creeper,* was presented at the Nottingham Playhouse, then transferred to the West End, where it ran for six months in 1965, at the St. Martin's Theatre, with Eric Portman as star. Her second melodrama, *The Astrakhan Coat,* also had its premiere at Nottingham, and in 1966 was produced by David Merrick on the Broadway stage.

For almost half a century, suspense plays—or, as they affectionately were categorized, plays of crime and detection—were popular and profitable staples of the American stage. Then, with little advance warning, they became nearly as extinct as the whooping crane. Their topple from theatrical grace has triggered an assortment of postulations, but it is the editor's belief that they reached their nadir not so much through audience rejection as through the dearth of contemporary American playwrights sufficiently skilled in the intricate art of mystery-weaving. The proof is in the records, for whenever an even middling specimen pops out from behind the seasonal shadows, it is zestfully greeted by a lurking public generally in contraposition to critical admonitions.

Apparently, the British theatre is not subject to this indigenous shortage, for hardly a season rolls by there without offering its fair quota of "chillers." (Coincidentally, Agatha Christie's prototypic *The Mousetrap* happens to be the longest-running production in the history of the London stage. It is now in its fifteenth year.)

Pauline Macaulay ranks high among Britain's newer purveyors of suspense. *Monica,* revealed in these pages for the first time in the United States, is an ingenious, tautly fashioned example of the genre, heightened by percipient overtones in its pitched battle between age and youth.

The authoress resides in London with her husband, director Donald McWhinnie, and their young son. In 1968, she temporarily will leave hearth and home again for the scheduled Broadway premiere of *The Creeper.*

SCENE. *Simon Elliott's apartment. Evening.*

The apartment consists of one room, quite attractively furnished in a rather haphazard fashion with things picked up in Portobello market. It is an obviously bachelor apartment, with nothing around except a few books and one or two silver cups won for rowing at a university. There is, however, one beautiful red rose lying on a table. In front of a rather ordinary gas-fire is a white polar bear rug. There is a divan couch, rather badly made-up, with a few cushions lying squashed at one end and at the other a paper bag. There is an abstract sort of painting on the wall up center. The window, up left center, is closed. Nothing much can be seen from it but some clouds and the tops of a few distant buildings. There is a very narrow balcony outside. The roof slopes towards this window, and towards the narrow alcove balancing it right center in which the divan is placed. The main door is down left. There is also a small door to the bathroom above the fireplace.

———

When the CURTAIN rises, SIMON ELLIOTT is discovered seated at the small desk writing a letter. He is an attractive young man, but takes himself a little too seriously and is a shade pompous. He wears a blazer, sports trousers and an old school tie. He finishes the letter, folds it up, and places it in an envelope on which he writes a name—Monica. He rises, leaving the letter on the desk, and goes to the low bookcase on which are several bottles of spirits, glasses, etc. He takes a swig from a bottle and wipes his mouth with the back of his hand. Then he goes to the divan, picks up the paper bag and takes out a giant roll of Cellotape and a pair of scissors. He blows up the bag, bursts it, and throws it into the waste-paper basket under the desk. He goes to the window, climbs on the chair below it and starts to seal it up with the Cellotape. For a moment he stops and gazes out into space with a morose expression, then returns to the taping, which he finishes quickly and not every efficiently. He cuts the tape with the scissors, then gets down, moves to a cupboard up left and throws the tape and scissors to join a pile of sundry articles inside. He then looks at his watch, pauses for a moment, then walks determinedly to the telephone on the desk and dials "TIM," checking with his watch as he holds the receiver to his ear. He replaces the receiver and goes to a small mirror on the wall above the low bookcase. He takes a comb from his pocket, combs his hair carefully, replaces it and flicks his shoulders. Then he goes to the desk, takes a fairly large safety-pin from a drawer, and pins the envelope on the front of his chest. He goes to the mirror, stepping back a pace or two to make sure the envelope is pinned dead centre. He then takes some of the cushions from the divan and places them at the downstage end of the polar bear rug. He picks up the rose from the table and lies down on the rug, head down stage on the cushions. He places the rose on his heart, lifts an arm carefully to look at his watch, reaches out slowly to the gas-tap of the fire, and turns it on.

There is a hissing sound of gas. SIMON's eyes stare vacantly towards the window. Suddenly he raises his head slightly, looking annoyed. At the window a large black cat with a misshapen fat face is looking in. SIMON turns off the gas-tap and sits up, holding the rose. He goes: "Psssssssh!" and the cat vanishes. SIMON lies down again, arranging the rose. He reaches out and turns on the tap.

The hissing noise starts again. SIMON's eyes stare vacantly into space. After a second or two his expression begins to look rather pleasurable. His eyes have a sleepy look and almost start to close. Suddenly they open wide. They look startled. His hand reaches out and turns off the tap. With his hand still on the tap he mutters: "Phew!" His other hand brings the watch up to his face. He looks at the time and replaces his arm. He lies still, as if listening for something.

There is a noise off left of a lift-gate clanging. SIMON's eyes alter and he again turns on the gas-tap. He looks towards the window with an expression of extreme sorrow carefully arranged on his face. The noise of the hissing becomes louder.

The doorbell rings. A look of annoyance crosses his face and his hand reaches out again to the tap and rests on it. The doorbell rings again. SIMON turns off the tap *and sits up, holding the rose. He looks at the door, puzzled and annoyed. The doorbell rings for the third time, more prolonged.* SIMON *looks very angry. He flings the rose away, gets up and wafts the air hurriedly with his hands. Then he crosses to the door and throws it open, speaking as he does so.*

SIMON. You bitch—you forgot your key!

(An immaculately dressed man is standing outside, wearing an expensive dark suit, bowler hat, and carrying an umbrella. He is verging on the elderly, his face a little podgy, his eyes a little sad. He has a very pleasant voice. He looks a well-dressed City business man.)

THE MAN. I haven't got a key.

SIMON *(in an embarrassed mumble)*. I thought you were somebody else.

THE MAN. Sorry to disappoint you. *(He smiles.)* May I come in? *(He crosses past* SIMON, *removing his hat, and turns to look at him.)*

SIMON *(still holding the door)*. Well, what is it?

(The MAN *says nothing, staring at* SIMON's *chest.)*

What are you staring at? *(Suddenly aware that he has left the envelope pinned to his chest)* Oh. *(He releases the door, which swings to, and begins to wrench at the pin. After what seems an eternity he gets it off, looks at the man and gives a nervous laugh.)* I'm rather forgetful. I pin these little notes on myself to remind me of things. You know what I mean—like putting a rubber band on your finger, only better—because with a rubber band—sometimes—you forget what it was meant to remind you of. . . .

THE MAN. You're very young to have such a bad memory.

(SIMON folds the envelope over in his hand.)

Aren't you going to read it?

SIMON. It's—all right. *(He moves up to the waste-paper basket.)* You see, I remember what it said. *(He throws the envelope into the basket.)*

(The MAN *moves quietly to the door and closes it with his foot.)*

(SIMON turns.) Now, what can I do for you?

(The MAN *doesn't seem to hear him. He is looking around and sniffing the air.)*

THE MAN. I can smell gas?

SIMON *(ingenuously)*. Gas?

THE MAN. Yes. *(Looking at the gas-fire:)* Perhaps you've knocked the tap on.

SIMON. Oh, I don't think so. I'll have a look. *(He goes towards the fire, and as he does so trips over the cushions. Discomfited, he picks them up and turns to the man.)* For the dog. *(He throws them on the divan and bends over the gas-tap.)* No, it's not on.

THE MAN. Well, you may have a leak. *(He puts his hat and umbrella on the table.)* We'd better open a window. *(He goes to the window and tries to open it. It does not budge. He pushes harder. With a sticky, tearing sound the window opens, pulling off some of the tape. He fingers the tape curiously, and looks round at* SIMON.)

SIMON *(moving up to him)*. It's for the draught. I tape it for the draught.

THE MAN. Oh, I see.

SIMON. Of course—on the Continent they have double windows. . . .

THE MAN *(gazing out)*. You're very high up here, aren't you? Where does that narrow balcony go to?

SIMON. I've never been out there.

THE MAN. Not a very impressive view, is it?

SIMON *(defensively)*. Well, you can see the sky—clouds and things.

THE MAN. You can see the sky from a prison cell sometimes.

SIMON *(pompously)*. Are you suggesting that my apartment is like a prison cell?

THE MAN *(turning)*. We all live in some kind of prison, don't we? *(He looks at the low bookcase.)*

SIMON. Look, I'm sure that's very profound, but I'm rather busy. So if you wouldn't mind telling me exactly what you want . . .

(*The* MAN *moves to the chair below the door.*)

SIMON (*raising his voice slightly*). Look, can I help you at all?

(*The* MAN *studies the chair, picks it up, turns it upside down, examines it closely.*)

THE MAN (*looking at Simon*). You've got woodworm in that chair. You'd better get rid of it before it spreads to the table.

(SIMON *takes the chair and replaces it.*)

SIMON (*sarcastically*). How very kind of you to tell me—how very kind. You're an antique dealer, of course.

THE MAN. No, no—not a dealer. Nothing like that. I dabble a little. I'm interested in furniture.

SIMON. I see. (*At the door*) Well, may I assure you I have nothing for sale—nothing at all.

THE MAN. You intend to take this furniture with you when you go?

SIMON. Go? Go where?

THE MAN (*pleasantly*). Well, that's entirely up to you, isn't it?

SIMON (*staring at him, then clearing his throat*). Er—I wonder—do you think, by any chance, you're in the wrong apartment?

THE MAN. Number fifty—Mr. Simon Elliott?

SIMON. Yes.

THE MAN (*moving up center*). Call me "Leonard." (*He stares at the painting, goes closer, then steps back and turns to* SIMON.) Slade School?

SIMON (*flushing*). Look, I wonder if you'd mind explaining exactly what you want. You ring my bell—at, I may say, a very inopportune moment—you walk in, a complete stranger—you walk in, criticize my view, condemn my furniture. . . . If you're not looking for antiques, what *are* you looking for?

LEONARD. A *pied-à-terre,* Mr. Elliott. Somewhere intimate—suitable for a quiet week-end—or an afternoon with a friend. (*Smiling:*) I live outside London, you see.

It would be ideal for my purpose. How much is it?

SIMON (*stiffly*). I think you've been misinformed. I don't let rooms.

LEONARD. Very well, I'll buy it. How much do you want for the lease?

SIMON. You're making some kind of a mistake, Mr.—er—Leonard. I'm not selling the lease. I live here.

LEONARD. But you were intending to vacate it, were you not?

SIMON. I certainly wasn't. Whatever gave you that idea?

LEONARD (*after a pause*). Are you sure you weren't intending to vacate it, Mr. Elliott?

SIMON. I . . . (*Looking slightly embarrassed:*) Well, of course, I don't intend to stay here for ever.

LEONARD (*musing*). How long is for ever? I sometimes ask myself that question. Perhaps you could give me some idea of when you might be going?

SIMON. No, I'm afraid I couldn't. I couldn't possibly.

LEONARD. What a pity. What a pity, Mr. Elliott.

SIMON. I wonder if you'd mind telling me who gave you my name?

LEONARD. Nobody gave me your name, Mr. Elliott. I came across it—on a piece of paper.

SIMON. What piece of paper? Where?

LEONARD. It was just lying about, Mr. Elliott—just lying about.

SIMON. I don't leave my name lying about on bits of paper, Mr. Leonard. Forgive me if I say that it sounds an odd and doubtful story. (*He looks at. his watch.*) Now, I wonder if you'd mind . . . my apartment is not to let, I'm not selling the furniture and I'm expecting someone. I wonder if you'd mind going? My friend will be here at any moment.

LEONARD. You can't rely on people, Mr. Elliott. You can't rely on people at all. They have a habit of letting you down when you least expect it. Don't you agree?

SIMON. Your friends, possibly. Not mine.

LEONARD. And the fair sex, without a doubt, are even less reliable than ours, wouldn't you say?

SIMON (*angrily*). No, I wouldn't say. (*He looks at his watch again.*) Now (*going to the front door and opening it:*)

would you mind leaving my apartment!
(*He holds the door back.*)

LEONARD (*picking up the rose from the
floor*). What a pity! (*He holds it up.*)
Such a beautiful rose. Some of its petals
have fallen off. It's sad, isn't it, how
quickly things die.

(SIMON *crosses quickly and snatches the
rose.*)

SIMON (*throwing it in the waste-paper
basket*). If you don't go I shall be compelled to call the porter.

LEONARD. Now now, Mr. Elliott, that's
not very hospitable of you. May we not
have a drink and a little chat?

SIMON. Chat? What about? I've never
seen you before in my life. I don't know
you from Adam. What could we possibly
have to say to each other?

LEONARD. We might discover that we
have something in common. (*He goes to
the drinks.*) You never know. (*He pours
himself a drink.*)

SIMON (*furious*). What *do* you think
you're doing?

LEONARD. Won't you have one with me?

SIMON. How outrageous! Now you've
really gone too far. (*He goes to the telephone, picks up the receiver and presses a
button. Several buzzes are heard. Turning
to LEONARD.*) I'm ringing the porter.

(LEONARD *sits above the table with his
drink.* SIMON *buzzes again furiously, without success. He looks at his watch. Rather
to his surprise, he cannot make out the
figures. He blinks, and brings the watch
closer. Then he wipes a hand over his forehead and buzzes again.*)

LEONARD (*pleasantly*). Perhaps he's
nipped out for a quick one.

SIMON (*muttering*). Unlawful entrance
—trespassing—(*He looks at* LEONARD's
glass.) stealing!

PORTER (*through the telephone*). 'Allo—
yes?

SIMON. Porter? This is Mr. Elliott, flat
fifty. I wonder if you'd mind coming up
here for a moment. (*He turns his back
to* LEONARD.) I'm—(*lowering his voice
slightly:*) it's rather urgent. . . . (*Raising
his voice slightly:*) I've got a little bit of

trouble here. . . . Yes, I appreciate that,
but if you could . . . No, I can't discuss
it. Come up right away, Porter. (*He puts
down the receiver and looks over at* LEON-
ARD *sitting calmly with his drink.*) If I
were you I'd leave now. Rather ignomi-
nious to be thrown out, isn't it?

LEONARD (*pleading*). Won't you join me
in a drink?

SIMON (*pacing between the fire and the
desk*). Don't think I like doing this, you
know. But really you leave me no alternative. I mean, you can't just barge into
someone's flat, try to intimidate them into
letting it to you, and, when they won't—
refuse to leave the premises, making yourself a nuisance into the bargain.

LEONARD. I shall be happy to pay for my
drink. (*He takes some change from his
pocket.*) One tot of whisky—at saloon-bar
prices— (*He puts two half-crowns on the
table.*) That should well cover it.

(SIMON *exits to the bathroom, runs the
cold tap, takes a couple of aspirin from a
bottle on a shelf, puts them in his mouth
and drinks some water. He can be seen by*
LEONARD.)

LEONARD. Headache, Mr. Elliott?

(SIMON *returns and closes the bathroom
door.*)

SIMON. You know, it's just occurred to
me. You might have just come out of
prison.

LEONARD (*looking at his suit somewhat
ruefully*). In that case I'd better see my
tailor.

SIMON (*resuming his pacing*). Something you were saying when you looked
out of that window—and—(*looking at*
LEONARD) a certain pallor.

LEONARD. I am not a young man, Mr.
Elliott.

SIMON (*pacing*). Prison—(*he mutters.*)
or some other place. (*He takes a cigarette
from a packet and picks up some matches
from the desk.*)

LEONARD. I wouldn't—if I were you.

(SIMON *turns.*)

Gas, you know—in the atmosphere. (*He

smiles.)

(SIMON *throws the cigarette down.*)

Where's your dog?

SIMON (*sharply*). What?

LEONARD. The dog you mentioned earlier.

SIMON (*nastily*). He's out. (*He resumes pacing.*)

LEONARD. By himself? (SIMON *continues to pace. There is a tap at the door.*) Perhaps that's him now—back from his walk.

(SIMON *strides across and opens the door.*)

SIMON. Ah, Porter—come in.

(*The* PORTER *enters. He is short, middle-aged, stockily built with powerful shoulders. Cockney or Irish. His face does not inspire trust.*)

PORTER. Good afternoon. (*Glancing at* LEONARD) 'Afternoon.

(LEONARD *inclines his head politely.*) (*To* SIMON) Now, sir, what's the trouble?

SIMON. Porter, I should like you to escort this gentleman off the premises.

(*The* PORTER *looks at* LEONARD. LEONARD *sits unperturbed.*)

PORTER (*faintly surprised*). Off the premises, sir?

SIMON. Well, out of my flat, anyway. And, I would suggest, out of the building. He's a public menace.

PORTER. May I ask what offence he has committed, sir?

SIMON. Trespassing! Trespassing on my property!

PORTER. A burglar, sir! (*He looks again at* LEONARD.) This gentleman?

SIMON. Well, not exactly a burglar, no. He hasn't actually stolen anything—apart from helping himself to my liquor. I suppose you'd call it "loitering with intent"—although what intent I'm damned if I know.

PORTER (*after a pause*). May I ask how he got *into* your apartment, sir?

(*There is a pause.* SIMON *hesitates.* LEON-

ARD *rises.*)

LEONARD. Tell the porter how I got in, Mr. Elliott.

SIMON. Well . . .

LEONARD (*to the* PORTER). Mr. Elliott let me in.

SIMON (*crossing below* LEONARD *to the* PORTER). Well, he rang the bell, so naturally I opened the door. I mean, it's the usual . . .

LEONARD. And what did you say when you opened the door?

SIMON (*flushing*). What do you mean?

LEONARD (*smiling*). Tell the porter what you said when you opened the door, Mr. Elliott.

SIMON (*discomfited*). "I was expecting somebody else." (*To the* PORTER) The point is—the bell rang and I opened the door. All right. This man, a complete stranger, walks in, makes himself at home and tries to intimidate me into letting my apartment. When I refused, he refused to leave. He seems quite impervious to reason. Will you kindly escort him off the premises? And I would suggest that if you see him around the block again, you call the police!

LEONARD (*sniffing*). Strong smell of gas in here, isn't there?

SIMON. Rubbish.

PORTER (*sniffing*). There *is* a smell of gas, sir.

SIMON. The gas-fire blew back, that's all. It's all right now.

PORTER. You want to be careful, sir.

SIMON. Yes, I know all about that. What I want now is for you to escort this man off the premises.

(*The* PORTER *looks past* SIMON *at* LEONARD. LEONARD *casually takes out his wallet and glances in it. Then he smiles at the* PORTER *and puts it back. The* PORTER *coughs.*)

PORTER (*to* SIMON). Of course, if you let him in, sir, he hasn't really committed any offence, has he, sir? Technically speaking, that is.

SIMON (*irately*). Of course he has! He refuses to go!

(LEONARD *picks up a book from the*

table. The PORTER *shifts his feet and glances across at him again.)*

Well, what are you waiting for? Kindly remove this man from my apartment.

(The PORTER *looks past* SIMON *at* LEONARD *again.* LEONARD *looks up from his book and once more takes out the wallet.)*

PORTER *(to* SIMON, *who has not observed* LEONARD). Well, I'd like to oblige you, sir, but the truth is, I've got a bad back—dislocations, I think I've got. You know—where you can't bend nor lift nothing. I'm afraid I couldn't be using any force at the moment, sir, or I might put myself out altogther.

SIMON. But it's part of your job. Do you mean to say . . .

PORTER. I'm very sorry, sir, it wouldn't be worth it—not with my back, you see.

SIMON. Oh, yes—I see!

PORTER. I'm very sorry, sir.

SIMON *(clapping his hands to his head).* Go away, man, go away! *(He moves away upstage.)*

PORTER. Yes, sir. *(He looks at* LEONARD.) I'm sure the gentleman will leave shortly, sir. *(*SIMON *swings round at him.)* Yes, sir. *(The* PORTER *exits quickly.* SIMON *waits for the door to close, then looks at* LEONARD. LEONARD *closes the book in his hand and puts it back on the table.)*

LEONARD. Interesting.

SIMON. You bribed him, I suppose—that porter—when you came in.

LEONARD. Bribed? Mr. Elliott! If by that you mean inducements offered to procure action or non-action in favour of the giver, I suppose I cannot demur.

SIMON. How despicable!

LEONARD. Of him, or of me? *(After a slight pause)* Of me, you may think what you will. Of him, I think you must be a little more tolerant. Some people, you must understand, are like machines. They work for those who know how to handle them. That's one thing we older men have learned, you know—how to keep people of a certain mentality happy and efficient. It's not their fault, you know. It's a certain robot quality. . . .

SIMON. He'll be reported.

LEONARD. I wouldn't advise that, Mr.

Elliott. He's probably been here longer than you have. What is his name?

SIMON. I have no idea.

LEONARD. Find out. *(Moving to the fireplace:)* Don't call him "porter"—it's pompous. *(*SIMON *glares.)* And what do you give him? Half a crown at Christmas? In future I would suggest a bottle of whisky and a small offering every Saturday. I think you'd find an extraordinary difference.

*(*SIMON *looks daggers at him, then goes to the telephone. He picks up the directory and thumbs through a few pages. He stops, peers hard at the page, then stops again with his finger on a place. He looks up.)*

SIMON. Mr.—er—Leonard, as you call yourself. If you were not an old man, I would throw you through that door myself.

LEONARD. Chivalrous.

SIMON. As it is, not only are you old, but you look sufficiently nasty to distort the story if I happened to break your nose. Therefore, unless you go through that door now, I intend to call the police station and have a policeman come up here and show you the way to go home. Perhaps you might also like to explain to him what you are doing in my apartment. *(Still looking at* LEONARD, *he picks up the receiver.)*

LEONARD. Well, of course, if it was necessary, I should simply say I was passing and smelt gas, rang the bell, and saved you from suicide—which, I believe, if unsuccessful, is a criminal offence, is it not? *(A slight pause)* You were about to commit suicide, weren't you?

SIMON. Don't be ridiculous.

LEONARD. Fake suicide, no doubt—but then I wouldn't be expected to know that. Nor would the porter. I'm sure the police would agree my motives were purely charitable. A man in a depressed state is better kept an eye on.

SIMON *(putting down the receiver slowly).* You seem to hold all the cards, Mr. Leonard. Although what the game is, only you seem to know. Well *(picking up a book from the desk:)*, as far as I'm concerned, you can play it by yourself. *(He lies down on the divan. He puts the book up to his face and turns a page or two, but is not really reading.*)

(*There is a pause.* LEONARD *picks up one of the silver cups on the mantelpiece and reads the inscription.*)

LEONARD. Bit of a sportsman, Mr. Elliott? (*He puts it down and picks up another.*) I used to be—in my younger days. Too old for it now. (*He puts the cup down and wanders over to the drinks.*) Too old for most things, I'm afraid. (*There is no response from the divan. Picking up the whisky bottle, looking towards* SIMON:) May I? (*Taking some silver from his pocket with the other hand:*) The same arrangement?

SIMON (*lowering his book*). The arrangements are all yours, Mr. Leonard. And since it looks as if you're here for the evening, just continue to make yourself at home. Only let me know if you're thinking of staying the night—because if you are, I shall have to go out. (*He raises the book.*)

LEONARD. I'll make a bargain with you, Mr. Elliott. (*Pouring himself a drink:*) I will stay only until your friend comes. (*He takes another glass and pours some whisky in it.*)

(*From behind his book* SIMON *brings his watch up to his face.*)

SIMON. My friend won't be coming—so one of us will have to go.

(LEONARD *puts some more silver down by the drinks and picks up the two glasses.*)

LEONARD (*going to the divan*). Since you are not expecting anyone, Mr. Elliott, why not have a drink with me? (*He stands there with a glass in each hand.*)

SIMON (*from behind his book*). You just carry on drinking by yourself, Mr. Leonard. (*Waving a hand towards the drinks:*) Empty all the bottles and drink yourself into a stupor. Then I can call an ambulance and have you removed painlessly.

LEONARD. Mr. Elliott, if I just wanted to drink I would have headed for the nearest bar. The drink is something to do with my hands, and a mild and rather pleasant form of anaesthesia. (*Gently*) I would just like to talk to you.

SIMON (*putting the book down and sitting up*). But you talk in riddles, Mr. Leonard! You've talked in riddles ever since you came into my apartment. What do you *suggest* we talk about?

LEONARD. We could draw some comparisons, perhaps—between your life and mine. The life of an old man and the life of a young man.

SIMON. What is this—market research?

LEONARD. Not for the market—just a little research of my own. What it's like to be a young bachelor in an apartment like this. I've forgotten, you see.

SIMON. Well, I'm terribly sorry, but . . .

LEONARD (*holding out the glass*). Have a drink, Simon, and talk to me.

(*There is a slight pause.* SIMON's *expression alters. He looks slightly puzzled, as if some chord from the past had been struck.*)

SIMON (*taking the glass*). You said that —as if you knew me very well.

(LEONARD *goes and fetches the soda syphon and offers it to* SIMON. SIMON *shakes his head.*)

LEONARD (*putting soda in his own glass, then returning the syphon to the bookcase top*). But I do know you very well. I've *been* you, or somebody like you, a long time ago. (*He walks back and sits beside* SIMON *on the divan.*) The gay days—just out of university—fit as a fiddle. My first job—my first apartment—my first mistress . . . (*He looks at* SIMON. SIMON *blushes and drinks hurriedly.*) They happened to me too, you know. (*He sighs.*) I sometimes think the young think the old have always been old. (SIMON, *embarrassed, knocks his drink back quickly.*) I envy you, you see. Your clean-cut looks, your nice healthy liver. I used to knock a whisky back neat like that, when I was your age. (*He looks at his glass and takes a sip.*) Now I have to dilute it. (*He takes* SIMON's *empty glass, rises, and moves to the drinks.*) I have to dilute everything. (*Pouring another whisky into* SIMON's *glass:*)

You'll have to, when you get older. (*Filling up his own with soda:*) Diluted pleasures. (*He goes back to* SIMON *and gives him his neat whisky, sitting beside him as before.*) What do you do, Simon? I mean, what is your job?

SIMON. I work in a publisher's.

LEONARD. Do you enjoy it?

SIMON (*guardedly*). Ye-es. It's all right.

LEONARD. But you're not crazy about it? You'd rather be driving about the Côte d'Azur in a nice white sports car. Or red—do you prefer red? (SIMON *grins boyishly.*) All that can be arranged, Simon, if you'd like to go.

SIMON (*sceptically*). Hah!

LEONARD. I remember my first sports car—well. Drop-head coupe, they called them then. I drove all the way from Nice to Ventimiglia on the wrong side of the road. (*He smiles.*) Of course, there wasn't much traffic in those days. Suicide now.

(SIMON *is not really listening. He looks thoughtful.*)

SIMON (*suddenly looking at* LEONARD). Do you know my father? (LEONARD *looks somewhat bewildered.*) I just suddenly wondered if you knew my father?

LEONARD. As far as I know, I've never had the pleasure.

SIMON. I thought he might have sent you here to—er—check up or something.

LEONARD. No. Why? Doesn't he trust you?

SIMON. I don't know, really. It just struck me that it was the sort of thing the old boy might do.

LEONARD. It's a tendency fathers have, I suppose. (*He pauses.*) Well, would you like to go abroad, all expenses paid?

SIMON. I've had my holidays.

LEONARD. Have another one.

SIMON. With you? (*He gives* LEONARD *a curious look.*) Is this some kind of proposition?

LEONARD. Not in the sense you're thinking of. (*He smiles.*) I wouldn't be going.

SIMON. Some kind of job? (*He takes a drink.*) Because I can assure you my father wouldn't . . . (*He drinks again, finishing the glass.*) Well, he placed me in this publisher's, and he'd be furious . . .

LEONARD. Not a job. Just a free holiday. (*He takes* SIMON'S *glass.*) Let me give you another drink—on me. (*He rises and goes to the drinks.*)

SIMON. Look, have I won some sort of competition? Because if I have, I'd rather have the money. (*He lies back on the bed and contemplates the ceiling.*) I'm thinking of getting married, you see.

LEONARD (*pouring the whiskies; his voice is sombre*). Some soda this time?

SIMON. No. *Have* I won some competition?

LEONARD (*putting more money down with the rest and moving back to the divan*). Well, that remains to be seen—but the offer is entirely from me. (*He holds out the glass.*)

SIMON (*sitting up and taking it*). You're so cryptic. Everything you say is so cryptic! I mean—why should you offer me a holiday abroad, all expenses paid? Why *me*, a complete stranger? You must want something in return.

LEONARD (*lightly*). I tell you what, Simon. If you tell me about your "suicide," I'll tell you what I really want with you. (*He sits beside him.*)

SIMON. Oh, that! That was just a joke. Can't think why you're interested.

LEONARD. Rather a macabre joke, wasn't it?

SIMON. I suppose so.

LEONARD. The young lady might have died of fright.

(*There is a slight pause.*)

SIMON (*mocking*). How do you know it was a "young lady"?

LEONARD. Well now, Simon, you don't look to me the sort of young man who'd go to all that trouble for anybody else. May I ask what it was you hoped to gain?

SIMON (*after drinking*). It's quite simple, really. I wanted her to get a divorce. (*He takes another drink.*) It sounds silly, but I thought if she saw I was prepared to die for her . . .

LEONARD. But you weren't prepared to die for her—were you, Simon?

SIMON. We—ell . . . (*He grins ruefully and slightly drunkenly.*)

LEONARD. There are very few young men today who are prepared to die for love, are there? If I thought that what I had discovered on entering this apartment had been anything but a little mock charade, our association might have been rather different.

SIMON (*puzzled*). What association?

LEONARD. No matter. Tell me about this young lady of yours. Where did you meet?

SIMON. The Tate Gallery. I went in one day in the lunch hour, and she was there. She . . .

LEONARD. Dropped her gloves?

SIMON (*scornfully*). *That* went out with Queen Victoria.

LEONARD (*murmuring*). Forgive me, I'm old-fashioned. (*He rises, moves to the table and puts down his glass.*)

SIMON. We both happened to be looking at the same picture.

LEONARD. "Woman Taken in Adultery"?

SIMON (*ignoring this*). It was a Picasso. And I just simply said to her: "Do you like Picasso?" and she said she did.

LEONARD. Ah, now that's something a young man can get away with—and an old man can't. If I went up to a young girl in similar circumstances and said: "Do you like Picasso?" she'd either look round for the attendant or use one of those modern phrases like "Get lost, Grandpa!" (*He smiles sadly.*) Anyway—you went on from there.

SIMON (*flippantly*). Never looked back. (*He lies back.*)

(*There is a pause.* LEONARD *moves to the window, then turns.*)

LEONARD. Tell me, Simon, how did you manage to conduct this *liaison dangereuse* without the young woman's husband finding out? I do remember, in my youth, that used to be one of my problems.

SIMON. Well, it was a bit difficult. We got fed up with the lunch hour.

LEONARD (*smiling*). Such a rush, isn't it?

SIMON (*sleepily*). Anyway, he used to go to his club every Friday night, so we started meeting then.

LEONARD. And that wasn't enough? You wanted to see her all the time?

SIMON. Well, it was a bit of a nuisance—being tied down to one evening a week—and Friday used to be my squash night.

LEONARD (*looking at him in some astonishment*). You know, I can't understand what any woman can see in a young man like yourself.

SIMON (*sitting up*). I beg your pardon?

LEONARD. You're so selfish. (*He moves to* SIMON.) I mean, we older men are so much more appreciative, so much more grateful for small mercies. We're not interested in sports evenings and nights with the boys.

SIMON. I say—look here . . .

LEONARD. But then we lose out physically every time, don't we? Receding hair —false teeth—tired legs . . . Not to be compared with a young man in his prime.

SIMON. But it's not just a physical thing. I'm perfectly serious about wanting her to get a divorce.

LEONARD. Are you sure she wouldn't lose just a little of her attraction if she did?

SIMON (*looking a little glassy-eyed*). Perfectly sure.

LEONARD. And why won't she get a divorce?

SIMON. Well—(*He swallows his drink.*) she married him when she was sixteen, you see—(*holding out his glass to* LEONARD) and she won't leave him—

(LEONARD *takes both glasses to the bookcase and pours two more drinks, putting down further money.*)

(SIMON's *voice a little slurred*)—father image, I suppose. You don't have to keep paying for those drinks, you know.

(LEONARD *returns with the drinks.*)

Anyway—(*Swinging his legs off the divan and sitting up*) she's married to this old fuddy-duddy—impotent, boring, falling-asleep-in-the-chair type. (*He takes the drink from* LEONARD. *As he does so, a faint kind of realization comes to him as to who* LEONARD *might be, but he cannot quite seem to sort out his thoughts. He drinks.*)

(LEONARD *moves away and sits above the table.*)

I said to her: "He's an old man—" he's quite well off, I believe, "—he can get a housekeeper." But she's sentimental. . . . (*He looks oddly at* LEONARD, *and blinks his eyes curiously a few times, as if there was something wrong with his vision again.*)

LEONARD. And she didn't turn up today.

SIMON (*yawning*). No. It's the first time —for ages. (*He blinks again.*) I ought to ring her and find out—but I can't—because of . . . (*He yawns.*)

LEONARD. Him?

SIMON. Yes. But I can't understand— she's always managed. . . . (*He takes a drink.*)

LEONARD. Perhaps he locked her in somewhere.

SIMON. Yes, that's more than likely. (*He wipes his hand across his brow.*) The old . . .

LEONARD. Buzzard?

SIMON (*grinning*). Yes. If I could only— I'd like to take her to the—you know what you were saying—the Côte—I'd like to take . . . (*He yawns again and blinks his eyes.*) Wouldn't go—on my own.

LEONARD. There are some lovely girls there, Simon.

SIMON. Yes, but not like her—not like— (*after the slightest pause*) Monica. (*Beads of sweat appear on his brow. He rises.*) I think I'd like more soda—(*He looks down at his glass.*) with my . . . (*He sways, as if unable to walk, then holds out his glass.*) Would you . . . ?

LEONARD (*rising*). Certainly. (*He takes the glass and moves to the drinks.*)

SIMON. You know—(*He sways again.*) you don't have to keep paying for all those drinks—you really don't. (*He takes a step or two and falls on his knees on the polar bear rug.*)

LEONARD. Is there something wrong?

SIMON (*muttering*). Dizzy—I feel— dizz . . .

LEONARD (*putting the glasses back on the tray*). You shouldn't play games with gas, Simon.

SIMON. Yes—it's the gas. The gas—and the drink—on top. (*He makes an effort to pull himself up, and keels over.*)

LEONARD (*crossing*). I am sorry. Let me help you. (*He tries rather ineffectually to get* SIMON *up.*)

SIMON. I feel so sleepy. I want to go to sleep . . .

LEONARD. Yes, well, if we could get you to the bed . . . (*He cannot succeed in getting* SIMON *to his feet.*)

SIMON. It's no use. (*He slumps down on the rug again.*) Let me go to sleep—please. . . . (*He lies full-length on the rug, his head upstage.*)

(LEONARD *looks at him for a moment, then turns.*)

LEONARD. I'll get you some cushions. (*He brings the cushions from the divan.*) Make you more comfortable. (*He puts them under* SIMON's *head, and straightens out his legs.*) There, that's better, isn't it?

(SIMON *looks at him glassily.*)

(*Straightening up and looking down at* SIMON). Do you feel a little cold? I'll shut the window. (SIMON *makes a feeble gesture, but* LEONARD *ignores it and moves to the window.*) It's getting dark anyway, isn't it? (*He shuts the window and closes the curtains, then turns on a small lamp on the mantelpiece and tilts the light deliberately towards* SIMON.) Not in your eyes, I hope?

SIMON (*blinking*). What time is it? (*His voice is far away.*) Is it time to go to sleep?

LEONARD (*gently*). It soon will be. Just lie quietly. Or would you like your book? (*He takes the book from the divan and gives it to* SIMON. *The book slips from* SIMON's *fingers, half on, half off his chest.* LEONARD *moves to the table and picks up his bowler and umbrella.*) A little quiet read . . .

(SIMON's *eyes half close, then open again. They follow* LEONARD *glassily.*)

SIMON. Are you going? Where—are— you . . . ?

LEONARD (*putting on his bowler*). Somewhere warm and sunny—like I was telling you about. You know, when I first came in I thought I might persuade you to go there. I even thought I might live here in your place. (*He goes to the mirror.*) Take over your existence. (*He gazes at his reflection—an elderly man with bowler and umbrella.*) But then, I don't look right, do I? (*He turns.*) Do you think they'll ever find the secret of eternal youth, Simon? (*He crosses and stands above* SIMON.) But then that sort of thought doesn't really worry you, does it? Youth is curiously uncurious about age. (*He looks down at him.*)

(SIMON's *eyes stare. His body gives a slight shiver.* LEONARD *takes a pair of gloves from his pocket and puts them on.*)

(*Moving round above* SIMON). Would you like the fire on, Simon? (*He bends down and turns on the gas-tap, but does not light the fire. The gas hisses faintly.* LEONARD *turns and looks down at* SIMON.) I'm going now.

SIMON (*in blurred speech*). You haven't . . .

LEONARD. I haven't . . . ?

SIMON (*his eyes beginning to close*). You haven't told me . . .

(*The gas hisses.*)

You never—told me—what—you want?

(*There is a pause.*)

(LEONARD *leans over him. His voice is more reminiscent of earlier on.*)

LEONARD. Mr. Elliott, I don't believe you could take it in.

SIMON's *eyelids flutter slightly and then slowly close. He lies very still. There is a pause, then* LEONARD *walks to the waste-paper basket and takes out the rose and the envelope. He puts the rose sadly to his nose, then gently places it on* SIMON's *chest. He looks at the envelope for a moment, then folds it over and puts it in his pocket. With his hat on and his umbrella over his arm, he turns and walks out of the room as—*

THE CURTAIN FALLS

THE WINDOW

Frank Marcus

RICHARD TREMAYNE   KEN
                                                    RALPH

FRANK MARCUS joined the inner circle of modern international playwrights with his "dark" comedy *The Killing of Sister George,* which scored heavily on both the London and Broadway stages with Beryl Reid as the title figure. At its opening in 1965, *The* (London) *Times* hailed the play as "the best comedy by a new writer to appear in the West End for a long time." To equalize matters, the *Evening News and Star*'s distinguished critic, Felix Barker, greeted the author as "a major playwright in the making."

A dexterous creator of unusual characters implicated in uncommonly provocative situations, Mr. Marcus also possesses that rare and enviable theatrical commodity: the ability to be both comic and affecting almost within the same breath. This striking characteristic is manifest both in *The Killing of Sister George* and his new short play *The Window,* published for the first time in this anthology. Similarly, both plays underscore Mr. Marcus' concern with the problem of illusion versus reality.

The author was born in 1928, in Breslau, Germany, and migrated to England just before the outbreak of World War II. After completing his education and a tenure at the St. Martin's Art School, he organized the International Theatre Group, an experimental company that performed in London's little theatres with Mr. Marcus functioning as actor, director, and designer.

His first West End play, *The Formation Dancers,* was presented at the Globe Theatre in 1964. Selected and published as one of the *"Plays of the Year, 1964–65,"* it also brought him to the attention of producer Michael Codron. The latter invited the promising young dramatist to write a play for his production auspices with a powerful part for a "star" actress. The resultant *The Killing of Sister George,* written in eight weeks, subsequently, won him a packet of "Best Play of the Year" awards, notably the prestigious seasonal citation from the London Theatre Critics.

Alerted, however, to the vagaries of the theatre, Mr. Marcus, who is married and the father of three, continued to operate a London antique silver shop (a family concern) until completely assured of the acceptance and success of *The Killing of Sister George.*

Frank Marcus' recent dramatic works include: *Studies In the Nude,* produced at the Hampstead Theatre Club in 1967; a new screen treatment of Ibsen's *Hedda Gabler;* and three original plays for television. He also provided the basic theme and concept of the mimedrama *Le Trois Perruques,* for his close friend Marcel Marceau, the celebrated French pantomimist.

SCENE. *The bedroom and ante-room of a small, modern flat. An early evening in June.* RICHARD TREMAYNE *sits propped up against his pillows, smoking a cigarette through a holder. The transistor radio by his side is switched on, playing the overture to* Orpheus in the Underworld. *A pleasant glow of sunshine comes from the window on the left; the window is open, and the curtains are slightly agitated by the breeze.*

There is a buzz from the front door, followed almost immediately by the sound of a key turning in the lock. KEN *enters: a small, youngish man in a raincoat, carrying a carrier-bag.*

———

KEN (*calling*). Mr. Tremayne? Are you there, sir?

TREMAYNE (*switching off the radio*). Hello! Come in, this way. (KEN *enters the bedroom.*) I've been expecting you.

KEN. I'm sorry I'm a bit late, sir. Ralph didn't tell me until Tuesday. . . .

TREMAYNE. No need to apologize. Make yourself at home. There's a plate of this frozen food stuff in the fridge. I think you'll find everything you want.

KEN. Thank you, sir. (*He goes to the kitchen.*)

TREMAYNE (*calling after him*). You'll find a can of beer there, too. Ralph got that in specially.

KEN (*from the kitchen*). Thank you. Yes, I can see it. (*He busies himself in the kitchen.*)

(*Pause*)

TREMAYNE (*calling*). I say!

KEN (*returning*). Yes, sir?

TREMAYNE. I don't know your name.

KEN. Oh, it's Ken, sir. I've known Ralph for some time. We were in the army . . .

TREMAYNE. I see. (*Pause*) Ralph's been with me for nearly four years, you know.

KEN. Yes, he often talks about you.

TREMAYNE. Not in a derogatory way, I hope.

KEN (*embarrassed*). Oh, no, sir. Far from it—

TREMAYNE. I was only joking.

(*Pause*)

KEN. Have you eaten, sir?

TREMAYNE. Yes, thank you. Ralph always brings in dinner, before he goes out. Just look after yourself; don't worry about me.

(KEN *goes back to the kitchen, and* TREMAYNE *switches on the wireless again.* KEN, *carrying a plate in his hands, stands uncertainly in the doorway.*)

TREMAYNE. Did you want something? (KEN, *startled, nearly drops the plate.*) You didn't think I could see you.

KEN. It wasn't that, sir—

TREMAYNE (*switching off the radio again*). Most people are surprised at the way I . . . sense where they are. You see, when one is blind, one develops one's other faculties to a very marked degree. I can almost—don't laugh—I can almost exactly visualise what you look like. By the way, do sit down by that little table and have your dinner. You see, I have a highly developed imagination.

KEN. That's . . . very interesting. (*He sits down, and starts eating.*) What do I look like, then? Let's hear the worst.

TREMAYNE. You are smallish—I can hear that from the direction of your voice: you are quite plump, I should say—

KEN (*laughing*). I could do with losing a few pounds!

TREMAYNE. Obviously, you must be about Ralph's age—twenty-eight?

KEN. Twenty-nine, actually. Still, that's near enough. . . .

TREMAYNE. I see you with brown, curly hair, with a sort of quiff—you know, a small cascade, in the middle—

KEN (*involuntarily putting his hand to his hair*). I say, I'm beginning to think you're pretending to be blind.

TREMAYNE (*a slight nervous laugh*). Yes, that's what many of them think. And you have a face like a coconut.

KEN. A coconut?

TREMAYNE. Please, don't take offence. I am in the habit of thinking of faces in terms of animals, plants, or fruit. The second I heard you I knew you had a fruit face. It was just a question of deciding. . . .

KEN. I don't know whether to be flattered, or what.

TREMAYNE. Coconuts are excellent: firm, nourishing, exotic really. Cigarette?

KEN (*helping himself*). Thank you, sir.

TREMAYNE. Meal all right?

KEN. Yes, thank you, sir.

TREMAYNE. There's a tin of fruit salad—

KEN. I'll have that later, if I may, sir.

TREMAYNE. As you wish.

KEN. May I ask you a question, sir?

TREMAYNE. Certainly, by all means.

KEN. If you're so good at guessing, or sensing, all this about people, why don't you get about a bit more? I mean, it would do you good to get out a bit. Lying in here, all cooped up—

TREMAYNE. Don't you like this flat?

KEN. Oh, no, it's not that! It's a lovely flat; very cosy, really, and convenient, I should say. . . .

(*Pause*)

TREMAYNE (*thoughtfully puffing on his cigarette*). The accepted thing to do is to try to overcome one's disabilities, eh? After all, there's some little thing wrong with almost everybody.

KEN. Quite, quite, that's just what I mean—

TREMAYNE. The gentleman in the queue walks with only the merest limp: one would never guess . . . a miracle of science . . . it's amazing what they can do nowadays. Teeth, eyes, limbs—in the safety of their bedrooms thousands of people disintegrate like badly constructed marionettes. And one would never guess! Where will it all end? Limbless pilots, blind motor-cyclists, bald beauty queens. (*In the tones of a television compère*) "This gentleman has been blind from birth. Give him a cheer! Hurrah!" And the ardent lover's hand shudders at the touch of his beloved's false bosom . . .

(*Pause*)

KEN. I can't say I've ever looked at it in this light. Of course, I used to do a bit of nursing. . . .

TREMAYNE. A male nurse?

KEN. I was never qualified, or anything. Just used to help out in an old people's home. And nowadays I look after my mother; she's bedridden, too.

TREMAYNE (*quietly*). So Ralph has left me in competent hands. . . .

KEN. I'll do my best, sir.

TREMAYNE. He told you, I take it?

KEN (*quickly*). Yes, sir.

TREMAYNE. And . . . what did you think?

KEN. Look, I'm here to do a job, to help out an old friend. It's not my place to probe into what people do, or want, or anything. As long as it's not illegal . . .

TREMAYNE. Admirable sentiments.

KEN. Would you like me to read to you, sir? The papers or anything?

TREMAYNE. You can read me a page of this. I got as far as "groundsel."

KEN. *The Oxford Dictionary!* Are you interested in words, then? I used to go to evening classes at the Polytechnic. . . .

TREMAYNE. "Groundsel."

KEN (*reading*) "Groundsel. (*archaic*) Timber serving as foundation, lowest part of wooden framework; threshold." Next: "Group. (*Fine Arts*) two or more figures or objects forming complete design or distinct part of one . . ."

TREMAYNE. Stop! I can't . . . I can't bear it. . . .

KEN. Anything wrong, sir? Are you in pain?

TREMAYNE (*shaking his head*). No, no, it will pass. (*Pause*) Sit down there, Ken. Make yourself comfortable.

KEN (*sitting down*). If there's anything you want . . .

TREMAYNE. It was the sound of your voice—I was trying to get used to it. After all, you'll have to do a lot of talking, afterwards. . . . I want everything kept quite impersonal, you understand? I shall want you to report quite unemotionally what you see, unadorned by sentiment or inhibition.

KEN (*nervously*). Yes, I know. Ralph told me.

(*Pause*)

TREMAYNE. What time is it?

KEN. Just on eleven, sir.

TREMAYNE. Good. That should give us another clear half hour. You seem to be a sensitive sort of chap, Ken. I think I shall tell you something about the background of this whole . . . thing. To try to make you understand.

KEN. That's very kind of you, sir, but I am really not at all curious. I'll just do what you ask me to do, without getting personally involved.

TREMAYNE. Have you ever been in love? (*No reply*) You consider this question as prying? Don't be afraid to tell me.

KEN. Well, yes, sir, I don't really see as it's got anything to do . . .

TREMAYNE. Your innermost feelings are your own, eh? An impenetrable citadel.

Splendid.

KEN. Well, I'm not asking *you* anything, so it's only fair . . .

TREMAYNE. Be quiet. You are being impertinent. (*Losing his temper*) You can leave, if you like! I can manage without you, or Ralph or anybody! Get out, you smug bastard! Do you hear me—get out!!

KEN (*pale and anxious*). I haven't said nothing!

TREMAYNE (*trembling*). Give me a light. (KEN *quickly holds a match to* TREMAYNE'S *cigarette.*) I'm sorry. I'm sorry—forgive me.

KEN (*relieved*). That's all right, sir. Don't worry, it's just that you're a bit on edge, like. It's not really surprising, after all you've been through.

TREMAYNE. Sit down. Are you quite comfortable?

KEN. Oh, yes, perfectly, sir.

TREMAYNE. Please, stop calling me "sir."

KEN. As you wish, s— Mr. Tremayne. Would you like me to go on with the reading?

TREMAYNE. No, thank you, Ken. Just sit still, and listen.

KEN. I'm listening, Mr. Tremayne.

TREMAYNE. I lost my sight in a car crash —Ralph will no doubt have told you—

KEN. A most unfortunate accident.

TREMAYNE. It was no accident: I had meant to kill myself. Does that shock you? It was in Cornwall—quite near where I was born. It seemed fitting to me, in keeping with my sense of style, that I should end where I began. It would have made an artistic whole.

KEN (*quietly*). I am sorry, sir.

TREMAYNE (*bitterly*). Your sympathy is entirely misplaced. Imagine for a moment —no, seriously, try to imagine—what makes a man attempt suicide. Imagine the days and nights spent trying to solve the insoluble, to resolve the unresolvable— for, make no mistake, I tried desperately to live, to find an excuse for living. But every time, turn how I may, the same stark conclusion confronted me at the end: death. I had to die—there was no other choice. For weeks I struggled to find an acceptable alternative—no good! Like a feared but familiar face, Death smiled at me from the darkness. Once I accepted it, I felt relieved, almost at peace. My time

was taken up with devising intricate ways of ending my life. Nothing hasty, nothing sordid; something that would sum up neatly my endeavours and my ideals. In the end I decided to crash my car through the sea-wall at dawn. I fixed the exact spot—a spot that held the most pleasurable recollections for me. By crashing there, I would destroy, but also in a way perpetuate, this recollection.

KEN. Might I ask what kind of recollection it was?

TREMAYNE. Yes, of course you may. It was the exact spot from which I first saw her.

KEN (*quickly*). Oh, I see. I'm sorry, I didn't mean—

TREMAYNE. That's perfectly all right: you are entitled to know. It was the spot directly in front of a beach hut rented annually by my parents. One day—I must have been about twenty—I stood idly gazing at the sea, when I heard a voice just below me, from the beach. It was a child's voice. She was squatting down, her legs like matchsticks, talking to herself while arranging pebbles and sea-shells in neat rows. I couldn't see her face—she had her back to me. Only the blinding glory of her long fair hair, reflecting the sun. I returned to the hut, thinking nothing more of it. (*He puffs at his cigarette.*) A week or so later, I saw her again. She came running up to the hut, tear-stained, heartbroken. "Please, please," she implored me, "my beach ball is floating away on the waves. It was all new—a birthday present!" I ran down to the sea. The beach ball seemed quite close, lightly riding the waves. I swam out after it, as fast as I could. Every time I came within grasping distance of it, it eluded me, by slipping away over an oncoming wave. There it was: glistening brightly in the sun. I can see it now: red, white, yellow, and green stripes. I must have swum after it for a long time—longer than was good for me; I had been recuperating from a serious illness. The next thing I remember was hearing her child's voice again. "Please, don't die, please, don't die" she kept repeating, like an incantation. I remember thinking: "How funny, whoever wants to die?" I opened my eyes. I was lying on the beach, and there was a small group of people standing around me, staring at me. It appears that I had lost consciousness in the water, and a passing fishing boat got to me just in time and picked me up. My first words were: "Where's the ball?" "What ball, what ball?" she said, uncomprehending. I scanned the horizon—there was the beach ball: a tiny black spot, gently bobbing up and down. If I had died that day, everything would have been perfect . . .

KEN. One never knows. It's not right to say things like that. . . .

TREMAYNE. Are you religious? (*No reply.*) You're lucky, really lucky. I could never manage it, and I tried hard.

(*Pause*)

KEN. Was that the . . . young lady. . . ?

TREMAYNE (*lost in reminiscence*). I referred to her jokingly as "my would-be murderess" . . . We became really good friends, although I was twice her age. . . . (*A clock strikes.*) It's half past; we must get ready!

KEN. Where shall I sit?

TREMAYNE (*indicating the window*). In that armchair. You'll find the binoculars at the side, on the window-sill.

KEN (*having settled in the chair*). I've got them, sir.

TREMAYNE. Quite comfortable?

KEN. Yes, thank you.

TREMAYNE. The glasses were adjusted to Ralph's requirements. I believe he has normal eyesight.

KEN. So have I, thank God.

TREMAYNE. Train them carefully on the ground-floor opposite, the fourth window from the left. Have you got that?

KEN. Yes, I have got that. There's nothing to be seen. (*He is relieved.*)

TREMAYNE. Describe the furniture.

KEN. Well, it's just an ordinary living-room: sideboard, dining table, chairs—

TREMAYNE. Television?

KEN. Yes, in the corner—

TREMAYNE. You are wrong: there is no television.

KEN (*stuttering*). Well, what is it, then? It looks like—

TREMAYNE. My poor Ken. You are short-sighted! Go on, lad, try again: adjust your binoculars. Go on.

KEN (*looking very hard*). It's a sort of . . . of cupboard.

TREMAYNE (*sighing with relief*). That's better. You mustn't think me pedantic, Ken, but exactitude of observation is essential in these matters.

KEN. I quite appreciate that.

TREMAYNE. Can you distinguish the picture above the sideboard?

KEN (*quickly*). Yes, it's a face: a clown's face.

TREMAYNE. Good! Yes! Yes, it's a Rouault print I gave her for her twenty-first birthday. . . .

(*Pause*)

KEN. There's nobody in there.

TREMAYNE. There wouldn't be, just yet. Maybe another twenty minutes or so. Keep looking, though. Don't shift your glance for a single moment—you must tell me the minute you see anything.

KEN. You can rely on me, Mr. Tremayne.

TREMAYNE. Help yourself to another cigarette.

KEN. Not just yet, sir, thank you.

TREMAYNE. How strange to think that you are about to see her for the very first time, and you're not even excited by the prospect. . . .

KEN. But I *am,* sir, I'm really curious—

TREMAYNE (*sharply*). Don't turn to speak to me—keep looking!

KEN. Sorry.

TREMAYNE. Do you believe in love at first sight? Don't answer. Of course, I had known her as a child; then, for almost five years, I lost touch with her. I sometimes thought of her—remembering her as a child. It never occurred to me that she must have grown up.

KEN. How did you meet her again?

TREMAYNE. By a complete coincidence. I had arranged to meet a friend at the theatre. He told me he'd bring a girl, but I had no idea who she would be. They were late. I sat in my seat, furious that they would disturb me and the other people in the row I was sitting in. The national anthem was played—still no sign of them. The house-lights dimmed, the curtain rose. The play was *Twelfth Night* —a miserable, stilted performance. Suddenly, very softly, hardly noticeably, I felt someone occupying the seat next to mine. I didn't even look. Then a very quiet voice: "Sorry we were late—my fault, I'm afraid." I turned. I didn't recognize her in the dark, but she immediately recognized me. From the moment she looked at me, she never took her eyes off me. I could feel them on me throughout the performance: I felt quite embarrassed, and ashamed for my friend. Large, blue eyes, at the same time liquid and steely. Extraordinary eyes. Then, suddenly, she whispered to me: "Please, don't die, please, don't die." (*He is very moved by the recollection.*) Why did you say that, my darling, in that tone of voice? It's what Beauty says to the Beast in the fairy-tale. What would you say to me now, my beloved, if you !new? (*A long pause.*) Anyone there yet?

KEN. No, sir, not yet. I haven't stopped looking.

TREMAYNE. I cannot think back on that meeting without pangs of nostalgia. You know, as one gets older, recollections can really hurt—in a physical way, I mean. I don't know what it is about one's youth that one misses so much: I think it is the quality of hope. Time never seems pressing—the future seems vast and promising. All one's ambitions and ideals seem fulfillable. Calamities are merely pebbles in one's path. The look she gave me that night in the darkened auditorium made my heart jump . . . I had the complete certainty that perfection was at hand . . .

KEN (*sighing*). I know just how you must have felt, sir.

TREMAYNE (*interested*). Really? You, too, have felt—

KEN. Many a time.

TREMAYNE. Tell me about it.

KEN. I can't, sir. You mustn't get angry, but I really can't express these things. Anyway, I should think most people have these high hopes at one time or another; if they didn't, hardly anybody would ever get married, now would they?

TREMAYNE. You don't like women, do you? (*No reply.*) Don't be ashamed to tell me; I am quite unshockable. We all have our little idiosyncrasies. . . . (KEN *gets up, and angrily puts the binoculars on the window-sill.*) Ken, what have you done? (*Very worried.*) What . . . are you doing?

KEN. I don't know what I'm doing here. I should never have come.

TREMAYNE. Get back to this chair! You can't leave now—it's nearly time.

KEN. I told you I didn't want to get personally involved—

TREMAYNE (*apologetically*). Yes, I know, I shouldn't have questioned you. I am really, deeply sorry. I have so little contact with people; I tend to get curious—not in any morbid way, I assure you. Please, stay, Ken, I beg you. I am completely in your hands: I entirely rely on you.

KEN. Why did you say that, then, about me?

TREMAYNE. I wanted to find out how you would look at her. I am pleased, really pleased, that you . . . are what you are. I like the commentary to be truly dispassionate, untainted—

KEN. In that case, why did you tell me all these stories, all this past history?

TREMAYNE. Because I wanted you to understand. My God, *don't* you understand? I have asked you to come here to do something that most people would regard as perverted, if not obscene: something morally reprehensible. By explaining to you, I tried to make you realize that what you are asked to do is not degrading, but part of an expression of love: a love without which I cannot live. The last remaining reason for my existence. Please, please, go back.

KEN. All right, Mr. Tremayne. If it's something you need—

TREMAYNE. Have you got the glasses? (*Anxiously.*) Are they adjusted?

KEN (*after giving* TREMAYNE *a long look, and shaking his head*). I'm focusing them now.

TREMAYNE. Well? Well, is anyone there? Why don't you speak? Has she come in?

KEN (*steadily*). She has just come in, sir.

TREMAYNE (*to himself*). Thank God, thank God . . . Tell me, tell me everything!

KEN. There's not much to tell, really. She's just sort of . . . tidying up.

TREMAYNE. What is she wearing? What does she look like? What do you think of her, Ken? Isn't she beautiful? Honestly now, as an impartial observer, have I exaggerated?

KEN. She's a very nice-looking girl, sir.

TREMAYNE. Yes . . . yes. Is she wearing her hair up or down?

KEN. She's wearing it up. She's just put on a house-coat, or dressing-gown, is it?

TREMAYNE. It's a dressing-gown. She has never owned a house-coat. She would regard that with contempt—women's magazine stuff. What is she doing?

KEN. Still tidying—papers and stuff.

TREMAYNE. Does she seem happy? Is she singing to herself?

KEN. She's gone to the kitchen—but that window's got curtains up.

TREMAYNE. Yes, I know. I know. She's probably preparing a meal. She usually has . . . someone round for dinner on Thursday night. I wonder who it'll be? And not only Thursdays. I'd better tell you, Ken, she has men calling on her. Regularly, you understand?

KEN. I understand.

TREMAYNE. Ralph knows them all by sight—he has nicknames for each of them.

KEN. Do the same ones always call on the same evenings?

TREMAYNE. Oh, yes, they are . . . regular . . . clients . . .

KEN. It's a shame, really, isn't it, sir, that a nice girl—

TREMAYNE. It had to happen. It was inevitable. It was in her nature. Nobody could have saved her—I realize that now—

KEN. She's come back again. . . . Looks like she's laying the table for dinner—

TREMAYNE. You see—I told you!

KEN. Dinner for two. A cosy little party . . .

TREMAYNE. Can you see her face? It should be quite clear: it's still light, isn't it?

KEN. Yes, I can see her clearly.

TREMAYNE. She's not beautiful, certainly not in a classical sense. Do you know what I used to like best about her face? Liked, you know, rather than admired? You will laugh—her nostrils! I used to say they were curved as delicately as those of a Dresden shepherdess. . . . Can you see her?

KEN. She's gone to the sideboard—wine glasses?

TREMAYNE. That's her attempt at gracious living. Nothing must ever be sordid. Although some of the men who call on her . . .

KEN. You can't always go by appearances.

TREMAYNE. I don't. But, sometimes, you know, they go to her bedroom—and in the heat of the moment forget to draw the curtains.

KEN (shocked). Surely Ralph doesn't—

TREMAYNE. He tells me everything. Detailed descriptions. You see, I have to know the truth.

KEN. I should have thought there were some things—

TREMAYNE (sharply). You are not here to think. What is she doing now?

KEN (slowly). She's making herself look pretty. I expect he's due any moment.

TREMAYNE. She's combing her hair?

KEN. At the moment, she's putting on some lipstick.

TREMAYNE. I wish she wouldn't do that. All the time we were together, she never used any make-up. It just wasn't necessary. Her mouth is beautifully shaped; she has a very well-defined upper lip. She had a habit of sucking it in when she had done something wrong. It made her look so childish and vulnerable that one instantly forgave her—it was completely disarming.

KEN (announcing). He's arrived.

TREMAYNE. What? Who has arrived?

KEN. The man. The visitor.

TREMAYNE. Who is it? What does he look like?

KEN. A young man—nice looking, really. One of those casual suede jackets—Italian, I think they are.

TREMAYNE. It must be Gerald. That's the name Ralph gave him.

KEN. That's the one—I mean, he looks like a "Gerald."

TREMAYNE. Please, confine your observations to what you see.

KEN. Well, they greeted each other very cordially—a nice hug, you know. He brought her a box of—chocolates, would it be?

TREMAYNE. Most probably. Yes, he's one of the . . . better-mannered ones. Gerald. Funny, I almost approve of Gerald. The sort of innocuous young man she might have married, if . . .

KEN. I don't think you would approve if you saw them now!

TREMAYNE. What—what are they doing? (KEN *sniggers*.) Speak, blast you!

KEN. Well, it's getting rather intimate. They're on the settee. She's lying across his lap.

(*Pause*)

TREMAYNE. Go on! (*Nothing from* KEN.) Go on!!

KEN. I'd have thought, with your highly developed imagination—

TREMAYNE. Please, Ken. Please. I didn't mean to antagonize you. I must know—can't you understand?

KEN. Oh, all right.

TREMAYNE. Well? He's unbuttoned her blouse?

KEN. She's taken it off. He's kissing her . . . all over. (TREMAYNE *hurls the dictionary in the direction of* KEN.) Steady, sir. (*He jumps up.*) That could have hurt me, if it had landed on my head.

TREMAYNE (*choked with anger*). It was aimed at her! False, false . . . she betrays me. Every day of the week she betrays me. Why does she do it? I gave her everything . . . (*He buries his face in his pillows, shaking.*)

KEN (*with a glance at the window*). Poor man.

TREMAYNE (*collecting himself*). Go . . . to the window. What are they doing now?

KEN (*quickly*). They have gone. I expect they have gone to her room now.

TREMAYNE. Are you sure? You're not just saying this to spare me?

KEN. There's nobody in the living-room, Mr. Tremayne, cross my heart and hope to die.

TREMAYNE. The bedroom? The window on the extreme right.

KEN. Curtains drawn, nothing to be seen.

TREMAYNE. The light on?

KEN. No light; there's nothing to be seen.

TREMAYNE. Give me a cigarette. (KEN *hands him a cigarette, and lights a match for him.*) Thank you. I ought to be used to it by now. It happens as regularly as clockwork. The same meaningless actions, again and again.

KEN. I don't suppose it's meaningless to the parties concerned.

TREMAYNE. That's where you are wrong. The moment it's over, it becomes meaningless.

KEN. Yes, but while it lasts . . .

TREMAYNE (*icily*). Get back to your chair, and watch, and report when you see something. (*He switches on the wireless, and smokes his cigarette in silence.*)

KEN (*with a smile on his face*). It is darkening. Soon I won't be able to distinguish anything.

TREMAYNE (*lost in thought*). What did you say?

KEN. Nothing. Nothing of importance. (*A long pause*)

TREMAYNE. Every time it's the same: the same anxiety, the same tension, the same despair . . . (*softly, to himself*) There's no shirking it: I must imagine it all. Every gesture, every look, every breath she takes . . . What am I hoping for? A miracle? That she will suddenly call my name? Loud enough for me to hear across the courtyard?

KEN. There's no sign of any activity, sir. (*An embarrassed laugh.*)

TREMAYNE. In the fairy-tale, the Beast is saved in the nick of time. Maybe one has to go to the very limit—to hold a knife to one's throat, and start counting to ten? And what happens after "ten"? One goes on counting: "ten plus one, ten plus two . . ." As long as there's the smallest glimmer of hope.

KEN. Can I get you anything? It seems pointless—

TREMAYNE. Stay where you are! You are not to shift your eyes from the room. What happens afterwards is as important. . . . One night, after he had gone, she sat and cried. For a long time. Ralph watched her, and she just sat there and cried, till it got dark and Ralph could not see her anymore. That night I wrote her a long letter. I told her everything; about the car crash, my sight, everything.

KEN. You told her that you were having her watched every night?

TREMAYNE. Yes, that too. But I never sent off the letter.

KEN. Why not?

TREMAYNE. Because I had to dictate the letter to Ralph. Imagine receiving a personal letter like this in someone else's handwriting? With spelling mistakes, and words crossed out?

KEN. Why should Ralph make spelling

mistakes?

TREMAYNE. Because he is careless, and half-educated.

KEN (*jumping up*). Mr. Tremayne, I'm not going to sit here and have my friend insulted—

TREMAYNE (*shouting*). You will sit there, and do as I tell you! You were hired to do a job, remember?

(*Pause*)

KEN (*picking up the binoculars*). They have just come out of her room. He's trying to put on his coat. She's pulling it off him again. She seems to be laughing. She's barring the door. He's getting nervous, pointing to his watch. They are having a sort of fight. They're on the settee now. He's got her across his knee, and is starting to spank her. Oh, dear me, what a carry-on!

TREMAYNE (*hoarsely*). You are lying!

KEN. Am I just? Why don't you get someone else from outside to confirm?

TREMAYNE. Go on—stop complaining.

KEN. He's taken some of her clothes off again. They seem to be preparing to make love again.

TREMAYNE. No! No!!

KEN. Would you rather I drew the curtains, sir? It's hardly decent to watch them, is it now?

TREMAYNE. Yes, no . . . I don't know. (*Pause.*) Watch them. Go on watching them.

KEN (*primly taking up his binoculars*). It's as I thought, Mr. Tremayne: they are making love.

TREMAYNE. Describe it. (*Long pause.*) Describe it, Ken. Describe it!

KEN. Surely you don't expect me to go into anatomical details?

TREMAYNE. I expect you to tell me what you see.

KEN. They are on the settee . . . she is completely naked . . . I—I don't know . . . it's getting rather dark.

TREMAYNE. You don't want to see a man and a woman together, do you? You think it abnormal, don't you? It makes you sick, doesn't it?

KEN. No need to get het up. They're both getting dressed now, anyway. I expect he'll be gone in a minute—what with looking at his watch.

TREMAYNE. Where is—she?

KEN. She's got her house-coat—sorry, dressing-gown—on now. She's giving him a kiss now; he's on his way. (*Getting up*) Can I have my fruit salad now, please?

TREMAYNE. Do what you damn well like.

KEN. Very polite, I'm sure. (*He goes off to the kitchen.*)

TREMAYNE (*exhausted*). Well, and where does that get you? You are alone again, just like me. . . .

KEN (*re-entering, holding a bowl of fruit salad*). Is there anything further you'll be requiring, sir?

TREMAYNE. I must thank you—and apologize.

KEN. No need to do that. You hired me; I did what you wanted, that's all. (*He eats.*)

TREMAYNE. I completely forgot to settle—

KEN. Don't you worry about that! Ralph said you'd see me all right.

TREMAYNE. Yes, I'll see you all right. . . . (*Pause*)

KEN. It's amazing how long it stays light—

TREMAYNE (*excited again*). It's still light? Why didn't you say so, you fool?

KEN. Don't say you want me to go back! You're not expecting any more fireworks from your little friend tonight?

TREMAYNE. Don't try to comprehend other people's thoughts and actions. (*Pointing to the window*) If you please.

KEN (*resuming his seat in the armchair with bad grace*). Of course, I'm only the hired help . . . I don't understand nothing, I don't.

TREMAYNE. What do you see now?

KEN. There's no one in the dining room, but there seems to be someone in the kitchen. Maybe she's washing up.

TREMAYNE. She never washes up in the evening; she always leaves it till the morning.

KEN (*maliciously*). Yes, I can believe that, having seen her, got to know her—as one might say—quite intimately.

TREMAYNE. You're trying to provoke me, aren't you?

KEN. Me provoke you? Dear me, no. What gives you that idea, Mr. Tremayne?

TREMAYNE. Because you hate me for loving a woman.

KEN. Oh, we're on that again! Quite a pet subject— (*Holding the binoculars to his eyes:*) Hold on, here's little Miss Sunshine again, all brisk and cheerful—

TREMAYNE. What—what is she doing?

KEN (*secretively*). Aha. No, don't worry, dear, she's only tidying up. Are you expecting another visitor to turn up, then?

TREMAYNE. That's the worst of it—that I have to place myself in other people's hands. People like you . . .

KEN. Beggars can't be choosers.

TREMAYNE. Describe what you see, while it's still light. Before the second blanket of darkness separates us.

KEN (*wearily*). She's just busying herself—ordinary household chores.

TREMAYNE. Her face? What does she look like? Sad, happy, anxious? . . . Fulfilled?

KEN. If you want my honest opinion, Mr. Tremayne, she looks just . . . ordinary, as though nothing very special had happened.

TREMAYNE. Just a normal sort of evening . . .

KEN (*triumphantly*). Hold on—not quite as "normal" as you might think, by the look of it!

TREMAYNE. What do you mean? (*A low chuckle from* KEN.) What are you hinting at? (*Urgently.*) Will you kindly tell me what's going on?

KEN. Another visitor, Mr. Tremayne. A girl friend, this time . . .

TREMAYNE (*pale and trembling; has got out of his bed*). Let me see! (*Shouting, and groping about:*) Let me see!! (*He has knocked over a chair.*) I want to see!!

KEN (*startled*). Mr. Tremayne, careful! You'll do yourself an injury—

TREMAYNE (*pressing his face against the window-pane*). I don't believe it, I don't believe it! (*Groaning:*) Let it not be true . . .

KEN (*anxiously*). Mr. Tremayne, sir, you must get back to bed— (*He takes his arm protectively.*)

TREMAYNE (*completely beside himself*). Is it true? Look—keep looking!

KEN. It's too dark—and they've drawn the curtains now . . .

(*Pause*)

TREMAYNE. Are you sure? A woman?

KEN. Positive, sir.

TREMAYNE (*turning his back to the window, begins to sob*). That was why, Ken . . . Guide me back to bed. . . . You understand now, don't you? . . . The pills—on the sideboard there—

KEN (*having helped* TREMAYNE *back into bed*). I'll get you a glass of water, sir. Just lie quietly. . . . (*He goes off to the kitchen.*)

TREMAYNE. Ken! Ken, are you there? (*Calling:*) You haven't left, have you? (*Frightened.*) Ken!

KEN. Here's your glass of water. Now— (*Reading the label of the box*)—it says here "to be taken two at a time." There we are. (*He gives the pills to* TREMAYNE, *and makes sure he drinks the water.*) You'll feel much better soon.

TREMAYNE (*lying back*). Yes, they work wonders. They send me to sleep. (*Pause*) Ralph will be here in a moment. He will settle with you. He'll see you all right.

KEN. Not to worry. Just relax and go to sleep.

TREMAYNE. You can switch the light out, Ken, and . . . sit and wait in the kitchen. You'll find newspapers—

KEN. I'll make myself comfortable, Mr. Tremayne.

TREMAYNE (*quietly*). Good night, Ken —and thank you. Maybe another time—

KEN. Good night, Mr. Tremayne. Happy dreams. (*He switches off the light, and leaves, shutting the bedroom door behind him. He sighs a sigh of relief.*)

TREMAYNE (*whispering*). My beautiful, my princess . . . Here, put your head on my shoulder . . . spread your hair over me . . . like a blanket of gold . . . (*He falls asleep, breathing regularly.*)

(*A long pause*)

(*There are three soft buzzes from the front door.* KEN *runs to open. It is* RALPH.)

RALPH. I'd completely forgotten that I gave you my keys. I hope he hasn't—

KEN. He's fast asleep.

RALPH. Well? Everything all right?

KEN. I've had a time of it, I can tell you. . . .

RALPH. Wait, let me just check up. (*He tiptoes into the bedroom, goes to the window, and slightly opens it. He tidies up one or two things, and picks up a blanket and replaces it on the bed.*)

KEN (*whispering*). I've had a narrow escape.

RALPH (*anxiously*). Didn't you remember?

KEN. Oh, I remembered, all right.

RALPH. The Rouault print?

KEN. Yes, of course.

RALPH. And Gerald?

KEN. Yes . . . but, you see, I also invented another visitor—a woman.

RALPH (*quickly*). You shouldn't have done that.

(*Pause*)

KEN. Sorry. It was an accident. And he'd been beastly. (*Pause.*) Still, he seems quite peaceful now. One would never believe . . . (*He walks across to the window.*) It's all . . . quiet now. Just one or two lights . . . I really thought I saw her, you know. . . .

RALPH. I see her . . . every night. . . . Of course, I have one advantage over you: I really *did* see her, months ago, before she moved. . . . A pretty little thing, she was . . .

(*Pause*)

KEN (*staring out into the darkness*). I wonder . . . I'd really be curious to know . . . where she's gone. . . .

(RALPH *and* KEN *leave the room quietly, and go into the kitchen.* TREMAYNE *is sleeping peacefully. From far away, there is the whistle of a train.*)

END

BIRDBATH

Leonard Melfi

Birdbath was first presented by Theatre Genesis on June 11, 1965, at St. Mark's Church in-the-Bowery, New York City, with the following cast:

FRANKIE BASTA Kevin O'Connor   VELMA SPARROW Barbara Young

Directed by Ralph Cook

Subsequently, *Birdbath* was presented by Theodore Mann and Paul Libin with the Circle in the Square on April 11, 1966, at the Martinique Theatre, New York City, as part of the bill, *Six From La Mama,* with the following cast:

FRANKIE BASTA Kevin O'Connor   VELMA SPARROW Mari-Claire Charba

Directed by Tom O'Horgan

THE PEOPLE OF THE PLAY

FRANKIE BASTA, *a poet in his late 20's.*
VELMA SPARROW, *26, a nervous and troubled young lady who is a rapid speaker and sometimes trembles.*

WHERE THEY ARE

New York City: a midtown cafeteria, the streets outside, and FRANKIE's basement apartment.

WHEN

Contemporary: a night in February. The action is continuous.

ON THE LOWER EAST SIDE of Manhattan, specifically between Seventh Street and St. Mark's Place on Second Avenue, an old frontage and a steep, ramshackle staircase lead to a long and narrow loft that would appear to the unconversant primed and begging for demolition. To the cognizant and faithful, however, its worn brick walls reverberate with the pangs of theatrical birth rather than the rattle of death, for these are the premises of Off-Off-Broadway's prevailing incubator of the "New Theatre": Café La Mama.

Since its inception in 1961, the renowned coffeehouse-theatre club—mentored and more or less subsidized by its founder, Ellen Stewart—has presented over two hundred new plays by more than one hundred writers to its "membership." (To avoid unpleasant hassles with municipal licensing officials and assorted theatrical unions, La Mama scrupulously functions within the framework of its charter as a private club. Membership involves personal registration and a one-dollar donation for the privilege of seeing each play.)

Characteristically, La Mama (as well as its leading competitors in the vaguely defined area of Off-Off-Broadway: Caffe Cino; Playwrites Workshop Club; Theatre Genesis; and Judson Poet's Theatre) specialize in what Miss Stewart has defined as "subliminal theatre." To codify the movement: "The New Theatre explores or seeks to manipulate man's inner emotion. Contemporary Theatre deals with man's conscious receptivity; the new art, the New Theatre, the new playwrights are interested in unconscious receptivity."

Aspirations often are diminished by accomplishment and, not surprisingly, the New Theatre is no less immune to failure than its uptown avuncular commercial theatre. But, unfettered by constrictive economics and safely beyond the shadow of Broadway's omnipresent noose of "succeed or perish," La Mama and its tribal colleagues can and do take their chances with plays and writers of glaringly disparate merit and ability.

Assuredly, Miss Stewart's track record must be the envy of her rivals, for in the six years of her reign along Off-Off-Broadway, La Mama has stripped the veil of oblivion from the shoulders of a galaxy of young playwrights, including: Jean-Claude van Itallie, Lanford Wilson, Sam Shepard, Rochelle Owens, Paul Foster, and, most recently, Leonard Melfi.

Until mid-1966, Leonard Melfi was regarded as something of an "added starter" in La Mama's blue-ribbon stable. Appreciated and admired for his plays and personal geniality, he was nonetheless temporarily obscured by his more prominently publicized colleagues. Then, as sometimes happens in the theatre, new or otherwise, a fateful bolt of lightning struck and illuminated both author and play. The memorable flash occurred in April, 1966, when the La Mama troupe commemorated its newly concluded European tour with a gala bill of six short plays at New York's Martinique Theatre. Though hailed abroad, the contingent's "welcome home" was disconcertingly lukewarm, except for one item: Leonard Melfi's *Birdbath*.

Acclaimed by the local press, *Birdbath* attracted the attention of Bennett Cerf, an inveterate theatregoer as well as publisher-panelist, and, in a somewhat rare move, he issued a collection of six short plays, *Encounters,* by the "unknown" Leonard Melfi. Its publication engendered unprecedented journalistic space for a young writer who still nightly plodded the limited path of Off-Off-Broadway.

In a theatrical area where four-letter expletives are fired about with all the abandonment of holiday rockets, and the clashing crudities of modern sex, inverted and otherwise, are considered gospel, Melfi's emergence came as a revelation to the inundated. This was propounded in *Life* by reviewer Joan Simon, who, after hailing *Birdbath* as "a minor masterpiece," added: "He is the first serious contemporary playwright, on or off Broadway, at home or abroad, who is focused on real people in an adult, heterosexual effort to save themselves by reaching for one another." Further approbation appeared in *Newsweek:* "Leonard Melfi, a Behanish fellow whose gift for comedy may make him, whether he likes it or not, the first OOB writer to land on Broadway." (Prognostically correct; his first full-length play, *The Jones Man,* has been optioned for Broadway production in 1968.)

The young author was born on February 21, 1935, in Binghamton, New York, and attended St. Bonaventure University. After spending two years with the United States Army in Europe, he came to New York City to study acting at the Herbert Berghof-Uta Hagen Studio. The determination to perform soon was superseded by a stronger ambition: writing. This led to poetry, then to plays that ultimately were seen at such experimental oases as Theatre Genesis, Circle in the Square, the Actors Studio and, of course, La Mama.

In 1967, Melfi was awarded a Rockefeller Foundation grant for playwriting. Now a dedicated New Yorker and staunch East Villager, he expressed his credo in a personal note to the editor of this anthology: "I am always taking off to go swimming, or running a motorboat, and learning how to water ski, but don't get me wrong: I still work on my new plays *every day*. I wouldn't know exactly what to do with myself if I missed a day at the typewriter. I'll tell you something: I think it bugs some of the people who now invite me to their places when all of a sudden I take off and write for a couple of hours. But I suppose that's their problem and not mine."

Evidently, sudden recognition and its inevitable collateral distractions are not about to dim Leonard Melfi's lamp of progress.

SCENE. *Hazy music coming from a piped-in system. The curtain rises. We are in a garishly-lit cafeteria. To our right we see* FRANKIE BASTA *behind the cash booth before the cash register. He lights a cigarette, eyes his wristwatch, and then begins to read a book.*

To our left we see VELMA SPARROW. *She is clearing off a table in her working-area. As she wipes the surface we are aware of her delicate, slow, and easy nature, fused together with strange anxiety. Ever so often she gives a quick look over at* FRANKIE. *He, in turn, does the same thing. But their eyes never meet. They never catch each other. It is almost as though they both know the precise moment when to steal their brief glances without being noticed. This little "game of glances" goes on for about two minutes before they are finally caught staring at each other, both face-to-face. There is a pause wherein they both seem semi-mesmerized, as they both continue to stare at each other.*

———

FRANKIE. Hi.

VELMA. Hi.

FRANKIE. How are you doing?

VELMA (*shrugging*). Okay . . . I guess. (*She goes back to her work;* FRANKIE *goes back to his book.*)

VELMA (*going over to him*). What's your name?

FRANKIE (*looking up*). Frankie. What's yours?

VELMA. Velma.

FRANKIE. I'm glad to meet you, Velma.

VELMA. Likewise, I'm sure.

(FRANKIE *smiles.*)

You jist started workin' here tonight, didn't you?

FRANKIE. Yeah. That's right.

VELMA. And you don't like it, do you?

FRANKIE. How can you tell that?

VELMA. By the way you look.

FRANKIE. How's that?

VELMA. Well, first of all, if you don't mind my sayin' so, you jist don't look like you belong in a lousy place like this. I think you look pretty high-class to me. My mother would really go for you.

FRANKIE. Yeah? How old is your old lady—I mean your mother?

VELMA (*giggling*). Oh, I didn't mean that way, Frankie! Now you got me blushin'. My face is red, huh? If my mother was here she'd really be blushin'. What I meant to say was she'd think you were jist *right.* . . .

FRANKIE. Right for what?

VELMA. I . . . I . . . oh, I don't know how to say it. Forget it . . . I guess. But do you know what, Frankie . . . ?

FRANKIE (*kindly*). What's that, Velma?

VELMA. Well, I used to be real skinny, you know what I mean? I used to be all bones, almost like one of them skeletons. But since I been workin' here for Mr. Quincy, well, I've been puttin' on some weight. (*She pauses.*) That's why, in a way, this job isn't really that bad—because of the free meal they let you have. My mother said to me, "Velma, you take advantage of that free meal. . . . You eat as much as you can. . . . When something's free you make use of it. . . . Take as much as they let you have." And so, I've been eating pretty good lately, and Mr. Quincy, he's a nice man, he never tells me that I'm eating too much. In fact, I think he's a real nice man, because he hired me without my having any experience at all. This is the first time I've ever had a job where I cleaned off the tables and everything when the people were through eating. Boy, at first I was real scared about this job. I didn't think I was gonna be able to do it right . . . you know?

FRANKIE. You're doing okay. . . .

VELMA. . . . Although, you know what? (*She starts to bite her fingernails.*)

FRANKIE. What's that, Velma?

VELMA. Well, sometimes Mr. Quincy says things to me . . . or he gives me certain kinds of looks . . . like for instance . . . (*Embarrassed*) . . . I was his . . . *girl-friend,* maybe. (*She looks at* FRANKIE, *waiting hopefully for him to agree with her.* FRANKIE *gives her a slight smile of comfort, but it is not a smile of agreement.*)

I told my mother about the way Mr. Quincy is to me sometimes, and right away she wanted to come down and meet him. She asked me how old he was and she wanted to know how he looked, and after I told her everything she wanted to know, she said that some night she would get all dressed up and then come down here and wait for me until I got off, and while she was waiting I could introduce her to Mr. Quincy. . . .

(*She walks away and begins to wipe the same tabletop over again.*)

. . . You know what she said to me, my mother? . . . she said that it was all up in my mind that Mr. Quincy might jist be . . . *interested* . . . in me. She said that it wasn't true and that I should jist concentrate on my job and forget about all those pipe-dreams, otherwise I would be gettin' fired. (*She pauses.*) Sometimes . . . sometimes it's so hard for me to figure my mother out . . . because right afterwards she's tellin' me that maybe I shouldn't eat so much after all because then I would be goin' from one extreme to the other. She said when I was real skinny I couldn't find a nice boy, and, well, if I kept on eating the way I've been doing lately I'd get real fat, and so it would still be the same old story for me.

(*She laughs, a desperate, frantic sort of laugh.*)

My mother . . . changes her mind so much sometimes . . . that it gives me a headache. . . .

(*She begins to wipe the tabletop with great pressure.* FRANKIE *watches her for a moment.*)

FRANKIE (*lightly*). Velma, what are you trying to do . . . ?

VELMA (*quickly*). What?

FRANKIE. Are you trying to wear that tabletop off?

VELMA. Oh . . . yes . . . I know what you mean.

FRANKIE. You can get a headache just by doing things like that, Velma.

VELMA. Yeah . . . I guess you're right. (*She goes back over to him.*) You know something . . . ?

FRANKIE. Yes? I'm listening to you, Velma.

VELMA. Oh, what a funny coincidence. That's what I was jist goin' to say to you, Frankie. I was goin' to say: you know something . . . ? You make me feel good, Frankie, because you're listening to me. And then I was goin' to thank you for it, and tell you how much I appreciated our conversation with each other. There's not too many people I can talk to. Or what I should say is that there's not too many

people who will listen to me because they think I talk too much. (FRANKIE *glances at his wristwatch.*) It's almost time to go, huh?

FRANKIE. Five minutes and we'll be free.

VELMA. You really don't like this job, I can tell. You can't wait to get out of here, can you?

FRANKIE. You know what you're talking about.

VELMA. But I don't know as much as you.

FRANKIE. You can't really say things like that.

VELMA (*after a pause*). What . . . do you do . . . when you leave here? I mean, if you don't mind my askin'. I know it's none of my business. . . .

FRANKIE. I would like to go out and get drunk!

VELMA. Boy, do you sound mad all of a sudden.

FRANKIE. That's the way I am sometimes.

VELMA (*rapidly*). Are you married?

FRANKIE (*trying to be pleasant*). Velma . . . I have a hard time just taking care of myself.

VELMA (*after a pause*). You know, you really look nice. You don't belong here, that's all there is to it. You should be in the movies. You know what I mean? You could be an actor. I always wanted to be in the movies. I'd love to be an actress, but my mother says I'm not pretty enough . . . and I guess she's right . . . or was she?

FRANKIE. Why don't you relax, Velma?

VELMA. How come you're telling me that?

FRANKIE. You're shaking. You should learn how to be calm. It would make things a lot easier for you.

VELMA (*very nervously*). Well, it's almost time, isn't it? It's almost midnight . . . time to quit and everything . . . so I better go and change. (*She starts to move away, but it is an immense effort for her to do so.*) I'll see you again tomorrow night, Frankie, okay?

FRANKIE. Sure . . . okay . . . Velma.

VELMA (*running off*). 'Bye! And nice talkin' to you. (*She is gone.*)

FRANKIE. 'Bye . . . (*Then, more to him-*

self) Nice talkin' to you, too. . . .

(*A quick blackout. The lights come up again. We are on the streets outside.* VELMA *is standing alone. She is out of breath. Then* FRANKIE *enters from our right.*)

VELMA. Hi, Frankie.

FRANKIE. What are you doing here?

VELMA. I . . . I . . . left . . . before you did! I've been standin' here waitin' for you!

FRANKIE. You're shivering to death.

VELMA. I was jist wonderin' if you would walk me to the subway. I'm usually never afraid, but tonight, well, I jist can't explain why I got the jitters.

FRANKIE. Where do you live?

VELMA. In the Bronx. It's pretty far. It takes about an hour on the subway. Where do you live?

FRANKIE. Around the corner.

VELMA. Oh, geez! You're lucky! I wish I lived near where I worked. My other job is jist as far away as this one. I never have any luck when it comes to my jobs.

FRANKIE. You mean you have another job?

VELMA. My mother wants me to. She says we need the money. For a while I only had the day job. But my mother said it wasn't enough. So then I got this job from Mr. Quincy about a month ago. He's a real nice man. I'll bet if you get to know him he'd be a lot like the way my father was.

FRANKIE. Your father dead?

VELMA. We really don't know. He might be. I ain't seen him since I was six years old. That's twenty years ago. I'm twenty-six.

FRANKIE. What did he do? Where did he go?

VELMA. He deserted us and no one's been able to find him since. But actually, he didn't leave me and my brother Herbert; it was my mother who he left. He said that if he didn't run away my mother would drive him nuts. But I don't think that would'uve happened because she didn't drive me and my brother Herbert nuts. We're both okay. Of course Herbert hasn't lived with us for a long time now. He got married when he was only nineteen and we hardly ever see him anymore. Do you know something? You're almost as handsome as Herbert. He's the most handsome person you ever saw. My mother always wanted him to be a movie star, and he could'uve been too if he didn't run away and get married like he did. My mother never stopped telling him that he was going to make a lot of money someday for all of us and that we would be so proud of him because he would be famous throughout the whole world. (*Very wistfully*) I wish he would'uve listened to her. Then I wouldn't have to work anymore.

FRANKIE. It's getting pretty cold standing here, Velma. One thing I don't like is cold weather. Let's start walking toward the subway.

VELMA. Okay.

(*They begin to walk.*)

FRANKIE. Wouldn't you know that I would be born during the month that has the lousiest weather?

VELMA (*after giving a long sigh*). We should celebrate, Frankie!

FRANKIE. Why?

VELMA. I was born in February, too.

FRANKIE. Congratulations.

VELMA. Ain't that a coincidence?

FRANKIE. Sure is. And it's also getting colder.

VELMA. When is yours?

FRANKIE. When is my what?

VELMA. The date. Mine's already gone. It was the seventh.

FRANKIE. Well, happy birthday, Velma. Mine hasn't arrived yet. It's the twenty-first.

VELMA. Well, then, when I see you on the twenty-first, I'll wish you yours, too.

FRANKIE. You do that.

VELMA. You jist sound so unhappy compared to when we first started talking tonight. February isn't that bad a month. I think it's the *best* month of all, Frankie.

FRANKIE. How do you figure that?

VELMA. Because of the people born in this month. There's George Washington, and Abraham Lincoln . . . and there's . . . *tomorrow!*

FRANKIE. What's tomorrow?

VELMA. Saint Valentine's Day!

FRANKIE. Oh . . . yeah. . . .

VELMA. You won't believe this . . . but . . . I never once got a valentine in my whole life.

FRANKIE (*after a long pause, uneasily*). It's getting colder by the minute, isn't it, Velma?

VELMA. But, do you know, Frankie, I didn't mind too much. My mother used to take me to Schrafft's and then afterwards we'd go to the Radio City Music Hall every Valentine's Day while I was still going to school. She said it would take my mind off not getting any valentines. My mother did good things for me except sometimes she would yell at me and say that I was homely and skinny and that I shook too much and it made her nervous and so she'd scream at me to go into another room so's she wouldn't have to look at me for awhile. . . .

FRANKIE (*quickly*). This is it! You want to come in for a minute? (*He stops and so does* VELMA.)

VELMA. Come in where, Frankie?

FRANKIE. This is where I live. Do you want to come in for some coffee? It'll warm you up.

VELMA. I really got to get back home. My mother will be waitin' up for me . . . and . . . oh . . .

FRANKIE. C'mon. Look, you're trembling because it's cold out here. It's even beginning to snow now.

VELMA. No, no. I'm not trembling because I'm cold. You know now how I tremble a lot, don't you? I'm really warm. I almost feel as though I'm beginnin' to sweat, as though it was the summertime, or because I was worried about something.

FRANKIE. What are you worried about, then?

VELMA. Well, I started to say before that my mother would be . . . waitin' up for me . . . but. . . .

FRANKIE. All right, then. C'mon, I'll walk you to your subway. I can't waste anymore goddam time!

VELMA. No, Frankie! I forgot! You see . . . my mother's not home . . . I mean she *is* home but she's not waitin' up for me tonight . . . and so . . .

FRANKIE. Yes? So?

VELMA. So I suppose it'll be all right if I come in for a few minutes. I guess I really would enjoy some hot coffee before I leave . . . for home.

(FRANKIE *takes out his keys and walks down the steps to his apartment. He opens the door and turns on the light.*)

FRANKIE. Well? Are you coming in, Velma?

(VELMA *is trembling almost violently.*)

VELMA (*standing on the stairs*). I . . . I . . . yes . . . I'm coming. . . .

FRANKIE. Jesus! Control yourself, will you?

VELMA. I'll be okay, Frankie, in a minute. It's jist that I've never been in a man's apartment before. It's jist that I've never been alone with a man before. Oh, I forgot . . .

FRANKIE. Hey! I don't have much patience left, Velma!

VELMA. I forgot that I *was* alone with a man before. My brother Herbert. But that doesn't really count, does it? Because he's my brother, huh, Frankie?

FRANKIE. If you don't come down here in one more second, I'm shutting the door on you and you're walking to the subway by yourself!

VELMA (*finally going down the stairs*). You know, Frankie, maybe instead of the coffee I'd better have hot tea instead. (*The lights are beginning to dim.*) My mother says . . . she *used* to say . . . that I drank too much coffee. Ever since I was a little girl I drank coffee, and she always told me that that was why I was so skinny and not very tall like most girls, and that's why I shake so much, and that's why I'll probably never find a nice man to marry me someday . . . but now I'm gaining weight and everything. . . .

(*Complete blackout. We hear music now. It is the old-time, dance-band type of music coming from a phonograph. The lights slowly come back up. We are in* FRANKIE's *apartment.* VELMA *is sitting on the edge of the bed drinking her hot tea.* FRANKIE *is standing up before the refrigerator with the door opened; he is drinking from a bottle.*)

VELMA. I don't wanna sound stupid or anything, Frankie, but what's the name of that record?

(FRANKIE *takes another long slug, puts the bottle back into the refrigerator, and slams the door shut.*)

FRANKIE (*turning around, facing* VELMA *with a smile*). "I Only Have Eyes for

You."

(VELMA *blushes and turns her face away; she stifles a giggle.*)

VELMA. It's a pretty song. . . .

FRANKIE (*with half a sigh*). It sure is! Makes me nostalgic. That's why I'm playing it, because I like feeling nostalgic. . . .

VELMA. I don't know what it means. . . .

FRANKIE. They used to play this song when I was in high school. It was the theme song of the ole' hometown band.

VELMA. I'll bet you had as much girls chasin' you as my brother Herbert did.

FRANKIE (*singing*). "Are the stars out tonight? I don't care if it's cloudy or bright . . ."

VELMA (*embarrassed*). It's certainly a romantic song. . . . (*She sips her tea.*)

FRANKIE. ". . . 'cause I only have eyes for you. . . ." (*He begins to dance.*) Would you like to dance with me, Velma? (*He bows to her.*)

VELMA (*really embarrassed*). Oh . . . I . . . I forgot to tell you. But I *did* get a few valentines when I was younger. My brother Herbert used to mail them to me.

FRANKIE. Jesus Christ! Will you shut the hell up about your goddam brother Herbert?!

VELMA. Geez . . . you get mad easy, don't you?

FRANKIE. And stop trembling like that. My bed's going to fall apart. (*He goes back to the refrigerator and takes out the bottle.*)

VELMA. You drink a lot, too, don't you?

FRANKIE (*drinking*). No shit, baby!

VELMA. And . . . when you drink . . . you curse a lot too, don't you?

FRANKIE. You don't like it?

VELMA. No.

FRANKIE (*pausing, then smiling*). I'm sorry . . . Velma.

VELMA. What's that you're drinkin'? If you don't mind my askin'?

FRANKIE. Ice-cold martinis. Already mixed. You can buy it in any liquor store, all prepared, ready and waiting for you. Saves lots of time, you know. Not too much time left . . . Velma . . . Sparrow!

VELMA. How . . . did you know my last name? I never told it to you.

FRANKIE. I guessed.

VELMA. Aw, c'mon, I don't believe you.

FRANKIE. Honest to God, I did.

VELMA. It's spooky then, don't you think?

FRANKIE. Not at all. It's a beautiful name, Velma. It goes perfect with you.

VELMA. I didn't tell it to you before because I've always been ashamed of it.

FRANKIE. How could you be?

VELMA. When I was in school the kids used to always whisper behind my back. They'd say: here she comes, here comes Velma the ugly sparrow.

FRANKIE. You forget about those creeps!

VELMA. Well, you know what I did? I quit school jist so's I wouldn't have to listen to them anymore. And I only had a year left before I would'uve got my diploma, too. Sometimes I think about going to night school, but my mother says it's all too late now. You know, my mother is a peculiar woman. First she's sayin' to me, "Velma, we gotta save money, that's all there is to it!" And then . . . the very next minute she's askin' me to loan her five dollars for the beauty parlor or something like that.

FRANKIE. Doesn't your mother work?

VELMA. You sound mad again.

FRANKIE. I am mad again! (*He takes another swig of the bottle.*)

VELMA. No, she doesn't work because she usually doesn't feel too well. That's why I have two jobs. During the days I work in a movie house in Greenwich Village. I'm an usherette. My mother didn't want me to work down there at first because she thinks the Village is dangerous. She doesn't like the idea of me being around all those fairies and those leprechauns. Well, I'm not afraid of the fairies but *those leprechauns* really scare me.

FRANKIE (*scratching his head*). What do you mean by leprechauns?

VELMA. You know what I mean: those girls who don't like men; they like to be with women instead.

FRANKIE. Uh, Lesbians, Velma, Lesbians. Not leprechauns.

VELMA. Oh, that's right, Les—bi—ans.

(FRANKIE *takes off his shoes and socks.*)

FRANKIE. I'm making myself comfortable, so don't worry about a thing.

VELMA. Oh, well, it's your apartment, so why should I mind, huh? Besides, I don't really mind anything right now. I'm having a good time here with you. (*She looks around.*) This is a real artist's apartment, isn't it?

FRANKIE. If you think so.

VELMA. So Frankie, what do you do? I know that being a cashier isn't your life. You're too handsome for that. And you're too smart. I've never seen so many books in all my life.

FRANKIE. I'm a writer, Velma.

VELMA (*thrilled*). Gee! You must have a big imagination! You'll probably be rich and famous someday, and then I'll be able to say that I knew you, won't I?

FRANKIE. I'm a poet, really. Poets don't make very much money, and they hardly ever become famous.

VELMA. Who's that on the wall? He looks real familiar to me.

FRANKIE. That's Van Gogh. A self-portrait.

VELMA (*excited*). Did he give it to you?!

FRANKIE. No, Velma.

VELMA. And who are these people in this picture? (*She looks closer.*) Oh! You're in the picture, too! It must be your family, huh?

FRANKIE. That's right.

VELMA. They all look so happy: your father and mother and sister and brother . . . and you! Are they all happy as the picture?

FRANKIE. Yes, they are, most of the time. I'm pretty proud of them . . . and they're pretty patient with me.

VELMA. You're sooooooo . . . lucky!

FRANKIE. Why's that?

VELMA. To be able to have such a nice family.

(FRANKIE *drinks some more.*)

FRANKIE. I'm getting stoned . . . drunk, Velma. Don't mind me if I do. I might get a little vulgar . . . a little truthful . . . I might start talking about myself . . . but I'll try to be nice . . . I really . . . *like you,* Velma!

VELMA (*nervously*). And do you know who else was born during this month?! My favorite actress! And you probably like her because she is the most beautiful woman in the entire world!

FRANKIE. Who's that?

VELMA. Elizabeth Taylor! What do you think of that?!

FRANKIE. Liz, huh? Marvelous! We're in good company, aren't we, Velma?

VELMA. I knew you'd like to hear that.

FRANKIE. Velma, I'm going to make myself some tea. I really shouldn't be getting this drunk. I'm a bad host, huh?

VELMA. Oh, no, I don't think so at all.

FRANKIE. Thank you. You're beautiful.

VELMA. I don't know what . . . to say. . . .

FRANKIE. You don't have to say anything. Just keep me company, that's all.

VELMA. I like you when you drink. It's like watching a show on TV or something. You never know what to expect next. First you're very funny and then you're very mad. In a way, it's fun. (*There is a pause.*) I'll bet I know why you don't have a TV set here.

FRANKIE (*trying to make some tea*). Why?

VELMA. Because if you had a TV set then you wouldn't write your poems, would you?

FRANKIE. You're very much on the ball.

VELMA. I wouldn't know what to do without a TV set in the house. My mother and me, we sit and watch all of the *love* stories! I used to go to Loeee's Paradise a lot. You ever been there?

FRANKIE. What is it?

VELMA. A movie house. It's just like a castle out of the fairy tales. You really dream there: Loeee's Paradise!

FRANKIE. It's *Loew's* Paradise, not *Loeee's,* isn't it?

VELMA. It is? Geez. My mother and me have always called it *Loeee's,* and we've been goin' there for years and years. But you must be right because you're educated and because you're an artist.

FRANKIE. Where is this place?

VELMA. It's in the Bronx. I used to go on Saturday nights. They have stars on the ceilings. Thousands of stars twinkling on and off. It's like another world. And if you sit right in the middle of the theatre there's a big full moon above your head. It's so romantic. You should see it! But . . . I stopped goin' because most of the girls and the boys go in couples and they all try to sit underneath the big full moon . . . and I was beginning to feel out of place.

FRANKIE. Velma, do you want more tea?

VELMA. I was thinkin' that maybe I'd like jist a little sip of that martini-mix, if you don't care, Frankie?

FRANKIE. Of course I don't care. It's my pleasure. (*He pours her a glass.*) Salut!

VELMA (*lifting the glass*). Cheers.

FRANKIE. Cheers, then. It's all the same. (*He drinks more too.*)

VELMA. It's strong . . . but I like it.

FRANKIE. Very good. Enjoy yourself.

VELMA. This is a real treat. I like treats. Every payday when I bring home the money, my mother decided that we both should have a treat, and so the next morning, every single week that I can remember, we have coffeecake and caviar for breakfast!

FRANKIE. Coffeecake and caviar?

VELMA. Oh, it's delicious together. Someday you'll have to come to our apartment for breakfast. You'll love it . . . (*She sips some more.*)

FRANKIE. Drink up, Velma. There's a lot more yet. Relax. (FRANKIE *flops down on the bed next to her.*) My head is beginning to spin.

(VELMA *immediately rises from the bed.*)

VELMA (*trembling*). I used to work at The Merry-Go-Round Club once. I was the hat-check girl, but my mother said they fired me because they wanted a girl who was prettier than me. Do you know that it was my favorite job, though, even if it didn't last very long. I saw all the stars and the celebrities. Once I even saw Ed Sullivan!

FRANKIE. Relax, Velma.

VELMA (*drinking some more*). Oh, I'm okay. I'm relaxed. (*She goes to his desk.*) This is where you write, huh?

FRANKIE. When I'm working on my book.

VELMA. You're writing a book too? You really are smart! I'll bet you're a good typist, too, aren't you?

FRANKIE. I never compose my poetry on the typewriter; only my book.

(VELMA *sits down at his desk.*)

VELMA. Well . . . anyway . . . (*She finishes the drink rapidly.* FRANKIE *sits up on his bed and stares over at her.*)

FRANKIE. You want more?

VELMA. I don't think I'd better. I'm gettin' sleepy now. Maybe I'd better go home . . . my mother is . . . well, she's *not!* . . . really . . .

FRANKIE. I would like to hug you, Velma. I would like very much to put my arms around you, and I would like to hold you ever so gently, and I would like to whisper tenderly in your ear; I would like to say to you: "Velma-honey, believe me, little-girl-Velma, things are not really that bad. Everything's going to be all right, okay, you just wait and see. Take my word for it, Velma."

(VELMA *does not know what to do; she glances back and forth at her wristwatch.*)

VELMA. Well! It's Valentine's Day now! I'll bet you have so many girl-friends, don't you? I can jist see it in the morning when you wake up. Your mailbox will be stuffed with hundreds of valentines, won't it? From all your girl-friends?

FRANKIE. It used to be that way once, but no more, and I like it that way. You see, Velma, most girls, after they flip their corks over me, find out pretty fast that they don't go for me anymore. They discover that there is competition. They believe I'd rather make it with my typewriter. Did you know that every chick I've ever sacked becomes insanely jealous of that innocent little machine over there on my desk? Isn't that the stupidest thing you ever heard of? Harmless portable! . . . inanimate black mother, old pawnshop object that never gives me any bullshit!

VELMA. You're really somethin'.

FRANKIE. Would you bother me if I sat down and typed away whenever I felt that I had to, whenever the urge was suddenly the most important thing in my life? You'd leave me alone, wouldn't you?

VELMA. Yes. . . .

FRANKIE. You wouldn't show any signs of bitterness, would you?

VELMA. No. . . .

FRANKIE (*drinking some more*). I knew you wouldn't let me down, Velma. You see, these chicks, almost all of them, they want all of your time and all of your attention. They say they understand you, but when it comes right down to the actual test, well, their lovely precious pussies panic! And so what do you do? You make it with a guy and there's just as much bullshit there too! (*Quietly*) The thing to do is to find out where the hell the right chick is . . . under my bed? . . . in the bathroom? . . . up in the Bronx, maybe? (VELMA *giggles.* FRANKIE *sips his drink.*) I'll tell you something: I'd rather *come* all over the keys of that hot typewriter . . . that's the way I feel sometimes! (*He gets up from the bed.*) Besides . . . (*He laughs bitterly.*) maybe it's not such a bad idea . . . it's a whole lot safer. No sweat. How can you knock up a typewriter? Oh, Jesus, I'm sorry, Velma . . . but I warned you: I told you that I get vulgar sometimes, when I drink on an empty stomach! (*He stops and stares at her.*) But . . . you don't even know what I'm talking about, do you? (VELMA *simply smiles back at him.*) Anyway, that answers your question about how many valentines I'll be getting in the morning. (*He begins to take off his shirt.* VELMA *gets up.*) Don't worry about anything. I'm only making myself comfortable, that's all. (*He takes off his pants.*) Will you please sit down? I'm not going to harm you. (*He goes into the bathroom.*)

VELMA. Please don't get mad at me, Frankie.

FRANKIE (*offstage*). I'm not getting mad at you. I'm just disappointed, that's all. (*He begins to sing and/or hum his song from the bathroom. Then he returns in a bathrobe.*)

VELMA (*after a moment*). Maybe I can stay here, jist for a little while? My mother won't even know about it . . . since she's not waitin' up for me . . . (*She begins to shake again.*)

FRANKIE. You're confusing me, baby, and I get confused enough when I got gin in my belly. Make up your mind. And forget about your mother. I'm sick and tired of hearing about your old lady!

VELMA. Okay.

FRANKIE. If I give you just a small glass of this martini-mix, it'll make you stop shaking like that. (*He goes and pours her some more.*) Now here. Take it and drink it in one gulp.

VELMA. Will it? Will it make my shaking stop?

FRANKIE. Don't ask questions. Just do as I told you.

VELMA. Okay. (*She manages to get it all down in one swig.*)

FRANKIE. You see? You did it. Now come over here and sit down like before

and make yourself at home. And take your coat back off. (VELMA *walks away from him and sits back down at the desk.*) Well, aren't you going to take your coat off?

VELMA. In a minute, Frankie, in a minute.

FRANKIE. Velma? You want to know something?

VELMA. What, Frankie?

FRANKIE. I'm glad that you came home with me tonight. You're the first woman I've had here in a long time.

(VELMA *shows signs of wanting to leave. She nervously notices a book lying on the desk.*)

VELMA (*reading, as she picks the book up*). "Poet in New York . . ."

FRANKIE. A great goddam good poet, too, let me tell you!

VELMA. Fed—er—ico . . . Garcia . . . Lorca . . .

FRANKIE. And God bless him! Amen.

VELMA. I . . . never heard of him. Is he a Puerto Rican?

FRANKIE (*softly*). Where did I find you?

VELMA. Does he still live in New York?

FRANKIE. Oh, sure. He's pushing boo up in East Harlem for the winter.

VELMA. Oh.

FRANKIE (*going to her*). Please . . . let me just hold you, Velma, okay? (VELMA *shows signs of wanting to leave again.*) Don't move! Stay where you are. . . . I'm not going to harm you. If only you'll believe that, then everything will be okay. Take my word for it, please . . . okay? (*He gives her a very honest smile.*)

VELMA (*after a moment*). Okay . . . I guess.

FRANKIE. Good, Velma. Besides, I need someone to talk to, and you need someone to talk to. Right?

VELMA. Right, I guess.

FRANKIE. In other words, we both need someone to listen to us.

VELMA. You mean those other women . . . I mean, didn't those other girls ever want to listen to you, Frankie? I mean the ones who used to come here?

FRANKIE. Never! That's the trouble, Velma.

VELMA. They just wanted to talk about themselves, huh?

FRANKIE. That's it, Velma. That's exactly it.

VELMA. And that's why you're not married yet, huh? Because maybe you can't find a girl who'll listen to you?

FRANKIE. Yeah, maybe it's one of the reasons. . . .

VELMA. It's so hard to believe that you're not married, though. I think you'd make a nice husband, and be a good father, too.

FRANKIE (*sharply*). Why would I make a nice husband and be a good father?

VELMA (*jittery again*). Well . . . because your kids would have so much fun with you. You'd make them laugh and everything. I never really had a father to make me laugh and have fun with because I hardly remember him.

FRANKIE. You're making me feel good, Velma. In a way, you're making me feel sort of happy. You see, about a year ago around this time I almost got married. I had this girl-friend, and . . .

VELMA. Was she pretty?

FRANKIE. It doesn't really matter now. It's not important anyway. Her name was Carrie, and we went together for over a year. Then she wanted to get married. I didn't. Remember, Velma: I have a very hard time just taking care of myself. Well, anyway, that's all she talked about was getting married. In a church. The whole works. And having lots of babies afterwards. It scared me, Velma. She was ashamed now. She didn't think we should go on living together. (*He laughs bitterly.*) We had to make it all legal! Carrie said some pretty stupid things to me. I was beginning to feel nervous and miserable. "Frankie Basta!" she screamed at me, "you're not a man! You can't face up to responsibilities!" Over and over again she said this to me. Christ, Velma, I couldn't even take care of myself then. Almost like now: no job, no prospects, no nothing. And I didn't know whether I was a good poet or a bad one. I still don't know. And so, I asked her to try and understand. I knew I would fail her then. I said to her: "Please Carrie-baby, just hold on and wait, and then we'll see, Carrie-honey . . . we'll see, okay?"

VELMA. But she didn't, huh?

FRANKIE. Didn't wait, you mean? No, she didn't wait and she wouldn't see. You can't do it, Velma, you can't do it! It's almost impossible to make people understand certain things, especially the people who you care so much about, the people who you love . . . or the people who you could care about and love. . . .

VELMA (*softly*). I . . . don't know what to say to you.

FRANKIE. You don't have to say anything, Velma. Just keep me company, that's all. (*He goes to the phonograph.*) What would you like to hear? Do you have any favorite songs, Velma?

VELMA. I like the one you played a little while ago.

FRANKIE. No, I mean one of your own. Don't you have one of your own favorites? That's *my* favorite song.

(*There is a short pause.*)

VELMA. Well . . . it's *mine*, too . . . now. (*She smiles faintly at him.*)

FRANKIE (*smiling back*). Then I'll play it again, for the both of us.

VELMA. It would make me happy, Frankie.

FRANKIE. What's the matter all of a sudden? I thought you *were* happy.

VELMA. I am . . . but I'm also worried . . . and . . . I'm getting tired. . . . I'm feelin' weak and everything. . . . (*The music begins to play softly.*) Oh, that's so nice . . . it makes me forget . . . things . . . easier. . . .

FRANKIE. And you're not trembling any more, either, are you?

VELMA. Geez, you're right! I never even thought of it.

(*He has somehow managed to get her to dance with him. It is all rather awkward: his drunkenness, her fear.*)

FRANKIE (*singing, dancing*). "Are the stars out tonight? . . . I don't care if it's cloudy or bright! . . . 'Cause I only have eyes for . . . *you!*"

VELMA (*pulling away, embarrassed*). This picture of you and your family sure is nice, don't you think? Don't you think so, Frankie?

FRANKIE (*singing*). "Dear Velma . . . Oh, the moon may be high . . ."

VELMA. . . . and you can tell that you're different from the rest of them. I mean, you look like an artist and everything. . . . All the rest of them look nice and ordinary.

FRANKIE (*singing*). ". . . Maybe millions of people go by . . ."

VELMA. . . . but you really stand out in the picture! You look nice and . . . *wild!* If you know what I mean? Frankie? Please, don't sing to me anymore, please! I'm getting to feel scared and I can't think when you keep singing to me like that, please!

FRANKIE (*turning off the phonograph*). I'm sorry, Velma. Look, anything to make you cozy.

VELMA. Boy, oh, boy, you really are drunk, aren't you?

FRANKIE. Why do you say . . . that?

VELMA. Well, because you're acting so funny.

FRANKIE. I know, I know . . . Velma. Look, from here on in . . . well, just don't mind me too much. . . . Excuse me if I seem . . . in any way clumsy to you, okay?

VELMA. Frankie?

FRANKIE. Let me have your coat. I'll hang it up for you.

VELMA (*motionless*). Frankie, I'm getting a tiny headache. . . . Do you think, Frankie, that you could keep a secret? I've never been so worried. . . .

FRANKIE. C'mon now: your coat?

VELMA. Yes. (*She hands her coat to him.* FRANKIE *goes and puts the coat on a hanger. He notices a newspaper half exposed in one of the pockets.*)

FRANKIE (*looking at it*). Velma, why are you reading a newspaper like this?

VELMA. You're mad again, aren't you?

FRANKIE. How can you waste money this way!?

VELMA. I buy it for my mother. She reads it.

FRANKIE. I don't want to hear another word about your *mother!* Do you hear me?

VELMA (*beginning to tremble again*). Yes, yes, Frankie.

FRANKIE. Yeah, sure! You buy this rag for your old lady, but you read it too, don't you?

VELMA. It . . . has lots of gossip in it . . . about all the stars and the celebrities . . . and *everything!*

FRANKIE (*reading*). "Mother Uses Daughter's Head for Hammer!" (*He rips the newspaper up with great fury.*) Velma, why do you read such shit?! What are you trying to do to yourself? (*Angrily*) "Mother Uses Daughter's Head for Hammer!" (*He moves closer to her.*) God, Velma, I mean *what's happening?* (*He makes an attempt at embracing her.*)

VELMA. Please, please! Oh, nooooooo! *I'm scared of you! I'm scared of everybody, of everything! (She tries to run from him.)* I never thought of it 'til now. . . . They'll do somethin' to me, won't they? I want my coat back! *I've never been alone with a man before!* My mother would think . . . *my mother!*

FRANKIE (*violently*). *Fuck your mother! Your mother is rotten!*

VELMA. I can't stay here tonight! Maybe it jist isn't right for me to stay here with you . . . not tonight!

FRANKIE. You've got to now. You're in no shape to go anywhere. It'll be all right, Velma. You'll sleep in my bed, and I'll sleep here on the floor. Nothing hard about that, is there?

VELMA. I can't, Frankie! *I've . . . got . . . to . . . be . . . there!*

FRANKIE. What are you talking about? (*He moves towards her again, his arms outstretched.*) Please, just let me hold you and whisper in your ear, Velma?

VELMA. *Nooooooo . . . ! (She pulls a small kitchen knife out of her pocketbook. It is partly caked with dried blood.) You stay away from me! I don't want you to touch me! We're not even married yet. . . . (She is trembling as she holds the knife toward* FRANKIE.) You leave me alone, Frankie . . . or I'll *kill* you! (FRANKIE *is motionless.*) When . . . we got up this morning, my mother and me, we had coffeecake and caviar for breakfast. It was a big surprise. My mother said that we were havin' the treat even if payday was three days away yet. She said it was sort of a special celebration. My mother said that she was leaving for the mountains this afternoon. She was going to a resort to meet a man. Harriet, my mother's friend who lives in the next apartment, she told my mother that there were a whole lot of available men at this certain resort up in the mountains, the Catskills, I think, and my mother said she was goin' no matter what, and that I must send her money every weekend until she has some luck. She said that I couldn't go because I would scare the men away, that I would ruin her chances, and that I was really such an ugly girl, and that I looked like the mother and she looked like the daughter . . . and then she said that was why we're havin' the treat early: to celebrate! The coffeecake and caviar . . . and then she asked me to cut her a big piece of the coffeecake and to cover it with a whole lot of caviar . . . and so I started to cut the coffeecake with this here knife, but . . .

(VELMA *trembles to such a degree that the knife falls from her hand and onto the floor. She runs to the bed and throws herself upon it in a burst of hysterical sobbing.*)

FRANKIE. Velma, what have you done? (*He picks up the knife and lays it on his desk.*)

VELMA. It's my mother's blood! I didn't know what to do. I don't . . . know why I did it! I don't even really remember that much, Frankie. When I got in the subway to come to work afterwards it was jist like nuthin' happened, nuthin' at all! But do you know? I thought, I thought when my mother asked me to cover her piece of coffeecake with a whole lot of caviar, I thought . . . my mother . . . she thinks that my head is a hammer! That's what she thinks! *And it isn't! It isn't!* Tell me, Frankie, please tell me that my head is not a *hammer!*

FRANKIE (*after a pause*). No, Velma, no: your head is *not* a hammer.

VELMA (*a brief pause*). Can I sleep here tonight?

(FRANKIE *goes to the bottle and takes the longest gulp he can manage. He falls, exhausted, into a chair. He closes his eyes.*)

FRANKIE. Sure . . . Velma.

(VELMA *continues to sob on the bed, but her crying is growing softer now.*

FRANKIE *gets up and turns off all the lights. The moon is shining in through one of the windows.*)

VELMA (*very quietly*). What will they do to me? I'm scared, Frankie.

FRANKIE. They're not going to do anything to you. I'll make sure of that.

(FRANKIE *goes and sits down at his desk. He begins to scribble swiftly on a piece of paper.*)

VELMA (*vaguely*). It makes me sleepy. . . . Alcohol . . . makes me sooooo tired. . . . I've never felt soooo . . . tired . . . before in my whole life. . . . (*She is no longer crying.*) Help me . . . help me . . . help . . . me.

FRANKIE (*still writing*). Yes, yes . . . *I will*, Velma Sparrow. . . . I promise you that *I will.*

(VELMA *is breathing heavily now.* FRANKIE *continues to write with great speed. He stops and then begins to read.*)

FRANKIE (*aloud, with a strange sobriety*).

"Dead birds still have wings
Dead birds, saddest-looking things
Because they are dead, on the ground
With their still wings, on the ground
Saddest-looking things
Dead birds with still wings,
Dead on the ground
Instead of the sky. . . ."

(VELMA *is sound asleep; her breathing is peaceful.* FRANKIE *turns and faces* VELMA'S *weary and forlorn figure. His eyes are full of tears. He stands up and lights a cigarette.*)

I have a treat for you in the morning, Velma. (*He turns out the desk lamp.*) I've just written you . . . a valentine.

CURTAIN

THE GOVERNOR'S LADY

David Mercer

The Governor's Lady was first presented at the Aldwych Theatre, London, on February 4, 1965, under the auspices of the Royal Shakespeare Company. Directed by David Jones, it had the following cast:

LADY HARRIET BOSCOE Patience Collier   SIR GILBERT BOSCOE Timothy West
AMOLO, *a native servant* Chris Konyils   JOHN MAUDSLEY Morgan Sheppard
CHARMIAN MAUDSLEY Elizabeth Spriggs   POLICE SERGEANT Mark Jones

Designed by John Collins
Lighting by David Read

DAVID MERCER joined the vanguard of Britain's outstanding new playwrights in 1961, when the British Broadcasting Corporation commenced televising his dramatic trilogy, *The Generations*. In 1962, he climbed another rung upward with a Screen Writers' Guild Award for his television play *A Suitable Case for Treatment*, but it wasn't until 1965 that Mr. Mercer firmly established himself in the theatre.

It was a memorable year for the author. The Royal Shakespeare Company introduced *The Governor's Lady;* Peter O'Toole starred in his West End success *Ride a Cock Horse;* and his subsequently hailed screen comedy *Morgan!* went before the cameras with David Warner and Vanessa Redgrave as an oddly matched pair.

Born in 1928, in Wakefield, England, Mr. Mercer originally trained as a medical laboratory technician, then turned his hand to painting. After studying art at King's College, Newcastle-upon-Tyne, he emigrated to Paris; two years later, he was back in London, teaching chemistry at the Barrett Street Technical College.

In 1961, Mr. Mercer finally found his proper niche with the telecast of *Where the Difference Begins,* the opening play of the aforementioned trilogy. An extremely ambitious work, it experimented boldly with new techniques and, as one journalist observed, even more boldly, in the context of everyday television, with *ideas*.

According to the author, it took five years for *The Governor's Lady* to travel from typewriter to stage: "It was commissioned by Barbara Bray at the BBC, but by the time I delivered it she had left, and it somehow never got done. I was delighted when the Royal Shakespeare Company suddenly wanted to do it, out of the blue; it came like an unexpected bonus. . . ."

The Royal Shakespeare Company was equally delighted. For, as it turned out, *The Governor's Lady* became the reigning success and leading conversation piece of their newly established Aldwych Theatre program, *Expeditions Two,* designed to introduce and encourage rising young British playwrights of exceptional promise.

With *The Governor's Lady* Mr. Mercer continues to explore dramatically a theme which, by his own admission, has most interested him in recent years: the expression of social alienation in terms of psychological alienation. This is manifest in his portrait of Lady Harriet Boscoe who resorts to hallucinatory episodes when she no longer can accept the fact that her glory, like her husband, has departed, and the African colony he had governed had been given its independence.

In 1966, Mr. Mercer and the Royal Shakespeare Company were reunited with the London presentation of his controversial drama *Belcher's Luck*.

Although three collections of David Mercer's plays have been issued in England, the publication of *The Governor's Lady* in this anthology represents his initial appearance in print in the United States.

The play is in one continuous act punctuated by blackouts or fades.

Exterior and interior of a bungalow in Africa surrounded by jungle.

The main stage is a composite set with the sitting room right with a round tea-table and two upright chairs.

On the left of the stage is the bedroom area, with a large double-bed covered with a white mosquito net.

On the left of the bed is a very high tall cupboard.

The forestage is a verandah area on which are two rush chairs and a drinks table.

On the right the jungle encroaches, and from one of the tall trees hangs a swing.

SCENE ONE

AFTERNOON BEFORE TEA

African music.

(HARRIET *is seated at the tea-table. She is writing in her diary.*)

HARRIET. May 15th . . . I cannot resist the temptation to anticipate Charmian's visit this afternoon, for the pleasure of writing my insights now and feeling them vindicated when she has gone. (*Pause*) Some women should not live in Africa, and Charmian is one of them. The heat withers her skin and the boredom withers her spirit . . . yet she still inspires in me that weary affection which passes for a bond between old women. (*Pause*) I wonder . . . I have no doubt she and John consider it eccentric of us to take this house on the plateau . . . what was it John said? Practically the jungle. (*Pause*) She will drive herself here in that ghastly what is it? Jeep? (*Pause*) And harass me with her inanities for two hours or more . . .

AMOLO. Mrs. Maudsley, Madam—

HARRIET. Surely not! What time is it?

CHARMIAN. Harriet, darling . . . I know I'm too early—

HARRIET. Of course not. How nice to see you. Such a wretched drive out here in the middle of the afternoon. Let's have tea at once, shall we? Amolo—tea. And you're just the person to help me, Charmian.

CHARMIAN. Help you?

HARRIET. I can't find Gilbert's gun.

CHARMIAN. I can't think why you should want Gilbert's gun. Are you going to attack somebody or are you expecting to *be* attacked? Anyway, how should I know where it is? (*Pause*) I came for tea, darling, since you invited me for tea.

HARRIET. You know you've always had a flair for finding Gilbert's things when he loses them—

CHARMIAN. That is true, but it is a flair of no practical value in the circumstances.

HARRIET. Circumstances?

CHARMIAN. Harriet, how could Gilbert lose *anything*, when Gilbert is dead?

(*Pause*)

HARRIET. Did I ask Amolo to bring in the tea? I am a good shot, you know, Charmian. And I feel safer when I have the means to protect myself. There *was* a time when a white woman in this colony could dispense with such vulgarities. Now, however—

CHARMIAN. One doesn't say "this colony" any longer, Harriet. Times have changed, my dear. Since they won their precious freedom you have to be careful what you say.

HARRIET. I have always thought . . . and I always shall think . . . that the natives are children. I know I am an old-fashioned woman, a stubborn old woman—

CHARMIAN. But you want to die in full possession of all your prejudices?

HARRIET. What's that, Charmian?

CHARMIAN. I said—

HARRIET. But I fail to see why they should wish to exchange their simplicity and innocence for *our* vices and machines. (*Pause*) Leave the trolley, Amolo . . . I shall not need you.

AMOLO. Yes, Madam.

HARRIET. I agree with Gilbert. Independence at this stage would mean anarchy. (*Pause*) Lemon?

CHARMIAN. Please. (*Pause*) Dear Harriet!

HARRIET. Why, Charmian . . . you are almost in tears!

CHARMIAN. Listen darling. You're quite sure you know when and where you are?

HARRIET. But why on earth shouldn't I?

CHARMIAN. Harriet, it is one year since this colony became independent. And six months since Gilbert died. Harriet, you are not the Governor's wife . . . You are the ex-Governor's widow. (*Pause*) I've . . . I can't go on pretending I don't notice that your mind is . . . wandering. There, I've said it. I've tried and tried to think of a kinder way of putting it. But there isn't one. Harriet, John and I think . . . we think you should consider going home. Have you seen a doctor?

HARRIET. My dear Charmian, I *am* at home. And I am perfectly well, thank you. (*Pause*) I think the drive must have tired you out. (*Pause*) And yet, it is so lovely up here. It has its compensations. Gilbert says that it is always five degrees cooler up here than anywhere else in the colony.

(*Pause*)

CHARMIAN. I meant—London, Harriet.

HARRIET. You don't know what you are saying, my dear. Leave Karalinga now? (*Pause*) You know, Charmian, Gilbert feels—and I couldn't agree with him more —that it is precisely now when they need us most. When they have to choose between *us* and those awful little demagogues of theirs with a degree from Manchester or wherever it is.

CHARMIAN. You can quote Gilbert till you're blue in the face, darling, but it won't do me a bit of good. And it makes *them* fractious. (*Pause*) Peter says they've got us by the short and curlies—

HARRIET. By the *what*?

CHARMIAN. It does sound ghastly, doesn't it? Children are so mature nowadays. John says when he was Peter's age he spent all his time reading Shelley and worrying about self-abuse. Thank God we only have one grandchild. I'd be prostrate by now if Tim and Mary had any more like Peter.

HARRIET. Short and curly indeed! A boy of sixteen—

CHARMIAN. Curlies, Harriet.

HARRIET. Well, I ask you!

CHARMIAN. It has a certain crude vigour, as dormitory language goes—

HARRIET. My dear Charmian, a boy who can be as facetious as that at sixteen can be a Socialist at twenty-one!

CHARMIAN. I don't *quite* see the connection—

HARRIET. From the moment they came to power in 1945, Gilbert noticed the prevailing tone in their dealings with him was one of disrespect . . . a, a want of feeling and discretion.

CHARMIAN. Well, darling, you remember what the Permanent Under Secretary said at the time—

HARRIET. I don't believe I do.

CHARMIAN. Uneasy lies the Red that wears a crown! (*Laughs*) No, Harriet, it won't do. Gilbert failed to adapt, and people who fail to adapt—especially in colonial matters—are, as I have no doubt Peter would say, sitting ducks.

HARRIET. I shall never understand you.

CHARMIAN. You talk as though it is all over and done with.

CHARMIAN. But isn't it?

(*Pause*)

HARRIET. So long as Gilbert is Governor of Karalinga, it is the *colony* that must learn to adapt.

CHARMIAN. Harriet—

HARRIET. Will you have some more tea?

CHAIRMAN. Harriet—

HARRIET (*petulantly*). Now what is it?

CHARMIAN. Gilbert is dead.

HARRIET. Then I have nothing more to say on the subject. We all have our, our idiosyncrasies, Charmian. You must cling to yours, and I must cling to mine.

CHARMIAN. I would hardly call it an idiosyncrasy, to ignore the fact that Gilbert caught pneumonia, and died, and has been buried nearly six months.

(*Pause*)

HARRIET. *I* was speaking of the subtleties of colonial administration, Charmian.

(*Pause*)

CHARMIAN. Look, darling, why not let John and me come and help you to pack? Have everything sent off by sea, and book you an air passage to London? (*Pause*) This house is too lonely, Harriet. Anything could happen to you out here, and none of us would know. (*Pause*) Living out here with two or three native servants . . . not even a telephone . . . must you, Harriet? At least, come and stay with us for a while—

HARRIET (*sharply*). Do *not* insist on treating me as if I were mentally infirm,

CHARMIAN. (*Pause*) Amolo can reach the town on his bicycle in forty minutes. Should I need you in any way during Gilbert's absence, I am grateful to think you would come if I sent for you.

(*Pause*)

CHARMIAN. Well, if you will insist on being indomitable—

(*Pause*)

HARRIET. Not indomitable, Charmian. Independent.

CHARMIAN (*jungle noises start*). Well, it's nice to know you're not entirely without faith in independence! (*Pause*) I think I'd better be going. Come out and see what I did, to the jeep thing on the way up here—

(*Exit both. Blackout.*)

SCENE TWO

MORNING: BREAKFAST

Fade-in Mozart piano concerto.
(AMOLO *is serving breakfast.* HARRIET *enters.*)

HARRIET. Good morning, Amolo. No, leave it. . . . I'll see to it myself. You can go now.

AMOLO. Yes, Madam.

HARRIET. Amolo—

AMOLO. Yes, Madam?

HARRIET. Where is that music coming from?

AMOLO. My nephew, Madam. He is visiting. Has gramophone.

HARRIET. I see. Your nephew is fond of Mozart?

AMOLO. Fond of all music, Madam. (*With pride*) He is a student.

HARRIET. A music student?

AMOLO. Go for engineer, Madam.

HARRIET. Ah! At Manchester College I suppose—

AMOLO. No, Madam. (*Pause*) Moscow.

(*Pause*)

HARRIET. That will be all, Amolo.

AMOLO. Yes, Madam.

HARRIET (*peevishly*). And ask him to turn the gramophone down, will you?

AMOLO.Yes, Madam.

(AMOLO *goes out. The music stops.*)

HARRIET. Absurd. Poor Charmian. (*Pours tea.*) She does not understand that they are . . . how can one put it? Biologically remote from us. Charmian will ramble. She rambles and rambles, which always infuriated Gilbert. I remember once during a lull at a Memorial Service in Westminster, she brayed out "When are you going to get that paunch of yours knighted, Gilbert?" So cruel! So unjust! (*She slices at an egg.*) The way a person slices an egg can be most revealing. There. Poor little embryo. I wonder if I—

(*Jungle noises as* GILBERT *enters. He is in full Governor's regalia.*)

GILBERT. Morning, Harriet.

HARRIET. Why, Gilbert! What time did you get back last night? I didn't hear you.

GILBERT. Small hours. No reason to wake you. Slept in the dressing room.

HARRIET. Will you have an egg?

GILBERT. I think, a banana.

HARRIET. A fresh egg—

GILBERT (*picks up an egg*). Frankly, I've always considered eggs to be messy things. (*Smashes it on the table.*) All that sog inside. No more eggs.

HARRIET. Did you have a good trip?

GILBERT. Arrived in Bonda just after a ritual murder. And in Kadun too early for the trials. All this rushing round from one province to another, ridiculous. A Governor should be . . . remote. Pass the bananas, will you, Harriet?

(HARRIET *passes the bananas. Noisy eating punctuated by snorts and grunts.*)

HARRIET. You must be very hungry, Gilbert.

GILBERT (*A growling belch*).

HARRIET. Really! Let me give you some tea. (*Tea poured.*)

GILBERT (*slurping*). They've actually asked me to let them have a report on the colony's fitness for self-government. Thoughtful of them, isn't it? Especially when they'll go straight ahead with it whatever I say. (*Pause*)

HARRIET. Charmian was here yesterday. For tea.

(GILBERT *knocks a cup off the table clumsily—it breaks.*)

Gilbert! What an extraordinary thing to do! That was one of my mother's breakfast cups. Gilbert, you deliberately broke it. Amolo!

GILBERT. Very odd, that. Had a sort of

. . . impulse.

HARRIET. And a very cruel one, if I may say so.

GILBERT. Now, Harriet—

HARRIET. My mother bought those cups in—

GILBERT. Oh, damn your mother's cups.

HARRIET. Gilbert!

GILBERT. You loathe those cups. You've said so before.

HARRIET. Civilisation, Gilbert, is the art of tolerating what we loathe.

GILBERT. Prissy old devil.

HARRIET. I think I shall go to my room and write some letters. You must have been out in the sun. We shall say no more about it.

(GILBERT *knocks off another cup.*)

GILBERT. Oh, God! Now, that *was* an accident—

HARRIET. Was it, Gilbert? (*Pause*) Where *is* Amolo? (*Pause*) It has suddenly gone very quiet—

GILBERT. I've never liked that boy. Imagine . . . imagine Amolo voting. Can you? Ridiculous.

(HARRIET *is uneasy.*)

HARRIET. It's so quiet, Gilbert.

GILBERT. Subhuman. Subhuman, the lot of them. Can't help it, but no use ignoring. It's a matter of evolution, Harriet. Brain pan's too small. (*Pause*) Ever seen one?

(HARRIET *goes to the door.*)

HARRIET. I believe . . . I believe there's no one there, Gilbert.

GILBERT. Now, what's the weight of the average human brain? In ounces. A *white* human brain.

HARRIET. Is there such a thing as a *black* human brain?

GILBERT. Ho-ho, you old liberal, you!

(HARRIET *comes back to him.*)

HARRIET. Gilbert, do not be jocose. I am trying to tell you that the servants, the servants have all disappeared.

GILBERT. Damn good riddance.

HARRIET. I don't know what it is, but I have the distinct impression that you are not yourself today. And what are we going to do for servants?

GILBERT. Get some more, Harriet. Get some more.

HARRIET. If it were not nine o'clock in the morning, I should say you had been drinking.

GILBERT. How like a woman!

HARRIET. We are too old for scenes, Gilbert.

GILBERT. Too old for too many things, if one listened to you!

HARRIET. I hope you are not going to raise *that* subject again.

GILBERT. What subject?

HARRIET. That subject.

GILBERT. You know, I sometimes wonder if you aren't getting just a bit senile, Harriet.

HARRIET. I shall go to my room. I will not listen to this.

GILBERT. And the servants?

HARRIET. I have managed your domestic affairs efficiently for forty years, Gilbert . . . I am not a spiteful woman, but what would you like me to do? Chase into the bush after them?

GILBERT. Don't think of it, Harriet. Don't think of it. (*Pause*) The proper setting for a colonial administrator's wife is, of course, a garden. Where everything is pruned . . . and sprayed . . . and kept under control. (*Pause*) So stick to the garden, there's a good woman.

HARRIET. Your mind is wandering, Gilbert. You ought to see a doctor. (*Pause*) Do stop scratching! It's hardly . . . Take a bath or whatever you like, but do not scratch. Gilbert!

GILBERT. It's that damned headman in Bonda. The feller's crawling. Now, you run along and write your letters, m'dear.

HARRIET. Perhaps by lunchtime you will be more yourself—(*Exits.*)

GILBERT. I hope so, Harriet. If that will please you. I hope so.

(*Fadeout.*)

SCENE THREE

EVENING

Fade-in nocturnal jungle sounds.

(HARRIET *at table writing*)

HARRIET. May 16th. The situation is maddening. The servants ran away this morning, for some inexplicable reason, and nothing will induce Gilbert to take the matter seriously. (*Pause*) An extraordinary change has come over my husband.

He seems . . . coarsened. Almost brutal, at times. It is perhaps one of the inevitable trials of old age that human dignity should prove so vulnerable to the malfunctionings of body and mind. (*Pause*) Gilbert is waging a struggle with himself in which I can take no part, except insofar as I can, and must, share his humiliations. (*Pause*) How one longs for white servants at moments like these; and despite one's love for Africa, there is always that sense of emergence from the primordial . . . that nostalgia for reason and order, which these poor people cannot achieve—no, not in a hundred years.

(*Pause. Creaking. Silence. Creaking. Silence. Creaking. Silence.*)

Gilbert . . . (*Louder*) Gilbert—Gilbert, where are you? (*Sound as of some kind of ring being thrown onto a post.*)

(GILBERT *on wardrobe*)

GILBERT. Now where the devil would you *expect* me to be?

(*Pause*)

HARRIET. *Not* on top of the wardrobe! And *not* rifling my jewel case! (*Pause*) What are my necklaces doing on this bedpost, might I ask?

(*Creak.* GILBERT *is throwing necklaces onto the bedpost.*)

Gilbert, come down here at once! Give me my jewel case. Come along. Give it to me.

(*Creak. Rattle.*)

GILBERT (*irritated*). Nearly missed that time! Go away, Harriet. Go away and write your blessed diary.

HARRIET. Not until you come down off that wardrobe and . . . (*Crying:*) Oh, Gilbert!

GILBERT. Harriet, you are trivialising our relationship—

HARRIET. Won't you come down? Just for me?

GILBERT. I can't imagine why you should think *you* are any sort of temptation!

HARRIET. Come down, my dear—

GILBERT. Ha! *My dear* now, are we?

HARRIET. Oh, this is futile.

GILBERT. You're not the woman I married, Harriet.

HARRIET. I am not indeed! I should like to think that nearly half a century had brought a little wisdom. Common sense, at least.

GILBERT. Who the devil wants wisdom in a woman? What about your woman's instincts, eh? What about them?

HARRIET. I have noticed before, that when you begin to talk like a character out of a Russian novel, it is best to leave you to your own devices.

GILBERT. A Russian novel? Me? I've never read one of those damned things in me life! All those vitches and ovnas . . . ukins and inskys.

HARRIET. It is your loss.

GILBERT. But, you wouldn't say I'm an *uncultured* man, would you, Harriet?

HARRIET. Until recently—no.

GILBERT. Now, they can say what they like but these people . . . these wretched natives . . . they're *all* instinct. Primitive. (*Pause*) I can admire instinct in a white woman of gentle birth. We have, we have centuries of slow, painful refinement behind us. But oh, my God, the unadulterated thing! The *thing* itself! Chaos! Absolute chaos! (*Pause*) If they knew what I really think about this situation . . . why, they'd have me out. Have me out, Harriet.

HARRIET. Gilbert . . . I do believe . . .

GILBERT. What's that? What?

HARRIET. Gilbert, are you—

GILBERT. Am I *what*?

HARRIET. A trick of the light.

GILBERT. Trick?

HARRIET. I had the distinct impression you were . . . salivating.

GILBERT. Salivating? What the devil do you think I am? *Animals* salivate, Harriet. Human beings spit. There's a world of difference.

HARRIET. Well, are you?

GILBERT. Or drool, I suppose.

HARRIET. There has never been the slightest confusion in *my* mind. A person who drools is not a person. (*Pause*) Which are *you* doing, Gilbert?

(*Pause*)

GILBERT. I'm spitting, Harriet. I'm spitting. I spit when I get carried away.

HARRIET. Then be good enough to regain control of yourself.

GILBERT. You know, there's something bloody odd about you this evening.

HARRIET. I have never known you lose control of yourself in forty years of Government service.

GILBERT. There's a difference between losing control and getting carried away. (*Pause*) In any case, the point is an academic one since I am not prone to either, when publicly fulfilling my obligations as a servant of Her Majesty's Government. (*Pause*)

HARRIET. What *resonance* there was in that phrase . . . once.

GILBERT. Oh, the *resonance* has gone, right enough!

HARRIET. When there was order in the world—

GILBERT. Law and order. Nowadays it's all, wha'do they call it? Pragmatism. Oh, there are people who regard me as a sort of living fossil! I know. I'm an enemy of pragmatism, you see. And it doesn't do these days, Harriet. It doesn't do.

HARRIET. It is satisfying to think that our kind have always acted . . . disinterestedly. That the instincts have been . . . sublimated.

GILBERT. You always were a clever woman, Harriet.

HARRIET. Do come down, my dear—

GILBERT. What about a nightcap?

HARRIET. On the balcony? As we . . . used to?

GILBERT. Right. I'm coming down then.

HARRIET. It's a lovely night— (*Pause*) Let me help you down, my dear!

(*Chattering of monkeys.* GILBERT *pours drinks.*)

GILBERT. It's a long time since we did this. (*Pause*) Life's too long, really. Ought to be cut off in the prime. (*Goes down to verandah in front.*)

HARRIET. I am not sure that a woman knows what . . . or when . . . her prime is.

GILBERT. Different for a woman.

HARRIET. That was how my father explained away a great deal in his declining years. Everything was . . . different for a woman. But he never mentioned his prime.

GILBERT. Great diplomat, your father. (*Pause*) The middle classes can run the Empire, he used to say, but it takes an aristocrat to run the middle classes. (*Pause*)Wouldn't recognise things as they are today.

HARRIET. I remember . . . at a week-end house-party once, he encountered that Lawrence person—

GILBERT. T.E.?

HARRIET. David Herbert—

GILBERT. Ugh!

HARRIET. We were strolling in the garden before dinner. Someone was talking about the Weimar Republic. Lawrence was being most tiresome, and my father said to him: Mister Lawrence, you stick to your solar plexus and leave Germany to the politicians—

GILBERT. Oh, splendid! (*Pause*)

HARRIET. Lawrence was a venomous little man, you know. He despised people like my father. He despised what we all stood for. But he lacked wit—

GILBERT. Worlds apart—

HARRIET. His reply must have been unexceptional, because I can't remember what it was.

GILBERT. Your father was in his prime then.

(*Chattering of monkeys outside*)

HARRIET. He was not a bigoted man. (*Pause*)

GILBERT. These young men *now* . . . They talk about the first war marking the end of an epoch. . . . They've no real idea what there, what there *was*. (*Pause*)

HARRIET. And yet . . . I sometimes think, Europe was besotted with sex after 1919.

GILBERT. Europe was in its prime, just before the First World War.

HARRIET. Well, we enjoyed some of the last of it, Gilbert— (*Pause*)

GILBERT. That's a pretty bowl—

HARRIET. Really! We have had that bowl for over twenty years.

GILBERT. Oh, it's pretty all right!

HARRIET. You gave it to me yourself.

GILBERT. Did I now? Did I?

HARRIET. You have always had exquisite taste, Gilbert.

GILBERT. Curious . . . don't remember it.

HARRIET. We have so many fine things. (*Pause*) I sometimes . . . even after all these years I still think how it would have been to have had children. Someone to pass these things on to. The sense of . . . continuity. It becomes more important as one grows older. (*Pause*) I don't like to think it might be . . . as if we had never existed.

GILBERT. Getting morbid, Harriet.

HARRIET. And these things will pass into the world after we are gone, and they will be . . . anonymous.

GILBERT. Morbid!

HARRIET. Oh, our lives have been rich, and full. I am grateful for that. (*Pause*)

GILBERT. Well, who mentioned not having children? Did I? Did I say anything about it? No. You raised the subject. (*Pause*) There's something . . . obscene about an old woman maundering over her sterility.

HARRIET. The question of whose incapacity was involved was never settled.

GILBERT. And why not? What in God's name is science *for,* then?

HARRIET. I have often put the same question to myself. Science illuminates, but it fails to explain. I believe that was the gist of *your* refusal to undergo a medical examination.

GILBERT. All this beating about the bush—

HARRIET. Gilbert, since you came home yesterday, I have had a strangely . . . cut-off feeling. Almost . . . almost the sensation that you wish to do me harm, Gilbert. Or, to put it another way, that you wish harm might come to me. (*Pause*) Everything was perfectly normal when you went away—

GILBERT. Everything is perfectly normal now, Harriet. Perfectly normal.

HARRIET. But, we don't appear to have quite the relationship that we had before. (*Pause*) The relationship that we have enjoyed since we were young people.

GILBERT. You mustn't allow yourself to feel guilty, Harriet. One has to adjust, as one gets older.

HARRIET. Guilty?

GILBERT. A more passionate woman might have . . . so to speak, disturbed the balance.

(*Pause*)

HARRIET. You are spitting again, Gilbert. Wipe your chin.

GILBERT. I'm going to shave this damned beard off. It gets . . . matted.

HARRIET. It is very distinguished. (*Pause*) You didn't tell me that you intended to grow one whilst you were away. (*Pause*) An imperial suits you.

GILBERT. It compensates somewhat for the waning authority of the Crown, don't you think? If Queen Victoria had had a beard the Empire would have lasted for a thousand years! (*Pause*) Still, they do . . . tend . . . to get . . . matted.

HARRIET. Never mind. It will photograph so much better than a . . . what does one say? A *naked* face? A bare face?

GILBERT. Nude face?

HARRIET. Most certainly not.

GILBERT. There, that's the last of the whisky.

HARRIET. Surely not? There was . . . surely, half a bottle?

GILBERT. Then Amolo must have been at it.

HARRIET. *Not* the sort of behaviour that goes with political maturity!

GILBERT. Ought to get back up the trees, where they belong.

HARRIET. Oh!

GILBERT. Now you're shocked.

HARRIET. I *am* shocked.

GILBERT. I can just tolerate the hypothesis that Amolo and I have a common ancestor in the lemur. Where I diverge from enlightened opinion is in the crass assertion that Amolo and I are the same beneath the skin. My remark was an attempt to be graphic about the divergence.

HARRIET. Nonetheless, it was the sort of remark one hears from gutter racialists—

GILBERT. Admirably put, Harriet, but you know me better than that.

HARRIET. I know you are not a racialist, Gilbert. (*Pause*) That I could *not* bear.

GILBERT. But you women . . . *you* know there's . . . something different about them. Now don't you? Something . . . attractive.

(*Pause*)

HARRIET. Attractive?

GILBERT. What do you mean, "attractive"?

HARRIET. You said: "something attractive."

GILBERT. I said repellent, Harriet.

HARRIET. I heard you distinctly. You said: "attractive."

GILBERT. And equally distinctly, I heard myself say repellent.

HARRIET. That must be what you intended to say.

GILBERT. Dammit, *I* know what I said!

HARRIET. Then we cannot profitably discuss the matter any further.

GILBERT. I *intended* to say "attractive," and I *said* "attractive."

(*Pause*)

HARRIET. There you go again!

(*Pause*)

GILBERT. You know, Harriet, it's just possible . . . it's just possible that *you* find them attractive!

HARRIET. I find them repellent.

GILBERT. Ah!

HARRIET. You needn't sound so pleased about it.

GILBERT (*shouting*). I am *not* pleased.

HARRIET. Oh? Aren't you?

GILBERT. I mean . . . I don't know where the devil all this is leading—

HARRIET. In my case—to bed. In your case, Gilbert, perhaps . . . up on the wardrobe, where you belong?

(*Monkeys. Fadeout.*)

SCENE FOUR

(*Fade-in* HARRIET.)

HARRIET. March 18th. I must force myself to put it down in writing: Gilbert is going insane. The evidence is overwhelming. He is gratuitously violent—so far, thank heaven, directed elsewhere, than at my own person. He has wilfully broken every bowl and vase in the house, and most of the cups. He appears to be losing control of his bodily functions and has also evolved the distressing habit of vomiting forth his bananas, then eating his vomit! In my last entry I spoke of sharing his humiliations! I see now that I was trying to conceal the truth from myself, for Gilbert and I are beyond sharing. . . . He has gone where I cannot reach him, and is so far in this that I cannot, I dare not hope for his return. (*Pause*) Yet, such is the resilience of human nature that I have already taken certain practical steps. (*Pause*) My poor Gilbert! I have unearthed the picnic basket which Charmian gave us last year, and I propose from now on to serve him his meals on plastic plates and his tea and coffee in a plastic beaker. (*Pause*) I found a set of clean dungarees in Amolo's room which, after some persuasion and cajoling, Gilbert consented to

wear . . . until I can have his ruined suits cleaned and pressed. When I look at Gilbert, my whole instinct is to weep and weep. (*Pause*) This must be conquered like any other.

(*Fadeout* HARRIET. *A long-drawn-out yell. Fade up into bedroom area.* GILBERT, *in semidarkness—a great hulking figure in dungarees. He is strangling Amolo. The body thuds onto the stage.* GILBERT *scuttles off.* HARRIET *enters, frightened. Enter* GILBERT *humming "The Teddy Bears' Picnic." He now has gorilla hands.*)

GILBERT. What's this?

HARRIET. Amolo . . . I think . . . I think his neck is broken.

GILBERT. Good God! (*Pause*) Dead as mutton.

HARRIET. His *neck* is broken—

GILBERT. Came sneaking back for the rest of the whisky, I suppose.

HARRIET. And broke his own neck?

GILBERT. One of the others did—

HARRIET. But why? Why?

GILBERT. This damned colony's seething. *Seething.* Tribal feuds . . . politics . . . communist agitators—

HARRIET. Not *Amolo*—

GILBERT. I shall declare a state of emergency throughout the province.

HARRIET. But—

GILBERT. Arrest the ringleaders . . . declare a curfew . . . soon put a stop to all *this.*

HARRIET. But Amolo—

GILBERT. What's that?

HARRIET. Wasn't mixed up in anything like that, Gilbert.

GILBERT. My dear Harriet, they are *all* mixed up in things like that.

HARRIET. What are we going to do . . . with Amolo's . . . body?

GILBERT. Have to be buried immediately, of course. Be stinking within twelve hours, poor fellow.

(*Pause*)

HARRIET. Do *you* intend to bury him, Gilbert?

GILBERT. *I*?

HARRIET. There is no one else—

GILBERT. I think I'll have a little swing, and think about it.

HARRIET. A swing?

GILBERT. You know what a *swing* is,

Harriet! A wooden seat suspended by two ropes from a—

HARRIET. Yes . . . I know what a swing is.

GILBERT. Then what are you looking so vacant about?

HARRIET. Nothing . . . nothing.

GILBERT. Nothing in that tone of voice means *something*. (*Pause*) This is not the time to be perversely feminine!

HARRIET. I think we had better go out into the garden. Amolo's body—

GILBERT. I've never thought of you as a *squeamish* woman, Harriet! The garden—

(*She exits fast out to garden and swing.* GILBERT *follows and sits on swing.* GILBERT *on swing, pushed by* HARRIET.)

GILBERT. Come on, Harriet, push me. Harder, Harriet! Push harder—

HARRIET. This is ridiculous—

GILBERT. Push, Harriet—

HARRIET. I am exhausted.

GILBERT. Feeble old woman!

HARRIET. I can bear no more.

GILBERT. Why, Harriet! Come now, I'll *stop* swinging—if you like.

HARRIET. Yes—do. For goodness' sake stop.

GILBERT. Didn't *you* ever like to swing?

HARRIET. Oh, yes! I liked to swing. Nearly sixty years ago!

GILBERT. In the privacy of one's own garden, Harriet . . . there are no limits. (*Pause*)

HARRIET. I think it is time you pulled yourself together and faced reality, Gilbert. The situation is intolerable. First the servants run away, then Amolo is killed—and you do nothing. Nothing. (*Pause*) For all we know, we are completely cut off. And once the killing begins—

GILBERT. They can tear themselves to pieces for all I care.

HARRIET. And what if they should tear *us* to pieces?

GILBERT. They wouldn't dare to lay a finger on us.

HARRIET. Revenge takes no account of the consequences.

GILBERT. Revenge? Good God, woman, what have we done to them except bring them a . . . a civilisation? Schools, roads, hospitals, technicians . . . government, Harriet. (*Pause*) If they remain savages, as they very obviously do—despite their gramophones and briefcases—then it is not a question of revenge, but of blind, gratuitous violence. And I know how to deal with that!

HARRIET. *Do* you, Gilbert?

GILBERT. Haven't I dealt with it before?

HARRIET. You have certainly shown that you know how to *eliminate* it. (*Pause*) Whether you have *dealt* with it, except in a very limited sense of the word . . . I don't know.

(*Pause. Distant sound of drums.*) Listen—

(*Pause*)

GILBERT. Listen to what? Can't hear a thing.

HARRIET. Sure . . . drums?

GILBERT. Nonsense.

HARRIET. I can hear drums—

(*Drumming stepped up slightly.*)

GILBERT. Blood pressure, more likely!

HARRIET. If I were the sort of person who hears things, Gilbert, I would know it!

GILBERT. Drums!

HARRIET. You *must* hear them.

GILBERT. But . . . I don't.

(*Pause. Drumming.*)

HARRIET. I am going into the house—

GILBERT. Well, then, you'd better be the one to bury Amolo . . . because I'm going for a walk.

HARRIET. I? Dig a *grave*? Bury *Amolo*? (*Pause*) How *can* you!

GILBERT. Harriet, you know perfectly well that I can't touch dead things. It's one of my, one of my . . . phobias. (*Pause*) On the other hand, you could simply let him rot—

HARRIET. Gilbert!

GILBERT. Leave him to the ants—

HARRIET. But . . . but Amolo is a *Christian*!

GILBERT. I shouldn't think the ants will mind, Harriet. Besides, being a Christian doesn't logically entitle anyone to a burial, now does it?

(*Pause*)

HARRIET. *We* are Christian, too.

GILBERT. Come now. Not *really* Christians. Eh? (*Pause*) There are other things besides being a Christian, you know.

HARRIET. Are you no longer a Christian, Gilbert?

GILBERT. Oh, come come come. I really

thought we were more sophisticated than that, Harriet! (*Pause*) Just a minute. What's that? Listen?

(*Pause. Silence.*)

HARRIET. Why . . . the drums have stopped.

GILBERT. *Your* drums may have stopped. (*Pause*) *Mine* have just started—

HARRIET. But . . . it's perfectly *quiet!* (*Pause*)

GILBERT. I think you'd better get started on that grave. On that *Christian's* grave.

HARRIET. I am sorry, Gilbert. . . . I will not do such a thing. How can you seem to . . . to expect—

GILBERT. You've had the poor devil at your beck and call for the last eight years . . . the least you can do is to bury him!

HARRIET (*moaning*). Gilbert . . . Gilbert . . . I won't, I can't—

GILBERT. I wish they'd stop those bloody drums. (*Pause*) Now Harriet, I'll find you a nice spade. I tell you what, I'll find some big stones as well. To put on top. If you don't, the hyenas'll get him, you know. (HARRIET *sobbing quietly*) Come along . . . that's right give me your arm . . . must get it done before sundown—

(*Fadeout* HARRIET *crying.*)

SCENE FIVE

LATER THAT EVENING

(*Fade-in* HARRIET *reading her diary. Muted drumming.*)

HARRIET. For what sin has my awful punishment been devised? (*Pause*) And what woman, grown old and experienced in the world, has had to take pen and record such vile assault on her whole being as I have endured today? (*Pause*) And Gilbert . . . Gilbert stood over me whilst I dug a grave. Under the hot sun, I took a spade, and measured the ground . . . and dug a grave for Amolo, whilst Gilbert watched . . . half smiling. (*Pause*) I half dragged, half carried the body to the grave, wrapped in a sheet. I read from the Book of Common Prayer (I cannot remember what) and lowered Amolo in, as gently as I could. (*Pause*) I was drenched with perspiration—and trembling . . . almost ready to die *then,* and have Gilbert bury me. (*Pause*) We came back to the house, and have not spoken since. . . . I feel . . . fanciful though it might be . . . that in burying that poor native boy, I have buried some angry devouring thing in my husband. (*Pause*) Now I must go to bed, for I ache both in body and heart . . . and the drumming out there in the hills is like the beat of evil itself. (*Pause*) Perhaps . . . we should give them their country, and go. (*Pause*) I can write no more. (*Pause*) God bring us peace with the morning light.

(*Gets into bed.*)
(*Fadeout.*)

SCENE SIX

(*Fade up bed in semidarkness. Low muted drumming. A clock strikes three. There is a scream, and we see* GILBERT *trying to climb into a bed. He does so, and* HARRIET *pleads with him.*)

HARRIET (*in bed; mosquito net over bed*). What are you doing? (*Pause*) Gilbert? Is that you? (*Creaking springs*) What are you . . . no, no . . . go back to your own bed and go to sleep. (*Pause. Silence*) Gilbert? (*Pause. Creaking springs*) Gilbert . . . we are old people. . . . This is . . . it is . . . you *shall* not! (*Pause*) Please . . . please, Gilbert—(GILBERT *grunts several times.*) How *dare* you, dare you attempt this disgusting behaviour! (*Pause*) Gilbert? (*Pause*) Be good enough to return to your own bed, and molest me no further. (*Pause*) It was . . . it was beastliness when we were young . . . and it would be . . . degraded beastliness now. Gilbert? You cannot. You must not. It was . . . *always* loathesome. There was never any response in me. You know that, don't you? (*Pause*) Never in me. *That* was not in me. (*Pause*) Gilbert? (*Pause*) Gilbert, I shall get up, and cross the room, and go out through that door . . . and *lock* it. I shall lock you up. Lock you in. (*Pause*) Lock you in alone with yourself, where you belong. (*Pause*) And perhaps tomorrow . . . if you are good . . . I shall let you out . . . and we shall say no more about it? Shall we? Not another word.

(*Massive jungle cacophony. Fadeout on bed.*)

Scene Seven

Next Morning: Breakfast

(*Long pause. Fade up* HARRIET *at breakfast. She has a rifle by her chair. Enter* GILBERT.)

GILBERT. Morning, Harriet. (*Pause*) I said Good morning, Harriet—

HARRIET. Yes. I heard you.

GILBERT. Well then?

HARRIET. You will understand if I find it difficult to engage in pleasantries this morning!

(*Pause*)

GILBERT. Dammit, you unlocked the door, didn't you?

HARRIET. As your presence at breakfast testifies!

GILBERT. Then we'll say no more about it.

HARRIET. *You* say that! (*Pause*) If it will reassure you . . . I do not propose to make an issue of what happened last night.

GILBERT. How are your drums?

HARRIET. I . . . I can't hear them this morning.

GILBERT. Mine have stopped, too. (*Pause*) It's a bit . . . ominous, isn't it? (*Pause*) The calm before the . . . attack . . . and all that.

HARRIET. Gilbert, why are you trying to frighten me? (*Pause*) What are you trying to do to me? (*Pause*) What have you become, Gilbert?

GILBERT. Now, Harriet, you unlocked the door of your own free will!

HARRIET. I unlocked the door . . . out of respect for *your* free will—

GILBERT. And why should *I* wish to frighten *you*?

HARRIET. If I knew . . . *I* would know how to help *you*—

GILBERT. The truth is, of course, that you are a cold, arrogant woman, Harriet. Something disturbs you . . . you find its source in me. And yet, when it comes to the natives you are . . . equivocal. If I were to put them down ruthlessly you would applaud me. Yet, secretly, you know that to have what you really want is an act of aggression against yourself. (*Pause*) I hope I am being lucid?

(*Pause*)

HARRIET. I . . . do not know you . . . any longer, Gilbert.

GILBERT. Which is why, I suppose, you are carrying that gun!

(*Pause*)

HARRIET. I . . . I am so tired of all this. (*Pause*) Do you remember what we were when we first came out here? Do you think I have not the pride of knowing that a few great families in one small country held out as long as they did? (*Pause*) Our motives have always been . . . beyond reproach. And to suggest that we were moved by the hungers and lusts which characterise *these* people is to put yourself . . . on the wrong side of the boundary of sanity.

(*Pause*)

GILBERT. A . . . few . . . great . . . families! What a felicitous way of understanding fifty years' precarious authority! (*Pause*) Isn't it time we did what we really want for a change? (*Pause*) Since we are virtually an extinct class . . . since we've let the *merchants* and *managers* and *technicians* capture the roost . . . we might as *well* go out with a bang! (*Pause*) And admit . . . that we are grateful . . . for the modest privilege of . . . destroying . . . each other!

(GILBERT *exits.*)

HARRIET. Where are you going? (*Pause*) Come *back*, Gilbert! (*Pause*) It's no use running off into the bush, you know—they'll catch you and tear you to pieces! You are behaving in a ridiculous manner, Gilbert. (*Pause*) You cannot possibly climb that tree. (*Pause*) Come down at once. Very well, then. If you will not—

GILBERT. There are some fine coconuts up here, Harriet . . . try one.

(*Pause. Crash of breaking coconut*)

HARRIET. I warn you, Gilbert—

GILBERT. Try another—

(*Coconut*)

HARRIET. Oh, I wish they could all see you now . . . in your tree, Gilbert. Like the beast you are. (*Coconuts thick and fast*) Like the ugly, monstrous creature you always have been. That is what I have lived with all these years, a monster!

I have the gun, Gilbert. (*Pause*) Come down, or I shall shoot . . . oh, I've wanted to, you know. I've wanted to. *Wanted* to shoot you. *Will* you come down or must I . . . (*She fires. Loud crash. Scream from* HARRIET.)

(*Blackout.*)

SCENE EIGHT

LATER THE SAME EVENING

(*Chattering monkeys. Fade-in. Breakfast things still there. Fade up sound of jeep. We hear it stop—its lights swing across the stage and come to rest. In half shadow there is a tree with the body of a huge gorilla lying beneath it. Voices off:* CHARMIAN, JOHN (*her husband*), *and a* NATIVE POLICEMAN.)

CHARMIAN (*off*). The place looks deserted.

JOHN (*off*). You take the back, Sergeant. I'll take the front.

(*They enter; the* POLICEMAN *first, carrying an electric torch, then* JOHN *and* CHARMIAN *together.*)

POLICEMAN. Mr. Maudsley—*you* will take the back.

JOHN (*irritated*). It's hardly an occasion for quibbling about protocol—

CHARMIAN (*frightened*). Poor Harriet—

JOHN. What do you mean? How do we know? She's probably in bed and asleep.

POLICEMAN. In Karalinga, Mrs. Maudsley, bad things no longer happen. We are not savages. Know how to behave. I am afraid, sir, this was not always the same with your own people.

JOHN. Oh, let's get on with it!

(JOHN *goes off. The* POLICEMAN *comes downstage flashing his torch, followed by* CHARMIAN. *He is near the tree.*)

CHARMIAN. I'm sure something's happened—

POLICEMAN. These men from the place of Lady Boscoe—good men, Mrs. Maudsley. Not liars. Thieves. They didn't have to come to me. Good cook, good houseboy.

(JOHN *enters. He takes* CHARMIAN's *arm. The* POLICEMAN *is wandering near the tree with his torch.*)

JOHN. She's on the verandah. Dead.

(*With a gasp,* CHARMIAN *makes to go towards the verandah.* JOHN *holds her back. Nods at the* POLICEMAN.)

JOHN. Best let him go first. His self-esteem, and all that. It's nothing violent. A heart attack, I should say.

(*The* POLICEMAN *has at last trained his torch on the gorilla.*)

POLICEMAN. Mr. Maudsley—

(JOHN *goes to him, followed by* CHARMIAN—*they look, and* CHARMIAN *screams.*)

JOHN. My God!

POLICEMAN. I have heard it said many times, Mr. Maudsley, they are the most intelligent, cunning of creatures. (*Pause*) And is it not known, sir, by your Darwin that they are our forefathers? Ancestors of black and white, red and yellow?

CHARMIAN. It's *huge!*

JOHN. And Harriet alone—

POLICEMAN (*slyly*). Perhaps he was a friendly fellow, sir—

JOHN. That's quite enough, Sergeant! Don't you realise what might have happened? Good God! Come away, Charmian. Ugly brute. (*Pause*) Gilbert told me himself . . . ages ago . . . the last, the last gorilla shot in these parts it was . . . surely it was before independence, wasn't it?

THE END

NANNIE'S NIGHT OUT

Sean O'Casey

MRS. POLLY PENDER, *proprietress of the Laburnum dairy*
Sweet on Polly:
  OUL JOHNNY, *a lodger*
  OUL JIMMY
  OUL JOE
IRISH NANNIE, *a young spunker*[1]
ROBERT, *Nannie's son*
A BALLAD SINGER and HIS WIFE
A YOUNG MAN
A YOUNG GIRL
CROWD

> SCENE: The premises of the Laburnum Dairy.
> TIME: The Present.

---

[1] Spunker: a drinker of methylated spirit.

To DWELL AT length upon the life and times of Sean O'Casey (1880–1964) would be as futile as transmitting a pot of shamrock to Dublin. A supreme artist and an incomparable man, he occupies a conspicuous and revered window in the tower of history's permanent dramatic literature. His writings and momentous passage through life have engendered scores of books, essays, analyses, and celebratory hymns; and as far as personal "background" is concerned, no one re-created it more eloquently than the master himself, in his two-volume autobiography *Mirror in My House,* published in 1956.

Born and raised in the tenements of Dublin, O'Casey knew intimately the people of whom he wrote and the events he covered in his plays, notably in his early Abbey Theatre dramas: *The Shadow of a Gunman,* his first play to be staged; *Juno and the Paycock;* and *The Plough and the Stars.*

He was a man who reflected in his life and work an infinite and passionate concern for humanity. As a person, he was a man of many moods and humors: witty, contentious, compassionate, challenging, and to those fortunate enough to have known him, a rare and lovable soul. As an artist, he belongs to a class of writers rare in all literature, perhaps rarer still in drama, the tragic satirists, in whom the comedy of satire points directly to tragic implications.

Nannie's Night Out represents something of a literary "find." Written shortly after *Juno and the Paycock* and just before *The Plough and the Stars,* the play was presented at the Abbey Theatre in 1924. Throngs attended the production, and a reviewer for the *Irish Statesman* wrote: "Take O'Casey's latest play—*Nannie's Night Out*—a rocking, roaring comedy—Dublin accents; queer 'characters'; window-smashing; burlesque lovemaking. Our sides ache, we laugh; we roar; we gasp—and then—a sudden feeling of discomfort, a queer, stupid feeling as if we wanted to cry. . . . He brings us to his plays and then he heaves life at us, with its sharp corners and its untidy jumble of laughter and tears. . . . And the worst of it is, that if we go on allowing him to make us laugh and cry together in this hysterical manner, we may end by insisting that he is a genius."

Oddly enough such strong sentiments and breathless praise did not impress or influence O'Casey, for as it has been recorded, he didn't much care for the comedy after he had seen it performed. On December 27, 1925, *The New York Times* printed an O'Casey letter in which he stated: "The Abbey directors finally allowed the author to withdraw the work because he felt the character of Nannie deserved the richer picture of a three-act play." Thus, Irish Nannie and her Dublin compatriots were banished from further public life by their creator. That is, until 1961, when O'Casey rescinded the banishment and permitted Robert Hogan to stage the play for the Lafayette (Indiana) Little Theatre. It was a long way from Ireland to Indiana and it took fully thirty-seven years before Nannie was allowed to make her second stage appearance in this world.

According to Mr. Hogan, the play came eminently alive on stage, "packed with the song, the dancing, the wild rhetoric, and the verve that have become O'Casey's trademarks."

Finally convinced that the play was "representative O'Casey," the author sanctioned its initial publication in Mr. Hogan's 1962 compilation of O'Casey's early writings: *Feathers from the Green Crow.*

With this volume, *Nannie's Night Out* makes its second appearance in print and its first in an anthology of plays. And again, to quote Mr. Hogan: "The text of the play is a recension of four varying and incomplete versions—the original typescript and three Abbey typescripts—and two pages of added material."

Three different endings to *Nannie's Night Out* remain in existence, and two are printed in this book. The unusual circumstances are best explained by an eyewitness, Gabriel Fallon, a director of the Abbey Theatre and a lifelong friend of the author: "I do recall a conversation in which Sean said there were *three* endings: the one he wanted, the one they (the Abbey people) wanted, and the compromise, which was the one used."

In an explanatory note to this editor, Mr. Hogan suggested printing two of the existing endings because "the third does not differ materially from the second, except for the excision of the gunman scene."

Whichever the preference, the true and most rewarding conclusion to *Nannie's Night Out* is that Sean O'Casey—shortly before his death in 1964—restored to public life a superb, even a masterly, piece of modern dramatic literature.

Two BALLAD SINGERS—*a Man and a Woman—are heard singing:*

> For Ireland is Ireland thro' joy an' thro' tears.
> Hope never dies thro' they long weary years;
> Each age has seen countless, brave hearts pass away,
> But their spirit still lives on in they men of to-day!

The curtain rises and shows:
A small dairy and provision shop in a working-class district. The shop is about as large as a fairly sized room; a small counter, on which are a crock of milk and a butter-weighing scale. At Back, a window filled with a medley of sweets, soap, penny toys, cigarettes, sauce, balloons, etc. At the end of counter, Right, is a railed-in till; on this is hanging a notice: "No Credit Given." Beside the notice is a price list, written with coloured chalks on black millboard. At Back, in a prominent position, are some small dressed dolls. The entrance from the street to the shop is on Right. On Left, a door leading to another part of the house. One electric bulb supplies the light. It is about eight o'clock, on a cold, wet, wintry evening.
Mrs. Pender, behind the counter, is weighing up sugar; she is a tall, straight, briskly moving woman, of about fifty; age hasn't yet taken all the friskiness of youth out of her. She is a widow, living alone—all her children being either married or dead—working from morning till night, the shop brings her in just enough to keep her going.
Johnny is standing beside Mrs. Pender, his hand on a newspaper that is on the counter. Johnny is an elderly, stout, rubicund-visaged man approaching sixty; his skin is tight on his body, like the tensely drawn head of a drum. His moustache is closely cropped. He is in his shirt sleeves, and is wearing a jerry hat. Beside him, on the counter, is a small cream jug.

JOHNNY (*looking up into Mrs. Pender's face*). An' she hot you right between th' two eyes with it?

MRS. PENDER. How do I know you got

th' egg here, or no, says I; d'ye doubt me word, says she; I don't doubt your word, says I, but I'm not goin' to take th' egg back. With that, she let it fly, an' hot me right between th' two eyes with it!

JOHNNY (*putting his arm around her neck*). As long as they know you're a lone widda, they'll stop at nothin'. The sooner you get buckled, Polly, th' betther.

MRS. PENDER (*slyly*). To you?

JOHNNY (*tightening his arm round her neck*). Polly—

MRS. PENDER (*taking his arm away*). Here, go on up, an' get your tea; I'll be wantin' you to take th' shop for a while in a few minutes.

JOHNNY (*taking up the paper and looking at it*). Heated scene in th' Doyle:[2] Deputy Morrison moved that th' Doyle end at six, instead of twelve, as th' Deputies were gettin' tired. Deputy Doran said they were sent here to do th' Nation's business; an' they could, an' they would do it, if they stopped up all night. It was like th' Labour Party, thryin' to do as little as they could. Labour Deputies, leppin' to their feet: withdraw, withdraw!

MRS. PENDER. Right between th' eyes I got it—

JOHNNY. Th' Cann Come-early,[3] ordher, ordher!

MRS. PENDER. What's th' Cann Come-early?

JOHNNY. Th' Sword Bearer, of course.

MRS. PENDER. Why do they be usin' names no-body understands?

JOHNNY. Everybody undherstands it; you might as well say that no-one ud undherstand Dunnlockairy meant Kingstown. I don't like th' idea of them goin' to inthroduce this new Divorce Bill—a nice thing if we had Free Love in this counthry.

MRS. PENDER. I don't know what th' Doyle is doin' at all; ah, I suppose th' only thing to do, is to put our trust in God.

JOHNNY. I betther be goin' up, or th' tea'll be stewed. (*Taking the cream jug, he goes out by door on Left. Mrs. Pender resumes the weighing of the sugar.*)

---

[2] Dail Eireann, the Irish legislative body.
[3] Ceann Comhairle, the chief counsellor, the Speaker of the House.

VOICES OF THE BALLAD SINGERS.

For Ireland is Ireland thro' joy an'
thro' tears.

Hope never dies thro' they long
weary years.

Each age has seen countless, brave
hearts pass away,

But their spirit still lives on in they
men of to-day!

(*A pause: then the Man Ballad Singer
enters. The under life of his profession
has soiled him a good deal; he has all the
cuteness of his class; there is a week's
growth of beard on his chin; he is sometimes deferential, sometimes defiant, timid
and bold. He wears a heavy, tattered top
coat. His battered hat is in his hand, and
he stretches it out in a suggestive, imploring and expectant movement. The woman's
voice can still be heard singing some distance away. "For Ireland is Ireland," etc.
There is a slight pause, which is broken
by a gentle cough from the Ballad Singer.
Mrs. Pender shakes her head. The Ballad
Singer holds the hat a little nearer. Mrs.
Pender shakes her head a little more vig-
orously. A pause.*)

THE BALLAD SINGER. It's a cowld night
an' a wet wan . . . me an' th' Mot [4] is
nearly drownded. . . . God an' the Holy
Angels bless you, ma'am. . . . It's cruel—
th' whole street to be able to spare only
tuppence—it's cruel. (*A pause.*) Tuppence!
Th' fourth part of th' price of a pint—it's
cruel!

MRS. PENDER. This is a bad place to come;
everythin' goin' out an' nothin' comin' in
—when all is paid, I don't have what ud
jingle on a tombstone.

THE BALLAD SINGER (*coming nearer to
her*). Eleven o' them me an' me Mot has
. . . eleven chiselurs [5] to keep . . . eleven
livin' an' two dead . . . now if it was only
two livin' an' eleven dead, I'd have an
aysier conscience.

(*A clamour of voices heard outside,
punctuated by shouts from Irish Nannie.*)

THE VOICE OF IRISH NANNIE. This is Irish
Nannie; out o' jail again an' lookin' for
throuble; let them send along their Baton
Men, Nannie's got a pair o' mits that'll
give them gib!

VOICES IN CROWD. Up Irish Nannie; give
us a song, Nannie; let th' poor woman
alone.

THE VOICE OF IRISH NANNIE (*singing*).

She's an' oul' fashion'd lady with
oul' fashion'd ways,

An' a smile that says welcome to
you.

An oul' fashion'd bedside where she
kneels an' prays,

When th' toil of th' long day is
through.

THE BALLAD SINGER (*as Nannie is singing
above*). If it was th' Summer, aself, it
wouldn't be so bad. . . . It's no laughin'
matther to be singing' "Kelly o' Killann,"
an' the rain beatin' into your dial. Cruel.

(*Irish Nannie enters singing. She is
about thirty years of age, well made,
strong, and possibly was handsome before she began to drink. Her eyes flash
with the light of semi-madness; her hair
is flying about her shoulders. Her blouse
is open at the neck. A much damaged hat,
containing flowers that once were brightly
coloured, but are now faded, is on her
head. Her manner, meant to be recklessly
merry, is very near to hysterical tears; a
shawl is hanging over one arm.*)

IRISH NANNIE (*singing*).

Tho' she wears no fine clothes, nor
no rich silken hose,

Still there's something that makes
her divine,

For th' angels above, taught th' way
how to love

To that oul' fashion'd mother o'
mine!

Irish Nannie's out again, an' as fresh as
a daisy; an' as full o' life, an' lookin' for
throuble.

THE BALLAD SINGER. I don't know how
we're goin' to live out th' winther. I
wouldn't mind about meself, if it wasn't
for th' Mot an' th' chiselurs. I'm waitin'
for th' first spring primrose to beckon me
back to th' counthry roads. . . . Th' Mot
an' chiselurs is too delicate for th' counthry, an' I'm too sthrong for th' city. . . .
Everythin' here—th' threes growin' in th'
streets; th' stars thryin' to shine in th' sky;
th' rain fallin' and th' win' blowin'—
they're all soiled with th' thrademark o'
Dublin. . . . It's cruel.

IRISH NANNIE (*giving her shawl a defi-*

---

[4] Wife.
[5] Children.

ant pull, and her voice a triumphant tone). I'm only afther comin' out o' the "Joy"—two months I done . . . assault an' batthery on a Polisman . . . me an' him had a hard struggle. . . . Th' same boyo'll think twiced before pullin' Irish Nannie again. . . . Be God, I didn't let him take me for nothin'—I bet him up in th' face!

MRS. PENDER. Wasn't that th' second time you were in Mountjoy, Nannie?

IRISH NANNIE. Second time me neck! Th' hundhred an' second time ud be nearer th' mark! Don't I know every stone in th' buildin'. Las' year ten months—it didn't take a feather out o' me—only a few o' th' wans in me hat!

MRS. PENDER (*to the Ballad Singer*). There's no use o' you waitin', me poor man, I can't give it to everywan.

THE BALLAD SINGER. You can't give it to everywan offen provides an excuse to give it to no-wan.

MRS. PENDER (*to Nannie*). Young Doran hopped over this mornin' with a bad egg, an' because I wouldn't change it, she let me have it between th' two eyes.

IRISH NANNIE. I'm tellin' you th' Polis is makin' a mistake if they think they can tame Nannie; Nannie's not like some o' th' Judies that's knockin' about, that has as much gizz in them as if they war afther a hundhred days' hunger strike! Irish Nannie has gizz in her, gizz in her, gizz in her! (*Singing:*) "For the angels above taught th' way how to love, to that oul' fashion'd mother o' mine!" (*Slapping the Ballad Singer on the shoulder*) A short life an' a merry wan, ay, oul' cock?

THE BALLAD SINGER. Oh, it's cruel, it's cruel. Yis, yis, a short life an' a merry wan—oh, it's cruel, it's cruel.

IRISH NANNIE (*coughing, sits down*). I'm dyin' on me feet . . . th' spunk has me nearly done for . . . Th' prison docthor told me th' oul' heart was crocked, an' that I'd dhrop any minute. . . . I'm afire inside . . . no-one cares a curse about Irish Nannie. . . . (*Screaming:*) I'll make a hole in th' river, I'll make a hole in th' river!

THE BALLAD SINGER. It's cruel, it's cruel.

IRISH NANNIE (*to the Ballad Singer*). Never say die till you're dead. . . . (*Singing:*) She's an oul' fashion'd lady with oul' fashion'd ways, an' a smile that says wel-

come to you. . . . If ever I meet that long-legged, counthry-faced bousey of a bobby that got me pulled, th' Lord look down on him; I'll batther th' helmet down over his head. . . . (*Going up to the door and shouting to the street:*) I'll kick th' shins off him! They're not bringin' a chiselur to school when they're bringin' Nannie to th' Polis Station. Five o' them it took, an' she sthrapped on a sthretcher, th' last time to bring her in! Nannie can tear an' kick an' bite! I'll die game. (*Screaming:*) I'll die game, I'll die game!

THE BALLAD SINGER. It's cruel, it's cruel.

MRS. PENDER. Go on home, now, Nannie, an' have a good lie down; you need it badly; go on home, Nannie—there's a good woman.

IRISH NANNIE (*coming back and sitting on the stool in front of the counter*). Nannie's no home. . . . Wan place is as good as another to Nannie. When Nannie was a chiselur any oul' hall she could find was Nannie's home—afther gettin', maybe, a morguein' from her oul' wan. Sleep? What does Irish Nannie want with sleep?

THE BALLAD SINGER. It's cruel, it's cruel.

IRISH NANNIE. It's merriment Nannie wants . . . singin' an' dancin' an' enjoyin' life. . . . What's the use o' bein' alive if you're not merry? (*Screaming:*) Merriment, merriment, merriment! (*Subsides with a cough.*) We'll be long enough dead. (*To the singer*) Nothin' like keepin' up th' oul' heart, ay?

THE BALLAD SINGER. Ay, if you had anything to keep it up with. Afther singin' your fill in a dozen sthreets, an' gettin' nothin'; findin' that half o' th' people was blind, an' th' other half deaf, you'd say it was cruel, cruel!

IRISH NANNIE (*catching him in her arms*). We'll be long enough dead, man. A short life an' a merry wan. (*Waltzing him round the shop, singing*) "She's an oul' fashion'd lady with oul' fashion'd ways, an' a smile that says welcome to you."

THE BALLAD SINGER (*in vigorous protest*). Ay, houl on there, houl on there. Me joints wasn't made for that gallivantin'; . . . will you houl on there, I'm tellin' you!

(*People gather at the door of the shop, amused at the sport; they offer encouragement with cries of, "Good man, Nannie; give him a good jazz; give him a balloon,*

Mrs. Pender.")

IRISH NANNIE.

> An oul' fashion'd bedside where she
>   kneels an' prays,
> When th' toil of th' long day is
>   through.

(*She suddenly releases the Ballad Singer, and seizing one of the balloons hanging up in the shop, she goes out singing and dancing, and can be heard going along the street, followed by the crowd.*)

THE BALLAD SINGER (*leaning against the counter, exhausted*). That's a wild animal, that wan.

MRS. PENDER. There's no use o' you waitin'. . . . Now an' again a coin comin' in between a finger an' thumb, an' people expectin' you to be givin' it back in handfuls.

THE BALLAD SINGER (*with a little bitterness*). Divil a much fear o' you givin' it back in handfuls.

MRS. PENDER (*briskly*). Fear or no fear, there's no use o' you waitin'. . . . Wan comin' in assin' you to give them a penny stamp . . . another thumpin' th' counther when you're upstairs, an' when you're afther breakin' your neck rushin' down, they'll ass you, "What's th' right time, Mrs. Pendher?" . . . an' someone'll folly them be a short head, assin' you for change of a threepenny bit!

THE BALLAD SINGER (*fiercely*). A penny won't break you, will it? If th' oul' spirit still lives on in th' men o' to-day, it doesn't look like as if it was livin' on in th' woman!

(*Mrs. Pender takes a brush from the end of the shop, and with the handle knocks at the ceiling. After a few moments oul' Johnny White enters by door on Left. He has a habit of catching the lapels of his coat and pulling at them with a jerk, ejaculating, "ayee" as he does so. His coat is on now, and he is still wearing his hat. He looks from the Ballad Singer to Mrs. Pender.*)

JOHNNY. Ayee.

MRS. PENDER. Here, take th' shop, Johnny, for a few minutes till I wet a cup o' tea.

(*Mrs. Pender goes out by door on Left; Johnny takes off his coat, and goes behind the counter.*)

JOHNNY (*looking at the Ballad Singer*). Well, sir?

THE BALLAD SINGER (*derisively*). Well, yourself, sir?

JOHNNY (*forcibly*). If you want nothin', you betther clear ou' o' this.

THE BALLAD SINGER. You don't own th' shop, do you?

JOHNNY. Own or no own, you clear ou' o' this.

THE BALLAD SINGER. Oh . . . are you th' cock lodger?

JOHNNY. Cock lodger or hen lodger, you clear ou' o' this!

THE BALLAD SINGER. Sure, isn't it all over th' neighbourhood, everybody talkin' about it . . . you an' oul' Joe an oul' Jimmy makin' a holy show o' themselves runnin' afther her. . . . You're a nice-lookin' thing to be lookin' for a woman to be sittin' on your knee . . . an' you afther berryin' two o' them.

JOHNNY. What is it to you if I berried a regiment o' them? Pop off ou' o' this, now, or you'll go out quickern you come in, I'm tellin' you!

THE BALLAD SINGER. Name some o' th' deadly sins, says a clergyman to a kid he was examinin' for Confirmation; Pride is wan, says th' youngster. Gwan, says th' priest, name another. Mathrimony, says th' chiselur—an' when I look at you an' think o' her, I wouldn't say but th' chiselur was right!

JOHNNY (*coming from behind the counter*). Right or wrong, you betther be gettin' out' o' this while you're safe.

THE BALLAD SINGER. More than me's been havin' a good laugh at yous; you that ud hardly be able to walk twiced round Nelson's Pillar without sittin' down for a rest. Oul' Jimmy that's so blind with age, that he wouldn't know a live bird in a cage from a dead wan, unless he heard it singin'. An' Oul' Joe so bent that he could pick a penny off th' ground without stoopin'. (*Mrs. Pender appears at door in a flame of indignation.*) Oh, it ud be hard to say which o' th' two plagues is th' worse—youngsters that you can't force into gettin' married even wanst, or oul' stagers that you can't keep from gettin' married three or four times. It's cruel, it's cruel.

MRS. PENDER (*going behind the counter*). Here, clear on ou' o' this y'oul scandal-giver. If a body wants to marry aself, we're not goin' to ass you for a special Dispensation. Buzz off, now; if th' man won't deal with you, th' woman will. Be off, now, an' take your spirit that still lives on in th' men o' to-day with you.

THE BALLAD SINGER (*to Johnny*). Why don't you put your arms round her an' give her a birdie? Isn't she waitin' for wan? You'd find Oul' Joe or Oul' Jimmy ud do it if they got th' chance. . . . Oh, me love is like a red, red rose! Wanst it was th' man that had to pick out th' best o' th' women, but now, it's th' lassie that has to pick out th' handsomest o' th' men —I wouldn't like her job, for there's none o' yous nice lookin'. I think meself, it'll be Oul' Joe. (*To Johnny*) Maybe you don't know she was at th' pixstures last night with him? Me an' th' Mot seen her hangin' on his arm, an' a bow in her hat as big as th' wings of an aeroplane! . . . Orange blossoms an' cypress trees. . . . (*He goes slowly to the shop door, lilting softly as he goes out*)

Th' mountain brooks were rushin',
    Annie dear;
Th' Autumn eve was flushin',
    Annie dear;
But brighter was your blushin',
    when first, your murmurs hushin',
I told me love out-gushin', Annie—

Oh, it's cruel, it's cruel! (*He goes out.*)

MRS. PENDER (*to Johnny*). You'll want to pull them up on you if you want your name over th' door. There's not much use of havin' a man like you about th' place, if any oul' thramp can come in an' say what he likes in th' shop.

JOHNNY (*going to her behind the counter*). Now, Polly, Polly, you didn't want me to go an' hit an oul' man, did you?

MRS. PENDER. An oul' man! Sure he wasn't any ouldher than yourself. I'm tellin' you if you're goin' to be in this shop, you'll have to be dealin' with more than cock-sparrows. A big fella like you to be afraid of a poor oul' scrawl that was thin to th' point of emancipation. If Oul' Joe had a been here, he'd ha soon sent him flyin'.

JOHNNY. Oul' Joe! I'd like to see him boxin' an' he half blind. Sure if he was lookin' at an elephant a few yards away, he'd think it was a fly! Oul' Joe, ayee! If you took Oul' Joe, it wouldn't be long till there was no name over th' shop.

MRS. PENDER. Well, there's Oul' Jimmy left. Not a bad oul' skin, now, since he's taken th' pledge.

JOHNNY. Ayee. He's a great teetotaler now—wild horses wouldn't drag him into a pub, an' in a day or two, wild horses won't be able to drag him out o' wan!

(*A commotion heard outside some distance away, and the voice of Nannie shouting.*)

IRISH NANNIE (*outside*). Irish Nannie's out again, out again . . . she's not dead yet . . . kept her crippled oul' fella for two years . . . a jib of a crane fell on his back workin' on th' docks, an' smashed his spine; two weeks' half pay he got from th' stevedore, an' then th' bastard went bankrupt . . . an' Nannie kep him for two years an' he lyin' on his back. . . . We'll all be long enough dead.

MRS. PENDER. She's full up o' methylated spirits again. She'll start smashin' windows in a few minutes.

IRISH NANNIE (*outside*). Nannie doesn't care a curse for anybody. . . . Let them send down their Foot, an' their Calvary— Nannie's waitin' for them; she'll give them somethin' betther than cuttin' down th' Oul' Age Pensions. . . . Republicans an' Free Staters—a lot of rubbidge, th' whole o' yous! Th' poor Tommies was men!

(*Oul' Jimmy is seen peering in through the window, shading his eyes with his hands; he presses his nose against the pane till it is flattened, desperately endeavouring to discover if Mrs. Pender be alone. Johnny perceives him, and moves to the end of the shop. Satisfied that a fair field is before him, he enters by the shop door. Jimmy is well over sixty, but he is hardy and lusty still. He carries himself with a jaunty air, but age has given a stiff and jerky action to his comical sprightly movements. His voice is a shaky treble. He carries a heavy walking stick under his arm. He is wearing a fancy waistcoat, a frock coat and a seal-skin cap, and has a flower in his buttonhole. He is painfully near-sighted, and peers closely at every-*

thing. He comes in whistling, but only succeeds in hitting a note of the tune here and there.)

JIMMY (*taking a bunch of flowers from under his coat, he does not see Johnny*). Them's for you, Polly . . . though a flower doesn't need a flower, sure it doesn't . . . I was afraid that other Ibex ud be here, annoyin' us, an'—

JOHNNY (*viciously*). Y'ought to open your eyes a little wider, for th' Ibex happens to be here. Maybe you ought to be a little more careful of what you're sayin', Mr. Jimmy Devanny, Esquire! Ibex, uh, be God, that's a good wan!

JIMMY. I, I didn't think you'd be hangin' around here—

JOHNNY. Haven't I as much right to be hangin' round here as you have? It's a dangerous thing for an oul' man to be looking for throuble, for he might get enough of it. . . . Ibex, be God, that's a good wan!

MRS. PENDER. Now, we want no fightin' here . . . Irish Nannie's enough, without havin' yous at it . . . Jimmy didn't mean any harm.

JOHNNY (*buttoning his coat, preparatory to going*). Oh, if he's your choice, I wish th' both of yous luck. But if I was you I'd keep him from callin' people Ibexes. I'm tellin' you no man is goin' to be let call me an Ibex! Flowers! Romeo an' Juliet! (*He goes towards the street door.*) It's sickenin' . . . Ibex, be God, that's a good wan! (*He goes out.*)

JIMMY. He doesn't like to hear th' truth. . . . He's lookin' terrible bad. His face is puffed like a purple balloon. . . . I wouldn't wondher if he dhropped down sudden, some day. . . . A woman ud be a fool to have anything to do with him.

(*Mrs. Pender takes the flowers with one hand, and Jimmy catches hold of the other.*)

MRS. PENDER. They're lovely, they're lovely, Jimmy.

JIMMY. Not half as lovely as little, little Polly herself.

MRS. PENDER. Young Doran hopped here this mornin' with a bad egg. How do I know you got th' egg here, says I; d'ye doubt me word says she; I don't says I, but I'll not change it; with that she let fly, an' hot me right between th' two eyes with it!

JIMMY. Oh, I wish I'd ha been here; you'll always have to put up with them things till you have a man about th' place.

MRS. PENDER. Here, let go me hand, Jimmy.

JIMMY (*slyly*). Oh, be th' way you don't like me to be holdin' it. Isn't it th' business? Who was it said that a woman's *no* meant *yis;* an' a woman's *yis* meant *no?* When are you goin' to put another little ring on th' little third finger of th' little left hand —wouldn't it be th' business?

MRS. PENDER. Now, don't be naughty, Jimmy, don't be naughty.

JIMMY (*elated at the idea of being naughty*). Naughty, ay; why not? Oh, women is cute, women is cute—isn't it th' business? We're not as ould as all that. (*Singing:*)

Ses herself to meself, you can court
    with th' rest o' them.
Ses meself to herself, sure I'm better
    than gold;
Ses herself to meself, you can court
    with th' rest o' them.
Ses meself to herself, sure we'll never
    grow ould!

(*He begins to cough with the singing.*) O, o, o, o, this cough has me nearly worn away!

(*A young girl enters. She is nicely dressed, and speaks in a gushing way.*)

THE YOUNG GIRL. How much is them dolls there? A little sisther o' mine is always assin' me to brin' her home a doll.

MRS. PENDER (*smilingly*). A shillin' each, me dear.

THE YOUNG GIRL (*astonished*). Only a shillin'! Would you please let me have a look at wan, ma'am?

(*Mrs. Pender hands her one of the dolls.*)

THE YOUNG GIRL (*examining the doll*). Oh, I'll have to take wan o' them. . . . Isn't it marvellous how they make them for a shillin'! (*Holding the doll flat.*) Closes its eyes, mind you, too. . . . (*Looking at the clothes:*) Everything perfect— tangerine undies an' all! . . . (*Turning towards the door and raising her voice:*) Maggie, look at this lovely doll—an' only a shillin'! (*She moves rapidly to the door and passes out. A pause*)

MRS. PENDER. What on earth's keepin' her?

JIMMY. Showin' it to th' other wan, I suppose.

(*A pause.*)

MRS. PENDER (*rapidly, her suspicions aroused*). Have a look out, Jimmy, an' see what she's doin'.

JIMMY (*going to the door and looking up and down*). God, I can see neither sign nor light of her.

(*Mrs. Pender runs to the door and looks up and down the street.*)

MRS. PENDER. Well, God Almighty, isn't that th' limit! An' no sign or light of a bobby, either. (*Comes back into the shop.*) Th' cool way that was done!

JIMMY. Now, would you put anything a past them, afther that?

MRS. PENDER. Who'd think a body ud be taken in with a body like that? Talkin' as if butther wouldn't melt in her mouth. . . . Everything perfect, says she, tangerine undies an' all!

JIMMY. Tangerine undies an' all. . . . It's marvellous how they make them for a shillin', says she.

MRS. PENDER. Please let me have a look at wan o' them, ma'am, says she.

JIMMY (*with a chuckle*). Be God, an' she's havin' a long look at it!

MRS. PENDER (*angrily*). It's very easy for some fools to be made to laugh. . . . It's no laughin' matther . . . a shillin' afther walkin' out o' th' shop. . . . It'll take a lot o' hoppin' about before I make a shillin' profit. . . . If you think it funny for divils like them to be comin' into th' shop, I can tell you I don't.

JIMMY. I wassen' laughin', I wassen' laughin' . . . but th' whole thing was done so cute, like, an' th' two of us lookin' at her!

MRS. PENDER. It was you gassin' here, out o' you, that made me take me mind off her, an' I knowin' th' sort o' billickers that's goin' about here.

(*Oul' Joe enters; he is about sixty years of age, very much bent in the body; he is dressed up to the nines—fawn coat, grey trilby hat, fancy muffler, brown boots and leggings. He carries a bunch of flowers.*)

JOE (*to Jimmy, stiffly*). Good evenin'.

JIMMY (*just as stiffly*). Oh, good evenin'.

JOE (*going over to Mrs. Pender*). There's a few flowers for another little flower.

MRS. PENDER (*irritably*). Ah, I don't want to be bothered with flowers now.

JOE. Why, what's up?

MRS. PENDER. A man about th' place! Faith, as far as I can see, a mouse about th' place ud be better than a man.

JOE. That all depends on th' kind th' man is. Why, is there anythin' wrong?

MRS. PENDER. A minute ago in sails a young whipster of a wan; let's look at wan o' them dolls, says she; how much is it, says she; shillin', says I; Oh, Maggie, says she runnin' to th' door, look a' th' lovely doll for a shillin', an' out she goes with th' doll, an' we're waitin' for her to come back ever since.

JOE. She did!

JIMMY. It was th' cleverest done thing I ever seen . . . marvellous value, says she . . . (*chuckling*) everythin' perfect, says she, tangerine undies an' all! It was th' business!

MRS. PENDER (*with cold dignity*). Mr. James Devanny, if you want to make a laugh of it, I'd be thankful if you'd make a laugh of it somewhere else, an' not in this shop.

JOE. People ought to show a little feelin', right enough.

JIMMY (*huffily*). Oh, I'll be off if I'm not wanted. . . . If yous settle anythin' between yous, maybe yous'll ass us to th' weddin'. . . . Dressed up to th' nines! . . . Puffed, powdhered an' shaved . . . oh, there's no fool like an oul' fool! (*He goes out.*)

MRS. PENDER. There now, that's what comes o' makin' too free with some people.

JOE (*looking after Jimmy*). Imagine a poor thing like that thinkin' he's a great man with th' ladies! Isn't it outrageous! . . . Well, every cripple has his own way o' walkin'. . . . Maybe it's a wife he wants! Love's young dhream, an' he totterin' to th' grave! It's sods'll be fallin' on him soon instead o' confetti. . . . Wife! . . . Oh, isn't he th' right oul' ram! (*Going behind the counter:*) Isn't it a wondher he can't see you're only havin' a laugh at him.

MRS. PENDER. Stop where y'are, now, jus' stop where y'are; I've had enough of that sort o' thing for wan night.

JOE. Sure, it isn't fair to be always

keepin' a man's heart in a frenzy of a flutter. Well, are you goin' to give us an answer wan way or t'other? What's th' use o' goin' on, buoyin' up men with false fancies? Can't you thry to come to a decision like th' Doyle, an' say either 'ta or nil? (*Coaxingly*) It's ten to wan on th' favourite, isn't it darlin'? (*Joe goes round the counter and with his arm around Polly, sings the following, his eyes fixed with fascination on her face.*)

> Gie me a quiet hour at e'en, me
> arms about me dearie o,
> An' worldly cares an' worldly men,
> may all gae tapsalteerie o,
> For Nature swears the lovely dears,
> her noblest work she classes o,
> Her prentice han' she tried on man,
> ah then she made th' lasses o.

Th' two of us nicely balanced, neither too ould nor too young. . . . Come now, isn't it soon going' to be for betther an' worse, for richer and poorer, come, say either 'ta or nil, dar-blast these chiselurs!

(*Robert, Nannie's boy, enters. He is twelve years old, and a hunchback, because of a spinal disease; pale and fragile, a half-cunning, half-wistful look in his eyes. His clothes are tattered, and his boots badly broken.*)

ROBERT (*handing Mrs. Pender a docket and a shilling*). Dandy Dinny sent me back with this—Gollywog didn't run. I couldn't come any sooner.

MRS. PENDER. Blast it! An' yesterday Kisser was beaten be a neck.

ROBERT. You can never depend on th' two-year-ouls.

MRS. PENDER. Have you anything good for to-morrow, Robert?

ROBERT. Well, now, it's a toss up between Noisy Oysther an' Batthery Smoke. I think Noisy Oysther'll about do it.

IRISH NANNIE (*in the street, some distance away*). There's th' Dublin Bobbies for yous. . . . Th' minute he clapped eyes on Irish Nannie off he skeeted. . . . Irish Nannie put th' fear o' God in his heart!

ROBERT (*running out*). God Almighty, here's me oul' wan, I'll have to skip!

MRS. PENDER. Poor little Robert . . . he's afraid of his life of her . . . she leathers hell out of him.

JOE. He's a crabby-lookin' little youngster.

MRS. PENDER. He couldn't be anything else; he lives on th' streets. When he was three or four he fell down a stairs an' hurted his back. . . . It's a wondher they wouldn't do something for poor little kiddies like him, instead o' thryin' to teach them Irish.

JOE. Oh, we've bigger things than that to settle first; we have to put th' Army on a solid basis, an' then, th' Boundhary Question has to be settled too—in comparisement with things like them, a few cripples o' chiselurs is neither here nor there.

NANNIE (*coming nearer, from Right to Left, till she is seen outside the window*). "She's an oul' fashion'd lady with oul' fashion'd ways, an' a smile that says welcome to you"—Nannie kep' her oul' father for years, an' he lyin' stretched out not able to stir a hand or foot . . . good money she earned for him, when it was to be got; an' bad money when there was nothin' else knockin' about. . . Th' Prison docthor says she'll dhrop any minute. . . . Well, we've only to die wanst, an' Nannie'll die game, die game, die game! (*She passes out of sight.*)

(*Jimmy and Johnny enter the shop from the Right; they stand for a moment at the door looking up the street. A crash of breaking glass is heard.*)

JOHNNY (*coming in, followed by Jimmy*). There, she must have afther puttin' in a window. She's outdoin' herself to-night. Ow, it's cowld to-night, mind you.

JOE (*coming from behind the counter*). Cowld? Maybe it is. . . . I don't feel cold meself, anyway. I never mind th' winther at all . . . other people have to be wrapped up in flannels.

JIMMY. You don't look very warm, then. . . . I don't feel cold meself. Indeed, it's a warm night . . . only for th' rain, I wouldn't have this coat on.

JOHNNY. Oh, I don't feel cold meself. . . . I was only sayin' what everybody's sayin'—doin' what th' Government wants us to do—fallin' in with th' will o' th' majority.

JOE. Th' heat has a drooth on me.

JIMMY. Here's th' same as that.

MRS. PENDER. There's plenty o' milk here to cool yous, if yous want to be cooled.

JOHNNY. Give's a glass of it.

JIMMY. Ay, an' me too.

JOE. I'll not be wan odd—give us another.

(*Mrs. Pender gives them the milk, and goes into the room Left. They take a drink in fear and trembling.*)

JOE. Oh, God, that's murdherin' cold!

JOHNNY. It's like ice goin' down!

JIMMY. It's not safe to be dhrinkin' milk in th' winther.

JOHNNY. It's not safe to be dhrinkin' it anytime. Didn't th' paper say there was only wan dhrink worse than milk, an' that was a dhrink o' th' Leffey wather at th' Butt Bridge. It's right enough for chiselurs.

JIMMY. I've had enough of it.

JOE. Same here.

JOHNNY. Me, too.

(*Mrs. Pender returns.*)

MRS. PENDER. Why don't yous drink your milk? That's th' stuff'll put th' gizz into yous.

JOE. Divil a much gizz I want; I'm as soople, nearly, as ever I was.

JOHNNY. It ud be a good job, then, to show your soopleness when you're leppin' off thrams.

JOE. Leppin' off thrams! Who was leppin' off thrams?

JOHNNY. Didn't I see you t'other day, an' you doin' th' big fella, leppin' off a goin' thram. (*To the others*) An' th' next thing I seen was me boul' boyo, an' he standin' on his ear!

MRS. PENDER. He'll have to be more careful—he'd be no use to poor Polly if he was a cripple.

JOE. If I was hurted aself, I wouldn't be long gettin' over it. (*Stretching out his hand:*) Look a' that, now! not as much as a sign, an' it was an ugly cut when I got it. U, u, u, ugh, says th' surgeon, that's a bad wan, as soon as he had a decko at it. Seven stitches, says he, I'll have to put you asleep. For what, says I? Th' pain, you wouldn't be able to stick it, says he. Gwan, says I, an' don't be keepin' me waitin'.

JIMMY. That's not th' story I heard from them that seen you runnin' like mad through th' streets to th' hospital; or Micky Mannin, that was there when you came beltin' in, an' th' eyes leppin' out o' your head with fright, an' you kickin' like a divil at th' first door you met, an' shoutin' —where's th' doctor, where's th' doctor;

am I goin' to be kep' waitin' till there'll be no use o' waitin' any longer; is there none o' yous gives a God's curse whether a man bleeds to death or no? (*He imitates the fright of Joe by clasping his left hand tightly with his right, as if it were badly cut, and kicking frantically at the counter.*)

MRS. PENDER. Aw, we don't mind Micky Mannin; he was jealous o' Joe, that's what it was.

JIMMY. Whether or no, a cut on th' hand isn't much to be blowin' about. It's not long ago since I was opened meself all around here (*His hand draws a circle round the middle of his body.*) an' everything inside o' me was as visible as th' works of a clock; there was only wan arthery that they didn't cut through— touch an' go, touch an' go, for days; an' here I am to-day as sound as a bell.

MRS. PENDER. An' lookin' for a wife.

JOE. Ay, lookin' for a wife.

JIMMY. An', maybe'll get wan, too; ey, Polly?

MRS. PENDER. Faith is able to remove mountains, Jimmy.

JOHNNY. Well, thanks be to God, I can say my inside was never out of ordher— I never took a spoonful o' medicine in me life. I believe in keepin' fit be exercise.

JOE. Exercise; walkin'?

JIMMY. Leppin' off o' thrams?

JOHNNY. Leppin' off o' thrams! Swedish Dhrill exercises; I'm that fit, now, that I'd tackle any young fella, an' more than hold me own with him.

MRS. PENDER. Unless he had a gun, Johnny.

JOHNNY. Gun or no gun, I'd chance it.

JIMMY. That wouldn't be much to do; th' most o' th' gunmen goin' now, are afraid to use their guns.

JOE. Go for them straight; tackle them, tackle them, an' divil a much fight any of them'll show.

JOHNNY. Not bendin' me knees, I can tip me toes twenty times without stoppin'.

JOE (*scornfully*). Oh, sure, anywan could do that.

JIMMY. Tcha, sure, you could keep that up all night, without feelin' tired.

JOHNNY (*challengingly*). Would either o' yous do it?

JIMMY and JOE. Of course we'd do it.

JOHNNY. Twenty times?

JOE. Ay, fifty times.

JOHNNY. Here, I bet yous anything yous like, yous won't do it twenty times.

JOE. Let's see you doin' it first.

MRS. PENDER (*interested, and seeing some fun in front of her*). The three of yous to-gether; gwan, I'll keep count; gwan, let's see which of yous is th' best man!

JOHNNY. All right; mind you, yous aren't to bend your knees.

MRS. PENDER. When I say wan, yous are all to start to-gether.

(*They form up, stretch their arms above their heads, and stiffly perform the exercises.*)

MRS. PENDER (*counting*). Wan, two, three, four—you're bendin' your knees, Joe—five, six—tip your toes, Jimmy—seven, eight nine.

IRISH NANNIE (*appearing at the window*). Irish Nannie wants nothin' from anybody, Free State or Republic. . . . Th' sharks hasn't left much for anybody to get. . . . As long as Nannie has her pair o' mits, she'll fight her own corner. . . . (*Passing:*) "For th' angels above taught th' way how to love . . . to that oul' fashion'd mother . . . o' . . . mine."

(*A young man in a light coat, and a cap pulled down over his eyes, enters; he looks at the exercising men for a moment.*)

THE YOUNG MAN. Are t'ould goin' mad as well as th' young?

(*Joe, Jimmy and Johnny rise, and stand together, a little embarrassed.*)

MRS. PENDER (*to the Young Man*). What d'ye want, sir?

THE YOUNG MAN (*quietly, drawing a gun*). I want all th' money you have in th' shop, quick!

MRS. PENDER (*appealingly*). I'm a poor lone widow woman, sir; you wouldn't rob a widow, would you?

THE YOUNG MAN (*snappily*). Come on, come on; I've no time to waste arguin'.

JIMMY. You'd betther, Polly, you'd betther.

JOE. Take him quietly, Polly, take him quietly.

JOHNNY. Oh, what's th' use o' thryin' to argue with a gun?

MRS. PENDER. I'm not goin' to let meself be robbed, I'll not let meself be robbed!

THE YOUNG MAN (*viciously, to Joe*).

Here, you, go behind, an' hand out th' cash. (*As Joe hesitates:*) Go on, y'oul' so an' so! (*Joe goes behind the counter, and Mrs. Pender bars the way to the till.*)

JOE (*imploringly, to Mrs. Pender*). Polly, what's th' use o' goin' again Providence! Sure, when it can't be helped, it can't be helped.

JIMMY. For God's sake, Joe, get th' money, an' let th' man go about his business!

JOHNNY. If y'ass me, she's lookin' for throuble!

(*Nannie rushes in like a whirlwind, carrying the balloon in her hand. Knocking against the Young Man, she catches him in her arms, and pulls him around the shop. Joe, Jimmy and Johnny duck behind the counter.*)

IRISH NANNIE. A short life an' a merry wan. . . . "She's an oul' fashion'd—"

THE YOUNG MAN (*struggling fiercely*). Blast you, you dhrunked oul' rip! Let me go, let me go, d'ye hear, or I'll—

(*He breaks away and runs precipitantly out of the shop.*)

MRS. PENDER (*enthusiastically*). Good man, Nannie; well done, Nannie. Bravo, girl, Nannie!

IRISH NANNIE (*wildly elated at realising, dazedly, that she has done something remarkable, catching Joe in her arms, and dancing with him*).

An' a smile that says welcome to
    you;
An oul' fashion'd bedside where she
    kneels an' prays,
When th' toil of th' long day is
    through—

JOE (*savagely, in degrees of crescendo*). Ey, ey, ey, ey, ey!

IRISH NANNIE (*releasing Joe, and seizing Jimmy*).

Tho' she wears no fine clothes, nor
    no rich silken hose—

JIMMY (*frantically*). Ey, houl' on there, damn you, houl' on there; d'ye want to shake th' little life I have in me out o' me!

IRISH NANNIE (*releasing Jimmy and catching Johnny*).

Still there's something that makes
    her divine;
For th' angels above taught the way
    how to love,
To that oul' fashioned mother o'

mine!

JOHNNY (*breathlessly*). Ey, houl' on, there, houl' on there; leggo ou' o' that! I'm not able to be leppin' about like this if you are—leggo ou' o' that, I'm tellin' you!

IRISH NANNIE.

She's an oul' fashion'd lady with oul' fashion'd ways,

An' a smile that says welcome to you.

An oul' fashion'd bedside where—

(*She suddenly stops singing; her body assumes a statuesque rigidity; a look of fear and terror flashes into her eyes; after the passage of a few moments, her body sways tremblingly, her arms are outstretched, and her hands paw the air as if feeling for support, and the realization of something terrible about to happen to her deepens in her face.*)

IRISH NANNIE. Christ Almighty! What ails me! Me head is whirlin', me heart is stoppin'. . . . Get me brought to th' hospital, quick. (*She grips the counter convulsively.*) I'll die game . . . I'll die game, I'll die game! . . . Will none o' yous go for a docthor . . . I'm dyin', I tell yous, dyin', dyin', dyin'.

(*She sinks down to the floor, and lies with her head and shoulders supported by the counter.*)

MRS. PENDER (*running over to her*). What's wrong, Nannie; what ails you?

IRISH NANNIE. For God's sake, some o' yous go for a priest. . . . I stuck be me oul' fella th' whole time he was crippled, till he died, till he died, till he died. (*Screaming feebly:*) I don't care, I don't care, I'll die game, I'll die game!

(*A crowd, which includes the Ballad Singer and Robert, Nannie's child, has gathered at the door.*)

ROBERT (*running over to Nannie*). What ails you, Mother, what ails you?

THE BALLAD SINGER. Aw, she's goin' right enough; I'm afraid this is th' end o' Nannie.

IRISH NANNIE (*feebly*). Tho' she wears no fine clothes, nor no rich . . . silken hose . . . still there's . . . something . . . that makes . . . her . . . di . . . vine . . . Jesus, I feel me heart stoppin'. . . . Is there ne'er a wan to go for a docthor? . . . Th' priest, th' priest. . . . God'll not

be too hard on poor Irish Nannie . . . poor Irish Nannie. . . . Say a prayer, will you . . . some o' yous . . . Nannie's goin' . . . she's goin'. . . . She'll die game, she'll . . . die . . . game.

ROBERT (*in anguish*). Mother, Mother!

JOE (*to Mrs. Pender*). Say a prayer, you, Polly.

MRS. PENDER. My prayers ud be no good, I only know Protestan' prayers.

THE BALLAD SINGER (*taking off his hat*). Look at her eyes, she's goin' fast; I'll say all I can remember. Lord have mercy on her.

THE REST. Christ have mercy on her.

THE BALLAD SINGER. Holy Mother o' God.

THE REST. Pray for her.

THE BALLAD SINGER. Virgin Most Merciful—

THE REST. Pray for her.

THE BALLAD SINGER. Health of the Weak—

THE REST. Pray for her.

THE BALLAD SINGER. Refuge of sinners—

THE REST. Pray for her.

THE BALLAD SINGER. May God look down on th' spirit of our poor sisther, that, feelin' th' wind, maybe got no message from it; that, lookin' up at th' sky, maybe seen no stars; that, lookin' down at th' earth, maybe seen no flowers. Rememberin' th' bitterness of th' shocks her poor body got, may God give th' soul of our sisther th' sweetness of eternal rest!

THE REST. Amen!

(*The sound of an approaching motor is heard, stopping near the shop. Nannie is lying very still.*)

JOHNNY. Here's th' ambulance comin'.

(*Two Ambulance Men enter; they carry a stretcher. One of them goes over to Nannie, and, bending down, gently places his hand on her breast.*)

THE AMBULANCE MAN. Aw, gone west! They all go like the snuff of a candle. She'll sleep in th' morgue to-night. . . . I suppose it's as good as any o' th' places she ever slep' in. . . . Catch a hold of her, Tom.

(*They swing Nannie on to the stretcher, and carry her out followed by Robert and the rest, except Mrs. Pender, Joe, Jimmy, and Johnny. The Ballad Singer lingers at the door.*)

JOE. Whoever ud a thought that she'd a

dhropped so sudden?

JIMMY. It's very hard to have any sympathy for that class o' people.

THE BALLAD SINGER (*turning round, and speaking passionately*). Yous gang o' hypocrites! What was it made Nannie what she was? Was it havin' too much money? Who gave a damn about her? It was only when she was dhrunk an' mad that anywan took any notice of her! What can th' like o' them do, only live any way they can? Th' poorhouse, th' prison an' th' morgue—them is our palaces! I suppose yous want us to sing "Home Sweet Home," about our tenements? D'ye think th' blasted kips o' tenement houses we live in 'll breed saints an' scholars? . . . It's a long time, but th' day's comin' . . . th' day's comin' . . . Oh, it's cruel, it's cruel! (*He goes out.*)

MRS. PENDER (*going over to the shop door, and standing at it*). Here, I'm goin' to shut th' shop; I've had enough for wan night. Addin' two an' two together, I think th' best thing Polly Pender can do, is to remain a bird alone.

JOE (*going out*). Good night, all.

JIMMY (*to Johnny*). Well, so long, Johnny. (*Goes out.*) Everything perfect, says she; (*with a chuckle*) tangerine undies, an' all! It was th' business!

(*Mrs. Pender closes and locks the door with a vicious movement.*)

JOHNNY. Give us a penny candle, an' I'll g'up an' go to bed.

(*Without a word, Mrs. Pender gives him the candle, and he goes out by door on Left.*)

VOICES OF BALLAD SINGERS (*some distance up the street*).

For Ireland is Ireland thro' joy an'
   thro' tears.
Hope never dies thro' they long
   weary years;

(*Mrs. Pender extinguishes the light and leaves the shop. The rain has ceased, and the stars in the sky seem to be peering through the window into the darkened shop.*)

VOICES OF BALLAD SINGERS.

Each age has seen countless, brave
   hearts pass away,
But their spirits still live on in they
   men of to-day.

THE CURTAIN SLOWLY FALLS

———

ANOTHER ENDING

IRISH NANNIE (*releasing Joe, and seizing Jimmy*).

Tho' she wears no fine clothes, nor
   no rich silken hose—

JIMMY (*frantically*). Ey, houl' on there, damn you, houl' on there; d'ye want to shake th' little life I have in me out o' me!

IRISH NANNIE (*releasing Jimmy and catching Johnny*).

Still there's something that makes
   her divine;
For th' angels above taught the
   way how to love,
To that oul' fashion'd mother o'
   mine!

JOHNNY (*breathlessly*). Ey, houl' on there, houl' on there; leggo ou' o' that! I'm not able to be leppin' about like this if you are—leggo ou' o' that, I'm tellin' you!

IRISH NANNIE. Nannie'll put gizz into you (*Singing:*)

She's an oul' fashion'd lady with
   oul' fashion'd ways,
An' a smile that says welcome to
   you.
An oul' fashion'd bedside where she
   kneels and prays,
When the toil of th' long day is
   through.

(*She releases Johnny, who sinks exhausted against the counter. Nannie catches up Jimmy's walking stick, dances round the shop and out into the street singing.*)

Tho' she wears no fine clothes nor
   no rich silken hose,
Still there's something that makes
   her divine,
For th' angels above taught th' way
   how to love,
To that oul' fashion'd mother o'
   mine!

JOHNNY (*with a gasp*). Every bone in me body's shook asundher!

JIMMY. Me heart's thumpin' yet like a piston rod; an' I'll never see me walkin' stick again, either.

MRS. PENDER. What does a frisky youngster like you want with a walkin' stick?

JOE (*going to the shop door and looking up the street*). The like o' them shouldn't be let out o' jail at all. . . . There she goes whirlin' th' stick. (*A crash of glass is heard*). O, o, oh, she's afther puttin' in th' window o' Doyle's! If you seen th' way she done it! (*Enthusiastically*) Drew back her fist with th' walkin' stick, let it fly an' gave it a larrup! It was th' business!

IRISH NANNIE (*up the street*). Nannie'll show yous whether she cares about yous or no . . . she'll make some o' yous put up your shutthers. . . . Nannie'll put th' fear o' God in some o' your hearts!

JOE. Aw, be th' holy, there's three Bobbies down on top of her! There's kickin' an' bitin' an' plungin'! God, it's th' business!

(*Jimmy and Johnny come to the door. Mrs. Pender looks out of the window.*)

IRISH NANNIE (*shouting outside*). Yous'll bring down Nannie, will yous? It'll take more than th' three of yous to pull her! Three agen' wan . . . three agen' wan! . . . Yous gang o' silver button'd bouseys! Th' poor Tommies was men, th' poor Tommies was men!

THE VOICE OF THE BALLAD SINGER (*evidently to the Police*). Have yous ne'er a bit o' spiritual or corporal charity left in yous? Don't be twistin' th' woman's arm!

THE VOICE OF A POLICEMAN. If I lay me hans on you, me bucko, I'll twist your neck!

IRISH NANNIE (*in the distance as she is being brought away*). Drag me down, drag me down. It's takin' three o' the' biggest bouseys in th' force to take Nannie. . . . I'll swing for wan o' yous yet . . . I'll swing for wan o' yous yet!

(*The clamour of bringing Nannie to the station dies away, and Jimmy, Joe and Johnny leave the door and return to the shop.*)

JOHNNY. It ud be a God's charity if that wan got about ten years!

JOE. I'm not over th' rattlin' she gave me yet. There's wan consolation—they'll knock hell out of her when they get her to th' station!

MRS. PENDER. They'll hammer hell out o' Nannie; but they weren't here to hammer hell out o' the gunman!

JIMMY (*half to himself*). Closes its eyes, an' all, too, says she; an' only a shillin'— it was th' business.

MRS. PENDER (*going over to the door and standing at it*). Comparin' Nannie with some o' yous is like comparin' a fly-wheel to a trouser's button—Here, I'm goin' to shut th' shop. I've had enough for wan night. Maybe there'd be another hold up, an' I don't want yous to be riskin' your lives. Yez are a nice gang of guardian angels for any poor woman to have hangin' round her. So th' whole of yous ud betther buzz off ou' o' this. I suppose when yous go out yous'll be sayin' Nannie got in the way; only for Nannie yous ud have stretched him out: that Nannie saved his life!

JOE (*going out*). I was jus' thinkin' o' goin' meself—good night all.

JIMMY. Well, so long. (*Going out.*) Everything perfect, says she; (*with a chuckle*) tangerine undies an' all—it was th' business!

(*Mrs. Pender closes and locks the door with a vicious bang.*)

JOHNNY (*meekly*). Give us a penny candle, an' I'll g'up an' go to bed.

(*Without a word Mrs. Pender gives him the candle, and he goes slowly out by door on Left.*)

THE VOICES OF THE BALLAD SINGERS (*some distance up the street*).

> For Ireland is Ireland thro' joy an' thro' tears.
> Hope never dies thro' they long weary years.

MRS. PENDER (*extinguishing the light and going out by door on Left*). Addin' two an' two together, I think th' best thing Polly Pender can do is to remain a bird alone.

(*The rain has ceased; the sky has brightened, and the stars seem to be peering through the window into the darkened shop.*)

THE BALLAD SINGERS.

> Each age has seen countless, brave hearts pass away,
> But her spirit still lives on in they men of to-day!

THE CURTAIN SLOWLY FALLS

A SUBJECT OF SCANDAL AND CONCERN

A Play for Television

John Osborne

The first performance in Great Britain of *A Subject of Scandal and Concern* was given on B.B.C. Television on November 6, 1960. It was directed by Tony Richardson, and the sets were designed by Tony Abbott. The cast was as follows:

GEORGE HOLYOAKE Richard Burton
MRS. HOLYOAKE Rachel Roberts
CHAIRMAN George Howe
MAITLAND Colin Douglas
MRS. HOLYOAKE'S SISTER Hope Jackman
BROTHER-IN-LAW Hamish Roughead
MR. BUBB Donald Eccles
CHAIRMAN OF THE MAGISTRATES Willoughby Goddard
CAPTAIN LEFROY David C. Browning
MR. PINCHING John Ruddock

CAPTAIN MASON Ian Ainsley
MR. COOPER Robert Cawdron
MR. JONES Charles Carson
JAILER John Dearth
CLERK TO THE ASSIZES William Devlin
MR. JUSTICE ERSKINE George Devine
MR. ALEXANDER Nicholas Meredith
MR. BARTRAM Nigel Davenport
CHAPLAIN Andrew Keir

THE NARRATOR John Freeman

To THEATRE HISTORIANS, May 8, 1956, forever will remain a decisive date in twentieth-century theatrical history, for on that now memorable evening, John Osborne's *Look Back in Anger* explosively took hold of the stage at the Royal Court, London, and as it ruthlessly swept away the cobwebs of the past, it detonated a new awareness and a strong, angered sense of protest in drama. Reflecting the nonconformity and the contradictory attitudes of the post-World War II generation, the play instantaneously established Osborne, at the time an actor, as a powerful and compelling new dramatist, and also triggered the extraordinary theatrical renaissance that followed in Britain and, subsequently, spread to other parts of the world. Through the fire and fury of his central character, Jimmy Porter, Osborne immediately became identified as spokesman for his complex and troubled generation, eager to grasp the hand of "one who speaks out of the real despairs, frustrations and sufferings of the age we are living in, now, at this moment."

Born in London, on December 12, 1929, Mr. Osborne came to the theatre as an actor after a brief tenure as a journalist. He made his first stage appearance in 1948, and later joined the Royal Court Company, where he remained until 1957.

In that same year, Mr. Osborne's *The Entertainer* commanded the West End season with its negative and tragic hero, a third-rate music-hall artist, brilliantly limned by Sir Laurence Olivier. More experimental in nature than its immediate predecessor, the play juxtaposed the music hall conventions with domesticity in order to eliminate the restrictions of the naturalistic theatre.

Two lesser works followed: *Epitaph for George Dillon* (in collaboration with Anthony Creighton) and a musical satire with the "sensational" press as target, *The World of Paul Slickey.*

In 1961, the trend-setting author regained a firm foothold in the theatre with his drama *Luther.* As anticipated, *Luther* did not emerge from his pen as a conventional historical epic of sixteenth-century Europe and the Reformation. Instead, Osborne illuminated the character and motivations of the man who tore Christendom apart, and in the process, himself, with his own fears, loneliness, and personal torment. With Albert Finney portraying one of history's most controversial figures, the drama was an international success.

A Subject of Scandal and Concern, written especially for television and now published for the first time in the United States, offers further evidence of the widening and deepening of Mr. Osborne's interests. The protagonist, George Holyoake, was the last person to be imprisoned for the crime of blasphemy in England, and in dramatically recreating the man and his epoch, Osborne has infused contemporary relevance as the young, accused schoolteacher questions: "What is the morality of a law which prohibits the free publication of an opinion?"

Unquestionably one of the world's most influential and popular dramatists, John Osborne has been accorded many international honors, including two "best play" awards from the New York Drama Critics Circle (*Look Back in Anger,* 1958;* *Luther,* 1964,†) and Hollywood's Academy Award for his screenplay *Tom Jones.*

Mr. Osborne's *Inadmissible Evidence,* with Nicol Williamson repeating his prize-winning London performance, was a Broadway success in 1965–1966.

* Season: 1957–1958
† Season: 1963–1964

ACT ONE

SCENE. *The stone corridor of a jail. A steel door opens and there is a sound of heavy boots walking smartly. The camera picks up the polished boots of a policeman, the boots only. Behind, a pair of civilian brogues come into vision. Presently both pairs stop outside a wooden door. The door opens and we see into a bare room, furnished only by a small wooden table and two chairs.*

As the camera tracks on to the table, the door is heard to slam, a briefcase comes into vision, is opened, and a thick typewritten manuscript is produced. The camera holds it in closer, the title page reads— "A Subject of Scandal and Concern." After a few moments, it is tossed with a thump onto the table, where it lies. The camera tracks back from it to take in the Narrator sitting on the table.

———

NARRATOR. Good evening. I am a lawyer. My name is unimportant, as I am not directly involved in what you are about to see. What I am introducing for you is an entertainment. There is no reason why you should not go on with what you are doing. What you are about to see is a straightforward account of an obscure event in the history of your—well, my—country. I shall simply fill in with incidental but necessary information, like one of your own television chairmen, in fact. You will not really be troubled with anything unfamiliar. I hope you have been reassured. Now; this concerns one George Jacob Holyoake, H-O-L-Y, as in spirit, and O-A-K-E, tree with an "e," a righteously English, comically English name. One May day in 1842, this George Jacob Holyoake, a poor young teacher, was walking from Birmingham to Bristol to visit a friend serving twelve months in jail for having set up a Journal which the authorities considered to be improper.

(Mix to:

(George Holyoake on the outskirts of Cheltenham.)

NARRATOR (*sound only*). His wife, Madeleine, was staying with her sister in Cheltenham, and Mr. Holyoake took this opportunity to visit her on his way, but apart from the pleasure of seeing his wife and child again, Mr. Holyoake was in Cheltenham for another reason. Being a member of the Social Missionary Society, and an unusually energetic man even for an earnest time, he had arranged to address a lecture to the local branch of the Society.

(Mix to:

(Poster)

NARRATOR. The subject being "Home Colonization as a means of superseding Poor Laws and Emigration."

(Mix to:

(A kitchen—early evening. Mrs. Holyoake is preparing soup. Mr. Holyoake is seated upon a bench by the fire. It must be noted that Holyoake has intense difficulty with his speech occasionally. For example, in his first line he has a considerable obstacle to overcome in the word "pleased." This defect must be emphasized sufficiently to appear painful when it happens, but obviously it must be exploited sparingly, and its later dramatic effectiveness must depend upon the nicest discretion of the actor and the director.)

HOLYOAKE. Your sister was not pleased to see me.

MRS. HOLYOAKE. I know.

HOLYOAKE. You seem frail, my dear.

MRS. HOLYOAKE. They are angry about your lecture.

HOLYOAKE. I see. Well—you are still a splendid sight for me.

MRS. HOLYOAKE. They say it is improper.

HOLYOAKE. I have missed you both.

MRS. HOLYOAKE. And further, that you are imprudent and ungracious to undertake such a thing while I am staying beneath their roof.

HOLYOAKE. Are you not giving them the twelve shillings a week I have been sending you?

MRS. HOLYOAKE. They do not think it enough.

HOLYOAKE. Not enough? A good lodging house would be cheaper but I thought you would rather be with your sister and her children.

MRS. HOLYOAKE. You are right, my dear, and I am grateful. George: they should have received you in the parlour.

HOLYOAKE. Cheltenham is a fashionable town and too genteel and thin for dusty boots in the parlour.

MRS. HOLYOAKE. I feel ashamed—

HOLYOAKE. Of your husband?

(*Mrs. Holyoake pours him his soup.*)

HOLYOAKE. I am sorry to see you so unhappy, Madeleine, I am indeed.

MRS. HOLYOAKE. There is some rice bread left. Will you have that?

HOLYOAKE. Thank you. I promise: you shall not stay here a day longer than necessary. I have applied for an appointment in Sheffield.

MRS. HOLYOAKE. Oh?

HOLYOAKE. To teach day school and lecture on Sundays.

MRS. HOLYOAKE. What is the salary?

HOLYOAKE. Thirty shillings a week.

MRS. HOLYOAKE. I do not mean you to think—

HOLYOAKE. The soup is good.

MRS. HOLYOAKE. To think I was ashamed of you.

HOLYOAKE (*smiling*). It is difficult when you have relatives such as yours.

MRS. HOLYOAKE. You allow them to be insolent with you, George. They treat you like a common innkeeper.

HOLYOAKE. I do not earn as much as a common innkeeper.

MRS. HOLYOAKE. You seem unable to speak up for yourself.

HOLYOAKE. That is true. I do find it hard. Very hard.

MRS. HOLYOAKE. Not merely your impediment—

HOLYOAKE. No.

MRS. HOLYOAKE. But you are a man. I cannot speak for you.

HOLYOAKE. I know.

MRS. HOLYOAKE. There is more soup.

HOLYOAKE. No, thank you. I must finish preparing my lecture. We can talk about these things later.

MRS. HOLYOAKE. George, the child is poorly.

HOLYOAKE. Why, what's the matter?

MRS. HOLYOAKE. The matter is simple. She is not getting enough to eat.

HOLYOAKE. But they are being paid.

MRS. HOLYOAKE. They keep me short and there is nothing I can do. I am alone here. I tell you there is much show of things here but it is mostly pantomime. And so it is with eating and drinking.

HOLYOAKE. Surely your own sister cannot see you going short—

MRS. HOLYOAKE. They will not listen to me. They do not want to hear and it is because of you. Their dislike for you is almost past belief.

HOLYOAKE. But we have never so much as argued—

MRS. HOLYOAKE. I know it is difficult but we need you to help us, George. We need you to be strong.

HOLYOAKE. I have promised you: you will not have to remain here.

MRS. HOLYOAKE. Will you speak to them?

HOLYOAKE. I will.

MRS. HOLYOAKE. Will you speak to them now?

HOLYOAKE. Later.

MRS. HOLYOAKE. Later!

HOLYOAKE. After the lecture.

MRS. HOLYOAKE. You are avoiding it.

HOLYOAKE. I will speak to them tonight.

MRS. HOLYOAKE. No.

HOLYOAKE. I have said I will.

MRS. HOLYOAKE. No, you will not speak to them tonight, you will fasten on some evasion and that will be an end of it.

HOLYOAKE. You have my word.

MRS. HOLYOAKE. You fly from brawling like a cat from the water; yet you can speak for others well enough.

HOLYOAKE. Not well enough, not well enough. As you know.

MRS. HOLYOAKE. Oh, you are no speaker, and it's idle to pretend otherwise (*She touches his shoulder*), but you will try your best. I am sorry.

HOLYOAKE. You are very patient.

MRS. HOLYOAKE. You will always recognize your duty and there it is. We shall all manage. (*She kisses his forehead.*) Forgive me, but you are not an easy man, and I am so anxious for the future.

HOLYOAKE. Please try to be patient. I, too, am anxious.

(*Mix to:*

The Mechanics Hall, Cheltenham. The Chairman of the meeting, a tall, glum, middle-aged man, is speaking from the platform. Holyoake is seated beside him staring down at his hands.)

NARRATOR (*sound only*). Mrs. Holyoake was right in saying that her husband was not an impressive speaker. He was easily flustered and if, as on some occasions, he was interrupted from the floor he would usually drop his notes or even, as on one agonizing evening, dry up completely. In spite of this deficiency, he was constantly being invited to speak. He persisted and for some reason, so did his audience. Besides, there was a considerable shortage of speakers on the subject.

CHAIRMAN. I am sure you will wish to join me in offering our thanks to Mr. Holyoake for a very stimulating, provocative evening (*light applause*) and now, I think, in conclusion, we may—yes? Do you want to ask a question, sir? Another question from the floor. I think it is a little late—ah, it is Mr. Maitland. Would you mind one more question, Mr. Holyoake?

HOLYOAKE. Well—

CHAIRMAN. Very well then, just one more, Mr. Maitland, and then we really should—

MAITLAND (*from the floor*). Sir, you have spoken at great lengths concerning our duty to man but what, sir, I would like to ask, of our duty to God?

HOLYOAKE (*uncertainly*). Yes?

MAITLAND. Shall we not have churches and chapels in community?

HOLYOAKE. I do not wish to—

MAITLAND. That, sir, is my question.

HOLYOAKE. I do not wish to mix religion—

(*Voice from the floor—"Can't hear!"*)

HOLYOAKE (*flustered*)—to mix religion with an economic and secular subject, but I will try to answer the question frankly.

(*Voice from the floor—"Hear hear!"*)

HOLYOAKE. Our national debt is a millstone around the poor man's neck, and our church and general religious institutions cost us about twenty million pounds annually. Worship is expensive, and so I appeal to your heads and your pockets: are we not too poor to have God? If poor men cost the state as much, they would be put, like officers, on half-pay. And while our present distress remains, it is wisest to do the same thing with Deity.

(*Scattered applause*)

MAITLAND. But, sir—

CHAIRMAN. What is it?

MAITLAND. My question has not been answered, sir.

CHAIRMAN. Come, Mr. Maitland, it is getting late.

MAITLAND. What of morality, Mr. Holyoake?

HOLYOAKE. I regard morality, but as for God, Mr. Maitland, I cannot bring myself to believe in such a thing.

CHAIRMAN. Ladies and gentlemen, it is past ten o'clock and I must declare the meeting closed. Good night and thank you.

(*The meeting breaks up.*)

NARRATOR (*sound only*). An orderly, somewhat dull meeting came to an orderly close and the few reasonable respectable citizens of Cheltenham, who had sat the most of a spring evening on hard benches in the Mechanics Hall, walked to their homes.

(*Mix to:*)

NARRATOR. The following day, this paragraph appeared in *The Cheltenham Chronicle*. (*He picks up a newspaper and reads from it.*) "On Tuesday evening last, a person named Holyoake, from Sheffield, delivered a lecture on Socialism, or, as it has been more appropriately termed, devilism, at the Mechanics Institute. After attacking the Church of England and religion generally for a considerable time, a teetotaller named Maitland got up and said the lecturer had been talking a good deal about our duty to man but he omitted to mention any duty towards God, and he would be glad to know if there were any chapels in the community. The Socialist then replied that he professed no religion at all and thought that they were too poor to have any. He did not believe that there was such a Being as God and impiously remarked that if there was, he would have the Deity served the same as the Government treated subalterns, by placing Him upon half-pay. To their lasting shame, be it spoken, a considerable portion of the company applauded these profane opinions." At the bottom of this paragraph is a note, signed by the Editor, saying: "We have three persons in our employ who are ready to verify on oath the correctness of the above statement. We therefore hope those in authority will not suffer the matter to rest here and that some steps will be immediately taken to prevent any further publicity to such diabolical sentiments." The methods of newspaper morality have changed very little.

(*Mix to:*

(*The home of Mrs. Holyoake's sister.*

Mrs. Holyoake, her sister and brother-in-law.)

NARRATOR (*sound only*). The next number of *The Cheltenham Chronicle* was able to announce:

BROTHER-IN-LAW (*reading aloud*). "In reference to a paragraph which appeared in the last *Chronicle* regarding the monster, Holyoake, the magistrates read the article alluded to and expressed the opinion that it was a clear case of blasphemy. In order to check the further progress of his pernicious doctrine, the Superintendent of Police was ordered to use every exertion to bring him to justice." (*To Mrs. Holyoke*) Read it for yourself.

(*Mrs. Holyoake takes newspaper and starts reading.*)

(*Mix to:*)

NARRATOR. By this time, Mr. Holyoake had reached Bristol, visited his friend Mr. Southwell in jail and, astonished to read the account of his meeting, set out on foot once again for Cheltenham. The evening after his arrival the owners of the Mechanics Institute, the Cheltenham Chartists, held a meeting, the subject being "Free Discussion."

(*Mix to:*

(*The Mechanics Institute. The platform. Holyoake is addressing the meeting.*)

NARRATOR (*sound only*). Mr. Holyoake was allowed to wind up.

HOLYOAKE. If you think it right to differ from the times and to make a stand for any valuable points of morals, do it, however rustic, however antiquated, it may appear.

(*Mix to:*

(*Mr. Russell, the local Police Superintendent. He has a dozen men with him who take up positions by the door, at the back of the little hall, and by the gangways.*)

HOLYOAKE (*sound only*). Do it not for insolence, but seriously.

(*Mix to:*

(*Russell observing the audience.*)

HOLYOAKE (*sound only*). As a man who wore the soul of his own in his bosom—

(*Mix to:*)

HOLYOAKE. —and did not wait 'til it was breathed into him by the breath of fashion.

(*Close-up of Holyoake struggling with the word "fashion."*)

(*Mix to:*

(*The Magistrates' Court, Cheltenham. Holyoake is in the dock. Mr. Bubb, a local solicitor, is speaking.*)

BUBB. I take my stand on the common unwritten law of the land. There have been a variety of Statutes based for punishing blasphemy, but these Statutes in no way interfere with the common unwritten law. Any person who denies the existence or providence of God is guilty of blasphemy and the law has an annexe to that offense; imprisonment, corporal punishment and fine. The offence is much aggravated by his having put forth a placard, announcing a lecture on a subject completely innocent and having got together a number of persons, has given utterance to these sentiments which are an insult to God and man.

(*Mr. Bubb sits down. The Chairman of the Magistrates looks across at Holyoake.*)

MAGISTRATE. Do you wish to add anything to the evidence you have already given?

HOLYOAKE. I should like to remind you, sir, that in any other town where they are better read in bigotry than Cheltenham, it is neither the custom nor the law to apprehend persons without the authority of a warrant.

MAGISTRATE. There is no justification for a warrant here.

HOLYOAKE. It is the practice for information to be laid and a regular notice to be served.

MAGISTRATE. We do not propose to argue with you. On the evidence we have heard, the case is clear. Whether you are of no religion is of little consequence to us, but your attempt to propagate the infamous sentiment that there is no God is calculated to produce disorder and confusion and is a breach of the peace. The entertaining of opinions is not opposed to law if people keep them to themselves. If they speak out of the way and seek to propagate them by undermining the institutions of the country, by denying the existence of a God, by robbing others of the hopes set before them, it is the duty of all to prevent this. And if there are any here present disposed to take up this unfortunate trade, I would assure them that as long as the law punishes and magistrates uphold the law, so long will they bring offenders to justice. So long as men say there is no God or that the religion of the state is a farce and a fallacy, these gentlemen shall not be deterred by any clamour. The prisoner will be committed to trial at the next Assizes and remanded on bail on his own recognizances of one hundred pounds and on finding two sureties of fifty pounds each.

(*Mix to:*

(*The jail, Cheltenham. Holyoake is being led into a small room where he is confronted by Captain Lefroy, the head of the Police, and Mr. Pinching, surgeon.*)

LEFROY. Now, sir, this is Mr. Pinching. Would you object to him questioning you on your opinions?

HOLYOAKE (*hesitating*). I—

PINCHING. Mr. Holyoake: even the heathen acknowledges the existence of a Deity.

HOLYOAKE. Yes.

PINCHING. If you entertain these opinions on your deathbed, you will be a brave man, will you not?

HOLYOAKE. Death is a hard thing for any man to face. And so is life, Mr. P-p-p— (*He stumbles on Pinching's name.*)

PINCHING. The name is Pinching, sir. But you will admit, surely, that you are actuated in all this only by a love of notoriety?

HOLYOAKE. I have no relish for argument, sir, but I must defend myself.

PINCHING. Notoriety is what you relish, Mr. Holyoake, even though you seem to have a poor spirit for it. (*To Lefroy*) This kind is familiar enough. (*To Holyoake*) Do you not believe in Jesus Christ?

HOLYOAKE. This is an historical argument, sir—

PINCHING. Historical argument you say, sir, and you shall have it. You are aware that there is the same mass of evidence for the existence of Our Lord as for that of Henry V?

HOLYOAKE. My argument is not whether he lived but what he said.

PINCHING. It is Robert Owen who has made you an Atheist, is it not?

HOLYOAKE. Mr. Owen is a Socialist. I do not believe he is an Atheist.

PINCHING. Why don't you answer honestly, sir, are you an Atheist or are you not? You hesitate, don't you, Mr. Holyoake?

LEFROY. I think we should give the prisoner some respite, Mr. Pinching. From the looks of him he must have had a disturbing morning, and this afternoon he must be on his way to Gloucester.

PINCHING. Your friend Mr. Southwell is in Bristol jail for the same offence, is he not?

HOLYOAKE. My position—(*difficulty*)

PINCHING. Your what? Can you not speak decently like a man, sir, and in a decent manly fashion?

HOLYOAKE. My position has been rather in defence of Mr. Southwell's right to—

LEFROY. You look tired, Mr. Holyoake, I should save your breath. Jailer!

HOLYOAKE. I am not to have time to obtain bail?

LEFROY. My instruction is to commit you forthwith to Gloucester county jail.

PINCHING. Good-bye, Mr. Holyoake. Unhappily the day has gone when we might send you *and* Mr. Owen *and* Mr. Southwell to the stake.

HOLYOAKE. You may well live to see that day, Mr. Pinching.

PINCHING. I hope so, Mr. Holyoake, indeed I hope so.

(*Mix to:*

(*Holyoake is leaving Cheltenham on the way to Gloucester jail. He is handcuffed and accompanied by two constables.*)

(*Mix to:*

(*The corridor in the county jail— Gloucester. The Governor, Captain Mason, Mr. Cooper and Mr. Jones, magistrates, are being escorted by the jailer to Holyoake's cell. They stop outside and the door is unlocked.*)

(*Mix to:*

(*Holyoake rising.*)

MASON. Holyoake, these gentlemen are Mr. Cooper and Mr. Jones. If you have any questions to put to them you may do so.

HOLYOAKE. I see. You are magistrates, are you not?

COOPER. Yes. Do you wish to tender any complaint, Mr. Holyoake?

HOLYOAKE. Only that I am a prisoner.

COOPER. Nothing else?

HOLYOAKE. I have been refused the note-book and papers which I need for my defence.

JONES. The prison chaplain does not think it necessary.

HOLYOAKE. It is necessary for him that I am deprived of them. I gave him a list of the books I wanted to read for my trial and he has only allowed me thirteen of them.

COOPER. Thirteen is a large enough number surely, Mr. Holyoake.

JONES. Besides, the chaplain has told me that the other books were of an unChristian character.

HOLYOAKE. They were, sir.

JONES. So—you see?

COOPER. The chaplain tells us you have refused any spiritual consolation.

HOLYOAKE. I would like my books.

JONES (gently). Do you not find this a hard course you have taken, Mr. Holyoake?

HOLYOAKE. I do, sir, I find it very hard. (Smiling:) It would be easier with the books.

JONES. Come now, you will be ill advised not to employ counsel.

HOLYOAKE. I shall defend myself, sir, as well as I am able.

COOPER. As well as you are able? And how well is that? Do let yourself be advised.

HOLYOAKE. I think a lawyer is not a good man to state a case of conscience.

COOPER. But able, Mr. Holyoake; how able are you?

HOLYOAKE. I shall try, sir.

COOPER. But what if you are not equipped to try? There are things some of us cannot do. What if your speech should fail you?

HOLYOAKE. I shall try, sir.

COOPER. Think on it, Holyoake. The judge will put you down and not hear you.

JONES (kindly). Come, boy. You are a deist, are you not? (Pause) You cannot be something else. Can you?

HOLYOAKE. I don't know, sir. I did not know before and I do not know now. But I do think that I am alone in this matter and will remain so.

(Fade)

END OF ACT ONE

ACT TWO

The Assize Court—Gloucester. Holyoake is in the dock awkwardly arranging a pile of books on the shelf in front of him. The Clerk reads the indictment as follows:

———

CLERK. The jurors for Our Lady the Queen, upon their oath, present that George Jacob Holyoake, late of the parish of Cheltenham, in the County of Gloucester, being a wicked and malicious and evil disposed person and disregarding the laws and religion of the realm, and wickedly and profanely devising and intending to bring Almighty God, the Holy Scriptures and the Christian religion, into disbelief and contempt among the people of this Kingdom on the twenty-fourth day of May, in the fifth year of the reign of Our Lady the Queen, with force and arms, at the parish aforesaid, in the County aforesaid, in the presence and hearing of diverse liege subjects of our said Lady the Queen, maliciously, unlawfully and wickedly did compose, speak, utter, pronounce, and publish with a loud voice, of and concerning Almighty God, the Holy Scriptures, and the Christian religion, these words following, that is to say, "I (meaning the said George Jacob Holyoake) do not believe there is such a thing as a God: I (meaning the said George Jacob Holyoake) would have the Deity served as they (meaning the Government of this Kingdom) serve the Subalterns, and place Him (meaning Almighty God) on half-pay." To the high displeasure of Almighty God, to the great scandal and reproach of the Christian religion, in open violation of the laws of this Kingdom, to the evil example of all others in the like case offending, and against the peace of Our Lady the Queen, her Crown and dignity.

NARRATOR (sound only). Mr. Holyoake, intent on speaking in a firm, manly fashion, pleaded not guilty and applied to have the name of the jury called over singly and distinctly.

(Mix to:
(Mr. Alexander, Counsel for the Prosecution.)

NARRATOR (sound only). Mr. Alexander,

Counsel for the Prosecution, said the offence only being a misdemeanor, the defendant had not right to challenge.

(*Mix to:*

(*Mr. Justice Erskine.*)

ERSKINE. Of course not, unless reasons are given in each case.

CLERK. The name John Lovesey is first.

HOLYOAKE. I object to Lovesey. He sat on the bench when I was before the magistrates at Cheltenham and approved the proceedings against me. He is not disinterested in this matter.

ERSKINE. That is not sufficient reason for challenging.

(*Mix to:*

(*Holyoake rearranging some of his books which have fallen down from his ledge into the dock.*)

NARRATOR (*sound only*). The names of the jury were called over and they each took their place.

(*The camera follows each jury man as he takes his seat on the benches.*)

NARRATOR (*sound only*). Thomas Gardiner, grocer, foreman.

James Reeve, farmer, Chedworth.

William Ellis, farmer, Chedworth.

William Matthews, poulterer, Cheltenham.

Simon Vizard, shopkeeper, Oldland.

Isaac Tombes, farmer, Whitcomb.

William Wilson, maltster, Brimpsfield.

Edwin Brown, farmer, Withington.

Bevan Smith, farmer, Harescomb.

William Smith, miller, Barnwood.

Joseph Shipp, farmer, Yate.

HOLYOAKE. Can I be allowed to read the indictment against me?

ERSKINE. Certainly.

(*A copy of the indictment is handed up to Holyoake.*)

ERSKINE. Do you require notepaper and pens?

HOLYOAKE. Thank you, sir, I do.

(*Mr. Alexander rises.*)

ALEXANDER. The defendant, on the twenty-fourth of May last, issued placards for a lecture to be delivered in Cheltenham. In this placard he announced, not the diabolical, the dreadful topics which he discanted upon, not anything which would lead the reader to imagine or to expect what really took place, but he gave out his subject as a lecture upon "Home Colonization, Emigration and the Poor Laws." Mark this, gentlemen of the jury, had he given in his announcement any hint of what was to have taken place, his end might have been defeated, and no audience attracted to listen to the blasphemous expressions you have heard set out in the indictment. But he did obtain an audience, a numerous audience, and then declared that the people were too poor to have religion. That he, himself, had no religion. That he did not believe in such a thing as a God, and—though it pains me to repeat it, that he would place the Deity upon half-pay. I shall call witnesses to prove all this and then it will be for you to say if he is guilty. It may be urged to you that these things were said in answer to a question, that the innuendoes must be made out. Innuendoes! I should think it is an insult to the understandings of twelve jury men—of twelve intelligent men—to call witnesses to prove innuendoes. But I should place the case before you and leave it in your hands. I am sure I need not speak, I need not dwell upon the consequences of insulting that Deity we are as much bound as inclined to reverence. Please call James Bartram.

(*The name of Bartram is called. Holyoake makes notes on one of his untidy sheets of paper.*)

(*Mix to:*

(*Bartram.*)

BARTRAM. I am a printer at Cheltenham, employed upon *The Cheltenham Chronicle.*

ALEXANDER. Did you attend the lecture, given by the defendant, on the twenty-fourth of May?

BARTRAM. I did, sir.

ALEXANDER. Did a placard announcing the lecture proclaim as follows, "Home Colonization, Emigration, Poor Laws Superseded."

BARTRAM. It did, sir.

ALEXANDER. At the very end of the evening was a supplementary question put to the defendant?

BARTRAM. Yes, sir.

ALEXANDER. What was that question?

BARTRAM (*glibly*). The defendant had been speaking of our duty to man, and at the end, Mr. Maitland got up, saying he—the defendant—had said nothing of our duty toward God. At this, the prisoner said, "I am of no religion at all. I do not believe in such a thing as a God. The people of this country are too poor to have any religion. I would serve the Deity as the Government does the Subalterns—place him on half-pay." He was the length of the room off; I heard him distinctly.

ALEXANDER. Thank you, Mr. Bartram.

BARTRAM. He spoke in a distinct voice.

HOLYOAKE. You say I said the people were too poor to have any religion. Will you state the reasons I gave?

BARTRAM. I think you said something about the great expense of religion to the country.

HOLYOAKE. Will you remember the other reason?

BARTRAM. I don't remember any.

HOLYOAKE. Now you have sworn the words are blasphemous—

ERSKINE. No, he has not.

HOLYOAKE. Will you state if the words are blasphemous?

ERSKINE. That question must be put through me. (*To Bartram*) Do you consider the words blasphemous?

BARTRAM. I do.

HOLYOAKE. Why do you think them blasphemous?

BARTRAM. Because they revile the majesty of Heaven and are calculated to subvert peace, law and order. They are punishable by human law because they attack human authority.

HOLYOAKE. Who has taught you to define blasphemy in this way?

BARTRAM. I have not been taught; it is my own opinion.

HOLYOAKE. During my examination before the magistrates you did not seem to be able to express these opinions. Can you swear that you have not concocted this answer for the occasion?

BARTRAM. I was not expecting to be catechized.

HOLYOAKE. Who advised you to come here as a witness?

BARTRAM. The magistrate, sir.

HOLYOAKE. On the night you attended my lecture, did you hear me speak against morality?

BARTRAM. No, you said nothing against morality.

HOLYOAKE. What is your opinion of morality?

ERSKINE. The question is irrelevant.

HOLYOAKE. Do you think I spoke my honest convictions?

BARTRAM. I thought you spoke what you meant.

ERSKINE. You must not ask the witness to give his opinions.

HOLYOAKE. Would you have lost your situation with *The Cheltenham Chronicle* if you had not come forward in this case?

BARTRAM. No, I would not. In my opinion you spoke wickedly as stated in the indictment. You spoke of the enormous sums of money spent upon religion, and the poverty of the people, and afterwards you said you would place God on half-pay as the Government did Subalterns.

ALEXANDER. Mr. Bartram, how long have you been employed by *The Cheltenham Chronicle*?

BARTRAM. For ten years, sir.

ALEXANDER. Do you give evidence from fear or reward?

BARTRAM. No, sir.

ALEXANDER. You give it from a sense of duty?

BARTRAM. I do, sir.

ALEXANDER. That is the case for the prosecution, my lord.

ERSKINE (*to Holyoake*). Now is the time for your defence.

HOLYOAKE. I am surprised to hear that the case for the prosecution is closed. I submit to Your Lordship, there is not sufficient evidence before the court,

ERSKINE. That is for the jury to decide.

HOLYOAKE. I thought, my lord, as the evidence is so manifestly insufficient to prove malice, you would have felt bound to direct my acquittal.

ERSKINE. It is for the jury to say whether they are satisfied.

HOLYOAKE. The counsel who opened the case did not state whether the indictment was as statute or common law.

ERSKINE. Common law.

HOLYOAKE. Then, gentlemen of the jury, I shall draw your attention to that, and I hope I shall be able to explain the law bearing on my case.

ERSKINE. The jury must take the law from me. I am responsible for that. If this is not an offence for common law, this indictment is worth nothing, I sit here not to correct the law but merely to administer it.

(*Holyoake is flustered.*)

ERSKINE. Continue.

HOLYOAKE. I— (*He flounders.*)

ERSKINE. You must see now that you should have given your case into the hands of counsel.

HOLYOAKE. I ask you to be p-atient, my lord. It is from no disrespect to the Bar that I did not employ counsel, but because they are unable to enter into my motives. There is a magic circle of orthodoxy they will not step out of. The intention of a libel constitutes its criminality. It is for you gentlemen to say whether I knowingly, wickedly, and maliciously offended the law. Malice is necessary to a libel. Conscientious words are allowable. What, then, is my crime? For my difference in opinion with you upon the question of Deity, I offer no apology. I am under no contract to think as you do and I owe you no obligation to do so. If I asked you to give up your belief, you would think it impertinence and if you punish me for not giving up mine, how will you reconcile it with "doing as you would (*struggles*) wish to be done to"?

ALEXANDER. My lord, I find it almost impossible to hear the prisoner. Might I suggest it would help if he were to slow down his delivery.

ERSKINE. We shall wait for you, Mr. Holyoake.

HOLYOAKE (*making more effort*). I have injured no man's reputation, taken no man's property, attacked no man's person, violated no oath, taught no immorality. I was asked a question and answered it openly. I should feel myself degraded if I descended to finding out if my convictions suited every anonymous man in the audience before I uttered them. What is the morality of a law which prohibits the free publication of an opinion?

ERSKINE. You must have heard me state the law that if it be done temperately and decently, all men are at liberty to state opinions.

HOLYOAKE. Then this liberty is a mockery. The word "temperate" means what those in authority think proper.

ERSKINE. An honest man speaking his opinions decently is entitled to do so.

HOLYOAKE. It must be already clear to you, gentlemen of the jury, that I am here for having been more honest than the law happens to allow. What is this "temperate"? What is "intemperate"? Invective, sarcasm, p—

ALEXANDER. Personality.

HOLYOAKE. Thank you, Mr. Alexander.

ALEXANDER. Pleasure.

HOLYOAKE. —and the like. But these weapons are denied only to those who attack the prevailing opinion. Is it intemperate to say the Deity should be put on half-pay? Did I do Him a disgrace if I thought He, who is called Our Father, the Most High, would dispose with one-half of the lip service He receives from the clergy, in order to give His creatures in poverty their due?

ERSKINE. If you can convince the jury that your only meaning was that the income of the clergy ought to be reduced and that you did not intend to insult God, I should tell the jury that you ought not be convicted. You need not go into a laboured defence of that.

HOLYOAKE. I see. (*Picking up again:*) There is a strange infirmity in English minds which makes them accept a bad principle which they, as Englishmen, are no longer bad enough to put into practice. So it is with this prosecution, which is no more than the poor rags of former persecutions. In this age, as often as men introduce new benefits so do others try to bring back old evils. Gentlemen, what is this p-rosecution?

(*There is some laughter.*)

ERSKINE. We shall have no repetition of that.

HOLYOAKE. "If any of you lack wisdom," says St. James, "let him ask of God but let him ask in faith." My prosecutors have asked, and Mr. Alexander has asked and they have put their faith in policemen and in the common law. A good Christian will be sure to leave the issue in God's hands. Not the will of God but the will of bigots has been done and the issue left in the turnkey's hands. A short time ago, it was argued that if the political squibs, which are seen in shop windows, were permitted to be published, they would bring Government into contempt. Soon you would have no Government. Well? Their publication has been permitted. Have we no Government now? So it is with religion. We might challenge all the wits and caricaturists in the world to bring the problems of Euclid into contempt. No man can bring into contempt that which is essential and true. Now, gentlemen, turn to the question. What is blasphemy? It is said to be "an injury to God." Men who could not string six sentences together have told me they would defend God—men I would be ashamed to have defending me. But blasphemy is an impossibility. What does it mean but an annoyance to God? To believe in this is to believe in the magical power of words and there is no magic in the words, neither yours nor mine.

(*Holyoake is beginning to find his way and collect himself. In the following speech he even attempts some lightness.*)

HOLYOAKE. This blasphemy, then, is an antiquated accusation. What a turmoil, what a splutter there was in this land when men first said they would not eat fish, that they would not bow down to priests, and that they would not confess except when they liked. What threats there were of Hell and flames, what splashing about of fire and brimstone, what judgment on these men choked with their beef steak on a Friday. Such frying, such barbecuing and everyone dripping in a flood of sin and gravy and not the smallest notion of a red herring anyway. How fathomless must be the patience of Heaven that this island is not swallowed up in the sea for it, when we know we shall appear in the next world with so much mutton on our heads! But we have tried to look into the rules with the intelligence that has been given to us and calculated the risk that eating mutton can no longer be a blasphemy. If God be truth you libel Him and His power! It is a melancholy maxim in these courts of law that the greater the truth the greater the libel, and so it would be with me this day if I could demonstrate to you that there is no Deity. The more correct I am, the severer would be my punishment because the law regards the belief in a God to be the foundation of obedience among men. I have been told to look around the world for evidence of the truth of the Christian religion; it is easy for those who enjoy good fortune to say so.

For them, everything shines brightly, but I can see cause for complaint, and I am not alone in the feeling. There are those here who think that religion can lead to general happiness; I do not, and I have had the same means of judging as yourselves. You say your feelings are insulted —your opinions are outraged; but what of mine? Gentlemen, I will not keep you much longer, but before I finish I must first give you some hint of my difficulties in this matter. What is Christian morality but the New Testament? Impressive it is, eloquent, poetic, but general and often impossible to be taken literally. You cannot eke out a whole man's morality from this. You are forced back to the Old Testament, which ethic is elaborate and specific but often barbarous and intended for a barbarous people. Your St. Paul rejected it, and was forced to draw on the Greeks and Romans even to the extent of sanctioning slavery. What you call your Christianity is not Christianity but your churches' work of two thousand years. I do not deny the goodness that is in it but I deny that it is more than a part of goodness. It is passive and obedient. "Thou shalt not" has precedence over "thou shalt." It has always feared the flesh and so it flees from life. It holds out hope of Heaven and the threat of Hell, indulging the fear in individual men, offering an investment instead of a contest. This is submission and I do not believe in it. Our obligation to man has come down from the Greek and the Roman. Whatever there is of personal dignity, honour, or magnanimity, comes from our human, not our religious education. You see, gentlemen, these difficulties have been insuperable for me. When I was in Cheltenham jail I was asked if I would be so brave on my death-bed. I cannot tell. My own supply of courage is hard to come by, but let me assure you that if men can expect to die in peace who can send their fellow men to jail for honest opinion, I have nothing to fear. Am I to count it a misfortune to live in modern times and among a Christian people?

ERSKINE. Gentlemen of the jury, I am not going to lay down as law that no man has a right to undertake opinions opposed to the religion of the state, nor to express them. Man is only responsible for his opinions to God, because God only can judge his motives. If men entertain sentiments opposed to the religion of the state, we require that they shall express them reverently. Christianity is ill defended by refusing audience to the objections of unbelievers, but whilst we would have freedom of inquiry restrained by no laws except those of decency, we are entitled to demand on behalf of a religion which holds forth to mankind assurance of immortality, that its credit be assailed by no other weapons than those of sober discussion and legitimate reasoning. What you have to try is whether the defendant wickedly and devisedly did intend to bring the Christian religion into contempt amongst the people. You are not called upon to say whether, in your judgment, the opinions of the defendant are right or wrong, but whether he uttered these words with the intent charged in the indictment. The question is whether the words spoken were uttered with the intention of bringing God and the Christian religion into contempt. Then the charge is made out, for I tell you that it is an offence at common law. If it is not an offence, the indictment is not worth the parchment it is written on. You have to consider the language and the passage read to you from the charge of a learned judge, "it may not be going too far to state that no author or preacher is forbidden in stating his opinions sincerely. By maliciously is not meant malice against any particular individual but a mischievous intent. This is the criterion and it is a fair one. If it can be collected from the offensive levity in which the subject is treated." If the words had appeared in the course of a written paper, you would have entertained no doubt that the person who uttered these words had uttered them with levity. The only thing in his favour is that it was not a written answer. The solution given by the defendant is that although, unhappily, he has no belief in God, he had no intention of bringing religion into contempt. He went on to state that he considered it the duty of the clergymen of the establishment to have their incomes reduced by one-half. If he had meant this, he ought to have made use of other language. You will dismiss from your minds all statements in newspapers or other statements made out of court and consider it in reference to the evidence. If you are convinced that he uttered it with levity, with the purpose of treating with contempt the majesty of Almighty God, he is guilty of the offence. If you think he made use of these words in the heat of argument without any such intent, you will give him the benefit of the doubt. If you are convinced that he did it with that object, you must find him guilty despite all that has been addressed to you. If you entertain a reasonable doubt of his intention, you will give him the benefit of it.

(*Mix to:*)

NARRATOR. Mr. Holyoake had finished, his voice notably stronger and his impediment astonishingly improved. He had little time to recover before the jury brought in their verdict.

(*Mix to:*)

FOREMAN. Guilty, my lord.

CLERK. And this is the verdict of you all?

FOREMAN. It is.

ERSKINE. George Jacob Holyoake, the arm of the law is not stretched out to protect the character of the Almighty. We do not assume to be the protectors of our God, but to protect the people from indecent language. Proceeding on the evidence that has been given, trusting that these words have been uttered in the heat of the moment, I shall think it sufficient to sentence you to be imprisoned in the common jail for six calendar months.

END OF ACT TWO

ACT THREE

NARRATOR. Mr. Holyoake's first trials after his committal to jail were the profusion of bells: dock bells, basin bells, jail bells, the bells of Gloucester Cathedral and prayer bells.

(*Mix to:*

(*The Common Room of the jail. A large grating overhead. A few prisoners eating gruel, including Holyoake.*)

NARRATOR (*sound only*). Bells and the itch. The itch being an ailment he was certain he had already caught from his fellow prisoners. More than the complaint he feared the cure. The cure being to be dipped naked into a barrel of brimstone and pitch. After this, the prisoner was left to lie for days in blankets already used by a hundred others smeared in the same way.

(*The heavy Cathedral bells are replaced by the prison prayer bell. The other prisoners get up and leave, and Holyoake is left alone with his bowl of gruel. He looks around cautiously and begins to scratch himself with rapt intensity. He is suddenly interrupted by the voice of the jailer.*)

JAILER. Holyoake!

(*Holyoake is startled, thinking he has been caught scratching.*)

HOLYOAKE. Yes.

JAILER (*entry*). Holyoake!

HOLYOAKE. I am here. (*Pulling down his sleeve hastily.*)

JAILER. Did you not hear the bell?

HOLYOAKE. I did.

JAILER. All the other prisoners have gone to prayer.

HOLYOAKE. What of that?

JAILER. I can't be talked to in this way. You must go.

HOLYOAKE. You are wrong. I must not.

JAILER. Don't you know where you are?

HOLYOAKE. I think I am aware of it.

JAILER. Don't you know you are a prisoner?

HOLYOAKE. I am sensible of that, too.

JAILER. Well, you must do as the others do and you must go to prayers.

HOLYOAKE. Then you must c— (*difficulty*)

JAILER. What are you trying to say?

HOLYOAKE. -c-carry me.

JAILER. I'll report you to the clergyman.

HOLYOAKE. Give the clergyman my compliments and say I'll not come to prayers.

(*Jailer is baffled and goes out. Holyoake makes sure he is really alone again and sits down painfully to scratch.*)

(*Mix to:*

(*Close-up—the Prison Chaplain. The Chaplain is serious, not a fool. He is merely humourless. Holyoake recognizes this immediately.*)

CHAPLAIN. Well, Mr. Holyoake, how is it you did not come to prayers?

HOLYOAKE. I am imprisoned on the ground that I do not believe in a God. Would you then take me to chapel to pray to one?

CHAPLAIN. If you attended the ordinances of grace it might lead you to believe.

HOLYOAKE. Then I am sorry for you, sir.

CHAPLAIN. I do not think you understand us, Holyoake, it is not you we prosecute—it is your opinions.

HOLYOAKE. Then I wish you would imprison them, sir, and not me.

CHAPLAIN (*more an unhappy bureaucrat than an evangelist*). But you must attend prayers. It is the rule of the jail.

HOLYOAKE. I will agree to this: that when on Sundays you preach and I shall hear something new. Then I will come.

CHAPLAIN. Well, if you don't come to prayers, you shall be locked up.

HOLYOAKE. Then, sir, you must give your orders.

CHAPLAIN. Well, you will at least allow me to present you with a Bible for your private reading.

HOLYOAKE. Thank you. I shall be glad of it.

(*The Chaplain hands him the prison Bible.*)

HOLYOAKE. This is the usual prison copy, is it not?

CHAPLAIN. Yes.

HOLYOAKE. And it will figure in the next jail report to the county magistrates, will it not?

CHAPLAIN. Yes, that is the form.

(*Holyoake hands it back to the Chaplain.*)

HOLYOAKE (*politely*). Then I should like to be presented with one worth acceptance or not at all. This book is like a dumpling. I could not endure it in my library.

CHAPLAIN. But this is the prison issue.

HOLYOAKE. The trade price is about ten pence. Surely special persons must present special needs. A thin copy bound in calf in pearl type with marginal references would be most acceptable.

CHAPLAIN (*concerned*). An edition like that would cost half a guinea.

HOLYOAKE. Yes, sir, it is a great deal.

CHAPLAIN. We shall see. (*At the door*) By the by, your friend Mr. Southwell is dead in Bristol jail.

HOLYOAKE. Southwell? When?

CHAPLAIN. Yesterday. He began to die

badly and then he started to curse your name.

HOLYOAKE. That is not true.

CHAPLAIN. And he recanted at the end.

HOLYOAKE. What?

CHAPLAIN. Why, he cried out like a child and begged forgiveness of his Father. He gave himself up.

HOLYOAKE. This is a crude strategy and I am tired of them. Please leave me.

CHAPLAIN. It is the truth, Mr. Holyoake. I swear it.

(*He goes out. Close-up of Holyoake.*)
(*Mix to:*
(*Holyoake's hand, slowly, carefully scratching at his bare shoulder. The sound of footsteps and he covers himself. Mr. Jones, the magistrate, enters.*)

JONES. Now, how are you, sir?

HOLYOAKE. I am well, thank you.

JONES. Yes. Yes, well I suppose you are looking well enough in the circumstances. Holyoake: I seem to remember your objecting to being called a fool by me for your opinions.

HOLYOAKE. I thought it a discourtesy, yes, sir.

JONES. I also remember you speaking with a surprising respect for some of the German theologians.

HOLYOAKE. Yes.

JONES. It might interest you to know that one of them has just published a new translation of the Psalms of David. I have brought it with me as a matter of fact. Now see there: the fourteenth psalm, "The fool hath said in his heart: there is no God."

(*Holyoake stares back at Mr. Jones.*)

JONES (*gently*). You see, Mr. Holyoake, David says you are a fool.

(*Holyoake looks at him with some affection.*)

HOLYOAKE. I do not respect rudeness in the mouth of David any more than in yours, Mr. Jones. (*He scratches surreptitiously.*)

JONES (*glad of the diversion*). Do you scratch, sir?

HOLYOAKE. No, sir. It is an old nervous impediment like my speech. Mr. Jones, will you be so good as to tell me the truth about my friend Mr. Southwell, in Bristol jail?

JONES. What have you heard?

HOLYOAKE. That he recanted on his death-bed.

JONES. It is true. (*Mr. Jones rises, troubled.*) I ask you to forgive me, Mr. Holyoake; I have conducted this interview very clumsily indeed and I am very sorry.

HOLYOAKE. Well?

JONES. Letters have come to the Governor's hands concerning your daughter.

HOLYOAKE. My daughter? Is she sick?

JONES. She is. To dying. If not already dead. I thought you would prefer me to tell you.

HOLYOAKE. Thank you.

JONES. I shall arrange for Mrs. Holyoake to come and see you as soon as she is able. You shall have the use of the Magistrates' Committee Room. It is a furnished cheerful apartment.

HOLYOAKE. Thank you.

JONES. Yes. Mr. Holyoake? (*Tentatively:*) Would you permit me to say a prayer?

(*Holyoake turns back to him.*)

HOLYOAKE. If it pleases you, Mr. Jones, if it pleases you.

(*Mr. Jones kneels while Holyoake stands beneath the cell window. The two figures are silhouetted.*)

JONES. O Almighty God with Whom do live the spirits of just men made perfect, if they are delivered from their earthly prisons; we humbly commend the soul of this Thy servant, our dear sister, into thy hands, as into the hand of a faithful Creator and most merciful Saviour; most humbly beseeching Thee that it may be precious in Thy sight.

(*Mix to:*
(*Close-up of Mrs. Holyoake, Magistrates' Committee Room.*)

MRS. HOLYOAKE. We made the arrangements for the burial at the Birmingham cemetery. The clerk asked whether we would provide a minister or whether friends of the deceased would do so, so I told him a minister was not desired.

(*The camera tracks back to take in Holyoake.*)

MRS. HOLYOAKE. Then the clerk said, "You mean you will provide one yourself?" so I said again we did not require one at all. Please send the beadle only. And on the day of the interment, the beadle came as you instructed. We did everything as you instructed. We told him to conduct the burial party direct to the grave and not into the chapel, and he did it without a word. The coffin was plain but very pretty, without tinsel or angels, and we all threw in a bouquet of flowers as it was lowered in. And when the grave was made up, we went home. She was buried without parade, without priest, or priestly ceremony. It was just as you instructed. (*Pause*) You may have your opinions, George, but I know now: this was not a manly thing to have done and I can't thank you for it. No, not that even. I cannot ever forgive you for it.

HOLYOAKE. I would rather regret my fortune—than—than be ashamed of my v-victory.

MRS. HOLYOAKE. There is no victory in this, George, and your future—you will regret that for the rest of your life. (*She rises.*) Except for two, none of your colleagues have sent a friendly word.

HOLYOAKE. What about Mr. Owen?

MRS. HOLYOAKE. Mr. Robert Owen. What a debt we owe to him! He has not recognized your existence, even by a single line. When you leave this place you will walk over the grave of your own child. Well? Where is your tongue now, Mr. Holyoake?

(*Close up of Mrs. Holyoake.*)

(*Mix to:*

(*The Prison Chapel. The Chaplain walks down the aisle, followed by Holyoake. He motions him into one of the spiked prisoners' pews and ascends into the pulpit. The Chaplain prays while Holyoake stands staring ahead of him.*)

CHAPLAIN. Hear my prayer, O Lord, and let me cry come unto Thee. Hide not thy face from me in the time of my trouble: incline thine ear unto me when I call: O hear me and that right soon. For my days are consumed away like smoke and my bones are burnt up as it were a fire brand. My heart is smitten down and withered like grass: so that I forgot to eat my bread. For the voice of my groaning: my bones will scarce cleave to my flesh. I am become like a pelican in the wilderness and like an owl that is in the desert. I have watched and am even as it were a sparrow that sitteth alone upon the house top and that because of thine indignation and wrath for Thou hast taken me up and

cast me down. My days are gone like a shadow and I am withered like grass. Do you not see what you have done? Can you not speak? But Thou, O Lord, shalt endure for ever and Thy remembrance throughout all generations. Holyoake, where are you?

(*Close-up of Holyoake.*)

CHAPLAIN. O Blessed Lord, the Father of mercies, and the God of all comforts; we beseech thee, look down in pity and compassion upon this thy afflicted servant. Thou writest bitter things against him, and makest him to possess his former iniquities; thy wrath lieth hard upon him, and his soul is full of trouble: but, O merciful God, who hast written Thy holy Word for our learning, that we, through patience and comfort of thy holy Scriptures, might have hope; give him a right understanding of himself and of thy threats and promises; that he may neither cast away his confidence in thee, nor place it anywhere but in thee. Give him strength against all his temptations, and heal all his distempers. Break not the bruised reed, nor quench the smoking flax. Shut not up thy tender mercies in displeasure; but make him to hear of joy and gladness, that the bones which thou hast broken may rejoice. Deliver him from fear of the enemy, and lift up the light of Thy Countenance upon him, and give him peace, through the merits and meditation of Jesus Christ our Lord. Amen. Do you see what you are and what you have done? Speak, Holyoake, why do you not speak?

(*Close-up: Holyoake makes an animal effort to speak, but nothing will happen.*)

(*Mix to:*

(*The courtyard, early morning. Inside the prison, Holyoake is being escorted to the reception gates. Captain Mason, the Governor, is waiting for him.*)

MASON. Good-bye, Holyoake.

(*Holyoake nods.*)

MASON. Good-bye and God bless you.

HOLYOAKE (*presently*). Good-bye. It has been a rare p-rivilege.

(*They look at each other, and Mason begins to laugh, in an uncontrolled, ironic sympathy. Holyoake smiles back at him. The outer gates open and he walks through into the cold December early morning as Mason's laughter follows him.*)

(*Mix to:*)

NARRATOR. This is a time when people demand from entertainments what they call a "solution." They expect to have their little solution rattling away down there in the centre of the play like a motto in a Christmas cracker.

(*He starts folding up a manuscript, and puts it into a briefcase.*)

NARRATOR. For those who seek information, it has been put before you. If it is meaning you are looking for, then you must start collecting for yourself. And what would you say is the moral then?

(*He picks up the case and starts to go.*)

NARRATOR. If you are waiting for the commercial, it is probably this: you cannot live by bread alone. You must have jam—even if it is mixed with another man's blood.

(*The door opens and a policeman's feet appear.*)

NARRATOR. That's all. You may retire now. And if a mini-car is your particular mini-dream, then dream it.

When your turn comes you will be called.

Good night.

(*He walks out. The camera follows him and pans up to a close-up of the policeman standing at the door. The Narrator walks deliberately down the prison corridor to his client.*)

THE END

BELLAVITA

Luigi Pirandello

Translated by WILLIAM MURRAY

BELLAVITA, *owner of a café and pastry shop*
DENORA, *a notary*
CONTENTO, *a lawyer*

MRS. CONTENTO, *his wife*
A CLERK
MR. GIORGINO
SEVERAL OF CONTENTO'S CLIENTS

SCENE: A sitting room in CONTENTO's house, in a small town of southern Italy.

In 1967, the world commemorated the one hundredth anniversary of the birth of the greatest of modern Italian dramatists, Luigi Pirandello. Awarded the Nobel Prize in 1934, Pirandello was, and still remains, a dominant force in the development of the modern theatre. The position he occupies at the crossroads of dramatic evolution and the impact his works have had upon succeeding generations of playwrights rank him as one of the giants of the theatre, comparable in status and influence with Ibsen, Strindberg, Chekhov, Shaw, and O'Neill.

Pirandello radically reformed the Italian theatre by giving it the power and substance to challenge the period's enervating supremacy of opera. More saliently, he revolutionized the presentation of human character on the stage with his masterly fusion of illusion and reality. His dramatic explorations of man's innate multiple identity and its concomitant "mask and face" technique have led directly into the antinaturalistic styles of much of our contemporary theatre.

How Man appears to others, and above all to himself, in an indifferent, insecure world is a major and recurring theme in most of Pirandello's plays. As a principal and lifelong concern of the author, he wrote: "We believe ourselves one person, but it is true to say that we are many persons, many according to the possibilities of being which exist within us. We are one for this and another for that person—always diverse and yet filled with the illusion that our personality is always the same for all."

Sicilian by birth (June 28, 1867), Luigi Pirandello began his literary career as a poet, and by the time he turned to the stage, he had already established himself as a major novelist (*The Late Mattia Pascal*), short-story writer, and critic.

It was in December, 1910, that Pirandello had his first encounter with the professional theatre when two of his short plays, *The Vice* and *Sicilian Limes,* were successfully presented in Rome. It was a significant and prophetic beginning of a new career for the forty-three-year-old author who, possibly unaware of it at the time, was to devote most of the rest of his life to writing plays.

An intensive writer, he seemed to have discovered in drama the perfect cathartic outlet for the turmoil of his own personal life. After the family's sulfur mines had collapsed along with their fortune, Pirandello's wife, for some years afflicted by hysteria, developed a mental illness bordering on insanity, and until her death in 1918, Pirandello devoted himself to her care.

From 1918 onward, he sought pacification from his domestic tragedies by dedicating himself to a prodigious output of plays, but it wasn't until 1921 that he became an international celebrity with the production of *Six Characters in Search of an Author.* During the years that followed, he wrote thirty full-length and thirteen short plays, of which the best known in this country are: *Six Characters in Search of an Author; Right You Are if You Think You Are; The Man with the Flower in His Mouth; As You Desire Me;* and *Enrico IV.*

Respected by his actors and associates as a born craftsman with an acute and remarkable awareness of the demands of the stage, Pirandello had an abiding and practical love for the theatre that never diminished. In 1925, he established (in association with his eldest son) his own art theatre in Rome at the Teatro Odescalchi and, later, undertook extensive and vigorous tours with his company in Europe and America. The venture was an artistic success but a financial disaster in which Pirandello himself lost a large sum of money. Yet this did not lessen his dedication to the theatre, and he continued to write plays until his death in 1936.

In *Bellavita,* originally produced in Milan, in 1927, Pirandello once more stresses that there is a mask over life that often causes droll comedy through the inconsistencies and incongruities between that mask and the face. The new and expert translation of *Bellavita* that appears in these pages was made in 1964 by the American novelist and short-story writer William Murray.

Although scores of professional critics, theatre historians, and academicians have attempted to characterize Pirandello's style of drama, it is most effectively defined, perhaps, in his own words: "A serious theatre, mine. It demands the complete participation of the moral-human entity. It is certainly not a comfortable theatre. A difficult theatre, a dangerous theatre. Nietzsche said that the Greeks put up white statues against the black abyss, in order to hide it. I, instead, topple them in order to reveal it. . . . It is the tragedy of the modern spirit."

By coincidence or historic design, Luigi Pirandello, master dramatist, entered the realm of the theatre in 1910 with two short plays; in 1937, the last of his works to be premiered in his native land also happened to be a short play, *I'm Dreaming, But Am I?*

SCENE. *A sitting room between* CONTENTO's *private living quarters and his professional studio. At rear there is an entrance opening into a corridor; at right, an exit leads into the lawyer's apartments; at left, two exits—one into a clients' waiting room, the other into the lawyer's office.*

As the curtain rises, the CLERK *is admitting the notary* DENORA. *The* CLERK *is young, shabbily dressed, but with a pretense at elegance. He has a small, sleek head on a long, scrawny neck.* DENORA *is fat, about forty, with thinning reddish hair and a large, purplish, pimpled face.*

CLERK. Make yourself comfortable in here, sir.

DENORA (*menacingly, barely able to control his agitation*). Will I have to wait long?

CLERK. Well, a few minutes, I'm afraid. But I'll tell Mrs. Contento you're here. (*He starts for the door at right.*)

DENORA (*detaining him*). No, never mind. What's she got to do with it?

CLERK. To keep you company.

DENORA. Thanks a lot! I can wait by myself!

CLERK. The lawyer's orders, sir.

DENORA (*shouting*). And I say the hell with them! (*Then, checking himself, contritely.*) I mean, I don't want to inconvenience her.

CLERK. No, not at all. You see, I have reason to believe that she herself—

DENORA. —wants to keep me company?

CLERK. Yes, because she said—

DENORA. —she wants to have a good laugh on me like everyone else? I see!

CLERK. No. How can you think that, sir? She told me to notify her as soon as you arrived, that's all. But here she is. (MRS. CONTENTO *enters from the door at right. She is about thirty, pretty, with a straight little nose and bright eyes. The* CLERK *exits at left.*)

MRS. CONTENTO. My dear Denora, so we've come to this, have we?

DENORA. For God's sake, Mrs. Contento, leave me alone or I'll go out of my mind!

MRS. CONTENTO (*taken aback*). Why? What did I say?

DENORA. Nothing, nothing. But I beg you not to ask me anything! I want you to bear in mind that if your husband's studio is full of clients and he's now doing so well, he owes much of his success to me! If I close up my office and go bury myself in the country, leaving you all without a notary public, he'll suffer as much as anyone. That's what I want you to keep in mind!

MRS. CONTENTO. I don't understand why you speak to me this way.

DENORA. Because I can tell from the way you came in here that you too want to bask in the spectacle of my exasperation.

MRS. CONTENTO. Not at all. You're not being fair to me, Mr. Denora. (*At this point,* CONTENTO *enters from his office. He is about forty, thin, all legs, with clear eyes that dart continually about as if he hears himself being called on all sides. He has a wide, wet, smiling mouth; gray hair worn rather long, bristly in front; and an abstracted, rather absent-minded expression.*)

CONTENTO. What is it? What is it, my dear fellow?

MRS. CONTENTO. I don't know! I came in to keep him company, just as you told me to—

CONTENTO. I still have so many people in there!

MRS. CONTENTO. —and he took offense.

CONTENTO. What? What?

MRS. CONTENTO. A suspicion—I'm sorry, my dear Denora—it really isn't worthy of you.

CONTENTO. A suspicion? What suspicion?

MRS. CONTENTO. He thinks we're all making fun of him, even us.

CONTENTO. Making fun?

DENORA. I didn't say that!

MRS. CONTENTO. You said we all want to enjoy the spectacle—

DENORA. Yes, that it amuses you. There. That's all!

CONTENTO. But where, for the love of God, did you ever get such an idea? How can you even think such a thing?

DENORA. Because it's only natural! Only natural! Do you think I don't know? This is the frightening thing, that I can see myself how ridiculous my position is. I'd be the first to have myself a good laugh on anyone else, even my own brother, if he were in the same position! The fact that I'm the victim, while I'd be among the first to laugh at anyone else—well, that's what is driving me crazy! Yes, crazy!

CONTENTO. But I'm here to help you, my dear Denora! To rescue you from this state of mind that distresses me so, as it distresses everyone who is fond of you and esteems you for the fine gentleman you are! Come, come. I've already sent for that bore in order to get rid of him for you. He'll be here soon. So you wouldn't have to wait alone, I asked my wife . . .

DENORA. Please forgive me, Mrs. Contento. Try to understand. I'm obsessed with this thing.

MRS. CONTENTO. Of course. I understand perfectly.

CONTENTO. Let me handle it. I'll have you free of him in a jiffy. Just as soon as he gets here. Yes, indeed! I've already arranged for him to be shown right in. You'll wait in there—(*Indicating the exit at right*)—with my wife, and I'll talk to him, as we agreed.

DENORA. The best school in Naples, tell him that!

CONTENTO. Leave it to me! I understand everything. And keep calm. (*He exits the way he came in.*)

MRS. CONTENTO. I don't think you ought to admit right away that the boy is your son. I'd at least express a few doubts. That's what I told my husband.

DENORA. No, no! It doesn't matter! Even if he weren't, it makes no difference! I admit everything! I accept everything!

MRS. CONTENTO. But why? If you could prove he wasn't yours—

DENORA. How can I prove it? It's not only the father, my dear lady, who can never know for sure. Not even the mother herself could say with any certainty whether her own son was fathered by her husband or her lover. It's all guesswork.

MRS. CONTENTO. Does the boy resemble you?

DENORA. So they say. Sometimes I think he does, sometimes I think he doesn't. You can't put much trust in resemblances. Anyway, as I said, I don't want to argue the point. I'm ready to do everything: adopt him, change my will in his favor, anything! I don't have anyone else. And I don't care any more about anything! I want to get rid of him—*the father,* I mean—at any cost! But the sound of money falls

on deaf ears with that man, and it won't do any good to try that tack. He's never acted for profit. That's why I'm so desperate.

MRS. CONTENTO. It's really unheard of!

DENORA (*leaping to his feet*). Unheard of! Unheard of! And it had to be just my luck to have to deal with a husband like him!

MRS. CONTENTO. Why do they call him Bellavita? It must be some kind of nickname, isn't it?

DENORA. Yes, given him out of envy. People used to pass in front of his shop and see it always full of clients, his wife sitting behind the counter like a great lady, and they'd say, "Eh, *bella vita! The good life!*" They've been calling him that ever since.

MRS. CONTENTO. I was by the shop only yesterday. It was pitiful. Those beautiful white counters and the coffee machine that used to be so bright and shiny, why you wouldn't recognize the place! Everything's yellow and dirty. And the sad, faded curtains, one pink, the other blue, stretched across those dried-up cakes and moldy pies! No one goes there any more. Was it you who kept the shop going for him?

DENORA. Me? Certainly not! Not a word of truth in it, if that's what you heard! He wouldn't even let his wife accept the time of day from me. He'd let me pay for an occasional coffee, when I'd show up there with my friends, because it would have been unnatural for him not to. But I'm sure he hated it.

MRS. CONTENTO. It seems hard to explain.

DENORA. What is there to explain, Mrs. Contento? Some things just can't be explained.

MRS. CONTENTO. How can anyone be like that?

DENORA. When we don't want to know something—it's easy—we pretend we don't know it. And if we're more concerned with fooling ourselves than others, believe me, it's exactly, exactly as if we don't really know. . . . He's even overflowing with gratitude for me.

MRS. CONTENTO. Gratitude?

DENORA. Oh, yes. For the way I stood up for him, from the beginning of the marriage.

MRS. CONTENTO. Yes, he was sickly-looking, always in poor health. . . . I don't know why she married him. She came from a good family.

DENORA. Fallen on hard times.

MRS. CONTENTO. I can't imagine what she saw in him.

DENORA. She used to accuse him of poor judgment, of being tactless with their customers, even of stupidity.

MRS. CONTENTO. Well, he really is stupid. . . .

DENORA. You're telling me?—The scenes they'd have!—Well, you understand, I was in the habit of dropping in with my friends for a coffee. . . . I'm a peaceful type—it used to upset me. . . . It began with my trying to make peace between them and . . .

MRS. CONTENTO. . . . peace today, a friend the next, and eventually . . .

DENORA. Unfortunately, these things do happen.

MRS. CONTENTO. Unfortunately. She was so pretty! I can still see her, sitting behind the counter, smiling and so full of life, with her pert little nose all powdered white and that red-silk shawl with the yellow moons on it around her neck, those big golden hoops in her ears and the dimples she had when she smiled! She was adorable! (*At this description of her,* DEN-ORA *begins to sob with his stomach, then, all choked up with emotion, to wheeze through his nose. He raises a hand to his eyes.*) Poor Denora, you really did love her!

DENORA. Yes, yes, I did! And I hate this man because it wasn't enough for him to poison my life; now he has to poison my grief at losing her! And you know how? By reveling in it! Yes. As if he were providing it for me to feed on, to suck on, like a mother offering her breast to her baby! That's why I hate him! Because he won't let me do what I want, to mourn her by myself! You can understand, can't you, the disgust I feel in having to share even her death with him? He came to see me before the funeral, with the boy, to tell me that he'd ordered *two* wreaths, one for him and one for me, and that he'd arranged for them to be placed next to each other on the hearse. He said they talked.

MRS. CONTENTO (*bewildered*). Who talked?

DENORA. Those two wreaths. Next to each other like that. He said they talked louder than words. He must have seen the hate in my eyes. He threw himself on my neck, crying and wailing at the top of his lungs, and he began shouting and begging me not to abandon him, for heaven's sake, and to have consideration and pity for him, because only I could understand him, because only I had had the same loss to bear. I swear to you, Mrs. Contento, that his eyes, as he spoke, were those of a madman, or I'd have been tempted to push him away and boot him out of my sight.

MRS. CONTENTO. I can't believe it! I just can't believe it!

DENORA. I can still feel the horror of touching him. I had to take him by the arms—they were like sticks under the furry cloth of that black-dyed suit of his —and free myself of that desperate grip he had around my neck! Funny, isn't it, how at certain times you notice little things that stay with you forever? There he was, crying on my neck like that. I turned toward the window, as if looking for a way out, I suppose, and somebody had traced a cross in the dust on the windowpanes. The whole sad business of this ruined bachelor life of mine, it was summed up for me in that cross, on the panes of that window, on that cloudy sky beyond. Ah, Mrs. Contento, that cross, those dirty windowpanes, I'll *never* get them out of my sight!

MRS. CONTENTO. Come now, my poor Denora, calm yourself! You'll see, my husband will—(*She is interrupted by the* CLERK, *who enters hurriedly.*)

CLERK. He's here! He's here!

DENORA (*leaping to his feet*). He is?

MRS. CONTENTO. Let's go in there. (*She points off right.*) Come on.

CLERK. Yes, madam. Your husband asked me to usher him in here.

MRS. CONTENTO. Let's go, then. Let's go.

DENORA. I could kill him! I could kill him! (*He follows* MRS. CONTENTO *out right. The* CLERK, *meanwhile, has exited through the rear door, and he returns a few moments later, followed by* BELLAVITA. BELLA-VITA *is almost disgustingly thin, waxily pale, with keen, smitten, staring eyes. He is attired in strictest mourning, in an old furry-looking suit, recently dyed, and he wears an old black wool scarf about his neck, its ragged strands hanging down before and behind.)*

CLERK. Make yourself comfortable, sir. The lawyer will be right with you. (*The* CLERK *exits again through the first door at left.* BELLAVITA *remains standing, motionless, spectral, in the middle of the room for a very long moment. Finally, with a sigh, he sits down on the edge of a chair beside a small table. After a minute,* CONTENTO *enters from the other door at left.)*

CONTENTO. My dear Bellavita! Here I am at last!

BELLAVITA (*jumping to his feet at the sound of his voice*). You're much too kind, sir! (*Immediately overcome by his sudden ascent into space, he covers his eyes with one hand and leans with the other for support against a table.*)

CONTENTO (*rushing to him*). My dear Bellavita, what is it, what is it?

BELLAVITA. Nothing, sir . . . sheer joy . . . when I heard your voice . . . I—I got up so quickly and . . . I'm so weak, sir, so weak. But it's nothing, it's all over now.

CONTENTO. Poor Bellavita! Yes, I can tell, you're very run down. Sit here, sit here, my dear man!

BELLAVITA. After you, after you. Please!

CONTENTO. Yes, of course. I'll sit here. Now then, I sent for you so we could resolve—or rather—so we could *finish resolving,* so to speak, a most painful and delicate situation.

BELLAVITA. What situation? Mine?

CONTENTO. Well, yes. Yours, the boy's, and the notary's. Both painful and delicate, my dear Bellavita. The—the—how shall I say it?—the *misfortune* you've both endured—yes, that's what I mean—this misfortune did, to some extent, suddenly resolve—brutally—at one blow—most painfully—but from a certain point of view—well, you could say, almost surgically!—you never wanted to—well, anyway, let's come to the point!

BELLAVITA. Yes, sir. Because I, you know —(*Tapping his forehead with one finger*) —my—my mind isn't what it was. Of this whole speech you've just been so kind as to make to me, I've understood absolutely nothing.

CONTENTO. I see, I see. Well then, I'll put it another way. It's going to be a great relief to you, my dear Bellavita. A great relief, which I know you'll welcome. You need it, I can see that. You need it as much as food.

BELLAVITA. Yes, sir. I haven't eaten for days, I can't sleep. I sit all day on one of those iron stools in my café.

CONTENTO. Yes, well—that's what I—

BELLAVITO. As if it weren't really me sitting there, you know?

CONTENTO. Of course!

BELLAVITA. As if somebody else had just propped me up and left me there, like a puppet.

CONTENTO. Now let's discuss—

BELLAVITA (*cutting him off with a gesture*). Wait a minute. They won't come.

CONTENTO (*confused*). What won't come?

BELLAVITA. The words, sir. And you want to discuss something with me. . . . I'm—I'm half deaf, half paralyzed. Let me try to get hold of myself a little. It's been so long since I talked to anyone! Now that I have the chance . . . Oh, you've no idea, sir, no idea what my days are like, sitting there in the café, at the table! I run my fingers over it like this, fingers full of dust. There's nothing but dust in my café any more!

CONTENTO. Well, it's a windy spot, our town! The dust blows all over the place.

BELLAVITA. And the flies. The flies eat me alive. I can hear them buzzing even in my head. I find myself shooing them away even when they aren't there. And I sit with my back to the counter, so I won't have to look at my scales. There's a single brass weight on one of the plates, the last sale my poor wife ever made—a *kilo* of sweets to the lawyer Giumìa. (*His thin face wrinkles up into a horrible grimace, and he begins to cry. He takes a black handkerchief out of his pocket and raises it to his eyes.*)

CONTENTO. My dear Bellavita, if you keep on like this, before the month is out you'll be going to join the poor soul!

BELLAVITA. If only I could! If it weren't for Michelino!

CONTENTO. Ah!—At last—that's it— Michelino!—You see, I sent for you—

BELLAVITA (*quickly, apprehensively*). —to discuss Michelino?

CONTENTO. I imagine the boy must be a great worry to you.

BELLAVITA. If you could see him . . .

CONTENTO. Naturally! Left motherless . . .

BELLAVITO. If you could see what's become of him, the poor little thing, in just a few days . . . All I can do is weep, weep, weep. . . .

CONTENTO. Well now, isn't that grand! I mean, I have a proposition to make to you, my dear Bellavita.

BELLAVITA. A proposition? Concerning Michelino?

CONTENTO. Exactly. On behalf of the notary.

BELLAVITA. What proposition?

CONTENTO. I'm getting to it.

BELLAVITA. But excuse me, the notary felt he had to come to—

CONTENTO. I'm his lawyer.

BELLAVITA. So much the worse!

CONTENTO. But I'm only acting for him as a friend in this matter.

BELLAVITA. That's what I mean! He goes to you and asks you to make a proposal concerning Michelino? Couldn't he come to me directly? (*Becoming excited:*) Good Lord, Mr. Contento—

CONTENTO. Don't get so excited until you hear what I have to say!

BELLAVITA. Why shouldn't I get excited? If the notary had to go to you—

CONTENTO. But I'm also your friend and—

BELLAVITA. That's very nice of you. My friend? No, that's too kind. My benefactor! But you see, I—oh—I'm—I'm fainting—I'm fainting. . . .

CONTENTO. No, no! Come now! What the devil! Listen to me!

BELLAVITA. Oh, God, I think you must be trying to take away even the air I breathe. . . .

CONTENTO. By proposing something for the boy's own good?

BELLAVITA. On behalf of the notary?

CONTENTO. Who's always been very fond of him—you can't deny that—and is *still* very fond of him!

BELLAVITA (*his eyes suddenly full of tears*). Really? But then why, why—

CONTENTO (*raising his hands to cut him off*). Let me finish, for God's sake! Mr. Denora proposes to send the boy to boardingschool, in Naples.

BELLAVITA. Send the boy to Naples?

CONTENTO. The best boardingschool in Naples.

BELLAVITA (*staring at him*). What for?

CONTENTO. What do you mean, what for? To give him a better education, of course.

BELLAVITA. In Naples?

CONTENTO. He'd pay all the expenses, that's understood. All you have to do is give your consent.

BELLAVITA. Give my consent? What are you saying?

CONTENTO. Well, why not?

BELLAVITA. Consent to send the boy away? My dear sir, what are you saying?

CONTENTO. That's what the notary proposes.

BELLAVITA. But why?

CONTENTO. I told you why.

BELLAVITA. But the boy is going to school *here*. He's doing very well. And the notary knows that. Send him to Naples? And what about me? Ah, so the notary doesn't take me into account at all any more!

CONTENTO. Who said so?

BELLAVITA. I'd die without the boy, sir! I'm dying now, dying of a broken heart, abandoned by everyone and I don't know why! What have I done to the notary that I should be treated like this, not only by him, but by all his friends?

CONTENTO. No one's mistreating you. You're just imagining it.

BELLAVITA. Then why doesn't he come to the café any more?

CONTENTO. Because he hasn't the time.

BELLAVITA. He always used to have the time.

CONTENTO. And now he doesn't.

BELLAVITA. Now that I've been overwhelmed by misfortune he doesn't have the time? And to top it all off, he wants to take the boy away from me?

CONTENTO. You won't let me finish!

BELLAVITA. What is there to finish? You shouldn't even have begun! You listen to me, sir! It's not true, you know, that he cares about Michelino's education. No. It's something else! And I know what it is! What? He talks about expenses? Him? He dares to talk about expenses to me? To me? When did I ever ask him for a cent to help bring the boy up? I did it, alone!

And the boy has had nothing but the best! As long as I live, he'll never have anything but the best, you tell him that! I can't send him to Naples. Even if I could, I wouldn't. Why does the notary force you to ask me such a thing? Was he afraid I'd show up with the boy to beg him for something?

CONTENTO. Such a suspicion is not only unworthy of the notary, but of *yourself!*

BELLAVITA. I'm sorry, but why does he do this, then? Doesn't he even want to see the boy any more? He's been avoiding me for some time now. You think the suspicion is unworthy of me?

CONTENTO. Unworthy and absurd!

BELLAVITA. Oh, no, not absurd! I understood, you know. I understood quite well that my visits to the notary were no longer welcome. I kept control of myself, bit my tongue not to scream, and I stayed out of sight. I'd send Michelino in to see him and I'd sit down, quiet as a mouse, in the anteroom—you know, where that green armchair is? Right next to it. You know how it is when you cry and you feel like giving your nose a good hard blow? Well, do you know how I'd blow mine? Very, very softly, so I wouldn't disturb him, so he wouldn't hear me. But you know how it is: the more you hold yourself in, the more you get to feeling sorry for yourself at the shabby treatment you get for all your trouble! I wouldn't want to cry and I'd find myself crying all the harder! I'm melting, melting in a pool of tears, my dear sir!

CONTENTO. That's enough now! Let's get to the point! I'm going to tell you once and for all, my dear Bellavita, what I have to say, and that will be the end of it!

BELLAVITA. Yes, sir. Fine. Speak out. I'm all ears.

CONTENTO. I'd like to ask you first, since I can see it isn't going to be easy, to please do your very best to understand without forcing me to be too specific. That's all. For your sake more than mine.

BELLAVITA. For my sake? What is it? Tell me what's happened!

CONTENTO. Nothing's happened! Except what *had* to happen. You know what I mean, I'm sure.

BELLAVITA. You're referring to my wife's death?

CONTENTO. Exactly. And now you ought to set your heart at rest!

BELLAVITA. How, sir?

CONTENTO. Make the sign of the Cross and put all this behind you!

BELLAVITA. Make the sign of the Cross? Behind me?

CONTENTO. I don't mean that you should stop mourning your wife. Mourn her all you want! I mean that your—what should I call it?—your forgive—yes, that's it—your *spirit of forgiveness,* my dear Bellavita, is a bit exaggerated in regard to the notary.

BELLAVITA. Forgiveness?

CONTENTO. Yes. It weighs, it weighs very heavily. Try to bear that in mind.

BELLAVITA. What do you mean, *spirit of forgiveness?* I'm sorry, I don't understand.

CONTENTO. For God's sake, try!

BELLAVITA. Is it because I've always respected him?

CONTENTO. Yes, partly! Too much!

BELLAVITA. Too much respect?

CONTENTO. And because you insist on keeping it up!

BELLAVITA. He doesn't want me to?

CONTENTO. No, he doesn't want you to!

BELLAVITA. It weighs on him?

CONTENTO. Yes, of course. Because the relationship, you see, had some substance and was tolerable, my dear Bellavita, while your beloved wife was alive. But now that, alas, she has been taken from us—well, be reasonable!—you can't expect the notary to go on being bound to you by your common grief, by the loss you've both sustained!

BELLAVITA. Why not?

CONTENTO. Because it's ridiculous!

BELLAVITA. Ridiculous?

CONTENTO. *Ridiculous! Ridiculous!* I can't understand why you don't see it!

BELLAVITA. And it weighs on him, you said?

CONTENTO. The death of your wife has altered the situation, my dear Bellavita! Try to understand! If the notary grieves for her, and he grieves for her, all right—

BELLAVITA. Oh, he does?

CONTENTO. But of course he does! And if he wants to mourn her—and he mourns her, all right, in his heart—there's no reason, let's be fair, *why he should mourn her with you!*

BELLAVITA. Because he's afraid of looking ridiculous? I see. I respect him and he's afraid of looking ridiculous! The man who for over ten years made me the laughingstock of the whole town, now *he's* afraid of looking ridiculous!

CONTENTO. The situation—try to understand!

BELLAVITA. I understand, I understand. And you can't imagine how sorry it makes me! So that's the reason he wants to wash his hands of me and Michelino!

CONTENTO. Not wash his hands of you!

BELLAVITA. Get rid of us! Get the boy off to Naples, and me—I'm supposed to pass him in the street and pretend I don't see him, pretend I don't know him, isn't that right? So people won't laugh if I tip my hat to him. . . . I understand, I understand. . . . Fine, Mr. Contento. Tell him, then, that as for going to see him at home, I won't go any more, either alone or with the boy. All right? . . . But as for showing my respect, well, as for that—I'm sorry —I can't do without that. Tell him so.

CONTENTO. What do you mean?

BELLAVITA. Ah, my respect for him—can he *stop* me from expressing it? I always respected him, I was always correct, at a time when it brought me nothing but shame and mortification. And now, this very moment, all of a sudden he expects me to stop paying my respects to him? Impossible, my good sir! I'll *always* respect him, I'll *always* honor him. I have no choice. Tell him so.

CONTENTO. Why? Simply out of spite?

BELLAVITA. No, what spite? Excuse me, but he himself shows me how to avenge myself and he expects me not to profit by it? (*At this point* DENORA *enters in a rage from the door at right, followed by* MRS. CONTENTO.)

DENORA. Oh, so you intend to get even with me, is that it?

BELLAVITA. Not I, Mr. Denora! I never wanted any such thing!

DENORA. You just admitted it to him!

BELLAVITA. Only because now you want me to, Mr. Denora! All *I* want to do is *respect* you, as I've always done, that's all!

DENORA. But it's to get even with me!

BELLAVITA. No, sir! It's genuine respect! But you're turning it into a vendetta by trying to stop me!

DENORA. *But I don't want your respect!*

BELLAVITA. You may not want it, but I want you to have it! I'm sorry!

DENORA. Oh, you do, do you!

BELLAVITA. How do you expect me to stop? I've always respected you.

DENORA (*trembling*). I warn you, Bellavita! I'll give you a good kick in the pants!

BELLAVITA. Go ahead, go ahead, Mr. Denora! You kick me! I'll let you!

DENORA. Watch out, Bellavita, or I'll really do it!

BELLAVITA. Go ahead, go ahead! I told you I'd let you, and I'll even *thank* you for it!

DENORA. Oh, you will, will you? (*He hurls himself furiously at* BELLAVITA.) You dirty rotten swine!

CONTENTO (*holding him off*). No, for God's sake! What are you doing, Denora?

BELLAVITA. Go on, go on! Let him kick me! I couldn't ask for anything better! And not only here, but out in the street! That's where he's got to do it! Come on! More! *More!* And I'll thank him in public!

DENORA (*raising his cane*). Get him out of here! Get him out of here or by the Madonna I'll break every bone in his head! (*Attracted by the shouting, seven or eight of the lawyer's* CLIENTS *rush from the first door at left. Among them is* MR. GIORGINO.)

CLIENTS. What is it? What is it? What's going on? The notary? With Bellavita?

MR. GIORGINO (*to* BELLAVITA, *kindly*). He's been kicking you?

BELLAVITA. Yes, you see? Because I want to *respect* him, he kicks me around!

DENORA. That's not true! He wants revenge! *Revenge!*

BELLAVITA. For what? For all the affection and kindness I've always shown him? You can *all* testify to that!

DENORA (*frantically*). Yes, yes, but that's *how* you revenge yourself . . . !

BELLAVITA. By repaying him with affection for all the harm he's done me?

DENORA. Yes, yes! I'm drowning in your stinking kindness!

BELLAVITA. Because it makes him look ridiculous? Oh, what a relief! What a relief, my friends! I can laugh, I can laugh again! All I've done is cry, and now I can laugh! Laugh and make everyone else laugh, too, for all the tears I've shed over this ingrate! Ah, what a relief!

CLIENTS. Why? What does he mean? What's he talking about? Has he gone crazy?

BELLAVITA. Revenge, the *new revenge* of all betrayed husbands! Don't you see? Mr. Giorgino, you, too! (*The other* CLIENTS *burst out laughing.*)

MR. GIORGINO. *Me?* What are you insinuating?

BELLAVITA. Yes, step out, step out! You, too! Come forward, Mr. Giorgino!

MR. GIORGINO. Me? What are you talking about? you . . .

BELLAVITA. Come on, Mr. Giorgino, *everyone* knows!

MR. GIORGINO (*furious, hurling himself at* BELLAVITA). Know what? you . . .

BELLAVITA. Come on! Don't pretend you don't know anything! Don't you hear? They're *all* laughing! And you know it, too! Come off it! Horns, the *same* horns I wear! We're a couple of goats, you and I! But don't let it bother you, it's nothing! You want revenge? *Worship, worship,* start worshipping, start bowing in public in front of your wife's lover! Watch, here's what I do with Mr. Denora! Watch, watch! Like this! You bow, you smile, you take off your hat—like this!

DENORA (*furiously*). Stop it! Stop it, Bellavita, or I'll kill you! (*He starts for him but is held back.*)

BELLAVITA. Yes, yes, kill me, *kill me!* I'll *bow,* I'll *scrape,* I'll *kneel!*

DENORA (*freeing himself*). Let me go! Let me go or I'll really kill him! (*Having freed himself,* DENORA *runs out, amid gales of laughter.*)

BELLAVITA. There, you see? He runs away! Laugh, laugh away! Let him run, and you all keep laughing! And now I'll go after him! Down every street, *nods, bows, curtsies,* until he hasn't a moment's peace! I'll go to my tailor! I'll order myself a mourning suit, something spectacular, and follow him around in it, impaled on my grief, two steps behind him all the way! He stops, I stop. He goes on, I follow. He the body and I the shadow! The shadow of his remorse! My new profession! Let me out! Let me out! (*He pushes his way to the door amid general joking and laughter.*)

CURTAIN

WHITE LIES

Peter Shaffer

White Lies was first presented by Alexander H. Cohen at the Ethel Barrymore Theatre, New York, on February 12, 1967, with the following cast:

SOPHIE: BARONESS LEMBERG Geraldine Page   FRANK   Donald Madden
TOM   Michael Crawford

Directed by John Dexter
Scenery and Costumes by Alan Tagg
Lighting by Jules Fisher

The play happens in the Fortune Teller's parlour of Sophie, Baroness Lemberg, on the promenade of a run-down seaside resort on the south coast of England. The time is the present, around six o'clock in the evening; mid-September.

IN ITS PERENNIAL pitch for box-office appeal, the theatre frequently yields logical mentation and creative concepts to waves of incredible reasoning. To cite one memorable philosophism: a prominent actress's assertion that she kept her distance from Shakespeare simply because she couldn't envision herself portraying characters written for male players. Obviously, that precious morsel never was digested by some of the lady's distinguished colleagues, including: Lynn Fontanne, Katharine Cornell, Helen Hayes, Judith Anderson, Blanche Yurka, Katharine Hepburn, Dame Peggy Ashcroft, Margaret Leighton, Flora Robson, Dame Edith Evans, Julie Harris, Siobhan McKenna, Dorothy Tutin, Claire Bloom, Rosemary Harris, or Irene Worth—all of whose frequent encounters with Shakespeare scarcely put a dent in their femininity or artistry.

It is a truism, of course, that most, if not all, of the Bard's women originally were limned by men, but this was in deference to an Elizabethan decretum forbidding women to appear on stage. Yet, genius and seer that he was, Shakespeare focused an eye on the future: by endowing his heroines with ample feminine sorcery, he perpetuated their irresistibility to leading ladies of oncoming centuries. A consummate man of the theatre, he undoubtedly also realized that casting absonant to a play's dimensions and demands tends to adumbrate its context and lessen its designed effect.

This preamble leads us, perhaps somewhat circuitously, to Peter Shaffer's *White Lies,* with its centerpiece of a challenging, almost classically proportioned role for a leading woman. Paired with the author's exceedingly popular *Black Comedy* during the 1967 Broadway season, critically it was relegated to the position of a consort whose presence was essential, though not overly welcome, to round out the evening.

To this admittedly partial observer, *White Lies* was shunted into its disproportionate position not so much because of script deficiencies, but rather by a lackluster production. With all due respect to the genuinely talented Geraldine Page, who originated the role of Sophie, Baroness Lemberg, this, as the saying goes, was not her dish of tea. She seemed curiously out of her element in the fortune teller's English seaside atelier, and since Mr. Shaffer's fundamentally introspective play is so dependent upon its central character, without the proper incumbent it comes closer in approach to a superficial lark than to what I assume was the author's original intent. Fortuitously, though, Mr. Shaffer, too, has had the foresight to enrich his heroine with theatrical sorcery enough to bewitch dozens of subsequent leading ladies, and ultimately *White Lies* should find its merited niche in the theatre.

Born in 1926, in Liverpool, England, Peter Shaffer's extraordinary range as a playwright has enabled him to write in many different forms with consistent success. This versatility and his command of craftsmanship have produced such diverse works as: *Five Finger Exercise,* a serious probing of a neurotic family; *The Private Ear* and *The Public Eye,* a tandem bill of sharply contrasting comedies; and *The Royal Hunt of the Sun,* an impressive epic drama dealing with the confrontation between Atahuallpa, the sixteenth-century Sovereign Inca of Peru, and the Spanish Conquistador leader Pizarro.

Black Comedy and *White Lies* represent Mr. Shaffer's most recent contributions to the theatre. The former originally was commissioned and produced by Sir Laurence Olivier for the National Theatre of Great Britain. *White Lies* was written expressly for the New York stage, and, in a reversal of tradition, later will be exported to London's West End.

SCENE. SOPHIE's *parlour is in fact a seedy living room facing the sea. One side of it is almost entirely occupied by a window, in which is spelt out in cheap gold letters (and in reverse, so that it can be read from outside):* BARONESS LEMBERG, PALMISTE. CLAIRVOYANTE. *And in smaller letters:* CONSULTANT TO ROYALTY. *Through this window you can glimpse a rusting iron balustrade, painted resort-green, and the bleak six o'clock sky of a disastrous English September.*

The entrance is on the other side, and leads into a sort of waiting room, partially visible when the door is open. A second door takes you from the waiting room into the streets; over it is suspended a loud bell to warn SOPHIE *if she has a client.*

The room is occupied by dusty, broken-down furniture. The most noticeable article of this is the fortune-telling table: an old chilblained Victorian thing, covered with baize and placed centrally on a rotting carpet. On either side of it stands an equally bunioned Victorian chair—and the same swollen decrepitude extends to the sideboard at the right and the little dressing table at the back.

There are two photographs in the room. One, on a wall, is of a huge man's hand and is clearly visible. The other—larger, and far more important to the action—stands on the side table with its back to the audience and, save for the frame, is invisible. This is a picture of Vassili, SOPHIE's *friend. It stands as far as possible from the other important friend in her life: Pericles the Parakeet—who is equally invisible inside his wire cage by the window. The* BARONESS' *life in this room alternates between these two poles, the photograph and the cage.*

As the curtain rises, the stage is apparently empty. Presently, however, we hear the sound of singing, issuing from one of the high-backed Victorian chairs facing directly upstage: "A Hard Day's Night" sung in a Germanic accent. Presently a hand lifts up and throws a whole fan of playing cards irritatedly onto the table. SOPHIE *has evidently been playing patience. She rises wearily and moves over to the window, through which the light comes drear and thick.*

SOPHIE *is a woman about forty-eight years old. Her appearance is rather neglected; bears the palpable signs of poverty; and is not enhanced by a German fondness for blouses and long woolen skirts. When she speaks her voice is marked by a marked, but never incomprehensible, German accent, and her delivery is mainly swift and vigorous.*

Now she stares through the window in bleak distress.

———

SOPHIE. Look at it. The sea. Like they've poured out ten million cups of tea. No wonder they call it the English Channel. Not one gleam of sunlight in ten days! Not one soul out. Not one miserable holidaymaker walking, jetty to jetty. Nothing but wet sand and rusty iron—and salt on the windows. Grinmouth-on-Sea: Fairyland of the South coast! Grinmouth-on-Tea! (*To the photo*) You hear that, Vassi, I made a joke. (*Sarcastic*) Oh no, don't laugh. We Germans have no sense of humour, it's well known. Only the Greeks are witty, ja ja, I'm sure. . . . (*To the cage*) Perry likes it anyway, don't you? No? . . . Are you sulking too? Well, I don't blame you. Poor little Pericles. Look, I'll tell your fortune—cheer you up? . . . Ja? . . . "You are to fly away on a long, long journey!" (*She laughs.*) . . . Only where would you go, poor little thing? Down the promenade to the chemist? Up to the Fish and Chips Shop? . . . One thing is sure, you'd never find your way home again . . . Never mind—soon, guess what? . . . They'll be putting the lights on. Red and blue lights under a sky like God's used handkerchief . . .

(*Gulls and wind*)

Beloved God, this silence! You would think someone would consult me, if only to ask should they kill themselves! . . . Do you realize there hasn't been an actual human being in this place for six days? And then it was only Mr. Bowler Hat— if you call him human! Next time he comes he'll close us: that's for certain. I haven't paid him a penny rent since June. (*Irritated*) Oh, Vassili, what's funny *now*? I'm in real difficulties, don't you understand? I owe two months' rent, and not a client for days. Is that so amusing? . . . Sometimes I think you're going to stay a child all your life. . . . (*She walks away from the photograph, then stops.*) What's that? . . . How charming! I suppose you think you're talking to one of your upstart ladies from Athens. Well, let me remind you who I am. (*Sharply*) You came here to learn history, well, so—here's some homework for you. My family was great under Maria Theresa. All you had then in your so wonderful Greece were goats. Human goats, my dear, living on curd milk! Alright? . . . (*Exasperated*) Oh, for God's sake now, are you going to sulk? Alright —join Perry. Sulks for the evening: how amusing! . . . I spend my life with a bird and a child, and I don't know which is the more boring! (*She sits. Her tone becomes penitent.*) I'm sorry, Vassi: my tongue runs off with me sometimes. I know how dreary it is for you in the house. Go out and see Irina. I tell you what: why don't you invite her here tomorrow for tea? . . . (*Sweetly*) Ja, of course I mean it! If you spent more time with people of nobility you'd know they always mean what they say. Hypocrisy is for the hoi polloi.

(*The bell clashes.* SOPHIE *is startled.*) Who is it? (*Silence. Then, speaking through the crack:*) One minute, please. Would you mind waiting in the room down the corridor? I'll receive you in a moment! . . . (*Shuts the door.*) Beloved God, there are two of them! Two whole clients. I don't believe it. And on a day like this—it's incredible! . . . That's two whole pounds—think of it. Four if they take the crystal ball. (*Sitting and fixing her hair:*) Well, they're going to take the crystal ball whether they like it or not. . . . I only hope I can remember everything. One gets so rusty! . . . (*To Vassili*) Oh, shut up, you!—that's not funny. . . . Ja, I have news for you. It takes a fraud to call a fraud: that's what I say! You were a liar in your baby carriage, I'm sure of it! . . . (*Addressing herself to the plants:*) Oh, don't droop so—boring middle-class plant! . . . Now—come on everyone!—buck up! A little regality around here, please! . . . Thank you. (*She opens the door.*) I'm ready now. Come in, please, one of you!

(*Enter* FRANK.)

SOPHIE (*very winningly*). Good afternoon. I am the Baroness Lemberg. Welcome and please sit down.

(FRANK *sits, examining her.*)

SOPHIE. Let me give you my scale of charges, mister. One pound for cards alone. Thirty shillings for cards and palms. Two pounds for the crystal ball. The ball of course is by far the most profound. It costs just a little more, it's true— but in this world if one wants the best one has to pay for it, doesn't one? (*She gives him a ravishing smile.*)

(*He returns it, thinly, nodding Yes.*)

SOPHIE. Good: You agree. So—you'll take the ball—ja?

(*He shakes his head: No.*)

SOPHIE. Oh . . . Which do you want then, please?

FRANK. None.

SOPHIE. I don't understand.

FRANK. I like your slogan outside. "Lemberg never lies."

SOPHIE. Thank you.

FRANK. Is it true?

SOPHIE. Of course.

FRANK. Pity.

SOPHIE. I beg your pardon.

FRANK. White lies never harm you. (*He examines the cage.*) Who's this? Your familiar?

SOPHIE. Please?

FRANK. All witches have familiars, don't they? Creepy little animals they share confidences with . . . ! I suppose you'd lose all your mystic powers without him, wouldn't you?

SOPHIE (*still sitting*). Stand away from there, mister, if you please. He's a very sensitive bird. . . .

FRANK. That's alright. I'm an expert on sensitive birds.

SOPHIE (*controlling herself*). Stand away, please, I asked you.

FRANK (*lightly*). Alright . . . Alright . . . !

SOPHIE. Now, mister, what do you want from me?

FRANK. A giggle, Baroness. (*He smiles at her, unexpectedly.*)

SOPHIE. A giggle? What is that?

FRANK. A laugh. A little fun. You look like you enjoy fun yourself. I hope you do.

SOPHIE. If the situation is amusing, sir, I imagine I can manage a—what?—a giggle.

FRANK. I'm glad to hear that, Baroness.

Because that's what I want to consult you about. That's what I want to create right here in this room—an amusing situation.

SOPHIE. Create?

FRANK. Exactly. For him—the boy who's come here with me. You see, him and me, we have this crazy relationship going, like, well, we kid all the time—have the laugh on each other: you know. What they call practical jokes. Some people think it's adolescent. I hope you don't.

SOPHIE. That depends.

FRANK. He's a clever kid—very impressionable. I got him here to see you by telling him you were one of the most famous fortune-tellers in the Western world. Doing a summer season for her health's sake. (*She lowers her eyes and makes modest noises.*) His name's Tom, and he's lead singer with our group. We're called The White Lies. I don't suppose you've ever heard of us.

SOPHIE. On the contrary, you are singing tonight . . . at the Holiday Camp.

FRANK (*impressed*). How d'you know that?

SOPHIE (*laughing*). I saw it on the poster! You're on the same bill with the Lettuce Leaves. That's a pity: they're lousy. However, you have the Serial Numbers to top the bill, and they're excellent.

FRANK. Well, well, a fan!

SOPHIE. A vulgar word, but true. Are you any good?

FRANK. He's good. A real talent. The girls go mad for him. . . .

SOPHIE. And you? Do you sing also?

FRANK. Me? No. I'm their manager.

SOPHIE. Well!

FRANK (*staring at her*). That's my scene, really. I manage.

SOPHIE (*nervous*). How interesting.

FRANK. It can be. It's why I'm here now —to manage this little scene. . . . (*He smiles at her again.*) When we drove into Grinmouth this afternoon and I saw your sign, I thought to myself immediately: Baroness Lemberg, you're the lady for me. In your mysterious parlour I could stage the best joke ever played. I could get him so brilliantly he'd never forget it.

SOPHIE. Really?

FRANK. With your help, of course. And with someone of your fame—consultant to royalty and all that—I wouldn't expect you to do it for nothing. I'm prepared to offer quite a large fee. I'll do anything for a giggle. I really will. (*He gives his smile.*)

SOPHIE (*interested despite herself*). What kind of giggle would this be exactly, mister?

FRANK. Well, it's sort of a game, really. I'd want you to tell him his past, present and future.

SOPHIE. Well, that's my profession, after all.

FRANK. I mean precisely. I don't mean to be rude—I'm sure you're fine on your own—but with me you'd be perfect, you see? No, you don't! In this envelope are the main facts of Tom's life—the things he's told me over the past year. No one else knows them but me. Some of it's pretty lurid stuff. Unhappy childhood. Coal-mining background. Drunken father who beat him and threw his guitar on the fire. It's all here.

SOPHIE. And are you suggesting I use it?

FRANK. Well now, listen. Tom's a bit dim but he's not an idiot. You'll have your work cut out for you to convince him you're genuine. That's where the fun comes in. By the time you've finished telling back to him what's in here, he'll be fish-mouthed, I tell you!

SOPHIE. Mister, I see no joke in this. It's not funny at all.

(*Pause*)

FRANK. To be honest, Baroness, this game isn't entirely for laughs. Mainly, but not entirely. I see it as a sort of warning game. Like I'm using it to say something to him. Do you understand? I mean, if you can get Tom to the point when he really believes you have the power to see his whole life, he'll really believe you when you see something a bit nasty in his future. It'll sort of scare him off a bit. Do you see?

SOPHIE. Scare him off what?

FRANK. A girl. I told you I was interested in sensitive birds. What are they? (*Staring at her necklace, which she is fingering.*)

SOPHIE. Greek worry beads.

FRANK. Are you worried?

SOPHIE. Why should I be?

FRANK. Her name's Helen, and she's the girl in our group. She's got a nice voice—

nothing special, but it can carry a tune and won't sour the cream. I've known her for a couple of years, on and off. Mostly *on,* if you follow me. In fact, these last eighteen months we've had what I'd call a perfect working relationship.

SOPHIE. It sounds very romantic.

FRANK (*lightly*). It isn't romantic: it works, or did till he came along. Tom the Talent, then things began to change. Mostly with her. She found she couldn't resist all that shy working-class charm. The downcast look . . . Yorkshire murmur, very trendy. . . . And when she looked . . . he looked. I don't exactly know what's been going on between them: nothing much I should think at the moment. She's too timid and he's too hung up on his loyalty to me, which he damn well should be by the way. I gave that boy a marvelous bloody chance. And this is his way of repaying me. He thinks I don't know, you know. Well, it's time we undeceived him, isn't it?

SOPHIE. You are in love with this girl?

FRANK. That word's rather got rigor mortis round the edges, hasn't it? (*He laughs.*) Look: the way we are is the way I like it. Cool . . . easy . . . nothing strenuous . . . Anyway, if there's any leaving ever done in my life I do it: do you see? (*Quietly*) Can't you leave them alone? (*She stops fiddling with the beads. He smiles.*) I suppose that's why they're called worry beads. Because they worry other people . . . (*She returns his smile even more uncertainly. A pause*) Well, let's get back to my little game, shall we? By this time you've done his past and present, and as far as he's concerned you're the hottest thing since the Witch of Endor. Right. Now you move in for the grand finale. I want you to have a vision, Baroness. A strange, symbolic vision. Let's set it right. . . . (*Slowly*) You look a little deeper into your crystal ball and you see pink. Shocking pink. Helen's dressing gown. Yeh, that's a good touch—very intimate. You see her wearing it, a pretty blonde girl lying on a bed. Describe the bed. Brass rails top and bottom, and above it, a picture on the wall: some droopy tart holding a lily and flopping her tresses over a stone balcony. It's called *Art Nouveau,* which is French for Sentimental

Rubbish. Helen loves it, of course! Anyway—use it. Establish the room. *My* room. You'll have him goggling! Now look deeper. "Good heavens, there's someone else on the bed! Why, it's you, Tom! And what are you doing, my dear? Gracious me, what a passionate creature you are. You're kissing her neck, running your fingers through her blonde hair. . . . (*Mockingly*) Inside that thin frame of yours is a raging animal, isn't there? . . ." (*He laughs.*) I'd love to be here during that bit. They've never even held hands, I shouldn't think.

SOPHIE. Go on, please.

FRANK (*carefully*). Well now, you'll have to darken it a bit, won't you? . . . Change the mood. I'd thought of something like this. I hope you like it. . . . The door opens. A man stands there. You can't see his face but he's wearing a green corduroy jacket, with black piping round the lapels. That'll get him best, a detail like that. The lovers look up, eyes wide and guilty! Corduroy begins to move towards them. They try to rise, but they're like glued on the bed. Slow motion. Him coming on—them tangled in the sheets—trying to escape. He arrives at the foot of the bed and suddenly—his hand shoots out—like an order!—and what? Why, the girl's whole manner alters at once. She smiles—takes the hand—allows herself to be lifted up, light as a pink feather—high over the brass rails to safety. Our Tom is left alone. . . . And now you see scare in the ball! Tom staring at them both. Them staring back, laughing. Yeh. And what's that now in her hands? Something —it looks like a metal can. Yes, a large metal can. She raises it—upends it—begins to pour from it over the sheets. And then, slowly, Corduroy raises his hands too—a matchbox in the air—strikes it—drops a match onto the bed. (*Very quietly*) Oh, look, the orange! Soft fire like orange squirrels running over the bed, over his legs, over his arms, up onto his head . . . his head bursts into flowers! (*Gesturing dreamily:*) The whole ball becomes orange—flame whirling, raging inside the crystal, obliterating everything. Then slowly it sinks in. Glass pales from orange to pink to grey, it clears. And then you see him. Tom the Talent. Still sitting upright on my bed—mouth open, one arm raised—like a salute to death. The only difference is—the whole figure is made of ash. (*Pause*) Interpret that vision, Baroness. Question it. "Who is this corduroy jacket?" "That's Frank," he'll say. "Well, know something, Tom. Frank and that girl are right together. Leave them alone."

SOPHIE (*softly*). Right together?

FRANK. If you come between them, it'll mean disaster for you. Maybe even death.

SOPHIE. "Right together."

FRANK. "Right together." "Belong together." What's it matter? Just so long as you scare him out of his wits.

SOPHIE. For a giggle.

FRANK. Yes, a joke, that's it. We all of us have different senses of humour, Baroness.

SOPHIE. Who am I?

FRANK. What's that?

SOPHIE. Who am I? Some silly gypsy bitch in a caravan you can buy for a couple of pounds?

FRANK. I was thinking of more than that.

SOPHIE. Four—five—what's the difference? It's what you think, I can see it: the mad old fake, she'll take anything I offer. Well, mister, let me tell you: you're dealing with a very different kind of lady, I assure you!

FRANK. Oh, come off it.

SOPHIE (*thrusts her hand at him*). Look at this! It has held the hand of a Grand Duchess in intimate spiritual communion! It has held those of Governors—Ministers of Justice—Princes of the Blood!

FRANK. Yes, I see them now—thronging the outer salon!

SOPHIE. Very amusing. Look, mister, I'm not mad, you know; there are no Duchesses out there, I know that. Mad spinsters, stinking of mothballs, and old red men with gin in their eyes, begging me to predict just one horse race to make them rich for life. Rubbish people, all of them, boring me to death with their second-rate dreams. Nevertheless, I make adjustment. Other years—other tears! I have to spend my life now casting prophetic pearls before middle-class swine. But one thing always: I may hate them, but I do not cheat them. *Lemberg never lies.*

FRANK. Is that how you think of me,

Baroness? One of the swine?

SOPHIE (*frightened*). Of course not.

FRANK. I hope not. I really do hope not.

SOPHIE. I merely say . . .

FRANK. What do you merely say?

SOPHIE. That if you think I betray my art for a few pounds, you are badly mistaken.

FRANK. Would I be equally mistaken if it was twenty-five pounds?

SOPHIE. Twenty-five?

FRANK. As you said, if you want the best, you've got to pay for it.

SOPHIE. I don't understand. Why don't you just tell him to leave her alone?

FRANK. If I do anything, Baroness, I do it with style. My own style. You do your job right, this'll work a treat.

SOPHIE. He may guess.

FRANK. And even if he does—he'll still get the message. What's your answer? . . . Look—we've kept him waiting long enough. Yes or no?

SOPHIE. Disgusting. It's disgusting! . . .

FRANK. Twenty-five quid.

SOPHIE. Alright!

FRANK. A sensible lady. I'll go and fetch him.

SOPHIE (*disturbed*). No—wait!

FRANK. What?

SOPHIE. Give me a minute, please, I must learn this. . . . (*She picks up the envelope.*)

FRANK. Alright. I'll keep him waiting, tell him how great you were, reading me. But hurry it up.

SOPHIE. Ja, ja . . . I'll call out when I'm ready.

FRANK. OK. (*He goes to the door.*) No tricks now, Baroness. I would hate you to try keeping that money without earning it. When he comes out of this room I want to see scare in his face, like I've never ever seen it. (*He goes out. She stares after him in horror.*)

SOPHIE. Beloved God! Beloved God, beloved God, beloved God! . . . (*Shouting at the photo*) Ja, I know, he's a nut— one more horror, so what? You've seen them before. The world is full of perverts. Business is business, for God's sake. And there's almost half the rent here—just for ten minutes' work! Anyway, what's it matter? He'll be another horror, just you see! A little backstreet nothing who wants to be a singer because he can't do a decent day's work! He'll deserve it. . . . Everyone deserves it! Look, everyone cheats a little, my darling, even your Greek witches. What do you think your famous oracle at Delphi was doing?—one silly cow sitting in a lot of smoke, saying exactly what she was paid to say! Anyway, I tell you once more and that's the end. It is the duty of the aristocracy to maintain itself, no matter what! Now kindly leave me to study these! (*She writes on the fan.*) "Born 1945 . . . Coal mines . . . Mother dead. Father drunkard . . . Guitar." Now! (*She tears open the envelope.*) Look! Do you see? I bet you've never seen so much money in all your life! Think what it means! More Beatle records, more little hats like you were starting the Russian Revolution! And next Sunday, if you are good, a taxi—and not a lousy bus! What do you say? . . . Alright, go to her! Always the same threat—the same threat. If that's the best you can manage—then go to her. See if I care! (*Opening the door:*) Misters! (*Returning*) Go—go—go—go!

(FRANK *returns with* TOM.)

FRANK. Mrs. Lemberg, this is my friend Tom. Tom, this is the Baroness Lemberg. The greatest fortune-teller in the world.

SOPHIE (*modestly*). Please! . . . How do you do?

TOM. Hallo.

FRANK. I've been telling him how incredible you are. I hope you don't mind.

SOPHIE. Such powers as I have, mister, I regard as a gift from the Lord God.

FRANK. Just what I was telling him. It's almost a religious experience, being read by you.

SOPHIE. I do my best to convey the truth as I see it.

FRANK. And lady, you certainly saw it! I was wondering actually if I could sit over here and listen to you read him. I'd be very quiet.

SOPHIE. Oh, no—no. I'm afraid that's quite out of the question. Your emanations would be very disturbing.

FRANK. Couldn't you just ignore my emanations?

SOPHIE. I appreciate your enthusiasm, mister. People of art are always nourished by enthusiasm. All the same, I have a basic rule. One client: one set of emanations.

TOM. Dead right!

FRANK. Very well.

SOPHIE. May I suggest you go for a promenade? When you return in fifteen minutes, you will be refreshed and your friend, I hope, satisfied.

FRANK. Fine. (*To* TOM) Good luck, then. Now that's silly to say. She's gonna tell ya if you got any or not. —But I hope ya have.

SOPHIE. So. Sit down, please. (*He sits.*) Such a flatterer, your friend.

TOM. No, I think he means it. I've never seen him so excited. He's not easily impressed, I can tell you.

SOPHIE. Nor you.

TOM. Me?

SOPHIE. You have disbelieving eyes.

TOM. Oh, yeah?

SOPHIE (*quickly*). You will take the crystal ball of course!

TOM. Will I?

SOPHIE. Of course, my dear. It's more profound. And I can see you deserve the most profound measures.

TOM. Thank you!

SOPHIE (*getting the ball*). You're a musician. (*He is startled.*) Oh, don't worry! Remember, I've just read your friend. I presume you are in the group he manages. It's an easy guess, after all. (*She sets the ball down on the table and uncovers it.*) There. Just a ball of glass. Except, of course, that nothing is *just* anything. Give me something you wear, please. A handkerchief will do. Thank you. You're very pale. Why?

TOM. No sun, I suppose.

SOPHIE (*sitting*). Yes, that can do it . . . Every day I look at the sea and hate it all over again. Not once this year have I seen it blue. I think: that's not a sea—it's a gutter between here and France. Hang your coat up: you're here for a few minutes, after all.

TOM (*rising*). Thanks.

SOPHIE. You like winter best, ja?

TOM. Could be.

SOPHIE. You're cautious with me. You have no need.

TOM. Well, Frank told me not to say anything.

SOPHIE. I think we can discuss the

weather without you thinking me a fraud.

TOM (*smiling*). Yeah, I think so, too. You're right. I love days like this. And seaside towns, too, but only out of season. When no one's there.

SOPHIE. Like here *in* season.

TOM. Oh, much worse! I mean, deserted. Dead, dead of winter, I tell ya. . . . I went to Herne Bay last March. It was so cold the rims of your ears felt like they were being gnawed through. The tide was out and there was snow on the seaweed.

SOPHIE. Snow?

TOM. Yes, it popped when you walked on it. All the sea-gulls were sitting in those little shelters that are for people in the summertime. They looked like rows of old convalescents, huddled down in their coat collars. (*She stares at him. Wind, outside the window*)

SOPHIE. Mister, I do not feel so well this evening. I'm afraid I won't be able to read you.

TOM. You won't?

SOPHIE. I have a headache coming. I feel it. In a minute it will be very painful.

TOM. How do you know?

SOPHIE. Migraine is one of the penalties of divination.

TOM. Oh, yeah?

SOPHIE. You'll have to go. You can wait for your friend in the room down the corridor.

TOM. Yes. Well . . . goodbye.

SOPHIE. Ja. (*He takes his coat and goes to the door. He hesitates.*) You want something?

TOM. No.

SOPHIE. Er . . . Your handkerchief.

TOM. Oh! Yes! (*He comes back to claim it. She hands it to him.*)

SOPHIE. Can that be only no sun—your paleness?

TOM. What else?

SOPHIE. You think I'm a fake. But somewhere in the back of your head, as you walked here tonight, you were thinking something. Well?

TOM. Well, I suppose what you always think about fortune-tellers. You read stories of people going in for a laugh, coming out changed for life.

SOPHIE. You want to be changed for life?

TOM. Sort of, yeah.

SOPHIE. Sit down again.

TOM. No, I'll be off now. . . . I think I'm a bit mad sometimes: honest . . .

SOPHIE. Sit, please.

TOM. No, really—

SOPHIE (*sharply*). Look, mister, what kind of a gentleman are you? You come here to ask my advice. I settle myself to give it. Then without a word of respect you turn your back and go!

TOM. You *told* me to go!

SOPHIE. Don't argue with a Baroness! Why do people know nothing of breeding?

TOM. I'm sorry—

SOPHIE. Then sit! (*Bewildered,* TOM *hangs up his coat again.*) Look, mister. Just for a giggle—you with your paleness —me with my headache—why don't we explore a little the possibility of changing your life? Alright?

TOM (*sitting*). Alright.

SOPHIE. I'll tell you a little your past, a little your present: then your future. (*She stares into the ball.*) Mmm. It's very disturbed. There's much confusion . . . 1945. You were born in 1945?

TOM (*surprised*). Yes!

SOPHIE. It's very ritualistic, the ball. Often first it gives the date of birth, then the place . . . Ja! Exactly! . . . Ah! I see now a place. A dirty street. A little narrow house: working-class. Somewhere in the North, maybe . . . In the background a wheel turning. A coal mine! Ja —a coal village. (TOM *reacts to this, very startled.*) I see I'm not too far from the truth. There's no woman in the house. Your mother is dead, ja? . . . Your father still alive. At least I see a man in working clothes—bad face—brutal face! . . . He ill-treated you? (TOM *stares at her, rivetted.*) And what's this now? I see a child. A little pale face—pale! Eyes frightened. Oh, mister, no! Such a frightened face! . . . He ill-treated you? (*She stares at him. He looks quickly away.*) Beat you, ja? . . . I must look closer here. . . . What's this now? A fire. On it I see something, burning.

TOM (*nervously*). What? . . .

SOPHIE. A guitar. Can it be a guitar? . . . What is it? A symbol perhaps of your music talent? (TOM *rises, terrified.*)

TOM. You saw *that*? . . .

SOPHIE. Very plain.

TOM. No—it's impossible. It *is!*

SOPHIE. I'm sorry. It was absolutely clear.

TOM. You can't. Just—not! . . . My head—it's here!

SOPHIE. And for me, it's there. You can lock nothing away, my dear. Time that happened once for you, happens now for me. . . . Why did he do that? To stop you from being a musician? . . . To hurt you? . . . (TOM, *who has been walking up and down the room, suddenly stops, and stands rigid, struck by something.*) What is it? Perhaps I should stop now?

TOM. No . . . Go on. . . .

SOPHIE. You are upset.

TOM. Doesn't matter.

SOPHIE. I stop.

TOM (*urgently*). No! What else do you see?

(SOPHIE *stares at him, then returns to the ball.*)

SOPHIE. Ah: it's better now. Happiness I think is coming. I see a dot of bright pink, moving towards me. It's a girl. On her a pink dressing gown. Very pretty: a blonde girl. You know her?

TOM. Go on.

SOPHIE. Now I see you. She is running to you—you reach out to stop her—but no: she runs right past you. Beloved God!

TOM. What?

SOPHIE. There's someone else. A man. I can't see his face. He wears a green jacket in corduroy. He puts out his hand. She takes it. They walk away together— leaving you alone.

TOM. Alone.

SOPHIE. Ja. The alone of alone. More alone than I've ever seen it.

TOM (*dead*). So that's the message. "Alone."

SOPHIE. Does this make sense to you, mister?

TOM. Oh, yes. It makes sense. It makes sense. . . . (*More to himself*) What a way to do it!

SOPHIE. To do what, please?

TOM. What a crazy way! To arrange all this—just to let me know—I suppose he set it up as a little joke!

SOPHIE. Who, please?

TOM. Then it was a few quid on the side.

SOPHIE. What d'you mean?

TOM. He's crazy!

SOPHIE. Young mister, are you suggesting I've been bribed?

TOM. No, I'm not suggesting it, I'm *saying* it.

SOPHIE. How dare you? How absolutely bloody dare you?

TOM. Because I absolutely know, that's why. There's only one person I've ever told about my childhood—and that's him.

SOPHIE. My dear, to a professional eye like mine, truth does not have to be told. It is evident.

TOM. I daresay. And what if it isn't the truth?

SOPHIE. What?

TOM (*embarrassed*). What if it's a zonking great lie? Like every word of that story.

SOPHIE. I don't believe it. . . .

TOM. Well, it's true.

SOPHIE. Impossible. You say this to discredit me.

TOM. Come on, why should I do that?

SOPHIE. Look, mister, what I see, I see. Lemberg never lies.

TOM (*gently*). No, well, I'm afraid I do. . . . The bit with the guitar I invented as late as last week.

SOPHIE. You mean your father is not a miner?

TOM. No. He's a very nice accountant, living up in Hoylake.

SOPHIE. And your mother isn't dead?

TOM. Not in the biological sense, no. She likes her game of golf and gives bridge parties every Wednesday.

SOPHIE. But your accent . . .

TOM (*letting it drop*). I'm afraid that's as put on as everything else. I mean, there's no point changing your background if you're going to keep your accent, is there?

SOPHIE. Beloved God! You mean to say . . . you live your whole life like this. One enormous lie from morning to night?

TOM. Yes, I suppose I do.

SOPHIE. Unimaginable.

TOM. Does it worry you?

SOPHIE. Doesn't it worry *you?*

TOM. Yes, sometimes, I guess. But not all the time. I've gotten used to it now— I regard the whole thing as a sort of . . .

SOPHIE. White lie?

TOM. Yes—that's good. A white lie!

SOPHIE. But why? Why? *Why* in heaven's name?

TOM (*with energy*). Because it's an image—and that's what people want! That's all they can cope with—images! And in the pop music world it's got to be working class: I soon found out. No one believes you can sing with the authentic voice of the people if you're the son of an accountant.

SOPHIE. Are you serious?

TOM. Believe me, Baroness: I've worked it out. Look—everyone makes images—*everyone*. It's like no one can look at anyone direct. The way I see it, the whole world's made up of images—images talking at images—that's what makes it all impossible!

SOPHIE. And do your parents know you've worked it out like this? Disowning them completely?

TOM. No. But they might as well. They've virtually disowned me, after all. Dad calls me "minstrel boy" now every time I go home, and mother has a whole bit with her bridge club that I'm in London "studying" music. Studying is a better image than singing in clubs. She can see herself as the mother of a student. Both of them are talking about themselves of course, not me. And I don't blame them. That's what I'm doing, too. All of us . . .

SOPHIE. What a complicated young mister you are.

TOM. Do you think I'm a bit mad?

SOPHIE. Because you choose to be somebody else? No, that's not mad. That's not mad. Not entirely.

TOM. I've never told anyone this before. You must have very special powers.

SOPHIE. Can you really believe that after the way I told your fortune?

TOM. Well, you were pretending then.

SOPHIE. If I were any good, would I need to pretend? Oh, come: it's me to be embarrassed, not you. It serves me right for playing silly games. Let's have a drink—what do you say? Cheer us both up!

TOM. I think it's more than a game to him.

SOPHIE. Why?

TOM. Well, he's always pulling gags, but he's never gone this far before. He can be really marvelous when he wants to. And then there's another side of him —like this . . . Alright, he's guessed about me and Helen—this is still a pretty weird way of telling me, isn't it? Is that all he asked you to say to me? That I was alone.

SOPHIE. Mister, please have a drink. I always take a glass of *retsina* about this hour in the afternoon. It tastes like gasoline, but it can be very encouraging.

TOM. Thank you. I think I will.

SOPHIE. My husband would never let me drink when he was alive. Mind you, he managed a luxury hotel—so he had to be careful.

TOM. It's so strange his coming here like this. What does he think's going on between Helen and me?

SOPHIE. You feel very strongly about this girl?

TOM. Yes.

SOPHIE. And she about you?

TOM. That's part of it.

SOPHIE. Are you afraid of him?

TOM. I don't know.

SOPHIE. Is she?

TOM. Maybe, I think so, yes.

SOPHIE. Well, that makes three of us.

TOM. You don't know what it can be like sometimes in that house.

SOPHIE. You all three live together?

TOM. Yes. Me upstairs, them down. I wake up every morning thinking of her in his bed. When I come downstairs, he's lying there smiling at me.

SOPHIE. Why don't you leave?

TOM. I can't.

SOPHIE. Why not?

TOM. I can't. Isn't it incredible? And every morning I get up and play that part: the coal miner's son frying up breakfast for three, and avoiding her eyes—her great green eyes.

SOPHIE. You mean you haven't told her the truth?

TOM. Why should I? The real me, as they say, isn't a wow with women. Look! Truth's the last thing she wants. She's "in love"—that's what she calls it! She's in love with a working-class boy—even though he doesn't exist. And I'm in love with feelings I see in her eyes—and I know they don't exist. I tell you that's what it's all about—images making noises at images: love—love—love—love— (*Pause*) But God, you should see those eyes. . . .

SOPHIE. Ja?

TOM. They're amazing! Like you said, the alone of alone. Well, these are the green of green.

SOPHIE. Eyes. It's always the eyes.

TOM. I don't know why I'm telling you all this.

SOPHIE. Green or black, it's always the same. (*Rises.*)

TOM. I can stretch out quite still for hours, and imagine I'm lying at the bottom of her eyes.

SOPHIE. With me it was black. Immense black, like the olives. He said to me once: "A Greek proverb for you, Sophie. 'Black eyes are the olives at the feast of love.'" He made it up, of course.

TOM. Who?

SOPHIE. Someone who was lied to. (*She indicates photograph.*)

TOM. He's got a marvelous face.

SOPHIE. Oh yes, white—quite white—with eyes stuck in it so huge. I remember the first time I saw him I thought: "Beloved God, he's dying!" He was paler even than you. He stood on my doorstep with a little suitcase in his hand, full of white shirts and a history of the Tudor kings. He was so polite and thin—like a breathing matchstick—like you—and he bowed so formal. "My name is Vassili. I am a student from Greece. Do you have a room, please? I regret I cannot pay more than three pounds."

TOM. When was this?

SOPHIE. Five years ago. I was a landlady then in Notting Hill. My husband had died penniless: I had to do something besides tell fortunes. Oh, well, other years, other tears. He was twenty-six years old, but still exactly like a child. Everything he felt, he gave you, like a present—shoved at you, a joy now, another joy, all day. He used to come into my room in the evening to watch the television. Always so neat and careful. "Excuse me, is there rock and roll entertainment tonight?" He was such a fan—he taught me everything: what groups were good or lousy, Top Ten, Pick of the Pops! Secretly I liked it, but it was vulgar to admit to. After all, I was the Baroness Lemberg. His own family was middle class. They sent him

what they could, but it wasn't much. In a while I stopped asking him for rent . . . and he spent the money instead on pink sweets, yellow beads, tributes to his lady. He lived for dancing and history, he was intoxicated by history! And because I was an aristocrat, I was supposed to know all about it. Every Sunday he went on a bus up to Windsor Castle, down to St. Paul's Cathedral. And what he never knew was every Saturday night I would sit up, secretly memorizing the facts—speaking them next day almost yawning. Tourism, after all, is a little common, my dear . . . typically I never looked at the buildings themselves. Only their reflections in his eyes. So one bright spring day, I saw St. Paul's—two tiny little cathedrals swimming in salt water—and I leaned forward and kissed them, and called him "*Mein liebe*" for the first time. (*Pause*) Can it be you have powers for me, too—to make me say things? . . . to make me see . . .

TOM. Go on.

SOPHIE. All along there was a fiancée. Maybe that's why I chose him to begin with. Her name was Irina—a slouchy little thing, living with her parents in London. She had been chosen for him by the two fathers, who were best friends. Such arrangements are common with Greeks; he was allowed to take her out for walks in the afternoon, but nothing more for two years, till he had finished studies and could marry. Over the months, just because he was forbidden to touch her, he started to whine. "Oh, Sophie, I need her so bad. Help me, help me, help me." And I—because it was so vulgar, you see, to show jealousy—I said to him—

TOM. Invite her home.

SOPHIE. Ja. "Secretly to your room, in the afternoon. If there are any questions, I shall have been chaperone."

TOM. And she came, of course.

SOPHIE. *Every week!*

TOM. And you?

SOPHIE. I served them tea. . . . Into their room with my little tray. "Hello, Irina: How are you? How well you look. How's your good father?" And underneath, the hate—I, who had never felt hate in my life before, wasted its first flood on her; a timid little nothing who never harmed me. Oh, that hate. Burning me so I would cry out to the wallpaper on the stairs—and then into them immediately—smiling, holding out chocolate biscuits. "Oh, Vassili, don't grab them like that. It's so rude at a lady's tea table!" I was you—frying your breakfasts!

TOM. Yes!

SOPHIE. Oh, mister, what pain comes when you start protecting white lies! (*The lights spring on. She moves towards the window, talking.*) Dishonest pain. Pain not earned. Pain like an escape from real pain . . . You know the terrible thing? Even now part of me wishes him unhappy, wherever he is, back in Greece. But then part of me wished *me* unhappy, and who can explain *that*? Always it escapes me. Though now and then, staring here across the water, I think I see the pattern. Then no. Like wrinkles on the skin of the sea, a cold wind rushes up and it dissolves. (*She stares out of the window.*)

TOM. What happened?

SOPHIE. One day he brought me a present. Him—in his little cage. He said: "Here, Sophie, this is Pericles. In Greece he is known as the bird of truth. No one must ever lie in his presence!" He made that up too, naturally. "What do you mean," I say to Vassi, "no one must lie?" He sits down, giggling. "Sophie, I was talking to Miss Steinberg, that friend who knew you in Germany before the war. She says you were not a Baroness at all. You were a Jewish girl from a poor family: a refugee who married a horrid Englishman who kept a pub. Not a grand hotel, like you said: a pub. And you were not a manageress in a great office. You were only a barmaid."

TOM. He made that up too?

(*Pause*)

SOPHIE. No . . . No . . . Now I am ice all over. "Darling," I say, "it is time we talked. The two years are almost over. Our relationship is not fair to Irina. You must think of your marriage." He smiles back—giving me his present, so happy! "I have thought, Sophie, and I tell you I do not wish to marry her. I cannot love someone chosen for me by my father." And now I the Baroness speak for the last time. "That's nonsense, Vassili. You are

both young. You are both Greek. You are right together. If you wish to make me happy—marry her."

TOM. No!

SOPHIE. Right together. Very, very right together!

TOM. But why?

SOPHIE. Because it was in his face—don't you see?

TOM. What?

SOPHIE. Love! . . . Not despising! Not anger with me! Just love, smiling in those black eyes. Now he could know me. Now we were equal! . . . (*Pause*) Intolerable.

TOM (*understanding*). Yes.

SOPHIE. You want advice from the witch by the sea? Dare to love, yourself. Go to your girl. Tell her all your lies! She'll laugh, I promise you.

TOM. And Frank? Will he laugh, too?

SOPHIE. What does it matter? You've never really been afraid of him. Only of yourself.

TOM. Yes, maybe! But still—

SOPHIE. What?

TOM. I owe him everything. When he found me singing in a Chelsea pub, I didn't have a penny to my name. He founded the group . . . he set me up . . . What kind of thanks is it to steal his girl?

SOPHIE. Mister, do you want to know what your friend really wanted me to see for you in that crystal ball? Him and your girl burning you to ashes. His word—ashes. . . . I'm sorry.

TOM. He said that?—You wouldn't lie. Not about this.

(*The bell sounds.*)

SOPHIE. No, I wouldn't lie to you. Go to her now, before the concert, take a deep breath—and tell her everything. I'll deal with him. Go now! . . . I said you had disbelieving eyes. It's not true. There is still a little hope in them. Don't let it fade out, mister, like the sky into the sea. All grey.

TOM. Goodbye, Baroness.

SOPHIE. Sophie!

TOM. Sophie.

(FRANK *enters*.)

FRANK. Tom: It worked, didn't it??? (*Pause*) What happened, then?

(TOM *silently leaves*.)

SOPHIE. I read his fortune.

FRANK (*excitedly*). I bet you did! Come on now—give me every detail, right from the beginning. Don't leave anything out!

SOPHIE. Mister, I'm afraid things have not gone as planned.

FRANK. What d'you mean?

SOPHIE. Your friend is more complicated than you think.

FRANK. Why? What happened?

SOPHIE. I don't know.

FRANK. Meaning?

SOPHIE. It grew dark; the lights came on.

FRANK. Look, Baroness, I'm in no mood for games. (*Her gaiety deserts her.*) Where was he off to in such a hurry?

SOPHIE. Mister, would you like a drink? Look, maybe I tell your fortune . . . for free!

FRANK. Where was he going, Baroness?

SOPHIE. To his concert, naturally!

FRANK. I don't think so. . . . You're lying, aren't you?

SOPHIE. No.

FRANK. Oh, yes, you're lying. . . . There's cheat in this room. I can smell it. It's hanging in the air like smoke. . . . Lady, you cheated me.

SOPHIE. No! I did exactly what you said. I earned my money!

FRANK (*disbelieving*). Lady, you cheated me! . . . He's gone off to—tell Helen, hasn't he? To tell Helen about all this.

SOPHIE. Of course not.

FRANK. To show me up in front of her —to show me up—to show me up. . . . You cheating old cow!!!

SOPHIE. Cheat? *Me*—cheat! Me! After what you asked me to do! . . . Fantastic! . . . (*Furious*) Listen, mister—Mr. Cool and Easy—nobody ever leaves you, do they? Well, news for you! Bloody marvelous news for you! They do. And they will! Tonight! (*Pause*) You've lost her. But then, did you ever really have her?

FRANK (*quietly*). Well, well, well. Who'd have guessed it? Here I was thinking Lemberg may be a bore, but inside that frumpy old bag is a real witch —and all the time she's only a provincial pocketbook psychologist. I think we really have to do something about this cheating, don't we? We have to stop you showing people up like you do. . . . (*He looks at the bird.*) I'm afraid we're going to have to take your license away, dear. No witch —no familiar. That seems fair, doesn't it? (*Moving to the cage, he grabs the bird in the cage.*)

SOPHIE. No!

FRANK (*taking the bird from the cage, walks to the window, which he opens; we hear the wind*). A bird for a bird. (*He throws the bird out the window. Pause. He moves to her.*)

SOPHIE (*icy*). I'm afraid you do not frighten me, sir. I told Pericles one hour ago he would be going on a long journey. Perhaps I am not so much a fake, after all.

FRANK (*ironically*). Very brave, Baroness. Very brave and gallant. Give me the money.

SOPHIE. I am not a Baroness. My name is Sophie Harburg. And maybe I am not a witch—but I can still read you, mister! . . . for free! (*Slowly she sits, looking at him.*) You want your money? Very well. (*She deals the cards.*) Five of pounds: card of vanity. Five of pounds: card of cruelty. Five of pounds: card of stupidity. Five of pounds: card of fantasy. Five of pounds: card of a loveless life! It's all there in the cards, mister. . . . Harburg never lies. (*She picks up photograph, looks at it and drops it gently to the floor.*) Never.

CURTAIN

THE TOWER

Peter Weiss

Adapted and translated by MICHAEL HAMBURGER

The Tower was originally performed in the English language on the B.B.C. Radio's "Third Programme," Great Britain, on July 3, 1964, with the following cast:

PABLO *Michael Bryant*

MANAGERESS *Beatrix Lehmann*

DIRECTOR *Felix Felton*

CARLO *Gabriel Woolf*

CONJURER *Nigel Davenport*

MIDGET *Timothy Harley*

FEMALE LION TAMER *Margaret Wolfit*

TRUMPET VOICE *Michael Kilgarriff*

NARRATOR *Kevin Flood*

SHADOW FENCER *Bruce Beeby*

ATHLETE *Gordon Faith*

FEMALE ARTIST *Patricia Leventon*

1ST MALE ARTIST *Glyn Dearman*

2ND MALE ARTIST *Wilfred Carter*

Produced by Martin Esslin

In 1964, a relative newcomer to the theatre gained worldwide attention and acclaim with a startling play. The man and the event: Peter Weiss and *Marat/Sade*—or, to give the play its full title, *The Persecution and Assassination of Marat as Performed by the Inmates of the Asylum of Charenton Under the Direction of the Marquis de Sade*. Hailed as "an electrifying experience" and "a superb once-in-a-lifetime stage presentation which remained uppermost in the mind," the drama instantaneously established Peter Weiss as a major new force in the modern theatre.

Born in Germany in 1916, Mr. Weiss left his homeland in 1934, shortly after the Nazis began to accumulate like vermin. After an agonizing period of deracination, he rejoined his parents, who had settled in Stockholm, Sweden, and since 1939 he has made that his home. Now a Swedish citizen, he continues to write in German.

Although he is an accomplished painter and has made many successful documentary films (as well as a full-length movie, *The Mirage*), his world renown has come as a dramatist. *Marat/Sade* had its premiere in April, 1964, at the Schiller Theatre in West Berlin. The English-language version opened in London in August, 1964, under the auspices of the Royal Shakespeare Company. Subsequently, this same production, directed by Peter Brook, was taken to New York, where it opened in December, 1965. One of the outstanding theatrical events of the decade, it swept the seasonal awards, including: The New York Drama Critics Circle citation as the year's best play; two major Tony Awards, for best play and direction; and seven categories in *Variety's* annual poll of the New York theatre critics.

Labeled by some as "theatre of cruelty," by others, "theatre of absurdity," it was director Peter Brook who came closest in defining *Marat/Sade* as "the theatre of disturbance." Mr. Brook's alarmingly vivid production—with its real and threatening madness —differed considerably from the Schiller Theatre staging, where the atmosphere of the play tended to be aesthetic and abstract. (A filmed duplication of the Royal Shakespeare Company's memorable production was released in 1967.) Parenthetically, Mr. Weiss designed his own setting for the German presentation, and his wife, Gunilla Palmstierna-Weiss, created the costumes for both productions.

On October 19, 1965, Peter Weiss's succeeding play *Die Ermittlung* (*The Investigation*), which he describes as "an Oratorium in 11 Cantos," had its simultaneous premiere in thirteen West German theatres, at the East German Berliner Ensemble, and a midnight play-reading by the Royal Shakespeare Company in London. Taken directly from German court records of the 1964–1965 trial of twenty-one persons who participated in the destruction of four million people at the infamous concentration camp at Auschwitz, this dramatic confrontation of man's inhumanity to man was presented on the New York stage in 1966. Well received, its stark and brutal truths of a disreputable and horrendous era were still too close for audience comfort, and the presentation expired after 103 performances.

Peter Weiss's *The Tower* is published here for the first time, in Michael Hamburger's poetic and arresting translation. As in his subsequent works, Mr. Weiss imaginatively and compellingly examines man's relation to the society in which he lives and by which he is cornered. A psychological allegory, *The Tower* and its inhabitants symbolize to Pablo, the play's protagonist, all the constricting barriers and strangulating bonds that man must overcome and unshackle before he can realize true liberty and personal freedom.

Included in this volume in its original "radio" form, *The Tower* is a transcendent play that would, and should, be equally impressive in any dramatic medium.

NARRATOR. Many years ago, Pablo lived in the tower. But later, in the outside world, he never quite got the tower out of his system. The tower is still present inside him like a great dead weight. Pablo can't get away from it. Only when he has the courage to penetrate deep into the tower once more and confront his past may he be able to liberate himself.

So he goes back and asks to be let in. It's as though he were making his way into his own self. There he finds the Director and the Manageress. It was under their supervision that he grew up. It was they who trained him for his part in the circus performances inside the tower.

There is also Carlo, a kind of brother, who stayed behind in the tower.

There is Nelly, the ghost of love.

Nelly is dead, driven to her death by the Conjurer. The Conjurer is the embodiment of every sort of deathwish. Seemingly idle, the Conjurer is the most powerful force in the tower. The lion, too, is dead. The lion stood for all that is wild and untamed.

The midget, who is crippled and misshapen, now takes the part of the lion.

In the past, Pablo used to do a balancing act on the giant ball in the tower. Now he has a new part—as an escapologist. Now he wants to have himself fettered here in the tower. He wants to expose himself totally to the tower's force.

Pablo takes the name "Niente" when he is readmitted. This means that he's a nothing, a nobody. Only when he's made his way out of the tower will he regain himself, and a name of his own.

(*Whirring, indistinct street noises. Footsteps coming nearer. They come quite close, and stop.*)

PABLO (*immersed*). The lion's head—with the hoop in his mouth—(*Knocks on the door three times with the iron ring.*) —how it reverberates all through the tower—they must be in—the others—I've come from outside—I must get in there—close to them. . . . (*Three more knocks. Now inside, with a resonant echo*)

MANAGERESS (*whispering*). There's someone outside.

DIRECTOR. Some drunk or other. Someone who's lost his way.

MANAGERESS. But it could be something important . . .

DIRECTOR. At this time of night?

(*Pause*)

PABLO. I see the door from the outside—I've come from outside—I'm no longer locked in—I know what it's like outside—(*Dragging steps. Rattling of keys*) I can hear her shuffling down the stairs—I can still get away. . . . (*The key grinds in the lock. The heavy door opens with a creak. Pause*)

MANAGERESS. Can't you speak? What do you want? (*Silence*) What do you want?

PABLO. I'm looking for work. . . .

MANAGERESS. At this hour of the night?

PABLO. It could have happened later still. . . .

MANAGERESS. We always need people. But we insist on quality. We maintain a high standard in our performances!

PABLO. Yes, I know. I've heard about the tower. . . .

MANAGERESS. Have you? Well, it all depends on what you can do. . . . (*She sighs.*) Good workers are rare these days.

PABLO (*matter-of-factly*). Escapologist. The untying act.

MANAGERESS. An escapologist? It's a long time since we had one of those. We could give it a try. Are you staying in the hotel?

PABLO. No. Can you put me up here?

MANAGERESS (*suspicious*). Haven't you any luggage?

PABLO. I don't need any luggage. I suppose you have such a thing as a rope. And someone to tie me up.

MANAGERESS. And is that all you need?

PABLO. That's all.

MANAGERESS (*hesitantly*). Come in, then. (*Locks the door.*) You can sleep here in the hall. You can kip down on that bench. I'll get you a blanket.

DIRECTOR (*calling out from upstairs, with an echo*). Who is it?

MANAGERESS (*calling back*). An artiste. Why don't you come down and say hello?

DIRECTOR. Why's he come at this hour?

MANAGERESS. He had nowhere to stay.

DIRECTOR. This place isn't a doss-house.

PABLO (*to himself*). I must stay here—must stay here now. . . .

DIRECTOR (*coming down*). Fancy arriving at this hour . . .

PABLO (*matter-of-factly*). My name is

Niente, sir. I do an escaping act.

DIRECTOR. How long have you been in the business?

PABLO. Ever since I was that high. Started with a balancing act. Then changed over to a hanging act. (*Tense*) You know, hanging from a noose that tightens at the slightest movement. I had enough of that. (*Challengingly*) Maybe you know the feeling, the way you suddenly get sick of a number you've been working at for a long time? It's a kind of disgust. You feel you've got to do something new. And I felt, if I do that once more, that's the end of me. Always that death leap. That sense of suffocating. (*Self-absorbed*) Now, I could think of nothing but how to get free. Let them bind me, so as to know what it feels like to get free. Even while they bound me my mind was full of the sense of escape. You have to be free before you start.

DIRECTOR (*who hasn't been listening. Out of his own thoughts*) Escapologist. We once had an escapologist.

CARLO (*his voice still far off, calls out*). Who is it, then? What does he want? Isn't the house full? Isn't the program complete?

DIRECTOR. Carlo? Aren't you asleep yet? Go to bed, and be quick about it . . . or you'll be in bad form again tomorrow.

CARLO (*coming nearer*). Who is that man?

MANAGERESS (*gently*). Go on, Carlo, go upstairs.

CARLO (*fading*). Who is that man?

MANAGERESS. And it's time we went, too. Here's the blanket.

DIRECTOR. Yes, let's go.

MANAGERESS. Good night.

DIRECTOR (*already distant*). Good night.

PABLO (*quietly*). Good night.

(*Silence. Then, some distance away, a challenging sharp whistle which resounds in the interior of the tower.*)

CONJURER (*still distant*). So, it's *you*? Why do you twitch like that? Could you be frightened of me? Though you've grown into such a big strong fellow! That can't be our little Pablo who ran away with the lion. . . .

PABLO (*emphatically*). Be quiet!

CONJURER. Me, be quiet? Wasn't it me who helped you to get away? Wasn't it me who unlocked the cage? What would

you have done without me?

PABLO. And why did you raise the alarm as soon as we'd got out?

CONJURER. Didn't I have to, so that they wouldn't suspect anything? And what more do you want, anyway—didn't you get out? The lion, of course—poor lion. Bang! And there he lay. I shall never forget how they dragged him away by his tail.

PABLO. I know why you unlocked the door. You wanted me to kill myself outside. You knew that I had the noose round my neck.

CONJURER. Really, Pablo—we were such good friends!

PABLO. You had captured me. I didn't know anything then—had never been outside. Yes, you were kind to me. You loved me so much that you gave me a knife to cut my wrists with. You told me to throw myself down the stairs. You told me to lie quite still and stop my breath—and I did lie still until something snapped inside me.

CONJURER. Pablo, how can you say such things!

PABLO. Wherever I went, you suddenly turned up with your whispering. In the dressing room, I suddenly saw you in the mirror. At night, I suddenly felt you sitting on the edge of my bed.

CONJURER. But you trusted me so much, Pablo.

PABLO. Out of fear, I put my trust in you. I was afraid of your white, expressionless face.

CONJURER. Pablo!

PABLO. *Conjurer* you called yourself. Clairvoyant! But you never appeared in the ring. Parasite! What do you do here, anyway? What did you do to me? And to Nelly? What did you do to Nelly?

CONJURER (*threateningly*). Have you come here to accuse me? You must have forgotten what you did with the lion-tamer girl? You must have forgotten *why* they locked you up in the lion's cage! There the two of you lay, beasts, both of you, and the rats whistled. You confessed to me, begged me to help you . . .

PABLO. I didn't tell you everything. . . .

CONJURER. I suppose you're going to say it was she who seduced you, is that it? Tore the clothes off you, is that it? Rolled about with you on the floor? And only screamed because she liked it so much?

PABLO. She screamed because I wouldn't touch her. Because I recoiled from her. I felt petrified all of a sudden. All I could see was Nelly—lying there in the ring. What did you do to Nelly?

CONJURER. Poor little Pablo. Pablo who never got out of the tower. Pablo doing his balancing act on the giant red ball. (*His last words have died away in a resounding echo. He continues in a spellbinding, hypnotic tone of voice.*) Come here, then—give me your hand—that's right—good boy—don't lose your balance now—clever boy—that's right—on tiptoe—now start moving forward—steady—forward—forward—round and round the ring—that's right—shoulders back—body straight—legs taut—quite taut—straight as a post—only your toes moving—quicker—quicker—that's it, Pablo—good—soon you'll be allowed to do it in public—ah—and your name will be carried through the streets outside—in great big letters—PABLO THE EQUILIBRIST—don't stop moving—on your toes all the time—your body quite straight—don't jerk your shoulders—

PABLO (*pulls himself free*). I'm not Pablo any more! I've come from outside. I know what the tower looks like from outside. I know what the street looks like—the town—the harbor—the sea—I know what other towns are like—I've been on mountains—in woods—on main roads—on boats—

CONJURER. You've never been outside. You're in the tower. (*Emphatically*) You are here because you have never been outside.

PABLO (*defeated*). You're right. All the towns and woods and seas were inside the tower. Walls everywhere. Whatever I touched—walls. Every word, every feeling—locked up in the tower. Yes, you're right! I never got free. (*More resolutely*) But I'm not Pablo any more. I don't balance any more on the ball. I don't hang myself any more. I'm here to get away.

CONJURER (*hypnotically*). Everything is unchanged here and everything has the same effect on you as before.

PABLO. No! Everything is changed. I shall open the door myself.

CONJURER. If you can get hold of the key!

PABLO. To walk out slowly. Not to rush out blindly. (*As though in sudden pain*) How it always hurts, to see myself running down the street. As though something was hitting me—everything blurs. To walk calmly out of the door . . .

CONJURER. Here everything is unchanged.

PABLO. No! Everything is different. I'm not afraid of you now. And the Manageress—how grey and tired she is. She used to come storming in—her hair like a black octopus. And the Director. When I saw him there on the stairs—with his trousers all creased—I was almost sorry for him. I asked myself—Was it for their sake, I came back here? Those two old people—what are they to me? Maybe they'll try to catch me again with their weakness—their feebleness and loneliness—their power won't get the better of me again!

CONJURER. Everything is as it used to be. Listen to the clock! Listen to the breathing! Everything is as before. Listen!

(*His last words have died away like a resonant echo. The muffled ticking of a clock can be heard. The clockwork rattles before striking. The broken sound of a gong. Then the ticking again. The* DIRECTOR *snores. The* MANAGERESS *moans in her sleep. The mattress creaks. Everything drowned as though in the swell of a great wave. Then silence again.*)

PABLO. Yes, I can hear it. The nights I crept to Nelly's room. Nelly—wake up! What did you do to Nelly?

CONJURER. Enough of that!

PABLO. She just lay there in the middle of the ring. Her horse vanished. You said she'd had a fall. But there were no hoofmarks near her. You stood beside her. Her face unrecognizable. The terrible silence up there in the empty auditorium . . .

(*Silence*)

CARLO (*his voice approaching from a wide echoing space*). I—Carlo—loved her most of all.

PABLO. I crept into her room when everyone else was asleep. . . .

CARLO. I—Carlo—was awake.

PABLO. I waited till I heard them snore upstairs. Nelly had left her door ajar—she sat up in her bed—waiting for me. . . .

CARLO (*his voice coming closer like a breath*). She was waiting for *me*. We lay in a close embrace. She said she loved me best. You want to steal everything I've got! You always get in my way! But she loved *me* best!

PABLO. You! Why, you were always clinging to the old woman's skirts!

MANAGERESS (*storming in*). Is he being cheeky again, that Pablo? Is he bullying you again? Just you wait! He'll be sorry when I tell your uncle of him!

DIRECTOR (*storming in*). What is it this time? What's going on?

MANAGERESS. It's Pablo, as usual!

PABLO. Yes, it's me, it's me! You couldn't get me down!

MANAGERESS. What's that you're saying? Wasn't I like a mother to you?

PABLO. But you aren't my mother. Not one of us has a mother! Not one of us was born here! We were all dragged in from outside. You, too, were dirty bundles left on the doorstep. There's no such thing as family ties! Only the tower. Only the tower keeps us together!

MANAGERESS. How can you be so heartless! You ought to be punished; punishment is what you need!

PABLO. That's right, punishment. I've punished myself. I was so obsessed with your power that every thought which turned against you ricocheted back on myself.

CONJURER. What does it really amount to? You got a few beatings; you were taught a bit of discipline. If the reins were held a bit tight at times, it was only to make you a really competent artist. What's all the fuss about?

PABLO. What *is* all the fuss about? Sometimes I feel my thoughts rising up out of a deep shaft before I can get hold of anything tangible. There's something unfathomable beneath every thought, something for which there are no words. And *that* was where I was made into what I am. When I first grew aware of the ball on which I was standing, I'd already been broken and tamed.

DIRECTOR. We were far too lax with you. You never learned to conform to the rules.

CONJURER (*hypnotically again: hollow, echoing*). Chest out—stomach in—shoulders back—that's right—arms stretched out—stick to the ball—that's better—faster—faster—run on tiptoe now—round and round the ring—always in a circle—

PABLO (*hypnotized, harassed*). Those faces up in the seats—all that hissing and mumbling and babbling—(*Sound of confused voices. Scraping of hands applauding*)—those terrible hands . . .

CONJURER. And then you'd bow so prettily. You were the public's darling. You looked so charming in your white blouse with your powdered face and your long black hair. You'd blow kisses at them.

PABLO. Out of fear! I was afraid of them. I thought they were animals. When I saw that they were like us, I thought there must be something wrong with my eyes. You'd told me that they'd tear me to pieces if I ever dared to mix with them. Why did you keep everything from me? Why wasn't I allowed to know anything about the world outside? When I asked you, you put a finger on your lips.

DIRECTOR (*hard and monotonously, rattling it off*). *This* is where we work and *this* is where we stay. First, you'll have to prove what you can do. Prove that you're equal to your duties, that you're capable of doing what is expected of you.

PABLO. Yes, that's the voice of the tower. But now I'm going to answer. I'm through with being seen and not heard. Even at that time, I revolted inwardly, I always knew that there's a world outside this tower.

CONJURER (*hard and monotonously*). For us there is only the tower. Out there everything is topsy-turvy. Only the walls of the tower are firm. Out there everything crumbles away. We rely on the law and order of the tower. (*Contemptuously*) And why do you think they come to us— those *people*? To draw strength from us. From us! We are the ones who give out strength!

PABLO (*obsessed*). But I've seen the world outside! I found the peep-hole up in the attic—a round white fire! It was just after I'd cut my wrists with your knife, when I was walking around with those thick bandages and I didn't have to work on my balancing act—you taught me that one has to kill oneself to get free; but there was another voice inside me—a voice that I couldn't yet hear—to answer you people with my stifled voice—that's what I came back here for, *had to come back here for!* It was that whisper that decided what I was going to do with my life. It was that voice, never yet heard, that drove me up to the attic, where I found that window. What was your power compared to that window! It only lasted a second. I was dazzled! I cried out! I felt an immense strength in face of that light! And then, you stood behind me—pulled me back—down the stairs—the attic locked up—the key thrown away!

DIRECTOR (*mechanically*). And now get a move on. Enough of your idling!

PABLO. That's it. You put me back on the ball. But I'd seen it! I'd caught a glimpse of the outside world. Up there I'd seen no more than a single white-hot chasm. But now, details emerged from the blinding light; I recognized more and more—new sights kept appearing—I saw a sea of rooftops—saw pillars—animals—smoke— brightly colored cloth flapping in the wind. I saw windows—behind the windows, rooms—in the rooms, figures—someone carried a glass ball—someone undressed—someone painted a wall with a wide brush—a giant rode by on a green horse, a sword in his outstretched hand—children played in the street—one was just disappearing in a ditch—people everywhere—alone or in groups. I saw a vast picture and looked for its meaning—discovered new meanings all the time—a great restlessness took hold of me—I wanted to get out—but I hadn't the courage yet—you still held me fast. . . .

CONJURER. You never had the courage . . .

PABLO. You don't understand what I'm saying. You can never understand me! There's nothing you can tell me, only what you've been hammering into me from the start. I can hear nothing but the echo of your words! Where are you—where are you?

VOICES (*replying in an echoing chorus*). All around you! All around you!

PABLO. I shall seize you, get to grips with you! I shall tear you out of myself!

VOICES. What have you got against us? We have our own lives! You couldn't see anything straight! You misunderstood everything! You can't blame us for everything!

PABLO. You penetrated right inside me. I was open to you. I'm permeated with you. I never hit back! Never kicked out at you!

DIRECTOR. That would have been the last straw!

PABLO. When you put me over your knee, I howled to put you in a better mood. And when you praised me for once, I forgot that my face was still smarting from your blows. . . .

MANAGERESS. How can you be so cruel! To us, who gave you food and work. I cooked a special gruel for you because you were so sickly—a nourishing gruel—don't you remember how much you liked it?

PABLO. It rotted in the dustbin every night. I spewed it up. And, in the night, I stole to the larder to grab what I needed. Those nightly journeys!

(*A muffled roaring fills the tower. The clock ticks. The snoring. The breathing of those asleep can be heard. A whizzing and rushing sound.*)

PABLO. As in a sinking ship, the water comes pouring in—my uncle and aunt up there—like hydraulic pumps. I glide through the house on the giant ball. I fly—whiz—down the stairs—through the passages—through the halls. How it whirs and roars—how large the place is! Whiz—down to the cellar—to the lion—*lion!* Are you there, lion? Lion! His eyes gleam—how still he lies! (*Mysteriously*) He's under a spell. I shall break it, lion! We shall run away together, see the world! We shall run—run—no one will stop us. . . .

CONJURER. Bang! There he lies! A bull's-eye! Right in his neck. I never miss the mark.

PABLO. The lion. The strong one. The wild one. The caged one. The killed one. Lion, I shall bring you back to life! Lion, come out!

(*A tittering growl is heard, a clanging of bells.*)

MIDGET. Here I come—here I am—

CONJURER. Come on, then, boy—come to your master—give me your paw—that's a good boy.

MIDGET (*tittering and growling*). So, it's our good friend Pablo—come back—come to save me, has he? Come to save the poor misshapen midget?

CONJURER. Yes, the great liberator has come.

MIDGET (*howling*). I'm free—free!

CONJURER. There's your lion for you, your new lion! A runt, a cripple, with bells on him. And Nelly—do you want to see Nelly again?

PABLO. Nelly . . .

CONJURER. Come on, lion—dance with Nelly!

(*Sounds of tittering, trampling, and rattling of bells.*)

PABLO. Nelly's frock—her white frock—

CONJURER. The last rags of her frock—

PABLO (*self-absorbed*). Is that all that's left of her?

CONJURER (*hard*). There never was more than that!

PABLO. But those nights—that I spent with her? (*In doubt*) That I spent with her?

CONJURER (*challengingly*). Well—so what?

PABLO. It was only once I went to her—but it seemed as though I'd always been with her. She showed me her breasts—

CONJURER. Well—and then what?

PABLO. Well— and then—

CONJURER. She asked you something—

PABLO (*whispers*). Yes—

CONJURER (*bluntly*). She asked you, can you do that thing—the same that Carlo can do?

PABLO. That's what she said. I heard her very clearly. I left. I never went back to you, Nelly. But, after you'd died, then I had you all to myself. Then I spent every night with you.

CARLO (*his voice drifting in from the distance*). She liked me best—me, Carlo—I spent the nights with her—

PABLO. And what did you do with your love—what became of you? (*The tittering and clanging of bells again*) Give it to me —give me the frock! (*Silence. Rustling of material*) Nelly—her scent—(*Whispering*) Nelly—Nelly—

(*The muffled roaring gradually rises again in the tower. The clock ticks. Deep, muffled breathing. After a while, the DI-RECTOR and MANAGERESS wake up. They stretch, groan, and yawn.*)

DIRECTOR (*still sleepy*). Yes—it's time—

MANAGERESS. I suppose it is—

DIRECTOR. Another day—

(*The mattress creaks. Yawning and clearing of throats*)

MANAGERESS. That's right—another day.

Better start making the coffee. . . . (*The shuffling of her slippers down the stairs. Yawns*) Lying there on the ground—didn't even use the blanket. What's that he's got over his face? What sort of rag has he got there? Do you mind getting up? I've got to lay this table—(*She rattles crockery.*)

DIRECTOR (*yawning, coming downstairs*). Right—here you are—brought the rope down for you—that suit you? What's the matter with him? Why's he still asleep? Who does he think he is? (*To the* MAN-AGERESS) Is the coffee made?

CONJURER (*from a distance*). Good morning, sir.

DIRECTOR. Ah—up early, as usual. But look at that one! Why doesn't he get up? We've got to take a look at him before we start rehearsing.

CONJURER. No need, sir, no need. Why, he's world famous. *Niente.* Escapologist. We can simply put his name on the program.

DIRECTOR. That one there world famous? Never heard of him!

CONJURER. But he is, he is. Quite a star, in fact.

DIRECTOR (*uncertainly*). Is that so—that fellow? Oh, well, if you say so . . .

(MANAGERESS *pours out coffee. Rattling of cups and spoons stirring. Confused hum of voices approaches. The* ARTISTS *come downstairs.*)

ARTISTS. Morning, sir. Morning, morning. Good morning, madam.

(*Scraping of chairs. Rattling of cups and spoons. Sound of sipping*)

DIRECTOR (*strikes a cup*). Today we're adding a new number to the program. Let's see, what have we got first? (*Turning over pages*) "Dramatic scene"—"Duel" —"Dancing Dogs" . . . All right, I think we'll put him in right at the start, to give them a novelty at once. (*Turning to the* CONJURER:) But you're quite sure, aren't you? I mean—

CONJURER. Absolutely sure, sir. Don't you worry.

MIDGET (*approaches, tittering*). Abso-lutely—don't you worry!

PABLO (*out of the confused hubbub, very close*). Now, it's going to start.

MIDGET (*close; hoarsely whispering*). Where am I—where am I?

(*During the dialogue that follows, rattling of cups. Sipping noises, murmuring in the background.*)

DIRECTOR. Whose act is first on the list today?

ATHLETE. Athlete!

DIRECTOR. With the heaviest weights.

ATHLETE. Heaviest weights!

DIRECTOR. Next?

SHADOW FENCER. Shadow fencer!

DIRECTOR. With new dueling postures.

SHADOW FENCER. New postures, sir!

DIRECTOR. And after that?

FEMALE LION TAMER. Lion tamer!

DIRECTOR. You're to use bigger whips—got that?

FEMALE LION TAMER. Bigger whips, sir!

MIDGET (*close; whispering*). What's going on here? What is it all about?

DIRECTOR. Then it's Carlo's turn.

CARLO. Right you are, Uncle.

PABLO. I'm inside the tower. . . .

DIRECTOR. And remember—more keenness—more enthusiasm!

MANAGERESS (*in the background*). Another drop of coffee?

PABLO (*whispering*). I've got to get out of the rope. . . .

MIDGET (*whispering, parrot-like*). Out the rope—out the rope . . .

DIRECTOR. More concentration! You've been getting slack lately. We mustn't forget the tradition of the tower!

MIDGET (*parrot-wise*). Tradition . . . tradition . . .

MANAGERESS. So you're up at last? Goodness me, you can sleep like a baby. A cup of coffee?

DIRECTOR. Well, how do you feel—Mr. Escapologist?

CARLO. Is that what he is, an *escapologist?*

FEMALE LION TAMER (*significantly*). It's a very long time since we had an *escapologist.*

CARLO. Is it Pablo you're thinking of?

FEMALE LION TAMER. And on top of it all, he *looks* like Pablo.

CARLO. And he's sitting at Pablo's old place! (PABLO *is startled.*)

CONJURER. Do remain seated, Mr. Niente!

DIRECTOR. What's all this talk about Pablo? I want no more of that!

PABLO. Who is Pablo?

MIDGET (*parrot-wise*). Who am I?

CONJURER. A splendid artist. The best we ever had. But he gave us the slip.

DIRECTOR. Not another word about Pablo, do you hear me?

CONJURER. And how good-looking he was—powdered white—enchanting.

MIDGET. The women's favorite!

FEMALE LION TAMER (*dreamily*). Yes—he was good-looking—our Pablo! Have you never heard of Pablo, the equilibrist? Did you never come across him outside?

PABLO. I don't know. I don't think I did. I don't remember. . . .

MANAGERESS. I wonder what became of him? I could never really understand him. He was so reticent. Couldn't get a word out of him.

PABLO. Why did he run away?

DIRECTOR. He didn't run away. He was sacked!

PABLO. Why?

DIRECTOR. Why, why! He was lazy! He was conceited! I tried to turn him into a conscientious artist, but he never knew what discipline meant!

MANAGERESS. He was always grumbling. Nothing was good enough for him.

DIRECTOR. He had no team spirit. He was disrespectful. But that's quite enough about Pablo! We've got to get down to the program now!

MANAGERESS. A drop more coffee?

PABLO. What did he do here?

FEMALE LION TAMER (*coquettishly*). He balanced on the ball.

MANAGERESS. By the way, didn't you say that you've been an equilibrist, too? Couldn't you do that act on the ball? We've still got the ball. And I'm not sure that people are all that keen to seen an escapologist. A bit too ambitious. We have to consider the taste of our public in this town.

PABLO. I'm an escapologist.

MANAGERESS. Why don't you think about it?

PABLO. I've given up balancing for good.

ATHLETE. I'm going to start my weight-lifting now.

(*Scraping of chairs. All get up. Rattling of crockery.*)

DIRECTOR. Hey! Where do you think you're going?

PABLO. Aren't we allowed to watch the

rehearsals?

DIRECTOR. That's not our custom here. Every man works by himself.

PABLO (*turning from one artist to the other*). Do you all work on your own, then? What do you do, then? And you—what do you do? Why don't you answer me? So you never talk about your work?

(*The* ARTISTS *go away. It becomes quieter.*)

FEMALE LION TAMER (*close*). My dear fellow, you can't hope to change anything in this place. It's obvious that you've come from outside. (*Nostalgically*) Did you see a lot of the world? Tell me about it.

PABLO (*self-absorbed*). I'm no longer sure I was ever outside. Maybe I only wished I were. What did I see? A landing pier—a beach—a sail—but myself, where am I?

CONJURER (*whispering*). You've got a whole tower around you. . . .

(*Once again, a crescendo of sound from the tower. Like a wave. Indistinct voices. Ticking of a clock. Noises of people at work: "Heave-Ho: Heave-Ho! One, two; one—two!" Then they fade out.*)

PABLO (*self-absorbed*). I remember the day when you arrived—I was standing here by the stairs— the door was locked behind you—you walked past me with your suitcase—I took it from you—carried it—wondered what was inside it. I followed you up to your room—stood at the door while you unpacked—I was startled to see that everything in the case was made of leather or metal. Then you came up to me—asked me my name—seized my arm—my hair . . .

FEMALE LION TAMER. You trembled all over.

PABLO. I was thinking of Nelly—couldn't get rid of the thought of Nelly . . .

FEMALE LION TAMER. You were quite beside yourself when you came to see me in the evening—oh—(*They embrace.*) Don't be so violent—don't be so excited—

PABLO. Your armor—you're armored—your whole body is armored—

CONJURER (*very fast, like a wrestling commentator*). Now she's kissing him—she tears open his shirt—she's biting him—she digs her claws into him—he puts his arms around her—she recoils—he pursues her— she's down—he hurls himself

on top of her—now it's warming up—(*Calling out, loudly*) now it's warming up—this is *it*, Pablo!

(*The word "Pablo" comes back from the tower as a great echo. From all sides, the hollow, echoing call of: "Pablo, Pablo, Pablo!"*)

PABLO. Yes! Here I am! Here I am! (*The word "am" re-echoes from all sides. Silence*) Is it time for me to start now?

DIRECTOR. Start what?

PABLO. Rehearsing.

DIRECTOR. No need.

PABLO. No need?

DIRECTOR. No need. We're absolutely confident—

PABLO. Absolutely confident—

DIRECTOR. The rope—is it all right?

PABLO. The rope?

DIRECTOR. Yes—this rope here. Didn't you ask for a rope?

PABLO. A rope? Yes, of course—a rope.

DIRECTOR. Is it thick enough, long enough?

PABLO. "Absolutely confident." You trust me because I'm a stranger to you. I've come from outside. If you knew who I am . . .

MANAGERESS (*gently; from far off, coming closer*). Don't you understand? We're only trying to do what's best for you. Where have we gone wrong, then? If only you'd consider how much trouble we've had with you—

PABLO. What was I to you, then—and Nelly—and Carlo?

MANAGERESS. Why, we did everything we could for you. You were entrusted to our care, both of you. We looked after you as though you were our own children. And what was the good of all that work? Not a word of thanks! Oh, how futile it all is! Night after night, I lay sleepless, wondering what I could do for you. And never a word of thanks. Only complaints. Where did I go wrong, then?

PABLO. It's the tower. Everything is due to the tower! You yourselves grew up in the tower. You wanted to get out, too. Even *you* wanted to get out. But an impulse like that—you would never face up to it. Didn't you beat me just because you knew—I wanted to get out? We were all so ingrown here. I was part of you—a rebellious part that had to be suppressed

—for the tower's sake. . . .

MANAGERESS (*startled*). Did you say something?

PABLO (*self-absorbed*). Did I say something?

MANAGERESS. What was I going to do? Where's the Midget? The posters must be put up—

MIDGET (*rattling his bells*). Right you are, Manageress—I've already started painting them! (*Slowly reading:*) THE STAR ATTRACTION—THE ONE AND ONLY APPEARANCE OF THE GREAT ESCAPOLOGIST!

PABLO. One and only?

MIDGET (*chanting*). The one and only—the one and only—

PABLO (*suddenly overcome by weakness*). How do I get out of here? The door —open the door—(*Beats on the door. Resounding blows*) I want to get out—*out!*

MIDGET (*parrot-wise, squeaking, screaming*). I want to get out—out! (*Dances, rattling his bells.*) Won't anyone help me! Oh, how sorry I feel for myself! Everyone clings to me—they pull me down—I'm quite lame already—and twisted—and crooked! Oh, poor wretch that I am! Won't anyone help me!! (*Then, business-like*) That's it—the poster is finished— THE ONE AND ONLY APPEARANCE OF THE GREAT ESCAPOLOGIST! (*Rattles keys.*) There—unlock the door and out we go!

PABLO (*runs after him*). Me too! I'm coming with you!

CONJURER (*sharply*). Stop! You're staying here! (*Scuffling and gasping*) That would suit you, wouldn't it, to give us the slip now!

(*The door is closed with a slam, then locked from the outside.*)

MIDGET'S VOICE (*from far away*). The greatest of all escapologists! One and only appearance tonight! Come and see him! Come and see the greatest of all escapologists! One and only appearance! Come and see him! Come and see . . . (*His voice fades out.*)

PABLO (*out of breath*). Oh—the tower —this tower—

(*The wave again from inside the tower. Voices. Footsteps. Ticking.* DIRECTOR'S *voice in the distance.*)

DIRECTOR. Carlo—start rehearsing now.

CARLO (*far off*). Right—I'm coming.

(*A door is slammed. The muted voice of the* DIRECTOR, *giving orders* . . .)

DIRECTOR. Head up—corners of your mouth down—turn your shoulders—dance now—that's it—that's it—legs higher—arms higher—that's it—can't see what's so difficult about it—(PABLO *flings open the door.* DIRECTOR *now is close.*) What's this —how dare you!

PABLO. I want to watch.

DIRECTOR. How dare you! Didn't I tell you, in so many words . . .

PABLO. Yes, you did. But I insist on my terms, too. I want to move about freely here—otherwise, I can't do my work!

DIRECTOR. You're dismissed! Get out of here! And make it quick!

CONJURER (*suddenly appearing*). But, sir—he's already been announced!

DIRECTOR (*indignantly*). In this place—sir—you have to conform to the rules! I'm the one who gives orders here!

PABLO. In that case I can't do my act!

DIRECTOR (*his voice breaking with excitement*). Filthy lot! Think they can hang around here and gape! But count me out! Count me out! (DIRECTOR *stamps out of the room.*)

CARLO. You've got a nerve—

PABLO. Come on—what about a bit of fresh air?

CARLO. Outside, you mean? You know that's impossible!

PABLO. Who can stop us? We're not convicts. We'll simply ask for the key. Demand it! (*Calling out:*) Director! We want the key! We want to get out! The key, do you hear? *The key!*

(*The Great Echo answers: "Key!* KEY! KEY!")

DIRECTOR (*resonant; from far off*). What's up?

(*Other calls from inside the tower blend in with the "Key!" echo.*)

VOICES. What's up? What's happened? What's the matter, then? Is the place on fire?—Yes, it's burning!—Fire! Fire!—It's burning!—Help! Help!

(*Amid the uproar, the words "Key!" "Fire!" "Help!" mingle. Footsteps come running down the stairs. The* ARTISTS *rush down.*)

DIRECTOR (*rushing in*). Who's got the key?

ARTISTS (*in a panic*). There's a fire! A fire! Open the door! We're locked in!

DIRECTOR. Where's the key?

CONJURER (*gloating*). The key's outside.

PABLO. Isn't there more than one key?

(ARTISTS *to the door, in a panic. Screams. Hammering on the door.*)

PABLO (*challengingly*). Where's the fire, then?

ARTISTS. That's right—where is the fire, anyway?

DIRECTOR. Did it start up there?

ARTISTS. No. Not up there. We thought it was down here. Where is the fire, then?

CONJURER. There's no fire at all. It was only a joke. Our distinguished escapologist permitted himself a little joke. You can all go back upstairs. Nothing has happened. Only a practice alarm, as it were.

(*The* ARTISTS *withdraw, grumbling, while, from outside, the* MIDGET'S VOICE *comes closer again.*)

MIDGET. His one and only appearance tonight! Jubilee performance in the tower!

(*Sound of the key turning in the lock. The door opens, creaking. Then it is slammed shut. The* MIDGET's *bells can be heard. The door is double-locked.*)

(*Silence*)

DIRECTOR (*close; threateningly*). What did you think you were doing—eh?

CARLO. But he only wanted the key— only wanted to take a turn outside with me—

DIRECTOR. How—how dare you interfere —are you still here? Off you go—upstairs, and be quick about it! (*To* PABLO; *close, threateningly*) Let this be a warning to you! Never again, do you hear?

MIDGET (*tittering*). But he can't help it —he isn't quite right in the head!

CONJURER. Never *was* quite right in the head. Always wanted to get out!

PABLO. Yes, I always wanted to get out. . . .

MIDGET. He hasn't been all there since he got that little bump on his head—

PABLO (*startled*). What's that? What's that you're saying?

CONJURER. Nothing—nothing at all—

PABLO. But—there was something— what was it?

MIDGET. Just a little bump. A little bump on the head!

CONJURER. Go away and shut up!

(*The* MIDGET *titters.*)

PABLO (*remembering*). Yes, of course . . .

CONJURER. Nothing at all. You just fell down, that's all.

PABLO. That's it—outside—outside in the street. I was outside . . .

CONJURER. Oh, nonsense—

PABLO. That's it! I got out once before —ran down the street—

CONJURER. Never—you must have dreamed that—

PABLO. That's it! I ran—I got out— down the street—but not fast enough. You came after me. That's it! I was outside—that's it! I'm outside—but not the time I ran away with the lion. Long before that. Long before. That's it! Now I know—I ran away once before.

CONJURER. You're only imagining it.

PABLO. No, I've always known what it was like outside. That's it—it was evening —the wet pavements—those great windows to the left and to the right—those enormous cars—those high masts—I run like mad—but not fast enough—you're after me—you catch me up—that's it— and then, the blow . . .

MIDGET. Just a little bump!

CONJURER. He doesn't know what he's talking about!

PABLO. Yes, I do! Now I do know it! At last I see everything clearly! Now I can see this tower. And I was outside. I know what it's like outside. In there nothing ever changes. When I came in here it was like going down into a well. The stale, stagnant air in this place. No window. The attic skylight boarded up. Now I can see this tower from the inside. Now I see it as it is! Now I know that I can get out!

CONJURER. You aren't out yet.

PABLO. I shall get out!

CONJURER. You'll have to prove that. We haven't bound you yet. We're going to bind you, my boy! Tonight we're going to bind you as you've never been bound.

MIDGET (*rattling his bells; echo-like*). Yes, we're going to bind you.

CONJURER. You'd better rest now and gather up strength. You'll need it tonight. Better have a good rest!

(*The wave of sound again from the tower. Ticking of the clock*)

CONJURER (*in a monotone, hypnotically*). Listen to time ticking—time running out for you—and you sit here—weary and listless—unending time—listen to it—hours —days—weeks—months—years—this is where you've always sat, waiting—wanting to get out—and never could get out— here you sit with your rope—time trickles away under your feet—nothing will come right—soon we shall tie you up—wind the rope round you—pull the rope tight round your chest—you'll never get free—very soon we'll throw the rope round you— start taking off your shirt so that we can bind you more securely—that's right— like that— and now we can start in a minute—but listen—(*A hubbub of many voices. A scraping of feet*) But look—the auditorium is packed—we sold out tonight—all those faces, all those hands—

DIRECTOR (*in a hurry*). Are you ready? It's nearly time.

(*The hubbub grows louder. A roll on the drums. Clapping. Then a trumpet joins the drum for a flourish. Now the drum provides a blurred rolling background for the* DIRECTOR'S *voice.*)

DIRECTOR. Ladies and gentlemen!

(*A trumpet-like voice echoes with his words.*)

TRUMPET. Ladies and gentlemen!

DIRECTOR. Permit me to introduce!

TRUMPET. Permit—introduce!

DIRECTOR. The great escapologist Niente!

TRUMPET. Escapologist—Niente!

(*Applause. Whistles. Stamping of feet.*)

DIRECTOR. You will see him bound!

TRUMPET. Bound!

DIRECTOR. From his neck to his toes!

TRUMPET. Neck—toes!

DIRECTOR. With this rope!

TRUMPET. Rope!

DIRECTOR. From which he will escape!

TRUMPET. Escape!

DIRECTOR. Without anyone's help!

TRUMPET. Help!

DIRECTOR. The Conjurer and the Midget!

TRUMPET. Conjurer—Midget!

DIRECTOR. Our familiar attractions!

TRUMPET. Attractions!

DIRECTOR. Will now begin to fetter him!

TRUMPET. Fetter him!

(*Applause*)

DIRECTOR. We beg our respected public to be absolutely silent!

TRUMPET. Silent!

(*Loud drum roll. Sighs and gasps. A muffled fall. Groaning. Silence. Then, only the subdued drum roll*)

MANAGERESS (*anxiously*). But that's impossible. He'll never get out of that.

DIRECTOR. But the rope is cutting into his skin.

MANAGERESS. But the rope is strangling him.

DIRECTOR. What a disgrace!

MANAGERESS. He should have done his balancing act after all.

PABLO (*with the utmost exertion*). Give me time!

DIRECTOR (*stepping forward*). Ladies and gentlemen, please!

TRUMPET. Ladies—gentlemen!

DIRECTOR. Please be patient!

TRUMPET. Patient!

(*Drum roll louder*)

PABLO (*whispering*). Give me time!

DIRECTOR (*whispering*). Think of our reputation!

MANAGERESS (*whispering*). Don't disgrace us!

PABLO. It'll take a little while yet—

DIRECTOR (*stepping forward*). Ladies and gentlemen!

TRUMPET. Ladies—gentlemen!

DIRECTOR. Rest assured!

TRUMPET. Assured!

DIRECTOR. He's doing his utmost!

TRUMPET. Utmost!

(*Drum roll louder. Murmuring. Laughter. A few whistles.*)

PABLO. Give me time!

CONJURER (*close; whispering*). You've got all the time you want—an endless amount of time—the whole tower is full of time for you!

PABLO. Leave me here. Put on the next act!

DIRECTOR (*nervously*). Ladies and gentlemen!

TRUMPET. Ladies—gentlemen!

DIRECTOR. We humbly beg you to be patient.

TRUMPET. Patient!

DIRECTOR. Meanwhile, we present—our phenomenal Carlo!

TRUMPET. Carlo!

(*Flourish of drum and trumpet. Applause. Whistles.*)

DIRECTOR. In a wordless mime!

TRUMPET. Wordless mime!

DIRECTOR. He dances genuine, deeply felt emotions!

TRUMPET. Emotions!

DIRECTOR. First—*Love!*

TRUMPET. Love!

(*Drum, trumpet, zylophone, and gong intone a whirring kind of music.*)

CONJURER (*close; whispering*). Do you see how he squirms with love—how he embraces the air and dreams of Nelly—how he bends his limbs—how he distorts his face—how he desperately searches for love—but here there's no such thing as love—he squirms like a worm on a hook—he squirms like you—and can't get free. . . .

(*The music fades.*)

DIRECTOR. And now—*Fear!*

TRUMPET. Fear!

(*The instruments begin again: scraping, scratching, grating, dragging.*)

CONJURER (*whispering*). Do you see how he crawls—how he runs this way and that, looking for a rathole—what's he afraid of, then? Eh? What are you people afraid of?

VOICE (*quite free and open; widely resonant*). Pablo, you're free! You must get out of the rope!

PABLO (*groaning*). Give me more time!

(*The grating music fades.*)

DIRECTOR. And lastly—*Humility!*

(*The music of the instruments is whining, wavering.*)

CONJURER (*whispering*). Do you see how he kisses the ground—how he wrings his hands—ah—he is completely at home here; he licks this floor out of devotion. Just look at him—the two of you—how the two of you kiss the ground—our good old stone floor. . . .

VOICE (*as before*). Pablo, you must get out! You're free!

(*The music fades out. Applause. Flourish. Then, drums begin again.*)

DIRECTOR. Ladies and gentlemen!

TRUMPET. Ladies—gentlemen!

DIRECTOR. While the escapologist summons his strength for the supreme effort!

TRUMPET. Effort!

DIRECTOR. Our much admired shadow fencer!

TRUMPET. Shadow fencer!

DIRECTOR. Will fight a duel with himself!

TRUMPET. Himself!

(*Applause. Drum louder.*)

DIRECTOR. Observe!

TRUMPET. Observe!

DIRECTOR. His new, unheard-of thrusts!

TRUMPET. Thrusts!

DIRECTOR. And parries!

TRUMPET. Parries!

(*While the drum rolls, a sound of violently clashing blades.*)

CONJURER (*hurriedly, like an announcer. With the drumming and clashing of blades behind him*). Meanwhile, the escapologist's struggle continues—desperately, relentlessly—the rope is still coiled tight around him; his skin has been rubbed away; you can see the superhuman exertion in his face—but he doesn't give in; still he's grappling with his fetters! Full of concern, we ask ourselves how much longer he will bear it—the veins on his forehead look as though they're about to burst—he's bathed in perspiration—his heart throbs furiously—

(*A couple of whip-like thrusts of the blades. Flourish. Applause.*)

DIRECTOR (*steps forward, flustered*). Ladies and gentlemen!

TRUMPET. Ladies—gentlemen!

CONJURER (*mumbling in the background*). It's a unique, exciting—

DIRECTOR. After the shadow fencer's victory over himself—

CONJURER (*in the background*). He was bound by powers of whose strength he had no inkling. . . .

DIRECTOR. As we tensely await the end of the escapologist's act—

(*Suddenly, a vortex of merry-go-round music. Fanfares. Singing voices. Bells. Rattles. Motor horns. Roaring of engines breaks out.*)

MANAGERESS (*screams*). The door—the door is opening!

CONJURER. The door—

PABLO. The outside world . . .

DIRECTOR. Who opened the door?

VOICE (*out of the uproar outside*). Pablo, you are free!

MANAGERESS. Carlo! He's running out! Carlo!

PABLO. Carlo is free!

DIRECTOR. Carlo!

MANAGERESS. Carlo's got out!

DIRECTOR. Why don't you stop him!

PABLO. Someone always gets away—

CONJURER. Someone always comes back again—

VOICE (*widely resounding out of the noises*). Pablo, you're free!

(*The door is slammed shut. Silence. Then the drum begins a new roll.*)

DIRECTOR (*exhausted*). Ladies and gentlemen!

(*Trumpet blows a single steady note.*)

CONJURER (*continuing his commentary*). He tenses himself for a last, for a final effort—drops of blood are already—

DIRECTOR (*breathless*). We will now present our next number—

(*Trumpet blows a drawn-out note.*)

CONJURER (*during the trumpet note*). —but now he seems to have realized that his efforts are hopeless—

DIRECTOR (*forcing himself, scarcely able to speak*). Our lion tamer in her famous act!

(*Trumpet blows single drawn-out tones. The* CONJURER *mumbles on unintelligibly. The trumpet utters what sounds like a distress signal, is submerged, then asserts itself again. The* LION TAMER's *whip: "Jump! Get moving, there! On your feet! Show them what you can do!" Cracks. Voices drone. Shouts of encouragement. Then, all is drowned again in a wave. Loud applause.*)

PABLO (*very close; whispering*). The landing pier—the beach—the sea—I'm outside—I'm in the open spaces—I'm beating the tower—I'm getting the better of it. . . .

CONJURER (*His voice fights its way through the din. He now speaks in a clipped way; groping, unsure*). To our astonishment we see him sit up! It must be the last reflex of life in him. In a minute, he will collapse—no, this is uncanny . . . (*His voice becomes blurred. The roar increases. The whip cracks.*)

PABLO. The whip can't reach me—nothing here can touch me any more—all is past—I'm free. . . .

CONJURER (*making a last effort*). The rope round his chest is slackening—his arms work themselves free of the fetters—and now . . .

(*The roaring increases. Hubbub of voices. Ticking of the clock. Loud, resounding beats on the drum.*)

DIRECTOR (*drowning*). The tradition of the tower . . .

MIDGET (*drowning*). Taradition—taradition . . .

MANAGERESS (*drowning*). Pablo—Carlo —Nelly . . .

CONJURER (*drowning*). Now he rises . . .

PABLO. The tower—where is the tower?

(*The great roaring swells once more. Then silence*)

VOICE (*very slowly, matter-of-factly, coolly*). The rope hangs down from him now like a navel string. . . .

THE END

MADAME DE...

Jean Anouilh

Translated by JOHN WHITING
Based on a story by Louise de Vilmorin

Madame de . . . was first presented at The Arts Theatre Club, London, on January 29, 1959, with the following cast:

A YOUNG MAN, *the pianist* John Warner	THE MAID Doris Groves
MADAME DE . . . , Elizabeth Sellars	VAN PUCK, *a jeweller* James Wellman
MONSIEUR DE . . . , *her husband* Douglas Wilmer	THE AMBASSADOR Geoffrey Keen
	1ST FOOTMAN Anthony Blake
	2ND FOOTMAN Norman Pitt

Directed by Peter Hall
Décor by Tom Keogh
Music by John Hotchkis

The action of the play passes in the year 1880.

UNDERESTIMATED during his lifetime both by the critics and by the public, John Whiting (1917–1963) is now praised as "a progenitor of the new British drama," and is regarded by some of his erstwhile disparagers as the most undervalued writer of his time. A man of imaginative ideas, sonorous dialogue, and dramatic power, Whiting's lifelong preoccupation with the nature of violence and of personal responsibility foreshadowed the concern of a younger generation of writers with issues of similar import and potency. Yet public acceptance scarcely touched him during his brief span as a dramatist, for his plays, at the time, were considered difficult and too clouded with ambiguities to induce instant audience-unraveling.

Born in Salisbury, Wiltshire, Whiting trained for the stage at the Royal Academy of Dramatic Art. His first produced play, *A Penny for a Song,* was presented at the Haymarket Theatre, London, in 1951, and while it drew a favorable press, it failed with the public. (Later, a revised version was presented in repertory by the Royal Shakespeare Company.) In that same year, 1951, the author's *Saint's Day* caused something of a furor in the London press. Winner of the Arts Theatre Play Competition (to celebrate the Festival of Britain), the play was violently attacked by the critics, but with matching vociferation, defended by the three judges of the competition: Christopher Fry, Peter Ustinov, and Alec Clunes. The caldron of controversy was to be stirred again in 1954 with another play: *Marching Song.* These events, coupled with the disturbing fact that a later work, *The Gates of Summer,* remained unproduced in London, discouraged the author, and he momentarily abandoned playwriting.

Ironically, it was an adaptation rather than an original play that restored him to his craft and elevated him to the front rank of British dramatists. Shortly after Peter Hall had taken over the direction of the Royal Shakespeare Company, he commissioned Whiting to dramatize Aldous Huxley's book *The Devils of Loudon.* Fatalistically, *The Devils,* as staged at the Aldwych Theatre, London, in 1961, turned out to be his culminating play and most significant achievement. (The play, with Anne Bancroft and Jason Robards in the pivotal roles, failed to duplicate its European success on the New York stage, where it lingered for sixty-three performances in 1965–1966.)

In addition to his works for the theatre, Whiting wrote a number of screenplays (notably, *Young Cassidy,* based on Sean O'Casey's autobiographical *Mirror in My House*) and several short plays, two of particular note: *No Why?* and *A Walk in the Desert.*

Madame de . . . , which John Whiting translated from Jean Anouilh's dramatization of Louise de Vilmorin's novel, is a delightfully stylized play with music by John Hotchkis. Its inherent charm and grace are expressively heightened by imaginative production devices; and setting it within the framework of a miniature theatre stresses the nostalgic theatricality of this fin-de-siècle bitter-sweet romantic fable, introduced to American audiences for the first time within these pages.

SCENE. *Paris, 1880.*

A grand piano and stool are set, right, on the stage, as if for a recital. Beyond is a front-cloth depicting the façade of a small town house in the period of 1880. This is like a little theatre set within a theatre.

When the curtain rises, the stage is empty. The YOUNG MAN *enters. He is very Proustian, and wears evening dress. He bows to the audience, crosses to the piano, sits, and casually starts to improvise a waltz, in the manner of the time, which will serve as a leitmotiv.*

MUSIC No. 1

(The YOUNG MAN *stops playing. A tumbler, center of the façade, is raised, revealing a boudoir, set behind a gauze. There is a dressing-table with its back to the audience. The mirror frame only is used and* MADAME DE *can be seen, sitting at the dressing-table, facing the audience.)*

YOUNG MAN *(nonchalantly).* In a society where a woman's success and reputation depend less on her beauty than on her elegance, Madame de—*(He plays a chord.)* was distinction itself. *(He plays a chord.)* She set the style for a whole day of life. Men believed there could be no other woman like her. So, of course, other women did their best to copy her. At least, they caught an echo of the compliments which were constantly being paid to her.

(As the YOUNG MAN *continues to speak, the following business takes place in dumb show.* MADAME DE *tries on a hat in front of her mirror. She is obviously delighted with it.*

MONSIEUR DE *enters, goes to* MADAME DE, *kisses her hand and congratulates her.)*

Monsieur de was a rich man. *(He plays.)*

MUSIC No. 2

(Over the music) He was proud of his wife, and allowed her anything. He never questioned the money she spent, so there was no reason to think that he might disapprove.

*(*MADAME DE *tries on a second hat.)*

Yet, like many people, she was driven by a weakness and bravado to pretend. *(He stops playing.)* When her husband admired something she'd bought, such as a new hat, she couldn't resist saying that it had cost a little less than the real price.

*(*MONSIEUR DE *exits.* MADAME DE *takes off the hat.)*

So Madame de kept from her husband just how much money she owed. *(He plays.)*

MUSIC No. 3

(The MAID *enters, and, in an embarrassed way, gives* MADAME DE *a bill, then exits.)*

(He continues, with an odd little tune.) After some years of this game she was faced with large debts. At first this worried her, then made her anxious, and finally she was in despair. *(He stops playing.)*

*(*MADAME DE *gropes in the drawer of her dressing-table and takes out a bundle of bills. As the* YOUNG MAN *continues,* MADAME DE *artlessly tries to think of a solution and mimes more or less what the Young Man says.)*

It was all the more difficult to tell her husband about the bills because she'd lied for such a long time, and he'd never been anything but generous. She didn't want to lose his admiration or his trust, and so there was only one thing to be done. She must sell some jewellery.

*(*MADAME DE *opens her jewel-box.)*

She opened her jewel-box. It would be unwise, she thought, to get rid of an heirloom: equally unwise to sell a quantity of cheap jewellery, for she would have to explain its disappearance. So she decided to sell a pair of ear-rings. They were diamonds—

*(*MADAME DE *holds up the ear-rings.)*

—cut in the shape of hearts—

MUSIC No. 4

—a magnificent present from her husband on the day after their wedding.

(The lights black-out except for the spots on the YOUNG MAN, *who continues speaking. During the black-out a front-cloth falls but the outline of the house remains. The cloth, painted in trompe*

l'œil, represents a jeweller's shop. MADAME DE, *at the same time, picks up her hat and cape, puts them on, collects her gloves and parasol, and exits. A* FOOTMAN *quickly sets an armchair, right, and exits. The lights come up.*)

She took them to the jeweller. He was a discreet man—friend as well as tradesman to the best people—

MUSIC No. 5

(MADAME DE *and* VAN PUCK, *the jeweller, enter.* VAN PUCK *sets the armchair for* MADAME DE, *who sits.*)

MADAME DE. You'll think I'm being very foolish, Monsieur van Puck.

VAN PUCK. That would surprise me, madame.

MADAME DE. I have decided to part with some jewels. (*She hands the ear-rings to* VAN PUCK.) These diamond hearts. I believe you sold them to Monsieur de on the day after our marriage.

VAN PUCK (*examining the ear-rings with his jeweller's glass*). That's so, madame. (MADAME DE *stares at him.*) Your decision distresses me—on your account. For myself, I'm rather pleased. They are lovely things. I regretted selling them.

MADAME DE. Then at least I've made you happy this morning. I won't ask how much they're worth. Monsieur de wouldn't like me to be told. (*She rises.*) Let me send my maid here tomorrow. You can settle the price with her.

VAN PUCK (*ill at ease*). Is your decision final, madame? I don't like the idea. . . .

MADAME DE (*smiling*). You must get used to it, Monsieur van Puck. I've already done so. It's always sad to get rid of something one loves, but it must happen to you more often than to me.

VAN PUCK. It's my business, madame. But losing some stones breaks my heart.

MADAME DE. Put these in its place, Monsieur van Puck. At least be wholehearted. I won't offend you by asking you to keep this secret.

VAN PUCK (*suddenly a little uncertain*). Madame, we family jewellers are rather like father confessors . . .

MADAME DE (*interrupting kindly but flatly*). Thank you. I'm already provided for in that way. All I ask is that you don't tell anyone that I've disposed of these.

VAN PUCK (*rather muddled, stammering*). I meant to say—I thought perhaps I might . . . Forgive a blunt question, but —what will you tell your husband, madame?

MADAME DE (*about to go*). I shall say . . . I shall say that I lost them. It would hardly be a lie. This is not being wise after the event, Monsieur van Puck, but one of the clasps holds very badly.

VAN PUCK (*the glass thrust in his eye; horrified*). Madame!

MADAME DE. Mind you don't lose them yourself. (*Crosses and exits.*)

VAN PUCK (*following* MADAME DE). Madame! Madame!

(*There is a short comic flourish on the piano by the* YOUNG MAN.)

MUSIC No. 6

(VAN PUCK, *worried, crosses to center, bent over the ear-rings, the glass in his eye.*)

YOUNG MAN. The clasp held perfectly well. And so the jeweller decided that Monsieur de must have secret money troubles and thought it best to negotiate through his wife. (*He plays.*)

MUSIC No. 7

The jeweller considered himself extremely tactful in pretending not to guess this. (*He stops playing.*)

(*The lights black-out except for the spots on the* YOUNG MAN, *who continues speaking. During the black-out the curtain of the jeweller's shop is raised and in its place is a window-frame filled with painted plants, beyond which a ball can be seen taking place in shadow play.* VAN PUCK *exits in the black-out.*)

Madame de paid her debts and her beauty seemed enriched.

MUSIC No. 8

(*A* FOOTMAN *quickly sets a chair, right, and exits. The lights come up.* MADAME DE *with her* PARTNER *is dancing, right, and* MONSIEUR DE *with his* PARTNER *is dancing, left.*)

There was a ball that night. Madame de

suddenly put her hands to her ears and cried out . . .

MADAME DE (*stopping dancing*). Oh, my God!

(*The* YOUNG MAN *stops playing;* MONSIEUR DE *stops dancing.*)

I've lost my ear-rings!

(*The* YOUNG MAN *resumes playing.*)

MUSIC No. 9

HER PARTNER. But, my dear lady, you were not wearing any.

MADAME DE (*putting her hands over her ears*). Yes, I was. I'm sure I had them. (*She runs to* MONSIEUR DE.) My ear-rings. The two hearts. I've lost them—dropped them somewhere. Look. Look. Oh, how wretched.

(*Everyone looks around, bending down. Only* MONSIEUR DE *stays upright, shrugging his shoulders. The* YOUNG MAN *stops playing.*)

MONSIEUR DE. You were not wearing ear-rings this evening.

MADAME DE. I was.

MONSIEUR DE. I'm quite sure of it. I noticed it as we were coming out, but I didn't say anything because we were already late.

MADAME DE (*plaintively*). You're wrong. As usual. I even hesitated between my hearts and my emeralds. And I chose my hearts.

MONSIEUR DE. Then you've left them on your dressing-table. Or you kept them in your hand, meaning to put them on in the carriage. You often do that.

MADAME DE. The carriage! Yes, I must have dropped them in the carriage.

(*The* YOUNG MAN *begins to play a sad version of the Waltz.*)

MUSIC No. 10

(MADAME DE *runs off.* MONSIEUR DE *very calmly follows her off. The couple remaining continue to dance.*)

YOUNG MAN (*over the music*). People were embarrassed by the incident. No-one liked to dance any more, the band stopped —(*he stops playing*) and the party ended.

(*The lights black-out except for the spots on the* YOUNG MAN. *During the black-out a front-cloth falls depicting* MON-

SIEUR's *library. It is painted in trompe l'œil. The* COUPLE *exit in the black-out. The* FOOTMEN *set a chair, right, and a chair and table, left. On the table are a pen, an inkstand, a box of matches and an ashtray. The* FOOTMEN *exit. A* NEWSBOY *is heard off, shouting.*)

NEWSBOY (*off; shouting*). Paper! Paper! Paper!

YOUNG MAN. The next morning the matter was in the newspapers. They let it be understood that the ear-rings had been stolen. The jeweller, who was very upset by this, decided to go and see Monsieur de, who received him at once. (*He plays.*)

MUSIC No. 11

(*The lights come up.* VAN PUCK *enters.* MONSIEUR DE *enters and crosses to* VAN PUCK. *The* YOUNG MAN *stops playing.*)

MONSIEUR DE. Good morning, van Puck. What brings you here? I suppose you've come to tempt me.

VAN PUCK. No, my dear sir. I'm sorry, but it's not that. I've never been in such a difficult position. Before I worry you, and perhaps annoy you, I must ask you to be discreet.

MONSIEUR DE (*crossing to the chair left, and sitting*). Good Lord, van Puck. A secret?

VAN PUCK. A secret and a matter of good faith, monsieur.

MONSIEUR DE. All right, I promise. Go on.

VAN PUCK. I received a visit from Madame de yesterday.

MONSIEUR DE (*a little surprised*). She wanted something mended?

VAN PUCK (*moving slightly*). Unfortunately, no.

MONSIEUR DE. She wanted to buy something? (*He pauses.*) Don't tease me, van Puck. I'm not at my best in the morning.

VAN PUCK. She wanted to sell something, monsieur. Madame de brought me these—(*He hands the ear-rings to* MONSIEUR DE.) two diamond hearts, saying that she wanted to get rid of them.

(MONSIEUR DE *examines the ear-rings.*)

I found it hard to believe that madame would dispose of something so valuable without your knowledge.

(MONSIEUR DE *puts the ear-rings on the*

table.)

I wanted to be of service to you, for we all have bills which fall due. On the other hand, I had to indicate to Madame de, who asked me to keep the transaction secret, that I must pretend to think that you were not concerned. I did this with just enough—not irony, I would not allow myself that—but just enough indifference to let her know that I knew very well that she would know that I knew. . . .

MONSIEUR DE (*laughing*). That was very good of you, van Puck, if a trifle involved. Rash, however.

VAN PUCK. I realized that this morning, when I read in the paper that they suspect the jewels to have been stolen.

MONSIEUR DE (*cheerfully*). There is a moral conclusion to this story, van Puck. It is that there are fewer thieves about than we are led to believe—and that should make us very happy. The actual conclusion should make us equally happy —you, anyway. I'm going to buy the jewels again.

VAN PUCK. I'm very unhappy having to sell them to you a second time.

MONSIEUR DE (*bursting into laughter*). Don't apologize. I'm very pleased to have them back. (*He takes out his cheque-book*.) I suppose the price is still the same.

VAN PUCK (*horrified*). Oh, monsieur . . .

MUSIC No. 12

(*The business of the cheque is con-cluded in mime.* MONSIEUR DE *and* VAN PUCK *continue to chatter happily*.)

YOUNG MAN. Monsieur de was sad to find that his wife had been lying to him for so long. By hiding her debts she'd harmed his credit and reputation. Her heartless deception the night before at the ball, when she pretended to be robbed, shocked him. (*He plays a few bars, then stops playing*.)

(MONSIEUR DE *rises and exits*. VAN PUCK *follows him off*.)

Yet he gave no sign of what he was feel-ing as he showed out Monsieur van Puck, but made a few masculine jokes about the fallibility of reliable women.

MUSIC No. 13

(*The lights black-out except for the spots on the* YOUNG MAN, *who continues speaking. During the black-out the* FOOT-MEN *enter, move the chairs of the previous scene and remove the table, and exit. The library cloth rises, revealing a screen be-hind which are silhouetted a* MAN *and a* WOMAN *sitting at a table at Maxim's. They talk affectionately. Only a maître d'hôtel who is serving them moves near them*.)

That night, at Maxim's, Monsieur de had a friendly farewell supper with his mis-tress. She was a beautiful Spanish girl. (*He stops playing*.) Monsieur de was be-ginning to fall violently out of love with her.

(*The* MAN *displays the ear-rings*.)

And also she was going to South America the next day. As his wife had shown she cared nothing for the diamond hearts, Monsieur de decided that it would be amusing—and just—

(*The* MAN *hands the ear-rings to the* WOMAN.)

to give them to this charming girl.

(*The* MAN *and the* WOMAN *pick up their glasses*.)

They were a present to thank her for leav-ing him before he was compelled to leave her.

(*The* MAN *and the* WOMAN *clink their glasses. The lights black-out except for the spots on the* YOUNG MAN, *who plays*.)

MUSIC No. 14

(*A black curtain falls. A small lighted packet-boat crosses the curtain*.)

(*Over the music*) So Madame de's two diamond hearts crossed the Atlantic on their way to a new destiny. (*He stops playing as the boat disappears*.)

(*In the black-out, after the boat has crossed, the black curtain is raised and the salon cloth is lowered. The* FOOTMEN *enter, set a footstool in front of the chair and a small table on which there are a cup of tea, an ashtray, a box of matches, a hand-bell and a magazine*.)

While this was happening, Monsieur de decided to have—well, not so frank a dis-cussion as would embarrass him as much as his wife—but at least to try to put an end, an end he could look upon as final, to this story.

(*The lights come up.* MADAME DE *is seated beside the table, drinking tea and reading a magazine.* MONSIEUR DE *enters, crosses to* MADAME DE, *kisses her hand, then collects the chair and sets it left of the table.*)

MADAME DE. Good gracious! Have you come to tea? It's so long since the last time that I've begun to think things. Have you any excuse?

MONSIEUR DE (*sitting*). What strange things you say. I like having tea with you very much. You are one of the few women of my acquaintance who drink tea in a proper way. Some women seem to be nourishing themselves, which is disgusting: others perform a rite, which is boring. But you seem to enjoy it.

MADAME DE. You're too kind. But it's true, I love tea. Let me ring for another cup.

MONSIEUR DE. No, thank you. I hate tea. I like to see you drink it, that's all. (*He leans forward.*) I want to talk to you about this unfortunate affair.

MADAME DE (*looking straight at him*). What affair?

MONSIEUR DE. The diamond hearts.

MADAME DE (*reassured*). Of course.

MONSIEUR DE. Don't you think too much fuss is being made about it? It's unfortunate, of course, but it only concerns us.

MADAME DE. I quite agree. I find it very tiresome.

MONSIEUR DE. Up to now our name has only been in the newspapers when someone in the family has married or died. Or sometimes when I've made a particular ass of myself at the Horse Show. Now it's on the front page, among the crimes. Although we're the victim and not the criminal, it's not very pleasant. You don't suspect anyone?

MADAME DE (*looking away*). No. (*She pauses and looks at him.*) Look, the more I think of it, the more I believe you're right. I lost the ear-rings. But if you'd only told me that I wasn't wearing them that night, I shouldn't have been so absent-minded. I was late, and I meant to carry them and put them on in the carriage. And then I forgot. You were talking, weren't you? It's a weakness of mine always to concentrate on what you're saying.

MONSIEUR DE. You are quite sure you lost the jewels?

MADAME DE. Quite sure.

MONSIEUR DE. Well, just say that you've found them.

MADAME DE. I hadn't thought of that.

MONSIEUR DE. One never thinks of the obvious. (*He rises.*) If you take my advice, you'll have the horses harnessed and go straightaway to tell our hosts. Apologize for the scene at their ball the other night. Perhaps you haven't thought about it—you were always ruled more by your heart than your head—but it was very unpleasant for everybody.

MADAME DE. You're right. (*She rises and crosses.*) It was unforgivable. I'll go at once. (*She turns, radiant*) But it would be a lie.

MONSIEUR DE. My dear, with things as they are . . . (*He picks up* MADAME DE's *cup and saucer.*)

MADAME DE. Do you want to know what I think?

MONSIEUR DE (*smiling; lightly*). Don't be absurd. I know.

(MADAME DE *hesitates, then exits.* MONSIEUR DE *tries to drink the dregs from the tea-cup. He grimaces, puts down the cup, and lights a cigar.*)

YOUNG MAN. Monsieur de did not like tea. And he did not know what his wife was thinking. All the same, he was satisfied. His cigar was excellent, and he believed he'd settled the exasperating business of the hearts in an intelligent way. (*He plays.*)

MUSIC No. 15

(*The lights black-out except for the spots on the* YOUNG MAN, *who continues speaking. The* FOOTMEN *enter and remove the table, footstool, etc., set the chairs, and exit.*)

But it was not settled—far from it. The beautiful Spanish girl in the Argentine found she missed Monsieur de. She'd never been in love with him, but there are other reasons for needing a man. She spent quite a time trying to find someone else with as little gravity and as much money. Bored, she gambled. And won. (*He stops playing.*) At first. It's the surest way of losing at roulette. And so lost. One day, penniless, she sold the hearts. The best jeweller in Buenos Aires kept them in his shop less than a day. An ambassador of a country near to France was leaving the Argentine and being appointed to Paris. He was a man of taste, and very rich. He saw the jewels, fell in love with them, and bought them before sailing for Europe. (*He plays.*)

MUSIC No. 16

(*The salon cloth is raised, showing the dining-room of an embassy. The scene is painted in trompe l'œil to show large tapestries hung with tassels. Also painted are green plants which prevent us seeing anything but a small part of the long table immediately beneath a painted chandelier.*)

Chance found the situation irresistible. A month later, at a dinner-party given in his honour by a colleague, the Ambassador was put at table beside Madame de. (*He continues playing.*)

(*The lights come up. The* AMBASSADOR *and* MADAME DE *are sitting at the table side by side, and with their back to us are* MONSIEUR DE, *a* WOMAN *and another guest. One or two* SERVANTS *stand about. The* YOUNG MAN *stops playing.*)

It was a great dinner. Madame de was at her wittiest that night. The Ambassador admired her very much. He had come to the dinner as a duty, but he found he wasn't bored. Far from it. He was fascinated, and showed it. Madame de knew how to interest men. And she was attracted, too. She liked to please people and from the first evening the Ambassador gave her the opportunity and provoked her vanity.

(*The lights black-out except for the spots on the* YOUNG MAN, *who continues speaking. The salon cloth is lowered. The* FOOTMEN *set a table and three chairs.*)

As they belonged to the same set of the same society, they often saw each other at dinners, balls and receptions. When they met they never offended convention by staying together too long in public. No, they would move away from the crowd as if they had something urgently important to talk about. (*He plays.*)

MUSIC No. 17

Monsieur de had the good manners not to be upset by this. He knew his wife was faithful. But, of course, after some months of these meetings, the Ambassador and Madame de ended by confiding in each other. (*He stops playing.*)

(*The lights come up on* MADAME DE's *salon.* MADAME DE *is seated by the table. The* AMBASSADOR *is standing. He has a slight and charming accent, perhaps Rumanian.*)

AMBASSADOR. It's become a pleasant habit to call on you late each afternoon. I am a man of habit. And it frightens me.

MADAME DE. Why?

AMBASSADOR. Each time we indulge ourselves, we die a little.

MADAME DE. Really, I find nothing so morbid in seeing you every afternoon in my drawing-room.

AMBASSADOR (*sitting*). My job makes for a nomadic life. I'm never sure where I shall be tomorrow. When a man has unlimited freedom forced on him he finds it difficult to found any lasting relationship. Who are you expecting today?

MADAME DE. No-one. I had the doorman told I was ill and that I couldn't receive anybody.

AMBASSADOR (*rising*). I'm so sorry. The doorman didn't see me come in. I walked here; it is such a lovely day. I'm sorry. I've disobeyed your orders, even though I didn't know about them.

MADAME DE (*rising; gaily*). My doorman was wideawake. He was told that I would receive you.

(*The* YOUNG MAN *plays a few notes.*)

MUSIC No. 18

AMBASSADOR (*blushing*). I'm so sorry.

MADAME DE. Again? What is it about today that makes you so repentant? (*She sits.*) I've also formed an agreeable habit. It is to be entertained by you.

AMBASSADOR (*sitting; laughing*). I've learnt to unravel the subtleties of most European diplomats. That's not so difficult. Few of them are Talleyrand, after all. But a Parisienne's wit still baffles me. The Republic should think of employing women like you.

MADAME DE (*carelessly*). It wouldn't occur to them. Nor to us. Women have plenty of other things to do. They must dress, please people, and kill time. All that takes ages.

AMBASSADOR. Do you like pleasing people?

MADAME DE. I've always thought, perhaps innocently, that diplomacy was the art of not asking certain questions.

AMBASSADOR. So far I've managed to hide this fact from various ministers. (*Softly*) I'm not a very good diplomat. Don't tell anyone. They'd send me God knows where and I shouldn't be able to see you.

MADAME DE (*with sudden tenderness*). Then I'll certainly not tell anyone.

(*There is a short, embarrassed silence between them. The* YOUNG MAN *plays a few notes.*)

MUSIC No. 18a

AMBASSADOR (*suddenly; with a change of manner*). I've been a very dull dog these last two weeks, all alone in Paris. Was it pleasant at Cap d'Ail?

MADAME DE. The sun was shining. I've never really understood why people think the sun so important.

AMBASSADOR. I met your husband several times at the club while you were away—he didn't understand why you'd gone, either—and he told me that you loved the sun.

MADAME DE. It's a rumour I put about so as to get away from Paris alone, in December.

(*There is another short silence. The* YOUNG MAN *plays a few notes.*)

MUSIC No. 18b

AMBASSADOR. How was the mimosa?

MADAME DE. The mimosa. It was yellow —it was—mimosa.

AMBASSADOR. I thought you loved that, too. I imagined it showering down on you as you sat writing letters. Funny thing—I don't suppose you noticed—but there were a few grains in your last letter. (*He pauses briefly.*) The one in which you told me about your solitary walks on the rocks in the rain.

MADAME DE. Oh, that was heavenly! I might have been in Normandy. For once the place stopped looking like the picture

postcards. But usually it's a setting for cut-and-dried feelings. They say that nine out of ten couples spend their honeymoon there. Imagine learning to love each other in such a place. No wonder most marriages fail.

AMBASSADOR (*thoughtfully*). Where can people learn to love each other?

(*The light begins to dim as twilight falls.*)

MADAME DE. In Paris, in dry dull weather, like today. Or in the country with a log fire and the rain tapping on the window. Do you know Grosbois? It's in the Beauvaisis. I'll ask my husband to invite you there for the boar hunting. I sometimes go alone for two or three days in the winter.

(*After a short pause the* YOUNG MAN *plays a few notes.*)

MUSIC No. 18c

AMBASSADOR (*suddenly rising; whispering*). I can't keep this up.

MADAME DE (*rising; simply*). Neither can I. (*She moves towards him.*) It's just a year ago today that we met for the first time. (*She is very close to him. The* AMBASSADOR *kisses* MADAME DE, *almost chastely, lightly touching her lips. A clock strikes the half hour. She nearly cries out.*) Ah! (*She smiles.*) It's that clock. Half past five already. Thursday then, in the country.

AMBASSADOR (*murmuring, as if bewildered*). Thursday! Three days. Oh, it's a long time—far too long.

(MONSIEUR DE *suddenly enters, rubbing his hands, noisy, frozen and happy.*)

MONSIEUR DE. Good evening. (MADAME DE *sits.*) I say, it's deliciously dark in here. My wife's not yet made up her mind to have electricity. Like her grandmother, she always waits for a footman to bring the lamps. (*He crosses to the table and lights the oil lamp. To the* AMBASSADOR) Good to see you. (*He turns to* MADAME DE.) My dear, Paris is in uproar.

MADAME DE (*lightly*). Has war been declared? And I am detaining an ambassador.

MONSIEUR DE. Worse than that, my dear. La Rascas won't be singing tonight. She muffed a note at this afternoon's performance and it made her so cross that she pretended the opera was bad. Garnier had foreseen it, God bless his top C. Just at the time we should be arriving like idiots, dressed up, to applaud her, La Rascas will be on the Milan express. If we want to hear her we must make for the Gare de Lyon to be at La Scala tomorrow. I shall need some blankets and sandwiches. Are you coming?

AMBASSADOR. Certainly.

MONSIEUR DE. Then fill your flask. It'll be a nice little trip. (*He pauses. Flatly*) I don't make you laugh. The trouble with you foreign diplomats is that you will bring Europe into everything. Like a woman who is always on your mind but with whom you can never have fun, because she is such a proper person. Has my wife ever mentioned Grosbois? (MADAME DE *turns away*.) Come down on Thursday for the boar hunt. It'll give you a rest. (*He crosses to* MADAME DE *and puts his arm around her.*)

AMBASSADOR. I'm sorry. I can't—I'm not free on Thursday. I've already accepted another invitation.

MONSIEUR DE. Then let's say the following Thursday.

AMBASSADOR. Why must it be a Thursday?

MONSIEUR DE. My wife and I have kept the habit since childhood. We always plan our amusements for Thursdays.

(*The* AMBASSADOR *glances suspiciously at* MADAME DE.)

AMBASSADOR (*moving to* MONSIEUR DE; *with sudden melancholy*). I spent my childhood at a boardingschool, under a guardian. The other boys always went out on Thursdays. It's a sombre day for me. I've always put it aside to daydream. The playground was full again on Fridays, which is the day I keep for my amusements.

MONSIEUR DE (*casually*). How odd! Friday always makes me think of codfish. I loathe it. (*The* AMBASSADOR *crosses and kisses* MADAME DE's *hand, about to take his leave.*) Anyway, we'll choose one of the other five days. And meet again.

(MONSIEUR DE *and the* AMBASSADOR *exit.* MADAME DE *is left alone, quite still, lost in thought. The* YOUNG MAN *plays a few notes.*)

MUSIC No. 18d

YOUNG MAN. "He didn't dare to look at me," thought Madame de. "He loves me."

(MONSIEUR DE *re-enters.*)

MONSIEUR DE (*crossing to* MADAME DE). Your suitor is charming. I know you're too sensible to encourage him if he wasn't. All the same, I find him rather a bore. Don't you?

MADAME DE (*casually*). No.

MONSIEUR DE. You've always had a liking for solemnity. So for us to get along together I'm the one who's had to be a little hypocritical. What do you think of the bombshell?

MADAME DE (*confused*). What bombshell?

MONSIEUR DE. La Rascas not singing at the opera tonight.

MADAME DE (*more and more confused*). What opera?

(MONSIEUR DE *puts in his eyeglass and stares in surprise at* MADAME DE. *The lights black-out except for the spots on the* YOUNG MAN *who, after a short pause, plays.*)

MUSIC No. 19

(*The* FOOTMEN *remove the table and one chair and set two chairs right and left. The gauze is lowered.*)

YOUNG MAN (*over the music*). Madame de spent a wretched night, neither happy nor guilty.

(*The lights come up behind the gauze.* MADAME DE *can be seen sitting in her salon, beyond the gauze, daydreaming.*)

She stayed at home all the next day, lazy with love, alone in her sitting-room. She relived the incident of the day before, and doubted if it had ever happened. The Ambassador, who was announced at five o'clock as usual, put her mind at rest on that point. It had all certainly happened. (*He stops playing.*)

(*A* FOOTMAN *enters and, in dumb show, announces someone. The* AMBASSADOR *enters and crosses to* MADAME DE. *The* FOOTMAN *exits.*)

The Ambassador was solemn and seemed deeply moved.

(*The* AMBASSADOR *kisses* MADAME DE's *hand.*)

"My love; my dear love," he began, "for some time now . . ."

(*The* YOUNG MAN *stops speaking, and it is the* AMBASSADOR *who can be heard continuing.*)

AMBASSADOR. . . . for some time now I've wanted to give you some jewels I have. (*He takes a jewel-case from his pocket.*) They might have been made for you, and you richly deserve them. (*He opens the case and goes down on one knee beside* MADAME DE.) You see these two hearts: they are ours. Keep them, hide them, and more than anything look on them as one. You can only wear them when we are alone. That makes me very happy.

MADAME DE (*bewildered and not believing her eyes*). Oh, it's impossible.

(*The lights black-out except for the spots on the* YOUNG MAN.)

YOUNG MAN. It was quite possible. For a moment, Madame de was lost for words. All kinds of thoughts, one as mad as another, came into her head.

(*The lights come up.* MADAME DE *and the* AMBASSADOR *are in an embrace.*)
Then she fell into the Ambassador's arms, murmuring "My love, my dear love!" with such sincerity that it brought tears to his eyes. All the same, he was rather taken aback that his present, magnificent as it was, had had such an effect on the woman he loved.

(*The lights black-out except for the spots on the* YOUNG MAN.)
For although he came of a cautious race and although the conversation which followed—if you could only have heard it—was extremely fatuous—it was all about love—he was deeply in love with Madame de. And Madame de loved him, too, more than anything in the world. The rest of the story, alas, will prove that. She'd never been in love before. The two kisses were the first she'd ever received. Yet there occurred to this sensitive and honest woman a most idiotic idea. One of those ideas—both silly and commonplace—which only women can have. It will offend every man in the theatre, as it was to mortally offend the Ambassador when he came to learn of it.

(*The lights come up.* MADAME DE *has her arms round the* AMBASSADOR's *neck.*)

Dreamily, Madame de said . . . (*He plays.*)

MUSIC No. 20

(*The* AMBASSADOR *and* MADAME DE *rise.*)

MADAME DE (*over the music*). Dearest, I want to wear these jewels proudly before the whole world. I want to have our two hearts always whispering of you in my ears.

(*The* YOUNG MAN *stops playing.*)

YOUNG MAN (*aside*). It was this that was so shocking.

MADAME DE. So let me tell a lie, since you will always know the truth.

YOUNG MAN (*softly*). And as she said this her eyes were as pure as water.

AMBASSADOR. A lie? What kind of lie?

MADAME DE. One which can easily be believed. (*She moves right and sits.*) My mother's cousin has already given me half the jewels from her very beautiful collection. No-one would be surprised if she should send me these ear-rings. She hates my husband; they're on such bad terms he never sees her. And she has nothing to do with the rest of the family. I'll go and see her tomorrow morning and take her into my confidence.

AMBASSADOR (*dropping on one knee beside her*). You frighten me, my love. Why do you need a confidante?

MADAME DE (*tenderly*). My secret is too heavy. I shall be happier sharing it.

AMBASSADOR. Darling, you're so silly. It seems that unless a woman tells someone she must doubt both her love and her lover.

MADAME DE (*putting a finger on his mouth to silence him*). Stop talking psychology. It's always gloomy and usually wrong. Just let me have my happiness. We're visiting your house tonight. When you see me come in wearing our two hearts you'll know that we are one and that I am all yours. (*She gives him a light kiss.*)

AMBASSADOR (*enchanted*). You're like a child. It's wonderful, just like a child.

(*The lights black-out except for the spots on the* YOUNG MAN. *The salon cloth is raised. A small inset is set behind the gauze.*)

YOUNG MAN. You must admit it was both very touching and very simple. Let me tell you how Madame de miraculously found her jewels again just as she was going out with her husband. They were in a pair of gloves she no longer wore, and which she'd sharply told her maid to find at the last moment. Now, Monsieur de knew quite well that he'd given those jewels to the Spanish girl some time before. And as he was less inclined than his wife to believe in miracles, he began to think the matter over—something he rarely did.

(*The lights come up behind the gauze.* MADAME DE *is in a ball dress. The* MAID *is beside her, holding* MADAME DE's *gloves and the ear-rings.* MONSIEUR DE *enters. He is in evening dress.*)

MONSIEUR DE (*as he enters*). My dear . . .

MADAME DE. My gloves. (*She takes the ear-rings from the* MAID.) Can you believe your eyes, my dear? My hearts.

(MONSIEUR DE *slowly puts in his eye-glass, looks at the ear-rings, then takes them from* MADAME DE *and puts them in his pocket.*)

What are you doing?

MONSIEUR DE (*coldly*). You cannot wear them. (*He takes her arm to lead her off.*)

MADAME DE. But really, it's ridiculous! Give me my ear-rings. Why can't I wear them?

MONSIEUR DE. You have your secrets: I have mine.

(MADAME DE *and* MONSIEUR DE *exit. The* MAID, *stupefied, is left alone.*)

MAID. My! (*She calls as she rushes out*) Juliette! Juliette!

(*The lights black-out. The* YOUNG MAN *plays.*)

Music No. 21

(*The gauze is raised and the black curtain lowered. In front of the black curtain is set an upholstered bench in front of the outline of a small carriage window. The lights come up.* MONSIEUR DE *and* MADAME DE *are seated, silent, gently bouncing in time to the music, on their way to dine with the* AMBASSADOR.)

YOUNG MAN (*over the music*). Madame de did not dare to ask for the jewels again. They arrived at the embassy without having exchanged another word. (*He stops playing for a few moments, then resumes.*)

Music No. 22

(*The lights black-out except for the spots on the* YOUNG MAN. *The ballroom window-frame is set. It is lit from behind to give a shadow-play effect. When the lights come up the* AMBASSADOR *is in silhouette, receiving guests who shake hands and retire.* MADAME DE *and* MONSIEUR DE *enter and are received by the* AMBASSADOR.) (*He stops playing.*) Monsieur de noticed the look which passed between his wife and the Ambassador. He was not spying on them and had no wish to see it. However, the look confirmed the conclusion he'd arrived at on the way to the *soirée musicale.*

Music No. 23

(*The silhouette of a violinist with his instrument is seen to enter. He bows and there is applause. The violinist then mimes "tuning-up" and playing the air played by the* YOUNG MAN. *At a diminuendo in the music the lights fade to black-out except for the spots on the* YOUNG MAN, *who, on the last note of the music, continues speaking.*)

He remembered that a year before the Ambassador had come from the same South American city where Monsieur de's former mistress had since been living. He thought it probable that she'd been short of money and had sold some jewels. He was not surprised that the Ambassador had bought them—Monsieur de's tastes did not incline towards platonic love affairs. All the same, he could understand that one day his wife had told the Ambassador how unhappy she'd been when, in debt, she'd had to sell some jewels she loved. And how, by an amazing coincidence—this was a little hard to find credible, but he must bring himself to believe it—the Ambassador, possessing those very jewels, had at once graciously offered to make her happy again. (*He plays.*)

Music No. 23a

(*The lights come up. The violinist is miming the last movement—played of course by the* YOUNG MAN. *At a short pause in the music, just before the end, there is applause by mistake. The final bar is then played. There is applause!*

The ambassador *sits down with* madame de *sitting left of him and* monsieur de *left of* madame de.)

Looking at the matter this way Monsieur de could see no reason to take it amiss. He knew how to distinguish between a friendly and an impertinent act.

(monsieur de *rises and looks at* madame de.)

He told himself that the Ambassador, far from having wished to offer Madame de a present that she could not have accepted, had only wanted to help her repair the damage done by the lie—of which they both supposed her husband was unaware.

(*The lights black-out except for the spots on the* young man.)

Even so, Monsieur de's honour would not allow him to admit that his wife had received such a valuable present from another man. So he took the Ambassador aside after the concert and led him into a drawing-room.

(*The lights come up. The* ambassador *rises and exits with* monsieur de. *They re-enter down right in front of the ball-room window.*)

monsieur de. My dear fellow, you couldn't have been more tactful. But, you see, I've good reason to know that my wife didn't find her ear-rings among some old pair of gloves this evening. I can understand how you were tempted to help her. You gave her the opportunity of erasing the unhappiness she'd caused me when she sold the jewels I'd given her as a wedding present.

(*The* ambassador *moves slightly.*)

I've not spoken to her about it, because I think some things can destroy the harmony between husband and wife. Now it will upset me very much to see her wearing these ear-rings knowing that she owes them to your generosity. On the other hand, I'd like to have these diamonds again. So, as the simplest and friendliest conclusion, I suggest—if you agree—that you entrust them to my jeweller and tell him what I owe him for them.

(*The* ambassador, *very pale, slightly bows. The lights black-out except for the spots on the* young man. *The* ambassador *and* monsieur de *exit in the black-out. The*

ballroom *window-frame is raised and the library cloth set. The* footmen *set chairs and a table. On the table are a pen, an ink-stand, an ashtray and a box of matches.*)

young man. The Ambassador was very hurt. He found it hard to forgive Madame de for accepting as a token of his love jewels which must have recalled her first love, her first favours, the intimacies of her married life. He felt himself in a ridiculous position. He saw insult and mockery in what she'd done. And all love died for Madame de. (*He plays.*)

Music No. 24

He went to the jeweller next morning and gave him the diamond hearts. Then, pretending that an official dispatch recalled him to his country, he disappeared without a word of farewell. (*He stops playing.*)

(*The lights come up.* van puck *enters.* monsieur de *follows him on. The* young man *plays a little tune to accompany* van puck's *nervousness, but this stops abruptly as* monsieur de *enters.*)

Music No. 25

van puck (*taking the jewel-case from his pocket and gesturing helplessly*). Would you believe it, sir?

monsieur de (*good-humouredly*). Yes, my dear fellow, I can believe it, because I know why you're here. (*He sits.*) Just tell me the price of what you have brought.

van puck (*moving to* monsieur de). In selling you these jewels for a third time— a lamentable and profitable business—I wish they could cost less than they do. (*He puts a bill on the table in front of* monsieur de.) But they have passed through the hands of one of my colleagues in Buenos Aires and, dear me . . . (monsieur de *puts in his eyeglass and looks at the bill.*) But what a coincidence, sir.

(monsieur de *removes his glass and philosophically takes out his cheque-book.*)

monsieur de. My dear van Puck, having established as a certainty that what is true is unlikely and that what is unlikely is true—nothing surprises me. Then we'll say . . . (*He fills in a cheque.*)

(*The* young man *plays.*)

Music No. 26

(MONSIEUR DE *hands over the cheque on the last note of the music.* VAN PUCK *exits. The lights black-out. The* FOOTMEN *remove the table and set the chairs.*)

YOUNG MAN. And so Monsieur de bought the ear-rings for a third time. How should one tell a story which ended so sadly? For it has all the appearance of a joke, as if fate were amusing itself—what is more, it's a true story. As soon as the jeweller had gone, Monsieur de rang for a footman and asked him if Madame de was at home. He was told that she had gone to her room. Her face was flushed, yet she complained of being frozen. She'd taken to her bed.

(*The library cloth is raised. The lights come up on* MADAME DE's *bedroom.* MADAME DE *is lying back on the pillow, pale and wan.* MONSIEUR DE *enters with the jewel-case hidden behind his back.*)

MONSIEUR DE. If I do you a favour, will you do the same for me?

MADAME DE. Of course. If any favour can still please me. (MONSIEUR DE *reveals the jewel-case and calmly puts the ear-rings into* MADAME DE's *trembling hands. She stammers, shyly, touchingly, like a bewildered child.*) Are they for me? Are they for me? Really?

MONSIEUR DE. Yes, but I insist that you come to the ball with me.

MADAME DE (*frightened*). What are you thinking of? I haven't been up for ten days.

MONSIEUR DE (*flatly*). You promised to do me a favour in return. If you won't, give me back the jewels.

MADAME DE (*pleading*). Please. Don't be cruel. Don't force me.

(MONSIEUR DE *sits on the edge of the bed, dry, elegant, almost mysterious in his clear-sightedness and refusal to dramatize.*)

MONSIEUR DE. Be sensible and consider. Think of the position you've put me in. Think of the position in which you've put our friend, the Ambassador, who only tried to help you. We agree on that, don't we? If you are seen wearing these ear-rings tonight you'll set his conscience at rest, as well as mine. You'll dispel this miserable atmosphere from which all three of us have suffered and for which you're entirely responsible.

MADAME DE (*whispering*). How will he ever know?

MONSIEUR DE (*dryly*). He has come back. He'll be at the ball where I want to take you tonight.

(*They stare at each other in silence for a long time.*)

YOUNG MAN (*softly*). Madame de knew the truth. She knew why the Ambassador had left her. She couldn't reveal this to her husband, but neither could she bear to part with the hearts which recalled her only two kisses. In a weak voice she answered . . .

MADAME DE. Very well. I will come.

(*The lights black-out except for the spots on the* YOUNG MAN, *who plays a brilliant version of the Waltz.*)

Music No. 27

(*The ballroom window-frame is set as before. The lights come up. The dancers are seen in silhouette. The* AMBASSADOR *is seen in silhouette down right.*)

YOUNG MAN (*over the music*). Madame de's health had been affected by her deep unhappiness and by being shut in her room for a month. Monsieur de took no notice of this nor of the bitterly cold February weather, and made his wife go to the ball.

(MADAME DE *and* MONSIEUR DE *enter in silhouette and cross to the* AMBASSADOR. *The* YOUNG MAN *stops playing.*)

She arrived smiling, the diamonds sparkling at her ears. An ultimate beauty gave her magnificence. She held herself all the more upright for being near to collapse. She was still smiling when her eyes met those of the Ambassador who had seen her come in. He misunderstood her smile and why she wore the diamonds. Both seemed an act of defiance to him. He believed that by wearing the jewels, about which he knew the truth, Madame de meant to sweep away the past because now she despised it.

(*The* AMBASSADOR *kisses* MADAME DE's *hand.*)

As he kissed her hand which she tenderly held out to him, he said: "I shall never forgive you." And while others crowded round her he turned away.

(*The* AMBASSADOR *exits.*)

Monsieur de was in a good humour. His vanity had been satisfied. He was ready to make a night of it and although usually very courteous he forgot his wife for once and let her go home without him while he went on enjoying himself. (*He plays.*)

MUSIC No. 28

(MADAME DE *exits. The ball goes on wildly around* MONSIEUR DE. *The* YOUNG MAN *continues to play for a little while. The dancers' silhouettes become imprecise and blurred as the lights dim out except for the spots on the* YOUNG MAN. *The gauze is lowered. The* YOUNG MAN *stops playing.*)

Madame de went to bed, sobbing, renouncing life and all wish for life. She wrote a line of humble prayer to the Ambassador, imploring him to come and see her. And in the dawn of that February morning— (*He plays.*)

MUSIC No. 29

(*A dim light comes up. Snow is seen to be falling.* MADAME DE *enters down left, crosses hurriedly, and exits.*)

—throwing her flimsy cloak over her shoulders she went from the house unseen and ran like a madwoman through the snow to the embassy. (*He stops playing.*) Frozen, she rang the bell for a long time.

(*The lights black-out except for the spots on the* YOUNG MAN. *The ringing of a doorbell is heard off.*)

At last the door was opened by a bad-tempered man, half-asleep, half-dressed in a forbidding uniform. He took the letter and slammed the door in Madame de's face.

(*A door is heard to slam.*)

The next day she died.

(*The lights come up behind the gauze, revealing* MADAME DE'S *bedroom.* MADAME DE *is lying on her bed, her eyes shut, as if dead.* MONSIEUR DE *is seated at the foot of the bed, watching her.*)

Neither health, love nor reason could tempt her to live. The Ambassador called that evening.

(*The* AMBASSADOR *enters in front of the gauze. He is sombre and handsome in a fur-lined coat. The sound of a doorbell is heard. A* FOOTMAN *enters and in dumb show informs* MONSIEUR DE *that the* AMBASSADOR *has called, and exits.* MONSIEUR DE *rises, leaves the bedroom, then enters down left and crosses to the* AMBASSADOR.)

MONSIEUR DE. My wife can't see anyone.

AMBASSADOR (*handing a crumpled letter to* MONSIEUR DE). She sent for me.

(MONSIEUR DE *looks wretchedly at the letter, then shrugs his shoulders.*)

MONSIEUR DE (*simply*). Come with me.

(MONSIEUR DE *and the* AMBASSADOR *exit, then enter into the bedroom, both silent. The* AMBASSADOR *stands above the bed,* MONSIEUR DE *at the foot of it.*)

YOUNG MAN. Madame de lay at the frontier of a new loveliness. The two men stood, motionless, looking down at her. She was still breathing, feebly and brokenly. Presently, feeling himself to be an intruder, the Ambassador was about to go, when Madame de, in a convulsive death agony, stretched out her arms—(MADAME DE *stretches out her arms.*)—gave a sigh, and died. Her hands opened a little and there were the two diamond hearts as if she wished to offer them to the unknown.

(*There is a long silence.* MONSIEUR DE *bends over, closes his wife's eyes, and takes the ear-rings from her hands.*)

MONSIEUR DE (*moving to the* AMBASSADOR). She is dead. (*He hands an ear-ring to the* AMBASSADOR.) Take this heart that she has given you. The other is her own. I'll dispose of it. (*The* AMBASSADOR *slowly bows, takes the ear-ring, goes down on one knee, kisses* MADAME DE'S *hand, rises, and exits.* MONSIEUR DE, *left alone, stands for a moment looking down at his wife. Then he crosses her hands on her breast. The* MAID *enters, trembling.*)

MONSIEUR DE (*simply*). Madame is dead.

(*The* MAID *sobs quietly. The lights dim slowly to black-out. The tumbler falls. The* YOUNG MAN *rises.*)

YOUNG MAN. So ends the story of Madame de and the two diamond hearts, which Monsieur de never had to buy again.

The YOUNG MAN *bows as—*

THE CURTAIN FALLS